Embassy's Complete Boating Guide to Long Island Sound

"All most skippers will want or need to know."
– Nelson Bryant, *The New York Times*

"A pearl of a book for a gem of a waterway."
– Paul Donnelly, *The New Haven Advocate*

"A definitive book...superb."
– Shale L. Tulin, President, *CT Boat Owners' Association*

**"Don't (!) miss getting this GUIDE...
Packed stem to stern with exceptionally readable,
easily referenced, and useful information."**
– Chris Percy, Executive Director, *The Sounds Conservancy*

Featuring:

✦ Dozens of new color photos and feature articles

✦ Embassy's Updated Tide and Current Tables

✦ More than 250 on-site LORAN waypoints

✦ More Than 300 Restaurant suggestions

EMBASSY

The Complete
Boating Guide
to

LONG
ISLAND
SOUND

Third Edition

Preface By
Tom and Betsy Whidden

Edited By
Mark C. Borton
Gene Mitchell
Antonio Jocson
Timothy Scannell

Embassy Marine Publishing
a division of
Embassy Imprint, Inc.

EMBASSY

Embassy's Complete Boating Guide to Long Island Sound, Third Edition

Copyright © 1990, Embassy Marine Publishing, a division of Embassy Imprint, Inc.

President & Publisher	Mark C. Borton
Managing Editor	Gene Mitchell
Assistant Editors	Antonio Jocson Timothy Scannell
Editor Emeritus	Ellsworth S. Grant
Navigation Editors	John Jensen-Outdoor Recreation Services, Fairfield, CT Paul Connolly-Connecticut Coastline, Rowayton, CT Bob Milne-Captain, *Volsunga III,* Stony Creek, CT
Original Book Design Cover Design	Susan Smith-Grandesign, New Haven, CT Peter Good Graphic Design, Chester, CT
Production Manager Production Assistant	Nancy J. Close Jeffrey Marsh
Typesetting	Comp One, North Haven, CT Brodeur Printing, Old Saybrook, CT
Printing	Singapore National Printers, Ltd., by arrangement with Palace Press, San Francisco, CA
Advertising & Book Sales	Kim O'Gorman-New York & Western Connecticut Michael McGuire-Eastern Connecticut, Rhode Island, and Massachusetts
Operations Manager	Irene L. Roy
Customer Service	Amy L. Perkins Ian Quarrier
Office Manager	Lucy Bakewell

Embassy Marine Publishing currently produces two editions of *Embassy's Complete Boating Guides* © – *Long Island Sound,* and *Cape Cod & Rhode Island. Embassy's Complete Boating Guides* to other areas on the East and West coasts and the Great Lakes are under development. Please call us toll-free at 1-800-999-1075 to order books, to place an advertisement, or for additional information.

ISBN 0-930527-09-7
Printed in the Republic of Singapore
First printing, February 1990

Embassy Marine Publishing, a division of Embassy Imprint, Inc.
37 Pratt Street, P.O. Box 338, Essex, CT 06426, (203) 767-1343

YOUR BOAT DESERVES QUALITY MOBILE COMMUNICATIONS: NYNEX

If you own a portable or mobile phone and aren't taking advantage of the NYNEX cellular system, it's easy to switch. And if you still haven't taken the plunge, so to speak, be sure to specify NYNEX cellular service.

Get the most powerful cellular system on the line.

Call 1-800-443-2355

For mobile communications, the answer is NYNEX.

Mobile Communications

An Introduction to the Sound

The Coasts of New York, Connecticut, and Rhode Island

The North Shore and Fish Tail of Long Island

Reference

C O N T E N T S

The Coasts of New York, Connecticut and Rhode Island

EMBASSY'S COMPLETE BOATING GUIDE TO LONG ISLAND SOUND

Chart Index

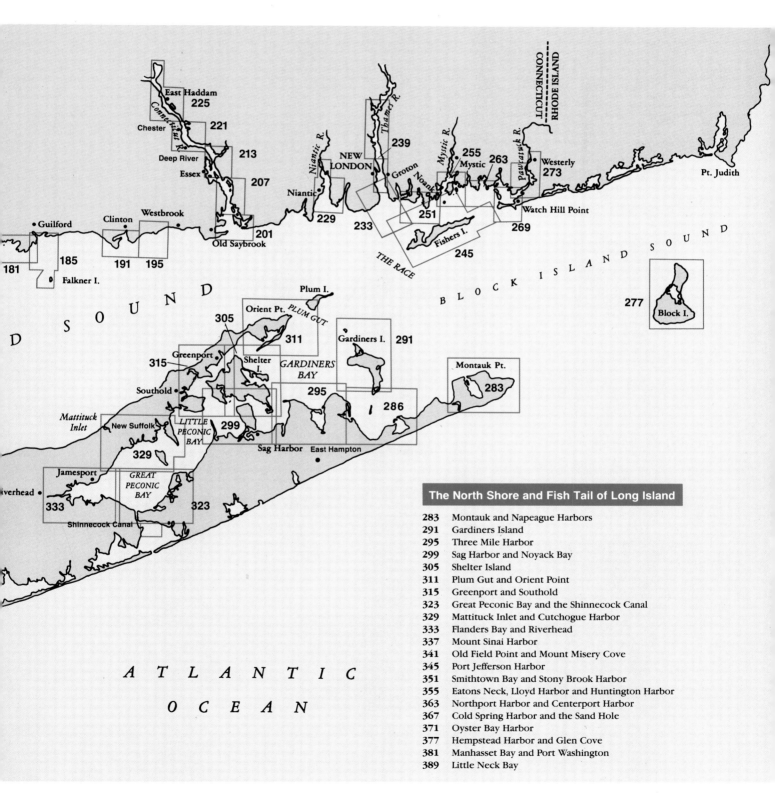

The North Shore and Fish Tail of Long Island

Acknowledgements

Embassy Marine Publishing would like to thank the following individuals and organizations for their invaluable assistance and expertise in producing *Embassy's Complete Boating Guide to Long Island Sound:*

Thomas Ashwell, Terry Backer, Henry Bakewell, Lucy Bakewell, Chandler Bates, Dr. Richard Benoit, Donald Blake, Michael Blanko, Bill Borchert, Terry and Debbie Borton, Julie Braun, Lauren Brown, Bill Browning, John Bullard, Howard Burdick, Bob Burns, George Cambell, Joan C. Carlson, Renwick Case, Cazart! The Wonder-Cat, Flex Clare, Dean Clarke, Pete Comstock, Francine Cornaglia, Frank Crawford, George Friend, Capt. Mary Ann DeGraw, Anthony De Ross, Joe Dolan, David Donald, Steve Dunwell, Bob & Naomi Eber, Tom Etchels, Lucy Fassel, Mike Flemming, Bill Finch, Jack Forehand, Jim & Barbara Fravel, Herbert Gardner, Susan Gardner, Ray Gay, Jr., Andy Geman, Andy Giblin, Sheldon Goldner, Steven R. Goldstein, Peter Good, Ellsworth S. Grant, Malcolm Greenaway, Clement Griscom, Ray Haney, Archibald Hanna, Eliot Harris III, Mary Jane Hayes, Karen Hayward, Robert J. Hefner, Joel Helander, Steve Henkel, Arthur R. Henick, Tom Hopkins, Jay Hostetter, Tom Jackson, Marilyne Johnson, Joseph Keating, Hubbard Phelps, Jim and Priscilla Keene, Janet Kepner, Nancy Kriz, Steve Krous, Adrian Lane, Tom Lenz, Ed LaFreniere, John Lockwood, Patrick Lombard, Jeffrey Marsh, Jim Marshall, John Marshall, Fran Martin, Nina Maurer, Jack McConnell, William McDermott, Roger McGrady, Michael McGuire, Paula McNamara, Edward Morrone, Lawrence Neidich, Michael Noyes, Dennis O'Brien, Kim O'Gorman, Mike O'Neill, Doug Oakford, Stan Ogilvy, Ed Oppenheimer, Halford Park, Amy Perkins, Bill Perks, Hubbard Phelps, Bill & Marie Pisani, Luca Point, Maggie Potapchuk, Ian Quarrier, Linda M. Rancourt, Ben Rathbun, Frank Raymond, Christopher Reaske, Lawrence Reybine, Sally Richards, Howard Richelsoph, Leah Ruth Robinson, John Rousmaniere, Irene Roy, Germaine Schumacher, Clayton Seelgen, Bob Shapley, Penny Sharp, Nina Shippen, Clyde Smith, Susan Smith, Richard Sisson, Charles Snow, I. Martin Spier, Rocket J. Squirrel, John Stellenwerf, Roy Tapio, Nancy Trimble, Gary Tuttle, Bill Vallee, Brian Valleton, Martin Waine, Tom & Betsy Whidden, Frank White, Tom Wilcox, Alice Wills, Capt. Al Wilson, Frank Wolcott, Robert Zwirner.

Mike Acebo	*Brewer Yacht Yard, Greenport, NY*
Harry Acker	*Senior Harbormaster, Halesite, NY*
Rufus Allen	*Harbormaster, Mystic River, CT*
Dick Alley	The Fisherman *Magazine*
John A. Amarilios	*Darien, CT Power Squadron*
Bill Ames	*Mystic Seaport Museum*
John Anderson	*Bay Constable, Southampton, NY*
Michael Anglin	*Jack's Marine, Shelter Island, NY*
Chester Arnold, Jr.	*UCONN Cooperative Extension Service, Sea Grant Marine Advisory Program*
Robert G. Bachand	*Long Island Sound Taskforce of the Oceanic Society*
Roger Balducci	*Harbormaster, Smithtown, NY*
Patrick Barry	*Harbormaster, Old Saybrook, CT*
Allen Berrien	*Milford Harbor Marina, Milford, CT*
Norman Boas	*Stonington Historical Society*
Nancy Bodick	*Milford Boat Works, Milford, CT*
Ray Bovich	*Connecticut Marine Trades Association*
Norman J. Brouwer	*South Street Seaport Museum*
Joanne J. Brooks	*Suffolk County Historical Society*
Tony Bruno	*Harbormaster, Stratford, CT*
Milan Bull	*Connecticut Audubon Society*
Tony Bullock	*Supervisor, East Hampton, NY*
Dave Burns	*State Harbormaster, Clinton Harbor, CT*
Carl Caldwell	*Harbormaster, Port Chester, NY*
John Clavin	*Harbormaster, Fishers Island, NY*
Floyd Carrington	*President, Shinnecock Marlin & Tuna Club*
Mark Champlin	*Harbormaster, Westerly, RI*
Roy Clark	*U.S. Army Corps of Engineers*
James Colbrook	*Dockmaster, Town Marina, Guilford, CT*
Paul & Kathy Connolly	*Connecticut Coastline, Norwalk, CT*
David Corrigan	*Museum of Connecticut History*
Rod Cook	*Stamford, CT Marine Police*
Bunny Cox	*Harbor Marina, Three Mile Harbor, NY*
Skip Crane	*Oceanographic Society*
Don Creller	*Harbormaster, Milford, CT*
Frank Crohn	*Connecticut River Books*
Ladd Cutter	*Harbormaster, Sag Harbor, NY*
Maureen Dacimo	*Narrow River Marina, Orient, NY*
Bob Dannewitz	*Modern Yachts, Hampton Bays, NY*
Albert Daniels	*Mamaroneck, NY Harbor Commission*
Barbara Davenport	*Ralph's Fishing Station, Mount Sinai, NY*
Edmund Delaney	*Connecticut River Watershed Council*
Elinor DeWire	*Mystic Seaport Planetarium*
Harriet Docteroff	*New York Marine Trades Association*
George Donnelly	*Mystic Aquarium*
Ed DuMoulin	*Sail America Foundation/Knickerbocker Yacht Club*
Donald Dzenkowski	*Senior Bay Constable, Southold, NY*
Tom Edwards	*Harbormaster, Montauk, NY*
Joan Feehan	*Clerk Treasurer, Sag Harbor, NY*
Lt. Wayne Fenelon	*Bay Constable, East Hampton, NY*
George Ferrer	*Police Chief/Harbormaster, Shelter Island, NY*
Debra A. Fillos	*Florence Griswold Museum*
George Finckenor Sr.	*Village Historian, Sag Harbor, NY*
Jim Flemings	*Manhasset Bay Marine Patrol*
Orion A. Ford	*Ford's Lobsters, Noank, CT*
Natalie Fox	*Shelter Island Chamber of Commerce*
Alex Galasso	*Larry's Lighthouse Marina, Aquebogue, NY*
Ann Gill	*The Whaling Museum, Cold Spring Harbor, NY*
Patrick Gillian	*Bay Constable, Smithtown, NY*
Arthur J. Gould	*West Shore Marina, Huntington, NY*
Sandy Grimes	*Harbormaster, Stonington, CT*
A. Christopher Gross	*Waterfront Commission Chairman, Northport, NY*
Averill Guess	*The Payne Historical Museum*

John Hall	*Harbormaster, Watch Hill, RI*
Carol Henkel	*Harbormaster, Darien, CT*
Thomas A. Hoctor	*Historian, City of New Rochelle, NY*
Robert A. Hogg	*SUNY Maritime College*
John H. Jensen	*Outdoor Recreation Services, Fairfield, CT*
W.C. Johnson	*Harbormaster, Southport, CT*
William Johnston	*President, Branford Historical Society*
Chris Joslyn	*Sachem's Head Yacht Club*
Peggy Joyce	*President, Montauk Historical Society*
Morgan Kaolian	*Long Island Sound America*
Daniel H. Kaplan	*Nassau County Museum*
Arthur I. Karpf	*West Harbor Yacht Service, New Rochelle, NY*
Brooks Kelly	*Cedar Point Yacht Club, Westport, CT*
Art Kelsey	*Sail Westbrook, Westbrook, CT*
Ed Kelsey	*Kelsey's Boat Yard, Branford, CT*
Bruce Killen	*South Minneford Yacht Club, City Island, NY*
Cathie Kossler	*Spicer's Marina, Noank, CT*
Mike Kurnides	*Manhasset Bay Yacht Club, Port Washington, NY*
Mike Lamperelli	*Marine Commerce & Development Commission, New London, CT*
Joseph Lewis	*Harbormaster, Noank, CT*
Ralph Lewis	*Connecticut DEP*
Chris Littlefield	*Harbormaster, Block Island, RI*
Jonathan Lovejoy	*Harbor Management Commission, Norwalk, CT*
Pat Logan	*Okeanos Ocean Research Foundation*
Mike Ludwig	*National Marine Fisheries*
Rob Lynch	*Harbormaster, Rye, NY*
James Mancusi	*Harbormaster, Mamaroneck, NY*
Norman H. Martin	*New York Sailing School, City Island, NY*
Norman Maurice	*Maurice Marine, Norwalk, CT*
Brad May	*Harbormaster, Clinton, CT*
Jerry McCarthy	*Town Historian, Greenport, NY*
Dennis McClean	*Barnum Museum, Bridgeport, CT*
Robert McKernan	*Guilford, CT Harbor Commission*
Kevin McKeon	*Federal Communications Commission*
Doris Meadows	*The Heckscher Museum*
Ann Mesnikoff	*National Audubon Society, New York, NY*
Len Mierzejewski	*Harbormaster, Westbrook, CT*
Brenda Milkofsky	*Connecticut River Museum, Essex, CT*
Dot Millen	*The Nature Conservancy, Connecticut Chapter*
Capt. Robert Milne	*Captain,* Volsunga III, *Stony Creek, CT*
Beth Mitchell	*Greenwich Harbor Club, Greenwich, NY*
Michael Nardella	*Harbormaster, Branford, CT*
Mary Newell	*The Museums at Stony Brook*
Joe Ochs	*Centerport Marina, Centerport, NY*
Norman Peck	*Harbormaster, Niantic, CT*
Robert Pelton	*Barnum Museum, Bridgeport, CT*
Chris Percy	*The Sounds Conservancy*
Lucy Picullo	*Cutchogue Harbor Marina, Cutchogue, NY*
Gloria Pritts	*Mamaroneck Historical Society*

Noble S. Proctor	*Southern Connecticut University*
George Prosser	*Harbor Square Marina, Stamford, CT*
Sidney Quarrier	*Connecticut DEP*
Bill Roesch	*Pequonnock Yacht Club, Bridgeport, CT*
Judy Raab	*Okeanos Ocean Research Foundation*
Nick Rascati	*New Haven Marina, New Haven, CT*
John Reid	*Wings Point Yacht Club, Three Mile Harbor, NY*
William Robbins	*Oyster Point Marina, New Haven, CT*
Michael Rowsom	*S.T. Preston & Son Inc., Greenport, NY*
Daniel E. Russell	*Harbormaster, Glen Cove, NY*
Joe Savino Jr.	*Harbormaster, Bridgeport, CT*
Richard Scalese	*Oyster Bend Marina, Norwalk, CT*
Jeffrey Shapiro	*Cedar Island Marina, Clinton, CT*
John Sheridan	*Harbormaster, Stamford, CT*
Ed Shimanski	*City Island, NY Power Squadron*
Ernst Shindele	Star of Life *Flotilla*
Wayland Shook	*Harbormaster, Westport, CT*
Joseph Siciliano	*Town of Greenwich, CT Parks & Recreation Department*
Clint Smith	*Harbormaster, Oyster Bay, NY*
Naomi Solo	*Danford's Inn, Port Jefferson, NY*
Paul Stag	*Long Island Sound America*
Larry Steadman	*1st. Assistant Harbormaster, Westerly, RI*
Joshua Stoff	*Cradle of Aviation Museum, Garden City, NY*
Bob Snyder, Sr.	*Dodson Boatyard, Stonington, CT*
Carol Traynor	*Society for the Preservation of Long Island Antiquities*
Bill Tuttle	*Sikorsky Aircraft*
George Utter	The Westerly Sun
John Volk	*Connecticut Department of Agriculture*
Tom Wall	*E.R. Strait Marina, Westport, CT*
Terry Walton	*The Vanderbilt Museum, Centerport, NY*
Dennis Watson	*Maritime Center on Long Island*
Bernard Weiss	*Halloween Yacht Club, Stamford, CT*
Wayne Wheeler	*U.S. Lighthouse Society*
Ed Wiegand	*Brewer's Yacht Yard, Mystic, CT*
Bruce Williams	*Captain's Cove Seaport/H.M.S.* Rose *Foundation*
George Wisker	*Connecticut DEP*
Lil Witzke	*Albertson Marina, Southold, NY*
Shirley Wood	The Block Island Times

Federal Communications Commission
National Park Service
Nautilus Memorial Submarine Force Library and Museum
New Rochelle Historical Society
New York Police Department Harbor Unit
New York Sea Grant Institute
Radio Technical Commission for Maritime Services
U.S. Coast Guard
U.S. Merchant Marine Academy
Walt Whitman Birthplace Association
Yale University Library

The best way to talk on water.

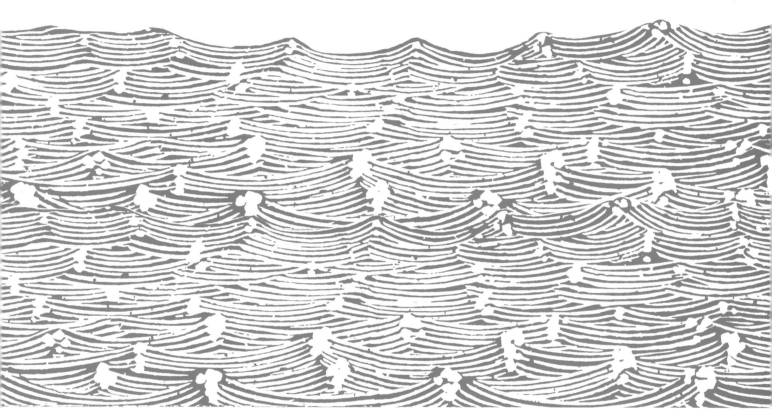

With Linx Mobile Phone Service.

Linx Mobile Phone Service is not just for cars. With a portable phone, you can take advantage of Connecticut's leading cellular service on the water too.

For more information about the unsurpassed clarity and coverage of Linx Mobile Phone Service, call SNET MobileCom at 1-800-922-LINX.

1-800-922-LINX

Preface

TOM WHIDDEN
Tactician, Stars and Stripes
Winner of the 1987 America's Cup

With Betsy Whidden

Long Island Sound has been good to me.

Beginning with my introduction to sailing in Lenny Raymond's Blue Jay when I was 10, to my preparation to win back the America's Cup from Australia in 1987, the Sound has taught me the subtleties of the sea. Needless to say, when Betsy and I were asked to write the preface for this book, we were delighted to help its readers share this very special part of the world, and learn from it as we have.

Little did Lenny know the monster he would create when he invited me out for an afternoon's sail some thirty years ago. His parents owned a cottage at Old Mill Beach, near Westport. I remember waiting impatiently for high tide to sail because at low tide his boat was perched high and dry on a sandbar, a fairly familiar sight along the coastlines of Connecticut and Long Island.

Tom and Betsy Whidden with their daughter Holly on board the *Stars and Stripes* in Fremantle, Australia, after winning back the America's Cup.

© *Leo Mason*

After that first afternoon, I sailed regularly with Lenny and we even competed in a few Cedar Point Yacht Club races back when the yacht club was located in Compo Basin. We did fairly well, although my greatest source of enjoyment was the freedom and independence I felt as a kid out on the water, doing something grown up.

I'm sure my parents appreciated the fact that the Sound's conditions were more gentle than those on open water. But back then, Long Island Sound could have been the Indian Ocean to me. I was in awe of its vastness. Yet I didn't understand what made it so unusual. I now appreciate the significance of the Sound's sailing environment – a very large, sheltered body of water like a lake, yet saltwater and tidal, like an ocean. That combination creates an ideal place to learn. Anyone with a real love for sailing and a keen desire to achieve can garner a wealth of experience under the Sound's varied conditions. The number of world-class sailors it has turned out is testimony to its greatness as a training ground.

By the time I was 12 years old, sailing was in my blood. I sailed every chance I could get in Sea Sprites and Blue Jays. I went to the Midget Championships in a Blue Jay and placed in the top five in Cold Spring Harbor, NY. Friends used to tease me that I had saltwater in my veins, and I guess to a certain extent it was true. By the time I was 14, I knew I wanted to be a sailmaker and compete in the America's Cup.

About that time I had my first big break. I crewed overnight on a wonderful old Concordia yawl named *Scotch Mist*, owned by the late Jim Rankin, and sailed out of Pequot Yacht Club in Southport. I had really arrived–or so I thought. A nice southwester blew as we set course for Stratford Shoals and beyond. This was to be quite an adventure. Up until then I had sailed only in daylight around local areas like Sherwood Island, Greens Farms and Compo Beach.

I remember quite vividly how strangely quiet it became on board as evening set in and we sailed on. It was a cloudless night, and the sky was packed with a million stars as a soft warm breeze pushed us past the shoals and on to the waters off the Thimble Islands and Faulkners. As daylight broke, we were headed for The Race. I was incredibly impressed by the amount of current. Once we were outside The Race, I had my first taste of "at sea" conditions. Heavy winds swept water over the bow and left me wet and miserable. I began to appreciate the gentler temperament of Long Island Sound!

But Lenny's monster grew. I spent countless hours in Lightnings, Thistles, and Atlantics. My dad presented me with an old, somewhat leaky Blue Jay that I named *Rebound.* It wasn't as fast as some of the fancier Blue Jays my friends had, but it taught me how to be more creative in the subtle Long Island Sound conditions.

My first taste in competitive, long distance racing came when I was in college. Art Tauck asked me to crew on his Palmer Johnson 36 named *Edelweiss* during the Block Island Race. The race course sent us from Larchmont, NY, around Block Island, and back. We were continually playing the currents and the winds. I learned that it was essential to read the charts and water to understand the strength and direction of the current in relation to where we were and where we were going. And I realized how important it was to look for the winds and read their shifts correctly. Long Island Sound is so warm that when the wind blows from the south it can bounce up over Long Island and come down in cat's paws, creating some of the most challenging conditions in the world.

When my former partner and I purchased Sobstad Sailmakers in Old Saybrook in 1972, my knowledge of the Sound really came into play. Not only was I expected to design and build state-of-the-art sails for customers, but I was also expected to get my customers around the race course—often on the Sound—in winning style. I found myself in countless discussions with other captains, trying to help them master the Sound's conditions, and win.

At the same time, I personally sailed in pretty nearly every Block Island Race and Vineyard Race (which involves long and tricky stretches on Long Island Sound) since 1973, and practically every other major other yachting regatta on the Sound. I've been fortunate enough to be in the winner's circle and, more times than not, in the top five.

My biggest achievement, and certainly my most rewarding, was out on the Indian Ocean on Gage Roads during the 1987 America's Cup, serving as navigator for *Stars and Stripes.* While the "Fremantle Doctor" made consistent housecalls with winds up to 30 knots, there were times when the desert winds prevailed, giving us light shifty air.

One race in particular comes to mind: the first race of the America's Cup on January 31. Instead of the brilliant blue skies and brisk winds we had experienced almost every day in Fremantle, that day dawned cloudy with shifty winds. On the way to the race course, Dennis Conner leaned over and said to me, "Sort of reminds me of Newport, or Long Island Sound."

I couldn't have agreed more. Drawing on all the hours and experiences I had accumulated out on the Sound learning to seek out the shifts and anticipate the tides, I was able to call the tactics that took us over the finish line 1:41 ahead of *Kookaburra III.*

During my five-month stint in Western Australia, I became President of North Sails, Inc., headquartered in yet another Long Island Sound community, Milford. Taking over the reigns of the world's largest sailmaker has allowed me to continue sailing in some of the world's most beautiful and exotic places. Yet I find myself being drawn back to those special qualities that lie here, in this wonderful school for sailing, Long Island Sound.

Most that I've learned about boating I've learned by experience, not from books. But you can be sure that *Embassy's Complete Boating Guide to Long Island Sound* will find a place in my chart locker. Its charts, harbor descriptions, entrance directions, and facility listings are accurate, clear, and easy to use–far and away the best available. They're essential tools for the inexperienced, and damn helpful, even for an old hand like myself. Just as important are the fascinating highlights in *Embassy's Boating Guide* of the geology, ecology, history, and culture of the Sound, many of which were new to me. Through its pages I've come to see the Sound with different eyes.

Once again, as it did in my childhood, this inland sea seems as vast as the Indian Ocean, waiting to be explored.

February 1, 1988
Essex, Connecticut   ◆

The Sound of Many Faces

JOHN ROUSMANIERE
Author of The Annapolis Book
of Seamanship

Having spent almost all my summers since early adolescence on Long Island Sound, I thought I'd seen everything the Sound had to offer. However, something new and marvelous appeared on a recent Fourth of July when the boat I was in pulled out of the East River into the Sound at sunset. Just as last light disappeared and the whole length of the Sound ahead faded into darkness, the shorelines to starboard and port suddenly burst into mammoth displays of fireworks. For the next two hours we took in this spectacle as we carefully worked our way east through a huge audience of drifting boats. As the last shooting stars fell, we anchored off the Connecticut shore in the sweet scent of the Arnold bakery that wafts downwind from Greenwich.

© Leah Ruth Robinson

The author at the helm.

That extraordinary night presented only one of the many faces that the Sound shows between its smoggy western entrance at New York City and its foggy eastern gate off Fishers Island. Consider the weather. One day there's a sultry calm flattening the water. The next there's a cold nor'east gale pushing up rolling, breaking seas reminiscent of the ocean's worst behavior. And then consider the strangely diverse geography. On the Long Island side, miles of sandy bluffs tower over a handful of deep embayments, like lovely Cold Spring Harbor, which has hardly changed since I sailed there as a boy more than thirty years ago. Yet only a few miles to the north, the other shore is a long stretch of low rocky islands guarding hundreds of coves and creeks.

For all the Sound's variables, there nevertheless is one constant everywhere from Execution Rock to Race Rock: the tide. Tidal currents are at their worst at either end, where the Sound alternately empties and is filled up. The fierce currents that blast through Hell Gate and The Race slam doors in the face of slow boats, whose crews are better off heaving-to for a sandwich than trying to fight it. A fast boat can make progress through a hard head current, but watch out if a fresh wind is running against the tide and they kick up a seaway vicious enough to break a hull (if it hasn't already shattered her crew's spirits).

I like the challenge of tides and tidal currents. That's one reason I've had so much fun in recent summers on the tricky waters near Stonington. My best friends in my constant battle to take advantage of fair currents and cut my losses in foul ones are tide tables and tidal current charts, like the ones in the back of this excellent guide to the Sound. Using the tables for The Race in coordination with the current charts, anybody can estimate the strength and direction of tidal currents anywhere on Long Island Sound and can predict how the boat will be affected as she moves toward her destination.

Though many people aren't familiar with it, there is a neat trick for figuring how to compensate for a current pushing a boat to the side. Using the current charts, estimate how many miles the current will push you to the side. Then employ a simple formula called the Rule of 60: divide that distance by the mileage to the destination and multiply the result by 60. The total is the required course alteration in degrees to make uptide.

I mention this practical tip not to distract readers from the pleasures of Long Island Sound but rather to make it easier to enjoy this wonderful body of water, which has been my playground for more than thirty years. I encourage you to sample the Sound in all its variety and charm. ◆

John Rousmaniere is the author of *The Annapolis Book of Seamanship, A Picture History of the America's Cup,* and other books on boating, and is a columnist for *Sailing World* Magazine. He lives in Stamford and sails out of Stonington, CT.

THE JOURNAL TALKS

Tune in to The Wall Street Journal Reports for the latest market information and business news. Hear the Reports on:

Introduction

ELLSWORTH S. GRANT

Long Island Sound is unlike any other large body of water in the world. Its winds are variable but generally not as boisterous as they can be in the Aegean. The weather of the Sound may not be as dependable as that of the Virgin Islands, but its expanse means more places to go and more to see. It has fewer coves and creeks than Chesapeake Bay, but fortunately it doesn't have the Chesapeake's violent storms and jellyfish. Nor is it as rocky or as covered with evergreens as the Maine coast, but its water is warmer and its fog less frequent.

What some call a curse and others a blessing, the Sound is accessible to 8.5 million people; an estimated 20 million throng its beaches each summer. The U.S. Power Squadron believes the number of boats on the Sound is close to half a million, but the Coast Guard says at maximum about 100,000 boats are actually on the Sound at any one time. Even with all this activity, the Sound offers you a fascinating variety of courses and destinations that let you escape the hurly-burly of daily living and get back to those elements from which the human race originally came: the sun, the salt, the sea, and – for sailors – the wind.

Called an "inland sea" or a "Mediterranean," roughly 100 miles long from Throgs Neck, NY, to Watch Hill, RI, with an average width of 15 miles, the Sound is almost entirely enclosed by Long Island to the south and the Connecticut and New York mainland to the north.

Through The Race at the eastern end, twice a day, a tremendous tidal surge from the Atlantic Ocean partly drains and then refills the Sound's 1,300 square miles. Freshwater from the rivers – mainly the Connecticut, the Housatonic, and the Thames – dilutes the inward flow of saltwater.

The Sound's tidal spigot is The Race, between Fishers Island and Little Gull Island. Within this 4-mile area, with depths as great as 350 feet, the current reaches a maximum velocity of 4 knots (and reaches 6 knots at a full moon). Over 5 million gallons per second pour in and out.

Because of the Sound's size and shape, the rise and fall of the tide is amplified as it moves westward. At New London, the tidal range is only 3 feet, while at Throgs Neck it is over 9 feet. The salinity at The Race is about 30 parts salt per 1,000 parts water, but 4 parts less at the western end. Since saltwater has a greater density, the fresh water emptying from the rivers floats on top. Every second about 120,000 gallons of freshwater enter the Sound, with the Connecticut River accounting for 70 percent of it. The variation in water temperature is as great as that of any body of water in the world; it ranges from 32° F in winter to 71.6° F in summer.

A yachter's paradise though the Sound may be – a haven of blue water, gentle waves, white sails, and cool breezes – experienced mariners know that it can at times become one of the most formidable marine highways in the world. Those who have braved New York's boiling Hell Gate or fought against the ebb in Plum Gut in a contrary wind or navigated Watch Hill Passage in dense fog understand some of the hazards. So do the hardy souls in the dark pilothouses, who, year-round, tow barges and steer tankers laden with oil for the homes of landlubbers.

In some ways, storms on the Sound can be worse than those in the open Atlantic, especially when wind and tide oppose each other. Former Chief Warrant Officer George Bannan of the Coast Guard at Eatons Neck once explained why:

> When I was in the Navy, I used to think of the Sound as a millpond, but since I've been stationed here in the Coast Guard, I've come to respect it. It's one of the most treacherous and dangerous bodies of water around. In less than an hour, it can kick up from glassy calm to waves 6-1/2 feet high. And what waves! Out at sea, the harder it blows, the longer the swells get, so you can ride up and over them without trouble. But the Sound is shallow – no more than 50 to 75 feet deep in most places – and in a blow you get a short, high chop that's really vicious. It knocks a boat around, makes it tricky to steer and almost impossible to sail, and slops right over you and threatens to swamp you.

To assist commercial operators and recreational boaters, the U.S. Coast Guard maintains some 975 buoys and other aids to navigation on the Sound. Because of cutbacks in funding, the Coast Guard has been forced to discontinue a number of the smaller buoys that yachters were accustomed to seeing, making it imperative to use the most up-to-date charts, and, of course, the current edition of *Embassy's Complete Boating Guide to Long Island Sound.* Safe boating is fun boating, so BON VOYAGE!

You're far offshore, and your engine just quit.

Now isn't the time to wonder about your engine dealer's parts availability or service reputation.

You need to know just how serious his committment is to keeping your vessel performing as it should, right from the beginning —before the sale is made. With H.O. Penn and Caterpillar® Marine Engines, there's never a doubt.

H.O. Penn and all our affiliated Marine Engine Parts and Service dealers are located conveniently throughout the Long Island, Connecticut and Hudson Valley regions, so you're never far from the genuine, high quality Cat® parts

and service you need, whether it be an emergency or routine procedure. Plus, our personnel are highly skilled, trained professionals, familiar with your engine and meticulous in their work.

Even more important, perhaps, is that Cat engines are designed from the beginning for dependability, longevity, and ease of maintenance, the same reasons that make Cat engines as popular on offshore industrial vessels as with pleasure craft owners.

So, if you'd like to know more about Cat Marine engines, parts, or service, stop in at any H.O. Penn or MEPS dealer location. Ask about scheduling advance maintenance, or about our fleet of field service trucks, available to travel to wherever you need them.

We'll have the right answers.

How to Use
Embassy's Complete Boating Guide

Embassy's Complete Boating Guide to Long Island Sound has been specifically designed to make your cruising as safe, interesting, enjoyable, and hassle-free as possible. This book represents our continuing effort to bring you authoritative, comprehensive, and easy-to-use information about our area. We believe *Embassy's Complete Boating Guide to Long Island Sound* is the finest guide available at any price, anywhere in the world, and we hope you will, too. It includes:

A COMPLETE INTRODUCTION TO THE COAST: When you enter the harbors and bays of our coast you enter a complex, fascinating ecological system with a long human history. The more you understand and appreciate the many aspects of the area, the more you will enjoy it. For that reason, *Embassy's Boating Guide* is much more than a compilation of charts, facility listings, and instructions. Seven separate chapters by acknowledged experts give you an in-depth understanding of the coast's geology and history as well as the fishing, birding, and scuba diving in the area. You'll also find articles on boating safety and first aid and the latest information on the health of the marine environment and what is being done to improve it.

HARBOR CHAPTERS: A separate chapter is devoted to each of the 59 harbor areas in Long Island Sound. These Harbor Chapters are organized in a clockwise fashion, starting from Throgs Neck, NY; moving across the coast of Connecticut to Block Island, RI; then to Montauk and through the Peconic Bay area; and finally west along the North Shore of Long Island. The Harbor Chart Index on pages 8-9 shows the area covered by each Harbor Chapter and its location in *Embassy's Boating Guide*.

TIDE AND CURRENT INFORMATION: In the back of *Embassy's Boating Guide* is a reference section that contains the most detailed tide and current information available anywhere. This section will be invaluable in planning your trip and in understanding the changing marine conditions that affect it.

LORAN INDEX: Also in the reference section of *Embassy's Boating Guide* is an index containing more than 250 LORAN waypoints. Most of the major offshore buoys are included, as well as the most important approach buoys in each harbor. These waypoints, all collected on-site by the editors of *Embassy's Boating Guide,* can serve as a valuable complement to your other aids to navigation. In addition, the waypoints are cross-referenced in the text and on the chart in each Harbor Chapter.

We named our publication *Embassy's Complete Boating Guide* because we want it to contain – in one easy-to-use package–all the important information that a boater will need. No single person could ever have provided such detailed data about so vast and complex an area. To give you the information condensed in *Embassy's Boating Guide,* we gathered dozens of feet of files and drew upon the expertise of hundreds of individuals and organizations throughout the region. This book is a testament to their knowledge and to their willingness to share that knowledge with others. We thank them wholeheartedly.

We plan to publish new editions of *Embassy's Boating Guides* regularly, updating them with the latest NOAA charts, marine facility listings, and advice from our Harbor Guides, as well as new photos, artwork, and Harbor Highlights. We hope you will join our current contributors and help to make *Embassy's Boating Guide* even better with each new edition. Send us your ideas for interesting articles – or write an article yourself!

If you don't want to write a whole article, you can still tell us what you've found on your boating expeditions. Please let us know of any improvements we can make in our harbor directions or listings. It is especially critical that these sections of *Embassy's Boating Guide* contain the most recent information, and those who cruise an area frequently are in the best position to notice changes and report them quickly.

To reach us, call our office at 1-800-999-1075 or "Tell Us What You Think" with the postage-paid form we have provided at the end of this book.

We'd like for you to keep your eyes open for *Embassy's Boating Guides* now being developed for other cruising areas around the country. Our second New England guide–*Embassy's Complete Boating Guide to Rhode Island and Massachusetts*–has just been published, and covers the cruising areas from Block Island, RI, to Marblehead, MA, including all of Narragansett Bay, Cape Cod, the North Shore and Boston. We're also starting work on an *Embassy Boating Guide* to the Florida Coast. Our goal is to bring you the finest guides in the world, wherever in the world your boating takes you. Call us for more information or to become involved in our continuing adventures.

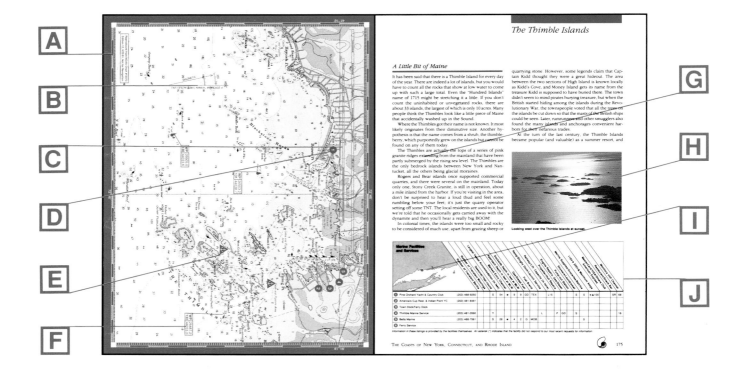

HARBOR CHARTS: Every Harbor Chapter in *Embassy's Complete Boating Guide* begins with a full-page, full-color section of the appropriate National Oceanic and Atmospheric Administration (NOAA) chart for the area. Information that we add to the chart is always printed in either blue (for Westchester County, Connecticut, and Rhode Island) or green (for Long Island). Our Harbor Charts are marked "Not for Navigation," as requested by NOAA of all private publishers. NOAA requests that this admonition be included on all charts that they themselves do not publish because they cannot control the reproduction and, hence, cannot guarantee its accuracy.

A Latitude and Longitude Border: Each Harbor Chart is surrounded by a latitude and longitude border, marked in degrees, minutes, and seconds for easy locating of landmarks and fixes.

B Compass Rose: Every Harbor Chart contains a segment of a compass rose showing the directions of true and magnetic north; the magnetic variation and annual increase.

C Distance Scale: All of our Harbor Charts are reproduced at exactly the same scale as the original NOAA charts. We never enlarge or reduce the charts, so you don't have to worry about nonstandard measures and can use your precalibrated navigational instruments.

D Marine Facility Locators: These show the location of virtually every marina, yacht club, boat yard, and dockside restaurant on Long Island Sound. The locators are cross-referenced to the Marine Facility Listings appearing on the opposite page.

E Anchorage Locators: These symbols show the location of good anchorages under normal conditions. Anchorages are detailed in the "Navigation and Anchorages" section of the text. Always take into account your boat, experience, and the weather before choosing an anchorage.

F LORAN Waypoints: We have collected more than 250 on-site LORAN waypoints in Long Island Sound. Each waypoint is numbered (e.g., **[WP-132]**) and located on the Harbor Charts. The waypoints are cross-referenced to the "Navigation and Anchorages" section of the text and listed at the back of the book in a special LORAN Index.

CAUTION: *Read the "Introduction to LORAN" at the back of this book before you use this information.*

HARBOR CHAPTERS: The Harbor Chapters in *Embassy's Complete Boating Guides* are designed for ease of use and maximum detail. Every chapter is organized in the same way so that you will know exactly how and where to find the information you need, no matter where you are.

Introduction: This section gives you some interesting historical and cultural background information on the harbor and the town, and a feel for what contributed to its development and unique character.

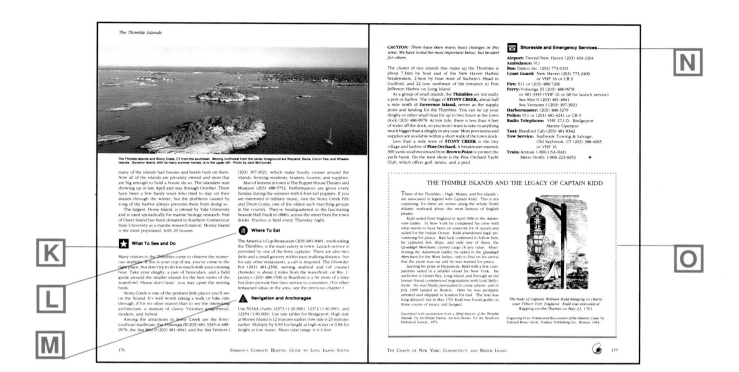

Color Photographs: "A picture is worth a thousand words," so we always give you at least one color aerial photograph of each harbor to show you what to expect and to point out local landmarks. The aerial photographs are always placed opposite the Harbor Chart or in the "Navigation and Anchorages" section of the text for easy cross-referencing.

Harbor Locators: To help you get a bearing on the location of the harbors, there is an outline map of the coast in the upper left hand corner of each Marine Facilties List. Chapter harbors are pinpointed here by a colored dot.

Marine Facility Listings: Here you'll find virtually every marina, yacht club, boat yard, and waterfront restaurant in the area, and the services and facilities they offer. Most of the categories are self-evident. However, it should be noted that facility operators sometimes report their approach and dockside depths optimistically.

What To See and Do: This section describes the most popular attractions and events in the area. Telephone numbers are always given, so you can get up-to-the-minute information about schedules, admission rates, and the like. We also alert you to some of the free attractions of the area such as beaches, wildlife preserves, parks, and good fishing holes.

Where To Eat: Culinary tastes and styles vary, so we try to give you lots of choices. We will mention most restaurants immediately accessible to the waterfront and get progressively more selective as you go farther afield, paying particular attention to restaurants that are recommended by our local Harbor Guides, as well as those that offer take-out, dockside delivery, or pick-up service for patrons.

Navigation and Anchorages: Read this section before you head for a new harbor. Here you will find lots of local knowledge about the tricks to dealing with the local tides, currents, or traffic; where the hidden rocks are and how to avoid them; and how to find the choice anchorages. Each section begins with a summary of the NOAA charts to use (in order of usefulness); the appropriate tide and current tables; and the distances by boat to the nearest harbors in each direction. The heart of the text is a detailed description of all the approaches and anchorages. All major landmarks, waypoints, and destinations are bold-faced for easy scanning. Also noted are the buoy changes and updates to charts as published in the Local Notice to Mariners as of our editorial closing date.

Shoreside and Emergency Services: Here are all the telephone numbers (and VHF channels) for important services ashore and afloat. Harbormasters often work part-time, so don't be surprised if you have difficulty getting through to them on summer weekends.

Harbor Highlights: We guarantee you'll have fun reading these short feature articles. We hope you'll begin reading the Harbor Highlight for the area you are visiting, and then read your way up the coast for a truly eclectic view of the people, ideas, and events that have shaped New England.

When your ship comes in, we have a perfectly beautiful place to put it.

About fifty feet from the terrace of your beautiful Caswell Cove condominium, in our equally beautiful marina.

With its own "Clubhouse".

And, all the very latest.

Like state of the art concrete floats and bubblers so you can keep your boat in the water year round.

In our own private, protected cove.

(People who know the Connecticut coast have been hiding from hurricanes here for over two hundred years.)

Caswell Cove.

The most romantic waterfront condominium in Connecticut.

The one "Sound" investment that's as rock-solid as the coast it's built on.

Very chic.

Very sleek.

Very zingy.

And, you won't need your dinghy.

Beautiful.

Call:1-800-727-COVE.

LITTLE HARBOR MARINE
at
TED HOOD MARINE COMPLEX
— A COMPLETE YACHT YARD —

- **100 Slips with Electrical, Water, Telephone Hook-Ups**
- **Ice, Laundry, and Shower Facilities on Site**
- **Inside and Outside Storage** • **30, 40, 160 Ton Travelift**
- **Workshops for Carpentry, Electrical, Mechanical, Custom Machine Work and Welding**
- **Extensive Paint Spray Capabilities**

ADDITIONAL SERVICES AVAILABLE at TED HOOD MARINE COMPLEX
LITTLE HARBOR CUSTOM YACHTS & LITTLE HARBOR YACHT SALES
BLACK WATCH CORP. (Sport Fisherman)
NEW ENGLAND BOAT WORKS — ATLANTIC TOWERS (Sportfishing Towers)
HOOD YACHT SYSTEMS — THE RIGGING COMPANY — ELECTRA YACHT
NEWPORT MARINE ELECTRIC — LIFERAFT & SURVIVAL EQUIPMENT, INC.
HOOD SAILMAKERS — S & S FABRICS (Canvas, Dodgers, & Cushions)

LITTLE HARBOR MARINE • PORTSMOUTH, R.I.
One Little Harbor Landing, Portsmith, R.I. 02871
TEL/FAX (401) 683-5700

The Geology of the Sound

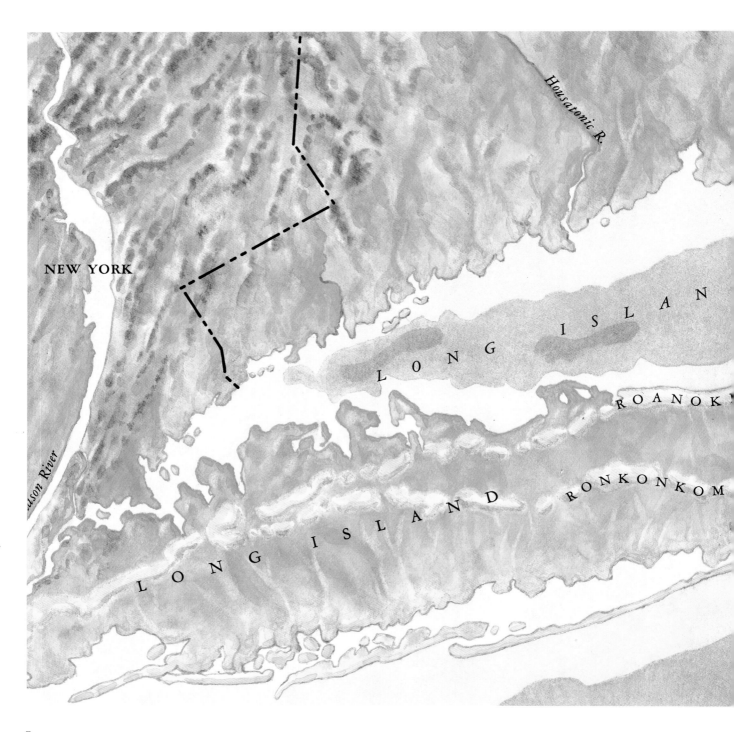

Long Island Sound is one of the most interesting geologic features of the eastern seaboard, but you'd never know it by just looking around today.

Ancient colliding continents and 1,000-foot-high glaciers are certainly not brought to mind as you savor a tranquil Long Island Sound harbor at dawn in summer. But as you read further, you'll come to appreciate the long chain of geologic events that culminated in the gentle vistas and snug harbors that presently characterize the Sound.

The story of Long Island Sound's development begins hundreds of millions of years ago, well before the North American Continent had taken its present shape. It begins

RALPH LEWIS
Marine Geologist
Connecticut Department of Environmental Protection

Illustrations by Dennis O'Brien

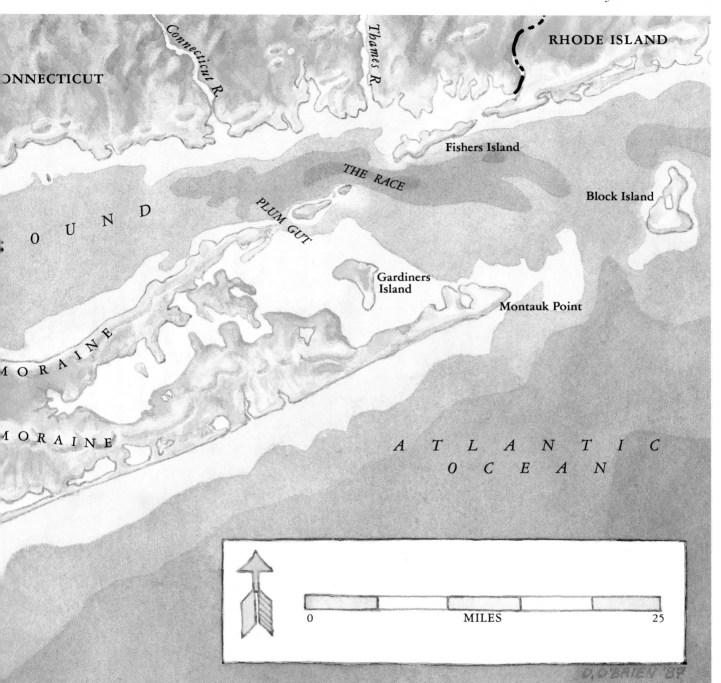

with the death of a very old ocean – an ocean that existed before the Atlantic, and with the formation of a supercontinent – one that no longer exists.

The length of time this story spans is important to keep in mind, because geologic histories are written in a context of time that is quite different from our everyday experience.

Geologists think in terms of millions or hundreds of millions of years. Their words and phrases are referenced against the 4.6 billion years (or so) that the Earth has been around.

For a geologist, terms like *continental collision* do not carry the immediacy of the Fishers Island Ferry splintering

*Eight Stages in the Geologic Evolution
of Long Island Sound*

200 Million Years BP

The eight cross-sectional diagrams shown here are schematic representations of important stages in the development of Long Island Sound. They are drawn from the perspective of a hot air balloonist who is looking westward while floating high over the middle of the Sound. The scale of these drawings is highly exaggerated and the topography has been generalized to show the major geologic components of the present Long Island Sound basin and their place in the overall story of its development. Bedrock is shown in brown and red. Coastal-plain sediments are shown in green. Tills and the moraines are shown in yellow and orange. The glacial lake deposits are shown in grey. Modern marine sediments are shown in purple. Glacial ice is white. Years cited are "Before the Present" (BP).

As Africa and America began to pull apart to form the Atlantic Ocean, the area that would eventually become Connecticut and Long Island was the tilted, bedrock surface of the Appalachian Mountains, which were being eroded by streams draining to the newly forming ocean.

the dock at Silver Eel Pond. In the context of geologic time, a continental collision refers to two land masses that inched toward one another over the course of tens of millions of years. In this same context Long Island Sound, as we know it, is a mere baby – only about 4,000 years old. But it does have a long and venerable lineage.

Earliest Beginnings In an Ancient Ocean

We can trace the Sound's earliest beginnings to a period from about 500 to 250 million years ago. During that time, the land masses that would ultimately become the African and North American continents were on a collision course. The ocean that separated them was slowly (several inches per year) growing smaller. This ocean pre-dated the Atlantic (named for the mythological Titan, Atlas), and is, therefore, called the Iapetos Ocean. (Iapetos was the father of Atlas). The closing of the Iapetos Ocean and the movements of the ancestral African and North American continents were part of a larger process that brought all of the major early land masses of the Earth together to form the supercontinent Pangaea (All-lands).

As the African and North American land masses came together, their colliding edges were crumpled, thrusting up the Appalachian Mountains. Pangaea survived as a super-continent for roughly 50 million years. But about 200 million years ago, a different set of forces started working on the joined land masses that made up Pangaea, and they began to move apart again. These movements initiated the development of Africa, North America and the Atlantic Ocean as we now know them. It was also at this time that the geologic foundation of Long Island Sound began to take shape.

Africa and North America split apart in a configuration that left the Appalachian Mountains as the western border of the emerging Atlantic Ocean basin. Stretching from Canada to Georgia, the Appalachian Mountain Belt at that time was much higher than it is now – a spectacular mountain range of towering snow-covered peaks, soaring as high as the Rockies of today. The constant attack of the elements over the last 200 million years has worn down these once majestic mountains so that only their core survives. Much of the sediment that was created during this long erosive process was carried eastward by streams to the edge of the expanding Atlantic Ocean. When the stream-carried sediment reached the ocean, it was deposited on top of the old, hard, crystalline rock that made up the eastern flank of the mountains.

(If you had taken a sail on the fledgling Atlantic Ocean every million years or so during this period, you would have noticed the changing horizons. The eroding but still majestic Appalachian mountains would have formed a beautiful western vista, and Africa would be fading away to the east. Changes in ocean spreading rates and various other factors would be contributing to many fluctuations in sea-level, radically altering the shoreline you followed on each visit.)

Stream Action on the Continental Shelf

Periods of lowered sea levels interrupted the buildup of sediment that was occurring along the expanding ocean's margins, but overall the sediment piles continued to build up and out (seaward). By about 3 million years ago, a seaward-thickening wedge of sediment buried most of the eastern flank of North America. Today we know the

Sediments eroded from the Appalachian Mountain chain built a huge seaward-thickening wedge of material on top of the old, bedrock surface forming the Atlantic coastal plain and continental shelf.

During the formation of the coastal plain and continental shelf, streams cut a drainage system into the surface of the coastal-plain.

landward, above-water portion of this wedge as the Atlantic Coastal Plain. Its thicker, submerged, offshore component forms the continental shelf.

For most of the nearly 200 million years that it took the continental shelf to develop, similar geologic conditions prevailed along the entire east coast of North America. With some local variations, the major force that worked to erode the coastal-plain sediment was stream action. If things had not changed dramatically as a result of the great glaciations of the last 3 million years, the story of Long Island Sound would be the geologic history of a river system, and Long Island itself would be part of the Connecticut coast.

The modern Delaware-Raritan River basin is a good example of what the Long Island Sound area would probably still look like if it had not been altered by glacial activity. A roughly northeast-southwest oriented main trunk valley, like the Delaware River Valley, would separate today's Connecticut from the coastal-plain to the south. The Long Island area would be situated seaward of the trunk stream in the same relative position that southern New Jersey (between Camden and Atlantic City) is to the Delaware River today. North-flowing drainage from what is now the north-shore area of Long Island, and south-flowing drainage from Connecticut would feed the main stream via tributary streams.

The present sharp contrast between Long Island Sound and the Delaware-Raritan drainage basin exemplifies the dramatic geologic changes that were brought about by the great ice advances of the last 3 million years. North of New York City the glaciers scraped away the thinner inland parts of the coastal-plain sedimentary wedge which once blanketed the entire east coast from Florida to Nova Scotia,

leaving exposed bedrock. Long Island Sound occupies the extensive lowland that lies where the old coastal-plain river system had been. The northern flank of this lowland (the Connecticut Coast) is primarily the crystalline rock of the Appalachian Mountains that has been re-exposed by ice action. The south flank of the lowland, the remaining coastal-plain sediments, is the foundation of Long Island.

The extent of the last ice sheet coincides with the most highly eroded segment of the coastal-plain wedge. The precise effect that each ice advance had on the crystalline rock and the coastal-plain wedge is not known. The exact number of ice advances is not really known either – there were at least two and probably more. What is clear, however, is that the combined erosive effect of the ice advances changed the landscape of the glaciated areas considerably. These changes involved wearing down and smoothing the crystalline rocks, cutting back and sculpting the coastal-plain wedge, and redistributing eroded material in the form of glacial deposits. As we will see, the net effect was that some areas were scooped out and other areas were built up.

Glaciers Build an Island

Initial glacial advances may have widened and somewhat deepened the pre-glacial river system that flowed through the Long Island Sound area. The last ice advance that began about 85,000 years ago (late Pleistocene time) probably moved perpendicularly across the east-west oriented Sound river system. The pre-existing lowland of the Sound and the higher ground of Long Island may have influenced how far south the ice advanced. Even the erosive power of the last glacier did not completely wipe out the basic fluvial (water

3 Million to 85,000 Years BP

85,000 to 19,000 Years BP

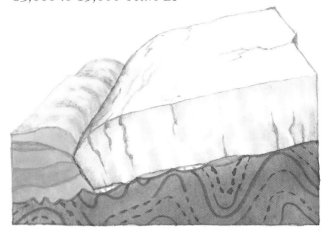

As the last great ice sheet advanced into the Long Island Sound area, it rode down the bedrock surface of Connecticut and into the Sound basin, eventually stopping its advance atop what remained of the coastal plain wedge. There it deposited the large end-moraines which now form most of the above-water portion of Long Island.

As more and more water was locked up in the glaciers, the sea level dropped further, exposing the coast plain and continental shelf. North of New York City glaciers worked to scrape away the thin inland parts of the coastal-plain wedge.

or river cut) aspect of the lowland. The eleven north-shore bays and harbors of Long Island from Little Neck to Mattituck Inlet are glacially modified tributary stream channels that once fed into the pre-glacial trunk river.

The crashings of continents and scrapings of glaciers laid the foundation for Long Island Sound, but the events of the last 19,000 years fleshed out its present configuration. The last glacial advance peaked about 20,000 years ago. At that time sea level was about 300 feet lower than it is now because ocean water was trapped in the ice sheet, and the ice margin had advanced to about the middle of Long Island. The glaciers deposited a pile of glacial debris there called *terminal moraines*. Some of this material was bulldozed, but most of it was carried in the ice and deposited as the ice front melted. The continental shelf was almost entirely above sea level, and that day's equivalent of an Atlantic coast beach like Fire Island was about 100 miles further south.

(You could not have sailed on Long Island Sound at this point because it was under more than one or two thousand feet of ice.)

By 19,000 years ago the ice could no longer maintain itself at its terminal position because it was melting faster than new ice was being pushed south. The ice front slowly

receded to the north. As the ice front retreated from its southernmost position, it stuttered and paused a few times. At each of these pauses (recessional positions) it left a pile of glacial debris known as a *recessional moraine*. The bulk of the above-water portions of Fishers Island, Plum Island, and northernmost Long Island are composed of this recessional moraine debris. From Plum Island westward, this glacial debris sits atop the glacially scoured erosional remnant of the coastal plain wedge and forms the high sandy bluffs of the North Shore of Long Island.

Because the glacier paused on the high portion of the coastal-plain remnant, it left a long, thin, high line of deposits called a recessional moraine which made an ideal dam. When the glacier resumed its northward recession, it began to back into the Long Island Sound basin that it had helped to create. This formed a low area between the ice front and the recessional moraine. The low area filled with melt water from the retreating ice and a glacial lake began to form.

The ice also stuttered as it retreated across the basin. It deposited a few small recessional moraines at Old Saybrook, Madison, and Branford near the Connecticut shore. These moraines may have offshore extensions in Long Island Sound: Kimberly Reef, Branford Reef, and Crooked S Shoal. The Captain and Norwalk Islands are also moraine segments. The familiar sandy bluffs of Falkners Island also have a glacial origin but they may be older than the most recent ice advance which left the other moraines.

By about 14,000 years ago the ice front had retreated out of southeastern Connecticut. The expanding glacial lake

19,000 to 11,000 Years BP

As the ice began to retreat northward the low area between the Long Island moraine dam and the retreating ice filled with glacial melt water, and a huge fresh water lake formed. Clay sediments were deposited in the lake, filling most of it.

11,000 to 10,000 Years BP

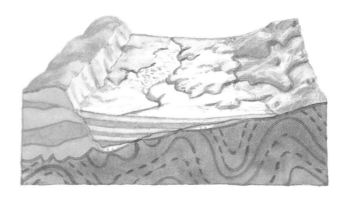

The retreating glaciers still held much of the world's water, so sea level was as much as 300 feet lower than it is now. By 11,000 years ago the lake had mostly drained away to the lower ocean, leaving a broad plain exposed to the air.

eventually filled the Long Island Sound basin, grew to about the same size as the present-day Sound, and began to fill in with clay sediments. At its maximum, this fresh water lake may have been connected with similar lakes in Block Island Sound and Buzzards Bay.

(Imagine a sail on Long Island Sound at this time! To the north, the horizon would have been covered by the dirty snow of the massive glaciers, several thousand feet high. Because the fresh-water lake was land-locked, there would have been no tides to worry about, but you would have needed to keep a sharp eye out for stray icebergs. And there would have been water, water everywhere – without a lick of salt in it! On shore, mastodons might have eyed you as you sailed by, just out of reach.)

The history of the glacial lake in Long Island Sound is not well understood. Up to 300 feet of glacial-lake clay deposits now partially fill the Long Island Sound basin, and it probably took several thousands of years for this sediment to accumulate. If the glacial-lake clay deposit had not partially filled the basin, Long Island Sound would now be much deeper than its present 64-foot average depth. Rather than a few very localized 300-foot maximum water depths that we see now, 600 to 700-foot water depths would be common.

Water Rises in the Recent Past

The lake is thought to have drained before sea-level had risen sufficiently to allow marine waters to flood the Sound. For a relatively short time the lake clays were exposed to the air, forming a broad plain which was cut by streams.

Ocean waters probably began to enter the Long Island Sound basin about 10,000-12,000 years ago. Sea-level rise associated with the glacial retreat was fairly rapid at first, so rapid, in fact, that tidal marshes did not have time to develop. By about 4,000 years ago, sea-level rise slowed and the tremendously fertile tidal marshes began to form.

In other areas of the world, we might expect the shoreline to have changed significantly over the last 4,000 years as the sea slowly rose. But as water bodies go, Long Island Sound has a fairly low-energy nearshore environment. This means that geologic agents such as wave action and near-shore currents have a hard time dominating the shoreline in a rising sea. It takes time and energy to build wide, extensive beaches, or large bars and spits. Because it is sheltered by Long Island, the Sound environment provides neither in great abundance. As a result, previous upland features such as glacially modified stream valleys and hills were not extensively changed as they were gradually submerged. Valleys became coves, harbors, and bays. Hills became headlands, promontories, or islands. Some beaches and spits did form but they did not really disrupt the overall shape of the submerged upland features that form the Sound shore of today.

If you sailed the Sound 4,000 years ago, only the major landmarks such as the Connecticut, Housatonic, and Thames Rivers or the high sandy bluffs of the North Shore of Long Island would be recognizable. The water level would be 20 feet lower than at present, so that hills and coves along the shore would look very different. The Thimble Islands would be a series of little hills with only their feet wet. Long

Sand Shoal between Westbrook and the Connecticut River might be known as "Long Sand Dune." Of course, there would be no man-made structures except Indian settlements along the shore – smoke rising from the lodges, piles of oyster shells glistening on the beach, men working the stone fishing weirs extending out into the water. Those fishing weirs are still there today – 20 feet under the surface of the Sound.

Continued sea-level rise, be it a natural occurrence, or man-induced by the "greenhouse effect" is a problem we will all have to live with. How much the sea will rise is an open and hotly debated question. In the natural scheme of things, beaches, tidal marshes, river mouths, and human settlements retreat before the rising sea. Modern man, with his sea-walls, jetties, and "permanent" structures has yet to learn the wisdom of such a strategic retreat.   ✦

4,000 Years BP to the Present

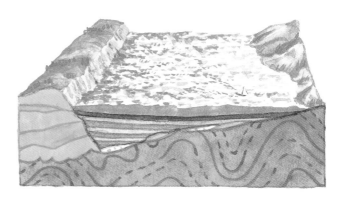

Further melting of the glacier caused sea-level to rise, and by about 10,000 years ago the sea was high enough to enter the Long Island Sound basin. Since then the sea has continued to rise, marine sediments have covered the lake clay and other glacial deposits, and Long Island Sound has taken its present form.

Guenster Rehabilitation Center, Inc.

When you need help coping in an imperfect world.

Alcohol and Drug Abuse Treatment Programs
Day & Evening

- *Confidential Assessment & Evaluation*
- *Individualized Treatment Planning*
- *Professional Family Intervention Service*
- *Certified/Degreed Counselors*

- *Family and "Significant Others" Program*
- *JCAHO Accredited*
- *Licensed by the State of Connecticut*
- *Treatment covered by most Major Health Insurance Plans*

(203) 384-9301

276 Union Avenue, Bridgeport, CT 06607

A Short History of Long Island Sound

ELLSWORTH S. GRANT
Former President,
Connecticut Historical Society

Archaeologists have determined that man first came to the coastal region of New England as early as 10,000 B.C., hard on the heels of the retreating glacier. By the time the European explorations began in the 16th and early 17th centuries, Indian life on the Sound was well established. Tribes belonging to the Algonquin family spent the summer months near the sea, fishing for herring and salmon and digging for shellfish in the bays. Often they ventured forth in birchbark canoes to set up fishing camps on offshore islands.

In 1524 Giovanni da Verrazano discovered New York harbor, Block Island, and Narragansett Bay. The Dutch sea captain, Adriaen Block, sailed along the Sound in 1614 in his 54-foot *Onrust*, discovering the Connecticut River, and sailing into Narragansett Bay, with the purpose of claiming the area for the Netherlands. Block Island, of course, is named for him. The same year Captain John Smith was hired to chart the coast of New England, and his subsequent book enthused over its beauty and the abundance of fish and timber.

Adriaen Block's 54-foot *Onrust* or *Restless*, from *Connecticut* by Albert E. Van Dusen.

The founding of the Dutch West India Company in 1621 soon led to trading posts being erected at New Amsterdam (now New York), Fort Orange (Albany) and as far east as the mouth of the Connecticut River where the Dutch carried on a brisk fur trade with the Indians. By 1630 there were 300 settlers living in New Amsterdam. Long Island Sound and the East River quickly became the best trading route between New England and Virginia. But the Dutch were no match for the influx of English settlers – who wanted land most of all – and in less than 40 years the Dutch had to abandon their hold on Connecticut and Long Island. The

final displacement came in March 1664 when the 30-year-old Duke of York sailed into New York harbor and, without firing a shot, forced the surrender of Governor Peter Stuyvesant. The Duke's royal grant included the present state of New York, the entire region between the Connecticut and Delaware rivers, Long Island, the Vineyard, and part of Maine.

The settlement of Saybrook in 1635 under auspices of the Warwick patentees, however, signified that Connecticut would develop as a separate colony. The 15 patentees commissioned John Winthrop, Jr. "the first governor of the river Connecticut," and he engaged an engineer, Lieutenant Lion Gardiner, to build a fort at its mouth. Though the local Indians gave a warm welcome to Gardiner's party – the fierce Pequots from the north – resented the arrival of the white men and kept Fort Saybrook in a constant state of siege. The beleaguered Puritans finally decided that they must wipe out their Pequot enemies or be exterminated themselves. In May of 1637 they attacked the Pequot stronghold near Mystic and killed more than 600 men, women, and children with a loss of only two Englishmen. In another battle in a swamp near modern Fairfield the remaining members of the tribe either surrendered or fled, and peace was restored to the Connecticut colony.

Eleven Generations on Gardiners Island

In 1639, Lion Gardiner, his four-year contract with the Puritan lords and gentlemen completed, purchased a lovely island from his good friend, the Montaukett Indians, as a permanent home for his family. Lying halfway between the jaws of the easterly end of Long Island – Orient and Montauk points – the island was known as Manchonake to the Indians, the place "where many have died." Some seven miles long, its 3,300 acres teemed with fowl and deer; it had plenty of fresh water, a lush meadowland and a virgin forest of white oak and wild grapevines. According to Gardiner tradition, the transaction was consummated for 10 coats of trading cloth, one large black dog, a gun and ammunition, and some rum – totalling about $20 in value, a little less than the Dutch allegedly paid for Manhattan.

For 11 generations the Gardiners have held the island, making them the oldest non-aboriginal landowners in America as well as the first American family to found a still-flourishing fortune based primarily on land. The year after Lion's death, with the departure of the Dutch, the English took over Long Island, and for the next century it remained a sparsely populated area in which a few hundred farmers struggled to wrest a living from the sandy soil.

36

EMBASSY'S COMPLETE BOATING GUIDE TO LONG ISLAND SOUND

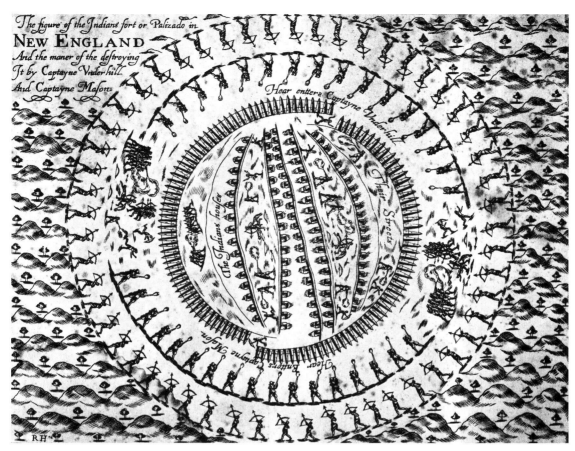

The raid on the Indian stronghold at Mystic in 1638. Drawing by Capt. John Underhill.

Battleground of the Revolution

During the Revolution the Sound was an indecisive battle-ground. Despite the enemy's control of New York and, until 1779, Newport, its attacks on seaports and its seizure of merchantmen, New England's maritime activity was never completely bottled up. Privateering was the most significant contribution to the fighting. Using New London as the main port, Connecticut provided over 200 armed merchantmen. New London's leading merchant, Nathaniel Shaw, alone accounted for 13 prizes in a two-year period. Altogether, nearly 500 British ships were captured, bringing back needed goods and greatly interfering with enemy operations along the Atlantic Coast.

When the British took possession of Long Island, hundreds of patriots fled across the Sound and sought temporary refuge along the Connecticut coast. Whaleboats from each side launched pesky raids that did little damage. There was also a profitable illicit trade. British goods, purchased in New York ostensibly for Tories, were taken to Long Island, smuggled across to Connecticut and traded for fresh provisions. Owners of Long Island stores sometimes connived to be "robbed" of goods which mysteriously reappeared in Connecticut. Lloyds Neck and Port Jefferson became notorious as bases for these illegal transactions.

Aside from Long Island itself, the British were able to occupy only Gardiners Island. In August 1775, 13 warships, led by *H.M.S. Rose* , anchored off the northeast shore and landed 200 redcoats. They found the island deserted but collected livestock, cheese, and hay. (A replica of the *H.M.S. Rose* is berthed at Bridgeport.) Five years later another British fleet, assigned to keep close watch on the French navy in Newport, hove into sight. The rest of that year and the following winter soldiers were stationed on the island, including several hundred sick and wounded.

As punishment for being the center of privateering, the English attacked New London in September 1781, in their most brutal and bloody foray against Connecticut. With the turncoat General Benedict Arnold (a native of Norwich) in command, the warships sailed boldly into the harbor, destroyed a great deal of shipping and recently seized goods, set the town ablaze, and landed 800 redcoats to capture Fort Griswold. After Colonel William Ledyard's surrender, the British, infuriated by the Americans' spirited defense, cut Ledyard down with his own sword and butchered 80 of his militiamen.

Ships Bound for the West Indies and China

As the "provision state" for the Continental forces, Connecticut paid a heavy price for the final victory that came in 1783. Its maritime trade was moribund, its ships and wharves badly in need of repair. But soon the state began to recover its reputation for being "a cask of good liquor, tapped at both ends, at one of which Boston draws, and New York at the other." For over a century the region's prosperous farms had been tied to the outside world by literally thousands of sloops, schooners, and brigs that plied the coast as far south as the West Indies and as far west as China. New Haven, New London and Stonington offered deep-water harbors. River ports like Derby, Middletown, and Norwich were marketplaces for the surrounding countryside. In 1784, when New Haven became a city (along with Hartford, Middletown, and Norwich), 30 vessels were berthed there, and weekly packets ran to New York and New London. To the east, the sandbar and lack of anchorage at the mouth of the Connecticut River prevented Saybrook from becoming a major port, the ocean-going brigs and schooners having to sail upstream to Essex, Middletown, and Hartford. Amazingly, in 1807 Middletown's customs house had the largest registered tonnage of all ports between New York and Cape Cod. Eastern Connecticut used Norwich and New London harbors to export its surplus produce and livestock, while Stonington and Westerly vied for domination of the communities along Fishers Island Sound.

Within a few years after colonization, shipbuilding developed into Connecticut's first real industry. Numerous small shipyards dotted the Connecticut River from Saybrook to Windsor. The first Continental warship, the 300-ton *Oliver Cromwell,* was built by Uriah Hayden in Essex in 1776; at the onset of the Civil War the Goodspeed yard in East Haddam turned out the gunboat *U.S. Kanaawha* in 90 days. Thomas Child's yards in Middle Haddam laid down 237 vessels, including the first Connecticut ships for the China trade and many of the first New York-to-London packets. During the 19th century it has been estimated that these yards produced over 4,000 ships. Equally important were the river-bred shipmasters. According to the historian

The American warship *Oliver Cromwell* (on right) in combat with the British warship *Beaver* in 1777.

Painting by Irwin J. Bevan, courtesy of the Mariners' Museum, Newport News, VA

Thomas Stevens, "these river towns contributed no less than a thousand captains – many of whom were of world renown whose exploits and records remain unsurpassed." Mystic and Stonington were also active shipbuilding centers. The former was noted for its clipper ships; in 1860, the *Andrew Jackson* set a record of 89 days and 4 hours from New York to San Francisco, breaking by nine hours the record made by the *Flying Cloud* in 1851.

Home of Whaling

Whaling made New London Connecticut's busiest and most colorful port. During the first half of the 19th century more ships were engaged in this rugged enterprise than in any other place except New Bedford, which in turn had displaced Nantucket, the mother-home of whaling. Other whaling ports in the Sound were Sag Harbor on Long Island, Mystic, and Stonington. The first whaler to clear from New London was the *Commerce* in 1794, and four years later she returned with a full cargo of oil. But whaling did not take off until after the War of 1812. When the industry reached its prime in the 1840's, New London was home to 70 of the tall ships, representing an investment of more than $2 million. Three thousand seamen were employed. During a 35-year stretch, the best known firm, Williams and Haven, sent out over 200 vessels fishing for whales, seals, and sea elephants from the Pacific to Greenland. In one year after the California gold rush, 26 ships brought in 67,500 barrels of whale oil and 2,900 barrels of sperm oil. During the Civil War whaling ceased almost entirely, and the discovery of petroleum in Pennsylvania in 1859 soon doomed the entire industry.

Blockaded in the War of 1812

Once again, during the War of 1812 enemy vessels blockaded Long Island Sound, destroying local shipping and frightening shoreline residents. None other than Sir Thomas Hardy of Trafalgar fame commanded seven ships of the line that anchored in Gardiner's Bay. In a rare display of military manners, Hardy purchased oxen from the proprietor, John Lyon Gardiner.

To discourage privateering, the English attacked the commercial fleet in the Connecticut River. On the evening of April 7, 1814, four sloops anchored off Saybrook bar and lowered into the water six boats carrying 136 sailors and marines. Piloted by an American turncoat, they proceeded quietly up the river to Essex. The marines searched the town for arms, burned a sail loft and then set fire to 27 ships at anchor or under construction. In August Hardy's fleet bombarded Stonington. The attack was a total fiasco.

Since that time, guns have been fired in anger on Long Island Sound only during the days of Prohibition. Fear of a Spanish invasion into the Sound during the Spanish-American War resulted in an attempt to fortify the north end of Gardiner's Island. The remains of this fortification were used for Navy bombing practice during the early days of World War II.

The British Raid on Essex, Connecticut in 1814

Painting by Kipp Soldwedell, courtesy of the Connecticut River Foundation, Essex, CT

The Steamboat Era

The coming of steampower ushered in a new era of transportation on the Sound that enjoyed a virtual monopoly for 20 years until the railroads were built. It all started in the spring of 1815 when the steamer *Fulton,* captained by the intrepid Elihu Bunker, left New York to make the 75-mile voyage to New Haven. Eleven hours later the wood-burning craft reached its destination, and two months later she astounded the populace by churning up the Connecticut River to Hartford. The next year, in the newly-launched *Connecticut,* Bunker successfully steamed through Hell Gate against the full force of the tide.

By 1817 there was regular steamboat service to New Haven and New London. After another captain dared to round Point Judith, where Block Island Sound and Narragansett Bay crash together, Providence, RI, temporarily became the chief terminus because of the short distance left to reach Boston by stagecoach. Norwich and Stonington were soon added as connections to Boston by railroad. In 1847 the Fall River Line began its famous 90-year career. Its reputation for regularity, safety, and luxury was unsurpassed.

Following the *Fulton's* debut, steamboats were soon running thrice weekly on the Connecticut River between Hartford and New York. The *Oliver Ellsworth,* in 1824, was the first of a long line of "floating palaces," 112 feet long and able to carry 400 passengers. Travel on the early side-wheelers, with their crude cross-head engines and undependable copper boilers, was at best a hazardous undertaking. Three years later, four miles off Saybrook, the *Oliver Ellsworth's* boiler exploded. She managed to sail to the dock, whence an excited post rider galloped to Hartford, burst in upon the legislature sitting in the statehouse, and shouted: "The Eliver Ollsworth...biled her buster!" Not long after the *New England* blew up at Essex, killing or maiming 15 out of 70 people. Before the Civil War, steamers were a link in the underground railway for runaway slaves. Afterwards they brought the carriage trade of New York to the summer resorts that sprang up across the coasts. The steamboat by then was fighting a losing battle against the railroad and the *Hartford* made its last trip in 1931, the end of the most romantic and elegant way of travel for business or pleasure.

From 1865 until the introduction of the internal combustion engine in the early 1900's the Sound also saw the development of specialized small sailing craft for the inshore fisheries. Today, the only active shipbuilders on the Sound is the Electric Boat Company, which has been located in Groton since 1924. Since the 1954 launching of the *Nautilus,* the first nuclear-powered submarine, Electric Boat has delivered to the U.S. Navy over 70 submarines.

During the steamboat era, many old skippers regarded the Sound as "one of the toughest runs in the world," because of the reefs and shoals, the many changes of course, the lack of searoom, the fog and ice, and the heavy commercial traffic. Nevertheless, they handled their giant passenger liners on rigid schedules with great skill, despite the lack of radar and LORAN. As an indication of the magnitude of sea traffic they contended with, in 1914 nearly 130,000 vessels were recorded as arriving or departing Hell Gate, carrying cargoes valued at $126 million and carrying 1.2 million passengers. Between 1831 and 1935 only seven marine disasters occurred in the Sound. One, claiming at least 30 lives, was the collision in dense fog in June of 1880 of the *Narragansett* and the *Stonington* near the Cornfield Point Lightship. The *Narragansett* sank but was later raised and rebuilt. The most recent collision also took place in very thick fog in July 1987 between two New London to Orient Point ferries as they tried to pass one another in Plum Gut; 18 persons were injured in the smaller vessel.

The rocky shore around Fishers Island has taken its toll in shipping. One of the worst wrecks on the Sound involved the steamer *Atlantic* in 1846, the pride of the Norwich and Worcester Railroad, which in her maiden year made a record run of six hours from Norwich to New York. Soon after leaving Stonington in a November gale, her steam chest was torn apart by heavy seas. Disabled, she tried to anchor, but the anchor failed to hold and the 320-foot vessel broke up on North Dumpling, drowning 45

passengers. As a result, the government bought the tiny island from a descendent of John Winthrop, Jr., the original proprietor of Fishers, and built a lighthouse. Recently, North Dumpling was turned into a private home.

Lighthouses for the World's Shipping

The appearance of lighthouses along the New England Coast in the 18th century represented the earliest efforts to reduce the dangers of seafaring. After the Revolution the new federal government was especially concerned with the approaches to New York and chose to locate its first lighthouse at Montauk Point in 1797. Both Presidents Washington and Jefferson took a personal interest in the light, an 80-foot-high structure atop a cliff that rises some 60 feet above the rocks. Until the 1860's it burned sperm whale oil. At that same time the government also assumed responsibility for placing buoys to mark navigational hazards.

Montauk, however, was not the first such beacon on Long Island Sound. New Londoners put up a stone tower at the western entrance to the Thames River in 1760. The money to build it was raised by selling lottery tickets, as the practical Puritans so often did in order to fund civic improvement. (Two decades later the "Saybrooke Bar Lottery" was held to remove the sand bar at the mouth of the Connecticut River, dredge a channel, and lay out buoys.) Other early lights still in service are: Little Gull (1806), Plum Island (1827) and Block Island Southeast (1875). From 1855 to 1894 there was also a light on the north end of Gardiners Island.

In 1939 the functions of the old independent Lighthouse Service were taken over by the Coast Guard, and today all

The Steamer *Hartford*

Photo courtesy of the Connecticut River Foundation, Essex, CT

of the beacons have been automated. Last to be de-manned was the 78-year-old New London Ledge in May of 1987. The lantern's classical 1890 Fresnel lens is now on display in the New London Customs House. The only thing the departing keepers will miss, so they reported, is the Ledge's notorious ghost, Ernie, who annoyed the occupants for decades by stealing tools, moving furniture, and passing them on the stairs in a cold, clammy rush of air.

In the past 50 years, the Sound has been hit five times by hurricanes. The most destructive was the one that swept in without warning on the afternoon of September 21, 1938, the first since 1815. It struck at full moon when the tide was highest. Pulverizing Long Island and cutting a swath across Connecticut, it killed nearly 700 people, injured as many more, and destroyed $400 million of automobiles, boats, and homes. The eastern end of the Sound was hardest hit: fires raged out of control in New London for seven hours, and ships torn from their moorings wrecked its wharves; 300 lost their lives in Rhode Island, as 121 mile-per-hour winds screamed up Narragansett Bay: Stonington's fishing fleet was wiped out; and a hundred yachts were sunk in Essex. The most recent hurricane, "Gloria," came through in 1985.

The Future

After a history of nearly four centuries of settlement and exploitation, today there is a good deal of environmental concern about the state of the Sound. Some pessimists claim that western Long Island Sound is "dead, dying, and devoid of life." Though an exaggeration, there are serious problems to be solved if the Sound's ecology is to be preserved and improved. The major concerns are sewage treatment plants, loss of marshland habitats, and areas with low dissolved oxygen levels. To which might be added the decline in certain species of fish, beach erosion, the overcrowding of harbors and marinas, and excessive noise from super speedboats. Obviously, all of these problems threaten the quality of life for both shoreline residents and yachtsmen.

Despite increasing concern about the environment in the last quarter century, the Sound has suffered from a lack of concerted, long-term research and monitoring programs. In 1985 Congress funded the five-year Long Island Sound Study administered by the Federal Environmental Protection Agency. For the first time, New York and Connecticut are working together toward the common goal of a comprehensive plan for managing the Sound and its resources, preserving its history for the future. ✦

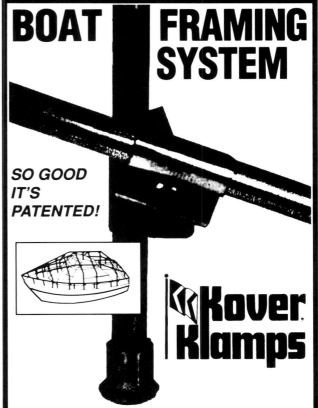

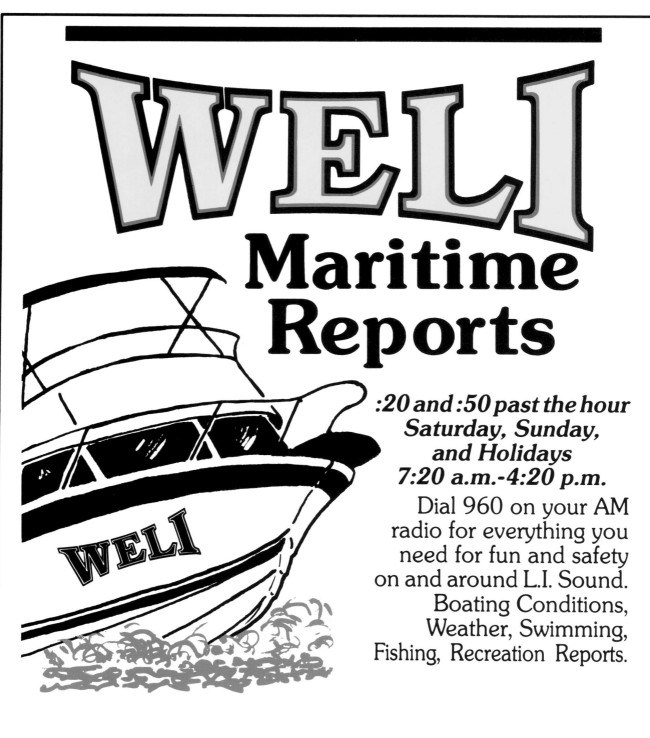

WELI

Maritime Reports

:20 and :50 past the hour
Saturday, Sunday,
and Holidays
7:20 a.m.-4:20 p.m.

Dial 960 on your AM radio for everything you need for fun and safety on and around L.I. Sound. Boating Conditions, Weather, Swimming, Fishing, Recreation Reports.

COUNT ON US! **WELI** 960 AM RADIO

First Step in Saving the Sound: The Long Island Sound Study

CHESTER L. ARNOLD, JR.
Connecticut Sea Grant

Long Island Sound has been much in the news these days – more often than not for alarming reasons. Medical waste is found floating in the water. Beaches are closed due to pollution. Lobsters are found dead in the pots. Is the Sound itself dying, as some have suggested? What can be done to combat the environmental problems that plague us?

The Long Island Sound Study is a major governmental and private effort to address these questions. It is a large bi-state research effort aimed at defining, understanding, and managing the environmental ills of Long Island Sound. The Study is federally funded as part of the National Estuary Program, created in 1984 by Congress in recognition of the increasing threat of pollution to the health of our invaluable marine resources.

In previous scientific efforts, the end product of the research was often just a collection of data, with little or no practical connection to the problems at hand. The end product of the LISS, however, will be a management plan for the Sound that will be implemented and enforced long after the Study itself is over.

When the Study began in 1985, the first task of the Study's Management Committee was to answer the simple question: What should we be studying? Unfortunately, this simple question had no simple answers. Although the $1 million a year Study budget may seem like a lot of money, it was clear that not all of the problems facing Long Island Sound could be studied. After long discussions with scientific and environmental experts, LISS decided to concentrate on the problems of toxic contamination and low oxygen conditions (hypoxia) in the water. These two areas include many of the major concerns of Long Island Sound users, such as fish and shellfish resources for commercial and recreational fishing, water quality for boating and swimming, and public health issues.

Where Does the Pollution Come From?

The first year's efforts in 1985-1986 concentrated mainly on collecting and evaluating the historical data base. As a first step to the study of contaminants, the National Oceanic and Atmospheric Administration (NOAA) compiled an inventory of pollutant inputs to Long Island Sound. Some of the results were surprising. For instance, the inventory found that, overall, industrial waste discharges into the Sound are relatively small. This is probably due to the closing of a number of polluting industries, such as metal finishing plants, and to the effects of treatment facilities mandated by the Clean Water Act of 1972. It is important to note, however, that while Sound-wide inputs are relatively low, local water quality can still be greatly affected by industrial waste.

Surprisingly, the largest source of pollutants to the Sound was found to be river drainage. This is a direct result of the huge volume of water discharging from the Connecticut and Thames rivers, which together account for about 80 percent of the freshwater entering the Sound. Although the contaminant levels are relatively low in these rivers (the Connecticut is perhaps the cleanest major river in the Northeast), the sheer volume of water discharged over the course of a year results in a high cumulative pollutant input. At this time, it is still unclear what effect these inputs have on the overall health of the Sound.

Perhaps the most eye-catching part of the NOAA inventory details the input of sewage treatment plants (STP's), which were found to be the second-largest source of pollutants to the Sound. There are 86 STP's operating in the area surrounding the Sound, with 44 discharging directly into its water. The average input from these plants, most of which is concentrated in the western Sound, is about 1 billion gallons every day! All of this sewage is treated to varying degrees, but many pollutants remain in the discharge. The environmental consequences of these discharges were strongly underscored by the surprising research results of the summer of 1987.

What Causes Water Without Oxygen?

Just as we need oxygen in the air we breathe, many marine organisms need oxygen in their water. Biologists generally consider dissolved oxygen concentration of 3 parts per million to be the minimum needed for sustained health of marine organisms. When dissolved oxygen falls below this level, hypoxia exists. During hypoxic episodes, stressed marine organisms may become ill, die, or move to more oxygen-rich waters.

Hypoxia can occur naturally during the summer in the deeper areas of coastal water bodies like Long Island Sound. During warm, stable weather, the surface waters heat up and form a distinct layer "floating" over the bottom waters, which are more dense due to their greater salinity and cooler temperature. The result is the formation of a sharp density gradient called a *pycnocline* (pick-no-kline), which prevents mixing between the two layers. Oxygen added to the surface waters by wave mixing and photosynthesis of marine plants is thus prevented from mixing into the depths, where it is needed to replace oxygen consumed by marine life and the decomposition of organic material on the bottom. Hypoxia is the result.

In the fall, cooling water temperatures and strong winds combine to dissipate the pycnocline and restore oxygen exchange throughout the water column. Although scientists have known about hypoxic episodes for many years, it is difficult to distinguish a "natural" episode from one that is significantly exacerbated by human activities. However, during the summer of 1987, Long Island Sound Study researchers found depletion of oxygen levels in the western Sound so severe that there is cause for deep concern.

In late July and August of 1987, LISS researchers, led by Dr. Barbara Welsh of the University of Connecticut's Marine Sciences Institute, found extremely low oxygen levels in the western Sound from the Throgs Neck Bridge to Greenwich, CT. At the mouth of Hempstead Harbor on the north shore of Long Island, there was literally *no* oxygen

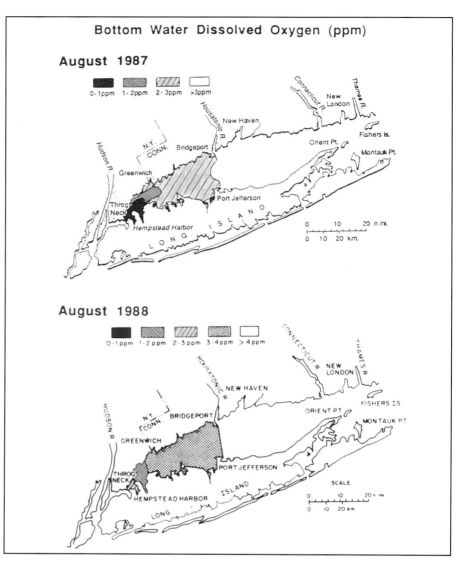

Comparison of the levels of hypoxia in August 1987 and August 1988.

in the bottom waters, and almost none at the surface. The results of fish sampling in this area graphically illustrate the impact of such severe hypoxia. Not one fish was found in any of the sample trawls, and 80 percent of the bottom-dwelling invertebrates (such as starfish and crabs) were dead!

During the same time period, there were reports by lobstermen in the area that dead lobsters had been brought up in their pots. Unlike the fish, the trapped lobsters had been unable to escape the low oxygen area and had suffocated. The hypoxia lasted well into August, eventually extending as far east as Bridgeport. Healthy dissolved oxygen levels in the area were not restored until mid-September. During the summer of 1988, hypoxia returned to the western Sound, although conditions were less severe than in 1987.

LISS scientists believe that the evidence points to nutrient input from storm water runoff and sewage treatment

plants as a major factor in hypoxia. The hypoxia of 1987 coincided with an intense "bloom" of tiny algae called *phytoplankton,* which, despite their small size, were so numerous that they turned the surface waters in the area into a reddish-brown soup – "red" or "brown" tide. Such a growth explosion can occur naturally, but as the algae use up the nutrients in the water, the growth slows down and the bloom soon collapses. However, in the western Sound it appears that the large nutrient input from sewage treatment plants and urban runoff fueled the algal blooms for a much longer period of time. As millions of the algae died each day during the bloom, they sank to the bottom and decomposed, using up all the oxygen. In this way, the prolonged algal bloom may have greatly increased the extent and severity of the natural summer hypoxia.

Historical data is too sketchy to be able to state with certainty that summer hypoxia in Long Island Sound is getting worse, although there appears to be no past record of such an extensive area experiencing low oxygen levels. It may be that a number of natural factors combined to make 1987 an unusual year. However, if the hypoxia continues in its severity in future years, for whatever reason, adverse impacts on the fisheries and shellfisheries of the Sound can be expected.

What Is the Current State of the Sound?

Just what is the state of the Sound? Is it getting better or worse? Long Island Sound Study participants are just beginning to form an answer to that complex question.

On the one hand, there is no doubt that there have been improvements in some areas since 1972 when the Clean Water Act first mandated the treatment of industrial and municipal wastewater. Levels of some toxic substances, particularly heavy metals, appear to have dropped in many species of shellfish and fish. Other contaminants such as PCB's appear to be more persistent in the environment and are still present in relatively high levels in some species. It is also true that because we are now studying Long Island Sound in unprecedented detail, we may be discovering long-standing conditions that had gone undetected in the past.

However, there is a growing feeling that the environmental impacts of the tremendous population boom in the area around the Sound have begun to outstrip many of the gains made in the 1970's. With over 5 million people living within 15 miles of its shores and a population of about 15 million living in its watershed, the Sound is perhaps the most urbanized major estuary in the country.

The stresses on the Sound received a great deal of attention during the summer of 1988 because of extensive media reports on medical waste and closed beaches. Despite this publicity, there is no evidence that there was more pollution in 1988 than usual, or that it was coming from "midnight dumpers," or that it was unusually dangerous. Conditions simply made it more evident. A series of spring storms flushed out the combined sewage systems that are typical in the cities along the shore, washing street debris into the Sound, and the winds were in the right direction to drive this debris onto the beaches. It was an unsightly mess of coffee cups and burger boxes, and mixed in was some medical waste – largely because the accepted disposal practice for such things as diabetic syringes is to flush them down the toilet.

There was virtually no chance of becoming infected from this medical waste, since very little of it was infectious to begin with, and infectious organisms cannot last long in the rigors of a marine environment. The beach closings – due to sewage overflows – were indeed indicative of a health hazard, but these too were much more isolated than the publicity suggested.

The medical waste and sewage pollution of 1988 may not have been unusual, but they did serve to remind the public that the Sound cannot absorb unlimited pollution. Ironically, the very resource that has drawn people to live and work along its shores is now clearly facing major threats from urban and industrial runoff, wastewater effluent, and the wetlands destruction that have historically accompanied such concentrations of population.

Why Is Action Needed?

Estuaries like the Sound pose a major dilemma: How can we continue to utilize their varied and unique marine resources without threatening the natural system that sustains them?

Scientific study is the first step toward finding an answer. Contrary to the belief of some, Long Island Sound has not been "studied to death." Rather, the Long Island Sound Study is just beginning to provide information that may lead to the solution of some of these problems. The Long Island Sound Study Management Plan is to be finished in the early 1990's. Although it is too early to be able to predict the contents of the plan, it is a sure bet that whatever the eventual recommendations, the management of the Sound will be a herculean effort, requiring large amounts of cooperation, foresight, and – you guessed it! – money. Upgrading sewage treatment plants alone could cost billions of dollars. However, the alternative is the degradation and eventual loss of Long Island Sound – our irreplaceable biological, commercial, recreational, historic, and aesthetic resource.

An economic evaluation of the resources of the Sound is difficult, but consider these conservative estimates for various uses of the Sound: 10,000 commercial fishermen, 200,000 recreational boaters, 300,000 sport fishermen, millions of beach goers and tourists. Linked with the human uses is the key biological role of the Sound as an enormously productive ecosystem supporting a wide spectrum of marine and terrestrial wildlife. About 70 percent of major commercial fish species on the East Coast rely on estuaries as their spawning and nursery grounds, and millions of birds either make their home in the surrounding salt marshes, or use the area as breeding grounds or fly over during migration. Lastly, no dollar figure can do justice to the value of the Sound as an integral and aesthetic part of our historical and cultural heritage - although it is a certainty that sky-high waterfront property values will plummet if the Sound becomes an aesthetic detriment rather than an asset.

What Can Be Done?

It is safe to say that the cost of cleaning up Long Island Sound is dwarfed by the cost of allowing the environmental degradation to continue. A comprehensive bi-state cleanup effort will be an ambitious social and political undertaking that must be fueled by the support of the populace. Obviously, there is a great need for awareness of the future of Long Island Sound. Public involvement, the third and last step of the study, is the critical link between scientific knowledge and political and social action. The public education campaign of the Long Island Sound Study, currently supervised by the Sea Grant Programs of Connecticut and New York, is working to increase the public's awareness and understanding of the pollution threat to Long Island Sound.

On the most basic level, homeowners within the drainage basin of the Sound must realize that the ultimate destination of most of their wastes is the Sound and, must accordingly adjust some of their behavior . For example, polluting substances such as waste motor oil and various household cleaners, adhesives, paints, and pesticides should be disposed of properly. On the local level, various municipal commissions and environmental groups are often excellent ways to have a hand in decisions affecting the Sound. In the political arena there has been a surge of interest in the Sound at all levels of government. Both state and federal legislative caucuses have been formed to address the problem of the degradation of the Sound and to respond to citizen concerns. In the end, the hard choices that determine the future of Long Island Sound will be dictated by the will of the people surrounding its shores.

For more information on the Citizen's Advisory Committee or on the public education campaign of the LISS, contact:

Connecticut Sea Grant Marine Advisory Program,
UCONN at Avery Point,
Groton, CT 06340
(203) 445-8664

or the

New York Sea Grant Extension Program,
Dutchess Hall
SUNY
Stony Brook, NY 11794
(516) 632-8737.   ◆

SAVE THE SOUND: AN EDITORIAL

The Sound faces a crisis.

That's common knowledge to every fisherman, yachtsman, beach stroller, and ecologist from New York to Boston.

What we all fear, quite simply, is that there may nothing left of the Sound for our children to enjoy in the future.

Within the next few years a combination of pollutants could cause the Sound to "crash," leaving a dead sea that cannot support oysters, fish, birds, or the millions of humans who seek refreshment and renewal on its beaches and in its waters.

Fortunately, scientists are now conducting a detailed, action-oriented study about the ecological crisis facing the Sound. We encourage you to read about this effort in Chet Arnold's "The Long Island Sound Study." It summarizes what has been learned about the health of the Sound, and what can be done to cure its ills. You will see that while the evidence is not all gloomy, the Sound needs our immediate help.

All of us are part of the Sound's problems. We are drawn to it in staggering numbers: 500,000 boats on its waters, 8 to 15 million people on its shores. We insist on developing the beautiful anchorages along the waterfront – the very marshes that are the most critical and fragile part of the Sound's ecology.

We love the Sound, and in our love, we abuse it. We are stressing it to its limits.

But we are also – each one of us – part of the solution to the crisis the Sound faces. It is true that coordinated governmental action and funding will be essential to preserve the Sound for future generations. And yet, it is a mistake to assume that government will take care of the problem for us. Each of us must make a conscious effort – first to slow the assault on the Sound, and then help to nurse it back to life.

We hope that through Embassy's Boating Guide you will become more aware of both the richness of the Sound, and of its ecological fragility. We encourage you to put that awareness into action – to join a recreational, environmental, or business organization working to protect this tremendous natural resource in our back yard.

In the future, perhaps your children will still be able to cruise the Sound's sparkling waters. Perhaps they will still be able to point out the fish swimming below and the birds flying above. And perhaps they will be able to tell your grandchildren the story of how the Sound almost died, and how you helped save it.

Mark C. Borton
Publisher
Embassy's Complete Boating Guide to Long Island Sound

Birding Ashore and Afloat

NOBLE S. PROCTOR, PH.D.

The waters of Long Island Sound have always held a wealth of birdlife, the dynamics of which are ever changing. Some species have disappeared, others have colonized, still others occur only on rare occasions or after severe storms. For the boater there is usually something to see at all times of the year and in all habitats.

A pair of binoculars, a good field guide, and a little patience will add greatly to your boating pleasure as you become more aware of your surroundings and the rich variety of birdlife that frequents Long Island Sound. One word about binoculars: remember that the higher the power the more difficult to hold them steady with the movement of the boat. As an upper limit, 10 power seems to be the cut off point and the standard 7 x 35 remains the favorite binocular for birders. There are a multitude of bird identification guides on the market but for the beginning birder, Roger Tory Peterson's *Field Guide to the Birds of Eastern North America* can't be beat. Identification features are pointed out for each species, allowing a quick identification. Because of the limited space available in this book, we have provided page references to Peterson's Field Guide after each species we mention.

Habitat

Birding can begin as soon as you arrive at the dock. There are many species that frequent the shelter of the dock areas taking advantage of the food either offered or created by man's presence. Ducks, gulls, and terns are groups that work this area to best advantage. Gulls in particular can become quickly habituated to feeding. This can cause problems for the boat owners on whose boat the gulls choose to roost. It is best not to feed birds in situations where they will cause a nuisance. Indeed, feeding birds adds little to their overall diet. Most birds are opportunistic; taking whatever is available. But if we were not there, they would survive as well.

As you head out of the harbor, the shoreline will often yield a rich variety of shorebirds and ducks that prefer embayments. These populations vary greatly depending on the time of the year. Migration periods of spring and fall will often bring masses of shorebirds, and dense flocks of ducks to coastal bays.

Long Island Sound contains a wide assortment of islands and offshore rocks, the bane of boaters but marvelous for bird life. Some islands have large tern and gull colonies, while on a few islands heronries have been established. Such heronries are rare in Long Island Sound and are vital to the survival of some species. *Please remember that eggs and young can be completely lost by one visit to such breeding colonies. Do not land. View the birds from your boat offshore.*

Open water is the realm of the deep divers; of species resting in migration or passing through; or of the rarity that is blown into Long Island Sound after severe storms off Massachusetts or Rhode Island.

In mid-summer, when most species are off on their nesting grounds, the open waters can seem quite sterile, but soon fall migrants and winter birds will be seen everywhere.

Timing

The time of the year you are boating will have an effect on the birds you will see. Mid-summer can be a bit slow on the open waters, but along shore the activity of birds feeding young on rocky islands or in coastal salt marshes is at its peak. Spring and fall boaters will see a wide selection of birds passing in migration. Hawks, landbirds, and shorebirds wing over the Sound's waters making their way north or south. Loons, ducks, and cormorants often pass in massive flocks. It is a time when just about anything can be expected. Take the case of the boater off Long Island who was surprised to see a tiny owl sitting on the foredeck – a Burrowing Owl from the inland prairies of Florida! Fall is a time of dispersal for this normally sedentary species which occasionally wanders far beyond its normal limits to the delight and surprise of this weekend boater.

Though not as many people ply the Sound's waters in winter, an abundance of birds use the area as a winter location. Greater Scaup, as an example, will winter in massive rafts, at times numbering in the thousands and forming one of the largest masses of birds wintering on the New England coast.

Migrants Aboard!

During migration periods it is not uncommon for tired birds to come on board boats for a rest before heading on, even while the boats are moving. Some may also take refuge on a boat to avoid the unrelenting pursuit of predaceous gulls. Gulls are constantly on the lookout for tired migrants as food, so do not be surprised to see a bird slip on board and seek shelter when aggressive gulls are nearby. If approached at this time they will fly off again usually into the mouths of the waiting gulls. Birds that stop simply because they are exhausted from a long journey over water, say a non-stop flight from Bermuda, are simply content to rest. They will not take food and water. Once rested they will head for shore at the first opportunity. They may spend some time with you and this will afford you an excellent opportunity to study them.

I remember being out with a birding group when migrants were coming on board. In one instance, a sleeping birder was brought to a quick awakening when a warbler

hopped on his knee and seeing its image in the mirror reflection of the man's sun glasses, attacked the "intruder" in defense of its new territory. As it crashed into the glasses, I am not sure which was more startled, the bird or birder.

Along these lines we are now seeing more and more rare species from distant lands arriving on our shores as "stow aways" on board large ships. Sedentary species normally resident in coastal Europe or the Far East have shown up very close to several coastal ports. One captain of a large tanker told us of a Peregrine Falcon that made three crossings with him, hunting petrels over the water during the journey. With the advent of the massive super tankers there are regions of the ships that no person goes near during a journey. These afford an excellent, predator-free, traveling sanctuary. Other, more social or tame species are fed by the crews and become the ship's mascot.

The following is a listing of some species of major groups you may encounter while boating. It is designed as an introduction to the groups as well as identifying some of the more commonly seen species. The page number following each species is in reference to Roger Tory Peterson's, *A Field Guide to the Birds Eastern North America*. You will undoubtedly encounter more species than those covered here but this will at least be a first step in expanding your knowledge and enjoyment of the birds of Long Island Sound.

Loons and Grebes

Loons and grebes belong to a primitive group of birds that superficially look like ducks. Their legs are positioned so far to the rear of their bodies that they are unable to walk on land. Both groups need to "run" over the surface of the

water before they can take off. Occasionally a storm-driven loon will land on an in-land body of water which is too small to allow a running takeoff. In such instances they have to be captured and taken to a large lake or shore to be freed. Fish are the major food source and long underwater dives in pursuit of prey are common. On the Sound two loons and one grebe are commonly seen.

Common and *Red-throated Loons* (p.32) can be seen from Fall through Spring. The Red-throated is the more abundant of the two. They are easily separated by color and bill size. The Red-throated has a small upturned bill and is basically grey in color whereas the Common has a large straight bill and is black above and white beneath.

Horned Grebes (p.34) arrive in the fall and overwinter on the Sound, staying until spring before heading north again to nest. It is basically a grey bird with a distinct black cap. In size it is smaller than a loon. By Spring it comes into a rich cinnamon plumage with bright golden "ear tufts" making them one of the handsomest birds on the Sound.

The small, plump *Pied-billed Grebes* (p.34) may be seen near marinas and on river dockings. Principally a fresh water species, it would be rare to see a Pied-billed Grebe any distance out on the Sound.

Cormorants

Cormorants, long-necked, fish-eating birds that can be easily identified by their vertical posture as they sit on breakwaters and navigational aids. They can also be seen with wings stretched out to the side drying in the sun after extended diving.

The *Double-crested Cormorant* (p. 40) is common on the Sound from April on through to fall. In April, massive flocks can be seen streaming over the water or flying overhead in loose V's. You may see several thousand pass within an hours time. Black in color with a yellow patch of skin, it is easily identified by posture alone. The young are brown with dark bellies. Cormorants have established themselves as nesters on offshore rocks during the last 10 years.

Great Cormorant (p.40) is as the name implies, the largest of the cormorants with the same basic features of the Double-crested. In adults, look for a white patch on the flanks. Immatures have a white underbelly. When the Double-cresteds leave for the winter, the Great Cormorant from Canada moves in. Widespread throughout the world, it is best known as the bird that the Japanese use for fishing. A ring is placed around the neck of the birds, preventing them from swallowing large fish. The birds are then released overboard with halter and line attached. Upon catching a fish they can be "reeled in," and the fish is taken from the bird's beak. When fishing is over for the day, the birds are rewarded with small fish that they can swallow.

Herons

Herons had a long history of involvement with man. In the early 1900's they were shot for the millinery trade. Whole Snowy Egrets were often placed on hats for ornamentation. It was the near extinction of this species and its close relatives that led to the founding of the National Audubon Society. Herons and egrets are now protected from such wanton destruction and have made a remarkable recovery.

Along mudflats, on island edges, or flying over the water, herons and egrets are a familiar sight in the summer.

The *Great Blue Heron* (p. 100) or "Great Blues" can be seen year round but are most abundant during spring and fall migration. They are the largest of the herons, and use their massive bills to secure a wide range of food from fish to crabs. I have even watched them spear rats and eat them! This is the bird most people refer to as a "crane" (which it is not) when they see it in coastal salt marshes. Its large size, (particularly long beak and legs) and overall bluish-grey color make it fairly easy to identify.

The *Black-crowned Night Heron* (p. 104) is most active at night feeding on crabs and fish at waters edge especially off islands and breakwaters. As you pass breakwaters look for them hunched over in the rocks. Grey in color with black crown and cap, they blend well with the background.

The *Great Egret* (p. 102) standing over three feet tall, has all black legs and a bright yellow bill. It will wade into water up to its belly while searching for fish and small crabs.

The *Snowy Egret* (p. 102) is a small egret which sports magnificent feather plumes during the breeding season. The bill is all black and fairly thin, and the legs are black with bright golden feet. It hunts by stirring up the shallow water with its feet, spearing fish that are chased out.

The largest heronry in the state is to be found on Chimon and Ram Islands of the Norwalk Island group. These islands are now part of the Coastal Wildlife Refuge and you *should not land here* during any part of the nesting season (May 15 - August 15). Even the slightest disturbance could cause nest abandonment. It is best to anchor just offshore and watch the birds through your binoculars. Other species that nest here are: *Cattle Egrets* (p. 102); *Glossy Ibis* (p. 108); *Green Heron* (p. 104); *Little Blue Heron* (p. 100 – rare); and the very rare nester, the *Louisiana* or *Tricolored Heron* (p. 100). Other island groups on the coast such as the Thimbles off Branford are now attracting herons and colonies are being established. *Again, please do not disturb the birds by going ashore on these islands.*

Ducks, Geese, and Swans

This group is represented by a great many species and there are usually some representatives to be seen in all habitats visited.

The *Mute Swans* (p. 42), with their elegant curved necks and white plumage, have become a very familiar sight in the harbors of the coast. Long Island Sound has the greatest population of this European import in its restricted East Coast range. Beware when feeding these birds as their wings and beaks can inflict serious injury if the birds become enraged. They are very pretty birds but not very pleasant.

Great Blue Heron *(Ardea heródias)*

The *Canada Goose* (p. 44) is familiar to everyone in New England. With the establishment of permanent populations throughout the state it has become difficult to determine which birds are year round residents and which are migratory birds. The wild population arrives in the fall, overwinters, and then heads north again in the spring. They tend to be inshore birds and favor protected coves of the shore or islands.

The *Brant* (p. 44), a close look-alike to the Canada Goose, is smaller, darker in color, and a true sea-going goose. They can be seen during the fall, winter, and spring but never in great numbers. This species is still recovering from the die-off of their favored food crop Eel Grass (Zostera). A fungal infection of the plants in the late 1940's led to a drastic drop in available food and hence the demise of the Brant. It only slowly adapted to other foodstuffs until the Eel Grass recovered and now the Brant population is on the increase again.

Black-crowned Night Heron
(Nycticorax nycticorax)

The ducks of the Sound are numerous and can be divided into two groups. The dabblers are the species of shallow water where they can "tip up" to feed on submerged plant and marine life. They can also "leap" into direct flight without first running over the water's surface. Divers are those which dive deep to secure food. This group needs considerable take off distance where they can run over the surface before taking flight.

Mallards and *Black Ducks* (p. 48) are two dabblers that are consistently seen in the harbors and just off shore. It is interesting to note that as a result of interbreeding and hybridization, the Mallards are slowly "swamping" out the Black Ducks so that a "full blooded" Black Duck is becoming harder to find. Hunting limitations have now been placed on the Black Duck until a better understanding of what is happening between these species is reached.

From fall through to spring the waters of the Sound play host to a great number of diving ducks. Typically these birds nest in Canada and overwinter each year in basically the same locations throughout southern New England.

Red-breasted Mergansers (p. 62) are common thin billed divers. The orange bill has serrations that act like teeth to hold fish after a long dive. The feathers of the head are swept back in a cowlick making this species easy to identify.

Common Egret *(Casmeródius álbus)*

Common Goldeneye (p. 60) flock up in large rafts. The green head with large white circle between the eye and bill make for an easy identification. When flushed from the water, their wings make a loud whistling sound which gives them their vernacular name of "Whistlers".

The *Great Scaup* (p. 58) gather in massive rafts that can be seen from shore as black lines out on the water. For the boater a flock moving from one feeding area to another can seem like an endless stream of ducks; groups in excess of 2,000 birds are not uncommon. One of the favored foods are crustaceans and the extensive blue muscle beds of the coast are the favorite feeding places for these birds. While resting they may raft-up anywhere on the Sound.

All *Scoters* (p. 54) are large and dark in color. The *White-winged Scoter* has large white wing patches that the other two species lack. The *Surf Scoter* has distinct white head patches which lead hunters to call them "Skunk-heads." The least common scoter is the *Black Scoter*. It is all black in color with a bulbous right yellow "nose like" lump on its bill called the operculum.

In addition to all of the preceding, look for small rafts of white, fast diving *Bufflehead* (p.60) and the swift flying, long-tailed basically white *Oldsquaw* (p.56). The Oldsquaw is the deepest diver of them all, reaching record depths in excess of 270 feet!

Shorebirds

Shorebirds are another group that has felt the impact of man over the years.

At the turn of the century hunting of shorebirds was common practice. At coastal sites, shorebirds were shot by the thousand and taken to market by the barrel-full where

Brant *(Bránta bérnicla)*

Red-breasted Merganser
(Mérgus serrátor)

Greater Scaup
(Aythya marila)

they were sold for one cent apiece! For several species the recovery has been slow and they still remain a rarity.

Shorebirds can be grouped into two major headings: Plovers and Sandpipers. Plovers tend to be chunky in build with short bills and fairly short legs. Sandpipers are slimmer with longer legs and certainly longer bills. More than likely the shorebirds you encounter will be on rocks, island edges, breakwaters, and mudflats. Over thirty species have been recorded in the state and many of them for the beginning birder fit into the category of "LBJ" or "Little Brown Jobs!" With patience they can be identified, and several that we deal with here can be learned quickly.

Killdeer (p. 120) are common nesting birds in gravel areas, often right in the boat launch area or parking lot edge of the marina. The double bands around the neck and orange tail contrasting to the brown back make them easy to identify.

Black-bellied Plovers (p. 118) are common in spring and fall migration. They show black underparts in breeding plumage and, in the fall, black under the wings and a white rump. The similar looking *Golden Plover* (p. 118) occasionally stops in the state especially if it encounters storms at sea. This bird normally fattens up on berries in Nova Scotia before jumping off on a three day non-stop flight to Argentina!

At several coastal areas you will see snow fence enclosures. This signifies a nesting area of rare and endangered *Piping Plover* (p. 120). Pale in color with a single neck band, this bird blends remarkably well with its sandy background. All terrain vehicles and the running of dogs on the beach during breeding season has severely affected the populations of the plover, however. *Under no circumstances* should people enter the fenced off areas during breeding season from late March through July.

Sandpipers often cover mudflats in dense concentrations. Species such as *Dunlin* (p. 132); *Semipalmated* (meaning a little bit of webbing between the toes) *Sandpipers* (p. 134); and *Dowitchers* (p. 124) are common. The *Sanderling* (p. 130) in its white winter plumage with black shoulders is familiar to all who have walked the beaches and seen them scampering about like little wind-up toys chasing the waves. Running about in the shallows will be both *Greater* and *Lesser Yellowlegs* (p. 128), a name befitting

their appearance. Look for *Spotted Sandpipers* (p. 132) on rocky shores and breakwaters. Heavily spotted below and with rich brown back, they "teeter" their body up and down as they walk about in search of small invertebrates.

Gulls

Of all birds, gulls are most often associated with the shore and boating. Like so many other groups, the influence of man has played an important role in their population dynamics. Being opportunistic, they have benefited from

Killdeer *(Charádrius vociferus)*

Great Black-backed Gull (*Lárus marinus*)

They have a yellow bill, on which there is a red spot during the breeding season. This spot elicits the pecking of the young when food is brought to the nest. Without the spot the young bird wouldn't peck and the adult wouldn't feed the young! The back is grey with black wing tips and the underparts white. Several large nesting colonies are to be seen on coastal islands. These birds are omnivorous and will eat anything.

Great Black-backed Gulls (p. 86) are very easy to identify by their large size (nearly a five foot wingspan), jet black backs, and white underparts. This is a top line predator at the shore and feeds on everything from fish to young Herring Gulls. It has made inroads as a nesting species in the last 25 years and has displaced many of the favored nesting tern colonies.

The *Ring-billed Gull* (p. 86) is a small, grey-backed, black-wing-tipped gull that is easy to identify in breeding plumage by the distinct ring around the bill. Though the species can be seen year round in the Sound they do not nest anywhere nearby. Nesting is on the large interior lakes to the North. It is one of the commonest gulls at coastal parking lots near restaurants.

The *Laughing Gull* (p. 88) is a bird of the summer and fall and it does not nest in this area. An adult is easy to identify with its all black hood and dark grey back. This is the most common gull on the Southern coasts and throughout coastal Florida.

Terns

Terns are sleek, long winged birds that give the appearance of diminutive gulls. Fishermen often use the term "Mackerel gull" in reference to these birds.

Only three species are seen with regularity from spring through to fall. Nesting areas are limited for these birds much the same way as they are for the herons. *Do Not Land* on any island showing tern activity. An island, such as Faulkners off Guilford is one of the last remaining strongholds for nesting Roseate Terns, an endangered species. One visit can disrupt nesting for the entire year.

The *Common Tern* (p. 96) as the name implies is the most common tern on the Sound. All white with a grey back and long reddish bill with a black tip, it can often be seen in large numbers diving for small fish off islands or in bays. Its loud "kee-arr" call is a familiar sound on the summer coast.

The *Roseate Tern* (p. 96) is an endangered species and has suffered from habitat loss throughout its North American range. Researchers are presently trying to enhance nesting sites such as Faulkners Island to improve population numbers. All nesting sites are under federal protection and are monitored for intrusion. One interesting and frustrating sidelight to this federal tern study was the unusual number of leg bands returned from South America. When investigated it was found that the natives had nets set over rivers and wintering Roseates were being captured and eaten. The bands were dutifully returned to Maryland's

man's residue! It is interesting to note that a survey of the coast from Milford to New Haven harbor in 1905 produced *two* Herring Gulls. The same route in a 1968 census produced over 38,000! The reason, open dumping! If food is available, the gulls will be there.

Gulls appear in a myriad of plumages. It takes three and a half years for a gull to go from the basically brown plumage of an immature to the characteristic plumage of an adult. It is easiest to identify adult birds at the outset.

The three species of gulls are found year round. The *Herring Gulls* (p. 86) are the most familiar along the shore.

Black-bellied Plover
(*Squatárola squatárola*)

banding station. Unfortunately, full protection in the United States doesn't always secure the status of a species in other countries. International agreements must be made for international birds.

The *Least Tern* (p. 96), a big fellow with all yellow bill and white forehead, is also suffering from disturbance on the sandy beaches of the state. Management programs have been set up and numbers of these birds appear to be increasing. Watch for these "mighty mites" as they plunge and dive along the shore or near their nesting islands.

We hope this introduction to the birds of the Sound has piqued your interest in birding both ashore and afloat. There are many organizations, and a wide array of books on all topics of birding, that are ready to answer your questions and help you enjoy the swooping, swimming, diving, and dabbling birds around you.   ✦

Photographs by Noble S. Proctor
Illustrations by Patrick J. Lynch

For more information contact:
Northeast Audobon Center, Sharon, CT
Connecticut Audobon Center, Fairfield, CT

Common Tern
(Stérna hirúndo)

Recommended Books:
Birds of North America, 2d ed. Washington, D.C.: National Geographic Society, 1987.

Eastern Birds - An Audubon Handbook. New York: McGraw-Hill, 1988.

A Field Guide to the Birds of North America, by Roger Tory Peterson, 4th ed. Boston: Houghton Mifflin, 1980.

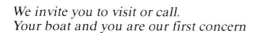

This Is The Life!
Lets Keep It That Way

To protect our waters and aquatic life
from possible boat and marina pollutants,
please:

 **DISPOSE OF
WASTE ENGINE
OILS IN PROPERLY
DESIGNATED
RECEPTACLES**

 **DISPOSE OF
USED ENGINE
ANTI FREEZE
PROPERLY**

 **WASH BOATS WITH
WATER PRESSURE:
USE MILD
CLEANERS ONLY
IF NECESSARY**

 **STORE AND
DISPOSE OF
ENGINE BATTERIES
PROPERLY**

 **PREVENT
PLASTICS FROM
ENTERING THE
WATER**

 **USE ONLY TBT
PAINTS THAT
COMPLY WITH
CURRENT
REGULATIONS**

 **DISPOSE OF
SANITARY WASTES
PROPERLY**

 **COLLECT
PAINT STRIPPING
AND SANDING
WASTES**

**For more information:
Department of Environmental Protection
Information and Education
165 Capitol Avenue
Hartford, CT 06106
(203) 566-5599 ● (203) 566-3489**

Fishing the Sound

Long Island Sound, nurtured by its many rivers and streams, dotted with islands and reefs, sparkling with currents and eddies, is a fishing wonderland. The sheltered estuaries of the Sound are a tremendously productive nursery for an exciting variety of food and gamefish.

Fat and tasty winter flounder seem to pave the bottom of the rivers and coves, in the spring and fall. Mackerel migrate northward from southern waters in early April, in time to provide bait for bass and bluefish anglers, and delectable taste treats from the backyard smoker.

Striped bass growing to trophy weights of 60 pounds and more move into western Long Island Sound from the Hudson River, while separate stocks from southern waters move up the Atlantic Coast to invade the eastern end. They remain through the hot summer months, and provide spectacular fishing action before departing around Thanksgiving. Bluefish explode onto the Long Island Sound scene in early May, ravaging bait schools, tearing apart tackle, and creating the incurable disease known as fishing fever.

Suit the Method to the Fish

Spinning equipment is the choice of most anglers who cast from boats. It's simple to use, relatively free of tangles and complications, and capable of handling a wide variety of lures and bait.

An ideal outfit is a six-foot, one-handed spinning rod, mounting a medium sized fast-retrieve spinning reel. Fishing natural baits requires heavier gear, but for fishing lures a 10 to 20-pound test line is best. This allows for good distance in casting, and has the strength to play and control big fish.

For bait fishing I switch to an 8-foot rod, with plenty of backbone, and line testing from 20 to 25 pounds. When bait fishing, line wear is compounded, and strong tackle is required.

Rate of retrieve and line capacity are prime considerations when choosing conventional tackle. Whether trolling, jigging, or bait fishing, the conventional reel with a star drag can be advantageous over spinning equipment. A level-wind feature is a valuable addition to the conventional reel. It ensures that the line is wound evenly onto the reel every time. While casting with conventional gear is more difficult to master, it is a skill to be proud of.

Trolling allows you to cover a lot of water in a short period of time. You can troll for bass, blues, and weakfish. You can troll with wire line, and with monofilament, with heavy lures, light lures, and natural baits like sandworms and bloodworms. You can troll on the surface or troll deep.

When it comes to fishing, there's nothing like the real thing – LIVE BAIT! Monster blues and trophy stripers are most often caught on live bunker by a method called live-

DICK ALLEY
The Fisherman Magazine

© Jack McConnell

Striped Bass   **Bluefish**

lining. Sandworms are a popular bait for striped bass, blackfish (in the early season), winter flounder and scup. Green crabs and fiddler crabs are the summertime favorite of the blackfish. Fluke prefer live minnows.

Simply put, natural baits are a sure bet when fish are around. Pieces of fish, referred to as chunk baits, have the odor and flavor to entice fish into feeding. Tackle for fishing baits varies from species to species, and method to method.

When big concentrations of fish are present in a given area, jigging is a sure-fire method of catching them. In Long Island Sound, spring mackerel and summertime blues are the prime targets of anglers who prefer this method. Jigging is the simple act of lowering a metal or lead jig into a school of fish, and them moving or jigging the rod in an up and down motion to make the lure dance about. Favorite jigging spots include Eatons Neck and Middle Ground, and party fishing boats catch thousands of fish every season using this method.

Years ago, fly-rodders were a novelty in the salt water. But today, it's hard to go on a trip without seeing someone wielding one of the long rods on the waters of the Sound.

The salt water fly rod should be at least 9 feet in length, and have the backbone to cast a number 10, 11, or 12 line – necessary to turn over a big streamer fly or popping bug. The reel should hold a couple of hundred yards of backing and should be equipped with a good drag system to fight heavy fish. A stripping basket or small tarp to toss over possible line-grabbing obstructions in the boat is also a must.

It's a relative term, depending on the size and species, but the challenge of catching, playing and boating over-sized fish on undersized tackle is exciting and rewarding. In 1986, Linda St. George of Huntington, CT, boated a 15 -1/2 pound bluefish on 4-pound test line, and received a check for $1000 from Berkley Line Company for setting a new line-class World's Record. The fish was caught in Norwalk, CT and Linda played it for over an hour before boating it. Catches like Linda's demonstrate that the average angler can take a favorite trout or bass rod from inland waters, and fish successfully for trophy fish on Long Island Sound.

What Fish Are Available When?

Striped bass again became legal in the State of Connecticut in the fall of 1987, ending a two year moratorium. Bass are now limited to one fish a day over 33 inches in length. The new regulation allows the taking of fish for mounting or dining while also allowing good numbers of fish to spawn and propagate the species. (Fishing regulations change frequently, so check at the beginning of each season.)

Poly-Chlorinated Biphenols, (PCB's) are known to be present in stripers of the Sound at levels deemed unsafe by the State Department of Health. They warn that striped bass should not be consumed by small children or pregnant women, and by adults no more than once a month.

Stripers feed on a variety of natural baits ranging from sand and bloodworms, through squid, sand eels, menhaden (bunker), and mackerel. They can be caught by fishing the bottom with worms or chunk baits, by trolling a variety of lures and worm-baits and by drifting and live-lining mackerel, bunker or seaworms.

They feed primarily during the night hours, and at dawn and dusk. Being anadramous, they survive equally well in fresh or salt water. Bass in western Long Island Sound come mainly from Hudson River stocks, while eastern parts of the Sound play host more to populations from the Chesapeake Bay and Atlantic Seaboard. Bass travel in dense schools, and have been caught weighing in excess of 70 pounds.

Bluefish make up the mighty armies of Long Island Sound. The blues arrive in May, and are believed to spawn in mid-Sound. They then settle in for the summer, where by day they haunt the trenches of the Sound, and at dawn and dusk raid the beaches and estuaries, providing abundant excitement for fishermen. Bluefish get bigger every season with choppers of 20 pounds and more being recorded each and every year. They're called choppers, and alligators, and gorillas, and tailors, and snappers, and harbor blues, too. Each nickname describes a different sized bluefish. Snappers for instance are the baby blues, available from the first part of August through September every year. Their growth rate is fantastic, and by the time they leave, many run to 10 inches in length. The lightest of fresh water tackle is ideal for these little scrappers, and they are the best of the bluefish family on the dinner table. Live or frozen small baitfish, and their artificial imitations, are the ticket to fast action for this favorite fishery.

Blues from 3 to 6 pounds are average fish these days, and provide the all-day action to trollers in mid-Sound in the heat of summer. They're savage fighting machines that will attack any splashing surface plug without hesitation.

Alligator or gorilla blues earned those names because they're strong and tough. The teeth on a bluefish over 8 pounds resemble those of an alligator, and their brute strength is that of a gorilla. Most big bluefish, those specimens reaching into the high teens and twenty-pound weight, are caught on chunk baits. Strong wire leaders, hook sizes 7/0 and 8/0, and special care in handling are standards for these trophies.

Wire-line trolling is the most productive method of summertime bluefishing for average blues. In western Long Island Sound, 100 yards of stainless-steel wire testing 40 pounds gets your lure down to the 30-foot mark, where the fish mostly lie. At the eastern end of the Sound in stronger currents and deeper holes, heavier wire is the norm.

Weakfish have become a sometimes seasonal fish. They'll practically disappear for a few years until the cycle turns, and then show up in good numbers, and in bigger sizes than ever. Resembling a fresh water rainbow trout, these fish are as delicious as they are physically attractive. Their relatively soft jaw requires a gentle touch by the fisherman, making them a favorite of the fly-rodder and the light tackle specialist. They'll feed on all the baits that striped bass and bluefish will.

Mackerel show up in mid-April, sometimes staying only a week or two, chased away by advancing hordes of hungry bluefish. These big Boston mackerel, running from 2 to 3 pounds, are a favorite of the fisherman with the backyard smoker.

Flounder are the definite favorite of the bottom fishing fraternity. Frostbite fishermen cut their teeth on first flounder in mid-March in the bays and rivers. From April to late May, they're found in every harbor and sandy cove on Long Island Sound. Connecticut State law sets a 10-inch minimum size limit on winter flounder.

Fluke are summer flounder. They must be 14 inches to keep. These fish also run in cycles, and the past couple of seasons have shown tremendous increases in the fluke populations at many spots in the Sound. Fluke are caught either by fishing live killies (baitfish) on a spinner fluke rig, or rigging a metal jig or bucktail, with a belly strip from a sand eel, or a strip of squid.

Blackfish are the bulldogs of Long Island Sound. The season begins in May, when they feed on worms, and then crab baits become best for fishing well into late June. In September, the fall run begins, and ends after the first snows of winter.

Porgies (Scup) are a scrappy little summertime species that run from half a pound to two pounds, and when they're here, from July to mid-October, the day's catch is measured by the bucketful than by the fish. They're very simple to catch, using worms or clam pieces and fished right on the bottom.

So-called trash fish like sea robins and sharks are usually incidental catches while fishing for other species. On occasion, some of the exotic species like wahoo, bonita, and albacore swing through, giving lucky anglers an exciting surprise.

Long Island Sound offers shoreline and surf fishing as well as fishing from boats. The boating angler however has a definite advantage, especially in western Long Island Sound where public access can be a problem.

Prior to World War II, the Sound had a flourishing oyster industry that produced almost three million bushels annually. Soft and hard shell clams, bay scallops, mussels, and whelks were also harvested for local consumption. Though pollution forced the closing of many bays and harbors to shellfishing, the industry is rebounding. Underwater oyster farms have been established in places like Huntington Bay, the Norwalk Islands, and Branford. Despite the abuse and neglect of the Sound's water quality, commercial fishermen are still able to land 7.6 million pounds of finfish and shellfish every year, a $30 million industry (at dockside), not including what is caught by sport fishermen.

On the Connecticut River the shad run every spring numbers 300,000 or more, providing an exciting sport for fishermen from Old Saybrook to Enfield. By the 1990s it is hoped that the salmon restoration effort will have sufficient fish returning to permit catches again for the first time in 200 years.

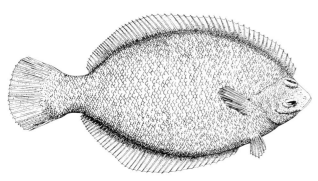

Winter Flounder

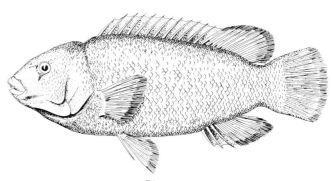

Blackfish

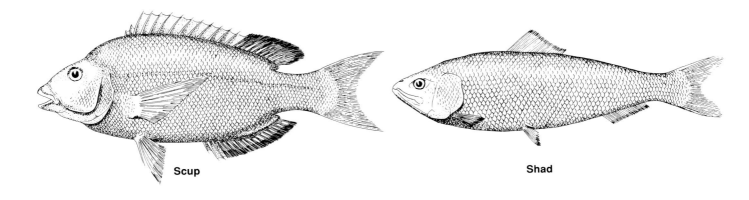

Scup

Shad

Where to Go

There's not a community on Long Island's north shore or along the Connecticut coastline that doesn't boast good fishing for one species or another over the course of a season. There are, however, several spots that provide consistently good fishing for many species.

The fishing around Huntington and Northport is excellent whether fishing for flounder inside the harbors in spring and fall; casting or trolling Eatons Neck for blues during the summer months; or fishing for porgies around Sand City and the Lilco Plant.

Further east, Cranes Neck is always the topic of conversation among fishermen, whether talking about trolling for blues, casting in among the rocks for big stripers, or simply bouncing the bottom for blackfish. Porgies are also caught here in good sizes and numbers. The busy harbor of Port Jefferson boasts excellent fishing inside the harbor, but buoy "11" outside the entrance is the spot where the talk turns to bluefish, fluke, and weakfish. A quick dropoff makes for some fine trolling, and often there's action on the surface at this spot, too. Wading River around can "9" is a recognized hotspot. Early mornings at this location are famous for lots of top-water bluefish action. The Orient Point area is another special spot for blackfish and porgies. This long held the reputation as one of the finest areas for blackfishing in Long Island Sound.

Sparsely settled eastern Long Island shows good fishing off Mattituck, which always had the reputation for the best sea bass, but also provides excellent bluefishing throughout the year as well as plenty of porgies and blackfish in season.

Plum Gut, complete with its fierce currents and ocean chop on a flat calm day, is a good spot to use heavy jigs and bucktails to pull up bass and bluefish.

The Peconic Bay area is noted for excellent spring weakfish runs, and summer and fall fishing for scup. This area also holds its share of bass, blues and blackfish, but the size of the May run of weakfish in Peconic Bay is an excellent barometer for the remainder of the season.

Montauk Point is the sport-fishing capital of the Northeast. It's the jumping-off point for offshore fishing for tuna, marlin, and big sharks. Closer to the Point itself there are daily sorties with big bluefish, some fine fluke fishing in the north rips, and some of the biggest porgies found anywhere. On crisp autumn nights, monster striped bass prowl the tidal rips, taking clam baits fished on the bottom.

Waters off Mamaroneck and Rye offer excellent fishing for flounder during spring and fall, but the big excitement for several summers now has been a huge concentration of big bluefish, invading the harbors and coves to feed on cornered schools of bunker.

The Greenwich area has also experienced excellent fishing in recent years. Hotspots include Great Captains Island, Greenwich Point, and Todds Point. Blackfish feed heavily around Cormorant Reef, Hens and Chickens, and Greenwich Point.

The reefs, sand bars, tidal rips, and sheltered coves of the Norwalk Islands provide fantastic fishing for most species from April to November. It would take a bigger volume than this to tell everything about fishing the Norwalk Island, but suffice to say that a couple of the top bass spots are Cockenoe Island, Sheffield Island, and Browns Point on Ram Island. Flounder are caught at near-record rates around Sprite Island, outside Calf Pasture Beach in the spring and fall, and outside Goose and Copps Island near buoy "26" during summer months. Blackfish may just be the best here, with Greens Ledge, Smiths Reef, Copps Island Rocks and buoy "24" off Cockenoe Island, some of the favorite spots.

One of Fairfield's prime fishing locations is Penfield Reef. This mile-long bar to the lighthouse is hot for bass, blues and weakfish. Fluke fishermen praise it often, and in the spring, it's one of the first spots to produce big flounder. The outer reaches near the light are studded with huge boulders, so caution is advised. But nestled among those boulders are some monster blackfish, and big stripers.

The Housatonic River is one of the hottest fishing spots in Long Island Sound. The mouth of the "Housy" provides good bass, bluefish and fluke fishing. When the exotics show up, you can bet it will be at this location.

Charles Island off Milford marks another spot that provides great fishing throughout every season. Then of course there's Middle Ground (Stratford Shoal), a place of bigger than normal bluefish and blackfish, where humpback porgies replace the sand porgies close to shore. Marked by the lighthouse, this area boasts strong tides and rough water.

There's good fishing in the New Haven area for blues, snapper blues, and blackfish. The latter cooperate well at Townsends Ledge, and the former invade the Quinnipiac and West Rivers and New Haven harbor in early fall.

The Connecticut River is the biggest, and probably provides the best and most consistent fishing for large numbers of species of fish throughout the season. 1987 saw more bass caught and released in this river than ever before. Bluefish cavorted almost daily at spots along the river. Spring shad runs, though not as popular as they were years ago, still provide lots of action at Enfield Dam in April and May. The Salmon Restoration Project for the Connecticut River continues, with results satisfactory some years, and disappointing in others. It is hoped that a salmon sportfishery will someday evolve in the river.

Connecticut communities at the eastern end of the Sound utilize the excellent fishing spots at Niantic, Noank, and New London to jump off to The Race for fabulous bluefishing, or offshore for tuna, marlin, and sharks.

A friend who's a charter boat skipper put it best last August when he said, "If there's a best spot for bluefish along the eastern seaboard, The Race has to be it." Race Rock Light is as famous for blackfishing as The Race is for bluefishing.

Niantic Bay bears mention, both for its excellent state ramp, and the fishing available. The Millstone Power Plant offers some very early bluefish, as well as good bottom

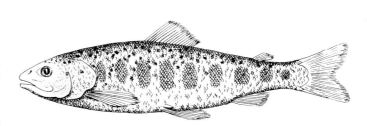

Atlantic Salmon

fishing for flounder, porgies, and fluke. But Niantic Bay is most famous for its scalloping season, which draws thousands each year.

Mystic is known for its fluke, flounder, and porgy fishing. Boat rentals are plentiful at this end of the Sound.

The many boat ramps and public access areas of the Sound provide easy means of reaching varied opportunities for great fishing, ashore and afloat. First-time anglers can have fun and learn from the experts at minimal cost aboard one of the party boats sailing from most of the larger ports. For even more fun and expert advice, charter boats are available at almost every harbor along the Sound.

Long Island Sound is a fine fishin' hole. Enjoy it!   ◆

Line Illustrations by Ronald Boisvert, courtesy of the Connecticut Department of Environmental Protection, Coastal Area Management Program.

Chartering: Another Way to Take to the Sea

ART KELSEY
President, Sail Westbrook, Inc.

"There is nothing – absolutely nothing – half so much worth doing as simply messing about in boats...or with boats...In or out of 'em, it doesn't matter."

–Kenneth Grahame, *The Wind in the Willows*

Regardless of prime rates, job-market statistics, gasoline prices, roofs that need repair, foul-weather reports, and all sorts of other stormy seas, there is still a great company of stalwarts who agree with Kenneth Grahame. These sturdy souls will always find a way to take to the sea.

Many will cruise in vessels they own. Others will find a vessel to rent or charter. Be they large or small yachts, power or sail, captained and crewed or bareboat, in dozens of locations all over the world, chartering is alive and well.

For the charterer there are many options. Likewise there are several questions that are asked, in one form or another, during the planning for that ideal vacation and challenge of the sea aboard a chartered vessel.

What Kind of Yacht Should We Charter?

Assuming that the decision for power or sail has been made, there are two important considerations pertaining to the size of the vessel.

The first is usually addressed in terms of the number of people involved and the length of the charter. Accommodations for eating, sleeping, and personal needs should be assessed carefully vis-à-vis the tastes and compatibility of your charter party. A party of six can have a great time for a three-day weekend aboard a 30-footer. An entire week aboard the same 30-footer might be a little taxing. Remember, on vessels of less than 50 feet there are rarely any secrets after the first couple of days.

The second, and more important, consideration is the skill of the skipper and crew members. Experienced boaters will swear that larger vessels are easier to operate than smaller craft. These same seasoned sailors will also readily agree that the larger the craft, the greater the skill required. Chartering a large vessel in the interest of obtaining privacy without adequate skill can result in some seriously strained muscles and psyches, not to mention bank accounts (marine damage is never cheap to repair).

Attention should be directed next to some specifics about the particular vessel. If your choice is a power boat, propulsion is certainly important. You will want to know whether it is a single or twin screw, diesel or gasoline, the fuel consumption, cruising range, and speed. In addition, electrical back-up systems should be assessed.

If your choice is an auxiliary sailing yacht, the same considerations are equally pertinent, though with two exceptions. Auxiliary sailing vessels are powered by single engines. Their cruising speed is dictated by their hull design and ranges between 5 and 8 knots regardless of the size or type of engine. Power becomes most critical when maneuvering in close docking quarters or if caught in a strong tide with little or no wind. Sail inventory, running rigging such as reefing and furling systems, and number and size of winches, are obviously more important.

Whether you are in a power or sailing vessel makes little difference to Neptune. He sends the winds and rains on the stink-potter and the rag-bagger alike. Simply be certain the vessel is appropriately equipped for the worst conditions imaginable. Then sail only when it seems sensible.

Basic navigational instruments and aids are absolutely essential. The exact kinds and quantities vary. Compasses, charts, parallel rules, dividers, pencils, and at least one good tide and current reference work should be minimum inventory on any vessel, charter or otherwise. Beyond these essentials are a VHF marine radio, radar, LORAN, knot meter and log, depth sounder. The list can become quite lengthy and some items are more useful than others, depending on the skill, preference, and experience of the user. However, there is no substitute for knowing the basics of navigation. There is nothing worse on the sea than not knowing whence you have come, whither you are bound, or where in the world you are.

Safety and emergency equipment are equally important. Safety harnesses, *life preservers,* fire extinguishers, flares, and basic spare parts are all items that can make a big difference in a crisis. If the charter-vessel inventory does not include these, a carry-on kit is a worthy investment.

Where Is the Yacht Berthed?

Preferably in the proximity of waters you'd like to sail. The southern coast of New England from New York to Nantucket offers some of the best boating in the world. There is a variety of wind and sea conditions from early May well into October. There are dozens of ports and equally dozens of places to see and things to do on land, or ample opportunities to set a long-distance course and drive hard from dawn to dusk just for the joy of working with the sea.

If you'd like comfortable day sails that put you in a different port each night, there are plenty of options from City Island to Block Island. The expanse can be conveniently divided into three overlapping cruising areas.

At the western end of Long Island Sound is City Island, with places such as Glen Cove, Oyster Bay, and Northport on the North Shore of Long Island and Larchmont, Mamaroneck, and Norwalk along the New York and Connecticut shore. In the middle of the Sound are Port Jefferson, Mount Sinai, and Mattituck on the island, with Stamford, Milford, New Haven, Branford, and the Thimble Islands on the northern shore. At the eastern end are Shelter Island, Sag Harbor, Montauk and the Peconic bays, with Guilford, Clinton, Duck Island Roads, Old Saybrook, Essex and the Connecticut River, Mystic, Stonington, and Watch Hill on the northern shore, with Block Island and possibly Newport at the end of the run.

The ports highlighted within each of the areas are generally a day's sail from one another. They are all yachting centers with a variety of interesting harbors and land attractions.

Select your point of departure with attention to the location and the kind of cruising you and your party will most enjoy. Remember also that boats go more slowly than cars. An extra hour on the highway may buy you a whole day on the water, making it a lot more feasible for you to tie up or drop the hook in some of those ports you've always dreamed about approaching from the sea.

Who's Offering the Boat for Charter?

Whether it be a private owner, a charter broker, or a full-charter company with whom you do business, choose someone who knows and cares about the vessel you are chartering. A fairly complete inventory and checklist of equipment and a set of clearly written operating instructions for the vessel are indications of responsible charter management and can make your vacation a lot more pleasant. Likewise, a walk-through of all operating systems followed by a short shakedown cruise with someone who knows the vessel is invaluable. It will steal a couple hours at the beginning of your vacation but is well worth the effort in the long run. Chartering a boat is sort of like making a new friend; it's always easier when a third party who knows you both can make the initial introduction.

Who Charters Boats?

People like you and I. It could be the owner of a vessel who has decided he'd like to cruise the waters and harbors in a location remote from where his own vessel is berthed and operated. It could be one who knows and loves the sea but doesn't own a vessel at all. The main questions the charter operator will have concern the qualifications of the individual to whom he is chartering.

Even the crewed-charter operator is concerned that the party on board his yacht respect the vessel. More than one charter skipper has remarked, after the charter party has left, "Look at this mess!" and then called his booking agent and said, "Don't ever book that bunch again."

The bareboat charter operator is usually even more concerned. He is, after all, trusting the charterer with a piece of equipment worth many thousands of dollars. There is no formal licensing in pleasure boating as there is in operation of automobiles or planes. Therefore, sailing histories, references, check-sails, and security deposits are essential. Ultimately, the charter operator is looking for the sailor who is knowledgeable, reliable, capable, and appreciative of the vessel and the sea.

How Do We Get Started?

There are many ways. One of the most frequent methods is to sail with a knowledgeable friend. Another is to enroll in some cruising and yachting courses, which are usually available in every yachting center. Many charter companies also offer formal instructions and training programs. Many can arrange for a skipper or instructor to sail with you for the first day or two of your charter until you and your crew are comfortable with the vessel.

Anyone with a little aptitude and a lot of desire can learn to operate a yacht efficiently and safely. It really isn't much harder than learning to drive a car. But as with any learning situation, the initial instruction is only the beginning. It is the experience that makes the difference.

Where Do We Find Charter Opportunities?

The boating periodicals carry advertisements regularly. Many carry directories of charter opportunities. An hour on the phone asking the appropriate questions will yield a host of possibilities. So why not spend some time "messing about" in a boat on Long Island Sound? ✦

Coastwise Distances: Cape Cod Canal, MA to New York, NY

(nautical miles)

To read this table:

The number at the intersection of the columns of the ports in question is the nautical mileage between the two.

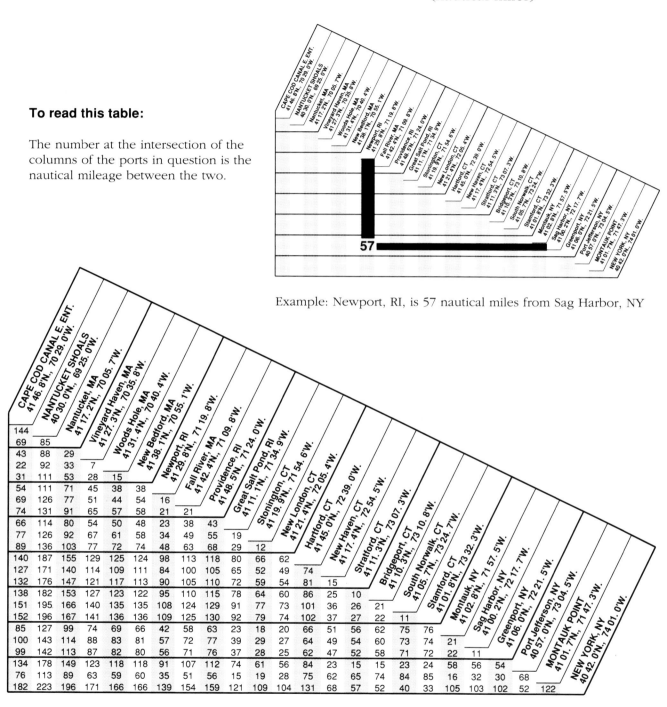

Example: Newport, RI, is 57 nautical miles from Sag Harbor, NY

Port coordinates:

- CAPE COD CANAL E. ENT. — 41 46.8'N., 70 29.0'W.
- NANTUCKET SHOALS — 40 30.0'N., 69 25.0'W.
- Nantucket, MA — 41 17.2'N., 70 05.7'W.
- Vineyard Haven, MA — 41 27.3'N., 70 35.8'W.
- Woods Hole, MA — 41 31.4'N., 70 40.4'W.
- New Bedford, MA — 41 38.1'N., 70 55.1'W.
- Newport, RI — 41 29.8'N., 71 19.8'W.
- Fall River, MA — 41 42.4'N., 71 09.8'W.
- Providence, RI — 41 48.5'N., 71 24.0'W.
- Great Salt Pond, RI — 41 11.1'N., 71 34.9'W.
- Stonington, CT — 41 19.9'N., 71 54.6'W.
- New London, CT — 41 21.4'N., 72 05.4'W.
- Hartford, CT — 41 45.0'N., 72 39.0'W.
- New Haven, CT — 41 17.4'N., 72 54.5'W.
- Stratford, CT — 41 11.3'N., 73 07.3'W.
- Bridgeport, CT — 41 10.3'N., 73 10.8'W.
- South Norwalk, CT — 41 05.7'N., 73 24.7'W.
- Stamford, CT — 41 01.8'N., 73 32.3'W.
- Montauk, NY — 41 02.8'N., 71 57.5'W.
- Sag Harbor, NY — 41 00.2'N., 72 17.7'W.
- Greenport, NY — 41 06.0'N., 72 21.5'W.
- Port Jefferson, NY — 40 57.0'N., 73 04.5'W.
- MONTAUK POINT — 41 01.7'N., 71 47.3'W.
- NEW YORK, NY — 40 42.0'N., 74 01.0'W.

Distance matrix (each row gives distances to the ports in preceding columns):

To \ From	Cape Cod Canal	Nantucket Shoals	Nantucket	Vineyard Haven	Woods Hole	New Bedford	Newport	Fall River	Providence	Great Salt Pond	Stonington	New London	Hartford	New Haven	Stratford	Bridgeport	S. Norwalk	Stamford	Montauk NY	Sag Harbor	Greenport	Port Jefferson	Montauk Point
Nantucket Shoals	144																						
Nantucket, MA	69	85																					
Vineyard Haven, MA	43	88	29																				
Woods Hole, MA	22	92	33	7																			
New Bedford, MA	31	111	53	28	15																		
Newport, RI	54	111	71	45	38	38																	
Fall River, MA	69	126	77	51	44	54	16																
Providence, RI	74	131	91	65	57	58	21	21															
Great Salt Pond, RI	66	114	80	54	50	48	23	38	43														
Stonington, CT	77	126	92	67	61	58	34	49	55	19													
New London, CT	89	136	103	77	72	74	48	63	68	29	12												
Hartford, CT	140	187	155	129	125	124	98	113	118	80	66	62											
New Haven, CT	127	171	140	114	109	111	84	100	105	65	52	49	74										
Stratford, CT	132	176	147	121	117	113	90	105	110	72	59	54	81	15									
Bridgeport, CT	138	182	153	127	123	122	95	110	115	78	64	60	86	25	10								
South Norwalk, CT	151	195	166	140	135	135	108	124	129	91	77	73	101	36	26	21							
Stamford, CT	152	196	167	141	136	136	109	125	130	92	79	74	102	37	27	22	11						
Montauk, NY	85	127	99	74	69	66	42	58	63	23	18	20	66	51	56	62	75	76					
Sag Harbor, NY	100	143	114	88	83	81	57	72	77	39	29	27	64	49	54	60	73	74	21				
Greenport, NY	99	142	113	87	80	80	56	71	76	37	28	25	62	47	52	58	71	72	22	11			
Port Jefferson, NY	134	178	149	123	118	118	91	107	112	74	61	56	84	23	15	15	23	24	58	56	54		
Montauk Point	76	113	89	63	59	60	35	51	56	15	19	28	75	62	65	74	84	85	16	32	30	68	
New York, NY	182	223	196	171	166	166	139	154	159	121	109	104	131	68	57	52	40	33	105	103	102	52	122

Scuba Diving in the Sound

You see a solitary sea horse, the tiny fin on its back beating rapidly, standing watch over its watery domain. Pink flower-like hydroids and bright-red, shell-less snails (nudibranchs) as pretty as any found on Australia's Great Barrier Reef, decorate the rock reefs. Red sea stars and foot-tall anemones cling to the stone surfaces. Schools of fish patrol the reefs above patches of small star coral scattered throughout the area. Are you diving in the Caribbean? Not at all. This is Long Island Sound!

As the near-freezing winter temperatures of the Sound's waters begin to warm in February, the Sound springs back to life with the bloom of astronomical numbers of microscopic drifting plants called phytoplankton. These plants, forming the base of the Sound's tremendously productive food chain, are responsible for fully one third of the reduction of the Sound's water visibility. The Caribbean, in comparison, is relatively devoid of these drifting plants and is thus much clearer. Visibility is further reduced in the Sound by an estimated seven million tons of sediments which is picked up and redeposited by the tidal currents each day. Most of the sediment finds its way into the Sound via rivers such as the Connecticut and Housatonic, accumulating at the rate of about one millimeter per year. If the Caribbean were faced with similar amounts of sediment, its corals and delicate ecosystem would not long survive, as is already evident in some Caribbean areas facing pollution.

The February burst of microscopic plant life is generated by the increased amount of sunlight and by winter storms that set free fertilizers from the bottom of Long Island Sound. The plants are soon followed by billions of microscopic drifting animals, zooplankton, which feed on the plants. They themselves become food for progressively larger marine animals.

A Garden In the Sound

During the colder months, beautiful pink flowerlike hydroids cover many of the rock reefs throughout the Sound. Related to jellyfish, coral and anemone, the pink hydroid, Tubularia, the most conspicuous of the hydroids, is in "bloom" until the water temperature approaches sixty degrees Fahrenheit. At that point this marine animal disappears, continuing to flourish only in the colder, deeper waters. Herds of shell-less snails, the prettiest of all sea creatures in the Sound, graze on hydroids, consuming their stinging cells without discharging them. The cells, which are like those of jellyfish and its other relatives, are then stored by the snails at the tip of each of their long back projections and are used for their own protection. These interesting animals, usually less than one inch in length, are literally what they eat, assuming the color of their food.

Patches of star coral, often no larger than a silver dollar, can be found at low tide in water less than one foot deep. Not capable of producing coral reefs such as those found in warm tropical waters, the cold water coral usually has about thirty individual "cups" forming its colony. Each of the calcium carbonate cups houses the coral's delicate polyp which ranges in color from a transparent pink to blue or green. The knoblike tip of each tentacle contains batteries of stinging cells which are used in capturing the coral's prey.

If you went swimming at Bluff Point State Park in Groton, CT you might be introduced to the graceful and pretty sea nettle, a jellyfish whose sting is seemingly out of proportion to its small size. The lion's mane or red jellyfish, ranging to a maximum of about one foot across, is ordinarily the largest jellyfish in Long Island waters. Juvenile butterfish seek shelter beneath the bell of the lion's mane, unharmed by its stinging tentacles. The same jellyfish, the culprit in a Sherlock Holmes mystery, grows in the Arctic to a phenomenal eight feet across, trailing two hundred foot tentacles. You can be glad the Sound is not colder!

Niantic Bay is host to the bay scallop, acclaimed as one of nature's best tasting seafoods. On the outer edge of the scallop's fleshy mantle is a row of about forty steel-blue eyes, each with a cornea, lens, and optic nerve. The eyes, however, are probably only capable of seeing shadows. The scallop swims rapidly by opening and closing its valves, producing jetlike pulses of water. When taken from the water the creature clatters away like loose-fitting dentures. A subject of mariculture research at the National Marine Fisheries Service in Milford, CT, the bay scallop grows quickly, reaching sexual maturity within one year and seldom living past two years.

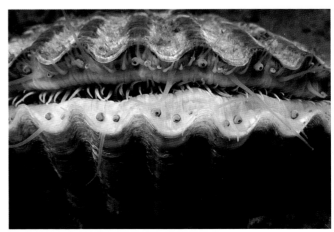

Blue-eyed scallop, *Aequipecten irradian:* **Niantic Bay, LIS.**

ROBERT G. BACHAND
Long Island Sound Task Force

Frilled anemone, *Metridium senile:* common throughout LIS on rock reefs. Penfield Reef Lighthouse, Fairfield, CT.

Purple sea star, *Asterias vulgaris:* Little Gull Island. This sea star occurs only from the extreme eastern end of LIS and northward into Fishers Island Sound, Block Island, and north of the Cape. It is rare east of Plum Island where it is replaced by the common sea star, *Asterias forbesii.*

In late summer, about one hundred yards off the beach at Woodmont, CT, sections of the bottom are carpeted by a stunning deep red sponge. The colorful red beard sponge is common along the entire coast, from Cape Cod to Texas. A species of yellow sponge, growing at times in clumps of one foot or more across, bores into oyster shells and other like surfaces. Though not considered parasitic, the boring sponge can weaken its host sufficiently to kill it.

Divers turning over small rocks at Woodmont and other areas of the Sound will usually find the ghost anemone, the lacy broyozoan, the fan worm, and a number of other interesting marine creatures. It is, however, good practice to roll the rocks back to their original position after inspection, since many of these animals choose the underside of rocks for protection. On large boulders, such as those supporting a breakwall or lighthouse, a diver entering the water at night can see the fully-expanded frilled anemone, the largest and most beautiful of our anemones.

The species of fan worms residing in the Sound, though much smaller than many found in tropical seas, are nevertheless as pretty. These segmented worms produce a tube of mucous and sand or calcium carbonate. Their featherlike appendages, varying in color from bright red to purple or light brown, protrude from the tube's opening. From that position, these appendages filter out food and oxygen from the surrounding water. If you disturb them, the animal quickly retreats to the safety of its tube.

Sea Stars: Scourge of the Oyster

The sea stars, universal symbols of the sea, abound in Long Island Sound. The common sea star, found in its greatest concentration in the Sound, is an active predator of oysters, clams, and other mollusks. Early oystermen, recognizing the sea stars' destructiveness, attempted to kill them by tearing the critters in half and throwing them back into the water. Their efforts were usually wasted as sea stars have enormous regenerative power. Tearing them in half simply doubles the population.

Responding to the concerns of the oystermen, the Connecticut State Legislature passed a law in 1901 making it illegal for anyone to help increase the range of the sea star. It read: "Every person who shall witfully deposit or assist in depositing any starfish in any navigable waters of the State shall be fined not more than fifty dollars, or imprisoned not more than six months." Modern oystermen control sea star predation by dragging a "star mop" over the oyster beds. The entangled creatures are then killed in boiling water. In case of heavy infestations of sea stars, a granular form of quick lime is spread over the beds at the

Blood star, *Henrecia sanguinolenta:* Smithtown Bay, NY.

Female sea horse, *Hippocampus erectus:* Scott Cove, Darien, CT.

rate of one ton per acre. This costly procedure does not harm the oysters but kills the voracious sea stars.

Possibly the most handsome species of sea star on our coast is the blood star. This beautiful little marine animal is found primarily at the eastern end of the Sound though it has occasionally been observed as far west as Smithtown Bay, NY. It is not a predator of oysters, feeding rather on sponges and organic particulate matter.

You can find colonies of star tunicates (sea squirts) in every corner of the Sound, encrusting rock surfaces, dock pilings, kelp, and any other available surfaces. These attractive creatures vary widely in color including gold, red, purple, blue, light brown, and white. Another species, perhaps more familiar to most, are the rather ugly looking sea grapes. You'll see these globular animals attached to the sides of boat docks. True to their name, they squirt water when lightly touched or squeezed. Distant–very distant – relatives of humans, this group of animals appears to have gone backward in evolution. Early in their lives, as tadpolelike larvae, they possess the primitive spinal cords of vertebrates, which are lost when they become adults. At metamorphosis, the mature animals are relegated to an existence of permanent attachment to the sea bottom, siphoning water for food and oxygen.

Long Island Sound has over one hundred species of fish, some of which are rare visitors, some seasonal, while others live here year-round. The Sound's most common sharks are the dogfish, sandbar shark, and possibly the brown shark. The brown is known to give birth to its young in the shallow bays of the Sound. One of the few recorded shark attacks in the Sound, according to the Office of Naval Research, occurred on August 4, 1960, at a Bridgeport, CT beach; the victim sustained only minor lacerations.

Other species of fish, well known to local fishermen, include the bluefish, striped bass, mackerel, menhaden, blackfish, cunner, and various flat fish. The sea horse, the darling of any aquarium, has on many occasions been picked up in the vicinity of Norwalk, CT, clinging to lobster traps, star mops, or oyster dredges. This intriguing fish, with

its grasping, prehensile tail, "sucks in" its food by forming a slight vacuum within its mouth. In an elaborate mating ritual, male and female swim around each other with their heads thrust slightly forward. They intertwine in an "S" fashion, whereupon the female transfers some of her eggs into the male's marsupial pouch. This can go on for several days, and it is the male who eventually broods the young.

The Sounds In the Sound

Take a dive in early June and you will be greeted by a chorus of frog-like sounds. The sea horse is one source. It is capable of producing a clicking or snapping sound, as is its close relative, the pipefish. Other sound producers in these waters include the grubby, sea robin, and blackfish. The oyster toadfish is the loudest fish on the coastline by far, producing a sound in excess of 100 decibels–the equivalent of a subway train. The male toadfish establishes a nest, often under a rock, beckoning to its mate with a series of "boat whistle" calls. Should another male or an unripe female approach the nest, the male produces a growl. A female, responding to his invitation, rolls herself over in the nest, depositing the eggs on the underside of the rock. Hatching occurs approximately 12 days later with the newborn emerging from, and remaining attached to, the top of the egg. The male parent remains with its brood and protects it from predators during the entire nesting period.

If you descend into the waters of Long Island Sound, you will not be immediately surrounded by a cornucopia of colorful creatures as in the Caribbean. Many of the marine animals are found only in certain areas of the Sound and at certain times of the year. With patience and careful search, however, you can see a multitude of these beautiful, delicate and interesting sea creatures – if you're willing to take the plunge. ✦

A Waterproof Companion

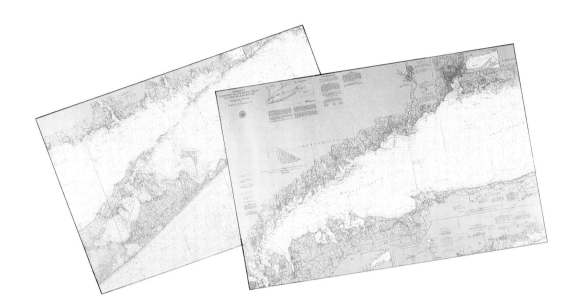

Embassy's Complete Waterproof Chart to Long Island Sound

$14.95

Call **1-800-999-1075**

Float Plan

Complete this page before going boating and leave it with a reliable person who can be depended upon to notify the Coast Guard or other rescue organization should you not return as scheduled. Do not file this plan with the Coast Guard.

1 *Name of person reporting:* _____ *Phone:* _____

2 *Type of boat:* _____ *Color:* _____

  Trim: _____ *Registration No.:* _____

  Length: _____ *Name:* _____ *Make:* _____

  Other info: _____

3 *Persons aboard: Name, Address, Telephone No.*

  _____

  _____

  _____

  _____

4 *Engine type:* _____ *H.P.:* _____

  No. of engines: _____ *Fuel capacity:* _____

5 *Survival equipment: (Check as appropriate)*

  PFDs _____ *Flares* _____ *Mirror* _____ *Smoke signals* _____

  Flashlight _____ *Food* _____ *Paddles* _____ *Water* _____

  Anchor _____ *Raft or dinghy* _____ *Other* _____

6 *Radio: Type* _____ *Frequencies* _____

7 *Trip expectations: Leaving time* _____

  Starting location _____

  Finishing location _____

  Expect to return by _____

  Return no later than _____

8 *Any other pertinent info:* _____

9 *Color, Make, Name of car:* _____

  License: Car _____ *Trailer* _____

  Where parked: _____

10 *If not returned by (time)* _____

  CALL: _____ *Phone:* _____

  _____ *Phone:* _____

  _____ *Phone:* _____

Copy this form as needed

First Aid

The following is provided as a reference only. If the situation is serious, take the victim to a hospital immediately.

Telephone numbers for emergency medical assistance are provided in each Harbor Chapter.

1 Breathing Difficulty

When Breathing Stops

1 Check for Unresponsiveness

Tap or gently shake victim. Shout, "Are you O.K.?"

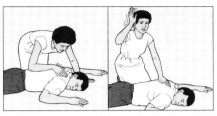

2 Shout, "Help!"

Get attention of people who can phone for help.

3 Position the Victim on His or Her Back

Roll the victim toward you by pulling slowly and evenly from the victim's hip and shoulder.

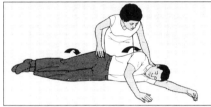

4 Open the Airway

Tilt head back and lift chin with fingers under bony part of jaw.

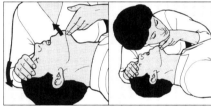

5 Check for Breathlessness

Look, listen, and feel for breathing for 3 to 5 seconds.

6 Give Two Full Breaths

Keep head tilted back. Pinch nose. Seal your lips tightly around the victim's mouth. Give 2 full breaths for 1 to 1½ seconds each.

7 Check for Pulse at the Side of the Neck

Keep head tilted back. Feel for carotid pulse for 5 to 10 seconds.

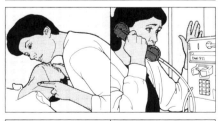

8 Phone EMS System for Help

Send someone to call an ambulance. Send 2 people if possible. Give location of emergency and condition of victim.

9 Begin Rescue Breathing

Keep head tilted back. Pinch nose. Give 1 breath every 5 seconds. Look, listen, and feel for breathing between breaths.

10 Recheck Pulse Every Minute

Keep head tilted back. Feel for carotid pulse for 5 to 10 seconds. If victim has pulse but is not breathing, continue rescue breathing.

Courtesy of the American Red Cross

First Aid for Choking

1 ....

ASK: Are you choking?

■ If victim cannot breathe, cough, or speak . . .

.... **2**

Give the Heimlich Manuever.

■ Stand behind the victim.

■ Wrap your arms around the victim's waist.

■ Make a fist with one hand. PLACE your FIST (thumbside) against the victim's stomach in the midline just ABOVE THE NAVEL AND WELL BELOW THE RIB MARGIN.

■ Grasp your fist with your other hand.

■ PRESS INTO STOMACH WITH A QUICK UPWARD THRUST.

3 ....

Repeat thrust if necessary.

If a victim has become unconscious:

.... **4**

■ Sweep the mouth.

5 ....

■ Attempt rescue breathing.

6 ....

■ Give 6-10 abdominal thrusts.

■ Repeat Steps 4, 5, and 6 as necessary.

Courtesy of the American Red Cross

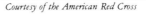

2 Bleeding

Bleeding may be stopped by applying firm pressure directly over the wound to form clotting or by digital pressure on a pressure point in the affected arm or leg or by a tourniquet (only if necessary) or by a combination of these.

3 Poisoning

First Aid for Conscious Victim of Poisoning

1. Dilute the poison by having the victim drink a glass of water or milk, if the victim is conscious and not having convulsions. Discontinue dilution if it makes the victim nauseous.

2. Save the label or container of the suspected poison for identification. If the victim vomits, save a sample of the vomited material for analysis.

3. Seek medical assistance by calling the poison control center or a physician. You should post the poison control center number for your region on your telephone. If you do not have the number, dial 0 (operator) or 911.

4. If the victim becomes unconscious, keep his or her airway open. Give artificial respiration or cardiopulmonary resuscitation (CPR), if indicated. Call an emergency squad as soon as possible. (Also see "First Aid for Unconscious Victim.")

First Aid for Unconscious Victim of Poisoning

1. Maintain an open airway.
2. Call for an emergency squad as soon as possible.
3. Administer artificial respiration and CPR, if indicated.
4. Save the container of the suspected poison.
5. If the patient has vomited, save a sample of the vomited material.
6. Do not give fluids to an unconscious person.
7. Do not induce vomiting in an unconscious person. If the victim is vomiting, position him or her on his or her side and turn the person's head so that the material drains out of the mouth.

4 Animal Bites

Wash wound thoroughly, using a solution of soap and water. Rinse with clean running water. Apply sterile dressing. Always consult a physician at once. Confine animal to escapeproof quarters. Notify police.

5 Bruises

Apply ice bag or cold pack. If skin is broken, treat as a minor cut.

6 Burns and Scalds

For burns of limited extent: Apply cold water. Cover with sterile dressing. For extensive burns: Treat for shock. Remove loose clothing. Do not remove clothing which sticks to burned area. Consult a physician. Never apply oil, butter, or any preparation to a burn. If burn covers a considerable area or if fever or blisters develop, see a physician.

7 Cuts

Wash with soap and water. Wash away from — not into — the cut. Apply direct pressure over cut with sterile gauze until bleeding stops. Apply antibacterial ointment and sterile dressing.

8 Eyes

Foreign bodies: Remove only those foreign bodies lying on the surface of the eye. Lift off with the corner of a clean handkerchief or flush eye with water, using eye dropper or bulb syringe. Do not rub eye. Never remove anything embedded in eyeball. Consult physician.

9 Fainting

Keep person lying down with head slightly lowered. Loosen any tight clothing about neck. If person does not respond within a short time, summon physician.

10 Fractures

Deformity of injured part usually means fracture. If fracture is suspected, do not attempt to move injured person. Call physician at once. Treat for shock.

11 Frostbite and Chills

Handle gently to avoid injury. Bring person into warm room and give warm drink. Immerse body part in lukewarm but not hot water or gently wrap in warm blankets. Do not rub or expose to stove or fire, nor put in hot water. Such procedures may cause serious permanent damage.

12 Heat Cramps

Symptoms: cramps in muscles of abdomen and extremities. Treatment: Same as for heat exhaustion.

13 Heat Exhaustion

Symptoms: Cool, clammy skin with body temperature about normal or below. Treatment: Keep person lying down with head lowered. If conscious, give saltwater solution to drink (1 teaspoon of salt to 1 glass of water) in small amounts at frequent intervals.

14 Heat Stroke

Symptoms: Hot, dry skin and extremely high body temperature. Treatment: Repeatedly sponge bare skin with cool water or rubbing alcohol or apply cold packs or place person in a tub of cold water (do not add ice) until body temperature is sufficiently lowered. Do not give stimulants. Consult a physician immediately.

15 Insect Bites

Remove stinger if present. Apply cold applications and soothing lotions, such as calamine. If person has history of allergic reactions to insect bites, get him to a physician at once.

16 Nosebleed

Place person in chair with head erect. Loosen clothing at neck. Saturate towel with ice water and apply over bridge of nose, at same time holding nostrils together tightly. Keep changing cold towels at intervals of one minute. If blood continues to flow freely, send for physician at once.

17 Poison Ivy

Wash exposed area well with naphtha (yellow) soap. Do not use brush or other rough material. Then use rubbing alcohol, if available. Apply calamine lotion. If area spreads, swells, or forms large blisters, see a physician.

18 Puncture Wounds

Encourage bleeding by mild pressure around the wound. Treat same as cuts. Always see a physician. A tetanus injection is usually necessary.

19 Scrapes

Wash with soap and water. Blot dry and treat the same as cuts. If scrape is deep and dirty, see a physician.

20 Shock

Keep person lying down. Cover only enough to prevent body heat loss. Get medical help.

21 Splinters

Wash area with soap and water. Sterilize needle point by passing it through a flame and use it to tease out splinter. Apply antibacterial ointment and sterile dressing.

22 Sprains

Elevate injured part to minimize swelling and apply ice bags or cold cloths immediately after injury. Cold applications of Epsom salts may be repeated every two hours. If swelling is pronounced, do not attempt to use injured part until seen by a physician.

23 Strains

Apply heating pad or heat lamp, then warm, wet application to affected area. Bed rest is indicated. If strained back, place board under the mattress for firm support.

24 Toothache

If cavity is present, moisten small piece of cotton with oil of cloves and apply to cavity. If no cavity is present, apply ice bag or hot water bottle to cheek for comfort. For any toothache, always consult your dentist.

25 Unconsciousness

Never attempt to give anything by mouth. Never attempt to induce vomiting. Place patient lying on side with head on arm. Loosen tight clothing; maintain body heat with blanket. Summon a physician at once. Be sure patient is breathing. If not, give artificial respiration. ◆

Illustrations reprinted with permission of the American Red Cross.

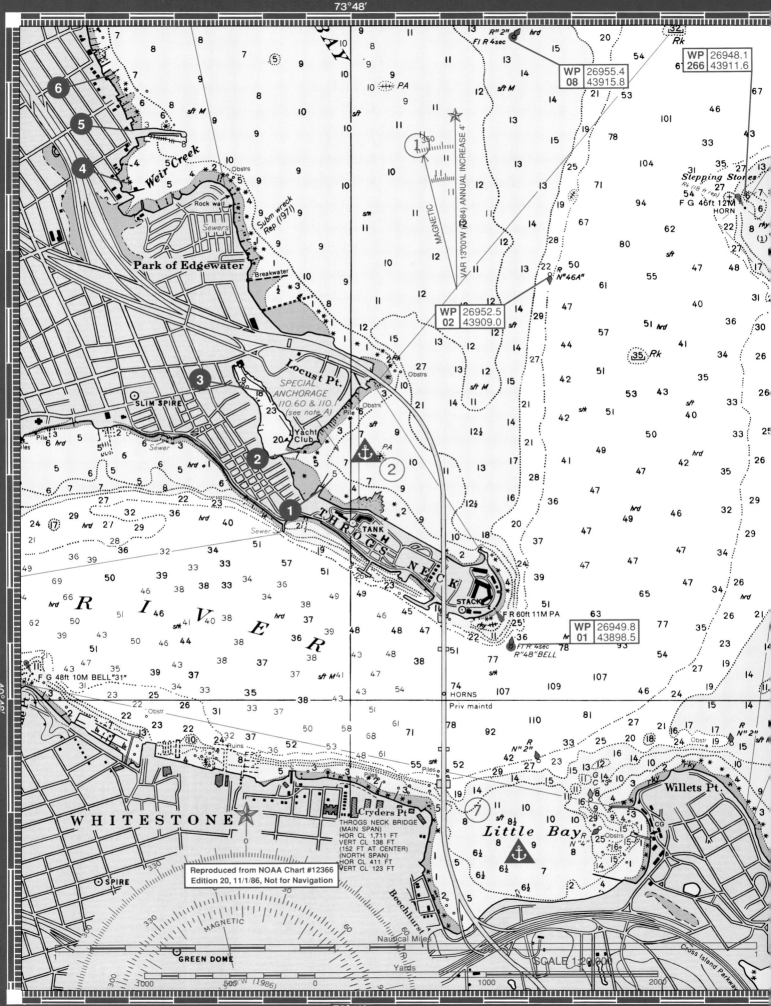

Throgs Neck and the East River

The Sound Begins

The entrance to Long Island Sound is as dramatic as the Sound itself. The 138-foot-high Throgs Neck Bridge, bedecked with lights, leapfrogs from Locust Point and across part of Eastchester Bay, drops onto Throgs Neck, leaps over the East River, and finally lands in Whitestone, NY.

Less than 7nm west is Hell Gate, the quirky, fast, and dangerous passage into New York Harbor. Hell Gate has been the death of hundreds of ships and thousands of people since it was discovered and aptly named by Dutch explorer Adriaen Block. The Race, the equally treacherous passage at the other end of Long Island Sound, is 84nm to the east.

Between Whitestone Point, a small bluff marked by a light and fog signal, and the Throgs Neck Bridge there are no public facilities for visiting yachters. On Throgs Neck itself you will see Fort Schuyler, now the home of the New York Maritime College. Fort Schuyler was built as a defense for New York City in the event that the British, or any other adversaries, should again make raids from Long Island Sound, as was done in the War of 1812. Although the fort was needed as early as 1818, construction was not started until 1833 and was not completed until 1856 – more than 40 years after the danger had passed.

Looking southwest across the Throgs Neck Bridge to the East River, Whitestone, NY, and the skyline of New York City.

 ## What To See and Do

In 1938 Fort Schuyler became the New York Maritime College (212) 409-7276. Tied up at the docks west of the bridge, you may see the yellow smokestacks and white hull of the college's 553-foot training ship, *The Empire State* – or you may not. The college is planning to replace her with a more modern vessel within the next two years. Tours of the college are available from September to April on weekends only.

The Throgs Neck area really isn't an anchorage, so there aren't too many attractions accessible by boat. The most interesting sights are the sweeping panoramas of the Throgs Neck and Whitestone bridges with the skyline of New York City in the background.

If you want to see the sights of New York City from your boat, take a trip a little way down the East River. You'll pass the World's Fair grounds and Shea Stadium in Flushing and see jets from LaGuardia Airport taking off over your head. One of our readers tells us his family enjoys leaving their boat at a marina in Flushing Bay and making the 20-minute walk to Shea Stadium (718) 507-8499 to catch a Mets game. The U.S. Tennis Association Tennis Center at Flushing Meadow (718) 592-8000 is next door to Shea, so if you're

	Marine Facilities and Services	Phone	Number of Transient Berths	Number of Transient Moorings	Seasonal/Year-round	Largest Vessel Accommodation (in feet)	Marked Entry Channel	Approach Depth (in feet)	Dockside Depth in feet at MLW	Gas/Diesel Fuel	Fuel Brand	Ramp/Dinghy Dock/Launch Service	Railway/Lift Service	Capacity (in tons)	Propeller/Hull Repairs	Engine Repairs: Gas/Diesel	Marine Supplies/Groceries/Bait/Ice	Showers/Laundromat	Pump-out Station	110V★ 220V▲ Maximum Amps	MasterCard/VISA/Diners Club	American Express	Restaurant/Snack Bar	Monitors VHF Channel
1	Marineland - Throgs Neck	(212) 824-4000			Y	30		5	5				L	15	PH		SI	S			V		S	68
2	Locust Point Yacht Club	(212) 822-9806	1	1	Y	40	●	3.5	12			R	L	20			I	S		★20			R	68
3	Locust Point Marina	(212) 822-7974			Y	50	●	5	17	G	LIB		L	35	PH		SI	S		★20				68
4	Bronxonia Yacht Club	(212) 822-9113		3	Y	38	●	3.5	3.5			RD	R	6			I			★▲				68
5	Shelter Cove Marina (p. 79)	(212) 822-3054			S	30		8	4	G	IND		L	6	P	G	SI				MV		S	68
6	White Cross Fishing Club	(212) 597-7347	PRIVATE CLUB - MEMBERS ONLY																					

Information in these listings is provided by the facilities themselves. An asterisk (*) indicates that the facility did not respond to our most recent requests for information.

in the area in early September you can check out some of the strokes at the U.S. Open.

For the adventurous sailor willing to brave the currents and traffic of Hell Gate, the reward is the most civilized approach to the world's most exciting city. The South Street Seaport (212) 669-9424/9400 near the foot of Manhattan is a fascinating place to visit. With reservations you can tie up at the Seaport's docks, but no services are offered. Even so, the Seaport, with lots of big old ships and a light and sound show about the early seaport, is a great gateway to those interested in sampling the infinite offerings of New York.

 Where To Eat

The marine facilities at Throgs Neck and to the north are surrounded by dense residential areas. The Locust Point Yacht Club (212) 822-9806 has some dining facilities, and two blocks up Pennyfield Avenue from Marineland is Buon Gusto (212) 863-2042, featuring medium-priced Italian. From any of the Throgs Neck marinas it's a short cab ride or a long walk to East Tremont Avenue, where you'll find small pizzerias, markets, and drugstores. There are small grocery stores near Marineland and the Weir Creek marinas; for variety, we recommend taking a cab to Manhattan or City Island.

 Navigation and Anchorages

Use NOAA Charts 12366 (1:20,000), 12364 (1:40,000), 12339 (1:10,000), 12327 (1:40,000) and 12363 (1:80,000). Use tide tables for Willets Point. High tide at Throgs Neck is 8 minutes later; low tide is 12 minutes later. Mean tidal range is 7.6 feet

The Throgs Neck Bridge is the generally accepted demarcation between the Sound and the East River. The tip of Throgs Neck, a narrow peninsula jutting southeast from the Bronx, is 2.0nm by boat south of City Island and 1.7nm east of the Whitestone Bridge. Opposite Throgs Neck, 0.7nm to the southeast, is the granite-walled Fort Totten Coast Guard Station (718) 352-4422 on Willets Point.

Willets Point forms the eastern boundary of **Little Bay,** the first anchorage in Long Island Sound. Little Bay (not to be confused with Little Neck Bay) has an average depth of 6 to 10 feet, with more anchoring room on the western side. Stay out from under the approach ramp for the bridge, which goes over the eastern part of the bay and marks the beginning of some shallow water. Also stay clear of the Coast Guard docks on the east side of the bay, and note that there is a visible wreck just southeast of nun "4" off the Coast Guard docks.

THROGS NECK AND FORT SCHUYLER

The original Fort Schuyler was constructed between 1833 and 1845 and named in honor of Major General Philip John Schuyler, commander of the northern army of General Washington in 1777. Built of Connecticut granite in the shape of an irregular pentagon, Fort Schuyler is now the site of the State University of New York Maritime College, which obtained the property in 1934. The original structure was designed to accommodate a garrison of 1,250 men. Fitted with 452 artillery pieces of all calibers, with two tiers of guns in casemates and one in barbette, the fort was an Army post until May 1, 1934, when Company A and the Headquarters and Service Platoon of the Twenty-Ninth Engineers were withdrawn.

The campus of the SUNY Maritime College, with the training ship Empire State, *a 553-foot converted passenger-cargo ship, on the left.*

Photo by Robert A. Hogg

Between 1934 and 1938 the old fort, which had never fired her guns in anger, was gutted: Thousands of cubic yards of earthen works were removed; dormitories, offices, a library, and classrooms were created within its pentagonal walls; and a pier and powerhouse were constructed. When renovated, the Fort was considered the finest physical facility for the training of Merchant Marine officers in the world.

The engineer in charge was later to pattern the world famous Pentagon in Washington, D.C., after Fort Schuyler.

Adapted from *Centennial: 1874-1974,* published by the SUNY Maritime College. Edited by Robert A. Hogg.

From the **Throgs Neck Light**, it's about 1.5nm north-northeast to the first major navigational aid in the Sound, the 46-foot green flasher at the **Stepping Stones Lighthouse [WP-266].** When rounding Throgs Neck, stay clear of the lighted red bell "48" **[WP-1]** that marks shoal ground off Throgs Neck.

Between the north side of **Throgs Neck** and **Locust Point** is a popular anchorage in the area enclosed by the north span of the bridge. Part of the bay is wide open to the east but is well protected by Throgs Neck from the prevailing southwesterly winds. The northern section, inside the Locust Point Yacht Club, is called **Hammond Cove** by the local residents, although unnamed on the chart. Hammond Cove is completely protected and has plenty of water, so it is likely to be crowded.

When passing under the north span of the **Throgs Neck Bridge** into this anchorage, you will have many channels to choose from between the bridge supports, but don't pass through the first five sections on either end, where shoals extend from the mainland. In the middle of this section of the bridge, the vertical clearance is as much as 60 feet. Less than 100 yards inside the bridge, close to the north side of Throgs Neck, is an uncharted wreck.

Once inside the bridge, getting into **Hammond Cove** can be tricky. Although the cove itself has plenty of water, the entrance channel is shallow and narrow (no more than 15 feet wide). The Locust Point Yacht Club maintains the channel markers, a tall pair of pilings painted red and green. Beyond these markers is another red piling, with deep water beyond. If you have a sailboat or other deep-draft boat, wait until high tide to attempt this passage.

To the north, between Weir Creek and **Locust Point,** watch out for stake buoys where tugs and barges often tie up. These buoys are 6-foot steel balls, and will win any battle you engage them in. Also, red nun "46A" **[WP-2]** northeast of Locust Point is difficult to see at night against the city lights.

If you're headed for **Hell Gate,** see the next page for a chart and navigational advice.

CAUTION: Remember that motoring through the tricky currents of Hell Gate will burn a lot of fuel. It's best to be smart and fill up at City Island or Port Washington before heading into New York Harbor, where running out of fuel will definitely be dangerous, and very embarrassing. Use the tide tables, current tables, and current charts at the back of this book to figure out the best time to run the Gate.

The **Throgs Neck** area can be mean and tricky. The tidal range is up to 9 feet, and the current can run 2 knots or more, with tide rips that mean business. The big commercial ships tend to hog the middle of the channel and swing wide when rounding Throgs Neck. Other commercial and recreational traffic runs in all directions, kicking up a confused sea. The traffic under the bridge can be particularly heavy. Cross-currents reminiscent of Hell Gate de-velop around the bridge piers, sucking small boats toward danger. To complicate matters further, the lighted aids to navigation in this area may be hard to pick out at night, obscured by the lights of the city in the background.

It is best to follow the buoys carefully, stay clear of the bridge stanchions, and keep well to starboard. Once past the bridge, heading west, keep an eye out for the large barges moored well off the north shore of the river, about a mile west-northwest of Fort Schuyler. You'll also see a lot of floating debris in the **East River,** so keep your eyes peeled. If winds are a concern for an overnight stay, find a lee of your choice; there is one within easy reach. But no matter where you hide, you probably won't be able to get away from the boat wakes.

CAUTION: Large commercial ships are hard to stop or turn quickly, especially when headed downstream in a stiff current. If evasive maneuvers are required, you'll be the one who has to make them.

 Shoreside and Emergency Services

Airport: Port Authority of NY/NJ 1-800-AIR-RIDE
Ambulance: 911
Bus: NYC Travel Authority (718) 330-1234
Coast Guard: Fort Totten (718) 352-4422/4423 or VHF 16
Fire: 911 or (212) 655-2201
Hospital: Westchester Square Hospital (212) 430-7300
Police: 911 or (212) 822-5411
        NYPD Harbor Unit (212) 993-0950 or VHF 16
Radio Telephone: VHF 25, 26, 84; I.D.: NY Marine
        Operator; VHF 86; I.D.: Mariphone
        Marine Operator;
        VHF 28; I.D.: WHU 738
Taxi: Zero's (212) 822-2222
Tow Service: Sound Tow Co., Bronx, NY (212) 885-3420
        or VHF 16
Train: Amtrak 1-800-USA-RAIL
        Metro-North 1-800-638-7646   ◆

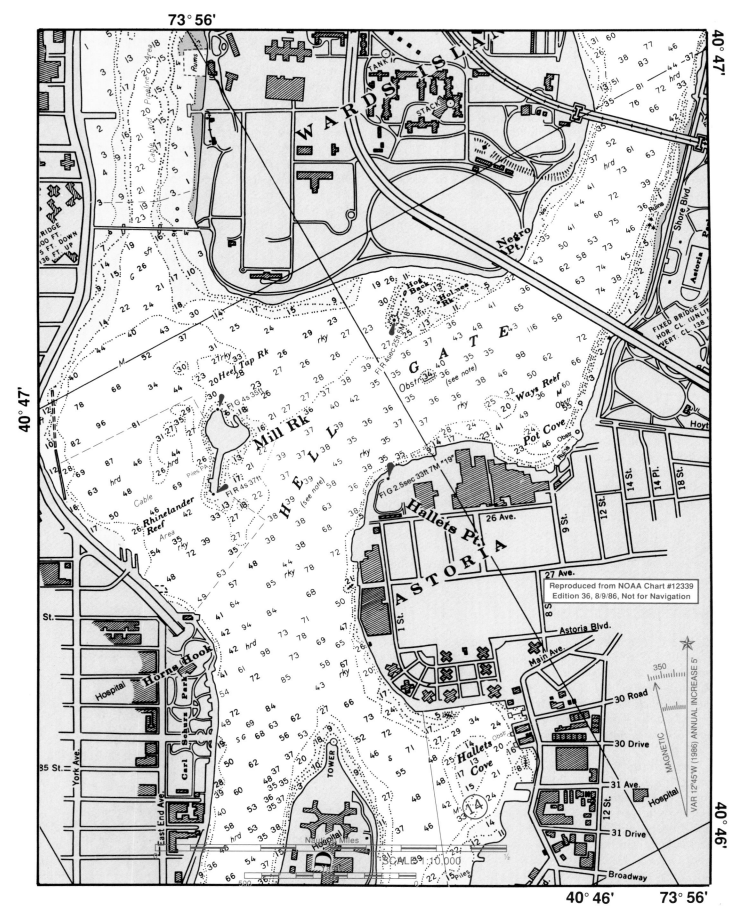

TAKING THE HELL OUT OF HELL GATE

The East River, the western gateway to Long Island Sound, is really a 14-mile tidal strait separating Long Island from the mainland. About halfway down the river is the infamous Hell Gate, where the strong currents of the East River combine with the waters of the Harlem River around Mill Rock.

The East River and Hell Gate have a reputation for strong reversing currents and large standing waves, and there are always (unfounded) rumors of whirlpools ready to swallow the unprepared. The river's reputation as a place to practice prudent navigation and piloting techniques *is* justified, however.

The tides and currents in the East River vary with location. Generally, flood currents set *eastward* into Long Island Sound and ebb currents set *westward* into New York Harbor, the opposite of Long Island Sound currents. At either end of the East River, currents are fairly weak. At Hell Gate, however, 4- to 5-knot currents combine with strong winds, heavy traffic, and fluctuating depths to make navigation difficult if you go through at the wrong time. Consult the Current Tables in the back of this guide for daily predictions for Hell Gate, and follow a few rules of thumb:

1. Go *with* the current and avoid maximum flood or ebb currents in Hell Gate, especially in small or underpowered boats.
2. Use proper charts and keep track of your position. (The bridges make great landmarks.)
3. Monitor VHF 13; commercial pilots will be making their passing agreements and position announcements as prescribed by law.
4. Wear lifejackets while on the river. Getting a person back aboard may take longer than in open water due to the traffic and currents.
5. In general, navigate to the right of center of the channels, but don't hug the edges. Realize that large vessels can't change course quickly, if at all.

Clearance is not a problem at any of the eight bridges crossing the river, with the possible exception of the vertical lift bridge at 36th Street on the east side of Roosevelt Island, with a clearance of 40 feet in the down position.

There can be a lot of debris in the water – everything from tires to railroad ties. It pays to keep a sharp lookout and travel at a safe speed. Rafts of debris tend to bunch together along the edges of the channels or where there is swirling action.

Heading westbound from Long Island Sound, the deep channel is nearly 1/2 mile wide from Throgs Neck to Rikers Island, where it narrows. Once past the Whitestone Bridge, you'll see the College Point Reef marker "CP" on a riprap island. You'll see and hear jets taking off and landing at LaGuardia Field to the south. North of LaGuardia is the green flasher "3." Stay 100 yards north of the buoy if your mast height exceeds 125 feet, unless you'd like a 747's landing gear as a souvenir.

Northwest of flasher "3" is the Hunts Point Sanitation Pier. Watch out for tugs and barges (loaded with you-know-what) maneuvering in this area.

To port is Rikers Island, where you can get long-term accommodations if you run afoul of the law in these parts. To the west you'll see North Brother and South Brother islands, with a shallow channel between them that can be very turbulent. Underpowered boats would do well to avoid this route, though it is shorter. The preferred channel runs north of North Brother Island, where "Typhoid Mary" was incarcerated for a time. There is a long bar stretching southwest from North Brother, where the currents can be turbulent at flood tide.

Vessels navigating Hell Gate on a rising tide often pass starboard-to-starboard because of the strong currents between Hallets Point and Negro Point. Outside this area the normal convention of port-to-port passing is observed.

On the north side of Hell Gate, in the middle of the Harlem River entrance, is Mill Rock, marked on both ends by lights. South of Mill Rock the channel splits at Roosevelt Island. The west channel is preferred because of the 40-foot clearance under the lift bridge on the east channel, and 35 feet of water. The bridge requires at least six-hours' notification to be opened. Currents in both channels can be swift; caution is required.

Once you've reached the tip of Roosevelt Island, don't cross between it and the 57-foot green flasher on Belmont Island because of shoaling. Just north of the Williamsburg Bridge, pass east of the red 2.5sec flasher "22." The deepest water is on the outside of the bend after the Williamsburg Bridge. By sticking to the deeper water you'll avoid some of the turbulent shallow areas.

One mile south of the Williamsburg Bridge is the Manhattan Bridge. A bit below that is the spectacular Brooklyn Bridge; soon after passing under it you'll see the tall ships docked at the South Street Seaport at the foot of Fulton Street. Watch out for the Governors Island and Staten Island ferries at The Battery, and enjoy the view!

Contributed by Captain John H. Jensen, president of Outdoor Recreation Services, a marine instruction and management company based in Fairfield, CT.

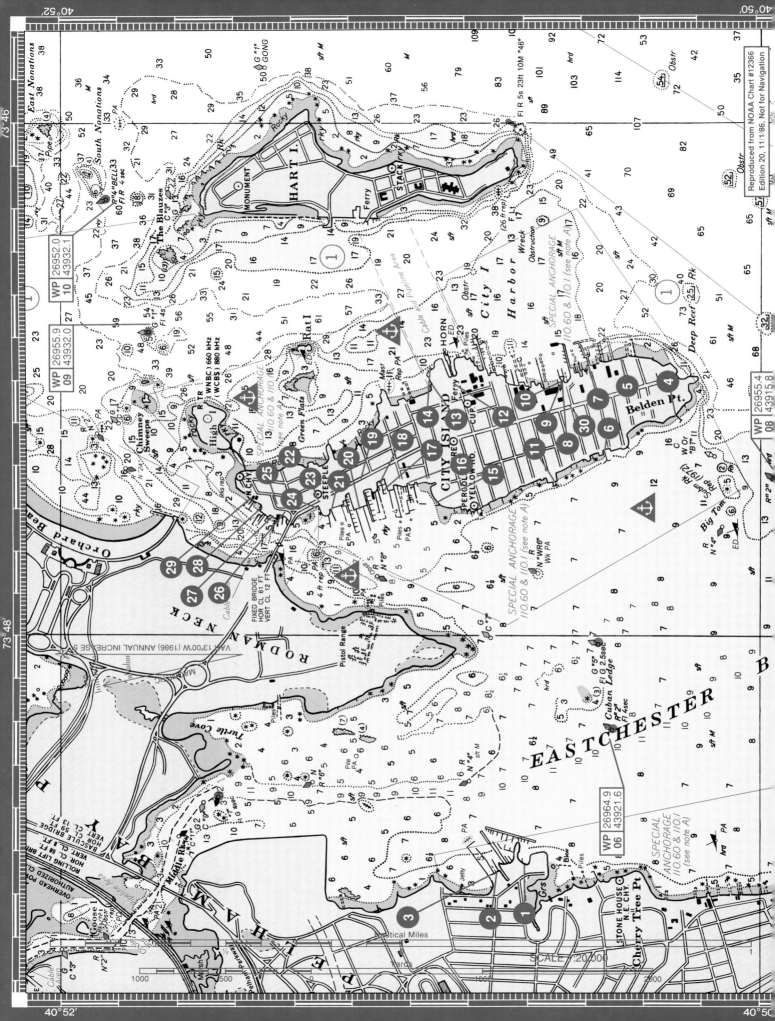

City Island and Eastchester Bay

A Lot on a Dot

City Island has the most heavily developed shoreline on Long Island Sound, with more docks per square mile than anywhere else. You get the feeling that without the money spent here by boaters, the island's economy would instantly dry up and blow away, so thoroughly is it dominated by the marine business.

The 1 1/2-mile-long island was first settled by the Dutch, who called it Minnewits Island. Later, the English took over, became Americans, and had to send two companies of fishermen/soldiers across Eastchester Bay to fend off a British raid on the island during the Battle of Long Island in August of 1776. The island slowly developed into a major fishing and shipbuilding area.

Not coincidentally, this little dot of land off the Bronx was famous for building some of the finest racing and cruising yachts in the world. Yachts designed by Sparkman Stephens were once built here, and Ratsey Lapthorn Sailmakers also plied their trade here. Minneford's Shipyard, builders of many America's Cup boats, was known worldwide for its craftsmanship. Although the shipbuilding industry has taken a beating in recent years from foreign competition, City Island still offers a wealth of excellent facilities for the yachtsman. Hell Gate pilots are stationed at City Island and board oceangoing vessels off Execution Rocks to steer them through the Gate and into New York Harbor.

The special anchorage on the northwest side of City Island, NY. In the upper left-hand corner is the WCBS radio tower on High Island. In the upper right is Hart Island.

Marine Facilities and Services

#	Facility	Phone	Number of Transient Berths	Number of Transient Moorings	Seasonal/Year-round	Largest Vessel Accommodation (in feet)	Marked Entry Channel	Approach Depth (in feet)	Dockside Depth in feet at MLW	Gas/Diesel Fuel	Fuel Brand	Ramp/Dinghy Dock/Launch Service	Railway/Lift: Capacity (in tons)	Engine Repairs: Gas/Diesel	Propeller/Hull Repairs	Marine Supplies/Groceries Bait/Ice	Pump-out Station	Showers/Laundromat	110V ★ 220V ▲ Maximum Amps	MasterCard/VISA/Diners Club, American Express	Restaurant/Snack Bar	Monitors VHF Channel
1	Evers Seaplane Base & Marina	(212) 863-9111	4		Y	80	●	6	6			R	L20	GD	PH	S			★5			
2	Pelbamar Corp.	(212) 882-8958	2	1	S	40		7	4				L10	GD	PH	S		SI	★30			
3	Sunrise Marina	(212) 823-3847			S	55	●	7	7			D	L	GD	PH	S			▲			
4	Morris Yacht & Beach Club	(212) 885-9814								*PRIVATE CLUB - MEMBERS ONLY*												
5	Transportation Services, Inc.	(212) 885-0110			Y	40		6	6				L30	GD								
6	City Island Yacht Club	(212) 885-2487		5	Y	45	●	7	6	*PRIVATE CLUB - MEMBERS ONLY*						S	I		▲		R	68
7	Consolidated Yachts, Inc.	(212) 885-1900	5		Y	110	●	7	7	GD			L60	GD	PH	S		SI	★	MV		68
8	Minneford's City Island Marineland	(212) 885-2000	5	5	Y	35	●	14	5	G		D	L20	GD	PH	SL		SI		MV		16
9	South Minneford Yacht Club (p. 86)	(212) 885-3113	4	6	Y	50	●	14	5			D					I		▲			71
10	North Minneford Yacht Club (p. 85)	(212) 885-3143			Y	60	●	15	6									SL				71
11	Stuyvesant Yacht Club	(212) 885-9840		5	Y	40		6	6			RDL	L15			S	I		★30		R	72
12	Hild Sails	(212) 885-2255			Y					*SAILMAKERS & CANVAS WORK*										MV		
13	Fenton Marine, Inc.	(212) 885-0844			Y	46	●	12	8				L20	GD	PH							
14	Barron Boat Yard	(212) 885-9802		50	Y	48		14	12			DL	L25	GD	PH				★			16
15	Harlem Yacht Club	(212) 822-1225								*PRIVATE CLUB - MEMBERS ONLY*												

Facilities listings continued on next page...

As elsewhere in New York City (and City Island is unmistakably part of the Big Apple), the locals have the appropriately hard-boiled exterior, but once they start to talk about their home you'll see the affection they have for the place. Those born and raised on City Island are known as "clam diggers" and are very proud of their heritage.

 What To See and Do

Anything you need, whether it be a chandlery, restaurant, supermarket, or laundromat, can be found within a few short blocks of the City Island docks. If you have some spare time when visiting the island, stop by the North Wind Nautical Museum (212) 885-0701 on City Island Avenue (which runs down the middle of the island) to see its fine whale exhibits and collection of nautical art.

The southwest side of the island is often called the "social side," where you'll find the Harlem, Stuyvesant, City Island, and Morris yacht clubs, as well as most of the island's residential areas. The east, or "commercial" side is jammed with marinas, boatyards, and outfitters, as is the northern half of the island. You'll also find the North and South Minneford yacht clubs on the east side, both of which cater to transient boaters. You'll have a hard time believing that so much could be crammed into so little space.

It's no surprise that an island with such intimate ties to the sea would be home to a great marine library. The tiny City Island Public Library (212) 885-1703, at 320 City Island Avenue, has the largest collection of maritime literature in New York City: over 2,000 volumes covering the past, present, and future of sailing and the sea. The library's hours vary, and they're closed Thursdays and weekends.

If you visit City Island on the first Sunday in June, you can take part in the blessing of the fleet. Early in the afternoon, boaters sail by the docks at Fordham Street and have their boats blessed by a local priest, rabbi, or minister. The event is organized by the City Island Power Squadron. For more information, call (212) 885-1559 or write the Power Squadron at P.O. Box 154, City Island, NY 10464.

If you cross the bridge connecting City Island to the mainland you'll be in Pelham Bay Park, New York City's largest. There's a driving range (212) 885-2646 and golf course (212) 885-1258 in the park, as well as the Pelham Bit Stables (212) 885-9723 or 0551 if you'd like some horseback riding.

The New York Botanical Gardens (212) 220-8777 and the Bronx Zoo (212) 367-1010 are relatively close by and easily accessible by bus or cab.

 Where To Eat

It only takes about 30 minutes to walk the length of the island, which is jammed with more than 20 restaurants in between the marinas, chandleries, and yacht clubs. Most of

Marine Facilities and Services		Number of Transient Berths	Number of Transient Moorings	Seasonal/Year-round	Largest Vessel Accommodation (in feet)	Approach Depth in feet at MLW	Marked Entry Channel	Dockside Depth in feet at MLW	Gas/Diesel Fuel	Fuel Brand	Ramp/Dinghy Dock/Launch Service	Railway/Lift: Capacity	Propeller/Hull Repairs	Engine Repairs: Gas/Diesel	Pump-out Station	Marine Supplies/Groceries/Bait/Ice	Showers/Laundromat	110V ★ 220V ▲ Maximum Amps	MasterCard/VISA/Diners Club American Express	Restaurant/Snack Bar	Monitors VHF Channel
16 Sagman's Marine, Inc. (p. 87)	(212) 885-1000	6	2	Y	85	●	6	6				L	L25	PH	GD		S	S	★▲50	A		16
17 Kretzer Boat Works	(212) 885-2600	6		Y	110		7	6					L60	PH	GD		S		★▲50	A		9
18 Stelter Marine Sales (p. 89)	(212) 885-1300			Y	35		5	4					L10	PH	GD			S	★30			
19 J.J. Burck, Inc.	(212) 885-1559			Y							MARINE SUPPLIES						S			MVA		
20 Maritime Landings/Thwaites Inn (p. 85)	(212) 885-1800	7	5	Y	85	●	6	6					L25	PH	GD		SL		▲		R	69
21 O'Keeffe's Marina	(212) 885-1692	4	3	Y	40	●	5	4					L7	PH	GD			SI	★30			68
22 New York Sailing School	(212) 885-3103		2	Y	35		10	6				L	R1.5	H					★	MVA		
23 Anna's Harbor Inn	(212) 885-1692			Y			8				RESTAURANT - DOCKAGE FOR PATRONS									MVA		
24 Sea Shore Restaurant & Marina (p. 87)	(212) 885-0300	25		Y	35	●	8	8				RD	R						★	MVAD	R	68
25 Bridge Boat Sales, Ltd.	(212) 885-2302			Y		●	8	6			NEW & USED BOAT SALES/ MARINE SUPPLIES									MVA		9
26 Ed Rosenberger Boat House	(212) 885-3453										BAIT, TACKLE, & SKIFF RENTAL											
27 City Island Yacht Sales (p. 86)	(212) 885-2300	5		Y	50	●	8	6	G	MOB			L30	PH	GD			SI	★30	MVA		9
28 Crab Shanty (p. 87)	(212) 885-1459										RESTAURANT - DOCKAGE FOR PATRONS											
29 Portside Marina	(212) 885-2211			Y	30	●	8	6					L	PH	G				★			
30 UK Sailmakers	(212) 885-1700			Y								L	SAILMAKERS								

Information in these listings is provided by the facilities themselves. An asterisk (*) indicates that the facility did not respond to our most recent requests for information.

© Mary Jane Hayes

the bigger eateries cater to tourists and as such aren't hard to spot – look for lots of bright lights, and *big* signs.

Several restaurants offer dockage for patrons. You can leave your boat at Maritime Landings/Thwaites Marina and cross the street to Thwaites Inn (212) 885-1023 for seafood and steaks in an elegant setting. Anna's Harbor Inn (212)

885-1692 offers indoor and outdoor dining and a float at O'Keefe's, next door. The Sea Shore Restaurant & Marina (212) 885-0300 offers fine dining on seafood and Italian. At the north end of the island is The Crab Shanty (212) 885-1459, formerly Lenny's Pier 1 Restaurant. Several of the yacht clubs also have restaurants.

If dockage isn't a problem, there are plenty of other choices along City Island Avenue, from seafood to Continental to Italian. Ask the marina operators or the island residents; nearly everyone has an opinion. If you're on a tight budget, try the small and unpretentious City Island Diner (212) 885-9867 at Fordham and City Island avenues, which is very popular with the local residents.

 Navigation and Anchorages

Use NOAA Charts 12366 (1:20,000), 12364 (1:40,000), and 12363 (1:80,000). Use tide tables for Willets Point. High tide at City Island is 3 minutes later; low tide is 5 minutes earlier. Mean tidal range is 7.8 feet.

City Island lies 2.0nm by boat north of Throgs Neck and 2.1nm by boat southwest of Davenport Neck. Between Throgs Neck and City Island lies Eastchester Bay, with depths of 7 to 10 feet in the southern part.

Caution is essential when navigating **Eastchester Bay.** The shores to the west are fringed with boulders, shoals, and wrecks and dotted with homes and apartment buildings. A dredged channel leads from Eastchester Bay north to the **Hutchinson River,** which has a controlling depth of less than 6 feet and nothing to offer the recreational boater, unless you like looking at oil and cement plants, and dodging barges. (We've heard, however, that a few fisherfolk were catching blue-claw crabs in the Hutchinson River in summer 1989.) The channel is narrow and has lots of obstructions.

Approaching City Island from the south or west, the principal hazards are **Big Tom,** a barely submerged rock about 700 yards west of Belden Point, and **Cuban Ledge.** Big Tom is well marked by a triangle of three buoys: flashing red "2" **[WP-8]** on the south, red nun "4" on the west, and an orange and white can "BT" on the east. The problem is that on a busy summer weekend the buoys may be "buried" by boats moored or anchored outside the special anchorage area, and thus difficult or impossible to spot. The same problem can occur with red nun "WR6," 1,000 yards to the north.

CAUTION: The other major hazard on this approach is Cuban Ledge, almost in the center of Eastchester Bay. The charted buoys at Cuban Ledge have been changed. The red 4sec flasher "2" [WP-6] on the west side of the ledge has been relocated slightly east, and the green 2.5sec flasher "5" has been removed and replaced by the red 6sec flasher "CL," about 400 yards to the southeast of flasher "2." Whatever you do, don't pass between the two buoys, or you'll be patronizing the nearest towing service. Also, be careful of the 5-foot spot about 0.3nm northeast of Weir Creek. You'll pass right over it if you leave Weir Creek and head directly toward the spire on City Island.

If you're anywhere around **Cuban Ledge,** keep a sharp eye out for the tug and barge traffic heading north into the Hutchinson River and for the air taxis that fly in and out of Evers Seaplane Base and Marina north of Cherry Tree Point on the mainland.

From the north or east, there are two approaches to **City Island:** around the southern end of **Hart Island,** or through the rocky but navigable waters to the north. The southern end of Hart Island was once a prison, then a drug rehabilitation center, and is now a prison once again. Potters Field on the northern part of the island is a cemetery for paupers from New York City. Some estimate that hundreds of thousands of people are buried there.

A cruise around the north end of **Hart Island** can be a pleasant trip. Some boaters are intimidated by the many rocks, but the area is well marked; go slowly and follow the aids. As you pass to the north of Hart Island, stay between red bell "4" **[WP-10]** at the South Nonations and can "3," swinging north and wide around The Blauzes.

CAUTION: Never try to go between the South and East Nonations to the north, or between The Blauzes and Hart Island to the south, where you can lose a hull with no trouble at all. Caution is also essential when heading down the channel north of Chimney Sweeps, to the north of High Island. Follow those buoys!

If you're heading for one of the marinas north of the bridge connecting City Island to the mainland, go carefully. There's plenty of water but the channel is unmarked. Aim for the middle of the bridge and stay in mid-channel. The longest of the piers to port come all the way out into the channel. On the north, the shore drops off pretty sharply into the channel.

If you're heading east, away from City Island, the channel north of **Hart Island** leads to the south entrance of **New Rochelle Harbor** and some very nice anchorages between Davids and Hunter islands.

If you want to anchor off City Island instead of staying at one of the marinas or yacht clubs, you can do so in

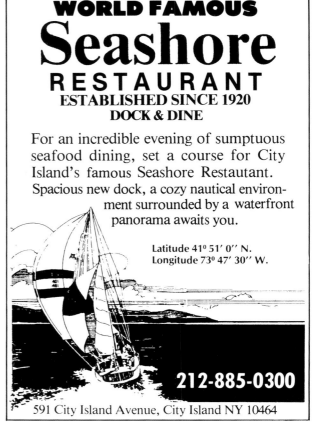

Eastchester Bay west of the island, although the anchorage is filled with yacht club and commercial moorings and is often packed with boats. Every year it seems that more moorings appear, spilling farther west out into the channel.

The most popular anchorage is south of the fixed bridge that connects City Island to Rodman Neck, in an area dominated by powerboats. If you're in a deep-draft boat, be aware of the 3- to 4-foot areas just off the shores on either side. Since the bridge has a vertical clearance of only 12 feet, circumnavigating the island is possible only for small powerboats. You may encounter currents of 1 or 2 knots in the area around the bridge.

You may find more room to anchor in **City Island Harbor,** also known as **Hart Island Roads,** to the east. City Island Harbor is somewhat better protected but has only fair holding ground. The best bet is south of the high rocks of **Rat Island.** Keep in mind that in a northeast or east wind, the area north of Rat Island is very exposed, and there's at least a good 50 miles of fetch behind those waves. The local residents tell us of seeing boats anchored north of Rat Island rocking hard on the high swells, while at the same time those anchored south of the island, protected by Hart Island, were rolling gently. Wherever you choose to drop a hook, you will have plenty of company.

Be sure to give **Green Flats,** just west of Rat Island, plenty of room. It's exposed at low water and always

dangerous. The fixed bridge connecting **High Island** and the WNBC and WCBS radio towers with City Island has no water under it at low tide.

Stay within the 5-mph speed limit around the island, or the NYPD Harbor Unit, which patrols these waters, may spoil your day. They are especially on the lookout for drunk boaters.

International Underwater Contractors (212) 885-0600 on Fordham Street has the only decompression chamber west of Norwalk, CT. Although mostly used by a local hospital for medical purposes, it is available to scuba divers in emergencies.

 Shoreside and Emergency Services

Airport: Port Authority of NY/NJ 1-800-AIR-RIDE
Ambulance: 911 or (212) 885-1116
Bus: NYC Travel Authority (718) 330-1234
Coast Guard: Fort Totten (718) 352-4422/4423 or VHF 16
Fire: 911 or (212) 566-3443
Hospital: Westchester Square Hospital (212) 430-7300
Police: 911 or (212) 822-5411
 NYPD Harbor Unit (212) 993-0950 or VHF 16
Radio Telephone: VHF 25,26,84;I.D.: NY Marine
 Operator; VHF 86; I.D.: Mariphone
 Marine Operator
 VHF 28; I.D.: WHU 738
Taxi: Zero's (212) 822-2222
Tow Service: Sound Tow Co., Bronx, NY
 (212) 885-3420 or VHF 16
Train: Amtrak 1-800-USA-RAIL
 Metro-North 1-800-638-7646
 Long Island Railroad (516) 794-LIRR   ✦

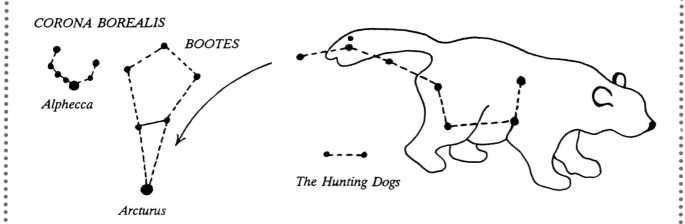

CORONA BOREALIS

BOOTES

Alphecca

Arcturus

The Hunting Dogs

JUNE SKIES:
The Herdsman and a Celestial Crown

Shortly after sunset on June evenings, the first star to appear to the naked eye will be Arcturus, a red giant some 36 light-years away. Arcturus is an aging star, swollen to nearly twenty-five times the size of our sun. Its name means "watcher of the bears," and it's the brightest star in the constellation Bootes, the herdsman.

The Greeks placed the herdsman in the sky to ensure that the mythical bears Ursa Major and Ursa Minor continually plod around the celestial pole. The herdsman has often been portrayed holding a staff in one hand and the tethers of two hunting dogs in the other hand. Bootes seems to walk behind Ursa Major, the Great Bear, nudging her with his staff, while the hunting dogs nip at her heels.

Bootes is easy to find on June nights. Sailors use an easy phrase to help them locate the herdsman: "The arc of the handle leads to Arcturus." Follow the curve of the Big Dipper handle, and not far off its tip will be the bright and coppery Arcturus. It forms a triangle with two faint stars to make the herdsman's legs. Atop the triangle is a circle of stars that form his torso. Actually, modern sailors may find Bootes more closely resembles an ice cream cone, with Arcturus at the tip of the cone.

Just east of Bootes is a pretty semi-circle of stars that looks like a smile. This is the constellation Corona Borealis, called the Northern Crown by sailors. The brightest of the stellar crown jewels is Alphecca, near the center curve of the crown.

Contributed by Elinore DeWire, Assistant at the Mystic Seaport Planetarium and a freelance writer.

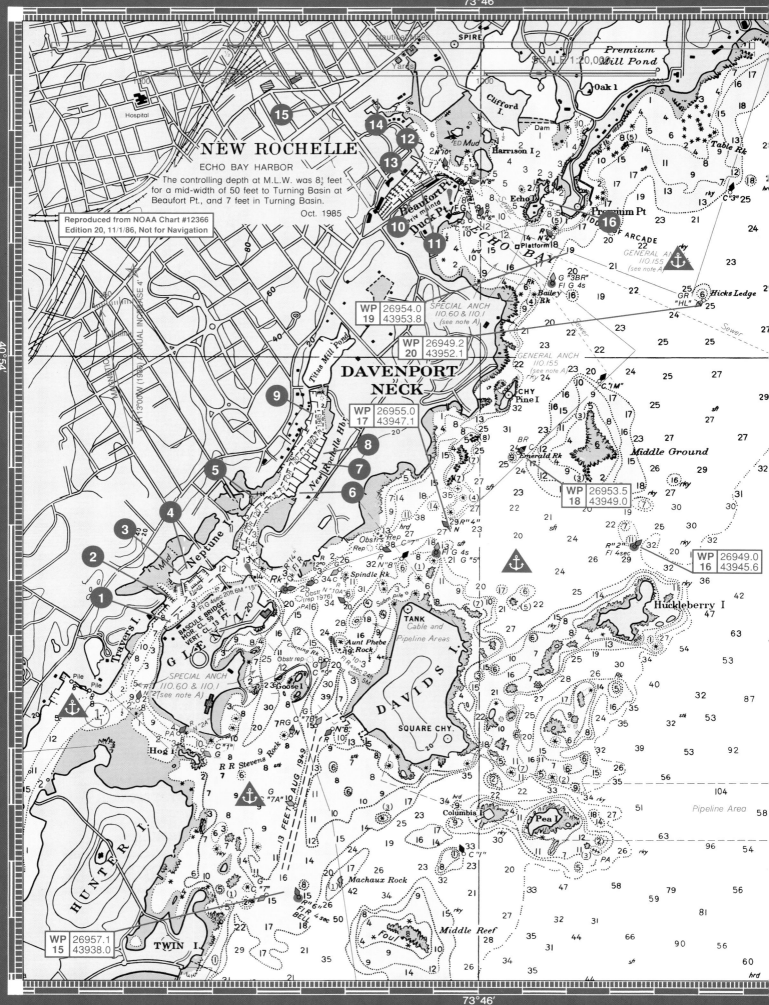

New Rochelle Harbor and Echo Bay

'Queen City of the Sound'

Islands count for a lot in these parts. In New Rochelle, tucked into the southeast corner of Westchester County, islands help to define the channels, protect the harbors and anchorages, and provide a place for a friendly fishing spot or a picnic.

For instance, if it's a park you want, try the wooded Hunter Island, a part of Pelham Bay Park, New York City's largest. Just across the channel is Glen Island, now a popular Westchester County park that also sports a casino (sans gambling) and restaurant. It was once actually five islands, in the days when it was a widely known amusement park.

If you're looking for a club or marina, just look across the channel to Travers Island, Neptune Island or Davenport Neck – a peninsula that may as well be an island for all its shoreline – full of homes, marinas, and private clubs.

Pretty cut-and-dried, to be sure. For the real action, however, you need look no further than Davids Island, to the east. At first glance, you'll see nothing but forbidding, crumbling buildings and a rusting water tower on the island. Ask almost anyone in New Rochelle, however; this 80-acre chunk of land is the hottest topic in town.

In the 1800s Davids Island was the site of Fort Slocum, built to defend the Sound. It served a variety of military

New Rochelle Harbor, NY (center) and Echo Bay (upper right) from the southwest.

Marine Facilities and Services

#	Facility	Phone	Number of Transient Berths	Number of Transient Moorings	Seasonal/Year-round	Largest Vessel Accommodation (ft)	Marked Entry Channel	Approach Depth (ft at MLW)	Dockside Depth (ft at MLW)	Gas/Diesel Fuel	Fuel Brand	Ramp/Dinghy Dock/Launch Service	Railway/Lift: Capacity (tons)	Propeller/Hull Repairs	Engine Repairs: Gas/Diesel	Pump-out Station	Showers/Laundromat	Marine Supplies/Groceries/Bait/Ice	110V★ 220V▲ Maximum Amps	MasterCard/VISA/Diners Club American Express	Restaurant/Snack Bar	Monitors VHF Channel
1	Glen Island Park Ramp		*LAUNCHING RAMP- RESIDENTS ONLY*																			
2	New York Athletic Club Yacht Club	(914) 738-2700	*PRIVATE CLUB - MEMBERS ONLY*																			
3	West Harbor Yacht Service	(914) 636-1524	2		Y	50	●	8	8				L25	PH	GD		SL	SI	★30			
4	Huguenot Yacht Club	(914) 636-6300	*PRIVATE CLUB - MEMBERS ONLY*																			
5	Wright Island Marina	(914) 235-8013	10	5	Y	65	●	11	11	GD	CIT		L50	PH	GD		SL	SI	★▲50	MV	SR	16
6	Imperial Yacht Club (p. 92)	(914) 636-1125			Y	65	●	13	13	GD	MOB		L70	PH	GD		SL	I	★▲	MV	R	16
7	Neptune Boat Club	(914) 636-9764			Y	35	●	8	7				L15	PH	G		S		★15			
8	Castaways Yacht Club (p. 93)	(914) 636-8444	2		Y	60	●	14	7				L35	PH	GD		SL	I	50		R	
9	Snug Cove Yacht Club	(914) 235-6200	*PRIVATE CLUB - MEMBERS ONLY*																			
10	Polychron Marina	(914) 632-4088			S	30	●	10	4				L5		G			I			R	
11	Hudson Park Bait & Tackle	(914) 235-0050			S		●	8		*FISHING STATION*								BI		A		16
12	New Rochelle Rowing Club	(914) 636-9717	*PRIVATE CLUB - MEMBERS ONLY*																			
13	New Rochelle Municipal Marina	(914) 235-6930	1		Y	50	●	10	5	GD	TEX		L20	PH	GD		SL	SIG	★15	MVA	SR	16
14	Echo Bay Marine	(914) 636-8334	4		Y	65	●	3	8				L15	PH	GD		S		★15			16
15	Defender Industries (p. 93)	(914) 632-2319	*MARINE SUPPLIES*																			
16	Echo Bay Yacht Club*		*PRIVATE CLUB - MEMBERS ONLY*																			

Information in these listings is provided by the facilities themselves. An asterisk (*) indicates that the facility did not respond to our most recent requests for information.

purposes until the 1960s, when the government sold the island to the city of New Rochelle, which has been trying ever since to figure out what to do with it.

Everyone, you see, has a plan for Davids Island. The latest proposal is to build a private community of high- and low-rise luxury condominiums, a heliport, an 800-slip marina, and a beach, all connected to the mainland by a 3,500-foot bridge and closed (entirely or in part) to the public. Estimated cost: $1 billion.

A lot of people, among them environmentalists and many local residents, say the development will increase traffic, create a "visual monstrosity," and strain the area's sewage facilities. Better, they say, that the island be turned into a public park, a wildlife sanctuary, a site for a new high-tech sewage treatment plant, or some combination thereof.

A lot of other people, among them the New Rochelle City Council, see the development as a creative and profitable use for the island. Throw in a host of local, state, and federal agencies with jurisdiction in the matter, and you've got an enormous free-for-all with very high stakes.

After more than three years of argument the issue is far from being settled. The final environmental impact statement was due out by Christmas 1989, and after that it was up to all those public agencies to reach a consensus. One thing there's no shortage of here is opinions. Public hearings on the proposal have been known to draw nearly 1,000 people.

 What To See and Do

Thomas Paine, the Revolutionary-War era author of *The Rights of Man, The Age of Reason,* and the famous *Common Sense,* once lived in New Rochelle. For more on Thomas Paine in New Rochelle, visit the Paine Monument, Paine Cottage, or the Paine Memorial House, open on weekends and maintained by the Huguenot/Thomas Paine Historical Association (914) 632-5376.

On Neptune Island north of the Huguenot Yacht Club, you'll see the dock for the *Klondike Princess* and the *Klondike IX* (914) 738-4593, excursion boats that offer cruises to New York City. The *Klondike IX* also doubles as an open-party fishing boat.

Of New Rochelle's two harbor areas, the larger and more popular is around Glen Island, a park and bathing beach for Westchester County residents only. But don't feel left out: friends tell us that you won't want to take a swim at the beach in either place, particularly in Echo Bay where the water quality is quite poor.

The city has plans to develop Five Islands Park on the north side of Echo Bay. Already there's a clubhouse and picnic area on Clifford Island. By the end of 1990 the city hopes to install footbridges from Clifford Island out to the two Harrison Islands to the south, where there will be trails and picnic sites. Once the park is developed, you'll be able to come ashore in a dinghy from your mooring.

Downtown New Rochelle, with an enormous shopping mall and a host of restaurants of every description, is on Main Street (Rte. 1), only 1/2 mile up residential Echo Avenue from the Echo Bay waterfront. You'll also find groceries and a laundromat on Main.

If you're staying at one of the marinas or clubs around New Rochelle Harbor and Davenport Neck, you'll find a supermarket, bakery, and a pizzeria on Pelham Road next to Snug Cove Yacht Club. There's another small strip mall with a deli, package store and meat market to the south, at Pelham and Town Dock Roads. Otherwise, it's more of a hike to any of the commercial areas. Consider taking a bicycle or cab.

 Where To Eat

Much of the waterfront area in New Rochelle is surrounded by neighborhoods, but there is a sprinkling of eateries relatively close by. At Polychron Marina is Dudley's (914) 636-9491, an unpretentious spot serving pub fare. Also, from Echo Bay it's a two-minute cab ride to downtown and Vincent DiOrio's (914) 636-6000, which specializes in ribs, steak, and seafood in a casual atmosphere. Lunch is inexpensive, dinner isn't, and take-out is available. There were plans to renovate and open the old restaurant at the Municipal Marina, but they seem to have fallen through in 1989. Keep your ears open for further developments.

To the south, between Echo Bay and New Rochelle Harbor on Pelham Road is Frank and John's (914) 636-6649, featuring steaks, seafood and Italian and prices from medium to expensive. Farther south on Pelham Road is Mamma Francesca (914) 636-1229, serving – you guessed it – Italian. The restaurant features a new deck overlooking the harbor.

On Davenport Neck, you'll find Serafino's (914) 636-9449 at the Imperial Yacht Club, serving steaks and seafood with a menu that changes daily. Finally, for a great location, elegant setting and prices to match, try the Glen Island Casino (914) 636-6500. You'll have an unobstructed view of Davids Island and a chance to formulate your own plan for it while you sample the Continental menu.

Navigation and Anchorages

Use NOAA Charts 12366 (1:20,000), 12367 (1:20,000), 12364 (1:40,000), and 12363 (1:80,000). Use tide tables for Willets Point. High tide at New Rochelle is 18 minutes earlier; low tide is 21 minutes earlier. Multiply by 1.0 for height at high or low water. Mean tidal range is 7.8 feet.

New Rochelle has two harbor areas, New Rochelle Harbor and Echo Bay. Both are strewn with rocks and small islands in addition to the larger islands. Davids Island, outside the entrance to New Rochelle Harbor, is 2.0nm by boat north of City Island Harbor, 1.9nm by boat northwest of Sands Point on Long Island, and 4.0nm by boat southwest of Mamaroneck Harbor. Echo Bay is about a mile to the northeast of New Rochelle Harbor.

CAUTION: *The number of obstructions around both New Rochelle harbors makes it dangerous to enter after dark if you are a newcomer. Even the local veterans get stuck now and then.*

The main approach to the area around **Glen Island** is between Middle Ground and Huckleberry Island. Be sure to keep the red 4sec flasher "2" **[WP-16]** to starboard. Another approach is to go via Echo Bay, past Middle Ground, to the narrow buoyed channel between Davids Island and Davenport Neck. If you're not interested in going ashore, there are fair anchorages northeast of Davids Island, northwest of Huckleberry Island, and just off the Glen Island Casino. Be warned, however: one of our readers tells us that the bird rookery on Huckleberry Island, which is owned by the New York Athletic Club, is the source of an incredible din during the nesting season.

Follow the chart closely. Once you're past **Middle Ground** on either approach, you'll be looking to shoot between red nun "4" and the green 4sec flasher "5" **[WP-17]** north of Davids Island. It's a straight shot west from red flasher "2" **[WP-16]**, but if you're coming south from Echo Bay, be sure to swing wide to the east to avoid the rocks immediately north of nun "4." From there follow the

buoyed channel, being careful to avoid Spindle Rock at all costs.

CAUTION: *Spindle Rock is well marked by green can "9," yet we're told that Spindle Rock is hit by boaters twice a day on some weekends!*

At the red quick flasher "14" between Davenport Neck and Glen Island, you turn to starboard. Dead ahead is Neptune Island, with a small pier for residents only. About 200 yards later, after passing the 20-foot green 4sec flasher "15," you have the choice of turning north to go into upper **New Rochelle Harbor** or south to go behind Glen Island in the lower harbor. If you need more than 13 feet of vertical clearance, you will have to give a long and a short blast of your horn to open the Glen Island bascule bridge.

From the south, there are two approaches to Glen Island and **New Rochelle Harbor.** If you're headed for New Rochelle Harbor, your best bet is to follow the dredged channel from the red flashing bell "6" **[WP-15]** west of Middle Reef, and then to head northerly between Davids Island and Goose Island. The area on the west side of the channel is an anchorage – very peaceful and fairly well protected.

A 19th-century poster advertising the Glen Island amusement resort off New Rochelle, New York. Note that bridges link the islands together. When Westchester County purchased the property in the 1920's, the gaps were filled in to make one large island – the present-day recreation area.
Photo courtesy of the New Rochelle Historical Society

GLEN ISLAND, AMERICA'S SHANGRI-LA

Old timers in New Rochelle used to say one could hear the lions roaring at feeding time on Glen Island, the famous 19th century amusement resort just off shore in Long Island Sound.

The Glen Island attraction was the creation of John H. Starin, former U.S. Congressman and New York transportation king, who bought five islands in 1870 and converted them into world attractions.

Starin's excursion boats brought thousands of people from New York City. A chain ferry provided access from the New Rochelle shore.

The islands were linked to a large island by bridges. Each island had its own attraction. There were restaurants, bathing pavilions, a zoo, an aviary, an aquarium and a replica of a German castle, "Little Germany."

The park probably reached its peak in the 1880's and continued to draw thousands through the end of the century. To boost trade Starin brought Indians from the West, and Filipinos and Puerto Ricans who caused the visitors of those days to gawk and marvel.

Starin died in 1904, and though the resort was continued by others for a while, it never was the same. Westchester County bought the islands in 1923, filled in the gaps and created today's Glen Island Park.

In the 1930s the island was a mecca for dancers, as Glenn Miller, Tommy and Jimmy Dorsey and Claude Thornhill ushered in the era of the Big Bands. Its casino still caters to those seeking refreshments and an occasional big band.

Contributed by Thomas A. Hoctor, New Rochelle City Historian

Head toward the 24-foot red 4sec flasher "10" at Aunt Phebe Rock, turn to port between it and green can "9," and head into the harbor. Beware of a number of charted but unbuoyed rocks in this area. You'll see a few of them if you're here at low tide.

The second approach is to the south of **Glen Island.** The controlling depth is only 6 or 7 feet, so again, a rising tide will help. The channel is very narrow, but big sailboats pass through it regularly. Keep it slow and watch the chart. The Bronx-New Rochelle border, incidentally, runs nearly right up the middle of the channel. On the south side of the channel you may see a few small "houseboats" or floating cabins, complete with porches and rocking chairs. Don't forget to wave as you go by.

There's a well-protected anchorage on the south side of **Travers Island;** one of our readers tells us that sometimes when he's anchored there it's so peaceful that he can't believe he's only 10 miles from Manhattan. On the other hand, the same area is not immune from waterskiers and the like, so you also might find the spot a little crazy.

The channel on the west side of **Glen Island** is crowded with assigned moorings and floats and is the home of the very exclusive New York Athletic Club Yacht Club (look for the huge white clubhouse with a red roof), the Huguenot Yacht Club, and West Harbor Yacht Service, which may have an available slip. There's a big sewer pipe going across the bottom of this channel – not a hazard for most of us, but big sailboats with drafts of 8 feet or more have been known to bump it on occasion at low tide.

CAUTION: Don't try to go around the eastern side of Davids Island. There is foul ground all around it. Also keep well clear of tiny Pea Island, owned by the Huguenot Yacht Club. The wreck to the southeast of Pea Island belonged to one of the many skippers who didn't realize how far the shoal extended. Note that can "1" off Columbia Island is now green.

Echo Bay is much easier to enter but offers fewer places to stay. The bay is generally shallow, except in the dredged channel, and usually is filled with local boats. Be especially watchful for the many small sailboats that shoot across the bay.

Approaching **Echo Bay** is much simpler than the approach to New Rochelle Harbor. From the south, you can go to the west of Middle Ground, marked by a green and red can at Emerald Rock **[WP-18]**. Once past tiny Pine Island, off Davenport Neck, it's a clear shot north-northeast to the green 4sec flasher "3BR" **[WP-19]** and the entrance to the channel.

From the east, approaching **Echo Bay** is even easier. The best landmarks are the gold-domed clock tower of the New Rochelle Rowing Club on Beaufort Point and the long red clubhouse of the Echo Bay Yacht Club on Echo Island. Start at the red 4sec flasher "2" **[WP-24]** about 1.0nm east of Middle Ground, and head west for the green and red can

"HL" **[WP-20]** at **Hicks Ledge.** Keep Hicks Ledge to starboard to avoid the 6-foot spot to the north of the can, and from there look for the green flasher "3BR" **[WP-19]**. If you pass closer to **Middle Ground,** note that can "1M" on the north of the shoal is now green.

After rounding Beaufort Point, to port you'll see (and hear) the New Rochelle Municipal Marina, which accommodates 600 boats and can be a little noisy. If you're headed for the Municipal Marina, get the fenders ready: The docks are steel, and very unforgiving.

Opposite the Municipal Marina on Beaufort Point is Polychron Marina, the Rowing Club, and a fishing station where you can rent small skiffs with outboards.

There is a 4-mph speed limit in the harbor. For a little more room to swing (or less commotion), try one of the general anchorages either northwest of Middle Ground or between Hicks Ledge and Premium Point, just outside the harbor.

 Shoreside and Emergency Services

Airport: Port Authority of NY/NJ 1-800-AIR-RIDE
Ambulance: 911
Bus: Westchester County Bee Line System (914) 682-2020
Coast Guard: Fort Totten (718) 352-4422/4423 or VHF 16
Fire: 911 or (914) 632-6700
Harbormaster: (914) 235-7339 or VHF 16
Hospital: New Rochelle Medical Center (914) 632-5000
Police: 911 or (914) 654-2229
Radio Telephone: VHF 25, 26, 84; I.D.: NY Marine Operator; VHF 86; I.D.: Mariphone Marine Operator; VHF 28; I.D.: WHU 738
Taxi: Blue Bird Taxi (914) 632-0909
    Deluxe Taxi (914) 632-8000
Tow Service: Sound Tow Co., Bronx, NY (212) 885-3420 or VHF 16
Train: Amtrak 1-800-USA-RAIL
    Metro-North 1-800-638-7646 ◆

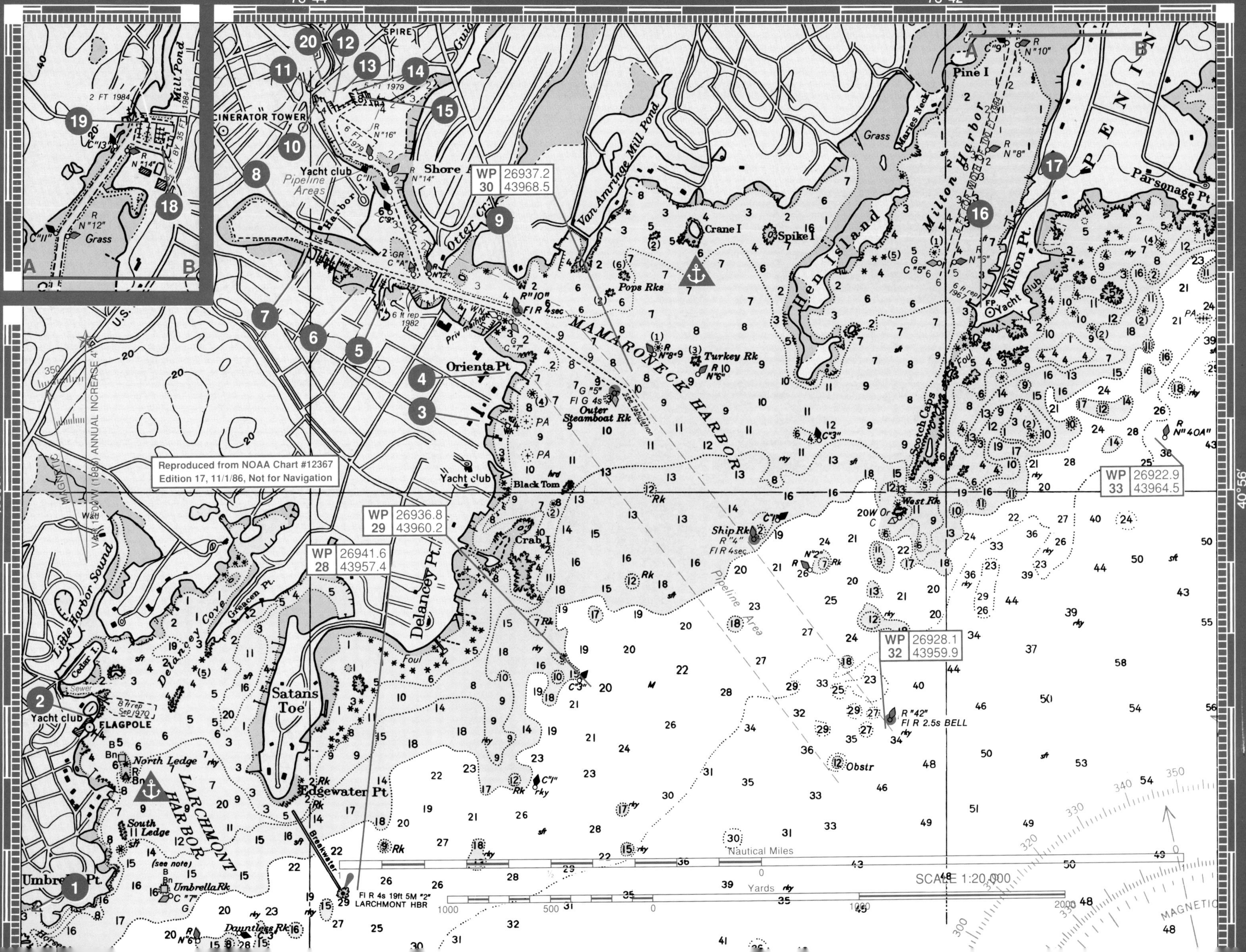

40°56'

73°42'

73°44'

PENINE

Parsonage Pt.

Pine I

Harbor

Milton Harbor

Milton Pt.

Yacht Club

Scotch Caps

West Rk

Harbor Island

Crane I

Turkey Rk

Pops Rks

Van Amringe Mill Pond

MAMARONECK HARBOR

Outer Steamboat Rk

Orienta Pt.

Black Tom

Crab I

Yacht Club

Ship Rk

Pipeline Area

Delancey Pt.

Gregson Pt.

Satans Toe

Breakwater

Edgewater Pt.

Yacht Club

Shore

Pipeline Areas

INCINERATOR TOWER

Mill Pond

Grass

Little Harbor Sound

FLAGPOLE

Yacht Club

LARCHMONT HARBOR

North Ledge

South Ledge

Umbrella Pt.

Dauntless Rk

Umbrella Rk

see tabulation

SCALE 1:20,000

Nautical Miles

Yards

MAGNETIC

Var 13°00'W (1988) ANNUAL INCREASE 4'

FI R 2.5s BELL

FI R 4s 19ft 5M "2" LARCHMONT HBR

WP 33 26922.9 43964.5

WP 32 26928.1 43959.9

WP 30 26937.2 43968.5

WP 29 26936.8 43960.2

WP 28 26941.6 43957.4

Of Moths' Wings and Mayhem

What did German emperor Kaiser Wilhelm, the financiers William K. Vanderbilt and J.P. Morgan, and Sir Thomas Lipton, the perennial challenger for the America's Cup, have in common? Well, apart from their considerable wealth, their power, their gender, and the fact that they're all dead, not much. Not much, that is, unless you live in Larchmont, NY, where you will be reminded that all were once members of the Larchmont Yacht Club.

The club is one of the oldest in the country and has sponsored Larchmont Race Week every July since 1895. During Race Week as many as 500 boats in every class will fill the waters around the harbor. One of our readers describes the scene as "a blanket of sails...like thousands of moths' wings in the harbor." Some would call it exciting, while others describe it as mere mayhem. Either way, be

Harbor Island and the west and east branches of Mamaroneck Harbor, NY.

Marine Facilities and Services

#	Facility	Phone	Transient Berths	Transient Moorings	Seasonal/Year-round	Largest Vessel Accommodation (ft)	Marked Entry Channel	Approach Depth (ft MLW)	Dockside Depth (ft MLW)	Gas/Diesel Fuel	Fuel Brand	Ramp/Dinghy Dock	Railway/Lift Capacity (tons)	Launch Service	Propeller/Hull Repairs	Engine Repairs Gas/Diesel	Marine Supplies/Groceries/Bait/Ice	Pump-out Station	Showers/Laundromat	110V★ 220V▲ Max Amps	MasterCard/VISA/Diners/AmEx	Restaurant/Snack Bar	Monitors VHF Channel
1	Horseshoe Harbor Yacht Club	(914) 834-9808											*PRIVATE CLUB - MEMBERS ONLY*										
2	Larchmont Yacht Club	(914) 834-2440		20	Y			4	4	GD			*PRIVATE CLUB - MEMBERS ONLY*				I				MVAD	RS	68
3	Orienta Beach Club	(914) 698-1900											*PRIVATE CLUB - MEMBERS ONLY*										
4	Beach Point Yacht Club	(914) 698-1600											*PRIVATE CLUB - MEMBERS ONLY*										
5	Total Yacht Sales of Mamaroneck	(914) 698-8930	2	1	Y	42	●	5	4				L15		PH	GD			S	★20			
6	Mamaroneck Boats and Motors	(914) 698-2700	6	2	Y	35	●	10	8	G	GUL		L30		PH	GD	SI	●	S	★30	MV		9
7	Nichols Yacht Yards	(914) 698-6065	5		Y	55	●	8	7	GD		D	L25		PH	GD	SI		S	★30	MV		
8	Harbor Island Municipal Marina	(914) 698-3142		2	S	22	●	7	7			RD								★			16
9	Mamaroneck Yacht Club	(914) 698-1130											*PRIVATE CLUB - MEMBERS ONLY*										
10	Global Yachts and Performance Boats	(914) 698-3893	2		Y	70	●	15	8						P				S	★			
11	Rad-Com, Inc.	(914) 698-6800			Y							*MARINE ELECTRONICS*					I						
12	Post Road Boat Yard	(914) 698-0295	5		Y	70	●	8	8	GD			L50		PH	GD	SI		S	★▲			
13	Robert E. Derecktor Shipyard	(914) 698-5020	5	2	Y	120	●	4	10				L20		PH	GD		●		★▲			
14	Orienta Yacht Club	(914) 698-9858			S	40	●	6	6			*PRIVATE CLUB - MEMBERS ONLY*					SI			★			68
15	McMichael Yacht Yard	(914) 381-5900			Y	50	●	6	9				L25		PH	GD				★30			16
16	American Yacht Club	(914) 967-4800											*PRIVATE CLUB - MEMBERS ONLY*										
17	Shenorock Shore Yacht Club	(914) 967-3700											*PRIVATE CLUB - MEMBERS ONLY*										
18	**The Shongut Marine (p.101)**	**(914) 967-3842**	1		Y	35	●	4	4	G	BP	D	L15		PH	G	SI			★	MVA		16
19	Rye Municipal Boat Basin	(914) 967-1440	1		Y	37	●	6	5			R						●		★			16
20	R.G. Brewer, Inc.	(914) 698-3232											*MARINE HARDWARE & SUPPLIES*										

Information in these listings is provided by the facilities themselves. An asterisk (*) indicates that the facility did not respond to our most recent requests for information.

prepared for lots of company if you plan to cruise here during Race Week. So strong is the racing fever that even in the dead of winter, you'll see the area's hardy "frostbiters," racing their tiny sailboats in the cold weather.

If it's facilities you're looking for, you'll have to head next door to Mamaroneck Harbor, which is almost entirely man-made. Harbor Island, home to the municipal marina and the sewage-treatment plant, was once called Quahog Island – not much bigger than a clam at only 4 1/2 acres. The East Basin was navigable only at high water and the West Basin was marsh. In 1912 the village dredged the East Basin and partially filled in the marsh between the island (by then called "Hog Island") and the mainland. Finally, during the 1930s the West Basin was dredged and the island was expanded to its present 44 acres to become Harbor Island.

Derecktor's, in the East Basin, built *Stars & Stripes,* the winner of the 1987 America's Cup, for Dennis Conner.

 What To See and Do

Unless you stay at the yacht club, there is no place to get ashore in Larchmont, so if you are in need of supplies or want to check out the restaurants in town, you would do better to head for New Rochelle or Mamaroneck. If you'd like to do some "real estating," however, you'll want to check out the neighborhood of palatial homes and tree-lined streets around Larchmont Yacht Club.

From Mamaroneck Harbor you'll have access to Mamaroneck Avenue and Boston Post Road, each loaded with shops and restaurants of every description. If that's not enough to sate your appetite(s), it's a quick cab ride to Larchmont, New Rochelle, or even White Plains.

If you're interested in fishing near Execution Rocks lighthouse, remember that it is surrounded by heavy commercial traffic, and occasionally, by currents strong enough to set you onto the rocks if you're not careful. The only safe place to come in close and anchor is on the south side. The rocks on the west side are particularly dangerous.

Playland (914) 921-0370, located between Peningo Neck and Port Chester, is touted as the largest city-owned amusement park in the world, with over 270 acres and a small artificial harbor. Good landmarks for Playland are a white tower, a blue and white dome, and the roller coaster. Just to the west you'll see the enormous white stucco pavilion at Rye Beach. For the past couple of years, Playland has put on a fireworks display every Wednesday and Friday night at 9:15 during the summer. From your boat you will have the best seat in the house and not have to pay admission to the park. Unfortunately, the pier at Playland is in disrepair and there is no docking here or at Rye Beach.

 Where To Eat

There are a number of restaurants within walking distance of Mamaroneck Harbor. Right at the entrance to Harbor Island Park, on the Post Road, is Lum Yen (914) 698-6881, a reasonably priced Chinese restaurant with the usual long menu. Just a block south on the Post Road is Seagull's (914) 381-5337, featuring steak and seafood, and a bit of history. The novelist James Fenimore Cooper, it's said, was married in this house in 1811. On the Post Road just north of Harbor Island is Charlie Brown's (914) 698-6610, specializing in steaks, chicken, and seafood in a casual atmosphere. Further north is The Mamaroneck Inn (914) 698-3564, which sports a diner-style menu and offers takeout.

Up Mamaroneck Avenue, within four blocks of Harbor Island Park, you'll find Luke's (914) 698-1011 tucked in among the storefronts. They specialize in Dutch Indonesian food at medium prices. Also on Mamaroneck Avenue, you'll find several diners, delis, and pizzerias; Tony's Pizza (914) 698-2829 delivers. For "do-it-yourselfers" there are also a couple of small markets on the same stretch.

Up at the head of Milton Harbor, your choices are more limited. Across the street from Shongut Marine and the Rye Municipal Marina there's a small deli (with seating) and Harbor Hut Pizzeria (914) 967-3347, but otherwise a cab will be necessary.

 Navigation and Anchorages

Use NOAA Charts 12367 (1:20,000), 12364 (1:40,000), and 12363 (1:80:000). Use tide tables for Willets Point. High tide at Mamaroneck is 2 minutes earlier; low tide is 13 minutes earlier. Mean tidal range is 7.8 feet.

Larchmont Harbor, a small, rocky harbor with almost no shore access, is 2.6nm by boat northeast of the entrance to New Rochelle Harbor, 6.7nm by boat southwest of Byram Harbor, and 3.0nm north of Sands Point on Long Island. Mamaroneck Harbor has a wide open entrance which it shares with Milton Harbor, and a well-protected, divided inner harbor. The entrance to Mamaroneck Harbor is 1.7nm by boat to the northeast of Larchmont Harbor.

Larchmont Harbor can be approached from either side of Hen and Chickens (off our chart), about 1/2 mile south of Umbrella Point. However, if you are a newcomer to the area, you would be much safer taking the main entrance by going between the Hen and Chickens bell "1" and the breakwater, marked by a flashing red 19-foot 4sec light **[WP-28].** Note that bell "1" now flashes green; it's been changed from white. Keep the green (formerly black) can "3" at Dauntless Rock well to port.

CAUTION: To port, opposite the inner end of the breakwater, is a pile known as Umbrella Rocks, the remains of an abandoned breakwater project. It is most hazardous when submerged at maximum tide, when its day beacon (spindle) has usually fallen over.

At the north end of the breakwater, the sand and mud bottom has shoaled, leaving considerably less water than

Execution Rocks Lighthouse
Photo by Robert G. Bachand

THE HOARY LEGEND OF EXECUTION ROCKS

Whoops! We hate to admit it, but we're guilty of publishing an untruth. Last year we found a great story, dutifully confirmed it with at least three different sources, and sent it off to the printers. To our surprise, we were summarily admonished by some historians in Westchester County, who informed us that our facts are, in fact, rubbish. Nevertheless, it's hard to let a good story die, so we once again present the horrible (but untrue) legend of Execution Rocks:

During Colonial times the British needed a quiet place to execute American patriots away from the emotionally and politically charged crowds that gathered at public executions. The British chose a rocky outcropping in the middle of the Sound where few curious landlubbers would bother, or dare, to interfere. Into the rocks they carved a small pit, fastening iron rings at low watermark. Condemned prisoners were taken to the rocks at low tide and chained into the pit, left to die a slow death as the tide rose slowly over their heads. The partially decayed remains of previous victims were sometimes left in the pit to add to the condemned prisoners' horror.

The history of Execution Rocks accounts for the unusual option that was established for the keepers when Execution Rocks Lighthouse was built in 1867. Part of the federal directive governing keepers' conduct declared that they would be free to request an instant, honorable transfer at any time. The American Government wanted to ensure that no one working on the site would ever again feel "chained to the rocks."

And now, the real facts: Execution Rocks was named for the many vessels and lives lost on the rocks, not for bogus British atrocities. The legend was apparently a bit of Colonial propaganda designed to whip up hatred for the British, although we don't know for sure where it comes from. In our defense we must note that the originators of the story must have been very effective propagandists, because the story is so widely believed to be true!

is shown on the chart. The mean tidal range is 7.8 feet, and often over 9 feet, so what looks good now may be bone-dry 6 hours later. Deep-draft boats should stay in the middle of the entrance.

Inside **Larchmont Harbor,** the depth is pretty good anywhere you see moored yachts. Spot the various rock spindles and avoid them. Going between the two spindles of North Ledge (directly off the yacht club) is a no-no; the rocks are exposed at low tide. You can't go very far into Delancey Cove except at high water. The cove between Greacen Point and Satans Toe is not worth trying because there is no room to anchor. Do your exploring in the dinghy, not with your keel.

There is good water for anchoring near the first moorings you come to, a few of which are guest moorings for the Larchmont Yacht Club. Moorings are available only to members or members of reciprocating clubs, and reservations are required. The club's main dock is off limits, even to members. Guests may tie up briefly at the work dock to the right of the club. At low tide there's about 6 feet of water at the work dock, but there's a small shoal before you get to the dock; call the launchman on VHF 68.

Mamaroneck Harbor, less than 1.5nm by boat northeast of Larchmont Harbor, encompasses everything from Delancey Point to Scotch Caps. The outer harbor is open to everything out of the south, but it's good in a northerly, and the area north of Turkey Rocks gives the best overall protection in the outer harbor. We don't recommend swimming in Mamaroneck. The water quality in the harbor is poor because Mamaroneck has only a primary water-treatment facility for its sewage. As we went to press, new sewer lines were being laid across the entrance to the West Basin, as well as in the marked "pipeline area" extending out into the Sound; the project was to be completed by March 1990. The treatment plant itself is also being upgraded, a project that will take several years.

The tricky part about entering **Mamaroneck Harbor** is that the buoys also serve Rye and Milton harbors. Coming from the east, the simplest and safest way is to observe the red flashing 2.5sec bell "42" **[WP-32],** which local boaters call the "42nd Street Buoy" because of all the traffic. Then turn and follow the main channel into Mamaroneck Harbor, leaving the reds to starboard. The confusing part is that you will be leaving a couple of greens to starboard in the process because they relate to Milton Harbor.

Heading into Mamaroneck, a good landmark from bell "42" **[WP-32]** is the pair of gray, cone-shaped towers of the Mamaroneck Yacht Club at the inner harbor entrance. The red 4sec flasher "4" at Ship Rock was temporarily changed to a red nun in 1989. Check your latest Notice to Mariners to find out when it will be changed back.

CAUTION: *On the trip into or out of the harbor, keep out of the little triangle of buoys marking Ship Rock. Every year, at least one preoccupied helmsman, spotting a red and a green ahead, steers between them before the rock serves as a rude*

reminder to keep the red on the right when returning. You can leave both to starboard or both to port, but don't go between them.

Observe the small green flasher "5" **[WP-30]** at Outer Steamboat Rock off Orienta Point. Even though you may see big boats moored to the west of it, it marks one bad rock. The harbormaster can show you a sonar image of it – tall and narrow like a chimney, and jagged! The rocks at nuns "6" and "8," northeast of Outer Steamboat Rock, show at low water.

Continuing into **Mamaroneck Harbor,** the first two marinas are private clubs. Farther in, the channel divides at the red and green can opposite nun "12." The channel to the **West Basin** is narrow and unmarked, but straight. At present, there is about 8 feet of water at low tide, but the channel may be dredged again in the next couple of years.

The Municipal Marina keeps a guest float in the **West Basin** on a first-come, first-served basis. The harbormaster can be reached on VHF 16, as can the Coast Guard Auxiliary (914) 698-0323, which maintains a base at the Municipal Marina. The Auxiliary also offers free safety examinations for your boat during the summer; call for more details.

The channel into the **East Basin** is deeper and buoyed. Do not cut the last nun. Between nuns "14" and "16" is a nasty reef very near the channel. All the water behind it is also bad as evidenced by the absence of moored boats in the area. You can come closer to the beach on the port side than you think, but your best bet is to stay in the middle of the channel.

Farther in, each "aisle" between the moored boats has deep water. There is obviously no room for anchoring, but you might have occasion to enter for service or repairs at one of the yards. If so, remember there is a 5-mph speed limit in the harbor.

CAUTION: *There is one rock off Derecktor's that gets hit by deep-draft boats. Use the outer aisle for McMichael's.*

In the northwest corner of the **East Basin,** next to the launching ramp, the harbormaster maintains a small dock for transients to tie up temporarily while picking up supplies ashore. It's an experiment for now – if boaters use but don't abuse the privilege, the dock will stay there.

Everything you need onshore is easily accessible from Mamaroneck Harbor. Mamaroneck Avenue has plenty of markets, delis, and drugstores, and a laundromat 3 blocks up the street from the Harbor Island Park entrance.

When leaving Mamaroneck Harbor to head east, many local skippers cut to the north of red bell "42" **[WP-32];** but as we said earlier, it's not something you want to try if you're unfamiliar with the area. Most of this channel is clear except for a couple of 6-foot-deep rocks (a lot shallower at new and full moons) southwest and southeast of West Rock, at the southern end of Scotch Caps. If you are determined to cut bell "42," stay well clear of the orange and white can at West Rock.

When entering **Milton Harbor** from the 42nd Street Buoy, you will head north between the red 4sec flasher "4" at Ship Rock and red nun "2," and then leave cans "1" and "3" to port. If you're coming from the east and you've cut bell "42" **[WP-32]**, keep in mind that the rock at nun "2" is to the east of the nun. In that case, stay midway between nun "2" and the white and orange buoy at West Rock.

Milton Harbor is full of moored sailboats. (If you can find a powerboat in there, let us know.) Up to Milton Point there is about 8 feet of water, and from there about 6 feet in the narrow, dredged channel. Be careful of the rock at

the green can "5" at the entrance to the channel, and don't miss the 5-mph speed limit sign.

In addition to the two clubs on the east side of Milton Harbor, you'll see the large brick clubhouse of the Durland Boy Scout Nautical Training Facility (914) 967-2770. It's one of the country's largest Sea Scout centers, where teenagers can learn day sailing, scuba diving, and snorkeling.

The trip up the harbor will be peaceful, and slow (remember that speed limit). You'll find the harbormaster at the Rye Municipal Boat Basin at the head of the harbor. You may go aground off the main dock, but it's soft mud.

📞 Shoreside and Emergency Services

Airport: Westchester County Airport (914) 328-1953
Port Authority of NY/NJ 1-800-AIR-RIDE
Ambulance: 911
Bus: Westchester County Bee Line System
(914) 682-2020
Coast Guard: Fort Totten (718) 352-4422/4423 or VHF 16
Fire: Larchmont 911 or (914) 834-0600/0016
Mamaroneck 911 or (914) 834-2100/9840
Harbormaster: Larchmont (914) 834-2440/8452
or VHF 9, 16, and 68
Mamaroneck (914) 698-3142 or VHF 16
Rye (914) 967-1440 or VHF 16
Hospital: New Rochelle Medical Center (914) 632-5000
Patrol Boat: Mamaroneck (914) 698-2400
Rye (914) 967-1234
Police: Larchmont 911 or (914) 834-1000
Mamaroneck 911 or (914) 698-2400
Radio Telephone: VHF 25, 26, 84; I.D.:NY Marine
Operator; VHF 86; I.D.: Mariphone
Marine Operator
Taxi: (Larchmont) Leon's Taxi (914) 834-4000
(Mamaroneck) Mamaroneck Taxi (914) 698-2000
Paramount Taxi (914) 698-2100
Tow Service: Sound Tow Co., Bronx, NY (212) 885-3420
or VHF 16
Train: Amtrak 1-800-USA-RAIL
Metro-North 1-800-638-7646   ◆

Greenwich Harbor and the Captain Islands

From Smugglers to Suburbs

The Byram River forms the lower boundary between New York and Connecticut, and supposedly got its name during Prohibition, when it was frequented by smugglers and was, therefore, a good place to "buy rum." Today the banks of the Byram River are lined with a mixture of marine facilities, industrial sites, and residential and commercial areas.

If you're headed into the Byram River you can dock your boat at a bit of living history. The aptly-named Tide Mill Yacht Basin was a working gristmill long before it became a haven for recreational boaters. The big red mill, now the marina office and storage building, was built in the 1770s and housed machinery that once enabled the mill to turn out more than 150 barrels of flour a week for New York City merchants. Unfortunately, the original machinery was removed and destroyed in the 1940s. All that remains are the two large millstones at the marina's driveway, and the wooden sluice gates that are still opened on occasion to drain Kirby Pond.

The Captain Islands and Captain Harbor are named in honor of "Captain" David Patrick, one of the original settlers of Greenwich, who was much respected for his bravery, but otherwise thoroughly disliked.

The town of Greenwich owes its transformation from farmland to suburb to the arrival of the railroad in 1848. On that momentous occasion, the *Stamford Advocate* reported that "animals of every description went careering around the fields sniffing the air in terror, and bipeds of every kind, condition and color set off at a full run for the railroad

© Robert G. Bachand

The old lighthouse on Great Captain Island, originally built in 1829 and rebuilt in 1868. The lighthouse was decommissioned in 1970.

Marine Facilities and Services

#	Facility	Phone	Transient Berths	Transient Moorings	Seasonal/Year-round	Largest Vessel (ft)	Marked Entry Channel	Approach Depth (ft)	Dockside Depth (ft at MLW)	Gas/Diesel Fuel	Fuel Brand	Ramp/Dinghy Dock/Launch Service	Railway/Lift: Capacity (tons)	Propeller/Hull Repairs	Engine Repairs: Gas/Diesel	Pump-out Station	Showers/Laundromat	Marine Supplies/Groceries/Bait/Ice	110V★ 220V▲ Max Amps	MasterCard/VISA/Diners/AmEx	Restaurant/Snack Bar	Monitors VHF Channel
1	Tide Mill Yacht Basin	(914) 967-2995	3		Y	60	●	8	8	GD	CIT		L25	PH	GD		S	SI	★▲100			
2	Port Chester Yacht Club	(914) 939-9687											*PRIVATE CLUB - MEMBERS ONLY*									
3	Pearl of the Atlantic Boatyard	(914) 939-4227	30		Y	35	●	15	15	G	BAR	D	L5					SI	★	MVA	R	16
4	Rudy's Tackle Barn	(203) 531-5928	1		S	25	●	12	4									SIB				
5	J. Catalano and Sons	(203) 531-9207			Y	35	●	6	6	G	AMO		L10	PH	G			S	★	MV		
6	Port Chester Municipal Marina	(914) 939-5226			S	25	●	12	5				*RESIDENTS ONLY*									16
7	Westchester Ave. Marina	(914) 937-1352	3		Y	55	●	6	6				L50	PH	GD			SI	★35	MVA		16
8	Byram Shore Boat Club	(203) 531-9858											R	*PRIVATE CLUB - MEMBERS ONLY*								
9	Byram Park Municipal Boat Basin	(203) 622-7818			S	20	●	3	3				R	*RESIDENTS ONLY*								
10	The Belle Haven Club	(203) 869-5014		2	S	70	●	7	7				RL				S	I	★		R	16
11	Greenwich Boat & Yacht Club	(203) 622-9558		2	Y	42	●	4	7								S	I				
12	Greenwich Fuel Dock	(203) 869-9689	2		S	40	●	6	4	GD	TEX	R	R10			●			★			16
13	Indian Harbor Yacht Club	(203) 869-2484											*PRIVATE CLUB - MEMBERS ONLY*									68
14	Showboat Hotel and Restaurant	(203) 661-9800											*DOCKAGE FOR PATRONS*								R	

Information in these listings is provided by the facilities themselves. An asterisk (*) indicates that the facility did not respond to our most recent requests for information.

depot." Ever since, Greenwich has been an affluent commuter's suburb of New York .City.

Despite its close ties to the Big Apple, Greenwich natives are very proud of their community's history and intent on preserving its uniqueness. By the way, the place is known as the *Town of* Greenwich, not the *City of*. We nearly had our heads taken off by some local dignitaries who heard us refer to it as the latter.

 What To See and Do

Unfortunately, unless you are staying at one of the marinas on the Byram River or in Cos Cob Harbor, access to the center of Greenwich is difficult from a boat. Other than the Showboat Inn and the few transient slips at the town fuel dock, it is hard to find a place in Greenwich Harbor to tie up your boat, or even your dinghy.

If you are successful in getting ashore, the shops and restaurants of Greenwich Avenue are very close by.

Greenwich Harbor from the southeast.

Surprisingly, Greenwich Harbor has no repair facilities or chandlery. The closest place to find such services is Cos Cob Harbor. (For more on what to do in Greenwich, see the next chapter on Cos Cob Harbor and Greenwich Cove.)

Due to its proximity to the Metro-North train station (less than 1/4 mile away) and other transportation services, the Showboat Inn (203) 661-9800 makes a convenient transfer point for guests. At the dock is the *Mark Twain,* a replica of a Mississippi paddlewheel steamer that seats 125 diners. *The Presidents,* the 93-foot motor yacht known as the *Honey Fitz* when used by President John F. Kennedy, and the *Dixie Belle* are both available for charter. Docking at the Inn is permitted for $20, but is free for restaurant patrons.

Just across the street is the Bruce Museum (203) 869-6376, with its exhibits of art and natural history. Of particular note is the museum's Nature Center, which offers exhibits on New England marine life.

Calf Island, the western boundary of Captain Harbor, is owned by the Greenwich YMCA (203) 869-1630 and may be used by visitors with permission. The 20-acre island is well equipped with a beach, campsites, a large barbecue, and refrigeration. There is a dock on the island; you are allowed to tie up for 30 minutes to load/unload. You can picnic at a campsite on a day basis or camp overnight for a fee. Groups can rent the entire island, and the YMCA will cater a clambake or roast pig luau.

If you have friends in Greenwich and you're willing to ride a ferry in return for a day at the beach, there is a municipal beach for residents only (and their guests) on

Great Captain Island. The island is served during the summer – as are Little Captain and Calf islands – by a ferry out of Greenwich Harbor (203) 661-5957.

The Audubon Center (203) 869-5272, with its 485-acre bird sanctuary and nature trails, is a 15-minute cab ride from the water and includes a section of the Byram River that's only a babbling brook. The Center is open six days a week year-round.

 Where To Eat

The part of Port Chester immediately surrounding the Byram River is full of delis and pizzerias, but not a lot of larger sit-down restaurants. The most notable exception is the Pearl of the Atlantic (914) 939-4227 at the boatyard of the same name, where you'll find medium- to high-priced Portuguese seafood, if you can get a spot to tie up at the marina. In downtown Port Chester on North Main you'll find Northern Italian at the Angsavanee Restaurant (914) 939-9645, and Spanish and Italian at the Mark Anthony (914) 937-3357. At the Rte. 1 bridge on the Byram side is Amerigo's (914) 531-9890, featuring reasonably priced Italian.

If you can get ashore at Greenwich Harbor, the Showboat Hotel and Restaurant (203) 661-9800 provides dockage for customers. The specialty is seafood, with prices ranging from medium to expensive, and you'll have a nice water view.

There are lots of other choices in the area. On Greenwich

Avenue, within walking distance of the harbor you'll find Restaurant Bertrande (203) 661-4459, recommended for its classic French menu. Even closer is The Chopping Block (203) 869-1700, serving medium-priced American and offering takeout, Benny's Italian Seafood (203) 661-6108, and the Thataway Cafe (203) 622-0947, featuring seafood and burgers.

If you've left your boat at Grass Island it's a short cab ride to the Conte Ristorante (203) 622-4387, featuring gourmet Italian at moderate prices, or Mhai Thai (203) 625-2602, featuring Thai food in an exotic atmosphere.

For more of a taste of the Orient, your choices are Maya of Japan (203) 869-4322, or La Maison Indochine (203) 869-2689 for Vietnamese. Both are fairly expensive and more than six blocks from Greenwich Harbor; a cab might be a good idea.

 Navigation and Anchorages

Use NOAA Charts 12367 (1:20,000), 12364 (1:40,000), and 12363 (1:80,000). Use tide tables for Bridgeport. High tide at Greenwich is 1 minute later; low tide is 1 minute later. Multiply by 1.1 for height at high or low water. Mean tidal range is 8.0 feet.

Your first or last stop in Connecticut is Greenwich, with four good harbors, except Indian Harbor, which should be avoided by because of mud flats. (See the following chapter on Cos Cob Harbor and Greenwich Cove for more information.) The entrance to the Byram River is 4.4nm by boat northeast of the Mamaroneck Harbor entrance and 1.7nm by boat southwest of Greenwich Harbor. Matinecock Point on Long Island is 4.8nm by boat south.

From the flashing red bell "32A" **[WP-300]** halfway between Captain Harbor and Oyster Bay, a course of about 315°m will bring you to the eastern entrance to Captain Harbor.

Coming into **Port Chester** from the south or west, it is safest to pass between the red bell "36" **[WP-39]** at Bluefish Shoal and Fourfoot Rocks, marked by a green and red junction buoy "F" (formerly black and red and unnamed). You should pass to the east of Bluefish Shoal, because hazards such as Glover Reef, farther to the west, are not buoyed. Keep an eye out for the large unlighted steel mooring buoys used by the commercial gravel barges. From Fourfoot Rocks, keep red nun "2" **[WP-43]** at **Great Captain Rocks** to starboard and the charted wreck to port.

Once past the wreck and Great Captain Rocks, swing to port around can "1," passing the 28-foot red 2.5sec flasher on the breakwater off **Byram Point.** The harbor entrance is between the breakwater to starboard and North Manursing Island to port.

From the north and east, you can enter **Port Chester Harbor** and the **Byram River** between Great Captain

WILLIAM M. 'BOSS' TWEED AND GREENWICH

A mong the most "illustrious" names in the Greenwich past was that of William M. "Boss" Tweed, the infamous Tammany Hall kingpin, who was a Greenwich resident from the late 1850's until his death in 1878.

A one-time bookkeeper who had risen steadily in New York City politics, by 1860 Tweed controlled Tammany Hall, the powerful Democratic machine that ran the city, and hence the state. Under Tweed and his cronies, the word *corruption* took on a new meaning. As head of Tammany's general committee, Tweed controlled the nominations to all city positions, and through fraud of every description stole a fortune. Estimates are that over the years the "Tweed Gang" plundered the City of New York of between $30 million and $200 million.

A good portion of Tweed's fortune was spent in Greenwich. Although he already owned a mansion in New York City, in 1865 he bought 80 acres on Putnam Avenue, on which he built his home, "Linwood." He also built a family bathhouse at Rocky Neck Harbor.

The Americus Club, a meeting place for his friends and political cronies, was begun in the 1850s and completed in 1871 on Round Island. Memberships went for $1,000, and a gold-and-ruby tiger's head membership pin went for another $2,000. In that same year, Tweed's gang managed to rig the town's vote in the election for state senator: the local winner? J.H. Woodward, an Americus Club member.

Finally exposed in New York City, Tweed was convicted of forgery and larceny and sentenced to prison in 1873. Released two years later, Tweed was again convicted on a civil charge. This time he escaped, passed through Greenwich on his way out of the country, and fled to Cuba and then Spain. There he was caught, extradited back to New York, and locked up in the Ludlow Street jail, where he died in 1878 at age 55.

The following year, the Tweed family left Greenwich for good when the Boss's widow sold the Linwood estate. The Americus clubhouse was demolished in 1892. All that remains today of the Tweed legacy is an obscure little island off the Greenwich coast.

Rocks and the unmarked Channel Rock, but it's tricky. If you have any doubts, don't attempt this shortcut. Be sure to stay clear of Channel Rock before heading west between can "1" and the breakwater. The tidal range here is about 8 feet, so if you are new to this area, come in on a rising tide.

Once in the main channel, there is a good, though small, anchorage south of the green 4sec flasher in the middle of the harbor. (There are mudflats north of the flasher.) Swimming is not recommended because Port Chester disposes of its sewage by pumping it into the river with only primary treatment.

The channel down to the Tide Mill Yacht Basin is newly dredged to 8 feet, and privately marked. The 12-foot-deep dredged channel up the river is about a mile long and reaches to the I-95 bridge, which has a vertical clearance of 60 feet.

CAUTION: *For such a narrow river, there's an amazing amount of commercial traffic here. Be on the lookout; you may see a few enormous barges tied up at the cement plants, further reducing the width of the channel. If you're a newcomer, wait for a rising tide to go upriver.*

The channel shallows to 5 feet or less at the turning basin in Port Chester. The Port Chester Yacht Club has a launching ramp available to non-residents for a $10 fee, although parking is a problem.

Byram Harbor, suitable only for shallow-draft boats in good weather, is about 2.0nm by boat northeast of the Byram River; another 1.0nm to the northeast lies Greenwich Harbor. Both Byram and Greenwich harbors are accessible only from Captain Harbor, which is bordered on the west by Calf Island and on the south by Little Captain and Great Captain islands.

Great Captain Island is to the west of Little Captain Island and is easily distinguishable by its 65-foot skeleton tower with a foghorn, a red and white flasher (now 14M instead of 12M), and a red and white diamond-shaped daymark on the eastern end of the island. Even easier to see is the island's old stone lighthouse tower. If you're sailing along the Sound, Captain Harbor is a good spot to tack into to get away from a contrary tide, or for protection in a blow. If you want to see just how much of a difference some protection from the tides can make, check yourself against Payea Reach, the measured nautical-mile course from Great Captain Island to Little Captain Island.

NOT-SO-LONE RANGERS

A man frantically radios for help after the swinging boom on his yacht has knocked his wife unconcious; about ten minutes later a white Uniflight pulls alongside, and the woman is rushed to a nearby hospital where doctors later admit that she would have died if help hadn't arrived so soon. Elsewhere, a young man is hauled out of the water into a similar white boat where he is resuscitated; a week later a grateful father begins a letter thanking a few men and women for saving his son from drowning.

If these episodes have the ring of a sea-bound lone ranger aiding people in distress, there is certainly some of that in an effective marine ambulance service aptly called the *Star of Life* Flotilla. Based in Stamford, Connecticut, the program's director, Ernst Shindele, graciously admits it was lucky the boats were in the vicinity when those calls came in. Luck or not, however, saving lives is what this team is all about.

Since its inception in 1976 as a one-boat medical assistance unit, the *Star of Life* Flotilla has grown to 34 volunteers and eight boats whose scope now extends beyond Long Island Sound and Amityville, south to Chesapeake Bay, then on to the Caribbean. These boats, each named *Star of Life* and numbered accordingly, are fully equipped for advanced life-saving and life-support situations. In addition to a Coast Guard-licensed captain and first mate, each vessel travels with at least two certified paramedics.

During the off-season each *Star of Life* is on stand-by at its respective home port. In the summers, however, they're usually on patrol, especially on beach and regatta days when accidents are more likely to happen. For the past three years the Stamford-based flagship, *Star of Life Number One,* has become a fixture in the annual power-boat races around Block Island in July. She is a twin-engined 32-footer, a high-performance craft capable of 34 knots when responding to an emergency.

Not all of the flotilla's boats are as large: based in St. John in the Virgin Islands, *Number 8* is relatively small at 23 feet, with a shallow draft appropriate for an area of gorgeous but shallow reefs.

While size may vary from base to base according to the peculiarities of the area, speed and efficiency are standard—Fast and Amazing. Being an auxiliary to the Coast Guard also enables the *Star of Life* to receive calls from the police and fire departments. The communications network makes for an average response time of 20 minutes; the flotilla has responded to 1,200 medical emergencies and save 23 lives since 1976.

Ernst Schindele hopes the *Star of Life* will become even more accessible and effective in the near future: there are plans to open the organization to the public by accepting charter members and their boats, thereby extending the program's reach. For the meantime the *Star of Life* will still make boat calls. Free of charge.

The two main approaches to **Captain Harbor** – and hence Byram Harbor, Greenwich Harbor, Indian Harbor, and Cos Cob Harbor – are from the east and west. If you're here for the first time, entering Captain Harbor from the east is the safest course. Use the passage between the green 2.5sec flashing gong "1" **[WP-51]** and red nun "2" off Flat Neck Point. Be sure to leave green can "1A" to port to avoid Hen and Chickens. Once past "1A" you'll be in Captain Harbor and will see Greenwich Harbor directly ahead to the northwest. Cos Cob Harbor will be to the north.

Entering **Captain Harbor** from the south or west, head north between the 25-foot 4sec green flasher at **Jones Rocks [WP-44]** and red nun "4" **[WP-45]** northwest of Cormorant Reef. The 25-foot skeleton tower and concrete base of Jones Rocks is easily spotted and makes a good landmark. An alternate route lies between Cormorant Reef and Great Captain Island, keeping can "1" close to port.

CAUTION: *While it is possible to enter Captain Harbor from between Great Captain Island and Little Captain Island, we concur with local wisdom and don't recommend this approach because of the lack of buoys. Many of the rocks you see exposed at low tide are deceptively covered much of the time.*

Once in **Captain Harbor,** you have easy access to Byram Harbor and Greenwich Harbor. Captain Harbor itself affords fair shelter and some good anchorages. Keep an eye out for Red Rock southeast of Tweed Island, which is a frequent cause of trouble for visitors. Tweed Island (named for the nefarious Boss Tweed) also marks the entrance to the very pretty Indian Harbor, which is too grassy and shallow to accommodate most cruising boats.

Two secluded anchorages can be found in the 7- to 8-foot area north of Calf Island and just outside Byram Harbor and in the 7- to 9-foot area west of the island. There is good fishing to be had here for winter flounder and blackfish. You can see one anchorage from the other, but don't try to get from one to the other in anything bigger than your dink unless you go all the way south of Jones Rocks. Reefs extend all the way from the mainland past the island and out to Jones Rocks.

A good daytime anchorage can be found northwest of Great Captain Island, although it is exposed to the prevailing southwesterly winds. One of our readers tells us it's a nice swim to the beach from there.

The approach to **Byram Harbor** and to the anchorage north of Calf Island is north of Bowers Island, between the red 4sec flasher "2" and can "1." The moorings you'll pass to starboard belong to the Belle Haven Club, which does not cater to transients but does offer reciprocating privileges to members of other clubs.

Don't try squeezing between tiny Bowers Island and Calf Island to get into this area or you will be in trouble. The town marina and the club in **Byram Harbor** are open to members and residents only. If you do enter the little basin at Byram Park, however, hug the Huckleberry Island side of the entrance to avoid shoaling on the south side.

The entrance to **Greenwich Harbor** is marked by red nun "2" **[WP-46],** well out in Captain Harbor. The mile-long channel takes you past the famous green-tile-roofed Indian Harbor Yacht Club, founded in 1889, which has guest moorings for members of other clubs. Advance reservations are usually necessary. On the west side is the fancy residential neighborhood of Belle Haven, which was developed in the last century. Passing can "3," you will see on the shore a scale model of the Brooklyn Bridge built by Roebling before he undertook the real thing.

You'll see plenty of boats moored in **Greenwich Harbor,** but if you're headed into the Greenwich Boat & Yacht Club, look for the row of white stake buoys with red tops, paralleling the western shore up to the club docks.

Farther into the harbor on the west side is Grass Island, and a town marina and fuel dock with 2 transient slips accommodating boats up to 40 feet. (Good luck getting one.) There is a 5-mph speed limit in the harbor. At the head of the harbor on the west side is the dock for the Greenwich Marine Police Boat.

 ## Shoreside and Emergency Services

Airport: Connecticut Limousine to JFK and LaGuardia (203) 327-5200
Westchester County Airport (914) 328-1953
Ambulance: 911
Coast Guard: Eatons Neck (516) 261-6868/6910 or VHF 16
Fire: Greenwich: 911 or (203) 622-7800
Port Chester: 911 or (914) 939-0700
Harbormaster: Greenwich: (203) 622-8044 or VHF 16
Port Chester: (914) 937-2433 or VHF 16
Hospital: Greenwich: (203) 869-7000
Port Chester: (914) 939-7000
Police: Greenwich: 911 or (203) 622-8000 or VHF 16 or CB 9
Port Chester: 911 or (914) 939-1000
Radio Telephone: VHF 27; I.D.: Bridgeport Marine Operator; VHF 25, 26, 84; I.D.: NY Marine Operator
Taxi: Greenwich Taxi (203) 869-6000
Tow Service: Southern CT Sea Tow, Bridgeport, CT (203) 331-0410 or VHF 16 or CB 9
Train: Amtrak 1-800-USA-RAIL
Metro-North 1-800-638-7646   ◆

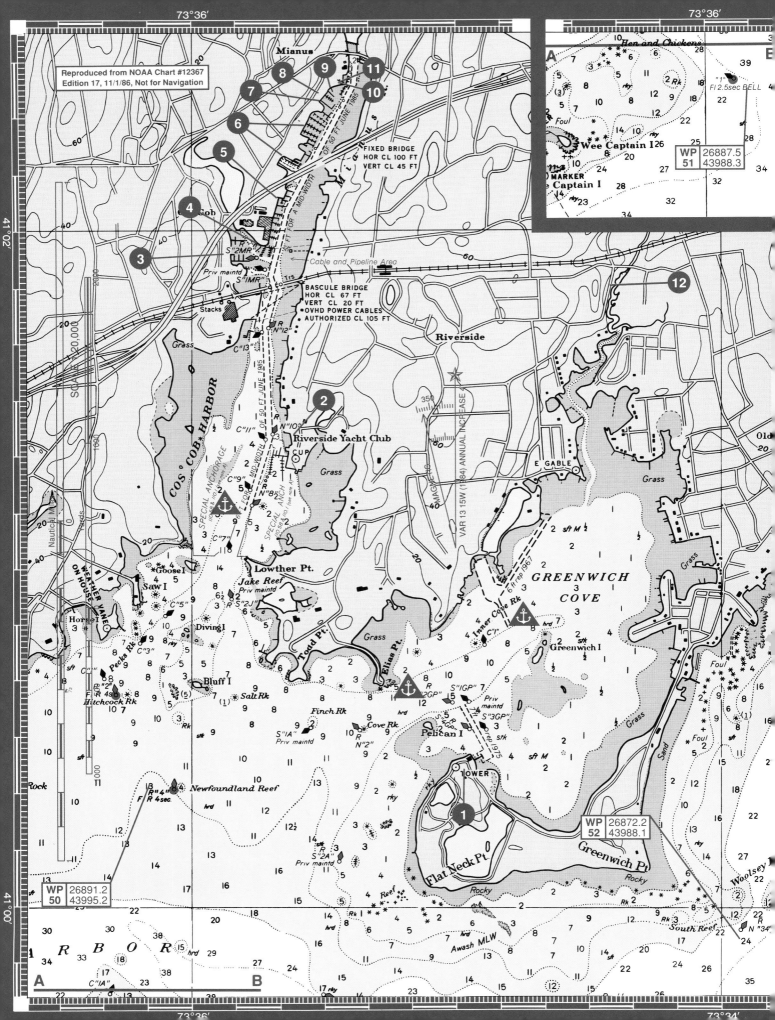

Strategic Salt and Summering Sketchers

None other than the intrepid Adriaen Block brought the first settlement to Greenwich in 1614, the same year the Dutch captain also discovered the Connecticut River. Named for Greenwich, England, the town was known for many years as "Horseneck" because of its fine grazing land. Legend has it that the land was bought from the Indians for 25 coats, making it one of history's greatest real-estate deals, since Greenwich today is one of the state's richest communities. The strategic location of Greenwich made it an important stronghold from the time of the French and Indian War right through to the War of 1812.

Cos Cob was a popular haven for artists in the late 19th and early 20th centuries. Many painters and writers from New York City summered in Connecticut to get away from the heat and stress of the city and to get their creative juices flowing again.

In Cos Cob, the center of the artist population was the Bush-Holley House, known then as the Holley Inn. Built in the late 1600's when Greenwich was still under the jurisdiction of New Netherland (later to become New York), the house was later used by the famous Revolutionary War General Israel Putnam, who, it's said, lived in it to keep an eye on the strategic saltworks nearby.

The British under General Tryon managed to plunder the saltworks and surrounding area anyway before being chased away by American troops. To this day there's a large saber gash in the front door of the house as a reminder of the conflict.

Today Greenwich's four harbors make it a busy and popular stop for boaters. As a result, finding a slip isn't easy, but with a pair of anchorages like Cos Cob Harbor and Greenwich Cove, the cruisers don't stop coming.

© Clyde Smith

Greenwich Cove (foreground), Todd Point, and the Mianus River entrance (background). The Old Greenwich Yacht Club is to the far left.

Marine Facilities and Services	Phone	Number of Transient Berths	Number of Transient Moorings	Seasonal/Year-round	Largest Vessel Accommodation (in feet)	Marked Entry Channel	Approach Depth in feet at MLW	Dockside Depth in feet at MLW	Gas/Diesel Fuel	Fuel Brand	Ramp/Dinghy Dock/Launch Service	Railway/Lift: Capacity (in tons)	Propeller/Hull Repairs	Engine Repairs: Gas/Diesel	Pump-out Station	Showers/Laundromat	Marine Supplies/Groceries/Bait/Ice	110V★220V▲ Maximum Amps	MasterCard/VISA/Diners Club	American Express	Restaurant/Snack Bar	Monitors VHF Channel
1 Old Greenwich Yacht Club	(203) 637-1961				*PRIVATE CLUB - MEMBERS ONLY*																	72
2 Riverside Yacht Club	(203) 637-1706				*PRIVATE CLUB - MEMBERS ONLY*																	9
3 Mianus River Boat & Yacht Club	(203) 869-4689				*RESIDENTS ONLY*																	
4 Palmer Point Ships Store	(203) 661-1243	5		Y	50	●	6	6	GD	TEX		L25	PH	GD		S	IG	★▲	MV	A		16
5 Riverscape Marina	(203) 661-4772	2		Y	50	●	6	6				L30	PH	GD		S	BI	★▲				16
6 Greenwich Harbor Club	(203) 869-8690	6		Y	80	●	6	6	GD		L	L35	PH	GD	●	SL	SI	★50	MV	A	R	
7 Mianus Marine	(203) 869-2253	6		Y	55	●	6	6				L25	PH	GD		S		★30				16
8 Albin Marine	(203) 661-4341			Y	*BOAT MANUFACTURING & SALES*																	68
9 Ole M. Amundsen (west)	(203) 637-0115	3		Y	35	●	6	6				L6	PH	GD		S	I	★30				
10 Drenckhahn Boat Basin	(203) 869-1892			Y	50	●	6	6	G	BP		L40	PH	GD		S	SIB	★▲				16
11 **Mianus Marine Engine Corp. (p. 113)**	**(203) 661-7678**			Y	100	●	8	8					P	GD		S		★▲				
12 Ole M. Amundsen (east)	(203) 661-5217			Y	22							L2	PH	G		S			MV			

Information in these listings is provided by the facilities themselves. An asterisk (*) indicates that the facility did not respond to our most recent requests for information.

What To See and Do

From the marinas in Cos Cob Harbor you can call a cab for a trip to the grocery stores, chandleries, tackle shops, and restaurants, of which there are plenty in Old Greenwich, Riverside, Cos Cob, and Greenwich, all part of Greenwich proper.

In a more cultural vein, there are many places to explore in the Greenwich area. The Greenwich Arts Center Gallery (203) 622-3998 is located in the former town hall building, offering monthly exhibits.

Bush-Holley House, a stone's throw from the marinas, is the headquarters of the Historical Society of the Town of Greenwich (203) 869-6899, and houses a fine collection of antique furniture and art, particularly works of the American Impressionists who summered here. The house has some secret passageways and trapdoors that lead to a dark and eerie cellar – gothic novel material, this.

Greenwich Cove is one of the most attractive, best-protected anchorages in Long Island Sound, unspoiled by any commercial wharves or buildings – or, for that matter, by any of the amenities you may desire while cruising. Ice, fuel, groceries, and repair facilites can be found in Cos Cob and Stamford, but not in Greenwich Cove. But for quiet beauty, Greenwich Cove is the place to be, especially on weekdays when there are few if any rafting boat parties.

Pelican Island and Greenwich Island are fair picnic grounds, but watch out for poison ivy and water rats on Greenwich Island. Alas, that tempting stretch of sand on the northwest shore of the cove is private property.

 ## Where To Eat

From the marinas around the I-95 bridge on the west side of the Mianus River, it's a short walk up Mead Avenue or Robertson Lane to East Putnam Avenue (Rte. 1), where you'll find several choices for dining. To the west is Le Shack (203) 622-9844, serving rich Belgian dishes in an intimate setting. Three blocks further west is Tumbledown's (203) 869-1820, with a widely varied American menu and medium prices. In between those two there's the unpreten-

tious Cos Cob Chili Station (203) 661-3911 for the boater in a hurry; strictly lunch counter fare here, and all available with – you guessed it – chili. Take-out is available. Across the street is a Friendly's (203) 661-9127.

On River Road north of Rte. 1 is Bruno's Mianus House (203) 622-9578, an 80-year institution in Cos Cob, open for lunch only. At River Road and Rte. 1 is Fonda La Paloma (203) 661-9395, serving reasonably-priced Mexican, and further east is Hunan Garden (203) 637-8773 at the Howard Johnson's Motel, serving medium-priced Chinese.

 ## Navigation and Anchorages

Use NOAA Charts 12367 (1:20,000), 12368 (1:20,000), 12364 (1:40,000), and 12363 (1:80,000). Use tide tables for Bridgeport. High tide at Cos Cob Harbor is 5 minutes later; low tide is 11 minutes later. Multiply by 1.1 for height at high or low water. Mean tidal range is 7.8 feet.

Cos Cob Harbor, where the Mianus River meets Captain Harbor, is the most popular destination for transient boaters among Greenwich's harbors, offering the most marine facilities and the best shore access. Hitchcock Rock, marking the outer entrance to Cos Cob Harbor, is 3.8nm by boat west of the Stamford Harbor breakwaters, 1.0nm by boat northeast of nun "2" at the entrance to Greenwich Harbor, and 2.7nm by boat northeast of Port Chester Harbor.

From the flashing red bell "32A" **[WP-300]** halfway between Captain Harbor and Oyster Bay, a course of about 315°m will bring you to the eastern entrance to Captain Harbor.

Approaching Cos Cob Harbor and Greenwich Cove from any direction, you'll first have to get into **Captain Harbor.** Your best and safest bet is to head south of the Captain Islands and enter between bell "1" **[WP-51]** at **Hen and Chickens** and red nun "2" off Flat Neck Point. Be sure to leave can "1A" to port to avoid Hen and Chickens. Once you're in Captain Harbor you have easy access to Cos Cob Harbor and Greenwich Cove as well as Greenwich Harbor and Byram Harbor.

If you want to try entering **Captain Harbor** from the west, do so between Jones Rocks and **Great Captain Island.** (See the preceding chapter for more information on the approaches to and anchorages in Captain Harbor, Byram Harbor, and Greenwich Harbor.)

Cos Cob Harbor looks tricky to enter but is perfectly safe if you follow the chart. As you enter Captain Harbor, look for the red 4sec flasher "4" **[WP-50]** marking **Newfoundland Reef.** Leave Newfoundland Reef to starboard and head for the red 4sec flasher "2" marking **Hitchcock Rock.** With Hitchcock Rock to starboard, pick up black cans "1," "3," and "5," leaving them to port, and follow the well-marked channel into the harbor. If you want to enter the "special anchorage" south of the Riverside Yacht Club, leave nun "8" to starboard; it marks a big rock.

The channel will lead you past the Riverside Yacht Club on the east bank. Riverside offers reciprocal privileges to members of other recognized yacht clubs, and there are a few guest moorings and/or berths in midsummer when members are away cruising. Launch service and basic supplies are available at the club, but you should call ahead to the dock captain.

There is a mooring area and a good anchorage opposite the club on the west side of the channel. If you want to drop a hook here, stay close to the channel or well south of the shoal in the middle of the "Special Anchorage" area. The deepest water in the anchorage is just northwest of can "7."

Powerboats with a vertical clearance of less than 20 feet and drafts of less than 4 feet can proceed up the **Mianus River** to the many marinas above the bascule railroad bridge. Sailboats will have to wait for the bridge to open; a long and a short blast of your horn should get the attention of the bridgekeeper between 5 a.m. and 9 p.m. Overnight, the bridge is usually not manned and will be opened only at the Metro-North railroad's discretion. Unless it's an emergency, you will have to stay put until morning. The dispatcher can be reached at (212) 340-2772, 340-3000, or 358-2512.

There is not a great deal of room to maneuver in the channel since the area near the bridge has silted up. Just upstream of the railroad bridge is the infamous Interstate 95 bridge, part of which fell into the river one night in 1983, killing several motorists.

If you haven't been here in awhile, you may be surprised to see some of the developments north of the rebuilt I-95 bridge. The old Greenwich Marine is now the Greenwich Harbor Club, an enormous marina and dockominium project. Scheduled to be open for business in Spring 1990, the Club also offers transient slips and daytime launch service. Fuel is available there or at Palmer Point Ships Store.

Once ashore, you can walk three blocks up Mead Avenue or Robertson Lane, where you'll find a laundromat, drugstore, and Post Office on East Putnam Avenue (Rte. 1).

SAILING SOLO AROUND LONG ISLAND

It's 10:00 p.m., and I'm alone on Long Island Sound. For more than an hour, I've been sailing into six-foot seas and a ten-knot wind. Hull speed drops steadily, and I fear mounting fatigue will soon overcome me. The C&C 29 I've dubbed *Course Correction* still seems unfamiliar to me in these heavy seas. I've sailed her for a season now, and I'm beginning the second with a solo trip around Long Island. It all seems too sudden. Between curses, I scan the chart and search east over my shoulder for the end of Long Island.

My problems begin early in the day. A water skier crosses the wake of a sport fisherman and tosses my boat like a cork on Montauk Lake. I quickly set anchor but continue to drift. A second anchor offers little help and then wraps itself tightly around the mooring chain of a channel marker. After untangling the mess, I'm forced to enter the chilly water and cut a dinghy painter that has grabbed hold of my prop. The cold water leaves me shivering and sets me to gulping the last cup of my coffee.

I spend the afternoon searching for a suitable anchorage behind Gardiners and Shelter islands. Weary of fighting the wind, I debate heading through Plum Gut for safe haven at Saybrook. I can see the breakwater lighthouse ahead, but *Course Correction* is bogged down and makes almost no headway. It seems I'll never reach my destination. With little patience left, I cut the wheel hard to starboard and look astern. More than 300 feet of anchor rode drags behind the boat. After an hour on the foredeck pulling up the loosed anchor, I again set sail for the Connecticut River.

My mind and eyes are now playing tricks. It seems I'm sailing uphill, toward formless blocks of black and grey. Suddenly the flasher is upon me, immediately to port, its white light glowing steadily above. The two lights are not at the ends of the breakwaters as I have imagined, and I find myself heading directly for the concrete wall on the east side of the channel. Turning the wheel hard to port, I narrowly miss becoming a permanent monument to miscalculation.

Two large marinas loom ahead to port, dark against the lights of town. I continue upriver until a small boat approaches and hails from about 50 feet. The local fishermen have set a gill net across the channel and are forced to escort me around their trap. Once free, I motor further north toward the railroad bridge, which is a clear and unbroken black line against the horizon. I circle for a few minutes while hailing the bridge by radio, but even after sounding my air horn and splitting the silent night, I receive no response. Unconsciously, I begin to swing in wider circles. Suddenly I run aground and am shaken alert

Happier days on board Course Corrections.

by the engine alarm. My prop is once again entangled with a nylon dinghy painter. I'm not ashamed to say that I'm forced to search for snorkel and mask through watery eyes.

The Connecticut River is cold and black tonight, and it quickly steals my favorite boatswain's knife right out of my hand. After climbing from the water, I'm not convinced the chill will ever leave my bones. I bundle up tight and tidy the cabin with fervor, hoping this will warm me while I wait for the tide to rise and carry the boat back into the channel. Slowly, she begins to rock, and then she swings hard on her keel. Once again, it's time to set off, but all I want is some sleep. Instead of heading further north, I drift back downstream and tie up at a fuel dock before succumbing to dreams.

Three hours later I awake and make breakfast. At first light the sky is overcast and still, but by midday I am anchored in Joshua Cove in Guilford, and can feel a heavy breeze coming up. The seas have begun to rise with the wind, and I break out wine and cheese to celebrate my escape from the river. Then, to the sound of approaching rain, I fall asleep. Though it's another three days to Sheepshead Bay and my walk for home overland, I'm certain the rest of my trip will be charmed. I dream of skidding the last few yards through Hell Gate and wonder whether I'll ever dare such a trip again. Then I imagine flying along at six knots on a sunny day, and I laugh. Of course, I'll travel this way again.

Contributed by Bill Browning, a Brooklyn resident and Sales Manager for a Manhattan electronics manufacturer. His most recent attempt to sail around Long Island – this time, *with crew* – failed.

There is another laundromat and a market on Rte. 1 at Riverside Avenue, on the east side of the river, a short walk from Drenckhahn's.

Back out in Captain Harbor, if you're heading into **Greenwich Cove,** give Cove Rock nun "2" a wide berth (its mooring sometimes drags), and leave Pelican Island to starboard. Don't try passing between **Pelican Island** and Flat Neck Point, because there is even less water there than the chart indicates.

Near the tall tower on the northwestern tip of **Flat Neck Point** is the Old Greenwich Yacht Club. The clubhouse has water, a telephone, and a head, but not much else. It's located on Greenwich Point, a town park that requires resident beach cards and closes at sunset (midnight on Saturdays), so it is no good as a landing for reaching town. However, if you just want to row your dink ashore to explore the park, no one will bother you. In the park, watch out for the hordes of joggers, walkers, and bicyclists soaking up the fresh air along the park's beautiful paths, lined with low stone walls. Across the road from the yacht club is a marker with the anchor from the *Sugar Boat* or *Tug Thames* which sank off Flat Neck Point in 1930, now marked by buoy S "2A."

Once you're in the cove, there is a no-wake speed limit, strictly enforced. Occasionally you'll see an intrepid water-skier dashing in from the outer harbor, but chances are that shortly you'll also see Greenwich's equally intrepid water police pounce on the culprit.

Inside **Greenwich Cove** you can anchor anywhere amidst the moored boats of your size, but stay out of the midcove channel. The holding ground in the cove is so good that if you feel you need a mooring, you really need a bigger anchor. Don't go too far north unless you like heeling over on the mud at low tide.

You should also resist the temptation to go east of **Greenwich Island.** There are numerous grass islands (only a few are indicated on the chart) that are barely submerged at high tide until late spring when the grass gets tall enough to show their locations. Don't be fooled by the natives who take their cruising boats inside of Greenwich Island at high tide. They know where the grass islands are; they have usually studied some of them at close range for four or five hours.

Because of its shallow waters, Greenwich Cove is alive with ducks, cormorants, loons, swans, graceful Great American Egrets, and the ubiquitous Canada geese feasting on the barely submerged marine life. If you see an egret stalking its dinner close to your boat, it's time to shift to deeper water.

 Shoreside and Emergency Services

Airport: Connecticut Limousine to JFK & LaGuardia (203) 327-5200
Westchester County Airport (914) 328-1951

Ambulance: 911

Coast Guard: Eatons Neck (516) 261-6868/6910 or VHF 16

Fire: 911 or (203) 622-7800

Harbormaster: Marine Police (203) 622-8044 or VHF 16

Hospital: Greenwich Hospital (203) 863-3000

Police: 911 or (203) 622-8006 or VHF 16 or CB 9

Radio Telephone: VHF 27; I.D.: Bridgeport Marine Operator; VHF 25, 26, 84; I.D.: NY Marine Operator

Taxi: Greenwich Taxi (203) 869-6000

Tow Service: Southern CT Sea Tow, Bridgeport, CT (203) 331-0410 or VHF 16 or CB 9

Train: Amtrak 1-800-USA-RAIL
Metro-North 1-800-638-7646 ✦

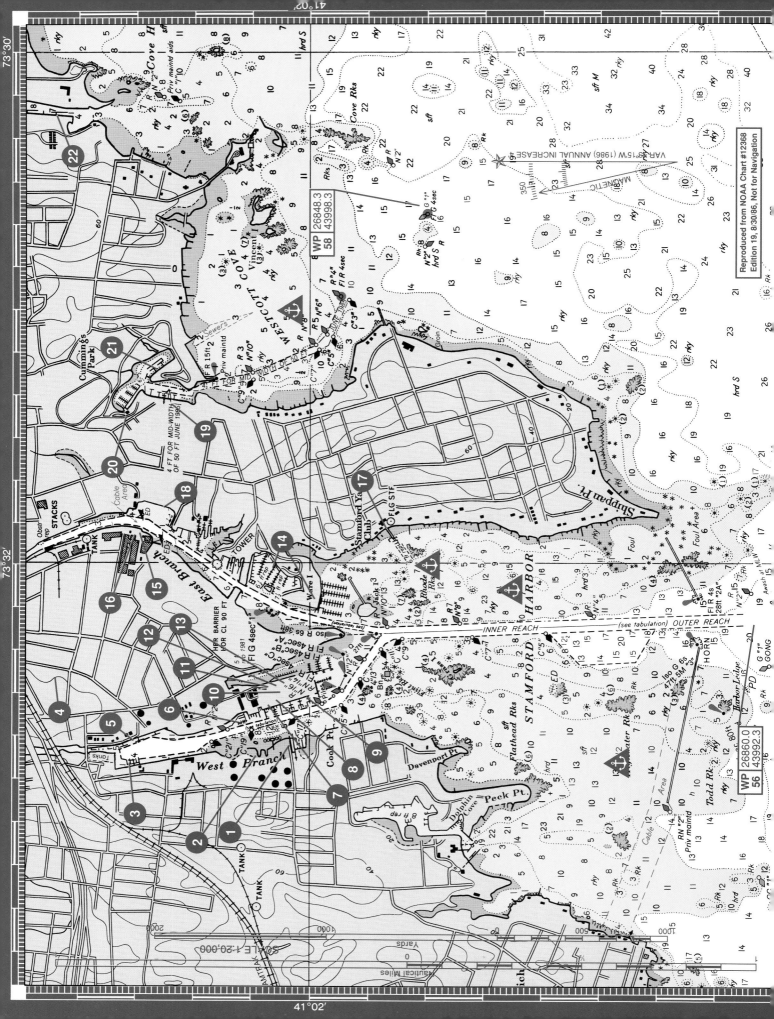

Stamford Harbor and Westcott Cove

Stamford, Inc.

On a typical summer's day you'll see more sailboats in Stamford Harbor than in any other port on the north shore of the Sound. Stamford is a major yachting center, and as its phenomenal downtown development will attest, a rapidly growing commercial center with the feel of a large city.

Settled in 1641 by families from Wethersfield, Stamford was a focal point for the supply, training, and encampment of American soldiers during the Revolution. The British never attacked its fort, though they did land raiding parties in search of cattle. In retaliation, the men of Stamford formed a whaleboat fleet to harass enemy warships in the Sound.

The towering masts and office buildings of Stamford Harbor, CT.

© Jack McConnell

Marine Facilities and Services

#	Facility	Phone	Transient Berths	Transient Moorings	Seasonal/Year-round	Largest Vessel (ft)	Marked Entry Channel	Approach Depth (ft)	Dockside Depth at MLW	Gas/Diesel Fuel	Fuel Brand	Ramp/Dinghy/Launch	Railway/Lift (tons)	Engine Repairs	Propeller/Hull Repairs	Marine Supplies Gas/Diesel	Pump-out Station	Showers/Laundromat	Groceries/Bait/Ice	110V★220V▲ Max Amps	Credit Cards	Restaurant/Snack Bar	VHF Channel
1	Southfield Park & Marina	(203) 977-4693						COMMERCIAL FISHING DOCK															
2	Stamford Landing Marina	(203) 965-0065	5		Y	50	●	12	8								●	SL	I	★50	MV	R	9
3	**Offshore Yachting Service (p. 120)**	**(203) 967-3856**	5		Y	70	●	15	10						PH	GD			BI	★▲30	MVA		9
4	Yankee Boat Works	(203) 348-4049						BOAT MANUFACTURER															
5	**Herbert's Landing Fuel Dock (p. 121)**	**(203) 325-9416**			Y	250	●	20	12	GD	MOB								I		MVAD		9
6	Ponus Yacht Club	(203) 327-8086						PRIVATE CLUB - MEMBERS ONLY														R	
7	Baltic Yachts East	(203) 353-0222			Y			YACHT SALES - NEW & USED															
8	Sailboats Northeast	(203) 353-0222			Y			YACHT SALES - NEW & USED															
9	Erik's Boat Works	(203) 359-3657			Y			REPAIR FACILITY															
10	**Yacht Haven West (p. 117)**	**(203) 359-4500**	70		Y	140	●	12	12	GD	TEX		L60		PH	GD		SL	SI	★▲50	MVA	R	9
11	Maritech Communications	(203) 323-2900			Y			MARINE ELECTRONICS													MVA		9
12	Hellier Yacht Sales, Inc.	(203) 323-5858			Y			YACHT SALES - NEW & USED															
13	MacDonald Yacht Rigging	(203) 323-5431						YACHT RIGGING															
14	**Yacht Haven East (p. 117)**	**(203) 359-4500**	100		Y	140	●	12	12										I	★▲50	MVA		9
15	**Harbour Square Marina (p. 120)**	**(203) 324-3331**	20		Y	120	●	15	8	GD	TEX						●	SL	SI	★▲50	MVAD	R	9
16	John G. Alden Yacht Brokers	(203) 327-2600			Y	50	●	6		YACHT SALES - NEW & USED													
17	Stamford Yacht Club	(203) 323-3161		10	S	60	●	6.5	7	D		PRIVATE CLUB - MEMBERS ONLY							I	★50		RS	9
18	Czesik Park Municipal Marina	(203) 977-4693			S	28		5	5								●						
19	Marina Bay	(203) 348-5341	25		Y	30	●	12	10	GD	TEX			R			●	SL	I	★▲	MVAD		
20	Halloween Yacht Club	(203) 348-5510		1	Y	37	●	5	8									S	I	★			
21	Cummings Park Marina	(203) 977-4693			S	22		2	2														
22	Cove Marina	(203) 977-4693			S	22	●	3.5	3														

Information in these listings is provided by the facilities themselves. An asterisk (*) indicates that the facility did not respond to our most recent requests for information.

The East Branch of Stamford Harbor, from the south. In the foreground is Yacht Haven East and the hurricane barrier; in the background is downtown Stamford.

Beginning with Linus Yale's invention of the first cylinder lock in Stamford in 1848, the city became a major manufacturing center. One peculiar local invention was the "Patent Swimming Baths" on Shippan Point. This contraption consisted of a pool over which was suspended a series of booms and harnesses that were used to teach the "most timid" of bathers the "art of swimming."

Today, Stamford is still an important business and commercial center and boasts of having more large corporate headquarters than any other city except New York. In Stamford, as a wealthy commuting suburb much like Greenwich and Westport, the average price of a residence now exceeds $300,000.

Coming into Stamford by boat, it's hard to imagine it ever having been a sleepy little farming town or its inhabitants tooling in and out of the harbor in whaleboats. From the mini- and mega-yachts in the harbor, to the factories, office buildings, condos, and the constant activity ashore, Stamford will make you feel *busy,* even if you're not.

⭐ What To See And Do

There is plenty to do ashore in this busy city of 107,000. Within a 15-minute cab ride is the Stamford Museum and Nature Center (203) 322-1646, with 118 acres of woodlands, a working farm, and many exhibits on the history of the area; the Whitney Museum of American Art (203) 358-7652, which hosts several exhibitions yearly as well as educational and performing-arts programs; and the Stamford Historical Society (203) 329-1183, with a public museum.

There are a number of annual festivals and shows in the Stamford area, and the Greater Stamford Convention & Visitors Bureau (203) 359-3305 is active in promoting them. One of the most popular is the city's annual July 4 seaside

celebration, complete with orchestral music and fireworks. You can enjoy the festivities from your anchorage in Westcott Cove or dink ashore at Cummings Park.

The Stamford Center for the Arts (203) 323-2131 and the Palace Theatre (203) 359-0009 are host to numerous plays and concerts throughout the year. Both are in downtown Stamford, 5 minutes by cab from the water.

If you're a devotee of ultramodern architecture, take a cab to downtown Stamford and check out some of the shapes, sizes, and colors you'll find there – not of people, but of office buildings! You'll think a few square blocks of Manhattan were picked up and transported 35 miles east.

There are many restaurants and shops along the waterfront if you can find a berth. Although the Stamford business district is only 5 minutes away by automobile, the cruising boater can find almost every necessity on the waterfront or within walking distance.

Racing is in the blood of the yachtsmen here. With six yacht clubs, there's plenty of competition on weekends and on Tuesday and Thursday evenings starting at bell "32" south of The Cows. The Stamford Yacht Club (203) 323-3161 sponsors two races: the Stamford-Denmark Friendship Race, a buoy race in the middle of Long Island Sound, and the Vineyard Race from Stamford to Martha's Vineyard and back each Memorial Day weekend. The Halloween Yacht Club (203) 348-5510 sponsors the Mayor's Cup Race every June.

Yacht Haven (203) 359-4500, always a busy marina, is also the home of the biggest sailboat show in the Northeast, held every September at the west yard. Visiting Stamford by boat during the show can be confusing and tiring because of the crowds, so you may want to come by car and kick some hulls with your shoe instead of bumping them with your boat. It is possible, however, to bring your dinghy

YACHT HAVEN ⚓ MARINE CENTER

Largest, Most Complete Marina on the East Coast

- 750 slips in two basins, west & east, for boats 30'-120'
- Wide floating docks, electricity & water at each slip
- 1000' work dock for in-water service, repairs
- 24-hour security
- Texaco gas & diesel fuel — ice
- Showers, heads, laundromat at both basins
- Ship's Store for gear & accessories
- Winter storage, covered & open

- Restaurants at Yacht Haven East
- Short cab ride from downtown hotels, restaurants, shops, RR station
- Haul-out to 60 tons
- Complete hull & engine service, machine shop, carpentry, rigging
- All-weather painting, Awlgrip fiberglass reconditioning
- Diesel and generator sales and service, all makes

Call or write to reserve space, Texaco, MasterCard, Visa and American Express Cards accepted

ON-SITE SPECIALTY SALES/SERVICE BY EXPERTS AT YHMC WEST

Navigational, communications electronics — **Maritech Communications Corp.**
Spars & rigging, all size yachts — **MacDonald Yacht Rigging, Inc.**
Yacht brokerage, boat sales — **Hellier Yacht Sales, Inc.**
New Boat Sales — **Sailboats Northeast/Baltic Yachts East**

"Best Bet for the Cruising Yachtsman on Long Island Sound"

YACHT HAVEN INC., Subsidiary of Marina America
P.O. Box 1435, Stamford, CT 06904   203-359-4500
FAX 203-359-1403

West: Ft. of Washington Blvd.
Exit 7, Conn. Tpke. (I-95)

East: Harbor Plaza
Exit 8, Conn. Tpke. (I-95)

(and only your dinghy) in to the gas dock at Yacht Haven West during the show.

 Where To Eat

Stamford is loaded with restaurants, some of the best right on the water. The inland restaurants, however, almost all require a cab ride. In the East Branch: at Yacht Haven East you'll find the Rusty Scupper (203) 964-1235, specializing in seafood and steaks at medium to expensive prices. Up the channel at Harbour Square is the Harbour Square Restaurant (203) 323-0044, offering a reasonably priced Continental menu with free dockage for patrons. Takeout is also available at lunch.

Less than half a mile east of Yacht Haven East is Catch-22 (203) 323-1787, offering live New Orleans jazz with your meal.

A few blocks east of the Czesik Park Marina on Shippan Avenue you'll find four casual places: the Continental Fast Food Restaurant (203) 324-1651 for the boater in a hurry; Monica's (203) 359-0678, specializing in gourmet pasta and offering takeout; the Shamrock Restaurant (203) 348-9003 (burgers and wedges for lunch, pizzas and salads for dinner); and Royal Guard Fish & Chips (203) 348-4653. The name says it all.

In the West Branch: Stamford Landing has two good restaurants, back-to-back: the Crab Shell (203) 967-7229, featuring reasonably priced fresh seafood (including live lobsters) and advertising weekly "Crab Bashes." Right next door is Rapallo (203) 967-8777, specializing in fine Italian cuisine at reasonable prices. Both restaurants overlook the harbor.

The Ponus Yacht Club (203) 327-8086 just north of Yacht Haven West serves lunches in the clubhouse; a dock is provided for patrons coming by water. A 1/2-mile walk up Washington Street from Ponus is Bill's Dockside Deli (203) 325-3595, a deli and convenience store offering takeout.

On Atlantic Street, a short walk from Yacht Haven West is Sai Wu (203) 348-3330, serving Chinese, or Tacos Guadalajara (203) 324-2204, serving homestyle Mexican. A bit further away by cab are more choices: The Brass Rail

(203) 324-5523 or Pellicci's (203) 323-2542, both serving fine Italian and offering takeout. Pellicci's also offers live entertainment. For a taste of New Orleans try Bourbon Street (203) 356-1467 for Creole and Cajun food.

From Westcott Cove you have easy access to any of the Shippan Avenue restaurants listed above, as well as to the Beach Cafe (203) 967-2860, featuring an inexpensive, varied menu of casual and not-so-casual American fare. Yes, there is a beach out front!

 Navigation and Anchorages

Use NOAA Charts 12368 (1:20,000), 12364 (1:40,000), and 12363 (1:80,000). Use tide tables for Bridgeport. High tide at Stamford is 3 minutes later; low tide is 8 minutes later. Multiply by 1.1 for height at high or low water. Mean tidal range is 7.8 feet.

Stamford Harbor is Y-shaped, including a large, relatively exposed outer harbor and two inner harbor channels, the East and West branches. The Stamford Harbor breakwaters are about 4.8nm by boat northeast of Greenwich Cove, and 2.5nm by boat southwest of Westcott Cove.

Approaching the breakwaters from the west, you have a clear shot from Greenwich Point 2.6nm to green gong "1" **[WP-56],** which marks rocks and a wreck, and then into the harbor.

CAUTION: *If you are coming from the east, don't be tempted to try to shave a few minutes off your run by cutting north of the red bell "32" [WP-57] at The Cows, off Shippan Point. As little as 2 feet of water covers the treacherous rocks that reach for 800 yards north of the bell. Likewise, rocks extend 800 yards south of Shippan Point, leaving not much room between the two shoals, and no buoys to guide you. The presence of many wrecks on these treacherous rocks should be enough to persuade any skipper to play it safe and go to the south of The Cows.*

While the rocks are troublesome for yachtsmen, they are a favorite hangout for blackfish, winter flounder, and striped bass, and – hence – fishermen.

From the two detached breakwaters the channel leads about 1 mile north through the outer harbor and then divides into the **East Branch** and the **West Branch.** The ideal range is the white flasher at the junction of the two branches and 38-foot red 6sec flasher immediately north of it on the mainland. You should have no trouble shooting straight up to the divide. There is a 6-mph speed limit throughout the harbor. Even with the breakwaters, the outer harbor is exposed to the south and can get uncomfortable during the summer since the prevailing winds are from the southwest.

There are a number of rocks in the outer harbor you will want to keep an eye on, but there is also room between them to swing at anchor. Remember, the average tidal range is 7.8 feet, so if you don't see the rocks now, just wait 6 hours.

One popular anchorage is just west of **Highwater Rock,** where the west breakwater offers protection from the southwest. You might also find anchoring room southwest of the Stamford Yacht Club, on the east side of the harbor, opposite where the channel divides. The area is not as well protected as the Highwater Rock area, and is often full of the yacht club's moorings. There is a channel marked with privately maintained red and green buoys from nun "8" in to the club's docks. The club offers launch service until late in the evening, free with a mooring rental.

Stay away from the commercial barge mooring area adjacent to the channel and south of can "5." A tug headed in there won't be inclined to make way for you.

The **West Branch** of the harbor is more commercial but has several marinas, a few fuel docks, and is home to the Ponus Yacht Club. The first facility you see to port is the Southfield Park Marina, which is operated by the city and is used mostly by commercial fishermen. You may see a few other boats docked there, but the place is in great disrepair, offers no security, and is generally a place to avoid.

The lights "A," "B," and "C" charted on the wooden tide barrier south of Yacht Haven West have been removed, and the wooden barrier isn't in such good shape anymore, either.

Note that can "21," near the head of the **West Branch,** has been removed. You'll also notice new condominiums (and, of course, dockominiums) under construction to port as you approach the head of the West Branch. If your boat uses more than 200 gallons of fuel a year you may want to stop at Herbert's Landing. They can give you information on how to get a substantial fuel-tax refund from the state of Connecticut.

The **East Branch** has a hurricane barrier that is designed to protect Stamford from unusually high storm tides such as those that flooded the town in the hurricane of September 1938. To the chagrin of the facility operators in the East

Branch, the hurricane barrier also intimidates some visiting boaters. But fear not; the channel is easy to navigate, 90 feet wide at the barrier, carrying 15 feet of water. It also offers the easiest access to downtown Stamford.

The town marina at Czesik Park is for residents only, but transients may tie up for 15 minutes for loading and unloading. A new slip basin was created at Harbour Square Marina in 1988, where fuel, supplies, and a pump-out station are also available. We encourage you to take advantage of the latter.

Westcott Cove is a snug little harbor about 2.5nm north and east of the Stamford breakwaters and 2.0nm east of Long Neck Point. It is the home of the Stamford municipal marina at Cummings Park, the Halloween Yacht Club, and a private facility, Marina Bay.

Coming from the west, keep south of red flasher "32" **[WP-57]** at **The Cows,** then head north-northeast toward the green 4sec flasher "1" **[WP-58]** south of **Westcott Cove.** After rounding the flasher, leave it to port and leave red nun "2" at Cove Rocks to starboard.

Don't confuse nun "2" at **Cove Rocks** with the nun "2" west of green flasher "1." You can safely pass on either side of the two buoys (green flasher "1" **[WP-58]** and red nun "2") marking the 4-foot rock, but don't pass *between* them. The Coast Guard is considering removing the western nun or putting an obstruction marker on the rock because so many boaters mistakenly pass between the two buoys. As one officer told us, "The prudent mariner will read the buoys properly, but on radar, it looks like a gate." The proposed buoy change is part of the review of all Long Island Sound buoys that's now underway. The Coast Guard invites public comment about buoys anywhere on the Sound; give them a call to impart your words of wisdom.

Coming from the east, keep south of the red flasher "30" **[WP-61]** at **Smith Reef** and then shoot between the red nun "2" at **Cove Rocks** and flasher "1" **[WP-58].**

Once past Cove Rocks, pick up the red 4sec flasher "4" at the entrance to the outer harbor and follow the channel into the marina at Cummings Park. (Note that the green can "3" opposite flasher "4" has been relocated slightly north

and west.) There's been some shoaling in the channel, especially between can "7" and nun "8," and at low tide, a sandbar blocks the channel 100 feet north of can "9" and nun "10," opposite the fishing pier. If you draw more than 4 feet you won't make it past the bar at low tide, so wait until high water to make the attempt. Stamford is considering dredging the channel within the next year.

The Cummings Park Marina is for residents only, but transients may tie up for 15 minutes to load or unload. The ramp on the west side of the **Westcott Cove** entrance may be used by anyone, but the further you live from Stamford, the higher the fee.

The float at the end of the ramp is also one of the two **emergency medical pick-up points** in Stamford; the other is at the Texaco fuel dock at Yacht Haven West.

The same restrictions apply to the Cove Island Park Marina, about 0.7nm northeast of Westcott Cove in **Cove Harbor.** Full of small to medium powerboats, Cove Harbor has some 3-foot spots at the entrance but carries 7 feet or more inside. If you draw more than 4 feet, don't try to get in there at low water. The inner harbor is a long, narrow channel neatly bordered by stone walls.

 Shoreside and Emergency Services

Airport: Connecticut Limousine to JFK and LaGuardia
(203) 327-5200
Westchester County Airport (914) 328-1951
Ambulance: 911 or (203) 357-1441
Coast Guard: Eatons Neck (516) 261-6868/6910
or VHF 16
Fire: 911 or (203) 323-3131
Harbormaster: Marine Police (203) 977-5720 or VHF 16
Hospital: Stamford (203) 325-7000
Saint Joseph's (203) 353-2000
Police: 911 or (203) 977-4444
Radio Telephone: VHF 27; I.D.: Bridgeport Marine
Operator
Taxi: Yellow Cab (203) 967-3633
Stamford Taxi (203) 325-2611
Tow Service: Southern CT Sea Tow, Bridgeport, CT
(203) 331-0410 or VHF 16 or CB 9
Connecticut Marine Towing, Stamford, CT
(203) 325-0368 or VHF 16
Train: Amtrak 1-800-USA-RAIL
Metro-North 1-800-638-7646 ◆

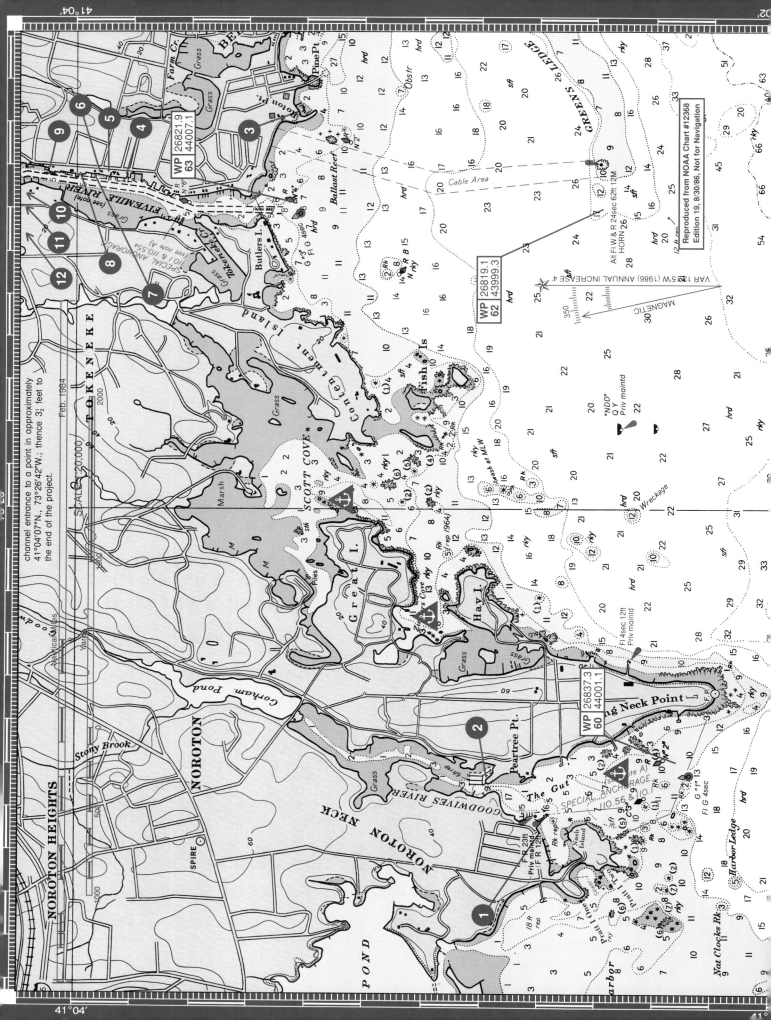

Darien and the Five Mile River

Gunkholes and Gold Medalists

Not many cruisers visit this part of Connecticut's coast because of the relatively small harbors, the lack of large-boat facilities, and the many rocks and reefs. Nonetheless, there are some very quiet, pleasant gunk holes and friendly marinas, and the surrounding residential neighborhoods add to the serenity. "Noroton" and "Rowayton" are anglicized versions of the original Indian names for this area, "Norsaton" and "Roaton."

Nash Island, Darien Harbor, and the Goodwives River from the southwest. Long Neck Point is to the far right.

Like their neighbors in Stamford, the Noroton Yacht Club's members are no strangers to yacht racing. The club is nationally known for its junior and adult sailors, including national- and world-class champions, Olympic medalists, and America's Cup sailors. Every Sunday during the summer months the club runs races for its one-design classes. The competition can get very exciting, setting even the hearts of the spectators...well, racing.

Greens Ledge Light, a prominent landmark for cruisers approaching Darien from the east, was built in 1902 as a replacement for the Sheffield Island Lighthouse of 1868, since few boats foundered on the island and many foundered on the reef that extends about a mile out from Sheffield Island.

 What To See and Do

As with any good gunkholing spot, many of the best things to see and do in Darien involve relaxing and taking in the surroundings, maybe taking a swim or doing some exploring in the dinghy. North of Fish Island, to the east of Zieglers Cove, is a favorite swimming spot for people with small boats. You will want to approach from the east because of the rocks on all the other sides. Plan your swim for high tide, or you'll be pushing your boat through the mud back to deeper water.

Marine Facilities and Services		Number of Transient Berths	Number of Transient Moorings	Seasonal/Year-round	Largest Vessel Accommodation	Marked Entry Channel	Approach Depth (in feet)	Dockside Depth in feet at MLW	Gas/Diesel Fuel	Fuel Brand	Ramp/Dinghy Dock/Launch Service	Railway/Lift: Capacity (in tons)	Propeller/Hull Repairs	Engine Repairs: Gas/Diesel	Pump-out Station	Showers/Laundromat	Marine Supplies/Groceries/Bait/Ice	110V ★ 220V ▲ Maximum Amps	MasterCard/VISA/Diners Club, American Express	Restaurant/Snack Bar	Monitors VHF Channel
❶ Noroton Yacht Club	(203) 655-7686			S		•	5	5	PRIVATE CLUB – MEMBERS ONLY												
❷ Darien Boat Club	(203) 655-1927			S		•	5	5	PRIVATE CLUB – MEMBERS ONLY												
❸ Roton Point Club	(203) 838-1606								PRIVATE CLUB – MEMBERS ONLY												
❹ The Boatworks	(203) 866-9295	3	5	S	45	•	10	8	GD	TEX	DL	L	PH	GD			SI		MVA		
❺ **The Bait Shop, Inc. (p. 124)**	**(203) 853-3811**			Y	25	•	10	10				L	PH	G				▲			
❻ Village Marine	(203) 866-1739			Y	25	•	10	10					P	GD				★	A		
❼ Rowayton Marine Works, Inc.	(203) 866-0251		1	S	45	•	8	8													68
❽ **Five Mile River Works (p. 125)**	**(203) 866-4266**	1	1	Y	50	•	7	7			D	L35	PH	GD			S	★▲50			16
❾ Conel, Inc.	(203) 853-6602	2		Y	60	•	8	8									S	★▲50	V		16
❿ W. Robert Haskell Marine Service	(203) 853-0088	1		S	38	•	5	5										★			
⓫ White Bridge Marina	(203) 838-9088			Y	30	•	6	6						D			S	★30	MV		16
⓬ B & G Marine	(203) 853-9599											L45	PH	GD							

Information in these listings is provided by the facilities themselves. An asterisk (*) indicates that the facility did not respond to our most recent requests for information.

Here, where residential neighborhoods dominate, it takes a bit of searching to find interesting spots to visit, but you will be rewarded for your effort. If you go ashore at one of the marinas on the east bank of the Five Mile River, you'll be on Rowayton Avenue (Rte. 136), which is lined with shops, restaurants, and delis. This is a quiet, low-key place, good for a relaxing walk or bike ride.

The Rowayton Arts Center (203) 866-2744 on Rowayton Avenue features multimedia art exhibits, as well as art and ballet classes. The Darien Dinner Theatre (203) 655-7667 on Tokeneke Road offers professional musical theater and good food: dinner and a show all in one. Reservations are recommended, at least two weeks in advance.

 ### Where To Eat

In Rowayton, next to the Boatworks, you'll find Rowayton Seafood (203) 838-7473, which has its own dock where boaters can tie up and buy fresh seafood. They'll even prepare a meal for you to take out if you call ahead. Just a crab's throw across the parking lot is Captain Henry's (no phone), serving seafood at the counter. To the north is the excellent 5 Mile River Grille (203) 855-0025, serving creative gourmet meals (including gourmet takeout baskets during the summer). For do-it-yourselfers, there's a deli and a market just across the street, next to White Bridge Marina.

For those with more casual tastes or smaller wallets, just down the street is Brendan's 101 (203) 853-1050 (a sandwich shop) right across the street from Rowayton Pizza (203) 853-7555.

On the Post Road in Darien (a cab ride away) you'll find Chuck's Steak House (203) 655-2254, featuring moderately priced steaks in an informal atmosphere. Also on the Post Road is the Newport Grill (203) 656-0383, recommended for good seafood at reasonable prices, and Bugbee & Brownell (203) 655-7481, for American fare served amid the ferns.

 ### Navigation and Anchorages

Use NOAA Charts 12368 (1:20,000), 12364 (1:40,000), and 12363 (1:80,000). Use tide tables for Bridgeport. High tide at Greens Ledge is 2 minutes earlier; low tide is 1 minute earlier. Multiply by 1.1 for height at high or low water. Mean tidal range is 7.8 feet.

The tip of Long Neck Point, marking the outer approach to the Goodwives River, is 3.7nm by boat northeast of the entrance to Stamford Harbor. The Greens Ledge Light off Sheffield Island is 1.6nm by boat east.

From the red 4sec bell "28C" **[WP-334]** at Cable and Anchor Reef, a course of about 340°m for 2.2nm will bring you to the **Greens Ledge Light [WP-62]** and the approach to the **Five Mile River.**

Darien Harbor, labeled **"The Gut"** or the **Goodwives River** on the charts, has a crowded anchorage between Noroton Neck and Long Neck Point. Long Neck Point, which has water on both sides, is one of the most beautiful places in Connecticut, with many fine homes and some private boat landings along the water.

Approaching **Darien Harbor** from the west, keep well to the south of the red 4sec flasher "30" **[WP-61]** marking **Smith Reef.** Don't cut inside the Smith Reef buoy at any time. Every year several boats get hung up there. Once past the reef, head for the east side of the green 4sec flasher "1," **[WP-60]** off Long Neck Point, 0.8nm to the northeast.

CAUTION: *If you're in a deep-draft boat, be sure to snuggle up toward nun "2" to avoid the 6-foot spot to the west before following the privately maintained midchannel buoys or range lights up to the Noroton Yacht Club.*

Coming into **Darien Harbor** from the south you have a clear shot up to the green flasher "1" **[WP-60]** so long as you stay a minimum of 400 yards off Long Neck Point. Between Nash Island and the yacht club is a small and crowded but well-protected mooring area.

Keep in mind that the entire area from Long Neck Point to Nash Island and up to the Darien Boat Club is a special anchorage, so moored or anchored boats will not be lighted. There is seldom space to anchor except near the tip of Long Neck Point. There is a 5-mph speed limit throughout the harbor.

Around the other side of Long Neck Point is the popular **Zieglers Cove,** named for the owners of an enormous estate that surrounds it. Zieglers lies to the north of Hay Island. It is a jewel of a gunkhole except in a strong easterly.

To get to **Zieglers Cove** from Long Neck Point, go 0.8nm north-northeast and look for the exposed rock off the east side of Hay Island. Head due north for 200 yards past the exposed rock before turning west into the cove, where there is about 9 feet of water waiting for you. The south side of Great Island is lined with a sheer rock cliff; boaters traditionally enter Zieglers Cove along this stretch, where there's 11 feet of water.

The marshes and wooded shores of **Scotts Cove** make it a beautiful gunkhole if you draw less than 3 feet. The chart shows as much as 9 feet of water due east of Great Island, but be sure to stay well off Great Island because of the nasty rocks on its east side. Scott Cove is a beautiful spot to explore in your dinghy, and we're told that in a dink you can go all the way up to the north end of **Contentment Island,** where there's adequate water at high tide.

The approaches to the **Five Mile River** from the east and west are pretty straightforward. There is an unnumbered red and green junction buoy (formerly red and black), about 0.3nm south of Butlers Island, that marks a nasty rock 2 feet under the surface. Give this buoy a wide berth.

The narrow channel up the dredged river carries only about 6 feet of water at midchannel for about 0.8nm until it fizzles out altogether. The channel begins at the green 4sec flasher "3" **[WP-63],** paired with red nun "4."

On the east bankof the river is Rowayton. The protection is excellent, and an assortment of restaurants, supplies, and other amenities are within walking distance of the marinas.

There are several facilities in the river for small- and medium-sized craft, although transient space is scarce. The lines of moored boats on the west side of the channel make turning a medium-sized boat difficult, even in the turning basin. It goes without saying there's no room to anchor.

☎ Shoreside and Emergency Services

Ambulance: 911
Coast Guard: Eatons Neck (516) 261-6868/6910 or VHF 16
Fire: Darien 911 or (203) 655-1216
    Norwalk 911 or (203) 866-3311
Harbormaster: Darien (203) 655-9028
Hospital: Norwalk (203) 852-2000
Police: Darien 911 or (203) 655-9239
    Norwalk 911 or (203) 866-4411
Radio Telephone: VHF 27; I.D.: Bridgeport
    Marine Operator
Taxi: Darien Yellow Cab (203) 655-8779
Tow Service: Southern CT Sea Tow, Bridgeport, CT
    (203) 331-0410 or VHF 16 or CB 9 ✦

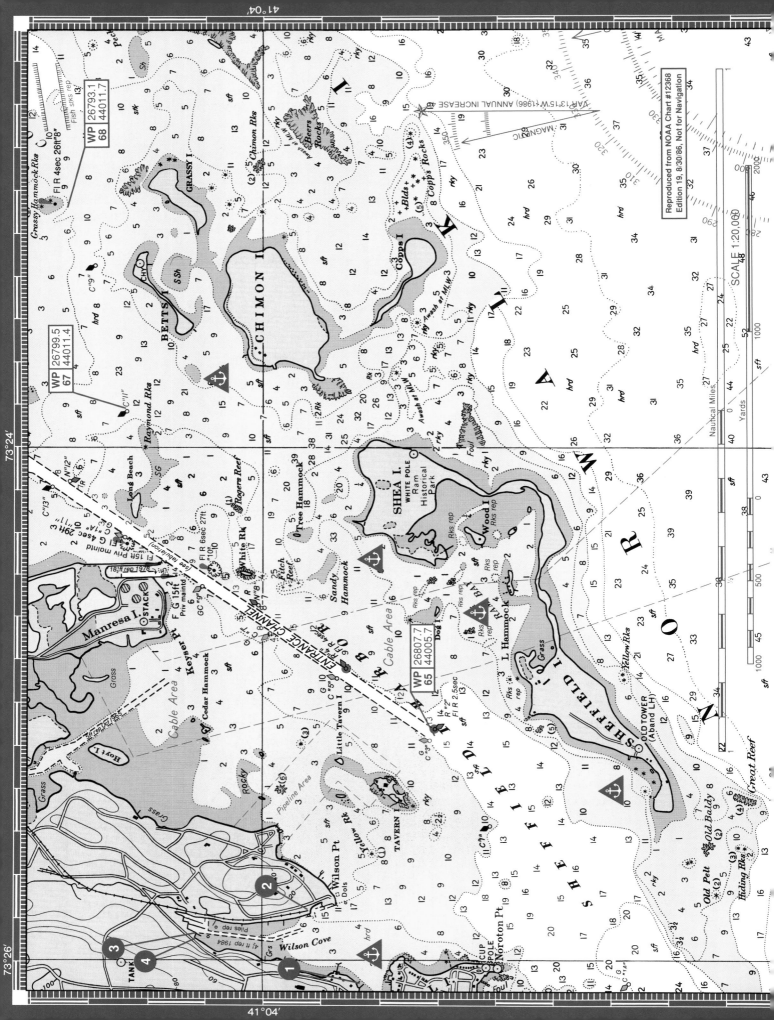

The Norwalk Islands

Islands of a Feather

The appeal of the Norwalk Islands stems from their history and beauty, and especially from their birdlife. Since 1984 Sheffield Island and Chimon Island have been the central parts of the Stewart B. McKinney National Wildlife Refuge. Comprising 145 acres of islands and coastlands in Connecticut, the refuge also includes Milford Point and Falkner Island, off Guilford. Chimon's 70 acres support the most important heron rookery in the state and one of the three largest wading-bird colonies in the northeast.

Like the Thimble Islands, some of the Norwalk Islands have been used over the last century as playgrounds for the rich (and the not-so-rich). Developers have always recognized the potential of the islands as resorts, and a few lavish clubhouses were even attempted, but these schemes were often doomed by storms, logistical problems, and last but not least, the lack of fresh water.

Chimon Island is the only one of the Norwalk Islands with a freshwater supply, so it was especially attractive to those wanting to build clubs or estates. The creation of the McKinney Refuge not only saved one of Connecticut's last relatively unspoiled ecological treasures but it also kept Chimon and Sheffield islands from being gobbled up by developers.

Tavern Island, once called Pilot Island, got its name during Prohibition, when it was reputed to have been a speakeasy. Now it is a favorite watering hole for herds of seahorses, as is Sheffield Island. The island has had many owners, but none more famous than Billy Rose. As a young man, Rose was a champion shorthander and typist who later became a major writer and producer of Broadway musicals. He was once married to comedienne-singer-actress Fanny Brice. Rose went to the altar many times—local savants say that there is a statue on Tavern Island for each of Billy Rose's five wives. Later Rose made a fortune as a Wall Street stockbroker, and at one time owned more AT&T stock than any other single person.

Three-quarters of a mile east of Chimon Island is Goose Island, which, according to legend, is bare because it was stripped of vegetation by treasure hunters madly searching for Captain Kidd's buried booty. Of course, there's not an island in Long Island Sound without a Captain Kidd legend attached to it, even though in truth he wasn't a very good pirate, nor did he spend much time in the Sound. The moral of the story is that if someone wants to sell you a tiny island with some of Captain Kidd's treasure supposedly buried on it, just offer to swap it for the Brooklyn Bridge.

Just north of Goose Island is the solar-powered Pecks Ledge Lighthouse, built in 1906 and said to be haunted by the ghost of one of the keepers. During World War II both the Pecks Ledge and Greens Ledge lighthouses were manned by Coast Guard personnel on the lookout for German submarines.

Windsurfing in the Norwalk Islands. Betts Island is in the background.

Marine Facilities and Services		Number of Transient Berths	Number of Transient Moorings	Seasonal/Year-round	Largest Vessel Accommodation (in feet)	Marked Entry Channel	Approach Depth (in feet)	Dockside Depth in feet at MLW	Gas/Diesel Fuel	Fuel Brand	Ramp/Dinghy Dock/Launch Service	Railway/Lift: Capacity (in tons)	Engine Repairs: Gas/Diesel	Propeller/Hull Repairs	Marine Supplies/Groceries/Bait/Ice	Pump-out Station	Showers/Laundromat	110V ★ 220V ▲ Maximum Amps	MasterCard/VISA/Diners Club	American Express	Restaurant/Snack Bar	Monitors VHF Channel
❶ Rowayton Yacht Club	(203) 854-0807	3	S	30		3	3						L		PRIVATE CLUB		S	I				68
❷ Norwalk Yacht Club	(203) 866-0941								PRIVATE CLUB - MEMBERS ONLY													
❸ Wilson Cove Marina	(203) 866-7020		Y	50	●	5	6						L25	PH	GD			S	★			
❹ Wilson Cove Yacht Club	(203) 853-8463								PRIVATE CLUB - MEMBERS ONLY													

Information in these listings is provided by the facilities themselves. An asterisk (*) indicates that the facility did not respond to our most recent requests for information.

© Robert G. Bachand

THE COASTS OF NEW YORK, CONNECTICUT, AND RHODE ISLAND

127

What To See and Do

Although the summertime traffic can be formidable, no one should miss exploring the Norwalk Islands. Most of the 16 islands are privately owned, but several of the larger ones can be explored by boaters, who will find many fine anchorages among the islands, bars, coves, and bays.

Sheffield Island, about 1.0nm east of Greens Ledge Light, is the westernmost of the Norwalk Islands. Most of the island is part of the McKinney Refuge, but the Norwalk Seaport Association (203) 838-9444 owns the old light-house on the western end. The lighthouse is now a museum and is listed as a National Landmark. It's open Memorial Day to Labor Day from 10:00 a.m. to sunset. Although restoration continues–the state has just chipped in $300,000 to help pay for the job–you can tour the lighthouse and view some of the workings and nautical artifacts collected by the group. Picnic tables, an old (but still functioning) hand-pump well, and other facilities are on the grounds. You can pull up to the docks on the north side of the island for mooring instructions. Launch service is available from the lighthouse to the Maritime Center in Norwalk (203) 852-0700 during the summer. Call the Seaport Association for more information.

The city of Norwalk owns a few acres on Sheffield, Shea, and Chimon islands, all open to the public for boating, swimming, and picnicking from dawn to dusk. There is a popular beach and camping area along the eastern shore of Shea. The area is marked by a tall white flagpole, which appears on the chart. On Sheffield and Chimon, hiking is prohibited from April 15 to August 15, the nesting season, as not to disturb the birds.

If you're in the area during the first weekend after Labor Day, you can visit the Norwalk Oyster Festival with its tall ships, continuous entertainment, arts and crafts shows, boat-building competitions, and, of course, oysters. The festival sports a new and rapidly growing boat show, also sponsored by the Seaport Association.

 Where To Eat

For restaurant suggestions in Norwalk Harbor, see the next chapter. Otherwise stock your galley.

 Navigation and Anchorages

Use NOAA Charts 12368 (1:20,000), 12364 (1:40,000), and 12363 (1:80,000). Use tide tables for Bridgeport. High tide at Greens Ledge is 2 minutes earlier; low tide is 1 minute earlier. Multiply by 1.1 for height at high or low water. Mean tidal range is 7.8 feet.

Greens Ledge Light, a red and white 24sec flasher on a 62-foot tower, marks the western end of the Norwalk Islands. The light is 5.2nm by boat northeast of the entrance to Stamford Harbor, and 7.5nm by boat southwest of the

entrance to the Saugatuck River. Eatons Neck Point on Long Island is 5.6nm to the south-southeast.

From the red 4sec bell "28C" **[WP-334]** at **Cable and Anchor Reef,** a course of about 340°m for 2.2nm will bring you to the **Greens Ledge Light [WP-62]** and the approach to Sheffield Harbor and Norwalk Harbor.

The eastern approach to **Cockenoe Harbor**–and, hence, Norwalk Harbor–goes past the flashing 4sec **Peck Ledge Light [WP-71]** just north of Goose Island. Even if you're coming from Westport or Southport, the only safe approach to Cockenoe Harbor from the east is to go outside Georges Rock can "1" **[WP-75],** the red flashing 2.5sec bell "24" **[WP-74],** and red nun "2" **[WP-73]** south of Cockenoe Shoal. Between any of these buoys and Cockenoe Island there are a number of dangerous rocks and shoals.

Once past nun "2," head northwest for **Peck Ledge Light [WP-71],** keeping both the light and green gong "5" to port and red nun "4" at Channel Rock to starboard.

After passing Peck Ledge Light, turn hard to port and head for the 28-foot red flasher "8" **[WP-68]** at Grassy Hammock Rocks. If you haven't started already, now's the time to start looking hard for oyster stakes and lobster pots, because there are many in this area.

Leave black can "9" and Betts Island to port, and make sure you continue toward can "11" **[WP-67]** marking **Raymond Rocks.** Then make a dogleg turn to starboard toward the 26-foot quick flashing red beacon "14" **[WP-66]** off Round Beach. Leave the tower to starboard and head up the main channel.

CAUTION: *This eastern approach to Norwalk Harbor is a pretty cruise when the weather is good. However, those unfamiliar with the area are advised against using the east approach during times of restricted visibility. Even when it's clear as a bell, it's a good idea to have at least one eagle-eyed crew member when taking this route. The aids to navigation can be hard to spot, and with the abundant shallows in this area, there's not much room for error. It's also very frustrating to have to follow such a narrow, winding channel through what appears to be such a wide-open harbor. Even so, those shallows are very real and especially dangerous at low water during a spring tide (when a new or full moon creates a greater-than-average tidal range). Take it slow!*

Although there is no speed limit around the islands, you should be on constant lookout for swimmers, windsurfers, and daysailers. (For more information on South Norwalk and Norwalk, see the next chapter on Norwalk Harbor. For information on Cockenoe Island, the easternmost of the Norwalk Islands, see the chapter on Westport and the Saugatuck River.)

To the west, **Wilson Cove** is the first shoreside anchorage east of **Greens Ledge Light [WP-62],** a 62-foot white and red flasher. The cove is lined with beautiful homes, two yacht clubs, and a marina. Unfortunately, it doesn't take much wind to make the cove uncomfortable.

The area just to the north and west of **Sheffield Island** and **Shea Island** makes a convenient stopover anchorage for those traveling along the Sound since it is easily reached and not far off the main east-west route. It is exposed to the southwest, but the holding ground is good. For best results, drop a danforth anchor into the soft mud.

It is not wise to cut between Sheffield Island and the **Greens Ledge Light** at low tide, particularly for newcomers. The ledge (i.e., rock, not sand) goes all the way from the island out to the light. However, many boats do pass over the ledge close to the east side of the light. If you want to try this, stay within 200 yards of the light or you will lose the bottom of your boat.

There are no marinas on the islands, so if you're looking for a slip, head up into Norwalk Harbor. The entrance channel for **Norwalk Harbor** begins 400 yards southeast of Tavern Island at green can "3" and the red 2.5sec flasher "2" **[WP-65].** The channel is also used by oyster boats, coastal oil tankers, and barges, along with all the pleasure boats. Give a wide berth to the 29-foot green flasher "11" off Manresa Island, because of a shoal reaching out from its base. The red lights on top of the tall stacks of the United Illuminating Company power plant on Manresa Island are excellent landmarks because they can be seen for many miles out on the Sound.

About 0.4nm northeast of green flasher "11," the channel turns to the north and then to the northwest before dividing into two channels at Fitch Point. (For more information on Norwalk Harbor and the entrance channel north of Manresa Island, see the following chapter.)

CAUTION: Stay completely out of the triangle between White Rock (red channel nun "8"), nun "12" on the Norwalk channel north of Long Beach, and Raymond Rocks (black can "11"). Lots of visitors find the shoal north of Long Beach at half tide.

Shea Island, formerly Ram Island, is named in honor of a Norwalk native who died in the Vietnam War. If you are traveling in a large boat and want to visit the island, you will want to anchor offshore and take your dinghy in. With a dinghy, you can approach from most directions. The easiest approach is from the north, followed by northeast, southeast, and finally south, by way of Wood Island.

The area between **Shea Island** and **Chimon Island** is known as the "Middle Passage." Like the Middle Ages, this is not something that you would want to go through. It is narrow, unbuoyed, and filled with rocks. Many of the local boaters zip between the two islands in their runabouts, but they already know where the rocks are and use them to scrape the barnacles off their hulls. If you want to try it in your dink, head north for the tombolo on the west side of Copps Island and turn to port, clearing the reefs off the southwest side of Chimon. Go on a rising tide and go slow.

If you've brought rod and reel with you, there's good fishing for blackfish and flounder on the south side of

Copps Island. Copps Island itself is privately owned and is none too inviting because of water rats.

CAUTION: If you're cruising outside the Norwalk Islands, be sure to keep well away from Copps Island. Copps Rocks extend almost 0.5nm to the southeast. From your boat, you may feel safe so far away from the island, but every year these rocks claim some unwary boaters.

In approaching **Chimon Island** from the north, you will want to stay at least 300 yards west of Betts Island and the same distance west of Chimon. Put can "11" **[WP-67]** at Raymond Rocks dead astern and aim for the flagpole on Shea Island until you're due west of the beach. Then make for land. This way you shouldn't go aground on the shoals that surround most of the island. The area northwest of Chimon is also a nice anchorage, well protected from easterlies.

 ## Shoreside and Emergency Services

Airport: Connecticut Limousine to JFK & LaGuardia (203) 327-5200
Sikorsky Memorial Airport (203) 576-7498
Ambulance: 911
Bus: Wheels Bus (203) 852-0000
Coast Guard: Eatons Neck (516) 261-6868/6910
or VHF 16, 22 and 83
Fire: 911 or (203) 866-3312
Harbormaster: (203) 847-0843
Hospital: Norwalk Hospital (203) 852-2000
Police: 911 or (203) 854-3010
Marine Unit (203) 838-0111 or VHF 14 or 16
Radio Telephone: VHF 27; I.D.: Bridgeport
Marine Operator
Taxi: Yellow Cab (203) 853-1267
Tow Service: Southern CT Sea Tow, Bridgeport, CT
(203) 331-0410 or VHF 16 or CB 9
Train: Amtrak 1-800-USA-RAIL
Metro-North 1-800-638-7646 ◆

Riverside Renaissance

South Norwalk, Norwalk, and East Norwalk, like many other coastal Connecticut towns, have been experiencing a revitalization of their waterfronts, but just how far this development should go is an on-going issue. In South Norwalk, the new Maritime Center opened in the Spring of 1988, built in a pair of 120-year-old former lock and iron foundries on the west bank of the Norwalk River, just above the railroad bridge. The $22-million center was eight years in the works and has become a symbol of the comeback in South Norwalk.

Known as "SoNo" by the local residents, South Norwalk was originally known as "Old Well" in the last century. It

Norwalk Cove Marina at Calf Pasture Park in Norwalk.

#	Marine Facilities and Services	Phone	Number of Transient Berths	Number of Transient Moorings	Seasonal/Year-round	Largest Vessel Accommodation (in feet)	Approach Depth (in feet)	Marked Entry Channel	Dockside Depth in feet at MLW	Gas/Diesel Fuel	Fuel Brand	Ramp/Dinghy Dock Launch Service	Railway/Lift: Capacity (in tons)	Propeller/Hull Repairs	Engine Repairs: Gas/Diesel	Marine Supplies/Groceries/Bait/Ice	Pump-out Station	Showers/Laundromat	110V★ 220V▲ Maximum Amps	MasterCard/VISA/Diners Club/American Express	Restaurant/Snack Bar	Monitors VHF Channel
1	South Norwalk Boat Club	(203) 853-8868								*PRIVATE CLUB—MEMBERS ONLY*												
2	**Defeo's Cove Marine (p. 134)**	**(203) 855-9870**								*YACHT SALES—NEW & USED*												
3	Harbor Watch Marina	(203) 853-0771	4	6	Y	55	10	●	7				L35	PH	GD	SI		SL	★50			16
4	**Rex Marine Center (p. 133)**	**(203) 854-5867**	5		Y	40	8	●	8				L35	PH	GD	SI		S	★▲50	MV		
5	Ischoda Yacht Club	(203) 853-8886	1	2	Y	34	7	●	7							I			★		R	67
6	**Norwest Marine (p. 134)**	**(203) 853-2822**	10		Y	50	15	●	8	GD			L30	PH	GD	SI			★	MV		68
7	Maurice Marine	(203) 866-5169		2	S	30	4	●	4			D	L5	PH	GD	SI			★30			16
8	Sono Seaport Seafood	(203) 854-9483	6		Y	40	20		6	*RESTAURANT—DOCKAGE FOR PATRONS*										MVA		67
9	Boat / US Marine Center	(203) 866-4426			Y					*MARINE SUPPLIES*								S		MV		
10	Norwalk Boat Club	(203) 853-8801	1		Y	25	4	●	4	*PRIVATE CLUB—MEMBERS ONLY*						SI					S	9
11	Coppola Marine	(203) 853-8343			Y		8		8						P	G			SB				
12	Neptune Boat Club	(203) 853-8526								*PRIVATE CLUB—MEMBERS ONLY*												
13	Wisner Bros. Boat Builders	(203) 866-2252	2	2	Y	40	5	●	5				L40	PH	GD				★30			68
14	Veterans Park Launching Ramp									*RESIDENTS ONLY*												
15	Pastime Marina	(203) 853-8613								*PRIVATE CLUB—MEMBERS ONLY*												
16	East Norwalk Boat Club	(203) 838-3184								*PRIVATE CLUB—MEMBERS ONLY*												
17	Overton's Boat Livery	(203) 838-2031			S	25	6	●	6				L5	PH	GD	SI		SL			S	67
18	Bloom Brothers Marine	(203) 838-9273			S	40	4	●	5	G	MOB		L15	P	GD	I			★			
19	Shore and Country Club	(203) 838-7507	2			42	6	●	6	*PRIVATE CLUB—MEMBERS ONLY*						I			★		R	
20	**Norwalk Cove Marina (p. 133)**	**(203) 838-2326**	50		Y	125	8	●	6	GD	TEX	L	L70	PH	GD	SI		SL	★50	MV	RS	16
21	Electra Yachts	(203) 866-1559								*MARINE ELECTRONICS—CELLULAR TELEPHONES*												
22	**Oyster Bend (p. 134)**	**(203) 854-6666**	12		Y	100	12	●	8							BI		SL	▲50			67
23	**United Marine, Inc. (p. 135)**	**(203) 853-1174**	4		Y	60	10	●	7				L35	PH	GD			S	★25	MVA		69

Information in these listings is provided by the facilities themselves. An asterisk (*) indicates that the facility did not respond to our most recent requests for information.

is changing from a run-down old neighborhood into a magnet for local and tourist dollars, and with the increased activity in the area comes the demand for more boating facilities to encourage more people to come.

There have been proposals to dredge the mud flats to the south of Veterans Memorial Park for a large new municipal marina. Environmentalists and commercial shellfishermen are concerned that Norwalk's famed oysters will be stressed if such a large part of their habitat is destroyed. On the other hand, the city, like other communities all around Long Island Sound, is feeling the pressure of the many boaters who want a place to keep their boats. Although the expansion proposal at Veterans Park has been shelved for the time being, the city is drafting a harbor-management plan that should set a clear direction for future development.

★ What To See and Do

There are plenty of things to do in the Norwalks. Finding a slip isn't always easy, though the addition of new transient facilities in the upper harbor should help. It's probably still a good idea to call ahead for a reservation.

Another way to visit is to use the launch service from the Sheffield Island Lighthouse Museum. Weekend service begins Memorial Day, with daily service from the end of June through Labor Day. The launch can ferry you to the island from your boat anchored off Sheffield, and for a small fare, the service will also take you from the island to the doorstep of the Maritime Center, from which you'll have easy access to the restaurants and shops of South Norwalk's restored waterfront. Call the Norwalk Seaport Association (203) 838-9444 for more information on the launch schedule.

The Seaport Association also sponsors the Norwalks' biggest event of the year: the Norwalk Oyster Festival, held the first weekend after Labor Day. The festival features tall ships, continuous entertainment, arts and crafts shows, international food, boat-building competitions, and, of course, oysters.

The restored SoNo shopping district features everything from antiques to books to ice cream. The restoration of the area has left intact the brick facades and gas lamps of the old district, which adds to the atmosphere. At Shenanigan's Nite Club (203) 853-0142 on Washington Street you'll find live entertainment every night, including well-known national performers.

You can easily spend a day at the new Norwalk Maritime Center (203) 852-0700. The center runs frequent features on its huge 6-story by 8-story IMAX screen every day. Inside the museum you'll find exhibits on boat building and Connecticut history, and there are lots of hands-on demonstrations available. The center includes aquaria showing the ecosystems of Long Island Sound and the Atlantic and tanks filled with seals, sharks, and fish of the Sound.

One of the most intriguing sights in Norwalk is the enormous Lockwood-Mathews Mansion (203) 838-1434. The 50-room mansion is the ultimate in Victorian architecture. The keeper of the National Register says: "The magnificent interior of the building has the best frescoed walls I have ever seen in this country, and the lavishness of the marble and wood inlay work almost defies description in the museum quality of its workmanship." To some it's beautiful; others would call it extravagant or gaudy, but everyone agrees it is unique. Way back in 1868 it cost $2 million to build. Almost lost to the wrecking ball, it was acquired by the city in 1938 and is now a museum.

Where To Eat

There are lots of restaurants in Norwalk, with two accessible by boat. You'll find Skipper's Restaurant (203) 838-2211 on the grounds of Norwalk Cove Marina, to starboard as you enter the harbor. Just before the auto bridge you'll spot an ornamental lighthouse to port, luring you to SoNo Seaport Seafood (203) 854-9483, where you can purchase fresh seafood or enjoy dockside dining. SoNo Seaport and Skipper's have a few slips for diners, but you can expect a wait. Just to the south, the Ischoda Yacht Club (203) 853-8886 serves American fare in a casual atmosphere.

If you've come by launch, there are lots of other choices from fancy/pricey to humble/inexpensive in the seaport area. Across the street from Veterans Park is Sunrise Pizza Cafe (203) 838-0166, which comes highly recommended for California-style designer pizza.

In the same block are the basics–basic Italian at Abruzzi Kitchen (203) 838-6776, and basic American at the Ocean View Cafe (203) 854-0770 (breakfast and lunch only).

The heart of the "SoNo" redevelopment is on Washington Street on the west side of the harbor. Among the assorted shops you'll have a number of choices. Pasta Nostra (203) 854-9700 offers sophisticated Italian. Just down the street is El Acupulco (203) 853-6217, serving Mexican, and Old Rialto (203) 852-7000 (formerly the Atlantic Club), serving fine American food in a nautical setting. In the same block is LaProvence (203) 855-8958, serving French for the gourmet in your crew. Reservations are a good idea at the latter two.

In East Norwalk, there is also a small snack bar behind Overton's Boat Livery, and right next door is Bar Harbour (203) 852-1257, serving seafood and other goodies.

 ## Navigation and Anchorages

Use NOAA Charts 12368 (1:20,000), 12364 (1:40,000), and 12363 (1:80,000). Use tide tables for Bridgeport. High tide at South Norwalk is 9 minutes later; low tide is 15 minutes later. Multiply by 1.0 for height at high or low water. Mean tidal range is 7.6 feet.

The main approach channel to Norwalk Harbor begins at the red 2.5sec flasher "2" between Sheffield and Tavern islands, about 2.0nm by boat southwest of Norwalk Harbor

itself and 6.8nm by boat northeast of the Stamford breakwaters. Huntington Bay on Long Island is 8.3nm to the south.

There are two approaches to **Norwalk Harbor:** from the west via **Greens Ledge Light [WP-62]** and from the east via **Peck Ledge Light [WP-71].** The commercial channel from Greens Ledge Light is much easier and is the only approach the newcomer should use if visibility is restricted.

CAUTION: Both approaches go through the Norwalk Islands; see the previous chapter for a complete description of the passages through the islands.

From red flasher "14" **[WP-66]** west of Round Beach, the dredged channel is well marked and easy to follow. **Charles Creek** has recently undergone extensive dredging (to at least 8 feet) to accommodate hundreds of boats, although Norwalk Cove Marina is the only commercial facility in Charles Creek. The docks farther up the creek belong to condo developments.

To get into **Charles Creek,** turn to starboard at green can "17" and follow the channel, staying in the middle between the bulkheads and docks on the right and the breakwaters on the left. Although the harbor is wide, it is shallow except at the main dock and in the channel.

Half a mile north of the entrance to Charles Creek is the **East Norwalk Channel** (unnamed on the chart), with an entrance marked by a 29-foot green 2.5sec flasher and red nun "2" and about 6 feet of water. There are several small-boat facilities up the channel. At Bloom Brothers Marine or Overton's you can rent small skiffs for fishing.

Once past the **railroad bridge** and the Maritime Center, there are more choices for the transient in search of a slip. Just south of the I-95 bridge is a new marina, Oyster Bend, which offers slips and other transient services. You'll find at least 8 feet of water in the channel nearly all the way up the harbor.

Farther north is a small boat club and a boatyard, Coppola Marine, near the head of the harbor. Keep an eye out for the occasional barge heading for the warehouses

and oil depots at the head of the harbor. (The barges maintain the channel by keeping the bottom clear.)

Both the Rte. 136 bridge and the railroad bridge can be contacted on VHF 13. The harbormaster monitors VHF 16, as does the Norwalk Police Marine Unit. If you don't have electronic means of communicating on board, one long and one short blast of your horn will signal your intentions.

 ### Shoreside and Emergency Services

Airport: Sikorsky Memorial Airport (203) 576-7498
Ambulance: 911
Bus: Wheels Bus (203) 852-0000
Coast Guard: Eatons Neck (516) 261-6868/6910 or
VHF 16, 22, and 83
Fire: 911 or (203) 866-3312
Hospital: (203) 852-2000
Police: 911 or (203) 854-3010
Marine Unit (203) 838-0111 or VHF 14 or 16
Radio Telephone: VHF 27; I.D.: Bridgeport Marine
Operator
Taxi: Yellow Cab (203) 853-1267
Tow Service: Southern CT Sea Tow, Bridgeport, CT
(203) 331-0410 or VHF 16 or CB 9
Train: Amtrak 1-800-USA-RAIL
Metro-North 1-800-638-7646   ◆

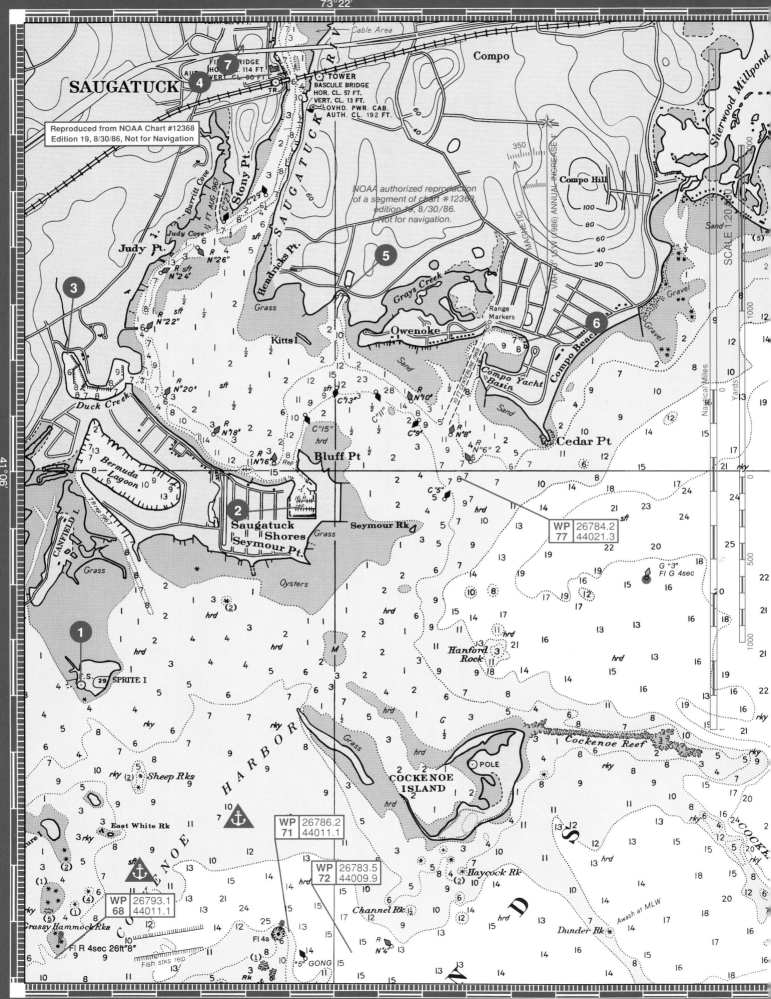

Westport and the Saugatuck River

Launching Patriots and Artists Alike

Like most other towns in western Connecticut, Westport began as a serene farming village which was transformed in the 19th century by the advent of the railroad into an I-want-to-get-away-from-it-all outpost for New York City.

The Saugatuck River north of the I-95 and railroad bridges. In the distance is the center of Westport, CT.

© Jack McConnell

In the fervent days of the Revolution, however, Westport was an outpost of a much different kind. In 1777, a couple of thousand Redcoats disembarked from a cluster of British warships at the mouth of the Saugatuck River, landed at Compo Beach, and marched inland to raid the supply depot at Danbury. From then on Saugatuck went on to become a favorite launching place for retaliatory raids by the Colonists against the British on Long Island.

Such a hostile demeanor did not last, and by the first decades of the 20th century Westport was little more than a few shops and homes along the Boston Post Road near the Saugatuck River. The town had even become a favorite among artists and writers who congregated at the Manor House, a local hotel. Today Westport is still the preferred home to a number of celebrities, among them actor, stock-car racer, and spaghetti-sauce mogul Paul Newman.

The lower Saugatuck River is lined with some very striking–and often palatial–modern homes that you'll get a good look at as you boat up the river. Westport is loaded with interesting architecture, so much so that the town conducted an architectural survey in 1988.

 What To See and Do

East of Compo Beach is Sherwood Island State Park (203) 226-6983. Established in 1914, the park was the first in Connecticut and one of the first in the nation. The park comprises 218 acres of sandy beaches, marshes, groves of linden and maple trees, picnic facilities, and a large pavilion with an observation deck. Because of the large number of bathers, landing at the beach is not permitted, although there are plenty of fishermen anchored just off the pavilion.

	Marine Facilities and Services	Phone	Number of Transient Berths	Number of Transient Moorings	Seasonal/Year-round	Largest Vessel Accommodation (in feet)	Marked Entry Channel	Approach Depth (in feet)	Dockside Depth in feet at MLW	Gas/Diesel Fuel	Fuel Brand	Ramp/Dinghy Dock/Launch Service	Railway/Lift: Capacity (in tons)	Propeller/Hull Repairs	Engine Repairs: Gas/Diesel	Pump-out Station	Showers/Laundromat	Marine Supplies/Groceries/Bait/Ice	110V ★ 220V ▲ Maximum Amps	MasterCard/VISA/Diners Club / American Express	Restaurant/Snack Bar	Monitors VHF Channel
1	Sprite Island Yacht Club	(203) 866-7879		3	S		•	5									S	I			S	9
2	Cedar Point Yacht Club	(203) 226-7411	3		S	45		7	9	GD		R					S	I	▲		S	16
3	Saugatuck Harbor Yacht Club	(203) 227-3607	10		S	55	•	7	6	GD	MOB	R					SL	I	★50			16
4	Coastwise Marine (p. 139)	(203) 226-0735			Y	24	•	8	6	G	GUL			PH	G		S	I	★	MVA		16
5	E.R. Strait Marina	(203) 226-3688			S	35	•	6	6	G	TEX							I	★30			
6	Compo Yacht Basin	(203) 227-9136			S	36	•	7	9	G	TEX	R						I	★30		S	16
7	Northrop Yachts*	(203) 226-1915																				

Information in these listings is provided by the facilities themselves. An asterisk (*) indicates that the facility did not respond to our most recent requests for information.

The second week in May is the annual Dogwood Festival (203) 259-5596. If the weather and the trees cooperate, it can be spectacular. A self-guided tour is mapped out through the northern section of the city, going through some of the most exclusive areas.

Other attractions in town are the Westport Country Playhouse (203) 227-4177, one of New England's best-known summer theaters, now in its 59th season. The Nature Center for Environmental Activities (203) 227-7253 is only a few miles from the river and offers 53 wooded acres of trails and streams, a natural science museum, a hands-on aquarium, and more–great for the kids.

The E.R. Strait Marina, located at the Longshore Club Park, is owned and operated by the town of Westport. The park also has tennis courts and an 18-hole golf course for residents only, but guest privileges are available from the town recreation department (203) 226-8311. To reach any of the shops, restaurants, or other facilities in town you may want to call a taxi.

 Where To Eat

Your easiest choices for dining are the Black Duck Cafe (203) 227-7978, located next door to Coastwise Marine on Riverside Avenue, serving a varied men, or the Arrow Restaurant (203) 227-4731, a stone's throw from Coastwise on Charles Street, where you'll find a Continental and Italian menu. Farther north on Riverside Avenue, on the other side of the I-95 overpass, you'll find DeRosa's (203) 227-7596, widely considered one of the best Italian restaurants in Fairfield County.

Staying on Riverside Avenue, north of DeRosa's is the Mansion Clam House (203) 227-9661 for seafood, and Manero's Steak House (203) 227-1500 for you-know-what. If your tastes run toward the hotter side, try Viva Zapata (203) 227-9988, also on Riverside Avenue, for Mexican food. Central Westport is also loaded with restaurants, if you're willing to take a cab.

 Navigation and Anchorages

Use NOAA Charts 12368 (1:20,000), 12364 (1:40,000), and 12363 (1:80,000). Use tide tables for Bridgeport. High tide at the Saugatuck River entrance is 2 minutes earlier; low tide is 1 minute later. Mean tidal range is 7.6 feet.

The mouth of the Saugatuck River, marked by the green 4sec flasher "3," is 3.1nm by boat west of the entrance to Southport Harbor. Peck Ledge Light, marking the eastern approach to Norwalk Harbor, is 3.2nm by boat to the southwest.

From the red and white Mo (A) whistle "BH" **[WP-87]** southeast of Penfield Light, steering a course of approximately 280°m should bring the green 4sec flasher "3" **[WP-76]** within sight; be sure to stay clear of Hanford Rock, east of buoy "3" **[WP-76].**

If you're coming from across the Sound, your sea marker should be the red 4sec flashing bell "2" **[WP-363]** at the southern tip of Middle Ground; steering a course of about 297°m should also lead you to the green flasher "3" **[WP-76]** outside the entrance to the Saugatuck River.

North of Cockenoe Island (pronounced *Ko-kee-nee*), between Bluff and Cedar points, the shallow **Saugatuck River** leads to **Westport.** You can't reach the river from the west inside the Norwalk Islands because at low tide there can be bare ground between **Cockenoe Island** and the mainland. If you're just harbor-hopping between Westport and Norwalk it can be frustrating to take the long but necessary trip around Cockenoe Island. You could probably walk between the two towns in less time.

If you're coming into this area for the first time, avoid going into the **Saugatuck River** at night, and be very careful. The channel is well-marked but extremely narrow and snake-like, slithering through the mud flats on either side. Generally, the channel follows the western shore.

Coming from the west, stay outside Cockenoe Shoal and reef, turn north at the red 2.5sec (formerly 4sec) flashing bell "24" **[WP-74]** and keep east of green can "1" **[WP-75]** at **Georges Rock.** (The can is now a 4sec flasher and has been moved slightly to the northeast.) Head for the green 4sec flasher "3" **[WP-76],** which will be in line with the first pair of river buoys, can "5" and red nun "6" **[WP-77].**

CAUTION: The green flasher "3" [WP-76] has been relocated at least 400 yards away from the location shown on the chart, to a spot just south of the 12-foot spot east of Hanford Rock. Because of the dramatic change in the placement of the buoy, we have published LORAN numbers for the new position in the "LORAN Index" in the back of this book. However, to avoid confusion we have elected to remove the LORAN placement from the chart in this chapter.

From **Cedar Point** on there is a 5-mph speed limit that the active marine patrols enforce. Because of the speed limit, the narrow channel, and the tremendous number of small single-class sailboats and windsurfers crowding the harbor, it can be a 20- or 30-minute trip up to the railroad bridge. Most of the marinas have floating finger piers because of the 8-foot variation in the tides.

Just inside **Cedar Point** is the Compo Yacht Basin (run by the town), which you may enter by rounding red nun "8." The basin can be congested, and anchoring is impossible. Just 800 yards to the west is the E.R. Strait Marina, also town-operated. At both facilities, guest berths are available only by chance. Calling ahead is recommended.

North of **Bluff Point** the channel twists in horseshoe fashion toward the west, then south, then west again, and finally snakes to the north. At Bluff Point the small basin southeast of red nun "16" is home to the Cedar Point Yacht Club. The entry is better protected than Compo or Saugatuck Harbor, but the basin is usually filled with the docks and boats of the yacht club.

The Cedar Point Yacht Club at Bluff Point, from the south.

Upriver to port you will see the Saugatuck Harbor Yacht Club at the head of **Duck Creek,** a nice little shelter. The Saugatuck River itself can be so filled with boats that it may discourage you from staying overnight. The river carries a depth of at least 6 feet at mlw up to the railroad and highway bridges. However, we once headed up the river at spring tide (when the moon is new or full, resulting in a greater than average tidal range) and found 4 feet or less in the channel at low water. North of the bridges, most of the depth disappears.

If you have a small boat, and/or you are adventurous enough, you can pass through the bascule railroad bridge and go upstream by signaling the bridge-tender with the usual long and short blasts of your horn. Just beyond the railroad bridge is the I-95 bridge; another 200 yards north is a small swing bridge that no longer opens. The vertical clearance of this bridge is only 6 feet at high tide. If this is enough overhead room for you, and you have a shallow-draft boat, you can proceed safely up the river right into downtown **Westport** at the Post Road. The depths in this part of the river are only 2 to 5 feet at mlw.

Back outside the Saugatuck River, the best-known and easternmost of the Norwalk Islands is **Cockenoe Island.** Owned by the town of Westport, Cockenoe is one of Long Island Sound's best picnic sites. You can reach the island only by dinghy, and the best approach is from the northwest side, directly into the embayment. It is shallow in the bay, but the bottom is hard sand and mud. If you have a very shallow draft, you can spend the night in the embayment: anchor at the mouth of the bay, toward the northeast fork. Deeper draft boats will want to anchor out in **Cockenoe Harbor.** Don't approach the island from the east: there are too many unmarked rocks and reefs.

Northwest of Cockenoe Island is **Bermuda Lagoon,** a privately dredged basin entered through Cockenoe Harbor, that is surrounded by private homes and docks. The lagoon itself is quite deep, but the entrance channel has been dredged only partway out into the shallow northern section of the harbor, so many boats can enter only at half tide or better.

Cockenoe Harbor, via Peck Ledge Light **[WP-71],** is also the eastern approach to **Norwalk Harbor.** Like the Saugatuck River, this is not a passage you will want to try for the first time at night. Aim for the green flasher atop the 61-foot tower at Peck Ledge **[WP-71],** swing to port, and head south of the 26-foot red 4sec flasher **[WP-68]** at Grassy Hammock Rocks.

CAUTION: Don't be tempted to run for the next red flasher you see off Round Beach: You will end up stuck in the mud. A better course is to head for can "11" [WP-67] off Raymond Rocks, and then turn northeast toward the red 26-foot quick flasher "14" [WP-66].

From here on, the channel is fairly well marked but can be tricky. (See the previous two chapters for descriptions of the channel up to the city of Norwalk and for more information on the Norwalk Islands.)

There is wonderful fishing and shellfishing in the Norwalk Islands, so beware of the many fish stakes placed throughout the harbor by commercial fishermen.

 ## Shoreside and Emergency Services

Airport: Sikorsky Memorial Airport (203) 576-7498
Ambulance: 911
Bus: Wheels Bus (203) 852-0000
      Westport Transit District Minibus (203) 226-7171
Coast Guard: Eatons Neck (516) 261-6868/6910
      or VHF 16
Fire: 911 or (203) 227-6673
Harbormaster: (203) 227-6002 or VHF 16
Police: 911 or (203) 227-4145
Radio Telephone: VHF 27; I.D.: Bridgeport
      Marine Operator
Taxi: Westport Star Taxi (203) 227-5157
Tow Service: Southern CT Sea Tow, Bridgeport, CT
      (203) 331-0410 or VHF 16
Train: Amtrak 1-800-USA-RAIL
      Metro-North 1-800-638-7646   ◆

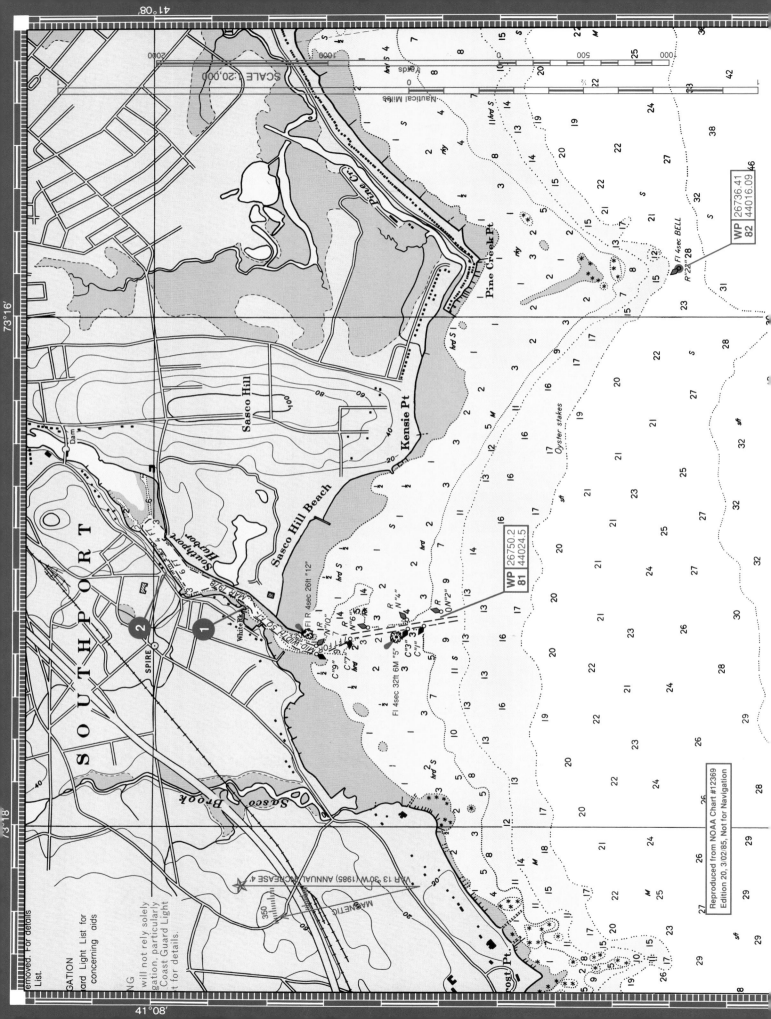

In The Cream

If all the harbors in Connecticut were milk, Southport would the cream; very rich, but not much of it. The harbor is quiet and beautiful, and you might feel as though you're in the middle of a picture-postcard, with the wooded residential areas on the west side and the wide spaces, rolling hills, and manicured greens of the Country Club of Fairfield's golf course to the east. The town is a cameo of the "good life" in Fairfield County.

You wouldn't think it, but this ground of gracious living was also the site of the Great Swamp Battle of 1637, when the last of the Pequot Indians, having escaped the massacre at Mystic, were run down in a Southport swamp and killed by the English settlers of eastern Connecticut.

In the Revolutionary days of 1779, General Tryon, the nominal British Military Governor of New York, and his Hessian troops burned 85 public buildings and private homes in the town of Fairfield. (The town was rebuilt, and now enjoys several beautiful old historical districts, one of which is the area on the west side of Southport harbor.)

Looking northeast into the small but beautiful harbor of Southport, CT. Sasco Hill Beach and the Country Club of Fairfield are to the right.

The subsequent history of the town is far from bloody—the settlers were farmers, and Southport was mostly onion fields. The Federal Government began making improvements to the harbor in 1831 so that more boats could reach Southport (and more people could enjoy Southport's onions). Teams of oxen pulled crude scoop buckets to dredge the river, and schlepped heavy wooden sleds loaded with granite boulders across the mud flats to build the breakwater.

All that hard manual labor has been much appreciated by the many recreational boaters, mostly sailors, who have since taken advantage of the small but snug harbor of Southport, and turned it into a charming port, smooth and rich like cream.

 ### What To See and Do

Only a mile away from Southport Harbor, Fairfield has a wide variety of businesses and industries, and is the headquarters of the Audubon Society of Connecticut (203) 259-6305, which runs the Birdcraft Sanctuary Museum (203) 259-0416 and the Larson Sanctuary, a nature preserve with 6 miles of nature trails that are open year-round.

The Fairfield Historical Society (203) 259-1598 operates a museum with art exhibits of the Revolutionary War, sea captains, and ships, including a collection of antique navigational aids. The other museum is the Ogden House, an 18th-century farmhouse furnished in period style. The society also hosts walking tours of historic Fairfield during the summer months.

There's not much in the way of shopping or restaurants right on the water. The center of the Village of Southport is a short walk from the town dock or the Pequot Yacht Club and offers a few shops, a grocery, two cafes, and a gas station.

If you're looking for a more developed commercial area, however, plan on taking a cab to downtown Fairfield.

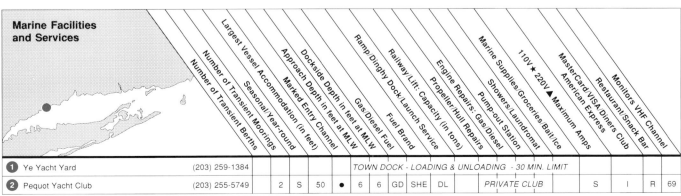

Marine Facilities and Services		Number of Transient Berths	Number of Transient Moorings	Seasonal/Year-round	Largest Vessel Accommodation (in feet)	Approach Depth (in feet)	Marked Entry Channel	Dockside Depth in feet at MLW	Gas/Diesel Fuel	Fuel Brand	Ramp/Dinghy Dock Launch Service	Railway/Lift Capacity (in tons)	Engine Repairs: Propeller/Hull Repairs	Marine Supplies/Groceries/Bait/Ice	Pump-out Station	Showers/Laundromat	110V ★ 220V ▲ Maximum Amps	MasterCard/VISA/Diners Club American Express	Restaurant/Snack Bar	Monitors VHF Channel
① Ye Yacht Yard	(203) 259-1384							*TOWN DOCK - LOADING & UNLOADING - 30 MIN. LIMIT*											
② Pequot Yacht Club	(203) 255-5749		2	S	50	●	6	6	GD	SHE	DL		*PRIVATE CLUB*				S	I	R	69

Information in these listings is provided by the facilities themselves. An asterisk (*) indicates that the facility did not respond to our most recent requests for information.

There you can eat or do some shopping at the excellent restaurants and stores surrounding the new gazebo on Sherman Green in the center of town. During warm months there is often entertainment at the gazebo. Off the green is the Community Theater (203) 255-6555 with a terrific old art deco-style neon marquee.

 ## Where To Eat

If you get ashore in Southport Harbor you'll be a 5-minute walk from the Driftwood Coffee Shop (203) 255-1975 and the Horseshoe Cafe (203) 255-8624, but for more substantial fare you'll still need a cab to get to your dinner destination.

In downtown Fairfield you'll find Tommy's (203) 254-1478 across from Sherman Green, specializing in Northern Italian cuisine. Reservations are recommended.

Gregory's Cafe & Bar (203) 259-7417 serves "New American" cuisine, and The Pie Plate (203) 255-5953 comes highly recommended for–you guessed it–pies, in a very casual atmosphere.

 ## Navigation and Anchorages

Use NOAA Charts 12369 (1:20,000), 12364 (1:40,000), and 12363 (1:80,000). Use tide tables for Bridgeport. High tide at the Black Rock Harbor entrance is 4 minutes earlier; low tide is 3 minutes earlier. Multiply by 1.0 for height at high or low water. Mean tidal range is 7.4 feet.

CAUTION: There have been many buoy changes in this area. We have noted the most important below, but be alert for others.

The entrance to the Southport Harbor channel is 3.1nm by boat to the northeast of the outer approach to the Saugatuck River, and 4.7nm by boat to the west of the outer entrance to Bridgeport Harbor.

From the red and white Mo (A) whistle "BH" **[WP-87]** southeast of Penfield Light, a course of approximately 285°m should bring you to the red 4sec flashing bell "22" **[WP-82]**. This position should put the entrance markers to Southport Harbor in clear view.

The approach to **Southport Harbor** is unobstructed except for the rocks off Frost and Pine Creek points and a few oyster stakes that are usually easily visible in the shallows of the bay. Make sure to stay south of the red (formerly white) flashing 4sec bell "22" **[WP-82]** off Pine Creek Point.

You have clear sailing up to the first buoys, green can "1" and red nun "2" **[WP-81].** All of the cans in the channel have been changed from black to green. Note, too, that the harbor entrance light "5," now a 28-foot 4sec green flasher, used to be a 32-foot white flasher. The red flasher "12" atop a 26-foot tower at the end of the breakwater is your next light on the starboard side as you enter.

The channel is very narrow–never more than 50 to 75 feet wide–until you reach the Pequot Yacht Club basin. The folks at the club tell us the main channel is shoaling, so after passing nun "10," favor the western side of the center of the channel for the deepest water. There you'll have at least 6 feet of water at low tide.

Unfortunately for transients, there's nothing here in the way of marinas. Unless you're a member of the Pequot Yacht Club, you'll need to head for Black Rock Harbor or Westport for fuel, service, or dockage. The yacht club does offer a few transient moorings, but don't expect them to be readily available. If you're looking for a slip or mooring, you should call ahead–perhaps saving yourself a trip into the harbor.

The harbor is less than a mile long and is usually full of moored boats. On the west side is the town dock–known locally and somewhat whimsically as "Ye Yacht Yard"–which has about 6 feet of water beside it at mean low water. You can tie up there for a maximum of 30 minutes to load or unload, but no overnight docking is allowed. Contact the harbormaster at (203) 259-0733 for information about town facilities. There is a no-wake speed limit in the harbor.

 ## Shoreside and Emergency Services

Airport: Sikorsky Memorial Airport (203) 576-7498
Ambulance: 911 or (203) 259-3311
Bus: Greater Bridgeport Transit District (203) 333-3031
Coast Guard: Eatons Neck (516) 261-6868/6910
      or VHF 16
Fire: 911 or (203) 259-1611
Harbormaster: (203) 259-0733
Hospital: Saint Vincent's (Bridgeport) (203) 576-6000
Police: 911 or (203) 259-3311/254-4800
Radio Telephone: VHF 27; I.D.: Bridgeport Marine
      Operator
Taxi: Fairfield Cab Co. (203) 255-5797
Tow Service: Southern CT Sea Tow, Bridgeport, CT
      (203) 331-0410 or VHF 16
Train: Amtrak 1-800-USA-RAIL
      Metro-North 1-800-638-7646 ◆

'MARKS OF HOSTILE IRE' IN FAIRFIELD

Though Fairfield was settled 350 years ago, few artifacts or buildings still survive from its first 140 years–thanks to a company of British soldiers under General William Tryon, who burned most of the town during a raid in 1779.
Tryon, the military governor of Long Island during the Revolutionary War, was widely known and hated for his many destructive raids on Connecticut towns from Westport to New Haven. The burning of Fairfield, however, earned him a special place in the heart of Col. David Humphreys, an American soldier. Humphreys composed a long poem, "Elegy on the Burning of Fairfield, in Connecticut." A sampling:

Ye smoking ruins, marks of hostile ire,
    Ye ashes warm, which drink the tears that flow,
Ye desolated plains, my voice inspire,
    And give soft music to the song of woe.

How pleasant, Fairfield, on th' enraptur'd sight
    Rose thy tall spires, and op'd thy social halls!
How oft my bosom beat with pure delight,
    At yonder spot where stand the darken'd walls!

How chang'd the blissful prospect, when compar'd,
    These glooms funereal, with thy former bloom,
Thy hospitable rights when Tryon shar'd,
    Long ere he seal'd thy melancholy doom!

That impious wretch, with coward voice decreed
    Defenceless domes and hallow'd fanes to dust;
Beheld, with sneering smile, the wounded bleed,
    And spurr'd his bands to rapine, blood and lust.

Vain was the widow's, vain the orphan's cry,
    To touch his feelings, or to sooth his rage–
Vain the fair drop that roll'd from beauty's eye,
    Vain the dumb grief of supplicating age.

Could Tryon hope to quench the patriot flame,
    Or make his deeds survive in glory's page?
Could Britons seek of savages the fame,
    Or deem it conquest, thus the war to wage?

Yes, Britons! scorn the councils of the skies,
    Extend wide havock, spurn th' insulted foes;
Th' insulted foes to tenfold vengeance rise,
    Resistance growing as the danger grows.

Long dusky wreaths of smoke, reluctant driv'n,
    In black'ning volumes o'er the landscape bend:
Here the broad splendour blazes high to heav'n,
    There umber'd streams in purple pomp ascend.

In fiery eddies, round the tott'ring walls,
    Emitting sparks, the lighter fragments fly;
With frightful crash the burning mansion falls,
    The works of years in glowing embers lie.

Tryon, behold thy sanguine flames aspire,
    Clouds ting'd with dyes intolerable bright;
Behold, well pleas'd, the village wrapt in fire;
    Let one wide ruin glut thy ravish'd sight!

Go, gaze, enraptur'd with the mother's tear,
    The infant's terror, and the captive's pain,
Where no bold bands can check thy curst career;
    Mix fire with blood on each unguarded plain!

These be thy triumphs! this be thy boasted fame!
    Daughters of mem'ry, raise the deathless songs!
Repeat through endless years his hated name,
    Embalm his crimes, and teach the world our wrongs.

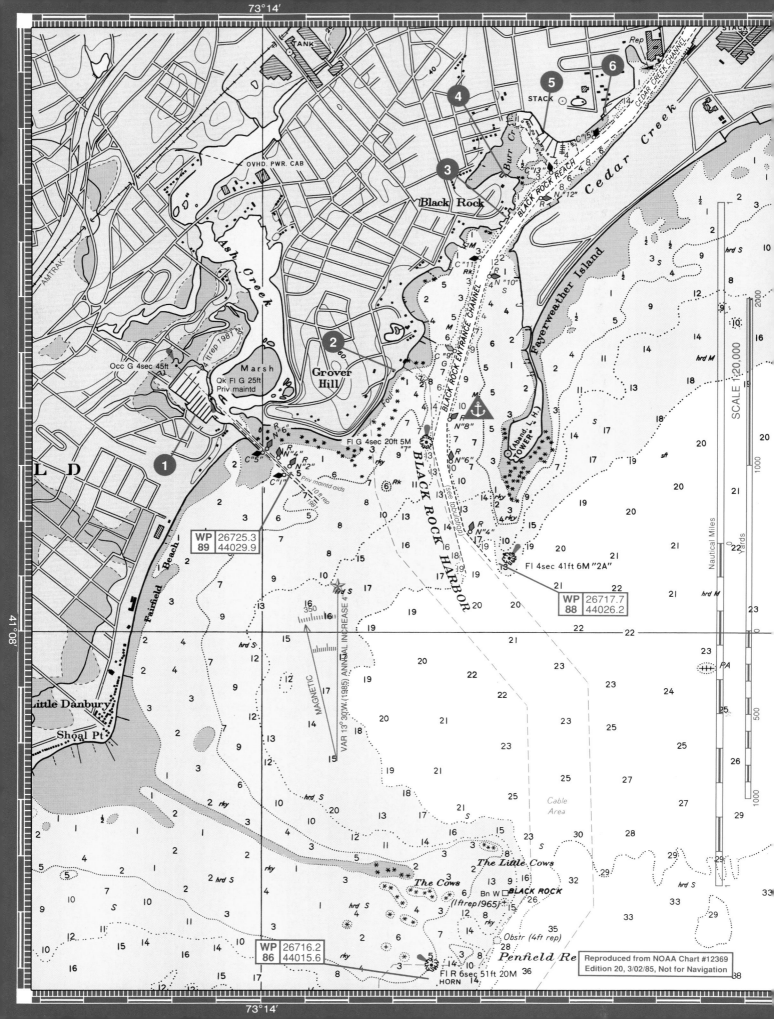

Cannon to Fire the Imagination

The village of Black Rock (first known as "Shipharbor") was settled in 1644 by some practical people who realized the value of the deep harbor. Until the early 1800s Black Rock Harbor and New London Harbor were the only Connecticut ports that could accommodate ships over 300 tons.

First among the settlers at Black Rock was Thomas Wheeler, who claimed the point of land between Black Rock Harbor and the cove now occupied by the Captains Cove Marina. There Wheeler built a stone house with a flat roof on which he mounted two cannon. One was aimed at the harbor to fight off Dutch invaders from New Amsterdam; the other pointed inland at an Indian encampment.

For the next century Black Rock was almost completely owned by the Wheeler clan, who made it into a trading port. Around 1760 its focus shifted rapidly, and the sleepy village began to grow into a shipbuilding center. During the Revolutionary War the harbor was home to privateers and was a launching place for raids on Long Island.

After 1800 Black Rock's fortunes declined as the unprotected harbor, which suffered catastrophic damage during hurricanes in 1811 and 1821, was eclipsed in trade by Bridgeport and Southport harbors. A short-lived shipbuilding boom began in Black Rock in the 1850s but was ended by the Civil War, never to rise again.

You can't miss the contrasts in Black Rock Harbor. To the east is P.T. Barnum's legacy–the beautiful Seaside Park stretching from Tongue Point all the way to the lighthouse on Fayerweather Island–but right next door is the old city landfill, now covered with grass. The west side of the harbor is home to two marinas and two yacht clubs, as well as the municipal sewage-treatment plant and some industrial sites. The masts of the spectacular tall ship HMS *Rose*, kept at Captain's Cove Seaport, tower over the harbor.

Thanks to Captain's Cove Seaport and the 24-gun *Rose*, Black Rock Harbor is once again a popular port of call. Unlike Bridgeport Harbor, Black Rock is predominantly a

© Jack McConnell

Ash Creek and the South Benson Boat Basin from the west. Fayerweather Island and the entrance to Black Rock Harbor are in the upper left corner.

Marine Facilities and Services		Number of Transient Berths	Number of Transient Moorings	Seasonal/Year-round	Largest Vessel Accommodation (in feet)	Approach Depth (in feet)	Marked Entry Channel	Dockside Depth in feet at MLW	Gas/Diesel Fuel	Fuel Brand	Ramp/Dinghy Dock	Railway/Lift: Capacity (in tons)	Launch Service	Propeller/Hull Repairs	Engine Repairs: Gas/Diesel	Pump-out Station	Marine Supplies/Groceries/Bait/Ice	Showers/Laundromat	110V ★ 220V ▲ Maximum Amps	MasterCard/VISA/Diners Club American Express	Restaurant/Snack Bar	Monitors VHF Channel
1 South Benson Boat Basin	(203) 254-2184	2		S	37	9	●	7	G	MOB						●	I		★		S	
2 Black Rock Yacht Club	(203) 335-0587				*PRIVATE CLUB - MEMBERS ONLY*																	
3 Fayerweather Yacht Club	(203) 576-6796	2		Y	50	25	●	15	G	TEX		L15	L				I		★		S	9
4 Fayerweather Boatyard	(203) 334-4403			Y	45							L25		PH	GD							
5 Captain's Cove Seaport (p. 147)	(203) 335-1433	20		Y	80	12	●	8	GD			L25		PH	GD		SL	I	★50	MV	R	18
6 Cedar Marina	(203) 335-6262	4		Y	50	25	●	15	G	TEX					GD		S	SI	★30		S	

Information in these listings is provided by the facilities themselves. An asterisk (*) indicates that the facility did not respond to our most recent requests for information.

sailors' port, helped in part by the sailboat races sponsored by the Fayerweather Yacht Club. These are held every Wednesday night during the summer and are open to all comers.

 What To See and Do

If you are visiting Black Rock Harbor, chances are you came to see the *Rose* (203) 335-1433. Along with dockside tours and sea chantey concerts, the seaport is offering school groups expanded tours that emphasize the Colonial maritime history of Black Rock Harbor and the surrounding area.

If you're looking for a charter, you've come to the right place. At the Seaport is a 70-foot party fishing boat, *Delmar IV* (203) 661-9166 available for charter, and two excursion boats: the 80-foot *Mr. Lucky* and the smaller *Island Girl* (203) 334-9166, now available for cruises on the Sound. Coastal Charter Company (203) 334-9256 also has a pair of power cruisers available for small parties.

You won't have much luck getting boat hardware at the seaport, although some supplies are available at the marinas. The seaport has about 20 specialty shops, a genuine fish market, and a restaurant with a patio overlooking the water.

The seaport is also home to a full-size replica of an aircraft built by Gustav Whitehead, the man who, some claim, was flying before the Wright brothers. The replica was built in recent years and has been flown at Sikorsky Airport. The controversy of the "first-in-flight" designation has led to some feuding between Connecticut and North Carolina, where the Wright brothers first flew their airplane. Unfortunately, the Whitehead aircraft is not available for public viewing.

If you want to get wet or just stretch out in the sand and bake, try Jennings Beach or Penfield Beach, both marked on the chart as "Fairfield Beach." The water, the sand, and the facilities all get better the farther south you go.

You can anchor overnight off the beach, but be sure to keep an anchor light burning–occasionally fishermen wait until after dark to troll for stripers or bluefish in this area. Refreshments, restrooms, and showers are all available at the public Penfield Beach pavilion. During the summer there are often free concerts at the pavilion in the evening. The Fairfield Chamber of Commerce (203) 255-1011 can supply a schedule of events. West of Shoal Point the beaches are all private.

Black Rock Harbor from the south.

 Where To Eat

If you want to stay in the harbor for a meal, the Black Rock Yacht Club (203) 335-0587 and Captain's Cove Seaport (203) 368-3710 both feature good restaurants (takeout is available at Captain's Cove), and the Fayerweather Yacht Club (203) 576-6796 has a good lunch menu at reasonable prices. The restaurant at Captain's Cove has a 40-foot model of the *Titanic* and the pilothouse of a steam tugboat, circa 1900, and we're told it's a hot spot for the singles crowd on weekends. Apart from the waterfront eateries, the harbor is surrounded by factories and warehouses, so a cab ride to Bridgeport or Fairfield is necessary.

From the South Benson Boat Basin in Ash Creek, you will be close to downtown Fairfield and within walking distance of the Grotto (203) 255-2624, serving Italian food, and the Pie Plate (203) 255-5953, famous, of course, for its pies. (For more on Where To Eat in Fairfield, see the previous chapter on Southport Harbor.)

 Navigation and Anchorages

Use NOAA Charts 12369 (1:20,000), 12364 (1:40,000), and 12363 (1:80,000). Use tide tables for Bridgeport. High tide at the Black Rock Harbor entrance is 4 minutes earlier; low tide is 3 minutes earlier. Multiply by 1.1 for height at high or low water. Mean tidal range is 7.4 feet.

CAUTION: There have been many buoy changes in this area. We have noted the most important below, but be alert for others.

The 41-foot red 4sec flasher "2A" at the entrance to Black Rock Harbor is 1.6nm by boat north of Penfield Reef Light, and 1.8nm by boat southwest of the red 4sec bell "10" outside Bridgeport Harbor. The breakwaters at Port Jefferson Harbor are 11.4nm to the south-southeast.

From the flashing red 4sec bell "2" **[WP-362]** at **Middle Ground (Stratford Shoal)**, a course of about 330°m will take you past the main Bridgeport channel and onto the approach to **Black Rock Harbor.**

CAUTION: When approaching Black Rock Harbor from the west or south, give Penfield Reef Light [WP-86] plenty of room, since it marks the southern tip of the reef and not the eastern tip where the Little Cows just break the surface at low tide. The Little Cows are marked with a round white daymarker known around the area as "the lollipop."

Stay to the east of the lollipop before turning north into Black Rock Harbor. Don't let the name fool you; the **Little Cows** are anything but little, and claim many boats every year. Occasionally a newcomer, traveling east after dark, will somehow mistake the red Penfield Reef Light for the white flasher at Middle Ground, 6.5nm to the southeast, and end up on the rocks.

Another problem is the bar extending from **Shoal Point** out toward **The Cows.** Every year, dozens of unwary boaters roar out of Black Rock Harbor toward the wide expanse of water west of Penfield Reef Light that beckons them out to the Sound, only to go aground on the bar. Lots of bets are made as to whether the fathometer or the captain will scream first. Pay attention to the charts: the rocks and the sandbar are real!

Note that the **Penfield Reef Light [WP-86]** has been changed from 20NM to 19NM.

If approaching **Black Rock Harbor** from the south, note that the whistle "BH" **[WP-87]** marking the Bridgeport channel approach is now red and white, not black and white as on some older charts. If approaching from the east, note that bell "18" **[WP-90]** south of Stratford Point is now flashing red 6sec; it used to flash white 4sec.

Fishermen with shallow-draft boats can anchor within 30 feet of the landing platform on the north side of the **Penfield Reef Light.** But be forewarned: the foghorn may drive you cuckoo. For greater stability, you can throw a grappling hook onto the riprap at the base of the light and a stern anchor off the other end.

Another cluster of rocks barely visible at low tide is off Saint Mary's, southwest of the 20-foot green flasher at the

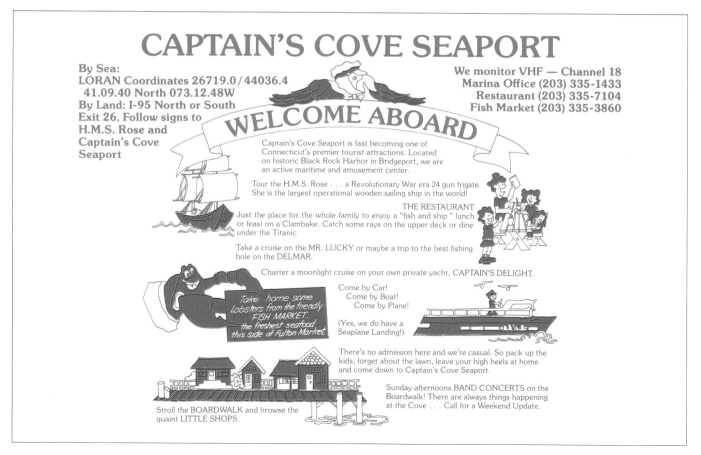

HMS Rose *in New York Harbor*
Photo © by Clyde Smith

HMS *ROSE*

The HMS *Rose*, docked at Black Rock Harbor in Bridge-port, is the largest operational wooden sailing ship in the world. She is a replica of a full-rigged, 24-gun British frigate that was sunk in 1779 at Savannah, Georgia after a long and distinguished career in His Majesty's service.

The original HMS *Rose* was built in 1756-57 at Hull, Yorkshire, England and first saw action in the French-Indian War (Seven Years War) from 1756-1763. She served in both European and American waters, with her first assignments in the English Channel against French ports. Arriving in the West Indies in 1761, she remained there until the end of the war, and then headed back to England for refitting.

By 1768 the *Rose* was back in America as part of the British fleet based in Boston. In April 1769, her First Officer, Lt. Panton, was killed trying to "impress" four sailors into service on the ship. The defendants were found not guilty by reason of self-defense. Their lawyer was the young John Adams.

In 1774, the *Rose* fought for the first time against the colonies when she set up a blockade in Newport, Rhode Island against molasses smuggling. That blockade led to Rhode Island's creation of the first state navy in the Colonies.

In 1776, the *Rose* was part of a fleet of 300 British ships attacking New York. She even sailed up the Hudson and

East Rivers at one point, where she was heavily bombarded by the Colonial Army under George Washington.

The end came in 1779 when the vessel was purposely sunk across the mouth of the harbor in Savannah, Georgia to keep out the Count d'Estaing's French invasion fleet.

One hundred ninety-one years later, a new HMS *Rose* was built from the original plans in Lunenburg, Nova Scotia by John Millar, who operated her as a museum in Boston, Newport, and other ports. In 1984 Kaye Williams of Bridgeport bought her and brought her to Black Rock Harbor for restoration from 1985-1987.

Like the original, the modern *Rose* has a foremast of 120 feet, a mainmast of 130 feet and a mizzenmast of 90 feet. She is 179 feet long with a beam of 32 feet, and displaces 500 tons. She can set as much as 13,000 square feet of sails and sail at 15 knots. In addition, her 24 working guns are fired regularly. She has made some concessions to twentieth century technology, however: above, she has sails of Dacron instead of canvas, and below, two diesel engines help the Rose navigate in port.

The *Rose* will soon be Coast Guard certified as a Sailing School Vessel, and will also be making "ambassadorial" trips to various ports.

For more information or for dockside tour schedules, call the HMS *Rose* Foundation (203) 335-1433.

head of the harbor. You can recognize Saint Mary's by the seawall supporting the road running along the shore and by the bright street lights that line the seawall.

Although the channel into **Black Rock Harbor** is dredged to a depth of 15 feet (shallowing to 9 feet at the sides), outside the channel there is considerably less water. Boats drawing more than 4.5 feet should honor the nuns and cans and stay in the channel. Cans "11" and "13," formerly black, are now green. Can "15" near Cedar Marina has been deleted. The average tidal range here is 7.4 feet, so all the marinas have floating docks.

The newly renovated Cedar Marina, north of the seaport, also caters to transients. Unfortunately, most of the nice parts of Bridgeport and Fairfield are not accessible by foot from Black Rock Harbor, so you will want to call a cab if you plan to go any farther afield than the seaport.

In **Burr Creek,** on the port side up by Captain's Cove, you'll find 4 to 5 feet of water. There are some muddy shoals in the creek, so you will want to enter with care. While the Seaport caters to transients, there are limited transient slips available on the Burr Creek side. If they are full, you'll be sent directly across the channel to another set of docks that do not have electrical hookups or water. Launch service is provided to the main Seaport facility.

Just to the south of Burr Creek the Fayerweather Yacht Club offers a few transient berths and moorings and is easily recognized by the Texaco sign. Club members are a hospitable, do-it-yourself type, and the club reputedly is a good place to pick up on the latest scuttlebutt from the area.

The large number of permanently moored boats leaves little room for anchoring in the inner harbor, but there is usually room in the excellent anchorage to the west of the old lighthouse on **Fayerweather Island.** Again, keep the anchor lights burning.

The area south of nun "10" off Fayerweather Island is full of private moorings. If you grab one, expect to be kicked off.

Directly to the west of this anchorage is the Black Rock Yacht Club, which offers some guest moorings, a restaurant, a pool, and tennis courts. Dockside depths at the club, however, can be skimpy at low tide. Best to call ahead on VHF 16 for advice.

For launching boats from trailers, there is a very weathered town ramp with a parking lot at the end of the road on **Fayerweather Island,** just north of nun "10." Also on Fayerweather Island, due east of can "9," is a fishing pier open to the public.

The harbor is open to the prevailing southwesterly winds, but otherwise offers good protection, thanks in part to the artificial windbreak of the old landfill. Since the old landfill has been completely covered with grass, you don't notice it, but because of the sewage-treatment plant, Black Rock still isn't the place to be on hot, windless days.

Although there has been a great deal of progress made in the last few years, it will be several more years before the water in the harbor is clean enough for swimming. The warm water from the sewage-treatment plant may keep the wintertime ice at bay, but it also promotes the growth of barnacles and such on the bottom of your boat.

Another protected spot is **Ash Creek.** Ash Creek has an approach depth of about 10 feet, but inside at the South Benson Boat Basin there is less than 4 feet at the docks. If you draw more than 3.5 feet, wait until at least 2 hours on either side of low water to approach the marina. The entrance buoys tend to go off station, so you should line up the two range markers, especially at night. The closest is a 25-foot green quick-flasher, and the other a 45-foot intermittent green flasher.

There is a no-wake speed limit in the dredged channel to the South Benson Boat Basin, which is owned and operated by the Town of Fairfield. The marina discourages transients, but may have a few slips in an emergency. The area just inside the **Ash Creek** entrance offers great protection in a blow. The marina sells gasoline, and snacks are available at the gas dock.

The area to the west of can "1" **[WP-89]** outside the entrance to Ash Creek is reserved for small-boat sailing, and power boats are prohibited from entering.

 ## Shoreside and Emergency Services

Airport: Sikorsky Memorial Airport (203) 576-7498
Ambulance: 911
Bus: Greater Bridgeport Transit District (203) 333-3031
Coast Guard: New Haven (203) 773-2400 or VHF 16
　　　　　　　Eatons Neck (516) 261-6868/6910
　　　　　　　or VHF 16
Fire: 911 or (203) 576-7692
Harbormaster: Bridgeport (203) 576-8163 or VHF 16
　　　　　　　　Fairfield Marine Patrol (203) 254-4866
　　　　　　　　or VHF 16
Police: 911 or (203) 576-7671
　　　　　　Marine Patrol Boat VHF 16 or CB 9
Radio Telephone: VHF 27; I.D.: Bridgeport
　　　　　　　　　　Marine Operator
Taxi: Fairfield Cab Co. (203) 255-5797
Tow Service: Southern CT Sea Tow, Bridgeport, CT
　　　　　　　　(203) 331-0410 or VHF 16
Train: Amtrak 1-800-USA-RAIL
　　　　　Metro-North 1-800-638-7646　　　◆

EAST BRIDGEPORT

NEWFIELD

EPORT

Pequonnock R.

UPPER REACH

LOWER REACH

Cable & Pipeline Area

BASCULE BRIDGE
HOR CL 71 FT
VERT CL 13 FT
(draw closed)

BASCULE BRIDGE
HOR. CL 70 FT.
VERT. CL. 18 FT.
OVHD. PWR. CAB.
AUTH. CL. 160 FT.

BASCULE BRIDGE
HOR. CL. 67 FT.
VERT. CL. 8 FT.

VERT LIFT BRIDGE
HOR CL 103 FT
VERT CL 8 FT DOWN
VERT 68 FT UP

TALLEST SPIRE

OVHD. PWR. CAB.
AUTH. CL. 150 FT.

FIXED BRIDGE
HOR. CL. 150 FT.
VERT. CL. 65 FT.

BASCULE BRIDGE
HOR. CL. 82 FT.
VERT. CL. 11 FT.

Yellow Mill Channel

MIDDLE REACH

UPPER REACH

FIXED BRIDGE
HOR. CL. 100 FT.
VERT. CL. 40 FT.

STACK

STACK
TANK

Bruce Pond

STACK

WHITE SPIRE

Hospital

STACKS

Steel

Cable &
Pipeline Area

LOWER REACH

BR
"YM" G C

Submpiles PA

STACK

Connecticut Turnpike

SWING BRIDGE
HOR. CL. 65 FT
VERT. CL. 7 FT

ANCHORAGE AREA
110,148 (see note A)
Cable & Pipeline Area

Johnsons Creek

Newfield Creek

R "N"8"

ENTRANCE CHAN

NEWFIELD REACH

R"N"4"

ANCHORAGE
107 FT. 1978

15 G
"9"
C "21"
16

"9"

34

BRIDGEPORT REACH

Tongue Pt.

Fl G 4sec 31ft "17"
Qk Fl G

33 FEET 1971
17

WP
92   26700.8
44034.5

Seaside Park

C "15"

Qk Fl G 50ft 5M
"13A"

ED

C "13"

MAGNETIC

VAR 13°30' W (1985) ANNUAL INCREASE 4'

R "16"
Fl R 2.5sec

R
N"14"

R
N"12"

C "11"

Fl R 4sec BELL
R "10"

Oyster stakes

Pleasure
Beach

RADIO
TOWERS
(WICC) 600 kHz

Long

Mars

hrd S

Fl R 4sec 25ft "12A"

WP
91   26700.9
44028.7

73°10'

41°10'

Bridgeport Harbor

Ferrying, Fishing, and Rehabbing

Although not as well-known as Hartford, the state capital, or New Haven, the home of Yale University, Bridgeport is Connecticut's largest city. Bridgeport is also one of the three deep-water harbors in Connecticut, maintaining a channel 35 feet deep all the way to the head of navigation at the Interstate 95 bridges. You will see many large oceangoing vessels in the harbor as well as the ferries of the Bridgeport and Port Jefferson Steamboat Company. Harbor pilots are required for all commercial vessels, so you may also see the 42-foot pilot boat snuggling up to one of the

big ships and letting off a pilot to guide the larger craft safely in.

Bridgeport got its start in the 17th century when farmer/fishermen from Fairfield and Stratford moved here. But it wasn't until the rise of manufacturing that the city really began to take shape. Elias Howe brought his sewing-machine works here in 1863 after successfully contesting patent infringements by several other manufacturers, including Isaac Singer.

Despite the urban blight that came with the decline of manufacturing, Bridgeport is determined to recover. One of the focuses of the rehabilitation effort has been the new Transportation Center, which includes the Amtrak and Metro-North railroad stations, local and long-distance bus service, and the ferry dock.

Hampering redevelopment efforts is the fact that Bridgeport is not in great financial condition, and funding large projects is difficult. One example is the ambitious Harbor Point plan to redevelop the area around the Carpenter Steel plant on the east side of the harbor. The idea has been kicking around for a long time, but prospects for its completion are very doubtful.

The Port Jefferson ferry arriving in Bridgeport Harbor, CT. To the right is the red and white stack of the United Illuminating power plant. In the center background is Johnsons Creek and Pleasure Beach.

 What To See and Do

There is a new bandshell at Seaside Park, originally designed by a Yale student and then built by student volunteers. Seaside Park offers a beautiful spot to picnic, get some sun, and enjoy the long beach.

Marine Facilities and Services		Number of Transient Berths	Number of Transient Moorings	Seasonal/Year-round	Largest Vessel Accommodation (in feet)	Approach Depth in feet at MLW	Marked Entry Channel	Dockside Depth in feet at MLW	Gas/Diesel Fuel	Fuel Brand	Ramp/Dinghy Dock/Launch Service	Railway/Lift: Capacity (in tons)	Propeller/Hull Repairs	Engine Repairs: Gas/Diesel	Pump-out Station	Marine Supplies/Groceries/Bait/Ice	Showers/Laundromat	110V ★ 220V ▲ Maximum Amps	MasterCard/VISA/Diners Club American Express	Restaurant/Snack Bar	Monitors VHF Channel
❶ Hitchcock Marine (p. 153)	(203) 334-2161	3		Y	60	●	22	20					L30	PH	GD		S	S	★30	MV		
❷ Pequonnock Yacht Club	(203) 334-5708			Y	50	●	4	6	GD		R					S	I	★▲	MV	S	16
❸ Riverside Marine	(203) 335-7068			Y	36	●	20	15	GD	TEX		L30		G			SI	★20	MV		9
❹ Ryan's Marine	(203) 579-1319	5		Y	45	●	15	7			RDL	L30	PH	GD	●		SI	★30			
❺ Sunnyside Marina	(203) 334-4412	6		S	50	●	27	7			D					SL	SIB	★60	MVA		16
❻ Lou's Boat Basin	(203) 336-9809			S	42	●	30	3	GD	SUN					●		IB	★20			6
❼ Miamogue Yacht Club	(203) 334-9882	2		Y	30	●	30	6	G		R							★20		RS	9
❽ Speer's Boat Yard				Y	30							L10		G							
❾ East End Yacht Club	(203) 366-3330	15	2	Y	40	●	7	6	G		RD					S	I	★30		R	9

Information in these listings is provided by the facilities themselves. An asterisk (*) indicates that the facility did not respond to our most recent requests for information.

P.T. BARNUM AND BRIDGEPORT

A pioneer showman, businessman, politician, and promoter par excellence, Phineas Taylor Barnum was one of the world's best-known figures, if not always the best loved. He was also a leading citizen of Bridgeport and a significant city developer.

A full recital of Barnum's accomplishments would take volumes, but his contributions to Bridgeport alone were significant. Born in Bethel, Connecticut, in 1810, Barnum resided the better part of his 81 years in Bridgeport and commuted to New York to run his museums and other business interests.

Although Barnum is known as a circus owner, a good deal of his fortune was gained through real estate in Bridgeport and investments in banks, utilities, and the Bridgeport and Port Jefferson Steamboat Company.

"The World's Greatest Showman" built four lavish homes in Bridgeport. The first, a bizarre mixture of Byzantine, Moorish and Turkish architecture, was aptly named *Iranistan*. Built on 17 acres overlooking the Sound, the spectacular mansion was enclosed in a park stocked with tame elk. The mansion burned to the ground in 1857 and was replaced by *Lindencroft*, erected just down the road in 1860. Barnum's next mansion, *Waldemere*, was a "sprawling, ornate gingerbread castle" near Seaside Park. Finally, in 1890, Barnum and his young second wife, Nancy, built a smaller house, *Marina*, a few feet to the east of *Waldemere*. The old site of *Waldemere* and *Marina* is now part of the University of Bridgeport campus.

An early photo of P.T. Barnum with
General Tom Thumb as a child
Courtesy of Historical Collections, Bridgeport Public Library

In honor of P.T. Barnum, Bridgeport throws the Barnum Festival each July, with a parade, fireworks, concerts, and other events. The festival is run by the Barnum Festival Society (203) 367-8495.

To get a better look at what all the Barnum hoopla is about, try visiting the Barnum Museum (203) 331-1104, reopened in June 1989 after more than a year's renovation. The museum's core exhibits center on Bridgeport and old P.T. himself, but you can also take the kids to the miniature 3-ring circus or check out the new exhibitions wing, which features several traveling shows a year. Admission is inexpensive, with discounts for seniors, young children, and students.

The Museum of Art, Science, and Industry (203) 372-3521 offers art, hands-on science exhibits, and planetarium shows on its 11-acre campus. The museum is especially popular with kids, and offers special programs for disadvantaged and disabled children.

Except for Seaside Park and Pleasure Beach, the heavily industrialized port can look rather intimidating to the recreational boater during the day. At night, however, with all the buildings lit up, it is quite attractive and is also a great landmark from the Sound.

 ## Where To Eat

There aren't a lot of eateries right on the water in Bridgeport, but there are lots of restaurants in town if you're willing to look. At the Hilton (203) 334-1234 on Main Street, just two blocks from the water, is the Parc 1070 Restaurant, featuring a varied menu, and The Arches, serving Continental cuisine. Also on Main are the Ocean Sea Grill (203) 336-2132 for seafood, and the Great Wall (203) 371-7211 for Chinese. For a bit more spice try the Italian food at La Scogliera (203) 333-0673.

 ## Navigation and Anchorages

Use NOAA Charts 12369 (1:20,000), 12364 (1:40,000), and 12363 (1:80,000). Use tide tables for Bridgeport. Mean tidal range is 7.2 feet.

CAUTION: *There have been many buoy changes in this area. We have noted the most important below, but be alert for others.*

The approach to Bridgeport Harbor, starting at the red and white whistle buoy "BH," is 4.4nm by boat east of the entrance to Southport Harbor and 5.8nm by boat southwest of the entrance to the Housatonic River. The entrance to Port Jefferson Harbor on Long Island is 9.2nm to the south-southeast.

From the flashing red 4sec bell "2" **[WP-362]** at **Middle Ground (Stratford Shoal),** a course of about 330°m will put you between the red and white whistle "BH" **[WP-87]** and the entrance to the main Bridgeport channel.

Bridgeport is hard to miss from the Sound. Even if you can't see its many large industrial and office buildings, you will see the red and white horizontally striped smokestack of the United Illuminating Co. (UI) power plant on Tongue Point.

Buoy "BH" **[WP-87]** has been fitted with a ball topmark, which identifies it as a fairway marker. About 1 mile north of "BH," lighted buoys begin at the red flasher "2."

The buoys marking the main channel have been changed as follows: nun "2" and can "5" are now 2.5sec flashers; nun "6" and can "9" are now 4sec flashers; red bell "10" **[WP-91]** now flashes 2.5sec; can "15" inside the breakwaters has been removed; and all black cans are now green.

Small craft need not run the length of the entrance channel; if you're coming from the east or west, just make for the red 2.5sec flashing bell "10" **[WP-91]** and then head into the harbor.

When approaching **Bridgeport** from the east, note two changes from the chart: red nun "20" south of **Stratford Point** no longer has a gong, and lighted red bell "18" **[WP-90]** is now a flashing 6sec light.

Tidal currents reach about 0.7 knots between the breakwaters at flood and ebb. To port will be the 200-acre strip of Seaside Park and the campus of the University of Bridgeport just behind it. To starboard, Pleasure and Long beaches stretch off toward Stratford and the east. The Tallmage Brothers Oyster Company has an arrangement with UI for storing oyster cultch on Tongue Point near the coal-fired power plant, so you may see huge piles of shells alongside huge piles of coal.

The first possible anchorage, protected from the north and east, lies inside the eastern breakwater off **Pleasure Beach.** The old pier from the defunct amusement park has been rebuilt and is now a public fishing pier. The sandy soil offers good holding ground.

Bridgeport Harbor has three channels, the first being **Johnsons Creek,** northward of Pleasure Beach and home of the Miamogue and East End yacht clubs. When entering the creek, do not cut the red nun "2" that marks the channel, as it also marks a shoal that extends north off Pleasure Beach. Note that nun "2" has been relocated slightly to the southeast.

The wooden swing bridge across **Johnsons Creek** has been rammed by many oil barges over the years, but has been repaired and is again open to automobile traffic. Call the bridge tender on VHF 13 or signal with the usual long and short blasts of your horn.

Opposite Johnsons Creek on the west side of the harbor is the Bridgeport "Bug Light" on **Tongue Point,** which gets its name for being as small as a lightning bug. Just to the west is an oil-barge terminal, which you would do well to avoid.

Farther up the harbor is the **Yellow Mill Channel,** home of the Pequonnock Yacht Club, Riverside Marine and a new marina, Ryan's. The yacht club and Ryan's both welcome transients. To avoid the infamous mud flats at the club, leave the green and red junction buoy "YM" (marked black and red on the chart) to port. Then, as you approach the club you'll see a new dock extending eastward from the charted docks. The people at the club tell us to avoid getting stuck, round the new docks closely to port and stay close, hugging the docks on into the marina. For more advice call the club on VHF 16.

Riverside Marine has a fuel dock, but offers no slips. To get upstream to Ryan's, you'll have to pass through or under the **Stratford Avenue bascule bridge,** vertical clearance 11 feet. Unfortunately, the bridge tender isn't always there, and you may have to give as much as *6 hours* notice to have it opened. Call the Pleasure Beach bridgetender on VHF 13 to make arrangements.

When in the harbor, be careful of the Bridgeport-Port Jeff ferries, which can kick up a considerable wake. Many boaters have complained in the past about the ferry wakes, and the harbormaster has managed to get the ferries to slow down, but you should keep alert just the same.

 ### Shoreside and Emergency Services

Airport: Sikorsky Memorial Airport (203) 576-7498
Ambulance: 911
Bus: Greater Bridgeport Transit District (203) 333-3031
Coast Guard: New Haven (203) 773-2400 or VHF 16 or CB 9
Ferry: To Port Jefferson: Bridgeport and Port Jefferson Steamboat Company (203) 367-3043
Fire: 911 or (203) 576-7320
Harbormaster: (203) 576-8163 or VHF 16
Police: 911 or (203) 576-7671
Radio Telephone: VHF 27; I.D.: Bridgeport Marine Operator
Taxi: Fairfield Cab (203) 255-5797
Tow Service: Southern CT Sea Tow, Bridgeport, CT (203) 331-0410 or VHF 16
Train: Amtrak 1-800-USA-RAIL Metro-North 1-800-638-7646 ◆

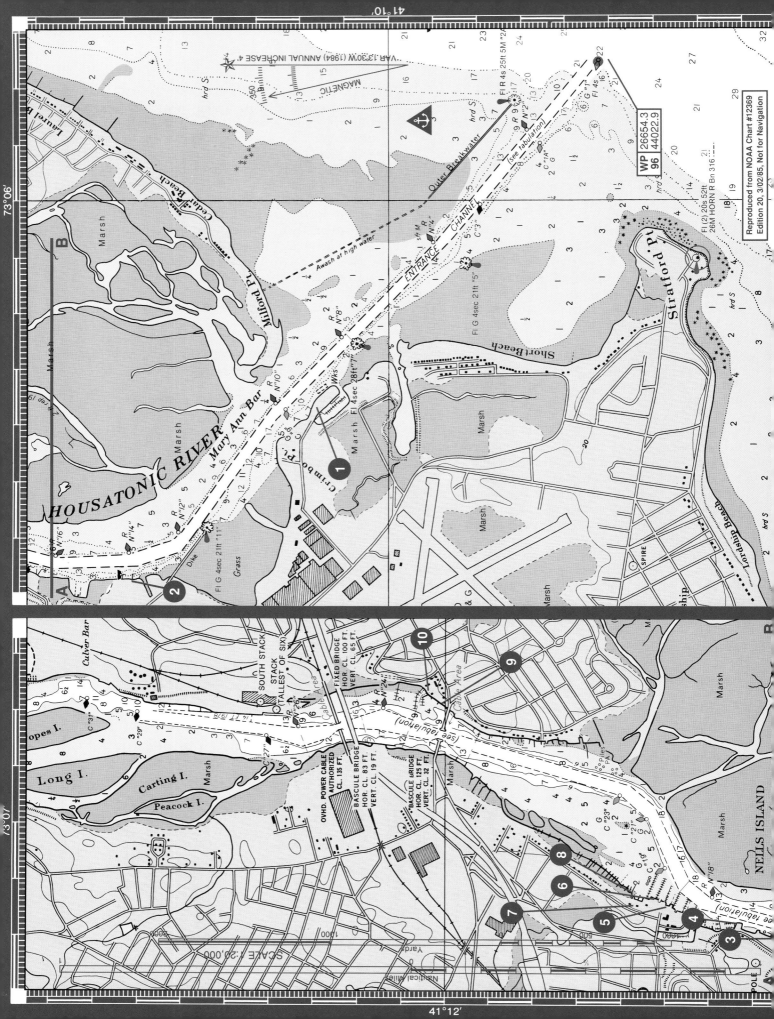

73°06'

41°10'

73°07'

41°12'

HOUSATONIC RIVER

Mary Ann Bar

Milford Pt.

Cedar Beach

Laurel B.

Marsh

Marsh

Marsh

Marsh

Grass

Dike

Crumbo Pt.

ENTRANCE CHANNEL

Awash at high water

Outer Breakwater

Short Beach

Stratford Pt.

Lordship Beach

SPIRE

VAR 13°30'W (1984) ANNUAL INCREASE 4'

MAGNETIC

Fl R 4s 25ft 5M "2"

Fl G 4sec 21ft "5"

Fl G 4sec 21ft "11"

Fl (2) 20s 52ft
26M HORN R Bn 316°

Fl 4s

(see tabulation)

WP 26654.3
96 44022.9

Long I.

Carting I.

Peacock I.

Culver Bar

opes I.

SOUTH STACK

STACK
(TALLEST OF SIX)

OVHD. POWER CABLE
AUTHORIZED
CL. 135 FT.

FIXED BRIDGE
HOR. CL. 100 FT.
VERT. CL. 65 FT.

BASCULE BRIDGE
HOR. CL. 83 FT.
VERT. CL. 19 FT.

BASCULE BRIDGE
HOR. CL. 125 FT.
VERT. CL. 32 FT.

Cable Area

Cable Area

(see tabulation)

Marsh

Marsh

Marsh

Marsh

Piers

NELLS ISLAND

(tabulation)

POLE

SCALE 1:20,000

Yards

Nautical Mile

1000

2000

3000

500

1000

Beyond the Mountains

Native Americans once referred to the Housatonic River as "the place beyond the mountains," because its headwaters are located in the Berkshires of western Massachusetts. The Housatonic runs through nearly 135 miles of Connecticut and pours more fresh water into briny Long Island Sound than any river but the mighty Connecticut herself.

Stratford, located along the shores of the Housatonic, was settled early in the Colonial period (1639). Today the town boasts the famous Sikorsky Division of United Technologies, named for the inventor of the helicopter. Still a leader in whirlybird production and design, Sikorsky is about 6 miles above the river's mouth, just beyond the Merritt Parkway bridge.

In the town of Stratford, you'll also find–appropriately enough–the American Festival Theater. Inspired by Lawrence Langher, who founded the Theater Guild, this Shakespearean stage was built to resemble the famous Globe Theater in London. The theater opened in 1955 and rode a long wave of acclaim and popularity until just recently. Now owned by the State of Connecticut and operated as a State Park replete with picnic benches for visitors, the theater reopened in 1989, showing several works of the master.

Between the river's mouth and the bridge are also some of the state's richest oyster beds. This estuarine section of the river produces huge quantities of seed oysters each year, and you'll often see small outboards dredging for the baby oysters here. There is plenty of beauty in this area and all the way to the head of navigation at Derby. Full of open spaces and endless marsh grass, the land is nearly as flat as the water, and most will find it a welcome change from overcrowded waterways in other parts of the state.

For many years, people have taken an active interest in preserving the 2,000-square-mile Housatonic River basin and fighting for its restoration. The Housatonic Valley Association (203) 672-6679 has played a key part in this struggle, working to end the pollution of the river with PCBs from industrial sites upstream. Despite this effort, it's

© Laura Barr

Stratford Shoal/Middle Ground Lighthouse, originally built in 1837, was automated in 1970.

Marine Facilities and Services		Number of Transient Berths	Number of Transient Moorings	Seasonal/Year-round	Largest Vessel Accommodation (in feet)	Marked Entry Channel	Approach Depth (in feet)	Dockside Depth in feet at MLW	Gas/Diesel Fuel	Fuel Brand	Ramp/Dinghy Dock/Launch Service	Railway/Lift: Capacity (in tons)	Propeller/Hull Repairs	Engine Repairs: Gas/Diesel	Marine Supplies/Groceries/Bait/Ice	Pump-out Station	Showers/Laundromat	110V ★ 220V ▲ Maximum Amps	MasterCard/VISA/Diners Club/American Express	Restaurant/Snack Bar	Monitors VHF Channel
① Breakwater Key								*CONDOMINIUM / DOCKOMINIUM*													
② Beacon Point Marine	(203) 378-4467			Y							R		PH	GD			S		MV		
③ Housatonic Boat Club	(203) 377-9195	1	3	S	40		20	7			DL										68
④ Brown's Boat Yard	(203) 377-9303	2		Y	40	●	5	9			R	L7			I			▲50			
⑤ **Stratford Marina (p. 157)**	**(203) 377-4477**	25		Y	80	●	13	7	GD	TEX		L35	PH	GD	SI		SL	★▲50	MVA	S	9
⑥ Maritronics Service Co.	(203) 377-8815			S	100	●	20	8	GD	TEX	R	L30	PH		SI		SL	★▲			
⑦ Housatonic Marina	(203) 375-1840			Y			*MARINE SUPPLIES*						PH	G			S		MVA		
⑧ Pootatuck Yacht Club *	(203) 377-9068																				
⑨ Rivercliff Yacht Club				S			6	6			R	L						★		MV	
⑩ Flagship Marina	(203) 874-1783	2		Y	32		6	6			R	L15	PH	GD	S		S	▲50	MV		

Information in these listings is provided by the facilities themselves. An asterisk (*) indicates that the facility did not respond to our most recent requests for information.

still recommended that you fish only for sport, being sure to release your catch rather than consuming it. The old Remington Gun Club on Stratford Point also contributed heavily to water pollution in the area; many thousands of pounds of toxic lead were shot from here into Long Island Sound, leading some to speculate that the waterway could now be mined.

As if that weren't enough, the state has proposed extending Rte. 7 across the Housatonic, which may threaten more of the fragile marsh ecosystem.

 ## What To See And Do

Although the navigable portions of the Housatonic are quite beautiful, the water quality is only "SC," suitable for recreational uses but not for bathing. If you'd like to do some shellfishing, take your dinghy into the winding side channels which run through the marshes.

Looking south down the Housatonic River. Between the railroad and I-95 bridges (foreground) and the Rte. 1 bridge to the south is Flagship Marina and the Tivercliff Yacht Club. Nells Island, Stratford Point, and Long Island Sound are in the background.

Beachcombers may want to stroll the intertidal zone along Short Beach, north of Stratford Point; joggers, however, should head out to the path along Lordship Beach, which is west of the point.

Spring, summer, or fall, you're bound to see a number of people fishing in this area. Depending on the season, they may be angling for blues, striped bass, fluke, or blackfish. For a guide to fishing the Housatonic, send a $3.00 check to the Housatonic Fly Fishermen's Association, Box 5092, Hamden, CT 06518.

A trip to the east side of the river in Milford will provide access to the excitement of Milford Jai-Alai (203) 877-4211. The west side of the river also offers excitement of various speeds: you can head into the Shakespeare Theater for rich enjoyment or perhaps wait until July for Bridgeport's Barnum Festival (203) 367-8495, which often features an air show leaving from Sikorsky Memorial Airport.

 ## Where To Eat

Stratford has the advantage of a small waterside town: there are several nice restaurants within walking distance of the docks. If you're staying at the Stratford Marina, we recommend you try the seafood at Schooner or Later (203) 377-2641. A walk up Broad Street to Ferry Boulevard will get you to the Blue Sky Diner (203) 375-5184, to Augustyn's Blue Goose (203) 375-9130 serving steak and seafood, or to Fagan's (203) 378-6560 offering a varied menu. Heading south on Stratford Avenue, you'll find China House of Stratford (203) 377-8570.

A bit further afield, requiring time in a taxi, you'll find two restaurants along the seawall at Lordship Beach offering good food and a view: the Seascape Restaurant (203) 375-2149 and Allen's East (203) 378-0556.

 ## Navigation and Anchorages

Use NOAA Charts 12370 (1:20,000), 12369 (1:20,000), 12364 (1:40,000), and 12354 (1:80,000). Use tide tables for Bridgeport. High tide at Stratford is 26 minutes later; low tide is 1 hour and 1 minute later. Multiply by 0.8 for height at high or low water. Mean tidal range is 5.8 feet.

The outer entrance to the Housatonic River, marked by the green 2.5sec flasher "1," is 5.2nm by boat northeast of Stratford Shoal, 2.6nm by boat southwest of Charles Island at Milford, and 5.1nm by boat from the entrance to Bridgeport Harbor to the west.

From red nun "20" south of **Lordship Beach** in Stratford, a course of about 60°m for 2.3nm will take you just outside of the green 2.5sec flasher "1" **[WP-96]** at the entrance to the **Housatonic River.** From the flashing red 4sec bell "16" **[WP-100]** south of **Charles Island** in Milford, a course of about 240°m for 2.4nm will also get you to the mouth of the Housatonic.

CAUTION: *There have been many buoy changes in this area. We have noted the most important below, but be alert for others.*

Built in 1822, the **Stratford Point Light** is a white conical tower with a brown band which makes an excellent landmark when heading toward the entrance of the Housatonic. Standing 52 feet above the water, this light—

flashing every 20 seconds–is the second most powerful beacon on the Sound and has recently been equipped with a radio signal.

Coming from the south, there is more than enough water around **Stratford Shoal,** but because the shoal itself is so shallow relative to the surrounding waters, a nasty chop often arises when the wind and the current are at odds. Note that black can "3" **[WP-363]** marking Middle Ground is now green, and that what was the red 4sec flashing gong "2" **[WP-362],** marking the south end of Stratford Shoal, is now a bell.

Coming from the west, look for the lighted red 6sec bell "18" **[WP-90]** (formerly a 4sec white flasher) south of Stratford Point. If you're passing this far south, you may want to head for red nun "20" (which was once a gong) south of Point No Point. From there, head for the green 4sec flasher "1" **[WP-96]** at the mouth of the river.

During the day, you'll see two black chimneys located 3.3nm up river in the town of Devon, which make excellent landmarks. Entering the river at night for the first time, however, can be risky. Make sure you heed flasher "1" at the channel entrance; there are several 6-foot spots between this buoy and green can "1A" ahead.

The breakwater extending from Milford Point is marked at its far end by a 25-foot red 4sec flasher "2A," and the channel leading upriver from this point is 200 feet wide with a depth of about 18 feet. Be sure to stay as close to the center of the channel as possible, because there are a few shoal spots along the edge leading to red nun "4." Also, part of the inner breakwater, marked by the 21-foot green 4sec flasher "11," is sometimes underwater at high tide. The chart also shows a green flasher "5" off Short Beach, which has been removed; and green can "3" on the west side of the channel has since been fitted with a green 4sec flasher and moved to take the place of buoy "5."

You must be cautious of the many oyster stakes marking the underwater shellfish beds; they are nearly as plentiful as the oysters themselves. Also be cautious of the current: though it normally runs at only 2 to 3 knots, it sets strong to the west at the river's mouth and quickens considerably during spring freshets or when the ebb tide is followed by a north wind. It's best to wait for an incoming tide or to enter under engine power.

CAUTION: *When tide and wind are opposed, you'll run into little hillocks of sea near the breakwater. Whether thrilling, challenging, or scary, these crazy waters should always be approached with care.*

East of the outer breakwater, you'll find a nice daytime anchorage. The water here is slightly deeper than the chart indicates, running sometimes to 5 feet, and is chock full of blackfish, blues, and spider crabs. The area is well-protected against weather from the southwest, but to the

The earliest and the latest in helicopter technology - Igor Sikorsky and the VS-300 in 1939 (left), and one of the new Coast Guard HH-60J Jayhawk Search-and-Rescue helicopters in action.

Photos courtesy of Sikorsky Aircraft

WHIRLYBIRDS OVER THE HOUSATONIC

Some great innovators in transportation technology have a strong Connecticut connection: First is David Bushnell of Westbrook who invented the first submarine, for use against the British in the Revolutionary War. Next is John Fitch, a native of South Windsor, who developed one of the first steamboats, although much of the credit went to others that followed. Third is Igor Sikorsky, who developed the first practical, mass-produced helicopter and started the company that bears his name in Stratford.

Igor Ivanovich Sikorsky was born in Russia in 1889. Encouraged by his parents, both professionals, in his scientific education, he built his first helicopter, a small rubber-band powered model, at the age of 12. In 1909 he constructed a 25-horsepower rotor helicopter that was, in theory, capable of vertical lift without a pilot. Unfortunately, in 1909 there were no engines powerful enough to lift the aircraft.

After the Russian Revolution, Sikorsky emigrated to the U.S., searched in vain for employment in his field, and ended up teaching. With a little help from his friends, he founded Sikorsky Aviation in 1923, and over the next 20 years developed large "flying boat" airliners.

But Sikorsky never shook the pesky helicopter bug, and in 1928 he began to experiment again. By 1935 he had secured a patent for the machine that was to become the *VS-300,* and in 1938 got approval from his firm's parent company, United Technologies, to produce a prototype. In September of 1939 at the old Vought-Sikorsky plant near the mouth of the Housatonic, the *VS-300* lifted itself a few inches off the ground and the age of powered vertical flight had begun.

The old Sikorsky plant moved to Bridgeport near Black Rock Harbor, and in the mid-1950s a new facility was built on the west bank of the Housatonic just north of the Merritt Parkway bridge, at the mouth of the Far Mill River. (Alert boaters will sometimes be lucky enough to see barges heading downriver, carrying Sikorsky aircraft.)

Today, Sikorsky is a major defense contractor, and test flights can often be seen over the Housatonic, Long Island Sound, and the surrounding area. Sikorsky tries to schedule test flights appropriately, but would like to be contacted at (203) 386-4000 if you are bothered by excessive helicopter noise.

east you'll find only water as far as Portugal, and that's an awful lot of fetch; we suggest you don't risk a wind shift by staying overnight.

Back in the channel, note that light tower "7," which once flashed in 4sec intervals, is now a flashing green 6sec light. To starboard, you'll see the extensive marshes which, because they developed in the last century, have fortunately escaped the fate of being sliced with mosquito drainage ditches. The buoy changes continue as you head further upriver. Red nun "14" has been moved slightly south of its place on the chart, and red nun "18" slightly southwest. Cans "27," "29," "31," "37," and "53" have each been changed from black to green.

Above red nun "16," you'll find the Housatonic Boat Club, offering guest moorings. Stratford Marina, located at green can "19," has more than 100 slips in addition to excellent facilities. Just north is the town launching ramp, but the price for use to non-residents is $100.00 per season. Contact the Stratford Recreation Department (203) 385-4053 for more information about the permit. Remember that there is an enforced 5-mph speed limit near all marine facilities and the bridge.

The Housatonic River can be explored as far north as Derby and Shelton, about 11.5nm by boat upstream of Stratford Point. You'll enjoy the scenery more and more as you head north, watching development drop off and nature re-assert herself.

High tide at Shelton is 1 hour 35 minutes later than at Bridgeport; low tide is 2 hours 44 minutes later. Multiply by 0.7 for height at high or low water. Mean tidal range is 5.8 feet.

You will have to wait for the bascule railroad bridge to open when you reach Devon. The bridgetender may be reached on VHF 13, or you may signal the bridge with your horn. The Connecticut Turnpike Bridge marks the line between saltwater fishing areas, where a license is not required, and the freshwater areas, where a license is required. South of the bridge, you'll see the state launching ramp on the east shore in Milford.

Above Devon, the river runs only 4 feet deep, and the hydroelectric dam near Derby is the absolute head of navigation. It's at this point that the heavily polluted

Naugatuck River runs into the Housatonic. Above the dam, the Yale crew team practices for its annual competition in the Derby Day races (203) 432-1412 during June.

If at any time during your trip you'd like to know the weather forecast, call the National Weather Service (203) 378-2344 at Sikorsky Memorial Airport, or listen to their pre-recorded weather message (203) 936-1212.

 ### Shoreside and Emergency Services

Airport: Sikorsky Memorial Airport (203) 576-7498
Ambulance: 911
Bus: Greater Bridgeport Transit District (203) 333-3031
Coast Guard: New Haven (203) 773-2400 or VHF 16
Fire: 911 or (203) 385-4070
Harbormaster: (203) 375-7597 or VHF 16
Hospital: Bridgeport Hospital (203) 384-3000
Police: 911 or (203) 385-4100
Radio Telephone: VHF 27; I.D.: Bridgeport Marine Operator
Taxi: Airport Taxi Co. (203) 377-8294
Stratford Taxi (203) 375-4445
Tow Service: Southern CT Sea Tow, Bridgeport, CT (203) 331-0410 or VHF 16; Saybrook Towing and Salvage, Old Saybrook, CT (203) 388-4065 or VHF 16
Train: Amtrak 1-800- USA-RAIL
Metro-North 1-800-638-7646   ✦

Milford Harbor

A Pearl Within

The humble oyster has been writ large in the economy of many shoreside Connecticut towns, but never more so than in Milford. The Gulf, with its shallow water, and the tidal flats of the Wepawaug River have been blessed with oysters, as though blessed by Mother Nature herself.

Native Americans consumed such quantities of the local mollusks that a huge pile of shells gathered at the mouth of the river. The English settlers followed suit, developing many ways of harvesting the bivalves. More recently, fishermen have tried some specialized vessels, the most spectacular of which was Simon Lake's tiny submarine, *Explorer*. Lake used it to catch the tiny critters hiding here. Lake built a submarine for military use, but because the United States Navy had no interest in the vessel, the inventor was forced to sell five of the craft—with their 3,000 mile range—to the Russians.

Another unique oystering boat went by the name *Shellfish*. Ordered by the state legislature in 1931 to purchase a boat suitable to their duties, the members of the shellfish commission designed a luxury cruiser with an oyster dredge on the foredeck—just big enough to haul in a few pounds of hors d'oeuvres. The boat served the commissioners well, until the state took it away and replaced it with a more useful craft. The state maintained it for many years until finally selling it a few years ago to a Connecticut boater. We once happened upon the beautiful old boat while on a visit to Block Island's Great Salt Pond.

Milford deserves credit for being one of the first towns in the state to develop a harbor management plan. The town shut down its two old sewage treatment plants and has opened a new one, leading directly to cleaner water in the harbor. Let's hope other towns follow suit, and soon.

Milford Harbor Marina (foreground) in Milford Harbor, CT. The red frame building in the background is Spencer's Marina on the east side of the harbor.

 What to See and Do

When in Milford do as Milfordites do: go oystering. West of the bar leading to Charles Island are some of the state's only shellfishing beds which are entirely open to the public. The only restriction here is that you use hand tools and restrict your take to a half bushel per person each day.

Charles Island belongs to the state and is open to the public. You may explore the ruins and daydream of the pirates who supposedly spent time here. As with many spots along this section of American coast, legend tells of Captain Kidd burying some treasure here. In recent years, the island has suffered at the hands of careless tourists, who have left behind their garbage, which soon attracted a herd of large rats. So remember, if you carry it in, carry what's

Marine Facilities and Services		Number of Transient Moorings	Number of Transient Berths	Seasonal/Year-round	Largest Vessel Accommodation (in feet)	Approach Depth (in feet)	Marked Entry Channel	Dockside Depth in feet at MLW	Gas/Diesel Fuel in feet at MLW	Fuel Brand	Ramp/Dinghy Dock/Launch Service	Railway/Lift: Capacity (in tons)	Propeller/Hull Repairs	Engine Repairs: Gas/Diesel	Pump-out Station	Marine Supplies/Groceries/Bait/Ice	Showers/Laundromat	110V ★ 220V ▲ Maximum Amps	MasterCard/VISA/Diners Club American Express	Restaurant/Snack Bar	Monitors VHF Channel
❶ Milford Yacht Club	(203) 877-5598			S	44	●			7	PRIVATE CLUB - MEMBERS ONLY					S	I	★15	MV	S		
❷ Port Milford (p. 163)	(203) 877-7802	4		Y	50	●	10	10					L35	PH	GD	S	SI	▲30	MVA		16
❸ Spencer's Marina	(203) 874-4173			Y	36	●	10	6	G	TEX			L12	PH	G	S	SI	★15	MV		
❹ Milford Harbor Marina	(203) 877-1475	20		Y	60	●	8	8	GD	TEX						S	SI	★50	MV		
❺ Milford Boat Works (p. 162)	(203) 877-1475	10		Y	65	●	8	8					L35	PH	GD	S		★30			

Information in these listings is provided by the facilities themselves. An asterisk (*) indicates that the facility did not respond to our most recent requests for information.

left back out again. Also watch for the tide change, as the bar leading to the harbor is fully covered with a swift current when the water's up.

Milford once had a deepwater port, and the town still maintains some of its old seaport atmosphere. With 14 miles of coastline and the Wharf Lane Complex of historic homes maintained by the Milford Historical Society (203) 874-2664, you'll have no trouble finding seaside enjoyment. The three houses were built in the 1700s and include a collection of over 4,000 Native American artifacts.

Anglers will want to drop a line into Gulf Pond. The tidal surge under the bridge makes this a favorite spot for bunkers and blues. Gulf Pond is also an excellent spot for birding; huge rafts of ducks collect on the safe waters of the preserve, and one resident claims that on any given day you can see every type of duck in Connecticut on Gulf Pond.

You will also find a number of grocery stores and a bargain-priced theater within walking distance of the docks. The train station is also about 4 blocks away, making it convenient to drop off or pick up passengers from your crew. If you'd like to watch a game of jai-alai at the fronton (203) 877-4211, you'll have to hail a cab.

 Where To Eat

Finding a restaurant close by the water in Milford is easy. Try the Saybrook Fish House (203) 878-2428 in Armory Square, serving seafood. Also within walking distance of Burns Point, you'll find seafood, pasta, chicken, and desserts at the Pilgrim by the Sea Restaurant (203) 874-9536.

Further from the water, probably requiring a cab trip, on Bridgeport Avenue is Armellino's (203) 874-6509, with an Italian menu. You may also want to try Chan's Inn (203) 877-3350 on Rte. 1, specializing in Cantonese and Mandarin.

 Navigation and Anchorages

Use NOAA Charts 12370 (1:20,000), 12364 (1:40,000), and 12354 (1:80,000). Use tide tables for Bridgeport. High tide at Milford Harbor is 8 minutes earlier; low tide is 10 minutes earlier. Mean tidal range is 7.6 feet.

The 25-foot 4sec red flasher "10" at the entrance to Milford Harbor is 4.3nm by boat northeast of Stratford Point Light and 6.1nm by boat west of the channel entrance between the New Haven Harbor breakwaters.

Coming from the east, one of your first landmarks will be the huge sloping seawall on **Pond Point.** From here ahead, you'll see **Welches Point,** which has a number of rocks just off its shores, so don't cut between the point and red nun "2" **[WP-107].**

You will also want to be careful of the shoals to the east and south of **Charles Island.** The old black can "1" **[WP-101]** east of Charles Island is now green, and bell "16" **[WP-100]** south of the island now flashes red to match its color.

CAUTION: You may see local boaters cutting across the bar to Charles Island, but we suggest you go your own way. No one's ever saved time by going aground.

At 10 to 16 feet deep, the body of water between Charles Island and Welches Point known as **The Gulf** is a fine anchorage, except in a south or southeasterly blow. The water shallows gradually leading to the north shore, except where the dredged channel leads into Milford Harbor. You'll find the most desirable anchorage north of Charles Island; anchor far enough offshore here that the mosquitoes don't arrive on the wings of a westerly breeze.

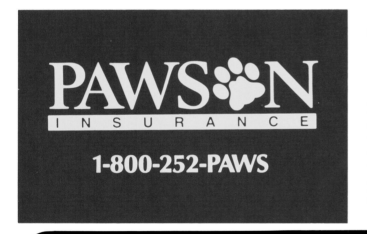

The further from shore you drop your hook, the more likely you'll encounter some swells; these will rock you to sleep, though some have met unexpected rotary currents in this anchorage. The bottom of **The Gulf** is hard sand, though it gets softer nearer shore. Be sure to watch for oyster stakes along both the east and west shores.

The channel leading into Milford's **Wepawaug River** is about 100 feet wide and is difficult to spot. The channel was last dredged in 1988 to a depth of 10 feet up to the Milford Yacht Club; it's 8 feet deep from there to the head of navigation. The new channel was moved slightly to the west. Heavy silting outside the channel has reduced depths to only about 3 feet, and you may still see an occasional fisherman propped against a buoy, rod in hand.

The Milford Yacht Club sponsors small-boat races, so on weekends expect the channel to be crowded with sailors on their way to the race course. Sailors entering the harbor against an ebb tide may have difficulty with the current. A strong southerly can cause waves to pile up in the channel, making it more difficult to enter. In either case, let someone bigger break the waves ahead as you follow close behind.

Gulf Pond empties into Milford Harbor just inside the eastern breakwater, which is marked by the 25-foot red flasher "10." When the tide changes, the rush of water forced under the bridge at the mouth of Gulf Pond is tremendous; if you are not careful or if your boat is underpowered, you may be pushed into **Burns Point.**

Milford Harbor is often filled with boats. A no-wake speed limit exists, while in the outer channel it's 5 mph. The bottom is a mixture of sand and mud, but space is limited. Many visitors moor fore and aft, as there is little room to swing. We suggest you call well ahead to reserve a slip. In any case, Milford Harbor is well protected in most weather, though Hurricane Gloria did take her toll.

 ### Shoreside and Emergency Services

Airport: Tweed-New Haven (203) 787-8283
Ambulance: 911
Bus: Connecticut Transit (203) 624-0151
Coast Guard: New Haven (203) 773-2400 or VHF 16
Fire: 911
Harbormaster: (203) 878-7784 or VHF 16 and 68
Hospital: Milford (203) 876-4000
Police: 911 or (203) 878-6551 or VHF 16
Radio Telephone: VHF 27; I.D.: Bridgeport
Marine Operator
Taxi: Milford Taxi (203) 877-1468
Tow Service: Southern CT Sea Tow, Bridgeport, CT
(203) 331-0410; Saybrook Towing and
Salvage, Old Saybrook, CT (203) 388-4065
or VHF 16
Train: Amtrak 1-800-USA-RAIL
Metro-North 1-800-638-7646 ◆

Where the Gargoyles Peer

Due to its striking size and success as a commercial port, New Haven is frequently overlooked by cruising boaters, and often for good reason; at times, it seems the harbor has been overrun with 500-ton tankers. Still, there are nearly 1,000 pleasure boaters based in New Haven, and there are many anchorages and marinas for these people to enjoy. So, while this harbor is surely not the best for gunkholing, it has more than its fair share of shoreside attractions.

When Adriaen Block arrived here in 1614, he was greeted by the Quinnipiac Indians and called the harbor *Rodeberg*, which means "Red Mount Place" in Dutch. Block attributed this name to the traprock mountains known to us as East Rock and West Rock, for their reddish color caused by the oxidation of iron trapped in the volcanic basalt layers.

When Block arrived, he probably found a harbor nearly half-again the size we see today. Silting over the years has led to large fill-ins of shallow harbor areas, all to meet the needs of the ever-expanding city. Not long ago, excavations of the foundation of Macy's department store led to the discovery of the original waterfront wharfs, now buried somewhere downtown near the town green.

Today, New Haven is most widely known as the home of Yale University. Ironically enough, the college was originally founded by a group of Harvard grads, way back in 1701, and was actually located in the town of Clinton. The school was then moved to Old Saybrook in 1707, and finally to New Haven in 1716. Yale's architecture now has great impact on the city's style, with buildings erected during the Gothic, Georgian, and Modern periods. Many residents would argue that the University also dominates the city's political, financial, and even social character.

During the 1900s, during the city's heyday, the *Neptune* sailed from New Haven Harbor under the command of Captain Townshend. She returned from her voyage to the West Indies, Falkland Islands, and Shanghai with a cargo

The Quinnipiac River in New Haven from the South. In the foreground is the Tomlinson Bridge and the I-95 "Q-Bridge."

Marine Facilities and Services		Transient Moorings	Transient Berths	Seasonal/Year-round	Largest Vessel Accom. (ft)	Marked Entry Channel	Approach Depth (ft)	Dockside Depth (ft MLW)	Gas/Diesel Fuel	Fuel Brand	Ramp/Dinghy Dock/Launch Service	Railway/Lift: Capacity (tons)	Engine Repairs: Prop/Hull	Marine Supplies: Gas/Diesel	Pump-out Station	Showers/Laundromat	Groceries/Bait/Ice	110V★ 220V▲ Max Amps	MC/VISA/Diners/Amex	Restaurant/Snack Bar	Monitors VHF Channel
1 West Haven Yacht Club	(203) 933-9825								*PRIVATE CLUB - MEMBERS ONLY*												
2 West Cove Marina	(203) 933-3000	7		S	56	●	8	6	G	TEX		L35	PH	GD		SL	SI	★50	MV		
3 City Point Yacht Club	(203) 789-9301		3	Y	43	●	8	8			L	L20				S	I	★			16
4 Oyster Point Marina	(203) 624-5895	10	5	Y	90	●	12	8	GD	BPS		L10				SL	IG	▲50	MVA	R	16
5 Waucoma Yacht Club	(203) 789-9530	3		S	36		4	4	*PRIVATE CLUB - MEMBERS ONLY*						S	I	★20			16
6 Fair Haven Marina	(203) 777-0523	4		S	40	●	4	4	G	TEX	RL	L10	PH	G		S	SI	★15		R	16
7 New Haven Yacht Club	(203) 469-9608		1	S	35	●	9	1			L	L2				S		★20			
8 New Haven Marina	(203) 469-8230	10		S	30		3	4	D			L5	PH	GD			SI		MV		16
9 Lighthouse Marina	(203) 468-2101			S	20		2	2	*FISHING STATION*										S	6	

Information in these listings is provided by the facilities themselves. An asterisk (*) indicates that the facility did not respond to our most recent requests for information.

EDIBLE AND INCREDIBLE DISCS

For most people New Haven brings to mind Yale University, but the "Elm City" owns some culinary claims to fame as well: As the birthplace of perhaps the two most popular foods in America, hamburgers and pizza. Another popular food in New Haven led to the invention of one of the country's favorite outdoor toys–the Frisbee.

It was here in 1900 that Louis Lassen chopped up the raw trimmings from steak meat and produced America's first hamburger sandwich. His eatery, Louis' Lunch, is still in business today, and has become a legendary New Haven landmark.

"We make 'em the same way in the same store today," says Kenneth Lassen, grandson of the restaurant's founder, as he promises a treat to the tastebuds for those game enough to give them a try.

The hamburger, which took its name from the German city where the meat was invented, actually came about as a by-product at Louis' from his own invention–the steak sandwich. Lassen sliced the steak thin and laid it on bread in layers. Not surprisingly, both the steak sandwich and the hamburgers made from the trimmings caught on.

"In the 1920s they both started to pick up real good," says Lassen, who today sells his hamburgers for $1.70, possibly the best bargain in town. No one today recalls just what Louis charged for the originals back in 1900.

Not long after the hamburger became a household word, pizza (or more correctly, "apizza") made its debut in New Haven. It's widely held that Italian immigrant Frank Pepe was first in the world to go commercial with pizza when he opened shop in the Wooster Square section of town in the 1930s. His 12-inch "tomato pies" were baked in brick ovens still used at Pepe's Pizzeria Napoletana today.

Salvatore (Sally) Consiglio opened shop eight years after Pepe and bakes pizza in similar fashion a few doors down. Long lines are standard fare at both Sally's and Pepe's pizzerias, which have spawned hundreds of thousands of pizzeria competitors nationwide. Tales abound of people boarding overseas-bound airplanes carrying New Haven pizza stacked high in white boxes.

In a very different sense, another food popular in New Haven made what is probably as important a contribution to American culture: the Frisbee.

The Frisbie Pie Company, bakers of Mrs. Frisbie's Pies, was actually located in Bridgeport, CT. In a nutshell, the story goes that in the 1920s Yalies took to flinging the empty pie tins–each one enstamped with the Frisbie name–across the New Haven green.

The sport caught on amongst the college set quickly, wherein its popularity still resides. Mrs. Frisbie's pies are long gone, but their legacy remains. Today's "tins" are plastic and manufactured by Whammo of San Gabriel, CA, but in New Haven lies their endearing origins.

Contributed by Patty Koller, a staff writer for Soundings *Magazine.*

worth $250,000, a full $50,000 of which went to the city in taxes.

 ## What To See And Do

While there are many ways to spend your time in New Haven, the most inspiring are the free tours of Yale offered by the Admissions Office (203) 432-2300. The history and architecture of the school are fascinating, and you'll be watched by the many gargoyles peering diligently from their cornice perches all over campus. Be sure to stop at both the Art Gallery (203) 432-0600 and the Center for British Art (203) 432-2800 for looks at two of the better collections in the state. Those interested in more dramatic renderings should spend an afternoon at the Peabody Museum of Natural History (203) 432-5050, offering displays of dinosaurs and whales. And the translucent marble walls of the Bienecke Rare Book and Manuscript Library (203) 432-2977 will surely attract your more studious crew members.

In addition to Yale and its many offerings, New Haven and its citizens are also blessed with more theaters any other city in Connecticut. In fact, many stars, including Meryl Streep, Dustin Hoffman, Joan Van Ark, and Jennifer Beals got their start at the Yale School of Drama. For excellent viewing, try the Schubert (203) 562-5666, the Long Wharf (203) 787-4282, the Yale Repertory (203) 432-1234, and the Palace (203) 624-8497. The Palace is also one of two excellent spots for great music in town. The other is Toad's Place (203) 777-7431, which books many of the hottest rock and blues acts in the business and is considered one of the hippest nightclubs in the northeast.

Landlubbers and sun worshippers will want to head to Lighthouse Point Park (203) 787-8005 on the east shore of the harbor, with its grand beach and beautiful old carousel. Swimming on the harbor side isn't all that appealing, but you'll surely enjoy it in the cleaner waters of the Sound. Even better, however, is a trip to Merwin Point in Woodmont, about 0.8nm west of the breakwater. The rocks about 200 feet off this public beach are great for snorkeling but should be approached in shallow draft boats only, and no one should cut inside them.

If you're more interested in New Haven's history than you are in getting a sunburn, head to the New Haven Colony Historical Society (203) 562-4183 or the Eli Whitney Museum (203) 777-1833, both on Whitney Avenue.

 ## Where To Eat

Any food you'd care to eat can surely be found in New Haven. Starting with the Chart House (203) 787-3466, located right on the water at City Point, you can treat yourself to excellent steak and seafood. Keeping up the tradition of nautical names, the Rusty Scupper (203) 777-5711 at the north end of Long Wharf serves very good seafood.

Lighthouse Point Park, Morris Creek, and Morgan Point on the eastern side of the entrance to New Haven Harbor.

But then again, if you're visiting this cultural center by boat, why not splurge? Take a cab ride into the city and sample the many fine eats downtown. We couldn't hope to name all the good restaurants there, but if you look long and hard enough, you'll find French, Italian, Jamaican, and Indian food, as well as everything in between. Here are some of our favorite spots: Modern Apizza (203) 776-5306 on State Street serves some of the best and most interesting pizzas around. The service can be slow, but the wait's worth it. Archie Moore's (203) 773-9870 is a tiny restaurant and pub tucked deep in the bosom of a homey neighborhood, where real food is cooked, so it's no surprise to find absolutely fabulous chicken wings there. The Foundry Café (203) 776-5144 offers live jazz for those who like to listen while they eat; and finally we list the most famous of them all and a local legend with college kids–a drum roll, please–Louis' Lunch (203) 562-5507, the reputed home of the first American hamburger.

If you're outside the city, at one of the marinas in or near Morris Cove, we suggest you try Alfano's Pizza and Pasta (203) 468-7969. In addition to the great Italian dishes mentioned in the name, you'll find excellent subs there, to go.

 Navigation and Anchorages

Use NOAA Charts 12371 (1:20,000), 12372 (1:40,000), and 12354 (1:80,000). Use tide tables for Bridgeport. High tide at New Haven City Dock is 1 minute later; low tide is 1 minute earlier. Multiply by 0.9 for height at high or low water. Mean tidal range is 6.4 feet.

The breakwaters marking the main entrance to New Haven Harbor are 4.1nm by boat west of Blyn Rock outside Branford Harbor, and 6.4nm by boat northeast of The Gulf at Milford Harbor. The Port Jefferson Harbor entrance is 17.5nm by boat to the south-southwest.

From the black and white morse code bell "NH" **[WP-118]** south of the entrance channel to New Haven Harbor, a course of about 350°m for about 2.2nm by boat will take you to a spot just between the middle and east outer breakwaters, marked by flashing green 4sec 29-foot tower "5" and the flashing red 5sec 57-foot Southwest Ledge horn respectively.

CAUTION: *There have been many buoy changes in this area. We have noted the most important below, but be alert for others.*

New Haven Harbor is the second largest commercial port in all of Connecticut, so you can expect that the channels will be well-marked and the water deep. While still in Long Island Sound on a clear day, you should be able to spot the Soldiers and Sailors Monument atop East Rock and the strobe marking the smoke stack of the United Illuminating power plant on the east shore. As you approach the harbor, also look for the brown towers of the Knights of Columbus Building and the new Maritime Center office next to the "Q Bridge."

Be cautious of the many commercial vessels you'll encounter in the area; they often have less steerage than a small boat, so try to give them the right of way. If you can't see the pilot house, they probably can't see you; if necessary, you can try calling a ship on VHF 13.

Coming from the south, range lights will guide you along the main shipping channel, which runs about 35 feet deep, from whistle buoy "NH" **[WP-118]** to the breakwaters **[WP-113];** from there, you will turn to starboard and head north up the channel. Note that buoy "NH" now has a ball topmark, and has the standard "morse alpha" white light flashing short-long as designation of entrance to a major harbor. Also, the red 4sec flasher "4" south of the breakwaters no longer has a bell. Most yachters can approach the entrance between the east and middle breakwaters from any angle; just be sure to stay near to the center of the channel, so as not to be set onto the breakwaters during a heavy tide change.

In good weather, cruising boats can avoid the traffic in the shipping lane by entering the harbor from **Quixes Ledge** and **Morgan Point** at the eastern end of the east breakwater. Just be sure not to cut inside of red nun "36" south of Round Rock or you will surely end up grounded.

ELI WHITNEY AND NEW HAVEN

History is written and taught selectively, and important details sometimes escape mention because they detract from popular legend. Take Eli Whitney, for example. Most people can give a rough biography of the man from what they learned in elementary school: he was the Yankee inventor of the cotton gin and the musket with interchangeable parts. People living in New Haven can't help but trip over his legacy when they drive down Whitney Avenue, through the suburb of Whitneyville, and past the old Whitney Armory site next to Lake Whitney.

But the dark side of Whitney's first major triumph isn't widely appreciated. Before Whitney invented the cotton gin in 1793, cotton was becoming nearly worthless to southern planters because it was so difficult to separate the cotton fibers from the sticky green seeds. Without a valuable, labor-intensive cash crop, owning slaves was impractical, and slavery was slowly dying out in the south.

Whitney's simple cotton gin changed everything. It could deseed 50 times the cotton a worker could process in a day. Suddenly cotton was gold. Within two years, cotton exports increased 11-fold and the price of slaves doubled. Slavery was unwittingly given its rebirth by a Yankee from staunchly abolitionist Connecticut.

Back in New Haven and looking for a new challenge, Whitney opened a gun factory in 1798 on the Mill River, and began his experiments with interchangeable parts. Here again, the textbooks mislead. True, Whitney did secure a contract with the U.S. Army to produce 10,000 muskets with interchangeable parts. But the idea didn't originate with him, and the parts weren't necessarily inter-

"Whitneyville"–now a New Haven suburb–as depicted in 1832 by J.W. Barber. To the right is the Whitney armory; to the left, workers' housing.

Engraving from *Windows on the Works: Industry on the Eli Whitney Site 1798-1979* by Karyl Lee Kibler Hall and Carolyn Cooper; the Eli Whitney Museum, 1984.

changeable. A Frenchman, Honore Blanc, made guns with interchangeable parts as early as 1785. (Fortunately for Whitney, Blanc turned down Thomas Jefferson's invitation to emigrate to the United States.) The poor precision of 18th-century manufacturing methods made uniformity relative, and gun collectors have since noticed that the parts of Whitney-built muskets do not always interchange. As often as not, parts were identical only because Whitney's workers did extensive filing and fitting by hand.

Despite the dents hammered into his legend, Eli Whitney *was* a mechanical genius, and rightly or wrongly, he became a symbol of the Industrial Revolution in America. Today, the Eli Whitney Museum is on the site of his original armory and informs the curious about the fact and fiction of Eli Whitney. The museum is free and open to the public. For more information call (203) 777-1833.

Follow the buoys east of Quixes Ledge and then pass between the breakwater and red nun "4," and then head directly for the red nun "6" off Lighthouse Point. You'll have plenty of water in this narrow channel, which is about 50 yards wide.

Rejoin the main channel near the red flasher "10A," which is now a 2.5sec flasher. Just keep an eye out for Adams Fall, marked by red and green junction buoy "A," as it is only about 5 feet deep; don't hug the buoy, and you'll be fine.

North of the east breakwater, you'll find a good anchorage. Also try **Morris Cove,** located north of the lighthouse, for its good holding ground; but be aware that the ride will be rough there in the prevailing southwest winds. The New Haven Yacht Club maintains many moorings in the cove; some should be available to members of other yacht clubs on a reciprocal basis. The yacht club also offers launch service during the summer daylight hours. Be aware that Black Rock, south of Fort Hale Park on the east shore and marked by a white and orange can, often grabs unwary visitors and keeps them grounded for a night or so.

When approaching **New Haven** from the west, you'll have plenty of room to enter the harbor between the mainland and the west breakwater. Hurricane Gloria destroyed many of the marks on the harbor breakwaters, and they have since been replaced with new navigational aids. The west end of the breakwater is now marked with flashing red 6sec light "2" on a 26-foot tower **[WP-108],** and can be seen for nearly 4 miles; the tower also carries triangular red daymarkers. New Haven Light on the east end of the breakwater now has a flashing white 4sec light on a 44-foot tower **[WP-112]** and is visible for 6 miles. The middle breakwater remains as charted, however, marked with a 29-foot red 4sec flasher on its west end and a 29-foot green 4sec flasher on its east end. You should note that the old black channel can "9A" has been changed to green.

Behind the breakwaters, you'll see a number of anglers fishing for blues. Except during bad weather, this is a decent spot to anchor for awhile, or to slip in out of the current during a tide change.

South of **Sandy Point,** New Haven looks like much of the rest of the Connecticut coast; north of the point, you'll surely notice the heavy industrialization. The inner harbor begins at Sandy Point and stretches from the west shore all the way to **Fort Hale** and the Coast Guard Station (203) 773-2400 on the east shore. Be aware that the waters outside of the channel in the inner harbor are often very shallow.

CAUTION: Do not stray from the channel when approaching the inner harbor. The breakwater at Sandy point is submerged at high tide, and many boaters have lost keels, rudders, or propellors when passing over this hidden obstacle.

Choices for anchorage in the inner harbor are mostly limited to the western side due to the many commercial facilities along the eastern shore. Note that black can "1" off **Long Wharf** has been changed to yellow 2.5sec flasher "A." If you'd like more comfortable accommodations, we suggest heading toward the facilities at **City Point** or continuing up the **West River** to one of the marinas there. This channel runs about 8.5 feet deep up to red nun "18." City Point is perhaps the quietest place in the harbor and offers easy access by cab to West Haven and downtown New Haven. You'll find a small deli and market at City Point, and there is courtesy dockage available through Oyster Point Marina. Because the tidal range throughout the harbor is 6.4 feet, you will often see small runabouts cutting across Shag Bank to City Point, but we suggest you go the long way around.

You may also want to anchor up beyond the Tomlinson Bridge on the **Quinnipiac River.** The bridge has a 12-foot vertical clearance when closed, but will open on demand if you call the bridgetender on VHF 13. The bridge, however, does not always work correctly, as it has been slammed quite frequently by tugs. In the summer, the bridge often overheats and gets stuck until the fire department can arrive to cool it down. Immediately following the Tomlinson Bridge is the I-95 bridge, often referred to as the **"Q Bridge,"** and this has a vertical clearance of about 60 feet at mlw.

The two other bridges upstream, at Ferry Street and Grand Avenue, now monitor VHF 13 and can be signaled with blasts of the old horn. The channel markers disappear after Grand Avenue; you should stay to the left side of the channel on your way to Fair Haven Marina or the Waucoma Yacht Club. Also be prepared to face currents up to 6 knots at times in this part of the river.

 Shoreside and Emergency Services

Airport: Tweed/New Haven (203) 787-8283
Ambulance: 911 or (203) 562-4107
Bus: Connecticut Transit (203) 624-0151
Coast Guard: (203) 773-2400 or VHF 16
Fire: 911 or (203) 787-6237
Hospital: Yale-New Haven (203) 785-4242
        St. Raphael's (203) 789-3000
Police: 911 or (203) 787-6316
Radio Telephone: VHF 27; I.D.: Bridgeport Marine
        Operator
Taxi: Metro Taxi (203) 777-7777
Tow Service: Southern CT Sea Tow, Bridgeport, CT
        (203) 331-0410 or VHF 16; Saybrook
        Towing & Salvage, Old Saybrook, CT
        (203) 388-4065 or VHF 16
Train: Amtrak 1-800-USA-RAIL
        Metro-North 1-800-638-7646 ◆

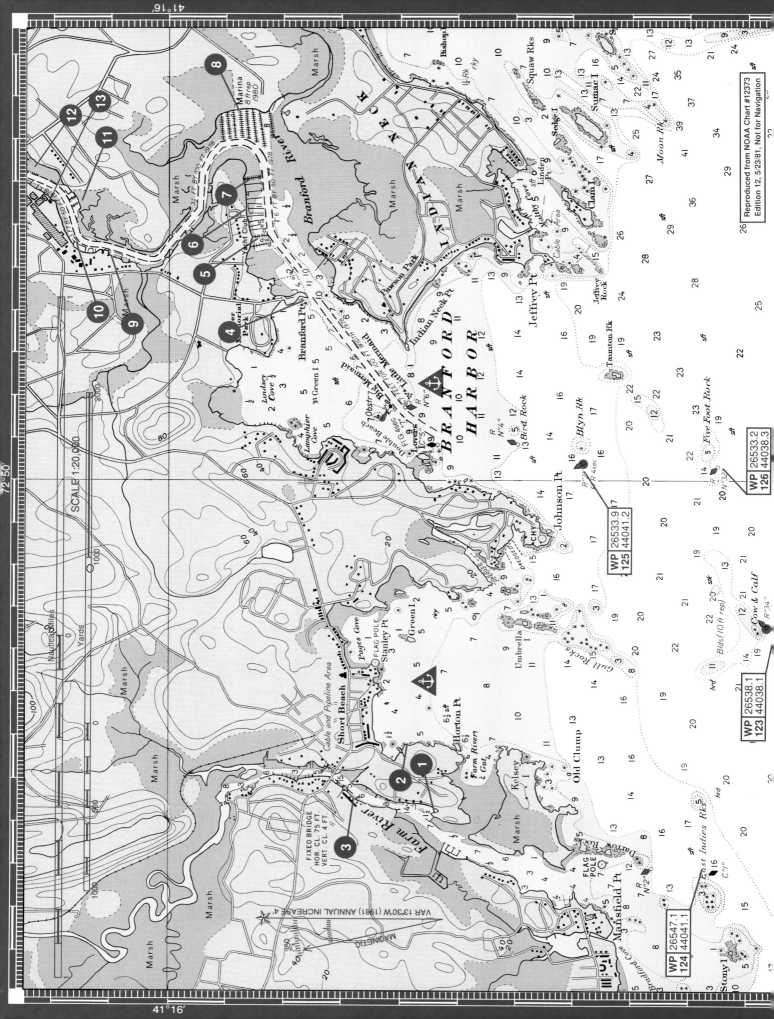

Branford Harbor

Small Town Granite

As best suits a coastal community without a deep water port, Branford was settled by farmers and fishermen. It was later discovered that the town's greatest natural resource lay not in the soil or water, but underground. The gray, white, and pink granite that forms the backbone of Branford Harbor and the Thimble Islands has been quarried for many years; it has been used for such New York City monuments as the abutments to the Brooklyn Bridge, the Statue of Liberty, and the facade of the new world headquarters of AT&T in Manhattan.

The inner harbor at Branford, CT, and Bruce & Johnson's Marina from the south over Indian Neck.

Those who come by water—whether to fish, explore tidal creeks, or water ski—will find Branford Harbor a nice place to play in a boat. Continue up the Farm River in your explorations, and you'll find all kinds of wildlife in the marshlands. Much of the marsh and the tidal flats along the river are owned by the town or the state and maintained as natural-bed oyster colonies. Although shellfish cannot be taken directly from this area, the beds are a tremendously productive nursery for young oysters.

 What To See and Do

While there are excellent marine facilities in Branford, the waterfront is surrounded by residential areas. You'll need a cab to go shopping or to find a restaurant. You can also catch a taxi or bus into New Haven, but if you're interested in staying put, you'll find plenty of choices in Branford. Try the Bittersweet Handcraft Village (203) 488-1599, which has 20 shops and artists' studios in a close setting. Featured crafts include glassblowing, painting, weaving, and leatherworking.

Marine Facilities and Services

#	Facility	Phone	Transient Berths	Transient Moorings	Seasonal/Year-round	Largest Vessel Accom. (ft)	Marked Entry Channel	Approach Depth (ft)	Dockside Depth at MLW (ft)	Gas/Diesel Fuel	Fuel Brand	Ramp/Dinghy Dock	Railway/Lift Cap. (tons)/Launch Service	Propeller/Hull Repairs	Engine Repairs: Gas/Diesel	Pump-out Station	Showers/Laundromat	Marine Supplies/Groceries/Bait/Ice	110V★/220V▲ Max Amps	Credit Cards	Restaurant/Snack Bar	Monitors VHF Channel
1	Kelsey's Boat Yard	(203) 488-9567	3	2	Y	40	●	3	3				L/R16	PH								68
2	Yale Corinthian Yacht Club	(203) 488-9330	*PRIVATE CLUB - MEMBERS ONLY*																			
3	C.T. Marina	(203) 481-3067	*PRIVATE BOATYARD / WINTER STORAGE*																			
4	Branford Town Dock	(203) 488-3279			Y	85	●	7	6													
5	Branford Yacht Club	(203) 488-9798			S	60	●	7	9	GD	MOB						S	I	★▲20	MV		
6	Pier 66 Marina	(203) 488-5613	4	2	S	45	●	8	6	G	TEX		L35	PH	GD		S	S	★	MVA	SB	
7	Goodsell Point Marina	(203) 488-5292	2		S	36	●	8	6				L50	H	GD	●						
8	Bruce & Johnson's Marina	(203) 488-8329	25		Y	65	●	5.5	6				L50	PH	GD		SL	SI	▲	MV		16
9	Branford River Marina (Marineland)	(203) 488-8921			Y	36	●	7	10				L	PH	GD				★15			16
10	Dutch Wharf Marina & Boatyard	(203) 488-9000	2		Y	60	●	8	8				L35	PH	GD		S		▲			
11	Indian Neck Yacht Club	(203) 488-9276			Y	36	●	5	2	G			L				S	I	★30			
12	Branford Marine Railway	(203) 488-2568			Y	30	●	6	6				L/L5	PH	G				★	MVA		
13	Branford Landing	(203) 488-3434			Y	50	●	6	6	GD	HSS		L35	P	GD	●	S	SI	★30			16

Information in these listings is provided by the facilities themselves. An asterisk (*) indicates that the facility did not respond to our most recent requests for information.

Branford's main attraction is the Shore Line Trolley Museum (203) 467-6927. Located on River Street (technically in East Haven), the museum has 90 trolleys and subway cars from around the country, and three miles of rails on which to clickety-clack down the track.

The Branford Historical Society (203) 488-4828 maintains the Harrison House, built in 1720, as a museum of period furniture and authentic farm implements. The backyard of the house contains what the historical society claims to be the oldest, and only, outhouse still standing in Branford. This simple structure has apparently caused a small controversy among local historians, who can't agree on its age. The queerest thing about this primitive commode is its door, which, for some odd reason, *faces* the house.

 ### Where To Eat

There's plenty to eat in Branford, but most of the food is at least a cab ride from the water. Lenny's Indian Head Inn (203) 488-1500 is a seafood house close by the Branford River that offers free limo service. Right across the street is the Backwater Tavern (203) 481-4086, a small restaurant and pub specializing in steaks, ribs, and fish.

About 4 miles from the harbor on Rte. 1, you'll find Casa D'Italia (203) 481-9525, which has excellent Italian-American cuisine. For Mexican, we suggest Su Casa (203) 481-5001 in Branford. The Indulge (203) 488-9457 is a vegetarian restaurant located at the Bittersweet Handcraft Village. For Chinese, you should try the Jade Pavilion (203) 481-3568.

 ### Navigation and Anchorages

Use NOAA Charts 12373 (1:20,000), 12372 (1:40,000), and 12354 (1:80,000). Use tide tables for Bridgeport. High tide at Branford Harbor is 8 minutes earlier; low tide is 18 minutes earlier. Multiply by 0.9 for height at high or low water. Mean tidal range is 6.2 feet.

The outer approach to Branford Harbor is marked by the red 4sec flasher "2" at Blyn Rock, which is 4.1nm by boat east of the New Haven Harbor breakwaters. Outer Island, the southernmost of the Thimble Islands, is 3.5nm by boat to the east.

From the flashing red 4sec gong "10A" **[WP-119]** at Townshend Ledge, a course of about 60°m for 2.3nm will bring you into the outer reaches of Branford Harbor, roughly south of red nun "32" **[WP-126]** at Five Foot Rocks.

The **Farm River,** known locally as the East Haven River, has not been dredged since the turn of the century. There was a time when coastal schooners could be pulled all the way up the river to the East Haven town green. Today the river is a pleasant gunkhole accessible to shallow- and medium-draft boats and includes two small-boat facilities and some private docks. You'll want to wait for high tide before entering the river if you draw more than 4 feet. At any tide, the river is difficult to enter because of the rocks

and the crooked channel. Stay close to the east of green can "1" **[WP-124]** at East Indies Rock, then steer west around red nun "2," leaving Darrow Rocks to starboard. From here on, the river is unmarked.

Most cruising boats will want to head for **Branford Harbor** proper, to the east of the Farm River, where there are deep-water anchorages and shoreside facilities. The area between the Farm River and Johnson Point, often called **Short Beach Bay,** is the headquarters of the Yale sailing team. In recent years, Short Beach Bay has gotten some of the overflow of boaters who didn't fit in Branford Harbor, but because it's wide open to the south it rarely attracts a large crowd. Short Beach gets its name from a series of beaches less than 100 yards long, wedged between the rocky outcroppings of the pinkish Branford granite. If you're headed there, you should keep an eye out for water skiers.

Coming to **Short Beach** from the west, you'll want to give East Indies Rocks a wide berth because of the 5-foot spot 500 yards east of can "1" **[WP-124]**. If you're coming from the east, even when exiting Branford Harbor, it's best to go south of the red 2.5sec flashing bell "34" **[WP-123]** at Cow & Calf. This way you'll be sure to stay off Gull Rocks, which extend 1/2 mile south and west of Johnson Point. **Farm River Gut,** the area between Kelsey Island and Horton Point, is also a good small-boat anchorage. At high

Doing it all at sunset in Branford Harbor, CT.

The town dock on Branford Point marks the beginning of the inner harbor, which offers complete protection and has excellent facilties. You can tie up for 20 minutes at this dock to load or unload, but the harbormaster will insist that the area around the dock remain uncongested. A no-wake speed limit is enforced upstream from Branford Point.

Although the staked channel up to Bruce & Johnson's on the east shore carries 8 feet of water, the marina operators tell us that dockside depth is 6 feet. If you'd like to explore, try taking your dinghy up the creek south of Bruce & Johnson's at high tide. There have been plans to dredge the channel to 8.5 feet mlw. The depths in the channel decrease as you go up, with at least 5 feet for 0.7nm upstream from the big marinas to the Indian Neck Yacht Club.

Most of the supplies and amenities in town are scattered about rather than centrally located on the water. You'll find a small market and a laundromat across the street from Lenny's Restaurant, but for most everything else, you'll have to hail a cab.

Shoreside and Emergency Services

Airport: Tweed/New Haven (203) 469-2364
Ambulance: 911
Bus: Connecticut Transit (203) 624-0151
Coast Guard: New Haven (203) 773-2400 or VHF 16
Fire: 911 or (203) 488-7266
Harbormaster: (203) 488-3279
Hospital: Yale-New Haven (203) 785-4242
Police: 911 or (203) 481-4241 (Patrol Boat) or CB 9
Radio Telephone: VHF 27; I.D.: Bridgeport Marine Operator; VHF 25, 26, 86; I.D.: New London Marine Operator
Taxi: Branford Cab (203) 481-8342
Tow Service: Saybrook Towing & Salvage, Old Saybrook, CT (203) 388-4065 or VHF 16
Train: Amtrak 1-800-USA-RAIL
Metro-North 1-800-638-7646 ✦

tide, small outboards can run across from Farm River Gut into the river itself.

From Mansfield Point at the mouth of the Farm River, it is 1.2nm by boat to Johnson Point, the southwest boundary of **Branford Harbor;** from there it's another mile to Branford Point and the inner harbor.

Coming from any direction, the only safe approach to **Branford Harbor** is between the red flashing bell "34" **[WP-123]** at Cow & Calf, and Five Foot Rock, marked by red nun "32" **[WP-126].** Keep the red 4sec flasher "2" **[WP-125]** at Blyn Rock to starboard. Local boaters will often shoot between Taunton Rock and Jeffrey Rock from the east, or between Gull Rocks and Cow & Calf from the west, but those approaches are best left to those who know them.

Once in the outer harbor, head for green (formerly black) can "5" marking the entrance channel off of **Lovers Island.** Stay between Big Mermaid and Little Mermaid, which are clearly marked, and you won't have any trouble going up the **Branford River.** Currents in the river reach 2 to 3 knots when the tide is at full flow.

The outer harbor area between Johnson, Indian Neck, and Jeffrey points has plenty of water and good holding ground, and it offers good protection except from the south. There are a few rocks in the outer harbor, but these are well marked. The area north of the **Mermaids** has a charted depth of about 5 feet; you would be wise to stay clear of this area except when exploring in a dinghy.

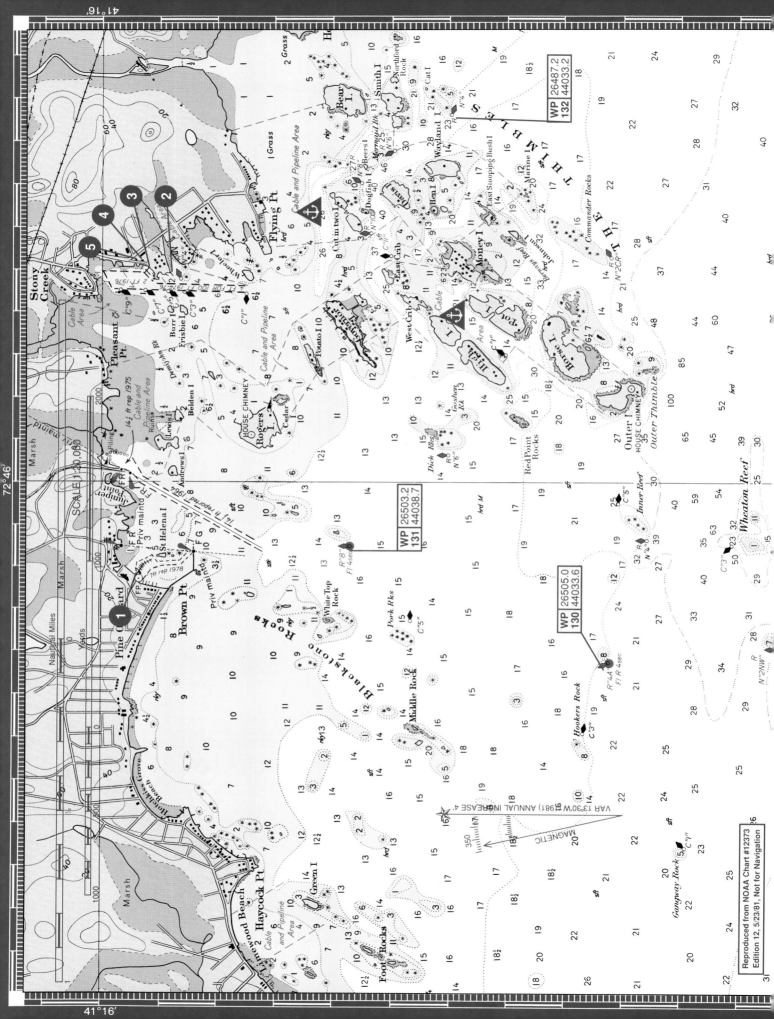

The Thimble Islands

A Wee Bit of Maine, Washed Up in the Sound

The Thimble Islands look like a piece of Maine coast that accidentally washed up in Long Island Sound. Some say there are islands enough to match each day of the year. To get that number, however, you'd have to count every rock and stone visible at high water. Even the name "Hundred Islands," coined in 1715, stretched the count a bit. If you ignore uninhabited or non-vegetive rocks, there are about 33 Thimble Islands, the largest only 10 acres.

How the Thimbles came by their name is unknown. Most likely, the title derives from the diminutive size of the islands, but could also refer to the thimbleberry, a shrub that purportedly grew on the islands at one time.

The islands are actually peaks along a pink granite ridge extending underwater from the mainland. This makes the Thimbles the only bedrock islands between New York and Nantucket–the others are all part of the glacial moraine.

In colonial times, the islands were considered too small and rocky to be of much use. A few settlers grazed sheep on the larger islands while others quarried granite, but for the most part the Thimbles went unused. Legend claims, however, that Captain Kidd found their seclusion ideal for hiding himself and his treasure. The area between the two sections of High Island is known locally as Kidd's Cove, and Money Island gets its name from the treasure Kidd supposedly buried there. While the locals didn't mind pirates burying treasure on their oases, they were inspired by the British presence during the Revolutionary War to cut down all of the islands' trees–so that enemy masts could be readily spotted in the local channels.

At the turn of the 19th century, the Thimble Islands became a popular and valuable summer resort, and many islands had houses or hotels built on them. Now the islands are all privately owned and the larger spits have at least one home on their shores. Islanders start arriving in late April and stay clear through October. A few hardy souls have even tried braving the winter, but problems caused by icing of the harbor have always made the stay impossible.

While Money Island is the most populated (the owners all hoping to find the treasure in a flower bed, no doubt), the largest island, called Horse, is owned by Yale University and is used for marine biological research. Part of Outer Island has been donated to Southern Connecticut State University and is also used as a marine research station.

The town of Stony Creek seems a quiet stepping-stone to the islands, but it still suffers from attacks of granite fever, so don't be surprised to hear rumbling beneath your feet. It's just Stony Creek Granite, the last remaining quarry in the area, cutting stone. Local residents are used to the tremors, but even they take notice when the blasters get carried away and set the window panes rattling.

Looking west over the Thimble Islands at sunset.

Marine Facilities and Services	Phone	Number of Transient Berths	Number of Transient Moorings	Seasonal/Year-round	Largest Vessel Accommodation (in feet)	Marked Entry Channel	Approach Depth (in feet)	Dockside Depth in feet at MLW	Gas/Diesel Fuel	Fuel Brand	Ramp/Dinghy Dock/Launch Service	Railway/Lift: Capacity (in tons)	Propeller/Hull Repairs	Engine Repairs: Gas/Diesel	Marine Supplies/Groceries/Bait/Ice	Showers/Laundromat	Pump-out Station	110V ★ 220V ▲ Maximum Amps	MasterCard/VISA/Diners Club/American Express	Restaurant/Snack Bar	Monitors VHF Channel
❶ Pine Orchard Yacht & Country Club	(203) 488-9250			S	54	●	9	9	GD	TEX	L	L4			S	SI		★▲100		SR	68
❷ America's Cup Rest. & Indian Point YC	(203) 481-8481	6	4	S	60	●	5	5	*DOCKAGE FOR PATRONS*						S			★120	MV	R	16
❸ Town Dock/Ferry Dock									*2 – HOUR TIE-UP FOR DINGHIES*												
❹ Thimble Marine Service	(203) 481-0590			Y					G				P	GD					MV		16
❺ Betts Marine	(203) 488-7061			S	28	●	4	2	G	MOB					S						

Information in these listings is provided by the facilities themselves. An asterisk (*) indicates that the facility did not respond to our most recent requests for information.

The Thimble Islands and Stony Creek, CT from the southeast. Moving northwest from the center foreground are Wayland, Davis, Cut-in-Two, and Wheeler islands. Governor Island, with its many summer homes, is to the upper left. *Photo © Jack McConnell*

 What To See and Do

The small town of Stony Creek is one of the prettiest places on the Sound, and it's well worth taking a walk or bike ride there, if for no other reason than to view the architecture–a mixture of Victorian gingerbread, modern, and hybrid. Among Stony Creek's other attractions are the ferry/tourboat/mailboats. The *Volsunga III* (203) 481-3345 or 488-9978, *Sea Mist II* (203) 481-4841, and *Sea Venture I* (203) 397-3921 each make hourly cruises around the islands, ferrying residents, boaters, tourists, and supplies.

Also of interest is the Puppet House Theater and Museum (203) 488-5752. Performances of popular plays and musicals are given here each evening.

If you're interested in military music, visit the Stony Creek Fife and Drum Corps, one of the country's oldest marching groups. They're headquartered in Seaside Hall, built in 1886 across the street from the town docks.

Many people visit the Thimbles to observe the seabirds. We suggest you use a dinghy, so you can make your way around the smaller islands. Also, bring a pair of binoculars and a field guide to identify the many waterfowl from afar. Please don't land, as you may upset the nesting birds.

 Where To Eat

The America's Cup Restaurant (203) 481-8481 on Indian Point overlooks the Thimbles and is Stony Creek's main eatery. Launch service is provided from the channel by one of the ferry captains. There are also two delis and a small grocery in town, all within easy walking distance of the water. For any other restaurants, a cab is required.

The Chowder Pot (203) 481-2356, serving seafood and, of course, chowder, is about 2 miles from the waterfront, on Rte. 1. They have a good brunch on Sunday and excellent bands for late-night dancing on the weekends. Lenny's (203) 488-1500 in Branford is a bit of a hike but provides free limo service to customers. For other restaurants in the area, see the previous chapter on Branford.

 Navigation and Anchorages

Use NOAA Charts 12373 (1:20,000), 12372 (1:40,000), and 12354 (1:80,000). Use tide tables for Bridgeport. High tide at Money Island is 12 minutes earlier; low tide is 23 minutes earlier. Multiply by 0.8 for height at high or low water. Mean tidal range is 6.0 feet.

As a group of islands, the Thimbles have no real port or harbor. The village of Stony Creek, about 1/2 mile north of Governor Island, serves as the supply point and landing for all the Thimbles. You can tie up your dinghy or other small boat for two-hour stays at the town dock (203) 488-9978. At low tide, there is less than 4 feet of water off the dock, so you won't want to arrive in anything other than a shallow-draft boat. Most provisions and supplies are available within a short walk of the town dock.

The cluster of islands that makes up the Thimbles is about 7.3nm by boat east of the New Haven Harbor breakwaters and 2.4nm by boat west of Sachem's Head in Guilford.

From the flashing red 4sec gong "10A" **[WP-119]** at Townshend Ledge, a course of about 80°m for 3.3nm will take you past the Branford Reef Light to a spot just south of the flashing red 4sec "28" at Negro Heads, which is west of the Thimble Islands. From the flashing red 4sec bell "10GI" **[WP-140]** off Goose Island, a course of about 305°m for 4.6nm by boat will take you to a spot south of Browns Reef, south of the Thimble Islands.

CAUTION: There have been many buoy changes in this area. We have noted the most important below, but be alert for others. Also note that buoys in this area can be difficult to follow, so study the chart before visiting.

The first thing to remember about cruising in the **Thimbles** is that the, and all their underwater obstructions are made of granite, not sand. Because most cruising boats weigh several tons, it's possible to build up a lot of momentum when traveling at only a few knots. So if you hit anything in the Thimbles, you're sure to hit it hard and suddenly, and you probably won't get off without some damage to your hull.

Approaching the islands from the east is no problem in daylight, but it can be difficult in fog or at night because there are no lighted buoys marking the way. When coming from Sachem's Head, pass **Goose Rocks Shoals** –which is marked at its southern end by the red 4sec flashing bell "22" **[WP-136]** –cautiously. Also beware of Leetes Rocks, which are totally unmarked now that red nun "2" to the southwest has been deleted.

You'll want to enter the channel at red nun "4" **[WP-132]** off **Wayland Island,** before passing red nun "6" at Mermaid Rock to starboard. Then head past Davis Island toward red nun "8." From there you have easy access to either Stony Creek or the anchorage between **Money** and **Crib** islands to the southwest. Note that red nun "10" south of Cut-in-Two Island has been moved and now hangs just south of Dogfish Point. Be sure to leave nun "10" to starboard before turning toward Stony Creek.

CAUTION: When heading southwest into the anchorage after rounding Davis Island, beware of the 3-foot spot opposite green can "11." Abeam of red nun "10," steer for can "11" rather than directly into the channel. Many boaters think they have clear passage and find out the hard way that the water shallows quickly to the south.

The anchorage, between green cans "11" off **East Crib** and "1" off **High Island,** is apt to be crowded on summer weekends. It's well protected except from the southwest, though even then the waves lose much of their force by the time they've rolled up between the islands. The bottom runs from soft to firm mud and offers a fair hold for most boats. This is the safest spot to anchor in the islands, but staying here may cost you the view of a spectacular sunset. Try to stay a bit to the northeast, so you can see the horizon between High and West Crib islands.

Much of the holding ground in other parts of the Thimbles is poor due to the rocky bottom. A strong northeast wind and an outgoing tide will give you problems, so after you've set anchor, be sure to observe your position periodically to make sure the boat isn't dragging.

There are underwater cables and pipelines everywhere among the islands. The only way you'll know you're over one is if you pull it up with your anchor. Because of the density of rocks, islands, and channels, the buoys tend to be close to the obstructions, so don't cut inside any of them. There can be strong rips on the eastern side of the islands when the tide is going out.

CAUTION: Coming from the west, tidal currents are not so strong, but the approaches are complicated by the many offshore reefs as well as the number and placement of local buoys. In this area the buoys seem to function more as obstruction markers than channel markers, so study the chart carefully and keep a sharp lookout.

Coming from **Branford Harbor,** your best course is to stay south of the red 4sec flasher "28" at Negro Heads and green can "1" at Gangway Rock. Be careful not to confuse the two channels ahead of you. To the northeast, both the green can "3" at Hookers Rock and the red 4sec flasher "4A" **[WP-130]** mark the approach to **Pine Orchard** and the Tilcon-Tomasso docks. The main approach to the **Thimbles** is farther east, south of Inner Reef.

Less than a mile west of **Stony Creek** is the tiny village and harbor of **Pine Orchard.** Heading for Pine Orchard, you'll cut northeast around can "1" at Gangway Rock before heading for the red 4sec flasher "4A." From here, make straight for the 4sec red flasher "8," and look for local aids to navigation taking you along the channel and into the harbor. A breakwater extends 300 yards southwest from Brown Point to protect the Pine Orchard yacht basin. On the west shore of the harbor is the Pine Orchard Yacht Club.

Anchoring is not permitted in the yacht basin. Just east of **Pine Orchard** is the Tilcon-Tomasso wharf, where gravel from North Branford is loaded on barges and shipped around the Northeast. The straight channel marked on the chart is for the barges, and you'll see three yellow flashing dolphins to lead the tugs into the wharf.

CAUTION: *When entering the Pine Orchard basin, be sure to avoid the chain of rocks south of Saint Helena Island. Stay close to the privately maintained marker at the end of the breakwater and give the tiny island a wide berth.*

Those who pass Pine Orchard in favor of the **Thimbles** and **Stony Creek** will continue between red nun "4" at Inner Reef and can "3" at Wheaton Reef. Both mark the channel heading east-west, not north-south, so keep both Inner Reef buoys—red nun "4" and green can "5"—to port.

Don't cut between Northwest, Browns, East, and Wheaton reefs, as many boats get hung up there. Past Inner Reef, steer northeast, keeping **Outer Island** to starboard. Then head for can "1" off **High Island.** Outer Island will be closest to you. Look for a cement seawall on its west side. Just scoot up the main channel between the two lines of islands, exiting around Davis Island (keeping it to starboard) or turning to port at can "11" to head into Stony Creek.

The same course is also best for those under sail who want to take a tour through the islands. Coming from the southeast, another approach is available. Keep East Reef green can "1" well to port and shoot between Inner Reef and Outer Island. When approaching Browns and East reefs from the south, note that lighted 4sec bell "26" **[WP-128]** has been changed from white to red.

Because of the highly variable tide and wind conditions caused by all the islands, we suggest that novices not try to sail through the **Thimbles.** Even expert sailors must proceed slowly. The channel requires precise handling because of the number of fixed and floating obstructions. It may prove safer to motor through, or at least to have the motor running, ready to pull you out of trouble.

There are many private moorings north of **Cut-in-Two Island,** but this area is unmarked and should be entered cautiously, with one eye on the depth sounder and the other on the moored boats. This is a good anchorage in early spring and late fall when fewer boats are moored.

Those boaters who are headed directly for **Stony Creek** and want to skip the islands should head northeast, being certain to keep Inner Reef and Dick Rocks well to starboard before passing between Governor and Potato islands.

CAUTION: *Red nun "6" off of Dick Rocks does not mark the passage into the Thimbles. Leave at least a 250-yard cushion to starboard when passing the buoy, and do not cut between Potato and Governor until you have left Dick Rocks well behind. Each year at least a dozen boats go aground here. In fact, you may recall seeing photos of a Coast Guard cutter sitting high and dry on these rocks in February 1989.*

Don't try passing between **Potato** and **Cedar** or **Rogers** islands, as there are too many rocks and shoals for safety. After passing between Potato and **Governor** islands, follow the marked and dredged channel up to the turning basin. Cans "1," "3," "5," and "7" leading into Stony Creek have been changed from black to green, and can "9" has been deleted.

The town maintains a no-wake speed limit within 100 yards of shore. You'll see water skiers and jet skiers around Stony Creek and the Thimbles, even in the anchorage between High and Pot islands, so keep an eye out and mind your speed.

 Shoreside and Emergency Services

Airport: Tweed/New Haven (203) 469-2364
Ambulance: 911
Coast Guard: New Haven (203) 773-2400 or VHF 16
Fire: 911 or (203) 488-7266
Ferry: *Volsunga III* (203) 488-9978 or 481-3345
 (VHF 16 or 68 for launch service)
 Sea Mist II (203) 481-4841
 Sea Ventures I (203) 397-3921
Harbormaster: (203) 488-3279
Police: 911 or (203) 481-4241 or CB 9
Radio Telephone: VHF 27; I.D.: Bridgeport
 Marine Operator
Taxi: Branford Cab (203) 481-8342
Tow Service: Saybrook Towing & Salvage,
 Old Saybrook, CT (203) 388-4065
 or VHF 16 ◆

THE THIMBLE ISLANDS AND THE LEGACY OF CAPTAIN KIDD

Three of the Thimbles–High, Money, and Pot islands–are associated in legend with Captain Kidd. This is not surprising, for there are stories along the whole North Atlantic seaboard about this most famous of English pirates. Born in Scotland about 1645, he became a ship owner and captain in New York. During King William's War, he and his ship performed valiantly against French privateers on the New England coast. As a result, when it was decided in 1695 to send a privateer against the pirates in the Indian Ocean, Kidd, who was in London at the time, was chosen to command the ship. The expedition was largely financed by a group of English nobleman headed by the Earl of Bellomont, newly appointed governor of New York and New England.

Kidd sailed from England in April 1696 in the *Adventure Galley*. In New York he completed his crew with what seems to have been an unsavory lot of rascals and sailed for the Indian Ocean. Here he was dogged by misfortune. His ship was leaky, cholera killed a third of his crew, and the rest, having been out nearly a year without pay or profit, turned mutinous. Whether under their threats or of his own free will, Kidd abandoned legal privateering for piracy. Bad luck continued to follow him; he captured few ships, and only one of them, the *Quedagh Merchant*, carried cargo of any value. Abandoning the *Adventure Galley*, he sailed in the *Quedagh Merchant* for the West Indies, only to find on his arrival that the alarm was out and he was wanted for piracy.

Leaving his prize at Hispaniola, Kidd with a few companions sailed in a smaller vessel for New York. He anchored in Oyster Bay, Long Island, and through an old lawyer friend commenced negotiations with Lord Bellomont. He was finally persuaded to come ashore, and in July 1699 landed in Boston. Here he was promptly arrested and shipped to London for trial. The trial was long delayed, but in May 1701 Kidd was found guilty on three counts of piracy and hanged.

Kidd's property was seized by the Crown and sold. As for the *Quedagh Merchant* and her cargo, they seem to have been sold in the West Indies by Kidd's abandoned crew and the proceeds rapidly dissipated. Nevertheless, perhaps because of Kidd's fame, which far outran his performance, within 50 years after his death there had sprung up a multitude of legends mainly concerned with treasure allegedly hidden by him. How many optimistic souls have spent time, effort, and money in chasing these will-'o-the-wisps in the intervening 300 years is beyond calculation.

Certainly by the year 1800 it was well established in local folklore that Captain Kidd had paid a visit to the Thimble Islands. There were circumstantial accounts of a mysterious ship that had lain concealed in the natural harbor at High Island, and of the unwary villagers who had rowed out, to discover almost too late to make their escape the true nature of the craft and its piratical crew. From here it was only a step to the belief that treasure must have been buried there, or on one of the neighboring islands. Many have searched, but with one small exception the only gold produced has been in the pockets of the hotelkeepers who kept the legend alive as an added attraction for visitors to the islands. In 1924, one Charles Burns, a New Haven fireman, found in the sand a curious gold ring, later pronounced to be of East Indian workmanship. Since he steadfastly refused to identify the spot on the island where he found it, the incident only seemed to reinforce the hopes of treasure hunters.

In the 1920s High Island was reputed to have served as a headquarters for rum-runners. It would indeed be strange if none of the Thimbles had served to alleviate the great thirst that arose during the Prohibition years.

Since 1909 the island has been owned by the Buccaneers Club, but there are no reports of passing ships having been seized piratically.

Excerpted with permission from a *Brief History of the Thimble Islands* by Archibald Hanna, Archon Books, for the Branford Historical Society, 1971.

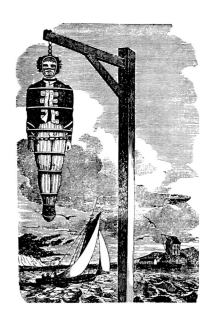

The body of Captain William Kidd hanging in chains near Tilbury Fort, England. Kidd was executed at Wapping-on-the-Thames on May 23, 1701.

Engraving from *Pirates and Buccaneers of the Atlantic Coast* by Edward R. Snow; Yankee Publishing Co., Boston, 1944.

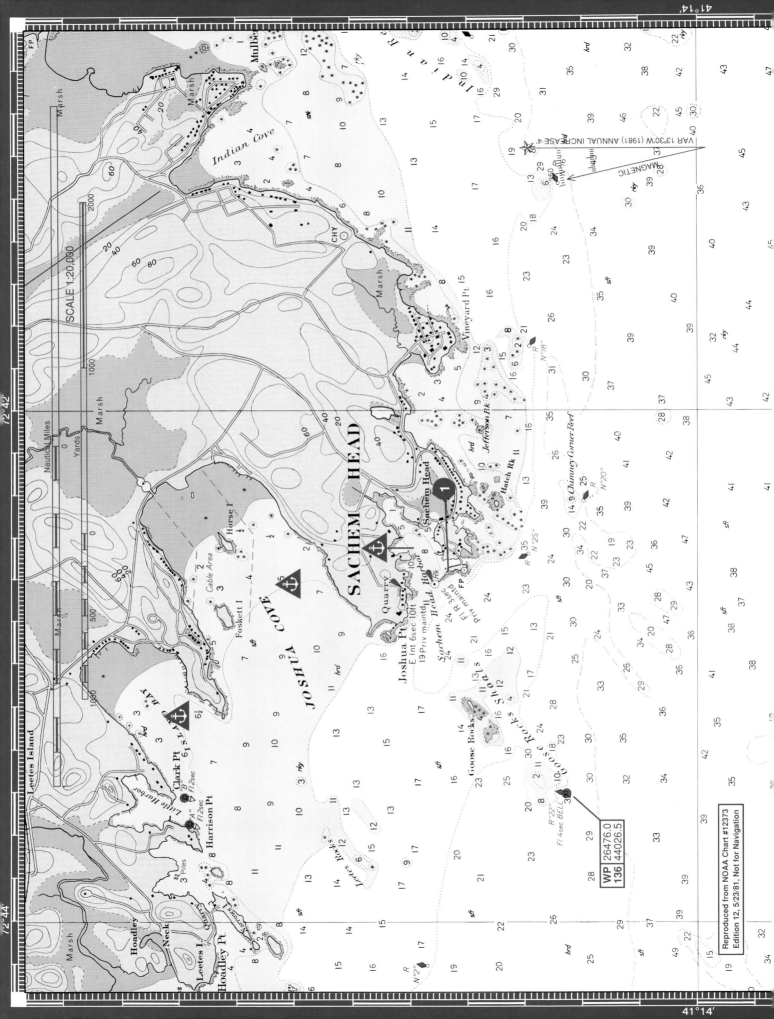

Tales You Hear, Heads You Lose

There are places all over Long Island Sound with names rich in lore and legend, but none with a bloodier story behind it than Sachem's Head in Guilford.

The time was the summer of 1637 and the circumstance was the Pequot War, by which means the English settlers of Connecticut intended to eliminate the aggressive and powerful Pequot tribe that controlled the eastern end of the state.

The remnants of the Pequot nation after the massacre at Mystic traveled westward down the Connecticut coast toward what is now Fairfield. The Pequot families could only move slowly and were forced to break up into separate parties to forage for food.

A pursuing force of Mohegans, under the leadership of the sachem Uncas, was gaining rapidly on the straggling Pequot survivors; and at the same time, an English force chased them by boat. Uncas and his warriors finally found a small party of Pequots camped at the head of what is now called "Bloody Cove" in Sachem's Head. One of the two lesser Pequot sachems there was killed, and the other, with

a few followers, escaped onto the peninsula that forms the western shore of Sachem's Head Harbor.

Pursued by the Mohegans, the remaining Pequots were forced to swim across the harbor from Prospect Point to Uncas Point, where Uncas and his men were waiting for them. The sachem was executed and the others taken prisoner. Legend has it that the sachem's head was placed in the fork of an oak tree overlooking the Sound, where it remained for years as a grisly reminder of Uncas' victory.

The end of the Pequot War came shortly after, in a swamp at Southport, where the remaining Pequots were killed by the English. As for the tree that held the sachem's skull on Uncas Point, it is long gone—as is the bluff on which it stood—destroyed by 19th-century quarrymen.

 ### What To See and Do

Sachem's Head is a small section of the larger town of Guilford, so for information about sights, activities, and restaurants, please see the following chapter on Guilford, Madison, and Falkner Island.

 ### Navigation and Anchorages

Use NOAA Charts 12373 (1:20,000), 12372 (1:40,000), and 12354 (1:80,000). Use tide tables for Bridgeport. High tide at Sachem's Head is 11 minutes earlier; low tide is 15 minutes earlier. Multiply by 0.8 for height at high or low water. Mean tidal range is 5.8 feet.

Sachem's Head Harbor is 2.5nm by boat from Flying Point in Stony Creek, 3.0nm by boat west of Guilford Harbor, and 23.6nm by boat northeast of Port Jefferson on Long Island.

From the flashing red 4sec bell "10GI" **[WP-140]** south of Goose Island, a course of about 340°m for 3.1nm by boat will take you to a spot just in front of the entrance to Sachem's Head Harbor. From the flashing red 4sec bell "26" **[WP-128]** south of Brown's and East Reefs, a course of

Sachem's Head Harbor from the south. The Sachem's Head Yacht Club on Prospect Point is to the left.

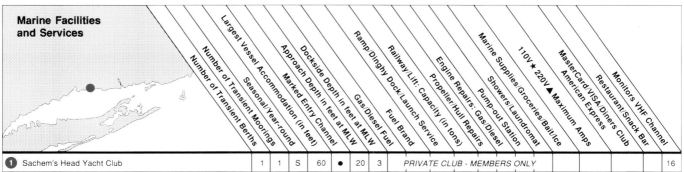

Marine Facilities and Services	Number of Transient Berths	Number of Transient Moorings	Seasonal/Year-round	Largest Vessel Accommodation	Approach Depth (in feet)	Marked Entry Channel	Dockside Depth in feet at MLW	Gas/Diesel Fuel	Fuel Brand	Ramp/Dinghy Dock Launch Service	Railway/Lift: Capacity (in tons)	Propeller/Hull Repairs	Engine Repairs: Gas/Diesel	Pump-out Station	Marine Supplies/Groceries/Bait/Ice	Showers/Laundromat	110V ★ 220V ▲ Maximum Amps	MasterCard/VISA/Diners Club American Express	Restaurant/Snack Bar	Monitors VHF Channel
① Sachem's Head Yacht Club	1	1	S	60	●	20	3	*PRIVATE CLUB - MEMBERS ONLY*												16

Information in these listings is provided by the facilities themselves. An asterisk (*) indicates that the facility did not respond to our most recent requests for information.

about 90°m for 2.2nm will take you to the flashing red 4sec bell "22" **[WP-136]** marking Goose Island Shoals; from here you will head to the red nun "2S" before swinging to a course of about 340°m and heading to the entrance of Sachem's Head Harbor.

CAUTION: *There have been many buoy changes in this area. We have noted the most important below, but be alert for others.*

All is quiet and civilized in **Sachem's Head** these days. With the old chief's skull long gone, the gracious Sachem's

Head Yacht Club presides over one of the quietest harbors you'll ever visit. The club is located on what is called **Prospect Point,** an island connected to the mainland by a footbridge just to the south of the harbor entrance. You'll find no place to land apart from the club, and if you head ashore, you'll find that the surrounding area consists of nothing more than beautiful woods and private homes. If you're looking for dinner or supplies, Sachem's Head is not the place to stop. Rather, you should head for Stony Creek to the west or for Guilford to the east.

Approaching **Sachem's Head** from the south, you have a clear shot up to the red 3sec flasher on the south side of

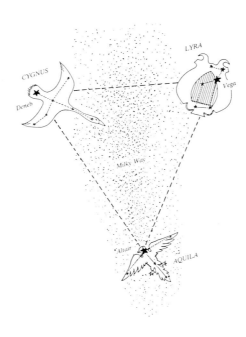

JULY SKIES:
The Summer Triangle and the Milky Way

High overhead on warm July nights, three bright stars twinkle in the shape of a huge triangle. To the south, at the tip of this Summer Triangle, is the star Altair. It's the eye of the eagle in the constellation Aquila. The two uppermost stars in the triangle are Vega to the west, part of the Lyra the Harp, and Deneb to the east, the tail feather of Cygnus the Swan. Cygnus is sometimes called the Northern Cross because its stars form a crucifix.

Notice the subtle color differences in these stars. Vega and Deneb are both hot, white stars, while Altair burns a cooler orange-red. Vega is the brightest of the three, and Altair the closest to earth at only 16 light years.

Luminous Deneb is the most fascinating of the three. It outshines most other stars in the July skies, though it's more than 9,600 trillion miles away. The light you see from it now took 1,600 years to reach Earth.

Running through the center of the Summer Triangle is a shimmering band of faint light called the Milky Way. The best time to see this is during a new moon, with a crystal clear sky. The hazy glow of the Milky Way is actually a view through the plane of our huge galaxy, including its dense starlit center.

Our solar system is located out along the edge of the spiral-shaped galaxy where there are fewer stars than in the center. But when we turn our gaze toward the galaxy's core, we see a concentrated region of stars, gas, and dust. The Greeks named this the Milky Way, believing their mother goddess, Hera, had squirted milk across the heavens.

Contributed by Elinor DeWire, assistant at the Mystic Seaport Planetarium and a freelance writer.

the harbor; this marker is maintained by the yacht club from June to September. From here, a turn to starboard will place you smack-dab in the tiny rock-ribbed harbor, which is about 0.3nm long, 300 yards wide, and has 5 to 10 feet of water at the floats and moorings. This snug size offers good protection except against southwesterly winds, which are prevailing during the summer. There is usually room in the harbor in the spring and fall, but during the summer, space is at a premium. There may be guest moorings available through the yacht club; we suggest you call ahead to avoid entering the harbor only to find no place to stay.

Heading in from the east requires some caution, since the Coast Guard has recently made several changes to the buoys shown on the chart. To begin with, can "1" at **Indian Reef** is now green and can be difficult to see. Your next marker is the red nun "16" southeast of **Vineyard Point.** The Coast Guard has removed nun "18"–which was due south of Vineyard Point–and nun "2S"–which used to lie 400 yards south of the yacht club. The rocks these buoys once marked are still present, however, so check your chart carefully and maintain your course.

Coming from the east, we suggest you head south of red nun "20" at **Chimney Corner Reef.** From here, you will continue west for a few hundred yards before heading north to the harbor in order to clear the rocks to the south of the yacht club.

Approaching the harbor from Stony Creek and the **Thimble Islands** also requires some caution. The Coast Guard has removed red nun "2," which was 0.6nm south of Hoadley Point. Your next concern will be the unmarked Leetes Rocks, which are exposed at low water, and another shallow spot 200 yards south of the rock. There is also a shallow spot 300 yards northeast of the northernmost rock.

If you are offshore and heading east into the harbor, you will want to pass south of flashing red 4sec bell "22" **[WP-136]** marking the southern end of **Goose Rocks Shoals.** In fact, you should stay at least 300 yards south and east of these rocks in order to avoid the extending shoals.

You probably won't want to anchor in **Joshua Cove, Island Bay,** or **Little Harbor,** all to the north and west of Sachem's Head. Just as the locals claim that the proper name for their harbor is the possessive Sachem's Head, so they argue that NOAA also misnamed "Joshua Cove," which should be "Great Harbor," as well as "Joshua Point," which should be "Uncas Point." It is the unnamed peninsula

between Great Harbor and Island Bay which is, in fact, the real Joshua Point.

Despite these debates, you may find fairly good protection in the area marked "Joshua Cove" on your chart, though it will get hairy in weather out of the south or southwest–which is prevalent during the summer. At low tide, you'll find about 6 to 10 feet of water up to **Foskett Island,** and then 2 to 3 feet in to the head of the cove. The soft mud bottom makes fair holding ground.

Island Bay can also be used as an anchorage, though not many people choose it as the waters get rough in a southwesterly breeze, as does the northern part of **Joshua Cove.** In the northernmost part of Island Bay is Shell Beach, which is run by the town.

Little Harbor is a snug little gunkhole just west of Island Bay, with 2 to 3 feet of water at low tide. Jetties protect both sides of the entrance between Harrison and Clark points. Unfortunately, it also gets rough when the winds blow out of the south, especially due to its shallowness.

If your boat draws less than 3 feet, you may want to head into the unnamed cove between **Harrison Point** and **Narrows Island.** Note that the rocks shown on the chart at the entrance to this cove are actually a bit further to the northeast.

 ## Shoreside and Emergency Services

Airport: Tweed/New Haven (203) 787-8285
Ambulance: 911
Coast Guard: New Haven (203) 773-2400 or VHF 16
Fire: 911 or (203) 453-8056
Harbormaster: Guilford (203) 453-8092 or VHF 16 or CB 13
Sachem's Head (summer) (203) 453-9207
Police: 911 or (203) 453-8061 or CB 9
Guilford Marine Patrol VHF 16
Radio Telephone: VHF 27; I.D.: Bridgeport Marine Operator;
VHF 25, 26, 86; I.D.: New London Marine Operator
Taxi: Guilford Cab and Transportation (203) 453-2264
Tow Service: Saybrook Towing & Salvage, Old Saybrook, CT (203) 388-4065 or VHF 16 ◆

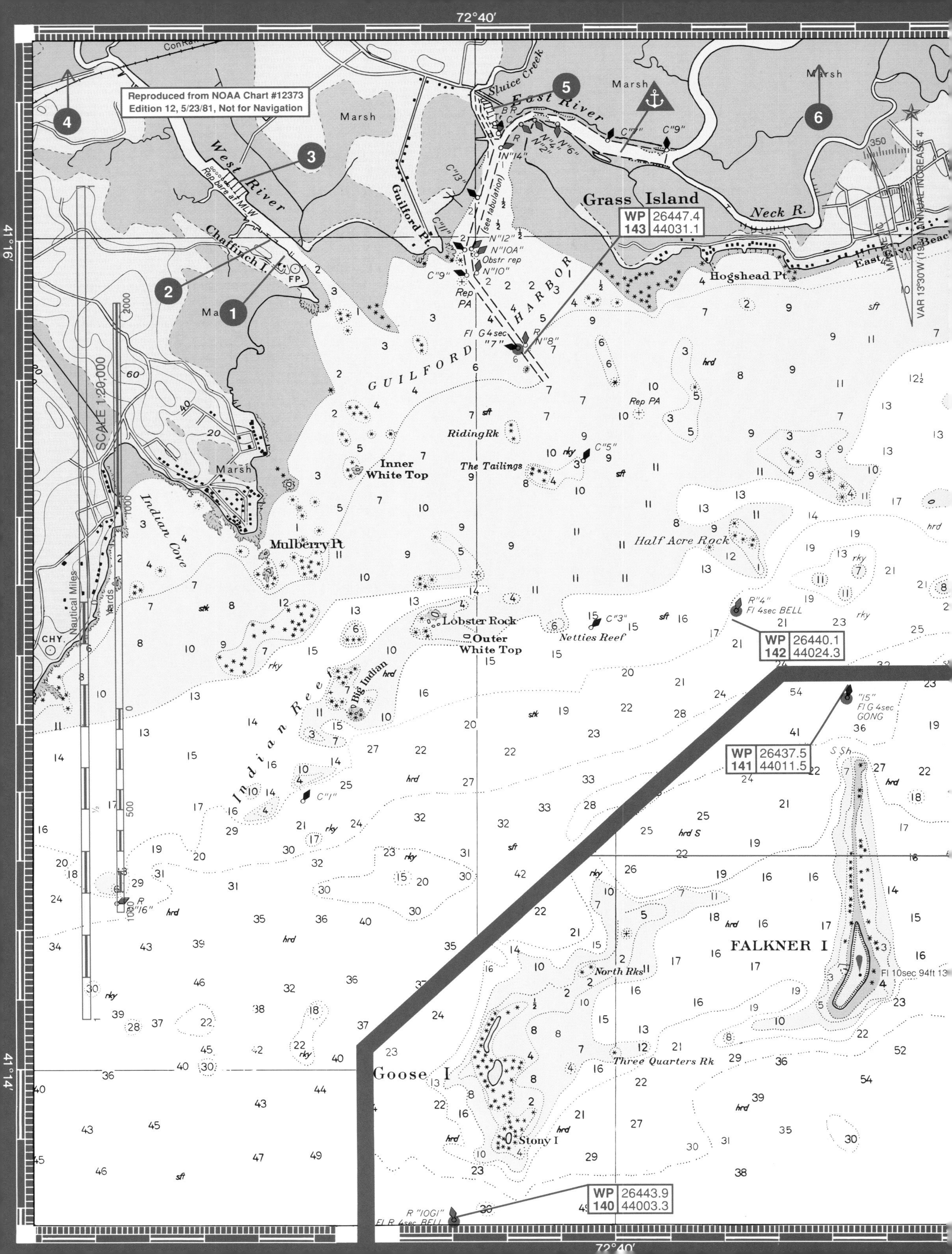

72°40'

41°16'

41°14'

Reproduced from NOAA Chart #12373
Edition 12, 5/23/81, Not for Navigation

ConRd.

Marsh

Sluice Creek

East River

Marsh

Marsh

West River

Red bare at MLW

Guilford Pt.

Grass Island

Neck R.

WP 143 | 26447.4 / 44031.1

Hogshead Pt.

East River Beach

VAR 13°30'W (10° ANNUAL INCREASE 4')

Chaffinch I.

FP.

Ma

GUILFORD HARBOR

Rep PA

Fl G 4sec "7"

N"8"

Riding Rk

The Tailings

C"5"

Rep PA

Half Acre Rock

rky

hrd

SCALE 1:20,000

Inner White Top

Indian Cove

Mulberry Pt

Marsh

CHY.

Nautical Miles

Yards

stk

rky

Lobster Rock

Outer White Top

Big Indian

Netties Reef

C"3"

sft

R"4" Fl 4sec BELL

WP 142 | 26440.1 / 44024.3

Indian Reef

C"1"

rky

hrd

"I5" Fl G 4sec GONG

WP 141 | 26437.5 / 44011.5

S Sh

FALKNER I

Fl 10sec 94ft 13

hrd

R "6"

hrd

North Rks

Goose I

Three Quarters Rk

Stony I

hrd

hrd

sft

R "IOGI" Fl R 4sec BELL

WP 140 | 26443.9 / 44003.3

72°40'

1 2 3 4 5 6

Guilford, Madison,
and Falkner Island

Shed No Teardwops for
Those Cwazy Wabbits

Led by the Reverend Henry Whitfield, the colonists who settled Guilford bought their land from the local Indians parcel by parcel. When a town was officially established out of these bits and pieces in 1639, it became the last independent colony in Connecticut, taking its place alongside Hartford, Saybrooke, and New Haven.

Rev. Whitfield also bought the town of Madison from the Menunkatuck Indians. Much like other coastal Connecticut towns, Madison went through a period, right after the Revolution, when fishing was crucial. The catch here was largely whitefish, used as fertilizer. A porpoise fishery also arose in Madison, providing lamp oil in the squalid tradition of whaling. During the 1800s, the town turned its focus to shipbuilding, making only a modest impact in comparison to more major ports like Essex. And today Madison is a quiet, residential town known for the extensive beaches and marshland at Hammonasset State Park.

Shaped like a teardrop and located more than 3 miles south of Guilford, Falkner Island gets its name from the many falcons which once lived there. The island's lighthouse, built on top of sand and boulders, was originally erected in 1802. After a serious fire destroyed the keeper's house in 1976, the light was fully automated. Today, you can still see the 46-foot white octagonal tower, the old fog signal building, and the boathouse by the breakwater, but you'll have to watch out for the many rabbits underfoot. It seems the island is overrun by the cute, furry beasts every few years. Environmentalists sponsor a round-up at these times and give the animals away to local children as pets.

Visitors to Falkner should know that the island is one of the most important tern nesting grounds in New England

What remains of the old lighthouse on Falkner Island. The island is now part of the Stewart B. McKinney National Wildlife Refuge.

and is now part of the McKinney Coastal Wildlife Refuge. No one is allowed on the island during the nesting season of May 15 to August 15, and camping at other times is discouraged. During the winter and early spring, harbor and gray seals occasionally visit nearby Goose Island, undoubtedly attracted by the plentiful fish.

 What To See and Do

Guilford's town green may be one of the most beautiful in New England. Surrounded by small shops and stores, the green hosts a continuous lineup of special events throughout the year, such as strawberry and apple festivals, fife and drum musters, concerts, a handicraft fair, folk dancing, and more. Cab service is available if the weather is bad or the

Marine Facilities and Services		Number of Transient Berths	Number of Transient Moorings	Seasonal/year-round	Largest Vessel Accommodation (in feet)	Approach Depth in feet at MLW	Marked Entry Channel	Dockside Depth in feet at MLW	Gas/Diesel Fuel	Ramp/Dinghy Dock/Launch Service	Railway Lift: Capacity	Engine Repairs: Propeller/Hull Repairs	Marine Repairs: Gas/Diesel	Pump-out Station	Showers/Laundromat	Marine Supplies/Groceries/Bait/Ice	110V ★ 220V ▲ Maximum Amps	MasterCard/VISA/American Express/Diners Club	Restaurant/Snack Bar	Monitors VHF Channel
❶ Browns Boat Yard (p. 189)	(203) 453-6283	2		Y	38		4	4	G			L15	PH	G			SI	★20	MV		16
❷ Bayberry Creek Marina	(203) 853-0874	1			30			4										★30			
❸ Guilford Yacht Club (p. 186)	(203) 453-8746	20		S	60	●	8	8		RD					●	SL	I	★50			16
❹ Guilford Boat Yards (p. 189)	(203) 453-5031			Y	35		1	6				L15	PH	GD		S	S	★	MV		
❺ Guilford Town Marina	(203) 453-8092	1		S	36	●	3.5	3.5		R								★30		R	16
❻ Beebe Marine	(203) 245-8665			Y	26		4	9		R		L7	PH	GD			S		MV		

Information in these listings is provided by the facilities themselves. An asterisk (*) indicates that the facility did not respond to our most recent requests for information.

Own a home for your boat as comfortable as your own.

That's what we offer at the Guilford Yacht Club Marina, a dockominium of 193 slips for 30 to 60 foot boats surrounded by beautiful tidal wetlands and unblemished waterviews.

Guilford itself is one of Connecticut's loveliest historic communities with quaint shops, antique homes and fine restaurants, just 12 miles from New Haven, less than 45 miles from Stamford and Hartford. A location with easy access to both your boat and open water.

For you and your family, dockominium ownership means more than boating. It includes membership in the Guilford Yacht Club and common interest ownership of the proposed clubhouse which will have an in-ground pool, sunning decks, kitchen, laundry and shower facilities.* *All the comforts of home away from home.*

The Guilford Yacht Club Marina offers:
- A beautiful natural setting
- New 1000 foot straight channel to Long Island Sound
- Draft of 8' at mean low tide
- No bridges
- State-of-the-art wooden docks
- Dockside storage lockers
- Utility columns for power, phone and cable TV hookup
- 35 ton lift and launching facility
- Pump-out facilities
- Fee simple title

379 New Whitfield Street, Guilford, CT 06437 (203) 453-8746

Sales Office open 9AM-5PM or by appointment

Directions: 1.8 miles south of exit 58 off I-95

This is a Connecticut Condominium Association and it is not registered in the State of New York. *Offered by Public Offering Statement only.

GUILMAR, INC.

◄ THE GUILFORD ►
YACHT CLUB MARINA

one-mile walk from the harbor is just too far. Buses also stop in town at the green; their schedules are available at the dockmaster's office (203) 453-8092, next door to the Coast Guard Auxiliary (203) 453-8046.

Guilford is quite proud of its heritage, and has several historical homes open to the public. Reverend Whitfield's stone house was built in 1639, making it the oldest house in Connecticut and the oldest stone house in New England (203) 453-2457. Located about half a mile up Whitfield Street from the town marina, the house is now preserved as a museum. Also visit the Hyland House (203) 453-9477 and the Thomas Griswold House (203) 453-3176, both located in town. Madison also has its share of historical attractions; both the Allis-Bushnell House and Museum (203) 245-4567 and the Tuxis Farm Center for Colonial Arts (203) 245-4798 are open to the public, and either will make for a nice day trip.

If you're more interested in crafts than in history, head on over to the Guilford Handcrafts Center (203) 453-5947 where you'll find a shop, gallery, and a handcraft school devoted to fine arts and handmade items.

There is also plenty to do down at the waterfront. The town beach, west of the town marina, is open to the public and often attracts a great crowd during the summer. You may also swim off the beaches on Grass Island, across from the town marina, though the north beach just up the turn of the East River has the best water. At high tide you can take your dinghy up into any of the local marshes to catch some crabs, or perhaps just to explore and watch the birds.

During the summer, the major draw in this area is Hammonasset State Park (203) 245-2785 in Madison. The beaches here are some of the the finest in Connecticut and are open year-round. Camping is also allowed during the summer. No docking or anchoring is allowed off the beaches, so you'll need to take a cab or ride a bicycle in order to reach Hammonassett.

 ## Where To Eat

Right down at the docks in Guilford, you'll find two restaurants, The Dock House (203) 453-6884 and the Little Stone House (203) 453-2566, serving seafood, steaks, and pasta at reasonable prices, and sometimes offering live entertainment.

Further from the water, to the east of downtown Guilford on the Boston Post Road, you can order sit-down or take-out meals at Ken's Pizza (203) 245-9742. Or try Chips Pub II (203) 453-0615 for great baby back ribs and other local delicacies.

Heading east to Madison, on West Wharf Road you'll find the Dolly Madison Inn & Restaurant (203) 245-7377 with a seafood, pasta, and chicken menu. You may also want to try the Wharf Restaurant (203) 245-0005, offering great seafood, steak, and chicken. Or head to the Hob Nob (203) 245-2043 for traditional American cuisine.

 ## Navigation and Anchorages

Use NOAA Charts 12373 (1:20,000), 12372 (1:40,000), and 12354 (1:80,000). Use tide tables for Bridgeport. High tide at Falkner Island is 14 minutes earlier; low tide is 25 minutes earlier. Multiply by 0.8 for height at high or low water. Mean tidal range is 5.8 feet.

The approach to Guilford Harbor, beginning at the red 4sec flashing bell "4" at Half Acre Rock, is 5.0nm by boat east of Outer Island in the Thimbles, and 5.9nm by boat west of Clinton Harbor. Mattituck Inlet on Long Island is 15.0nm to the south-southeast.

From flashing green 4sec gong "15," a course of due north magnetic for 1.7nm by boat will take you to flashing red 4sec bell "4;" from here, a course of about 335°m for 0.8nm will take you to the green 4sec flasher "7" **[WP-143]** at the mouth of the Guilford Harbor entrance channel.

CAUTION: There have been many buoy changes in this area. We have noted the most important below, but be alert for others.

Entering **Guilford Harbor** will offer no problems as long as you follow the buoys, though there are some rocks and other foul ground outside the harbor entrance. When coming from **Sachem's Head Harbor,** 2.9nm by boat to

CONNECTICUT YANKEES IN KING GEORGE'S PORT

One of Connecticut's most glorious moments in the Revolutionary War was the daring and successful raid on a British fleet anchored at Sag Harbor, Long Island that was launched from the shores of Guilford in 1777. The raid was in retaliation for a British attack on Darien a month earlier, and the prime mover in the episode was Colonel Return Jonathan Meigs of Middletown.

Embarking at New Haven with about 230 men in 13 whaleboats protected by two armed sloops, Meigs' force sailed to Guilford, where they picked up another 170 men. On the afternoon of May 23, the force left from Sachem's Head for Sag Harbor, arriving at Southold at 6 o'clock. The boats were carried overland to Shelter Island Sound and proceeded on to Sag Harbor.

There the dauntless Colonials hid the boats in the woods and broke up into several smaller groups, coming within 200 yards of the British encampment before being noticed. In the ensuing battle, the Americans sunk a dozen British ships at anchor in the harbor. Some of those ships went to the bottom with large stores of supplies for the British army of occupation in New York. Six Redcoats were killed and 90 more were captured and taken back, along with a healthy load of provisions.

Twenty-four hours after they had left Guilford, Colonel Meigs' force arrived back in Connecticut, having suffered no casualties, and were cheered as heroes of the Revolution. Congress later awarded Meigs a sword and memorial as reward for his work.

Less than a month later, the British took their revenge. On June 17, troops landed at Sachem's Head and burned a house and two barns belonging to Solomon Leete, one of the large clan of Leetes settled in the Guilford area. The British also carried off some livestock.

It wasn't only the soldiers that behaved bravely in defending the young nation against the British. People like the Leetes living on the Connecticut coast during the war were constantly on guard against British raids. Those property owners who braved the danger by staying put and acting as lookouts for the neighboring towns were among the unsung heroes of the Revolution.

---

the west, you will want to keep red nun "16" to port and stay to the south of green can "1" (formerly black) at Indian Reef. Remember that nuns "2S" and "18," south of Sachem's Head, have been removed. From Indian Reef it is about 0.8nm northeast to green can "3" (formerly black) at Netties Reef and the approach to the harbor.

CAUTION: *Do not let the strong wind and currents in this area set you inside the buoy line and onto Indian Reef or The Tailings.*

When coming from **Clinton** and other points east, your safest route follows a path south of Madison Reef and red nun "14" **[WP-147]** at Charles Reef. Note that if you're using an older NOAA chart, can "1" and red nun "2" at Madison Reef have now been eliminated. Always pass red flashing bell buoy "4" **[WP-142]** marking Half Acre Rock to the left, and don't round it too sharply. Note that bell "4" has been relocated slightly to the south.

Turning north toward the harbor, you will pass The Tailings green can "5" (formerly black) to port before making your turn into the dredged channel. If you are boating late in the season, you may not see the lighted green 4sec buoy "7" **[WP-143]** at the entrance, since it is

removed by the Coast Guard in December. Watch out for shoaling around red nun "10."

All boaters should note that nuns "8," "10A," "2," "4," and "6," as well as cans "7" and "9" in the **East River** have been removed. The black and red split-channel marker at the entrance to Sluice Creek is also gone.

The channel into the marinas and the harbor of refuge in the **East River** carries about 4 feet of water at low tide. However, at the approach to the town marina on Sluice Creek, there is shoaling to about 2.5 feet in the channel, so it's best to go in at high water. All slips and moorings at the town marina are reserved for residents, but the dockmaster may be able to find a place for you if someone is away cruising. If no room is available at the inn, just drop your hook beyond the town moorings in the dredged basin up the East River, where you will have plenty of company on weekends. You can then take a dinghy into the town launching ramp and tie up behind its floating dock.

Use the same approaches and cautions for the **West River** as for the **East River,** but head northwest from Netties Reef green can "3."

The new Guilford Yacht Club dockominium project begun in 1988 is nearly completed. New range lights should be installed by spring of 1990. The privately-marked channel has been dredged to 8 feet and the bar at the river mouth has been removed. Dredging in the spring and fall will continue to widen the channel from 60 to 80 feet. GYC (203) 453-8746 will have some transient docking space.

Both the outer harbor and the East and West rivers are patrolled by police boats from Guilford and Madison. A speed limit of 4-mph is strictly enforced in the channel and the rivers. The only gas available in the Guilford Harbor area is at Brown's Boat Yard on the west side of the West River. Beyond the Guilford Yacht Club there's shallow water at low tide up to the railroad bridge and beyond to the Guilford Boat Yard. The current here runs about 1 knot.

Falkner Island Light stands 94 feet above the water and lies about 3.5nm south-southeast of the Guilford Town Marina. The light is 3.1nm southeast of Sachem's Head Harbor and 6.7nm southwest of Cedar Island in Clinton.

A depth of over 10 feet can be carried between **Falkner** and **Goose** islands by staying in the center of the passage and following a course of about 40°m to gong "15" **[WP-141]**, or 220°m from the gong. This should keep you clear of the 8-foot and 11-foot spots.

CAUTION: If you want to go between the islands, go slowly. Divers tell us that there are many uncharted rocks and plenty of wrecks. You also have to be careful of the tidal *currents of 1 to 2 knots, which can set you well off course. Many boaters regret trying to cross the bar that extends almost half a mile north of the island to the green flashing 4sec gong "15" [WP-141].*

The west side of **Falkner** is a nice place for a swim on hot summer afternoons, but again be careful of the currents–the mainland is a long way off. On relatively calm nights you can settle into the lee of one of the islands for an anchorage, but the islands don't offer much protection. Note that the red 6sec flasher "KB" at **Kimberly Reef** to the east of Falkner Island is now red and green.

☎ Shoreside and Emergency Services

Airport: Tweed-New Haven (203) 787-8285
　　　　　Action Airlines 1-800-243-8623
Ambulance: 911
Coast Guard: New Haven (203) 773-2400 or VHF 16
Fire: 911 or (203) 453-8056
Harbormaster: (203) 453-8092 or VHF 16 or CB 13
Police: 911 or (203) 453-8061 or CB 9
　　　　Guilford Marine Patrol VHF 16
Radio Telephone: VHF 27; I.D.: Bridgeport
　　　　　　Marine Operator
　　　　　　VHF 25, 26, 86; I.D.: New London
　　　　　　Marine Operator
Taxi: Guilford Cab and Transportation (203) 453-2264
Tow Service: Saybrook Towing & Salvage, Old
　　　　　Saybrook, CT (203) 388-4065 or VHF 16
Train: Amtrak 1-800-USA-RAIL
　　　　Metro-North 1-800-638-7646　　◆

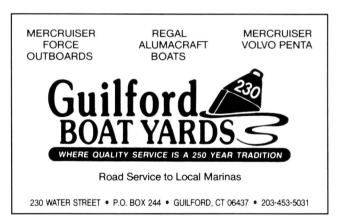

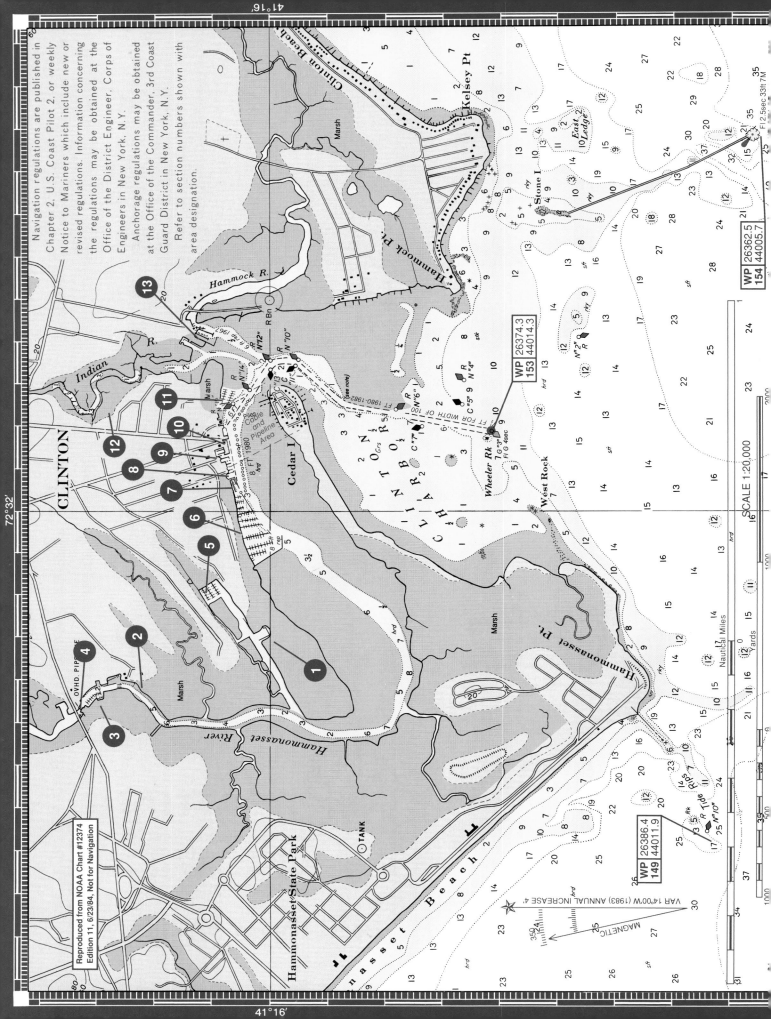

To Preach, Teach, and Captain Ships

In its early days, Clinton was graced with the presence of two outstanding citizens; both were men of the cloth. The Reverend Abraham Pierson held classes in the local parsonage of the "Collegiate School" during the year 1701; classes which turned out to be the first in the long and distinguished history of Yale University.

Clinton's other outstanding man of the cloth was Reverend Jared Eliot, a preacher said to have delivered more than 4,000 sermons, never missing a Sunday in nearly 40 years. Beyond his sermons, Eliot achieved fame as one of New England's leading physicians and as the discoverer of a way to convert black sand, found on many coastal beaches, into usable iron. This breakthrough earned Eliot a membership in the Royal Society of London.

The area we now call Clinton was originally called *Homonoscitt*. By the time the village was incorporated as a township in 1667, the name had been changed to Kenilworth. Over the next century the small settlement became Killingworth, and that name stuck, at least in part. In 1838 the township split in two, the northern retaining the old name while the southern half became Clinton, named after DeWitt Clinton, the Governor of New York who was largely responsible for the Erie Canal.

Cedar Island and Clinton Harbor, CT.

Like many coastal Connecticut towns during the 19th century, Clinton had a sizable shipbuilding industry. At one time there were three shipyards located along the Indian River in the center of town, which is now mostly marsh, one local resident even became famous as a captain: Charles W. Morgan led the ship that bears his name on many a voyage around the globe's oceans in search of the great leviathan. Today, his vessel, the *Charles W. Morgan*, is the last

Marine Facilities and Services		Number of Transient Berths	Number of Transient Moorings	Largest Vessel Accommodation	Seasonal/Year-round	Approach Depth in feet	Marked Entry Channel	Dockside Depth in feet at MLW	Gas/Diesel Fuel	Fuel Brand	Ramp/Dinghy Dock/Launch Service	Railway/Lift: Capacity (in tons)	Propeller/Hull Repairs	Engine Repairs: Gas/Diesel	Marine Supplies/Groceries/Bait/Ice	Pump-out Station	Showers/Laundromat	110V ★ 220V ▲ Maximum Amps	MasterCard/VISA/Diner's Club American Express	Restaurant/Snack Bar	Monitors VHF Channel
❶ Clinton Yacht Haven	(203) 669-7254	25		Y	50	●	4.5	5					L30	P	GD	●	S	SI	▲80	MV		
❷ Ritt's Seaport Marine (East)	(203) 669-5359	2		Y	44	●	8	3					L25	PH	GD		S	S	★30	MV		16
❸ Ritt's Seaport Marine (West)	(203) 669-5359	2		Y	44	●	8	3					L25	PH	GD		S	S	★30	MV		16
❹ Needle Loft	(203) 669-8065						*CANVAS & INTERIOR DECORATING*														
❺ Riverside Basin Marina	(203) 669-1503	4		Y	39	●	3	8					L16	P	G		S	SI	★20			16
❻ Cedar Island Marina	(203) 669-8681	70		Y	120	●	8	8	GD	GLF			L35	PH	GD	●	SL	SGBI	★▲100	MV	SR	16
❼ Holiday Dock*																					
❽ Clinton Town Marina	(203) 669-2621	4		S	30	●	8	8				R	*TOWN DOCK*						★30			
❾ Harborside Marina	(203) 669-1705	30		Y	65	●	6	6				RL	L12	PH	GD		S	SI	★30	MV		69
❿ J&J Bait	(203) 669-6440	9		S	45	●	5	8										I	★			16
⓫ **Port Clinton Marina (p.193)**	**(203) 669-4563**	6		S	50	●	6	5					L50	PH	G	●	S	SI	★▲50			16
⓬ Indian River Marina *	(203) 453-9343																				
⓭ Old Harbor Marina	(203) 669-8361			Y	100	●	10	10					L10	PH	GD		S		★	V		69

Information in these listings is provided by the facilities themselves. An asterisk (*) indicates that the facility did not respond to our most recent requests for information.

remaining wooden whaling ship in the world and is the centerpiece of the wooden boat collection at the Mystic Seaport Museum.

Clinton is now a quiet New England town, though it does have a curious distinction as headquarters of a major cosmetics firm. Chesebrough-Pond's is located in town, an operation which began years ago by making Pond's Extract from witch hazel cut in the surrounding woods.

The harbor here is also one of the better cruising stops in Connecticut; as a result, problems arise concerning attempts to accommodate the heavy demand for dock space. Recently the town has been enmeshed in a controversy over the proposed conversion of mudflats into marina slips. The DEP had denied the request of a local marina to expand its dock space, but that decision was overturned by the U.S. Commerce Department. While several other stages of approval must be met before expansion can begin, it looks as though Clinton will soon be even more appealing to the cruising boater. Still, the controversy is bound to continue, as some local residents feel the harbor is already overcrowded.

 ## What To See and Do

Located between New York and Newport, Clinton is one of the most-visited ports on Long Island Sound. During the summer, the waterway is often busy with sail and power boats stopping over for supplies. A 15- or 20-minute walk into town offers access to a variety of shops, restaurants, grocery stores, and a laundromat.

Just west of Clinton Harbor is Hammonasset State Park (203) 245-2785, one of Connecticut's three state-owned saltwater bathing beaches. The beaches are open year-round, and camping is allowed during the summer, all for a small fee. From the Sound, the park can easily be recognized by the large pavilion and flagpole, as well as by the throngs of surf and sun gods. The straight coastline along the beach lets the current pick up speed, creating tide rips off Hammonasset Point. When swimming or diving there, be careful of the undertow. Underwater visibility is also poor here, due to sediment brought down by the rivers emptying into Clinton Harbor and the Connecticut River to the east; if you snorkel on a good day, however, you may get to see a few squid and even some seahorses.

In mid-August, Clinton becomes the "Bluefish Capital," celebrating sport fishing for three days with parades, antique shows, concerts, raft, inner tube, and canoe races, and, of course, fish bakes. If you are interested in either the fishing or the festival, call the Chamber of Commerce (203) 669-3889. They will be happy to send you a map of good fishing spots as well as more information about the festival.

Historical attractions in town include the Stanton House (203) 669-2132 (built c.1790), which is maintained by Connecticut National Bank as a museum of American antiquities, and the historical room at the town hall with its collection of china, dolls, glass, and silver.

 ## Where To Eat

Just a step from your boat to the docks of Cedar Island Marina will bring you to Kristopher's Pier (203) 669-7808, a restaurant specializing in steak and seafood; but that's as far as service on the water goes. For more selections, you'll have to head into town, about 1/2 mile up Commerce Street.

On East Main Street in Clinton, you'll find Yesterday's (203) 669-4993, which serves seafood, poultry, and Italian dishes. The King's Garden (203) 669-7775 is the local Chinese restaurant, offering a Szechuan and Cantonese menu. Also on East Main is Clinton Pizza (203) 669-5422, which we hear is quite good. On Boston Post Road in Madison, we suggest you try Lenny & Joe's Fish Tale Restaurant (203) 669-0767, serving excellent local seafood.

 ## Navigation and Anchorages

Use NOAA Charts 12374 (1:20,000), 12372 (1:40,000), and 12354 (1:80,000). Use tide tables for Bridgeport. High tide at Duck Island is 26 minutes earlier; low tide is 35 minutes earlier. Multiply by 0.7 for height at high or low water. Mean tidal range is 4.8 feet.

The entrance to Clinton Harbor at Wheeler Rock is 3.8nm by boat west of the entrance to Westbrook Harbor and 5.9nm by boat east of the approach to Guilford Harbor at Half Acre Rock. Mattituck Inlet on Long Island is 14.8nm to the south-southwest.

From the flashing 2.5sec 33-foot Kelsey Point Breakwater Light **[WP-154]**, a course of about 325°m for 1.2nm by boat will take you past a white caution marker "2" reading "ROCKS"–which you must keep to starboard–to the green 4sec flasher "3" **[WP-153]** at the entrance to the Clinton Harbor channel.

When approaching Clinton from the east, beware of lobster-pot markers in the outer harbor area, particularly around Kelsey Point Breakwater. The current is strong enough to pull the markers under the surface, making them hard to spot, so stay at least 50 yards off the breakwater and keep your eyes peeled.

CAUTION: *Once past the breakwater, keep in mind that red nun "2" southwest of Hammock Point has been changed to a white CAUTION marker that reads "Rocks," and that red nun "4," 700 yards to the north, has been eliminated. It's best to stay well south of that entire area, which develops a nasty chop in a southerly wind.*

The approach from the west is mostly open, though the problem areas are well-marked. You can pass both **Falkner Island** and **Kimberley Reef** to either side. When passing Falkner to the north, don't cut inside the red 4sec flashing gong "15" **[WP-141]**. Once at Hammonasset Point, also remember to stay south of red nun "10" **[WP-149]** and to give the point a wide berth in order to avoid the heavy tide rips you'll find there.

Entering **Clinton Harbor** is straightforward as long as you follow the buoys closely. The outer harbor is shallow, but the channel leading in is well-marked and charted. When entering the channel, give lighted green 4sec buoy "3" [WP-1**53**] fair berth, as it marks Wheeler Rock, which is covered by only about 1 foot of water at low tide. When passing red nun "6," do not stray even slightly from the channel as there is heavy shoaling east of this area. Just ahead, you will have to watch for the bend in the channel as it begins to round **Cedar Island;** this is now marked by green can "9" and red nun "8." On a clear day, you may also use the church steeple in town to guide you from buoy "3" up to these new buoys.

Also note that red nun "10" opposite the island has been replaced with can "11A," located between cans "11" and "13" on the port side. Though it is connected to the mainland by a sand spit, **Cedar Island** has no road access, so as you'll see, most of the summertime residents commute by boat.

Once inside the harbor you have your choice of several marinas, each offering a full range of services and facilities. The channel was dredged in 1987 to a depth of 8 feet as far as Cedar Island Marina, which has 400 berths and caters to transients. When the tide and current are opposed, docking along the **Hammonasset River** can be quite difficult and

requires care. There are also four slips available at the town dock. Call the town dockmaster (203) 669-2621 to see if one is available. Also, near the town dock, you'll find a paved launching ramp.

The river is a complex waterway that demands attention. First off, note that a 6-mph speed limit is in effect beginning at Wheeler Rock, though you won't see anything posting this until you reach green can "9." If you have a deep-draft boat, you should be aware of encroaching mud 1 foot inside the row of moorings on the south side of the channel. And keep an eye out for water-skiers near the "Cable and Pipeline Area" north of Cedar Island.

There are several more facilities up the **Hammonasset River,** but you shouldn't try taking a cruising boat up the channel until high tide. This same precaution applies to the **Indian River,** which has one small-boat facility and a lot of mud at low water.

 ## Shoreside and Emergency Services

Airport: Action Airlines 1-800-243-8623
Ambulance: 911
Coast Guard: New Haven (203) 773-2400 or VHF 16 or CB 9
Fire: 911 or (203) 669-8686 or VHF 16 or CB 9
Harbormaster: (203) 669-9684 or (203) 669-2621 (dockmaster)
Hospital: Shoreline Clinic (203) 767-0107
Police: 911 or (203) 669-0451
Radio Telephone: VHF 27; I.D.: Bridgeport Marine Operator
Taxi: Clinton-Madison Taxi (203) 669-5677
Tow Service: Saybrook Towing & Salvage, Old Saybrook, CT (203) 388-4065 or VHF 16; Marine Rescue Services, Wickford, RI (401) 295-8711 or VHF 16
Train: Amtrak 1-800-USA-RAIL Metro-North 1-800-638-7646 ◆

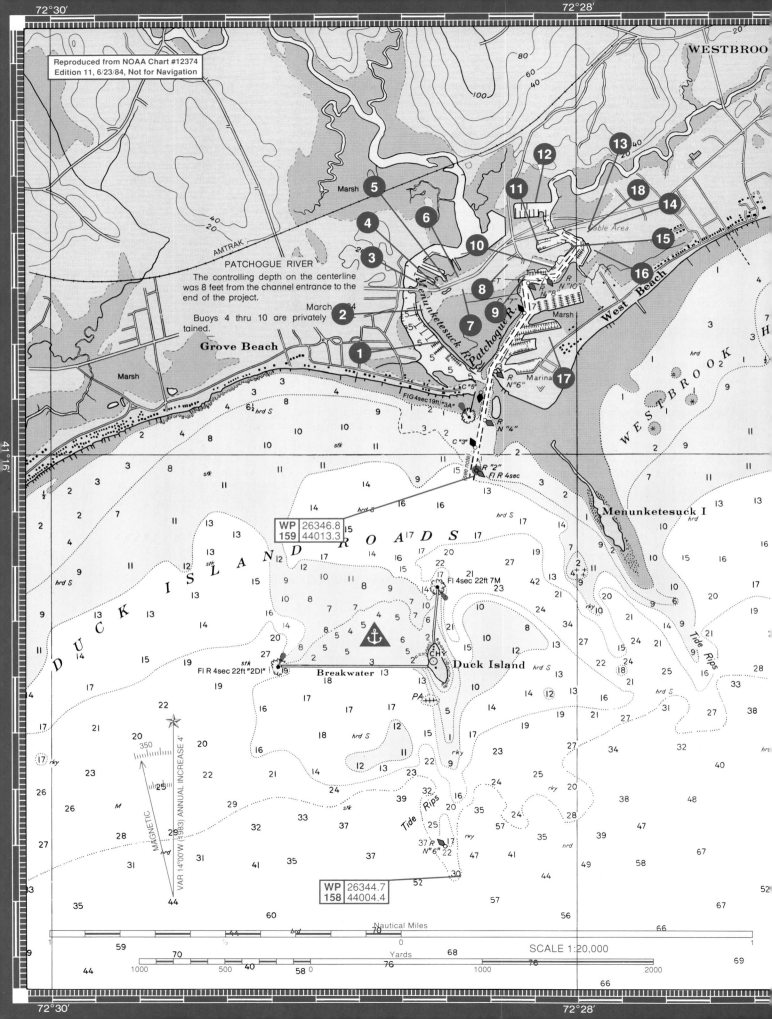

WESTBROO

WESTBROO

AMTRAK

PATCHOGUE RIVER
The controlling depth on the centerline
was 8 feet from the channel entrance to the
end of the project.

March 1984
Buoys 4 thru 10 are privately
tained.

Grove Beach

Marsh

Marsh

Menunketesuck R.

Patchogue R.

Marina

Marsh

West Beach

Cable Area

WESTBROOK H

Menunketesuck I

FI G 4sec 19ft "3A"

C "5"

R N "4"

C "3"

R "2"
FI R 4sec

WP 159 | 26346.8 / 44013.3

D U C K   I S L A N D   R O A D S

FI 4sec 22ft 7M

Breakwater

FI R 4sec 22ft "2DI"

Duck Island

CHY

PA

Tide Rips

Tide Rips

R N "6"

WP 158 | 26344.7 / 44004.4

MAGNETIC

VAR 14°00'W (1983) ANNUAL INCREASE 4'

350

Nautical Miles

SCALE 1:20,000

Yards

1000   500   0   1000   2000

The Great American Turtle

Originally called *Pachogue,* which meant "at the confluence of two rivers" in a local Native American dialect, the town of Westbrook wasn't settled until 1648, relatively late for these parts. The town remained part of greater Saybrook for nearly 200 years until finally breaking away in 1840.

During that time, however, Westbrook made great use of its coastal location. With 4 miles of shoreline, freshwater rivers, and direct access to the Sound, Westbrook grew into an early shipbuilding center. The related businesses of smelting and salting also thrived. Though he came along much later, the greatest shipbuilder in the town's history was David Bushnell, who invented the submarine–called *The American Turtle*–and was born here in 1740. Bushnell has long gone unrecognized as one of the great mechanical minds in American history, and has only recently begun to take his place among the other geniuses of invention, Benjamin Franklin and Thomas Edison.

The Patchogue River in Westbrook, CT from the northeast.

© Jack McConnell

Marine Facilities and Services

#	Facility	Phone	Number of Transient Berths	Number of Transient Moorings	Seasonal/Year-round	Largest Vessel Accommodation (in feet)	Marked Entry Channel	Approach Depth in feet at MLW	Dockside Depth in feet at MLW	Gas/Diesel Fuel	Fuel Brand	Ramp/Dinghy Dock/Launch Service	Railway/Lift: Capacity (in tons)	Engine Repairs: Gas/Diesel	Propeller/Hull Repairs	Marine Supplies/Groceries, Bait/Ice	Pump-out Station	Showers/Laundromat	110V★ 220V▲ Maximum Amps	MasterCard/VISA/Diners Club / American Express	Restaurant/Snack Bar	Monitors VHF Channel
1	Pilot's Point Marina, North	(203) 399-7906	10		Y	60	●	8.5	9				L30	GD	PH	SI		S	★▲50	MVA		9
2	Menunketesuck Yacht Club		*PRIVATE CLUB - MEMBERS ONLY*																			
3	Dick's Marina	(203) 399-6534			Y	26		4	4			R						S	★20	MV		
4	Fishing Unlimited	(203) 399-6194			Y							R				SIB				MV		
5	Ol' Salt Harbor Marina *	(203) 399-6684																				
6	Basset Boat Co.	(203) 399-5935			Y	*BOAT SALES & SERVICE*																
7	**Sedgwick Marine (p. 197)**	**(203) 399-9943**			Y	*MARINE SUPPLIES*														MV		
8	Colvin Yachts	(203) 399-9300			Y	42	●	12	7										★▲50	MV		
9	Westbrook Town Dock	(203) 399-6084		2	Y	40	●	7	7			R										
10	Harry's Marine Repair	(203) 399-6165	3		Y	40	●	7	8	G			L10	G	P	S	●	S	★	MV		
11	Westbrook Lobster Co.*	(203) 399-9414																				
12	Pier 76 Marina	(203) 399-7122	20		Y	33	●	4	3			R			PH	SI				MV	R	
13	Bassett Boat	(203) 399-5581	*BOAT SALES & SERVICE*																			
14	Custom Navigation Systems	(203) 399-5511			Y																MV	9
15	Duck Island Yacht Club	(203) 399-9083	6	1	S	40	●	9	6					D				S	★30			
16	Pilot's Point Marina, East	(203) 399-7906	5		Y	50	●	7	7				L25	GD	PH	S			★▲50	MVA		
17	Pilot's Point Marina, South	(203) 399-7906	15		Y	100	●	10	12	GD	MOB		L70	GD	PH	SI	●	S	★▲50	MVA	R	9
18	Sail Westbrook	(203) 399-5515	*YACHT CHARTERS*																			

Information in these listings is provided by the facilities themselves. An asterisk (*) indicates that the facility did not respond to our most recent requests for information.

Westbrook also has another claim on maritime history. The Cornfield Point lightship marking Long Sand Shoal, about where Qk Fl red bell "8A" floats now, was one of five lightships on the Sound. Long Sand Shoal was first marked by a lightship in 1856; but the ship with the most character went by the romantic name *LV48* and was rammed twice in one day before finally being ripped in half and sunk in eight minutes flat by an oil barge in 1919. The seventh and last ship to serve off Cornfield Point was a direct descendant of this great combatant, and was named *LV118*. Finally removed in 1957, the ship is now owned by a historical society in Lewes, Delaware.

Today, Westbrook is a summer beach and boating town. If you care to take a walk from any one of the marinas, you will find a town whose streets are literally crammed with boating facilities–there are more in this small space than many large harbors claim. The coast itself is mostly marshland, home to waterfowl, crabs, and innumerable other marine beasties, though humans have clearly laid claim to the long, sandy beaches.

 What To See and Do

Westbrook is a small town with many marine facilities and a fine selection of restaurants. However, most of the activities in this area occur outdoors. First, we suggest you spend some time exploring both the Patchogue and Menunketesuck rivers. There are several pairs of osprey nesting in the extensive marshes just upstream of the Rte. 1 bridges. In addition, swans, geese, terns, and heron can be seen swimming, wading, and swooping about these waters. If you'd like to poke about, you may even find some blue crabs in early summer.

If you're interested in seafood with fins rather than claws, the Westbrook Economic Development Commission (203) 399-6236 provides maps showing where to find the fish. And if you'd like to prepare your own meal but don't care to catch it first, you'll find several places on the waterfront selling fresh lobster, shellfish, and fin fish.

Long ago, Duck Island may have been used as a hospital for smallpox and tuberculosis patients. Others claim the island's most interesting history occurred during Prohibition when rumrunners dropped their goods here. You can visit the island by dinghy and explore the remains of an old building or walk the small beach; just be careful not to disturb the terns who nest on the island from May through August, and be aware that much of the island is covered with poison ivy.

Military buffs may want to visit the Company of Military Historians Museum (203) 399-9460 and view the war memorabilia. Or, perhaps, you'd rather spend some time at the annual Westbrook muster and parade, held on the fourth Saturday in August. The event is usually attended by fife-and-drum corps from all over Connecticut and other parts of the United States, as well as from countries as far away as Switzerland. Even if you're not into this sort of

© *Steven R. Kraus*

thing, you'll surely enjoy the eating, drinking, and general merriment. For more information about this and other events, call the Town Hall (203) 399-6236.

 Where To Eat

Right as you come into Westbrook Harbor, you'll find Gourmet Galley (203) 399-5751 at Pilot's Point South, with a varied menu. Also amongst the many marinas and supply stores in Westbrook, you'll find Bill's Seafood Restaurant (203) 399-7224, where you can dine on the patio while watching the birds on the river. Also try Luciano's Boat House Restaurant (203) 399-5923 nearby, specializing in seafood and Italian cuisine.

Further from the water, we suggest you try Lenny & Joe's Fish Tale Restaurant (203) 669-0767 in Clinton, 1.5 miles to the west. Or head to Frankie's (203) 399-5524 which specializes in seafood and steak. And, of course, you'll find many restaurants along Rte. 1 east of the marinas. My Dad's Place II (203) 399-6896 serves seafood in an informal setting, while the Library Limited Edition (203) 399-7078 also specializes in seafood and has dancing in the evenings. Water's Edge Inn & Resort (203) 399-5901 offers seafood and continental food in an elegant setting. For more spice, we suggest you try the Mexican and Cajun food at the Cuckoo's Nest (203) 399-9060 in Old Saybrook.

Navigation and Anchorages

Use NOAA Charts 12374 (1:20,000), 12372 (1:40,000), and 12354 (1:80,000). Use tide tables for Bridgeport. High tide at Duck Island Roads is 24 minutes earlier; low tide is 32 minutes earlier. Multiply by 0.6 for height at high or low water. Mean tidal range is 4.4 feet.

The red 4sec flasher "2" marking the entrance to the Westbrook channel is 6.6nm by boat west of the breakwaters at the entrance to the Connecticut River, and 3.4nm by boat east of Clinton Harbor. Plum Gut and Orient Point on Long Island are 14.0nm by boat to the southeast.

From the red and green flashing (2+1) horn "W," a course of about 0°m for 2.4nm will get you to the red 4sec flasher "2" marking the entrance to the channel leading into Westbrook. From the 33-foot 2.5sec flashing Kelsey Point Breakwater light **[WP-154]**, a course of about 65°m for 2.1nm will take you to the red 4sec flasher "2" in Westbrook.

CAUTION: There have been many buoy changes in this area. We have noted the most important below, but be alert for others.

Most people think of the **Patchogue** and **Menunketesuck** rivers as Westbrook Harbor. Technically, however, Westbrook Harbor is the bight just east of **Menunketesuck Island.** This area is not used much as an anchorage because it is unprotected and is scattered with many large boulders.

CAUTION: To supply all the lobster pounds in town, there are many lobster pots along the waterways of Westbrook, particularly near the breakwaters and Menunketesuck Island. Tidal currents are often strong enough there that pot markers ride below the surface, making them hard to see.

Approaching Westbrook from Clinton and the west, you will have to pass to the south of the **Kelsey Point Breakwater,** which protects Duck Island Roads from winds out of the southwest. Normally you'll want to stay south of red

nun "8," 400 yards off the breakwater, since there can be tide rips to the north.

When arriving at night, look for the 33-foot 2.5sec white flasher **[WP-154]** on Kelsey Point Breakwater as a landmark, but be sure to keep at least 50 yards off of it. Then swing to port and run about 500 yards to the 4sec red flasher "2DI" on the end of the breakwater off **Duck Island,** keeping it well to starboard. There are strong tidal currents around the Duck Island breakwaters, so give them fair berth at all times.

When coming from the south, pick up red and green buoy "W" **[WP-164]** at the end of **Long Sand Shoal** and follow a course of due north magnetic up to the buoys at the rivers' entrance. Don't cut between red nun "6" **[WP-158]** and **Duck Island.** The water is only a few feet deep for more than half the distance out to this buoy, and there are strong tide rips, especially when wind and tide are opposed. If you're looking for blackfish, blues, or bass, however, and have a shallow draft, this is the place to be.

Coming from the east, the major obstacle when approaching Westbrook is **Long Sand Shoal.** Generally speaking, the tides are slightly stronger south of the shoal, so when heading against the tide, stay north; and when going with the tide, stay south. Depending on the draft of your boat, you may not want to cross the 6-mile-long shoal, which can be as shallow as 4 feet and has a hard, lumpy bottom. Assuming the tides are favorable, most mariners will opt to sail along the north side of Long Sand Shoal while keeping south of the red 4sec bell "2" **[WP-166]** at Cornfield Point Shoal, as well as Hen and Chickens, and Crane Reef which is marked by red nun "4" **[WP-165].**

There is a passage inside **Cornfield Point Shoal** (which was once marked with a lightship) that is close to shore and has a depth of about 15 feet. Passage here can be more interesting than a trip outside but requires careful navigation and a sharp lookout for **Halftide Rock.** Usually awash, Halftide Rock shows a white and orange daymark "A." **Cornfield Point** in Saybrook is a good landmark when approaching Westbrook from the east and is easily recognized by the huge stone walls and red tile roofs of the Castle Inn.

Closer to **Duck Island Roads,** you will want to stay well south of Menunketesuck Island, which is often confused with Duck Island, but can be recognized as the island *without* a tall chimney. Shallow ground extends about 500 yards south of the island, causing yet another set of nasty tide rips.

When heading for the rivers, keep at least 400 yards off **Menunketesuck Island** to avoid a patch of rocks that lies southwest of the island. These rocks are now marked by two privately maintained white buoys labeled "ROCKS." One buoy is about 350 yards west-southwest of the southern tip of the island; the other marks the 6-foot spot 400 yards southeast of the island. Between these buoys there are many lobster pots, so you should definitely stay clear of this area unless you want to risk both hull and prop.

Heading into the rivers, don't cut any of the buoys or you'll get stuck in the mud. The red 4sec flasher "2" **[WP-159]** can be difficult to see, since it is only 3 feet off the water and is often confused with the red flasher at the west end of **Duck Island Roads,** which has the same pattern. Once you've entered the channel at red flasher "2," a no-wake speed limit is in effect. You'll see that can "3" at the river channel entrance has been changed from black to green.

Although the currents in the rivers are not usually swift, you should be aware that when traveling up the channel at ebb tide the currents will be working to set your vessel onto the rocks to the east. Note that can "5" is about 20 yards south of the Menunketesuck River channel, so if you turn to port at the buoy, you will bury your keel in mud.

DAVID BUSHNELL AND *THE AMERICAN TURTLE*

It is fitting, although only a coincidence, that the nation's submarine fleet is based in the home state of the submarine's inventor: David Bushnell of Westbrook, CT. Born in 1740, Bushnell entered Yale at the age of 31. During his senior year, he astonished classmates and professors by exploding two ounces of gunpowder underwater. At the time of Bushnell's graduation in 1775, hostilities between the American colonies and the British were growing steadily. Bushnell's patriotism led him to apply his knowledge of underwater explosives to the development of underwater mines and a means of getting them to their targets. The result was *The American Turtle*, the first successful submarine.

Bushnell's submarine was named *The American Turtle* because it resembled two tortoise shells bolted together. It was built of oak and steel, similar to a large wine cask, and was propelled by means of hand-driven propellers. It could submerge or rise by turning a vertical propeller or by pumping water into or out of the bilge. The operator navigated by the phosphorescent tips of a compass and depth gauge. *The American Turtle* was also outfitted with a sharp steel screw that could be screwed into the bottom of enemy ships. A mine with a timing device was attached to the screw and set to detonate after the submarine had escaped.

Bushnell made the first trial run of *The American Turtle* on the Connecticut River off Ayer's Point. He was then sent by General George Washington to New York Harbor to sink the 64-gun British flagship, *The Eagle.* Unfortunately, the usual operator of the submarine fell sick and had to be replaced by an inexperienced Ezra Lee. Lee managed to get under *The Eagle,* but was unable to attach the mine. As daybreak was coming, he decided to retreat and try again another night. However, his retreat was seen by the British and in order to escape, he set off the mine, keeping the British at bay, but revealing to them the intentions of the strange Yankee craft. *The American* *Turtle* went on several other missions, all with similar results.

Perhaps Bushnell did not receive the credit he deserves because *The American Turtle* did not succeed in sinking any major British ships or because of Bushnell's own secrecy. Bushnell's lack of recognition may also be because Robert Fulton later laid claim to the invention and had to be publicly denounced by Thomas Jefferson. Fulton did, however, succeed in taking credit for the invention of the steamboat, which was, in fact, developed by John Fitch of South Windsor, CT, and by Samuel Morey of Orford, NH.

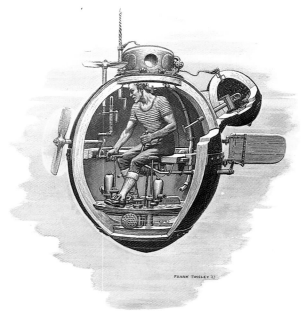

Cut-away illustration of The American Turtle
by Frank Tinsley.
Courtesy of the Connecticut River Foundation

The **Menunketesuck River** tends to shoal on the west side and is less than 5 feet deep at mid-tide. However, if you stay close to the marina slips, you'll find deeper water. The Rte. 1 bridge prematurely cuts off the river for most cruising boats, but there are plenty of smaller boats berthed upstream. The chart doesn't show it, but the 5-foot-deep channel up the **Menunketesuck** is marked by privately maintained buoys. Also note that there is now a green and red junction buoy where the two rivers meet, with the green on top of the red to signify that the preferred channel is up the **Patchogue River.**

Of the two rivers in Westbrook, the **Patchogue** is more heavily developed. There are several marinas, boat yards, a commercial fishing wharf, and a town dock along this channel, which has been dredged to 8 feet. Note that can "7" and red nuns "8" and "10" by the town dock have been replaced by daymarkers in the same spots. You may tie up at the town dock for as long as 2 hours, but cannot stay overnight. The town also supplies two free bow-and-stern moorings directly across the channel from the dock. You may have to compete for space with commercial fishermen unloading their catches here.

Westbrook is something of a boater's dream: you will find restaurants, chandleries, fishing stores, and grocery stores to fill your belly, tool box, tackle box, and ice chest, and a laundromat to empty your hamper. It's also hard to miss Pilot's Point Marina; with nearly 1,000 slips at three locations, this is one of the largest marinas on the Sound. In addition to this, the many other marinas, full-service boat yards, and repair facilities in Westbrook can handle just about any marine job you can name.

Traveling up the **Patchogue,** the Boston Post Road "Singing Bridge"–listen when a car crosses the bridge at 40 mph and you'll understand its name–cuts off river travel for large boats but doesn't stop the smaller ones.

No anchoring is allowed on either of the rivers themselves. If you'd like to anchor outside the rivers, head for the triangle formed by the breakwaters at **Duck Island.** It's protected except in weather from the northwest, which may blow you onto the breakwaters or Duck Island if you're not careful. Also be cautious of the 3-foot spot inside the "triangle;" it's just south of the midway point between the two flashers on the breakwaters. Long ago the area inside the Duck Island breakwaters was dredged to a depth of 15 feet, but in places it has silted up. The mud bottom does give a pretty good hold for your anchor, but again, be careful of the hordes of lobster pots all around the area. If you're planning to anchor here under any conditions, leave yourself plenty of room and scope, because you're sure to swing at least 180° when the tides change.

When the wind is blowing from the northwest, either the east side of the north breakwater, or the east side of Kelsey Point Breakwater will offer some protection.

 Shoreside and Emergency Services

Airport: Action Airlines 1-800-243-8623
Ambulance: 911
Coast Guard: New Haven (203) 773-2400
or VHF 16 or CB 9
Fire: 911 or (203) 399-7921
Harbormaster: (203) 399-9406
Hospital: Shoreline Clinic (203) 767-0107
Police: 911 or (203) 399-7304
Radio Telephone: VHF 27; I.D.: Bridgeport
Marine Operator
VHF 25, 26, 86; I.D.: New London
Marine Operator
Taxi: East Shore Cab & Transportation (203) 388-2819
Tow Service: Saybrook Towing & Salvage,
Old Saybrook, CT (203) 388-4065
or VHF 16; Marine Rescue Services,
Wickford, RI (401) 295-8711 or VHF 16
Train: Amtrak 1-800-USA-RAIL
Metro-North 1-800-638-7646 ◆

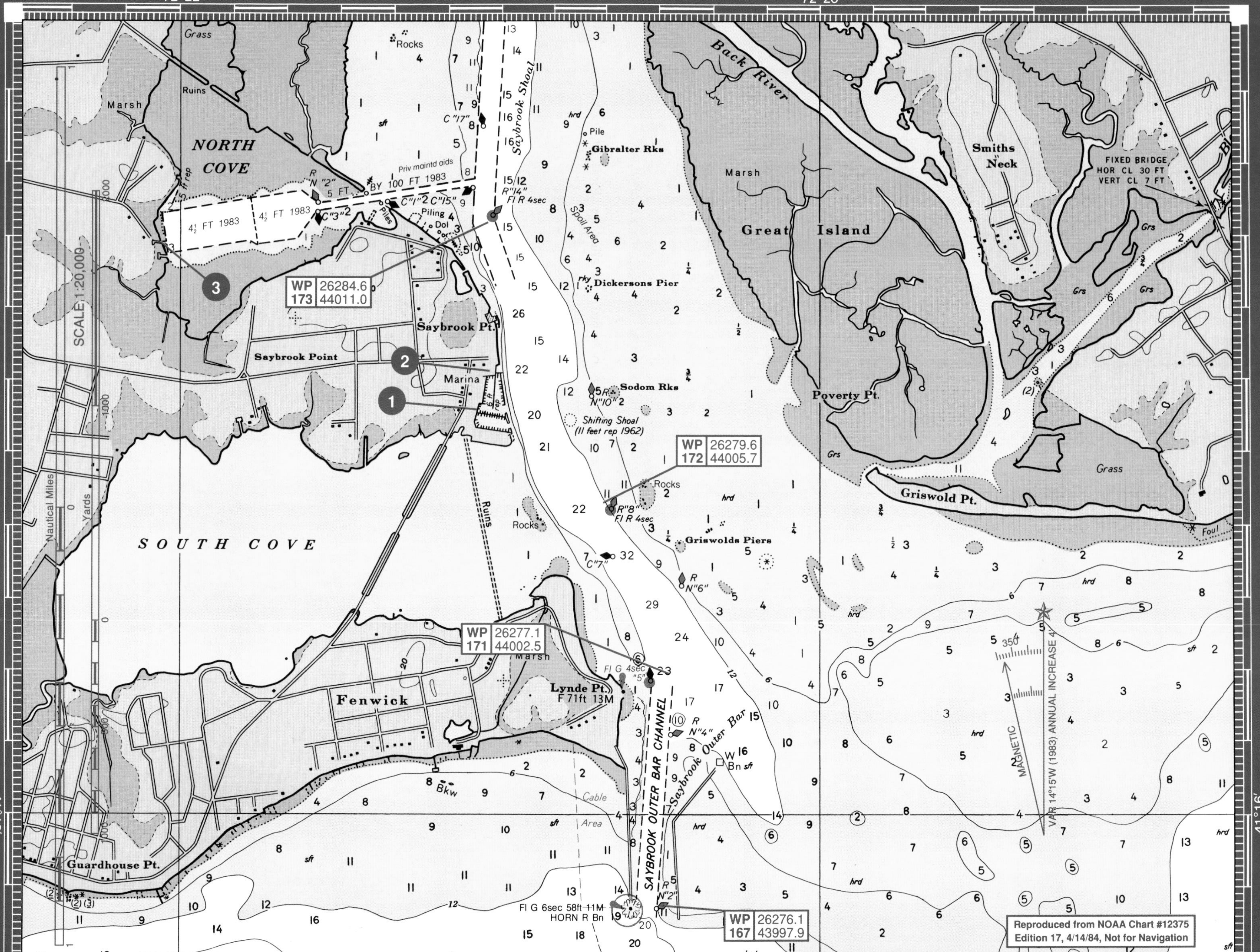

72°20'

72°22'

FIXED BRIDGE
HOR CL 30 FT
VERT CL 7 FT

Smiths Neck

Grs

Grass

Griswold Pt.

Poverty Pt.

Great Island

Back River

Marsh

Grs

VAR 14°15'W (1983) ANNUAL INCREASE 4'

MAGNETIC

350

Griswolds Piers

R "6"

Rocks

WP 26279.6
172 44005.7

R "8"
Fl R 4sec

Sodom Rks
R "10"

Shifting Shoal
(11 feet rep 1962)

Dickersons Pier

Gibralter Rks

Pile

Spoil Area

hrd

C "7"

Saybrook Shoal

Priv maint aids

R "14"
Fl R 4sec

15/2

C "11"
C "9" "5"
C "2"
Piling
Dol

Piles

R "2"
5 FT 1983
C "3" "2"

BY 100 FT 1983

WP 26284.6
173 44011.0

NORTH COVE

Ruins

Marsh

Grass

4½ FT 1983

Saybrook Point

Saybrook Pt.

Marina

Ruins

SOUTH COVE

Fenwick

Bkw

Guardhouse Pt.

Lynde Pt.
F 71ft 13M

WP 26277.1
171 44002.5

Marsh

SAYBROOK OUTER BAR CHANNEL

Saybrook Outer Bar

R "4"

W 16
Bn sf

WP 26276.1
167 43997.9

R "2"

Fl R 5

R "12"
Fl G 6sec 58ft 11M
HORN R Bn

C "7"

N "4"

Fl G 4sec
R "5"

hrd

Foul

Cable

Area

SCALE 1:20,000

Nautical Miles

yards

Rocks

Rocks

Saybrook Point
and the Connecticut River

Einstein's Miscalculations

It seems that although Albert Einstein was comfortable in a laboratory, he was a bit perplexed by sailing vessels. While visiting Old Lyme in the summer of 1935, the professor spent some time on the river, messing about in a small sailboat, and apparently he had more than his share of troubles. Caught between the wind, the tide, and the shoal, it seems the professor spent more time aground than afloat. Our readers know that the mouth of the Connecticut River causes problems for even the most experienced navigators, so they will surely forgive the scientist his mistakes, but the *New London Day* was not so considerate. Wasting no time, the newspaper gleefully trumpeted Einstein's misadventures the next morning under the headline: "Einstein's Miscalculations Leave Him Stuck on Bar of Lower Connecticut River."

In fact, Einstein had simply rediscovered what residents of Old Saybrook knew many years ago: the sandbar at the river's mouth is a pain in the neck. Unlike most other major rivers of the world, the Connecticut has never been open to much heavy shipping, and for this reason has never developed a major metropolitan port along its banks. Instead, you'll find the estuary lined with small towns and wildlife preserves, and the waters dotted with peaceful anchorages.

Adriaen Block first explored this "long tidal river" in 1614. Poking about in his 50-foot *Onrust* with its shallow 6-foot draft, Block had little trouble crossing the infamous Saybrook Bar. In fact, the stout boat made of oak garnered from the wooded isle of Manhattan carried Block a full 60 miles upriver, to Enfield Falls. Of course, he had much more experience than Einstein–and sailed freely, without the added pressure of performing for a curious public.

The Connecticut River is the longest and largest river in New England. From its source just south of the Canadian

Sailing south through the Connecticut River breakwaters at Fenwick Point in Old Saybrook, CT.

border, the river runs 410 miles through Vermont, New Hampshire, Massachusetts, and Connecticut. At the same time, it drops 1,800 feet over 16 dams, drains 11,000 square miles of land, and pours an average of 10 billion gallons of fresh water per day into Long Island Sound.

During the colonial period, the river provided New Englanders with both transportation and food. At one time, Middletown, just 30 miles north of the mouth, attracted more business than any other port between New York and Boston; and fish enough could be caught during the annual Spring shad and salmon runs to supply settlers with food for months.

Over the years, however, the river's tributaries were dammed one by one, cutting off spawning grounds for most of the shad and all of the salmon. As a result, the shad run has been cut to a fraction of its original size, while salmon have become extinct along the river. In addition, the increasingly concentrated population along the banks

Marine Facilities and Services		Number of Transient Berths	Number of Transient Moorings	Seasonal/Year-round	Largest Vessel Accommodation (in feet)	Approach Depth in feet at MLW	Marked Entry Channel	Dockside Depth in feet at MLW	Gas/Diesel Fuel	Fuel Brand	Railway/Lift: Capacity (in tons)	Ramp/Dinghy Dock/Launch Service	Propeller/Hull Repairs	Engine Repairs: Gas/Diesel	Pump-out Station	Marine Supplies/Groceries/Bait/Ice	Showers/Laundromat	110V ★ 220V ▲ Maximum Amps	MasterCard VISA/Diners Club American Express	Restaurant/Snack Bar	Monitors VHF Channel
❶ Harbor One Marina (p. 205)	(203) 388-9208	15		S	250	●		25	10	GD	TEX				P	GD		SL	SI	★▲200	MVA		16
❷ Saybrook Point Inn & Marina (p. 203)	(203) 388-0212	25		Y	300	●		20	16	GD	MOB	D			P	GD		SL	SGBI	★▲200	MVDA	SR	16
❸ North Cove Yacht Club	(203) 388-9087			S	45	●		6	6			L				S			I				68

Information in these listings is provided by the facilities themselves. An asterisk (*) indicates that the facility did not respond to our most recent requests for information.

of the Connecticut led to a steady worsening of water quality, until the river became known as "the nation's most beautifully landscaped sewer."

In the 1950's, a group of concerned citizens formed the Connecticut River Watershed Council (203) 293-0227, dedicated to restoring and preserving the river. Thanks to their efforts, and to the Federal Clean Air and Water Acts, the Connecticut has undergone one of the most successful restoration efforts in the country. Twenty-five years ago, only 20% of the river was suitable for swimming and fishing; now, 80% of the water is at least that clean or cleaner. The shad run has rebounded, and salmon have been reintroduced with some success. Between the Sound and East Haddam, 16 miles upriver, the Connecticut is also protected by a unique regional agency called the Gateway Commission (203) 388-3497. Established by local towns, this group works to limit development along the river in order to preserve its scenic beauty.

 ## What To See and Do

Many of the attractions at the entrance to the Connecticut River are provided by nature. Griswold Point and Great Island on the eastern side of the river contain the largest nesting population of ospreys in Connecticut and are two of the best bird-watching sites in the state. Remember to keep your distance from the birds so as not to disturb them.

The 2-mile-long beach at Griswold Point is a favorite swimming spot and early morning jogging route. Pets are not welcome at the preserve because of the trouble they can cause for the nesting birds. If you want to cross from one side of the spit to the other, please use one of the designated trails in order not to trample the dune grass that helps stabilize the spit. Actually, nothing really holds the glacially deposited spit in place; it has been continuously moving north and getting longer, as is evidenced by its vastly different size and shape on early navigational charts.

Great Island and the Back and Black Hall rivers are fun to explore by dinghy or canoe, which you can rent at the Old Lyme marinas. You'll see ospreys, egrets, sandpipers, and herons stalking the tidal flat at low tide and peering through the marshes at higher water. On sunny weekends from June through October you'll see someone on every bridge, angling for the blue crabs that live in the brackish water below. Some use special folding traps, but most use the traditional net and a chicken wing or some other leftover tied to a string.

You can take canoes and dinghies well into Great Island by entering any of the side channels. You may feel lost and alone, however, in the reeds that rise above head height. When poking around in the tidal marshes, remember to go in on a rising tide. Although the tidal range is only about 3.5 feet, it's still enough to leave you high and dry on wet mud—a sloggy walk back to deep water.

On the western side of the river is the borough of Fenwick, a beautiful and exclusive summer community.

Fenwick has a public golf course (203) 388-2516 that's open only to local residents during the summer.

Many people remember the old Terra Mar Marina and Hotel that once stood on Saybrook Point. In its heyday, it was the glitziest resort on the Sound. It closed a decade ago and was left to rot. A new group of investors has bought the property, completely rebuilt the marina, torn down the old hotel, and built a new luxury hotel, condominiums, and conference center named Saybrook Point Inn and Marina.

If you are a Yale graduate or a lover of history, you will want to stop off at Saybrook Point to see Fort Saybrook Monument Park, the statue of Lion Gardiner, the tomb of Lady Fenwick, and the boulder marking the site of Yale University from 1707 to 1716. Legend has it that there was a riot when the books were removed from the library here to Yale's new location in New Haven.

The town of Old Saybrook bought several acres on Saybrook Point in early 1989, which it plans to add to the park. The land includes a miniature golf course, which the town will operate for the time being.

 ## Where To Eat

If you're staying at one of the Saybrook Point marinas, your most convenient dining choice is Saybrook Point Dock & Dine (203) 388-4665, where you can get your land legs back on the dance floor after your meal.

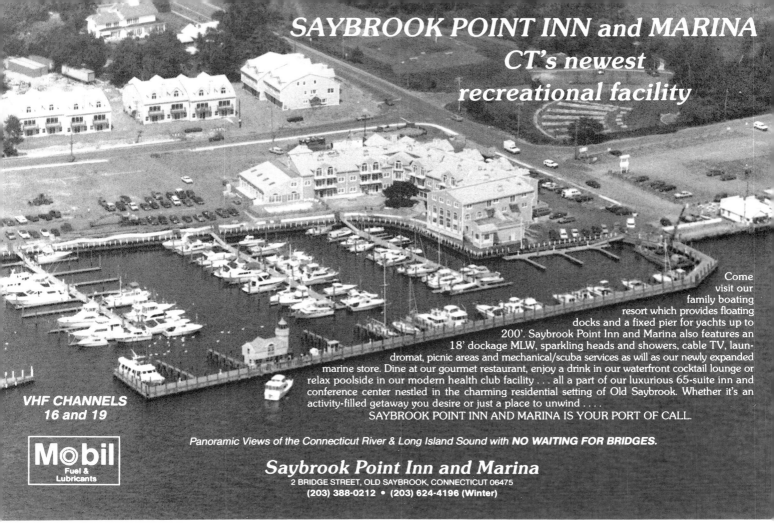
Downtown Old Saybrook is less than a mile away. We suggest Wine & Roses (203) 388-9646 on Main Street, specializing in regional American cuisine. Also on Main Street is Orsini's Grinder Shop (203) 388-5937, featuring take-out sandwiches.

Pat's Kountry Kitchen (203) 388-4784 and O'Brannigan's (203) 388-6611 are both more than a mile from the waterfront, but they feature a wide variety of food at reasonable prices. For more on Where To Eat in Old Saybrook, see the following chapter.

 Navigation and Anchorages

Use NOAA Charts 12375 (1:20,000), 12372 (1:40,000), and 12354 (1:80,000). Use tide tables for New London. High tide at Saybrook Point is 1 hour 11 minutes later; low tide is 53 minutes later. Multiply by 1.2 for height at high or low water. Mean tidal range is 3.6 feet.

The 58-foot green 6sec flashing light on the Saybrook breakwater is 6.2nm by boat east of Duck Island in Westbrook, and 8.6nm by boat west of Black Point and the entrance to Niantic Bay. Plum Gut is 8.1nm by boat to the southeast.

From flashing red 4sec bell "8" **[WP-181]** southeast of the mouth of the Connecticut River, a course of about 320°m for 1.5nm will take you to a spot between red nun "2" and the 58-foot flashing green 6sec horn at the outer bar channel to the river. From here you will follow the buoys upriver, being sure, especially at night, to avoid floating debris.

CAUTION: *There have been many buoy changes in this area. We have noted the most important below, but be alert for others.*

Approaching the **Connecticut River** from the west, look for the 58-foot green 6sec flasher **[WP-167]** on the outer lighthouse at the southern end of the breakwater. On a clear day, you can see the white tower for many miles. The light also emits a continuous RDF signal, which can be received for a range of 11 miles and is helpful when the visibility is poor. West of the breakwater is an anchorage nice for lunch and a swim. It is unprotected, however, so don't stay overnight.

When coming across the Sound from **Plum Gut,** or coming from the west and going around the south side of **Long Sand Shoal,** note that the red and green nun "E" at the east end of the shoal has been changed from red and black. Coming from these directions, one of the first things you'll see is the large white house with two chimneys in Fenwick. Be sure not to confuse the 71-foot inner light on **Lynde Point [WP-171]** with the shorter outer light on the breakwater.

The 71-foot Saybrook Inner Light on Lynde Point, from the north.

As you head north through the breakwaters, keep red nun "2" **[WP-167]** to starboard, as it marks a shoal area on the eastern side of the channel. On weekends, the mouth of the river will be heavily congested with all types of boats. And during an ebb tide, the current can run anywhere from 4 to 5 knots. You will also face some cross current at the southern end of the breakwater, so take care not to drift into the rocks. The only other consideration is a set of earplugs. Once the cigarette boats are past the outer light–and sometimes before–they have the throttle wide open and are hoping everyone within three miles is listening.

Give a wide berth to large commercial vessels, as they aren't very maneuverable and can't really alter course once within the restricted width of the dredged channel. A "steerage only" speed limit exists from the breakwaters up to the red flasher "14" **[WP-173]** opposite **North Cove.**

When coming from the east, we suggest you pass south of Hatchett Reef red nun "6" **[WP-183]** off Old Lyme Shores. Then head for the red 4sec bell "8" **[WP-181]**, formerly flashing white, before swinging to the north and heading for the breakwaters.

CAUTION: *Adventurous souls often try passing over the infamous Saybrook Sand Bar. They line up red 4sec flasher "8" [WP-172] north of Lynde Point and red nun "6," just to the south, and then follow the natural course of the river. You should not attempt this stunt unless you draw less than 3.5 feet and are quite sure of your navigating skill. Even then, don't try it at anything less than half tide.*

The 71-foot **Lynde Point** inner light **[WP-171]** was erected in 1803, making it the second oldest lighthouse in Connecticut. After you pass both the light and green can "7," which was formerly black, Old Saybrook's **South Cove** will be just to port. The remains of an old railroad causeway at the mouth of this cove make it accessible only to dinghies and other small boats. At exceptionally low tides, you'll be able to see the remains of the steamboat *Granite State*, which sank in 1883 near the mouth of the cove.

CAUTION: *The ruins of the old shad fishing piers on the east side of the river–Griswold Piers, Sodom Rocks, Dickerson Piers, and Gibraltar Rocks–are real. You may see commercial fishing boats heading through here, but do not follow them. At least one boat a week goes aground here, so unless you want to be next, obey the buoys.*

Saybrook Point is located between South Cove and North Cove. There are two marinas and a restaurant here, which, because of their closeness to the open water of the Sound, are favorite stopovers for large cruising boats on their way to Newport or New York.

North Cove in Old Saybrook has a dredged channel with a depth of 6 feet, making it accessible to most cruising boats. At green can "15" (formerly black) turn sharply to port and stay between the local markers. There are some 100 permanent moorings here, so you'll find precious little space to drop a hook. Both the town of Old Saybrook and the North Cove Yacht Club maintain one guest mooring

THE FINEST FISHIN' ON THE EASTERN SOUND

Anglers in eastern Connecticut and Rhode Island are lucky; fishing in some of the most fertile waters in the world, fed by a North Atlantic biomass that sustains fish in variety and number. Along with the usual flounder, fluke, blackfish and porgy, the most popular gamefish are the bluefish and striped bass. Because of their strength and size, blues and stripers attract the serious and the not-so-serious sport anglers.

Pat Abate knows all this. That's why he's been a fisherman for 40 years, the last 18 in and around the Connecticut River in Old Saybrook and points east.

Abate, 44, is a friendly sort who doesn't mind dispensing advice. Yes, it's part of his business, but he also does it for love. He's co-owner of the Rivers End Tackle Shop in Old Saybrook, a meeting place for anglers from New York to Rhode Island. He let us in on a few of his favorite spots.

If you're not intimidated by the tide rips and strong currents, try The Race or Plum Gut. Stripers and blues like it here where they can pounce on the weaker food fish (including, presumably, the ones on the end of your line). In The Race, wait for an ebb tide; in Plum Gut, often less crowded than The Race, look for an incoming tide.

Farther east, try the rip just off the north tip of Block Island. If you're really committed, rent a house in the fall on Block Island and fish through the night for blues and stripers. There are other species too: off Southeast Light for pollock; off the east side of the island in the spring for cod; and off southwest point for cod and blackfish. Closer to home, try Hatchett Reef off Old Lyme, CT. Look for red nun "6" and the blues and stripers surrounding it.

Finally, if it's protected waters you want, head for the railroad bridge on the Connecticut River. Fishing is good on both sides of the river, but avoid it on weekends when heavy boat traffic scares the fish away.

Contributed by Arthur R. Henick, a freelance writer from Chester, Connecticut.

each. At the head of the cove, there is also a town dock where you can tie up for a limited time. If you are moored in the cove or have found an open spot for anchoring, a short half-mile walk along Sheffield Street will bring you to downtown Old Saybrook.

Note that when continuing upriver from North Cove, can "17" is now green.

 Shoreside and Emergency Services

Ambulance: 911
Coast Guard: New London (203) 442-4471 or VHF 16
New Haven (203) 773-2400 or VHF 16 or CB 9
Fire: 911 or (203) 388-3508 or VHF 16
Harbormaster: (203) 388-4059 or VHF 16
Hospital: Shoreline Clinic (203) 767-0107
Police: 911 or (203) 388-3500 or VHF 16
Radio Telephone: VHF 27; I.D.: Bridgeport Marine Operator; VHF 25, 26, 86; I.D.: New London Marine Operator
Taxi: East Shore Cab & Transportation (203) 388-2819
Tow Service: Saybrook Towing and Salvage, Old Saybrook, CT (203) 388-4065 or VHF 16; Marine Rescue Services, Wickford, RI (401) 295-8711 or VHF 16; Southeastern Marine Towing, Groton, CT (203) 445-8381 or VHF 16
Train: Amtrak 1-800-USA-RAIL
Metro-North 1-800-638-7646 ◆

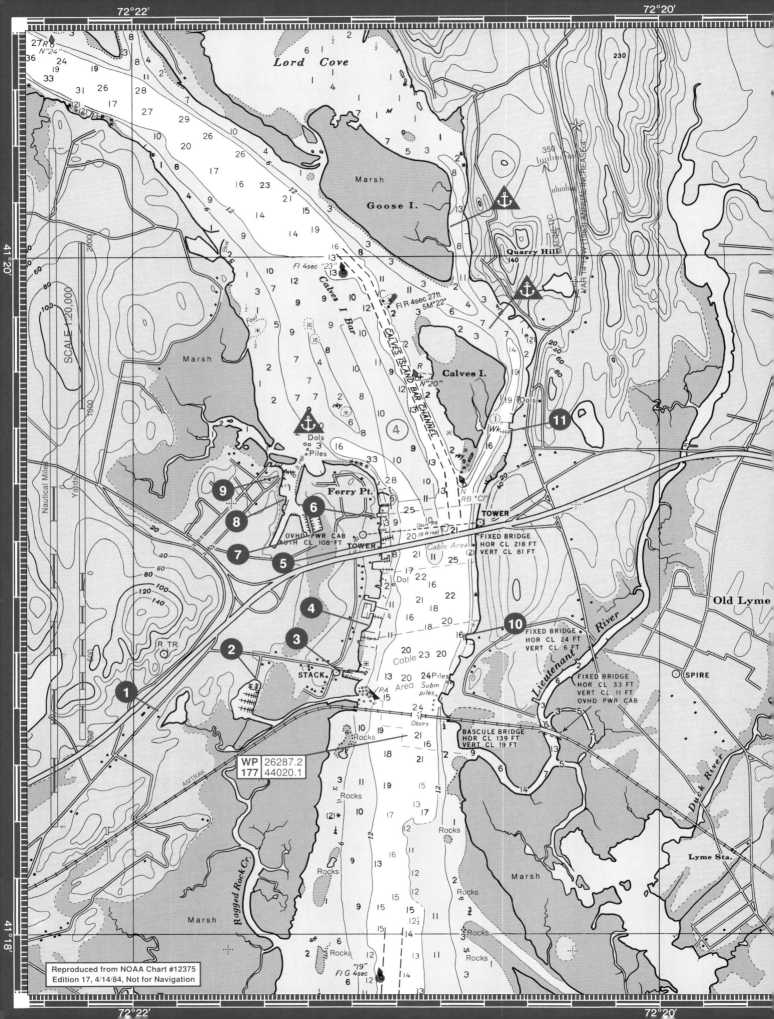

Lord Cove

Goose I.

Marsh

Quarry Hill

Calves I Bar

Calves I.

CALVES ISLAND BAR CHANNEL

Fl 4sec "23"

Fl R 4sec 27ft 5M "22"

N "20"

Dols

Wk

Ferry Pt.

Dols
Piles

Marsh

SCALE 1:20,000

OVHD PWR CAB
AUTH CL 108 FT

TOWER

TOWER

N
RB "CI"

Cable Area

FIXED BRIDGE
HOR CL 218 FT
VERT CL 81 FT

Cable Area
(2)

Dol

STACK.

Cable
Area

PA

Piles
Subm
piles

Obstrs

WP 26287.2
177 44020.1

Rocks

Rocks

Rocks

Rocks

Rocks

Rocks

Rocks

Ragged Rock Cr.

Marsh

AMTRAK

"19"
Fl G 4sec

Lieutenant River

Old Lyme

SPIRE

Duck River

Lyme Sta.

Marsh

FIXED BRIDGE
HOR CL 24 FT
VERT CL 6 FT

FIXED BRIDGE
HOR CL 33 FT
VERT CL 11 FT
OVHD PWR CAB

BASCULE BRIDGE
HOR CL 139 FT
VERT CL 19 FT

Nautical Mile
Yards

Old Saybrook and Old Lyme

Puritan Lords and Pugilists

The settlement of "Saybrooke" was first conceived by 15 English lords of Puritan descent. Given a large tract of land along the lower Connecticut River by the Earl of Warwick, these gentlemen determined to create a colony for "men of distinction and qualitie." Namely, themselves. They intended to cover the land with large estates so that they might continue to live a comfortable life, safe from the anti-Puritans back in England. Two of the 15 gentlemen, Lord Say and Lord Brooke, lent their names to the colony, though only one of the founders ever visited the settlement. He was Colonel George Fenwick, for whom the elegant shore section of Old Saybrook was named.

In 1635, soldiers employed by the founders landed near the mouth of the river, and within a year, Lion Gardiner, of Gardiners Island, had built a fort on Saybrook Point. While Saybrooke never developed into the elite haven envisioned by its founders, the huge tract of land did become some of Connecticut's most beautiful property.

By 1663, Lyme had split from the rest of the colony; and over the next 300 years, the remaining land would be broken up into five smaller towns: Chester, Deep River, Essex, Old Saybrook, and Westbrook. Even today, Old Saybrook remains the hub of the region from Chester to Old Lyme and west along the coast to Clinton. This status may be partly due to the town's historical role as the center of the colony, but it's also because of the town's strategic location at the junction of Interstate 95 and Rte. 9. Zoning laws have also allowed Old Saybrook more commercial development than other towns, with small shopping malls, auto dealerships, fast-food restaurants, and even some light industry.

While Old Saybrook has managed to retain much of its charm despite this growth, especially along Main Street and the shore roads, it can't hope to compare in beauty with Old Lyme, its neighbor just across the river. Gracious captains'

Ferry Point on the Connecticut River from the north.

#	Facility	Phone	Number of Transient Moorings	Number of Transient Berths	Seasonal/Year-round	Largest Vessel Accommodation	Marked Entry Channel	Approach Depth (in feet)	Dockside Depth in feet at MLW	Gas/Diesel Fuel	Fuel Brand	Ramp/Dinghy Dock/Launch Service	Railway/Lift: Capacity (in tons)	Propeller/Hull Repairs	Engine Repairs: Gas/Diesel	Marine Supplies/Groceries/Bait/Ice	Pump-out Station	Showers/Laundromat	110V★ 220V▲ Maximum Amps	MasterCard/VISA/Diners Club · American Express	Restaurant/Snack Bar	Monitors VHF Channel
1	Connecticut Marine Center	(203) 388-9300						*OUTBOARD SALES / SERVICE*															
2	Ragged Rock Marina	(203) 388-1049	10		Y	65		5.5	10	GD	CHE		L20			SI		S	★30	MV		16
3	Saybrook Marine Service	(203) 388-3614			Y	50		10	10	GD			L30	H	GD	SI		S				13
4	River Landing Marina	(203) 388-1431	20		Y	200		20	15	GD	TEX		L60	PH	GD	SIG	●	SL	★▲50	MVA	SR	16
5	**Oak Leaf Marina (p. 211)**	**(203) 388-9817**	10		Y	100	●	10	8	GD	MOB		L25	PH	G	SI		SL	★100	MVA		16
6	Seth Persson Boat Builders	(203) 388-2343			Y	35		4	4				R25	H	*BOAT BUILDERS*							
7	Ferry Point Marina	(203) 388-3260			Y	45	●	8	4	GD	TEX		L25	PH	G	S		S	▲30			16
8	Offshore East	(203) 388-4532	2	2	S	50	●	7	5				L20	PH	D	SI		S	★30			
9	Island Cove Marina	(203) 388-1275	5		Y	50	●	9	8				L35	P	GD	SI		SL	★▲	MV		16
10	Old Lyme Dock Co.	(203) 434-2267	4	1	S	150	●	16	13	GD	TEX			P		SI		SL	★▲200	MVA		16
11	**Old Lyme Marina (p. 209)**	**(203) 434-1272**	5	5	S	50	●	16	16			D	L25	PH	GD	SI		S	★50			16

Information in these listings is provided by the facilities themselves. An asterisk (*) indicates that the facility did not respond to our most recent requests for information.

homes still sit back from tree-lined streets, and the town possesses a sense of pace, never hurried or ruffled. On a summer weekend, it's hard to pass through town without meeting a wedding party, usually gathered on the lawn and stone steps of an old church, its white steeple reaching beyond the old oaks to the sky. Over the years, Old Lyme has been home to many artists, especially some American Impressionists around the turn of the century. There is still a fine arts academy in Old Lyme today, and the town retains much of the character that first attracted these painters—it is easily one of the most pristine and beautiful villages in Connecticut.

Lest you mistake Old Lyme for an effete place suitable only for the sophisticated, we tell the story of one of the town's earliest boundary disputes. In 1670, Old Lyme laid claim to a 3-mile stretch of land also claimed by New London. Rather than taking their quarrel to the British courts, the towns agreed to settle the disagreement by way of a fist fight. Champions were chosen from each village, and the rules were set: the last man left standing secured the land for his hometown. After a grueling match with much bloodshed, Old Lyme won.

 ### What To See and Do

While Saybrook claims most of the marinas and a fair number of restaurants, it comes up a bit short on things to see and do. Lyme, on the other hand, has a fair number of sights and diversions, but can't boast too many marinas nor all that many restaurants.

In Old Saybrook, you're sure to find any supplies or equipment you'll need for your boat, though you'll need to take a bike or taxi into town from the marinas. To while away an afternoon, however, you'll probably find yourself heading up to Essex or across to Old Lyme. Most of Old Saybrook's beaches are private and there aren't any public athletic facilities nor any historical sites in this part of town.

Coming up the Connecticut River, don't be in such a hurry that you simply pass Old Lyme by. The opportunities for viewing art and nature are greater here than at any other point along the river. In addition to the town's fine architecture, be sure to see the Florence Griswold Museum of American Impressionist paintings (203) 434-5542. The Lyme Art Association (203) 434-7802 and the Lyme Academy of Fine Art (203) 434-5232 are also located in town, and both have rotating exhibits of contemporary work and welcome visitors.

For those who prefer the out-of-doors, Lord Cove's marshes offer fantastic bird-watching. You will see many ospreys, herons, egrets, hawks, kestrels, and other shore-side birds here. If you happen to be in the area during the winter, keep your eyes peeled for bald eagles who visit here when the river is frozen farther north. They ride the ice floes, hunting for big fish swimming just below the surface.

In June, the marshes are filled with yellow and purple flag in bloom. By summer, the pink flowers of the swamp rose mallow burst into blossom. At dawn and dusk, muskrat, deer, and foxes can be seen coming to the water's edge, and recently there have been a few coyotes in town. Back in 1962, there was a moose.

North of the Old Lyme drawbridge is considered inland Connecticut—i.e., freshwater—so you'll need a fishing license to capture those blues. Call the Old Saybrook (203) 388-2029 or Old Lyme (203) 434-1655 town clerks for license information. South of the "draw," as the bridge is known locally, is still marine—i.e., saltwater—so no license is required.

Where To Eat

In Old Saybrook at River Landing is Basem's Restaurant (203) 388-4212, specializing in continental cuisine and boasting a deck with a water view. Just a couple of blocks away, you'll find the Saybrook Fish House (203) 388-4836, which is one of the finest seafood restaurants in the state.

Downtown Old Saybrook is about a mile from the marinas and should be reached by cab. On Main Street, you'll find Wine & Roses (203) 388-9646, specializing in regional American food. For bakery, try Vanderbrook Bakers (203) 388-9700 across the street. O'Brannigan's (203) 388-6611 at Saybrook Junction, has a varied menu at reasonable prices, and nearby is Pat's Kountry Kitchen (203) 388-4784 for homestyle meals. And finally, for good pizza, head to Two Brothers Family Pizza (203) 388-9794.

On the other side of the river, there are two fine restaurants. Both the Old Lyme Inn (203) 434-2600 and the Bee and Thistle Inn (203) 434-1667 serve excellent food in elegant and comfortable settings. Reservations are suggested for both since there is no "season" for fine food.

Navigation and Anchorages

Use NOAA Charts 12375 (1:20,000), 12372 (1:40,000), and 12354 (1:80,000). Use tide tables for New London. High tide at the Baldwin Bridge is 1 hour 25 minutes later; low tide is 1 hour 10 minutes later. Multiply by 1.2 for height at high or low water. Mean tidal range is 3.4 feet.

The I-95 bridge between Old Saybrook and Old Lyme is 2.9nm by boat north of Lynde Point at the river's mouth; from the highway bridge, it is another 2.6nm by boat north and west to the Connecticut River Museum docks at the foot of Main Street in Essex.

There are two separate waterfront areas in Old Saybrook. One, around Saybrook Point, is discussed in the previous chapter; the other, around Ferry Point, is often referred to as "that place up there by the bridges."

The Amtrak railroad crosses the Connecticut on the **Old Lyme Drawbridge [WP-177],** about two miles from the river's mouth. More often than not, there are more boats trying to make their way along the river than there are trains trying to cross it, so the bridge is usually open. All except the largest powerboats will be able pass beneath the bridge even when it is closed, as it has a vertical clearance of 19 feet. Smaller powerboats may even want to pass between a span other than that along the main channel.

The bridgetender may be contacted on VHF 13, but will only answer if you ask for the *Old Lyme* drawbridge, not *Old Saybrook.* You may also contact the bridge with one long and one short blast of your horn; if you receive a similar horn signal, then the bridge will open shortly; if, however, you receive a single, long 5sec blast, then the train is on its way, and you'll have to wait.

Just north of the railroad bridge, you will pass beneath the **I-95 bridge,** with a vertical clearance of 81 feet. Passing under the bridge, you will see a state-owned launching ramp on the Saybrook shore. Automobile traffic crossing the river during the summer is quite heavy, so plans have been made to replace the existing bridge with a much larger thoroughfare. So far, no work has begun, but one of the marinas just south of the present bridge has been bought by the state, and a model of the proposed replacement span is on view at the Old Saybrook Town Hall (203) 388-3401. You will also notice that around the bridges, the Old Saybrook shoreline is packed with marinas, equipped to handle any of your repair needs.

An early 20th-century postcard of a steamer visiting Government Landing in New London, CT.
Photo courtesy of the Connecticut River Foundation.

MAJESTIC MONARCHS OF PLEASURE AND COMMERCE

One hundred years ago steamboats ruled Long Island Sound. They were the majestic monarchs of pleasure and commerce, carrying passengers and freight from New York to Bridgeport and New Haven, up the Connecticut River to Essex and Hartford, eastward to New London, Norwich, Fall River, and New Bedford, and back.

They were floating pleasure palaces as long as a football field, with grand ballrooms and restaurants serving haute cuisine. Many were owned by the likes of the Morgans and the Vanderbilts, whose names and reputations attracted New York, Boston, or Hartford swells trying to impress their dates, and lower rollers looking for transportation to a big city.

Oliver Jensen remembers the steamboats' allure. As a youth in the 1920s, he took the steamboat to New York with his father. Passengers in New London would board the boat south of what is now City Pier at 9:00 p.m. for the 11-hour trip.

"I'd walk around," recalls Jensen, an author, editor, and railroad and steamboat buff who lives in the Fenwick borough of Old Saybrook. He remembers admiring the boat's grand salon, gilded woodwork, Persian carpets, and decorative pottery.

"It had a sort of faded Victorian grandeur," Jensen said. One-way fare was one dollar each, plus an extra 50 cents if you wanted a berth. The Jensens did. Young Oliver got the top bunk. They would wake up the next morning as the boat steamed down New York's East River. Normally a slow riser then, Jensen had no trouble getting out of a steamboat berth. "I got up, bang, as soon as it was light. I wanted to watch the world go by."

It was some world to see. There were streams of steamboats arriving in New York Harbor, all dropping off passengers for a day of business, shopping, or sightsee-ing. The steamers came down from the Hudson, up from New Jersey and south from New England.

"When you are a boy," Jensen reflects, "you think this is the way the world has been and always will be." And why not? By then, steamboats had been around for a century.

The first Sound-going steamboat, the *Fulton,* named after steamboat pioneer Robert Fulton, made the run from New York to New Haven in 1815. The last passenger steamboat left the Connecticut River in 1931. Buffeted by the Depression, the success of railroads and automobiles, and a crippling strike, the famous Fall River Line folded in 1937.

In his book *Floating Palaces: New England to New York on the Old Fall River Line,* the eminent steamboat historian Roger Williams McAdam described the last hours of the Fall River Line, fought in federal court in New Haven, where the line's owners petitioned for abandon-ment.

"Sentiment and economics were to engage in a death struggle," McAdam wrote. "Futility and hope were ar-rayed against each other. Ledger figures, red; brilliantly and boldly red; stood out against broken spirits and veritably bleeding hearts. Could it be that the fate of the once omnipotent Fall River Line rested here? Life or death–that was plainly the issue." Death won.

More than 50 years later, why do people still recall the steamboats' grandeur? Oliver Jensen knows: "You're probing the human spirit. There will always be people who feel that the old ways are interesting and sometimes better. And that their departure is something to be mourned."

Contributed by Arthur R. Henick, a freelance writer from Chester, CT.

North of the highway bridge, you'll find several nice anchorages. Medium-draft boats will want to check out the area east of **Calves Island;** this is a pleasant place to drop a hook and is away from the heavy wash that creeps up so steadily near the main channel. You may have a fair number of neighbors while visiting there, so you'll probably be best off using a Bruce or fisherman's anchor for their short scope. Note that the junction buoy "CI" at the southern tip of Calves Island has been changed from red and black to red and green.

For more privacy, head about 0.25nm into **Lord Cove,** just east of Goose Island. You'll have good water up to the northeast corner of the island, but then the shallows take over, making it possible for exploration by dinghy only. You may also want to anchor north of **Ferry Point,** across from Calves Island. You'll have more water here, but also more noise and more wake from traffic in the channel. Note that green 4sec flasher "23" just across from Goose Island was formerly a black can.

 ### Shoreside and Emergency Services

Ambulance: 911
Coast Guard: New London (203) 442-4471 or VHF 16
New Haven (203) 773-2400 or VHF 16
or CB 9
Fire: 911 or (203) 388-3508 or VHF 16
Harbormaster: (203) 388-4059 or VHF 16
Hospital: Shoreline Clinic (203) 767-0107
Police: 911 or (203) 388-3500 or VHF 16
Radio Telephone: VHF 27; I.D.: Bridgeport
Marine Operator
VHF 25, 26, 86; I.D.: New London
Marine Operator
Taxi: East Shore Cab & Transportation (203) 388-2819
Tow Service: Saybrook Towing and Salvage,
Old Saybrook, CT (203) 388-4065
or VHF 16; Marine Rescue Services,
Wickford, RI (401) 295-8711
Train: Amtrak 1-800-USA-RAIL
Metro-North 1-800-638-7646 ◆

Essex and Hamburg Cove

A Town of Masts

Though it's on a river, many consider Essex the quintessential sea-side New England village. With its many marinas and narrow, one-way streets, the town has maintained a great deal of its maritime heritage. In the last 300 years, more than 500 vessels have been built in Essex, including the 24-gun *Oliver Cromwell*–the United States' first man of war, which was designed by the local Uriah Hayden in 1775. Testament to the town's enduring commitment to the sea, Hayden's house at the foot of Main Street is now home to the Dauntless Club. Essex is known today as a yachting capital, comparable in all respects except size to Newport and Annapolis.

Essex played a large role as a shipbuilder during the War of 1812. In fact, the British launched a midnight raid against the town in order to destroy the local warships while also hindering future production. While no one was hurt during the twelve-hour raid, 23 vessels at anchor or under construction were burned, and the British managed to commandeer a great many supplies from local chandleries, including all the town's rum. Legend has it that a British officer even left his sword in a local home after imbibing too freely during the brief occupation.

The foot of Main Street from the Essex, CT town dock.

During the Age of Steam, Essex was busy with visits from the Connecticut Valley Railroad as well as the 243-foot sister ships *Middletown* and *Hartford,* which stopped at the foot of Main Street on daily runs between New York City and Hartford. Although the steamships offered the most glamorous means of transportation in that time, they were also quite dangerous. Two ships suffered boiler explosions

Marine Facilities and Services		Number of Transient Berths	Number of Transient Moorings	Seasonal/year-round	Largest Vessel Accommodation (in feet)	Marked Entry Channel	Approach Depth (in feet)	Dockside Depth in feet at MLW	Gas/Diesel Fuel	Fuel Brand	Ramp/Dinghy Dock/Launch Service	Railway/Lift: Capacity (in tons)	Engine Repairs: Gas/Diesel	Propeller/Hull Repairs	Pump-out Station	Showers/Laundromat	Marine Supplies/Groceries/Bait/Ice	110V★ 220V▲ Maximum Amps	MasterCard/VISA/Diners Club American Express	Restaurant/Snack Bar	Monitors VHF Channel
1 Essex Yacht Club	(203) 767-8121	2	10	Y	60	●	8	8								S	I	★30	MV	R	16
2 Essex Corinthian Yacht Club	(203) 767-3239			Y	40	●	7	7	GD	*PRIVATE CLUB - MEMBERS ONLY*							SI	30	MVA		9
3 **Brewer's Chandlery East (p. 219)**	**(203) 767-8267**	10	10	Y	65	●	8	8	GD	MOB	L					S	SI	★▲50	MVA		9
4 Connecticut River Museum	(203) 767-8269	2		Y	80		4		*PUBLIC MUSEUM*												
5 Middle Cove Marina	(203) 767-2641	5		Y	40	●	4	5								S					
6 **Essex Boat Works (p. 218)**	**(203) 767-8276**		2	Y	80	●	10	10			D	L50	GD	PH				★▲50	MV		16
7 Essex Island Marina	(203) 767-1267	75		Y	150	●	7	7	GD	TEX	L	L30	GD	PH		SL	SIG	★▲50	MVA	S	16
8 Essex Boat House	(203) 767-1781			Y					*MARINE SUPPLIES*										MVA		
9 **Embassy Marine Publishing**	**(203) 767-1343**			Y	*PUBLISHER OF EMBASSY'S BOATING GUIDES*														MVA		
10 **Thomas Clark Sailmakers (p. 215)**	**(203) 767-8278**			Y	*SAILMAKERS*														MVA		
11 Brewer's Dauntless Shipyard	(203) 767-2483	10		Y	115	●	12	12				L25	GD	PH		S	I	★▲50	MV	S	16
12 Pettipaug Yacht Club	(203) 767-8893			S	*PRIVATE CLUB - MEMBERS ONLY*																
13 Cove Landing Marine	(203) 434-5240		15	Y	70	●	6	8				L15	GD	PH	●	S	SIG	★▲			16
14 Reynolds Garage & Marine	(203) 434-0028			Y	50	●	5	5					R								

Information in these listings is provided by the facilities themselves. An asterisk (*) indicates that the facility did not respond to our most recent requests for information.

SONGS ACROSS THE WATER

The first half of the 19th century, often considered the golden age of sailing ships, was also the golden age of sea chanteys–shipboard work songs sung while hauling anchor, hoisting sails, or performing many other tasks requiring gangs of men.

Sea chanteys first came into widespread use in the early 1820s and were most widely sung between 1860 and 1880. As steam overtook sail and fewer men were needed to operate ships, some chanteys were adapted for new uses, but on the whole, the manly art of chanteying began to decline. Today it's a rare sailor who knows any of the old tunes.

With many exceptions, a chantey usually consists of a one-, two-, or four-line verse paired with a chorus or alternating refrain. The chanteyman, usually a veteran sailor familiar with many chanteys, would lead with a verse, while the gang of sailors would reply in rhythm at each pull of the line or turn of the capstan.

The subjects of sea chanteys are many and varied, but the basic themes are woven around the life of a sailor. It goes without saying that rum and women figured prominently in the subject matter, and that the language was....well, salty. Different occupations had different chanteys. Like other oral traditions, sea chanteys leave plenty of room for improvisation. No two chanteymen sing a tune the same way, and lyrics from one song often appear in different forms in many others.

It's easy to romanticize the great age of sailing ships, but for the common sailor, life at sea usually meant dangerous, backbreaking work, harsh discipline, poor food and miserable living conditions. Music was one of his few leisure-time options. Chanteys sung for entertainment were often called "fo'c'sle" chanteys after the part of the ship where the crew bunked. One example is *The Jolly Roving Tar.*

THE JOLLY ROVING TAR

Now ships may come and ships may go
But the sea doth always roll.
Each sailor lad, just like his dad
He loves that flowing bowl.
Each trip ashore he does adore
With a girl so plump and round.
When his money's gone, it's the same old song,
"Get up, Jack; John, sit down."
CHORUS:

Come along, come along,
Me jolly brave boys,
There's lots of grog in the jar.
We'll plow the briny oceans
In the Jolly Roving Tar.

When he gets ashore he'll head for the door
Of some old boarding house.
They'll welcome him with rum and gin,
They'll feed him on pork souse.
He'll lend and spend and not offend
Till he lies drunk on the ground.
When his money's gone it's the same old song
"Get up, Jack; John, sit down."
CHORUS

And then he'll slip aboard some ship
For China or Japan.
In Asia there the ladies fair
They love that sailor man.
He'll go ashore and he won't scorn
To buy some girl a gown.
When his money's gone, it's the same old song,
"Get up, Jack; John, sit down."
CHORUS

When Jack gets old and weatherbeat,
Too old to knock about,
They'll turn him out to some grog shop
Till 8 bells calls him out.
He'll raise up high and loudly cry,
"Great God, I'm homeward bound!"
When his money's gone, it's the same old song,
"Get up, Jack; John, sit down."
CHORUS AND END

The *Jolly Roving Tar* is a ship, although it can be taken as a reference to British sailors, who were commonly known as "tars" for their habit of wearing tarred hats or tarred pigtails. Those with tarred tails often wore a collar with a square of cloth hanging from the back to protect their shirts from the sticky tar. The square hanging collar later became a standard part of naval uniforms.

Even though this chantey characterizes sailing rather favorably, it still shows a sailor's rather sad view of the pleasures and perils awaiting him ashore after months at sea. (It should be noted that this version has been cleaned up considerably to make it fit for publication.)

Sea chanteys are not dead in the 1980s. A good many collections have been published, and chanteymen still ply their trade, though more often in pubs than on poops. The Griswold Inn (203) 767-1812 in Essex, CT, has hosted chanteymen every Monday night for years. The Mystic Seaport Museum (203) 572-0711 hosts a Sea Music Festival every June.

The chantey and information for this article were provided by Norman Ott, Chanteyman for the Ancient Mariners, an International Fife and Drum Corps.

off the Essex shore: the *Ellsworth* in 1827, and the *New England* in 1833.

The saddest day in Essex history was September 21, 1938, when the great hurricane hit without warning. One hundred yachts, which constituted almost the entire fleet, were destroyed in that storm. In fact, the only local boats that survived the storm were those anchored in Hamburg Cove, about 1.5nm northeast of town and across the river. Protected on all sides and anchored on a soft bottom, all of these boats rode out the storm with ease. Since then, Hamburg has been known as "Timid Cove," because it's where you run and hide when the wind comes blowing.

★ What To See and Do

One reason Essex has remained associated with yachting throughout its history is its location on a peninsula. Surrounded by water on three sides, the village offers cruising boaters all they need within a short walk of the water. Lined with beautiful Federal and Colonial period homes and shops, the town attracts hoards of visitors during the summer. For those who want to explore further afield, the Sew & Sew Shop (203) 767-8188 rents bicycles.

Despite its small size, the Connecticut River Museum (203) 767-8269 at the foot of Main Street, right next to the town dock, is one of the finest little museums you will ever visit. Along with the best view of the harbor, the museum has outstanding exhibits on the geology of the Connecticut River Valley, native Americans, shipbuilding, brownstone quarries, and more. The pride of the museum is a working, full-size replica of the *The American Turtle*–the first submarine, invented in 1776 by David Bushnell of Westbrook. The museum docks are also popular with fishermen and crabbers plying the brackish waters for their prey.

The Valley Railroad Company (203) 767-0103 has a large collection of old steam and diesel locomotives, as well as freight and passenger cars, and other pieces of machinery associated with a working railroad. Daily train rides bring passengers upriver with the option of joining a sight-seeing boat for a cruise along the river. The railroad also offers fall foliage rides and a special Christmas trip. The railroad museum is about a mile from the waterfront on Rte. 154. A witch riding a broomstick on the weather vane of the E.E. Dickinson Witch Hazel Company watches over the yard, so don't try any tricks.

Also of interest is the local Jazz Festival (203) 767-0237 held each August, when half a dozen or more bands ride the Valley Railroad trains to various locations where picnickers wait to hear them. A little farther down the road in Ivoryton is the Company of Fifers and Drummers Museum (203) 767-8825. This part of Connecticut is a hotbed of wailing fifes and pounding drums–they come out to strut their stuff and make "joyful noise" at every opportunity.

The mooring area at the foot of Main Street in Essex, CT. Brewer's Chandlery East is to the left; Essex Island Marina, Essex Boat Works, and Brewer's Dauntless Shipyard are to the right.

 ### Where To Eat

There are only two restaurants in the village of Essex itself. The Griswold Inn (203) 767-1812 is known locally as "The Griz" and has been in continuous operation since 1776. A sign over the taproom door reads, "Because we cater to yachtsmen, a coat and tie are not required." The interior of the Griz is filled with a fine collection of authentic marine paintings and prints, as well as an excellent collection of antique firearms. The restaurant has recently been renovated, and is usually packed, so reservations are suggested.

Half a block further up Main Street is the Black Seal Seafood Grille (203) 767-0233, with a pub and dining room. The restaurant serves good food at reasonable prices, and the bar is popular without being rowdy.

There are also two sandwich shops in Essex. She Sells Sandwiches (203) 767-3288 at the Dauntless Shipyard serves everything from the titled sandwiches to homestyle soup, salad, and desserts. The Cheese Shop (203) 767-8172, just across the street from the Griswold, also serves sandwiches, quiche, salad, and soup. Farther afield, a cab ride will get you to Oliver's Taverne (203) 767-2633, with a varied American menu at reasonable prices, or Fine Bouche (203) 767-1277 in Ivoryton, offering expensive French cuisine.

Those who find price no object should certainly try the Copper Beech Inn (203) 767-0330. This extraordinary restaurant is one of the finest in the state. Located on Main Street in the village of Ivoryton, you'll have to take a cab to get here from the water. While the prices are not all that high by New York City standards, they are high for around here; but the food is probably worth the bill.

 ### Navigation and Anchorages

Use NOAA Charts 12375 (1:20,000), 12372 (1:40,000), and 12354 (1:80,000). Use tide tables for New London. High tide at Essex is 1 hour 39 minutes later; low tide is 1 hour 38 minutes later. Multiply height by 1.2 for height at high or low water. Mean tidal range is 3.4 feet.

You can't miss Essex when coming by water–there are boats everywhere, most sporting masts. You'll see large mooring areas on either side of the marinas and will be forced to cut in from the main channel to reach the town. At night, the lights of town are alluring, and without the sound of speedboats on the river, this can be an extremely peaceful place.

The dock at the Connecticut River Museum, at the foot of Main Street, is 6.0nm by boat upriver of the Saybrook Breakwater Light, and 2.6nm by boat upriver of the I-95 Baldwin Bridge.

Approaching **Essex** is a piece of cake. Coming from the south, follow the Coast Guard buoys up to Haydens Point, where you'll leave the 30-foot 4sec green flasher "25" to port, and then follow the private buoys past the moored fleet into the marina or club of your choice.

South Cove, with an entry between Thatchbed Island and Haydens Point, is too shallow for anchoring but is home to a diversity of wildlife. **Middle Cove,** lined with beautiful homes, a marina, and the town green, is much more hospitable, and has a dredged channel about 6 feet deep. Some silting has occurred recently, so sailboats will want to enter on a rising tide.

Essex Island Marina, at the entrance to **North Cove,** is almost a resort, complete with pool, tennis courts, snack bar, and a private ferry that runs a continuous 1-minute commute to the mainland. Essex Boat Works and Brewer's Dauntless Shipyard on the mainland can handle any type of service your boat requires. Although there are many types of boats in **Essex,** it remains mostly a die-hard sailor's port. Several of the yacht clubs have small-boat racing groups–frostbiters–active throughout the winter.

Due to the large number of moorings between the river channel and the marinas, there is little room for anchoring here. If you find an open spot be sure to use a plow or kedge anchor to secure your boat in the thick eel grass. There is a 6-mph speed limit in effect between the 30-foot green 4sec flasher "25" at the **South Cove** entrance and red nun "28" at the north end of the main mooring area.

If you want a quiet anchorage away from it all, try the far side of **Nott Island,** a.k.a. **"Six Mile Island."** Most boats will only be able to approach the anchorage from the south due to the shoals and marshes at the north end of the island, but there is 7 to 12 feet of water here, and usually lots of solitude. There's also a nice beach on the northwest side of the island. The water in this part of the Connecticut River is "Class B," acceptable for both swimming and fishing.

Approaching Essex from the north, be sure to keep an eye out for the rocks and sandbars that surround **Brockway Island:** insurance has paid for far too many boats beached and broken on this island. Take note of the two wrecks charted on the east shore.

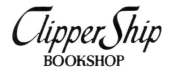

Hamburg Cove from the west.

Brockway Island is opposite the entrance to **Hamburg Cove,** which is 1.5nm north of **Essex.** The entrance to the cove is unimpressive, with a grass island right in the middle. Note that can "1" at the entrance to the cove has been changed from black to green.

Once past the narrow buoyed channel, the cove opens up to a deep hemlock-lined bowl. The channel inside the cove is marked by a series of greens to port and red daymarkers to starboard. Heed the buoys but stay well channel side, and proceed cautiously. What's revealed inside is worth the trip.

CAUTION: The red daymarkers in Hamburg Cove are poles driven into the mud about 10 to 15 feet outside the channel. If you hug them you'll end up in the mud, so favor the port side of the channel.

Because of the many swimmers and moored boats, there is a 5-mph speed limit throughout **Hamburg Cove.** The tide range is under 3 feet, but the tidal and river currents can add up to 4 knots in the entrance channel. When under sail, plan your trip to take advantage of the tides, and take care when docking.

Surrounded by hills and completely protected, **Hamburg Cove** is an excellent hurricane hole, but it often gets extremely crowded during the summer, with rafting parties or club rendezvous almost every weekend. Almost no wind gets in here, so it can get hot, too, and there's nothing to blow the mosquitoes away. One of our readers claims the cove is also her favorite spot to ride out a thunderstorm, because of the way the sound bounces off the hills along the shore. The near lack of current inside the cove helps to make the water very warm.

There isn't much in the town of Hamburg itself, but you'll find a genuine old-time general store at the head of the cove, famous for ice cream, and an annual country fair held during the third weekend of August (203) 434-2494.

Continuing south to **Essex,** you'll see the lights of town ahead once you leave the entrance to Hamburg Cove. Proceed until you see the "no wake" markers and then begin to look for the private markers leading you through the mooring area to the marinas. Because of the town's popularity, it's best to call ahead to reserve a mooring or slip.

 Shoreside and Emergency Services

Airport: Chester (203) 526-2555
Ambulance: 911
Coast Guard: New London (203) 442-4471 or VHF 16
New Haven (203) 773-2400 or VHF 16
Fire: 911 or (203) 399-7921
Harbormaster: (203) 767-0504
Hospital: Shoreline Clinic (203) 767-0107
Police: 911 or (203) 399-6221
Radio Telephone: VHF 27; I.D.: Bridgeport Marine Operator
VHF 25, 26, 86; I.D.: New London Marine Operator
Taxi: East Shore Cab and Transportation (203) 388-2819
Tow Service: Saybrook Towing and Salvage, Old Saybrook, CT (203) 388-4065 or VHF 16 ✦

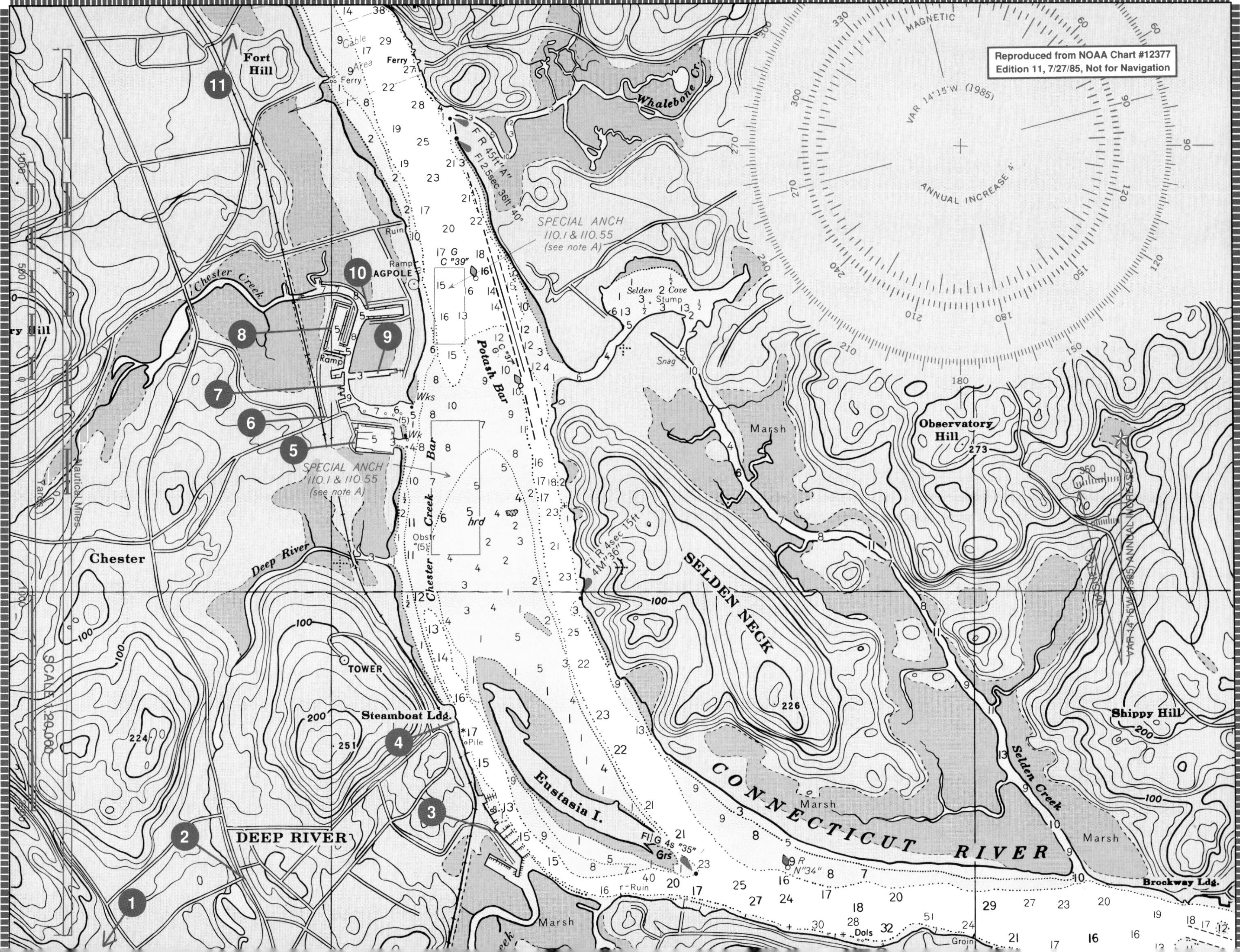
Reproduced from NOAA Chart #12377
Edition 11, 7/27/85, Not for Navigation
72°26'
72°24'
41°24'
CONNECTICUT RIVER
SELDEN NECK
Selden Creek
Selden Cove
Shippy Hill
Observatory Hill
273
Brockway Ldg.
Eustasia I.
Potash Bar
Chester Creek
Chester Creek Bar
Steamboat Ldg.
DEEP RIVER
Deep River
Chester
Fort Hill
Whalebone Cr.
TOWER
Marsh
SPECIAL ANCH
110.1 & 110.55
(see note A)
MAGNETIC
VAR 14°15'W (1985)
ANNUAL INCREASE 4'
Nautical Miles
Yards
SCALE 1:20,000
1
2
3
4
5
6
7
8
9
10
11

Chester and Deep River

The Power of Water

Wherever you find industry, you'll also find a power source, and until recently that usually meant flowing water. The force of a river running downhill toward the ocean generates more tappable energy than just about any other act of nature; so it's not surprising that of all the towns in the original Saybrook Colony, Chester and Deep River were the two which developed the most industry. Not that these towns ever resembled Pittsburgh, but the cataracts on the Chester, Deep River, and Pattaconk creeks did generate enough power to fuel 50 small factories. Brushes, combs, knitting needles, single twist shipbuilding augers, ink wells, and lace were all produced here at one time. And long before anyone thought to worry about extinction of the world's largest land mammal, elephant tusks were off-loaded in Deep River for use by Pratt Reed & Company, the largest piano key manufacturer in the world. Predictably, the factory is now used as condominiums.

The small town of Chester also has its claim to fame: the ferry which runs from here across the river to Hadlyme has been in continuous operation since 1768, making it the second oldest ferry in Connecticut. (The oldest crosses the Connecticut River 25 miles further north at Glastonbury.) The ferry doesn't run in the winter, because the river ices up this far north. So you'll have to count on the swing bridge at East Haddam, as it is the only crossing between Old Saybrook and Middletown. Even after major renovations, however, the bridge isn't that reliable and was stuck open for a few days in March of 1989.

Gillette Castle State Park and the Chester/Hadlyme ferry, the *Seldon III*, crossing the Connecticut River.

© Jack McConnell

★ What To See and Do

If you like the theatre, you've come to the right place. A renovated mill in the center of Chester is home to the National Theater of the Deaf (203) 526-4971; and in an old

Marine Facilities and Services	Phone	Number of Transient Berths	Number of Transient Moorings	Seasonal/Year-round	Largest Vessel Accommodation	Marked Entry Channel	Approach Depth (in feet)	Dockside Depth in feet at MLW	Gas/Diesel Fuel	Fuel Brand	Ramp/Dinghy Dock/Launch Service	Railway/Lift: Capacity (in tons)	Propeller/Hull Repairs	Engine Repairs: Gas/Diesel	Pump-out Station	Marine Supplies/Groceries/Bait/Ice	Showers/Laundromat	110V★ 220V▲ Maximum Amps	MasterCard/VISA/Diners Club; American Express	Restaurant/Snack Bar	Monitors VHF Channel
❶ Outboard Service Center (p. 222)	(203) 526-4774											BOAT & ENGINE SALES & SERVICE									
❷ H & L Diesel	(203) 526-5941			Y								DIESEL SALES & SERVICE									
❸ Deep River Marina (p. 223)	(203) 526-5560	12	4	Y	50	●	15	12	GD	TEX		L15	H			S	SI	★▲50	MV		9
❹ Deep River Navigation Co.	(203) 526-4954											SIGHTSEEING CRUISES									
❺ Connecticut River Marina	(203) 526-9076	4	1	Y	40	●	6	6				L25	PH	GD			SI	★		S	
❻ Chester Auto & Marine	(203) 526-3823			Y									PH	GD			S				16
❼ Chester Marina	(203) 526-2227	10		Y	40	●	6	5				L30	PH	GD		S	SI	★▲30			16
❽ Hays Haven Marina	(203) 526-9366	10		Y	48		5	6	G		R	L15	P			S	SI	★	MV		
❾ Springfield Yacht & Canoe Club												PRIVATE CLUB - MEMBERS ONLY									
❿ Pattaconk Yacht Club	(203) 526-5626											PRIVATE CLUB - MEMBERS ONLY									
⓫ Chrisholm Marina (p. 223)	(203) 526-5147	2		S	45	●	5	5	G	TEX	●	L7	PH	GD		S	SI	★30	MV		16

Information in these listings is provided by the facilities themselves. An asterisk (*) indicates that the facility did not respond to our most recent requests for information.

knitting needle factory is the Goodspeed at Chester (203) 873-8668 (a branch of the Goodspeed Opera House in East Haddam) where you can see new and experimental plays.

Atop one of the "seven sisters," a row of seven hills on the east side of the river, sits Gillette Castle (203) 526-2336. This stone castle was built by Shakespearean stage actor William Gillette. We recommend a visit for the spectacular views of the river as well as the opportunity to spend time in the unique building this man called home.

The big event in Deep River is the annual Ancient Fife and Drum Muster (203) 399-6665, held on the 3rd Saturday in July. Thousands of people and dozens of drum corps

from as far away as Ohio and Virginia turn out each year to watch the parade and join the fun. You may also want to take a trip on one of the excursion boats operated by Deep River Navigation (203) 526-4954, which meet up with the Valley Railroad steam train from Essex and go up river to East Haddam.

 Where To Eat

Chester and Deep River host a number of fine restaurants. Two favorites are Fiddlers (203) 526-3210, serving seafood and great desserts, and the Inn at Chester (203) 526-4961, offering Continental and American cuisine. The Pattaconk Inn (203) 526-9285 serves seafood and steak and has both a patio and take out. The Restaurant Du Village (203) 526-5301 offers a fine French menu; reservations are suggested.

If you're in the area for lunch try the Deep River Inn (203) 526-3500, with some of the best, least expensive, most enormous, mouth-watering burgers in the world.

 Navigation and Anchorages

Use NOAA Chart 12377 (1:20,000). Use tide tables for New London. High tide at Hadlyme is 2 hours 19 minutes later; low tide is 2 hours 23 minutes later. Multiply by 1.1 for height at high or low water. Mean tidal range is

The marinas at Chester Creek are 5.0nm by boat north and west of the docks at the foot of Main Street in Essex, and 3.4nm by boat south and east of the East Haddam Bridge.

This well-marked section of river is easy to navigate. Coming from the south, you may approach **Deep River** from either side of **Eustasia Island.** On the western side of the island is an old steamboat channel. The concrete base of the old light marking this channel still stands, though the light has been removed. There is plenty of water here for all but the largest boats, but you will want to favor the western shore to avoid the moored boats and the sandbar which extends 0.5nm north of the island. There is a 6-mph speed limit in the channel, and around the marinas at **Chester Creek.** The imposing structure on top of the hill in Deep River is Mt. Saint Johns, originally a monastery, and now a home and school for troubled boys. About 3/4 of a mile from the water is downtown Deep River, where you can purchase anything from fresh pasta to tattoos.

About 0.7nm north of Steamboat Landing are the marinas at the entrance to **Chester Creek.** Wait until you are due east of the marinas before heading for the docks. Selden Cove is opposite Chester Creek at green can "37."

CAUTION: If you draw less than four feet, you can probably circle Selden Island, but be sure to go slow in Selden Creek

to avoid the many stumps and snags. The cove itself is shallow, with some deep water near the island.

If you are looking for a nice gunkhole, your best bet is to approach **Selden Island** from the south and go 0.8nm up the creek. The water is good and deep, and the protection from the wind is complete, but there is no room to swing at anchor and little room to turn around. It will probably be best to anchor and tie a line to a tree on shore.

Another beautiful spot to explore by dinghy is **Whalebone Creek,** just to the south of the ferry slip on the east side of the river. On one side of the entrance to the creek is a high rock wall of convoluted granite, and on the other is a small sandy beach, at the point of which is the 45-foot steel tower of the red range light "A." The paired red 2.5sec 36-foot range light "40" stands just to the south.

When heading up river, be sure to leave the ferry plenty of room, and stay away from its backwash, which can easily flip a dinghy. North of the ferry slip in **Hadlyme** is a ramp at Gillette Castle State Park. You can swim off the beach at the park, and canoes are available for rent (203) 526-5492 at the landing, where there are also portable toilets.

 ### Shoreside and Emergency Services

Airport: Chester (203) 526-2555
Ambulance: 911
Coast Guard: New London (203) 442-4471 or VHF 16
New Haven (203) 773-2400 or VHF 16
Fire: 911 or (203) 526-5321
Harbormaster: (203) 526-3688
Hospital: Shoreline Clinic (203) 767-0107
Police: Deep River 911 or (203) 526-3200
Chester 911 or (203) 526-3605
Radio Telephone: VHF 25, 26, 86; I.D.: New London Marine Operator
Taxi: East Shore Cab and Transportation (203) 388-2819
Tow Service: Saybrook Towing and Salvage, Old Saybrook, CT (203) 388-4065 or VHF 16 ◆

East Haddam and Middletown

Would Nathan Hale Have Enjoyed a Musical?

William Goodspeed was a real hard-core American entrepreneur who believed in vertical integration of his businesses; not only did he own a major shipyard and manage a large warehouse in East Haddam, he also ran a steamboat line from New York that stopped at his shipyard, picked up freight from his warehouse, and let passengers off to see a show at *his* opera house–after, of course, they did some shopping at his store and had a drink at his bar.

East Haddam also has some other interesting historical claims. During the winter of 1773-74, the patriot Nathan Hale taught reading, writing, and arithmetic to children in a one-room schoolhouse; and just next door, at Saint Stephen's Episcopal Church, there is an old steeple housing a bell reportedly cast in A.D. 815, which would make it the oldest bell in North America.

The Moodus section of East Haddam also has some history, though not so distant as that bell nor so dominating as the name Goodspeed. No fewer than a dozen mills were established along the Moodus River, which drops nearly 300 feet in only three miles. All of these mills made cotton twine, most of which was used to construct fishing nets; and one of them, the Brownell Mill, was the first mill in the world to spin nylon. Today, Brownell is the only one of the Moodus mills still in operation, and is still making nylon fishing nets.

Sailing past the Goodspeed Opera House in East Haddam, CT.

© Clyde Smith

Approaching East Haddam from the south, you will pass Rich Island. The island was created in the 1800s by a hurricane that left a huge raft of floating debris, which eventually coalesced into a permanent land mass. Just across from the island is Chapman Pond, which is uniquely freshwater *and* tidal, though only hurricanes carry salt water so far north.

Marine Facilities and Services

#	Facility	Phone	Number of Transient Berths	Number of Transient Moorings	Seasonal/Year-round	Largest Vessel Accommodation (in feet)	Marked Entry Channel	Approach Depth in feet at MLW	Dockside Depth in feet at MLW	Gas/Diesel Fuel	Fuel Brand	Ramp/Dinghy Dock/Launch Service	Railway/Lift: Capacity (in tons)	Propeller/Hull Repairs	Engine Repairs: Gas/Diesel	Marine Supplies/Groceries/Bait/Ice	Showers/Laundromat	Pump-out Station	110V ★ 220V ▲ Maximum Amps	MasterCard/VISA/Diners Club/American Express	Restaurant/Snack Bar	Monitors VHF Channel
1	**Chrisholm Marina (p. 223)**	(203) 526-5147	2		Y	45		7	5	G	TEX		L7	PH	G		S	SI		★30	MV		16
2	Middletown Yacht Club	(203) 526-5634	2	2	S	46	●	6	6	*PRIVATE CLUB - MEMBERS ONLY*						S						
3	Camelot Cruises	(203) 345-8591								*SIGHTSEEING CRUISES*												
4	Andrews Marina	(203) 345-2286	3	1	S	46	●	6	6	G						S	SI		★30	MV	RS	
5	Damar Ltd./Midway Marina	(203) 345-8052	2		Y	50		14	6			R	L10	H	GD	S	SI		★30	MV		
6	Goodspeed Opera House	(203) 873-8664			S	167		15	10													
7	Petzold's Marine Center	(203) 342-1196		6	S	55	●	15	4	G	GUL		L35	PH	G				★	MV		16
8	Portland Boat Works	(203) 342-1085			S	75		12	10	G	TEX		L50	PH	GD			S	★▲50	MVA		
9	Yankee Boat Yard Marina	(203) 342-4735	8	8	S	45		15	12	G		RD	L	PH	GD	S	SI		★30	MV		19
10	Crowley & Holmes Riverside Marina	(203) 342-7911	3	1	Y	48		15	12			D	L30	PH	GD	S	SI		★	MV		
†	Wethersfield Cove Yacht Club	(203) 563-8780	4	6	Y	40	●	5	15	G		D				S	S		★30			

Information in these listings is provided by the facilities themselves. An asterisk (*) indicates that the facility did not respond to our most recent requests for information.
† indicates that the facility is located upstream, off of our chart.

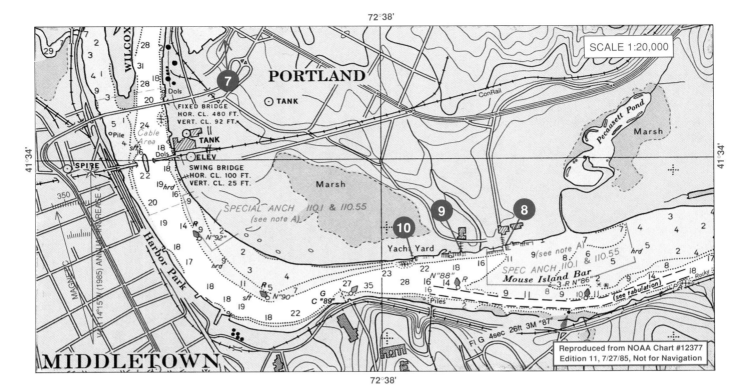

Most boaters think that navigation ends at the East Haddam Bridge; but if you have the time and the desire, you can continue up to Middletown, a dozen miles further north, or even up to Hartford, which is nearly 30 miles north of the bridge and is the official head of navigation. Above East Haddam, the Connecticut River is not quite so idyllic as it is to the south; still, the river is remarkably pristine, much of it bordered by nothing more than state parks.

★ What To See and Do

The town of East Haddam offers the pleasant opportunity to browse for antiques or pick up supplies at the local grocery store. You may also want to head for the famous Goodspeed Opera House (203) 873-8668, a 400-seat theater dedicated to the American Musical. Basic marine supplies or hardware items can be found about 1/2 mile west, in the village of Haddam. You can also take in a wonderful view of the river in a plane leaving from the Goodspeed Airport (203) 873-8568.

One of the most interesting events in Haddam is the Quinnehtukqut Rendezvous and Native American Festival (203) 347-6924 held on the third weekend in August at Haddam Meadows State Park. The festival includes dance competitions, a demonstration village, Colonial crafts, and a black-powder musket shoot.

Haddam Meadows is also the terminus of the zany Connecticut River Raft Race (203) 887-6969, usually held on a blistering hot Saturday at the end of July or the beginning of August. Dozens of homemade rafts compete for prizes given to the fastest raft, the funniest-looking, and the raft most in the spirit of Tom Sawyer and Huck Finn.

Other races to watch for are the annual Pearson Sunfish regatta that sails from Hartford all the way to Haddam in June, and the Head of the Connecticut rowing regatta on Columbus Day weekend in Middletown (203) 347-6924.

🍴 Where To Eat

Restaurants aren't easy to come by in Haddam and East Haddam. Fortunately, the best-known local eatery, The Gelston House and Summer Garden Café (203) 873-1411 in East Haddam, is back in business. For a pleasant dinner on the water, try Camelot Cruises' (203) 345-8591 dinner voyages on its 400-passenger ship.

Should you continue upriver to Middletown, however, you'll find many fine restaurants. Harbor Park (203) 347-9999 is right on the river and offers a spectacular view from its patio. A local favorite is Ziti's (203) 346-3217, where we suggest you try the "stone pies." To get to Ziti's you have to walk through La Boca (203) 346-4492, serving spicy Mexican dishes. On the east side of the river, in Portland, try Farrell's (203) 342-4589, serving seafood and steaks, or J.T. Reilly's (203) 342-2498, with an American menu.

⚓ Navigation and Anchorages

Use NOAA Chart 12377 (1:20,000). Use tide tables for New London. High tide at East Haddam is 2 hours 42 minutes later; low tide is 2 hours 53 minutes later. Multiply by 1.1 for height at high or low water. Mean tidal range is 3.2 feet.

The East Haddam Bridge is 3.4nm by boat north and west of Chester Creek, and 8.4nm by boat north and west of the

Connecticut River Museum Docks at the foot of Main Street in Essex. The Arrigoni (Rte. 66) Bridge in Middletown is 12.6nm by boat to the north and west.

This section of the **Connecticut River** is easy to navigate. There are quite a few shoals, but the channel is well marked and easy to follow, with the deepest water on the outside of the turns. The first anchorages you'll encounter are to the west of **Rich** and **Lord** islands. Between the islands, you'll find a beautiful spot to drop a hook, though it's best left to those in shallow-draft boats. The tides rise only about 3 feet here, so don't expect too much of a lift if you go aground.

Chapman Pond and the little creek that starts at its southeast tip are too shallow for anything larger than a canoe or dinghy, but the trip around the unnamed island is a pleasant escape from the traffic in the main channel.

Short-term tie-up space is available at the Goodspeed Opera House wharf, but you must call first. If you want to stay longer, you should dock at Andrew's Marina on the west side of the river and walk across the bridge. From Andrew's you have easy access to the Opera House, groceries, and a laundromat. Maintain "steerage only" speed in the "Cable Area" near the **East Haddam Bridge.**

On the east side of the river, below Goodspeed's Landing, is Goodspeed Airport (203) 873-8568; docking arrangements vary here each year, so call ahead.

The state launching ramp at the mouth of the **Salmon River** is 0.9nm north of the East Haddam Bridge. Deep-draft boats can go about half a mile into the cove, but should not pass Cones Point because the channel is nearly impossible to see, and the mud is thick enough to grab your keel and hold it for life. However, the bottom does give a good hold, and many local boats successfully weathered hurricane Gloria in here. Note that black can "47" south of the Salmon River entrance is now green.

Shallow-draft boats and dinghies are a great way to explore the **Salmon River** 4nm up to the head of navigation at the Leesville Dam and fish ladder. The Salmon River is Class "A" water, the cleanest in the state, and one of the focuses of the Atlantic Salmon restoration effort. There is a small display at the fish ladder explaining the project, and if you're lucky, you may see one of the state biologists working with the big fish at the counting station. And incidentally, if you love tubing, the upper Salmon River is one of the most beautiful and fun spots to float in the state.

Just above the **Salmon River** is the Connecticut Yankee Atomic Power Station discharge canal. The canal is blocked to boats, but fish are attracted to the warm water, and so fishermen follow close behind. The Connecticut Yankee's Energy Information Center (203) 267-9279 at the north end of the property has a dock and picnic facilities for visitors arriving by boat, as well as a new series of nature trails.

Directly across the river from the power plant is the launching ramp at Haddam Meadows State Park. Be careful of the shallow water near **Haddam Island**–you can reach the island by foot at low tide. There are two sets of range

lights on the east bank above Haddam Island. The first pair is opposite green can "55." The 44-foot light "B" has been changed to a 2.5sec red flasher. North of **Rock Landing,** the 54-foot 2.5sec light "C" (front) is now yellow. The 70-foot rear light "C" is also scheduled to be changed to yellow.

If you're headed upriver to **Middletown** and **Portland,** you'll find that the river is well marked with buoys and lights at every bend. There have been two buoy changes above East Haddam: red nun "62" at Higganum has been relocated 500 yards to the north, and red nun "78" at The Straits has been moved slightly north.

The trip upriver will take some time, as it is nearly 12nm by boat to the three marinas in Portland (and a good two miles more to Petzold's, futher upstream). All the service you'll need can be found up there, and the trip will reveal a wholly new side to the river. Be sure to keep an eye out for the buoys and heed them as you go. The channel is deep, as it runs mostly on the outside corners, but there are shallow spots and rocks outside of the channel all the way. We suggest you don't make this trip at night unless you've already made it once before in daylight. The river gets mighty dark after sunset, and it can be tiring and dangerous to strain your eyes looking for buoys on such a long trip.

 Shoreside and Emergency Services

Airport: Goodspeed Airport (203) 873-8568
Chester (203) 526-2555
Ambulance: 911
Coast Guard: New London (203) 442-4471 or VHF 16
New Haven (203) 773-2400 or VHF 16
Fire: 911 or (203) 537-3411
Hospital: Middlesex Memorial (203) 347-9471
Police: Middletown 911 or (203) 347-4333
Radio Telephone: VHF 25, 26, 86; I.D.: New London Marine Operator
Tow Service: Saybrook Towing and Salvage, Old Saybrook, CT (203) 388-4065 or VHF 16 ✦

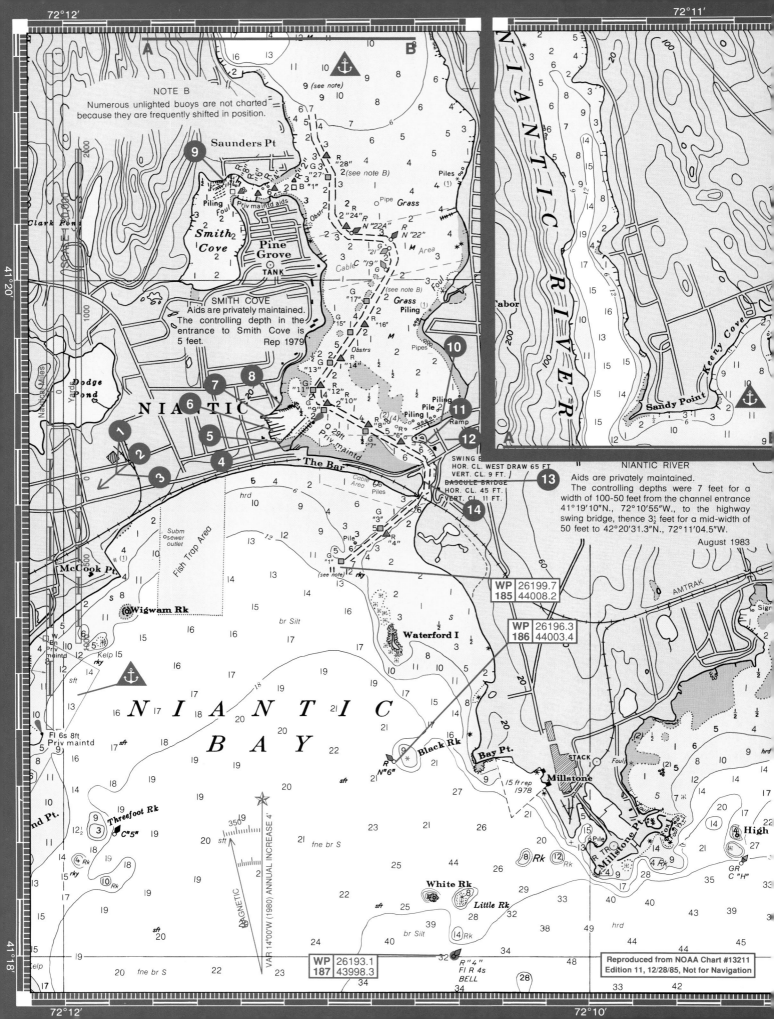

Niantic Bay and the Niantic River

A Look Beyond the Tower

Traveling between Mystic and Saybrook, you'll surely see the 389-foot stack at the Millstone Nuclear Power Station on the east shore of Niantic Bay; and on a good day, you can see that stack from 10 miles or more. It rarely draws boaters in, however, as most are hell-bent on reaching the Saybrook breakwater to the west or the large port of New London to the east.

Their haste is also their loss, as many feel the Niantic River is as nice as Hamburg Cove on the Con-necticut–a beautiful gunkhole with wooded shores and clear water–though Niantic is roomier and less crowded. The river itself is cut off from the bay by a sand bar, keeping it sheltered from overuse. The mouth of the river was once a summer camp for the Nehantic Indians, a local tribe who had been easily pushed out by 1807, when the Boston Post Road opened. The town then became a popular stopover for passengers waiting to cross on the ferry, and grew to its present modest size.

Today's visitors won't find Niantic all that different, except for the bridges. If you look hard enough, you'll find the Pattagansett Marshes, tucked quietly behind the bluffs of Black Point on the southwest side of the bay. The nature preserve here includes the Watts Island wetlands and the rockier Long Ledge. The marshlands are protected by a primary sand dune that is itself stabilized by rocky outcroppings from the west end of Black Point. Nesting platforms there have long attracted ospreys, who thrive on the wide variety of life flourishing in the marsh ecosystem.

The marinas on the west side of the lower Niantic River, from the northwest. In the background is the Millstone Nuclear Power Station.

Marine Facilities and Services

#	Facility	Phone	Transient Berths	Transient Moorings	Seasonal/Year-round	Largest Vessel Accommodation	Marked Entry Channel	Approach Depth (ft)	Dockside Depth (ft at MLW)	Gas/Diesel Fuel	Fuel Brand	Ramp/Dinghy Dock/Launch Service	Railway/Lift: Capacity (tons)	Propeller/Hull Repairs	Engine Repairs: Gas/Diesel	Pump-out Station	Showers/Laundromat	Marine Supplies/Groceries/Bait/Ice	110V ★ 220V ▲ Max Amps	MasterCard/VISA/Diners Club · Amex	Restaurant/Snack Bar	Monitors VHF Channel
1	Niantic Bay Yacht Club	(203) 739-7311	→ *PRIVATE CLUB - MEMBERS ONLY*																			
2	Four Mile River Marina	(203) 434-7283			S	23	●	1	3	G	TEX	R										
3	South Lyme Marina *																					
4	Bayview Landing	(203) 739-6604	6		Y	45	●	3.5	3				L30	PH	GD		S	S	★30			16
5	Boats, Inc.	(203) 739-6251	10	4	Y	30	●	6	6	G	MOB	R	L8	PH	G	●	S	SI	★30	MV		71
6	Harbor Hill Marina	(203) 739-0331	20		Y	35	●	5	4			R						S	★			16
7	Port Niantic, Inc.	(203) 739-2155	4		Y	36	●	3.5	3				R15	PH	GD			S	★15			16
8	Niantic Dockominiums *																					
9	Bayreuther Boatyard	(203) 739-6264	5	2	Y	50	●	5.5	5	GD		R	L30	PH	GD		S	SI	★15	MV	S	16
10	Waddy's Dock	(203) 443-7259	2		S	40	●	5	5	GD	CHE	R	L50	P	GD		S	SI	★15			88
11	Niantic Sportfishing Dock	(203) 447-3635	1		Y	60	●	10	10	GD	MOB	R						BI	▲50	MVA		88
12	Captain John's Sport Fishing Center	(203) 443-7259	2		Y	40	●	5	5	GD		R					S	SI	★15			88
13	Mijoy Dock	(203) 443-0663	→ *DEEP SEA FISHING PARTY & CHARTER BOATS*																			
14	Black Hawk Dock and Market	(203) 443-3662			S	100	●	10	10	*FISHING STATION* →									★60	MV		

Information in these listings is provided by the facilities themselves. An asterisk (*) indicates that the facility did not respond to our most recent requests for information.

What To See and Do

Niantic Bay is one of the few areas on Long Island Sound where water visibility is clear enough for snorkeling. On a good day, you'll be able to spot objects 5 to 7 feet away. Keep an eye out for the blue-eyed scallops in the eel grass around the shallows. Peering up from the bottom with 40 dangling "eyes," these guys may seem bizarre. The "eyes" are actually light sensors, not so different from our own.

Groups can visit the Millstone Nuclear Power Station on weekdays with prior reservations. An Energy Center (203) 444-4234 associated with the station provides computer games on energy creation and use, as well as films, exhibits on solar, nuclear, and hydro power, and a bicycle generator that lights up a small house with only pedal power.

East of the bay, on Goshen Point, you'll find the 231-acre Harkness Memorial State Park (203) 443-5725, dedicated to handicapped children. Set amid extensive gardens open to the public, the 42-room Harkness mansion harbors the original watercolors of Rex Brasher, an artist who painted more than 1,000 species of birds, published in a 12-volume work titled *Birds and Trees of North America.* The mansion itself is currently scheduled for renovation, but luckily the park's real beauty is the outdoors. Enjoy the huge lawns and white beaches any time, and look forward to the summer music festival sponsored at the park each year.

The Eugene O'Neill Memorial Theatre (203) 443-5378 also isn't far from Harkness. The theater's graduate program for actors, producers, and playwrights provides an excellent opportunity to see dramatic readings of works-in-progress.

Near Black Point to the west, Rocky Neck State Park (203) 739-5471 is often less crowded than Harkness. Relax in the sun, sink your toes in the sand, swim in the clear waters, or hike the trails to a private, unknown camp, all for free.

 Where To Eat

Like any good port, almost all of Niantic's eateries are within easy walking distance of the marinas, which are themselves conveniently bunched at the river entrance. On the river's west shore, you'll find The Morton House Resort (203) 739-8564, an old Victorian hotel and restaurant with more than its share of charm and a full menu. Dad's Restaurant (203) 739-2113 is more informal, but has good food and is barely a hop, skip, and a jump from Boats, Inc. China Pavillion (203) 739-8901 serves fine Chinese dishes, while those more interested in the catch of the day should head to Constantine's (203) 739-2848. You'll also find three pizza parlors, several delis, and a Friendly's in this area.

The east shore may have sparser pickin's, but the food is just as good. Try Capt. Ahab's (203) 442-1444, Moby Dick's (203) 444-0237, or Unk's (203) 443-2717, for seafood. Or hunt for the lunch stand, which serves burgers and grinders during the day.

 Navigation and Anchorages

Use NOAA Charts 13211 (1:20,000), 12372 (1:40,000), 12354 (1:80,000), and 13205 (1:80,000). Use tide tables for New London. High tide at Millstone Point is 9 minutes later; low tide is 1 minute later. Multiply by 1.1 for height at high or low water. Mean tidal range is 3.0 feet.

Niantic Bay is 8.5nm by boat east of the Saybrook breakwater and 4.7nm by boat west of New London. Plum Gut is 8.1nm to the south-southwest of Niantic Bay. The 389-foot red and white stack at the Millstone Nuclear Power Station makes a good landmark coming from any direction.

From the 35-foot flashing 5sec horn **[WP-191]** at **Bartlett Reef,** a course of about 330°m for 3.2nm by boat will take you past flashing red 4sec bell "4" **[WP-187]** at White Rock into the center of **Niantic Bay.**

To avoid the shoals at the mouth of the Connecticut River when coming east from the breakwaters, resist any temptation to turn to port until you've gone at least a mile offshore and also passed the flashing red 4sec bell "8" **[WP-181].** Once past bell "8," **Hatchett Reef** is the principal hazard offshore of Old Lyme and East Lyme, which are both crowded with summer enclaves. The reef is well-marked by red nun "6" **[WP-183]** to the south and green can "1" to the north, and there is plenty of water·between it and the mainland, but not between those buoys.

As you approach **Black Point,** keep an eye on the chart and locate the Brothers, a cluster of rocky islets inshore. If you're heading into the bight west of Black Point, watch for red nun "2" and heed the aids on the way in. East of the Brothers there's a nice daytime anchorage and picnic spot. The water and sandy beach here are good for swimming, but the spot is too exposed for an overnight stay.

There are three small islands west of Black Point, none open to visitors. Both Griswold Island, to the southwest of Watts Island, and Huntley Island, due west of Watts, are privately owned. Watts Island itself is part of a nature sanctuary, and not open to the public.

There are two approaches to Niantic Bay from the east. First, you may approach via **Twotree Island Channel** north of Bartlett Reef, being sure to go south of the red and green junction buoy "R" **[WP-195]** at Rapid Rock and green can "3" at Little Goshen Reef. Keep green can "1" north of Bartlett Reef and can "3" off Twotree Island to port, and you'll have a clear shot at the flashing red 4sec bell "4" **[WP-187]** that marks the outer part of Niantic Bay.

You may also head south past **Bartlett Reef,** which is marked by a 35-foot flashing white light, a fog signal, and a red and white diamond on a skeleton tower **[WP-191].** There is a strong current around the light; and just to the east, you'll see green can "1A." As you round the reef, it's wise to stay fairly close to it on an ebb tide so that the 4- to 5-knot current won't suck you out toward The Race. Remember that tides turn about one hour earlier along the coast than out in the middle of the Sound.

Coming into **Niantic Bay** itself, stay well west of White Rock and Little Rock off the eastern shore, marked by red flasher "4" **[WP-187]**. Niantic Bay is wide enough (1.5nm) for seas to build up, making for an uncomfortable night if the wind is blowing from any direction but the north. There is a special anchorage on the west side off Crescent Beach, about 0.4nm northwest of Threefoot Rock, with good holding ground. The anchorage is marked by an 8-foot, 6sec flasher, maintained by the Niantic Bay Yacht Club at the end of the curving breakwater.

The **Niantic River** is entered by a narrow channel, with a controlling depth of 6 feet up to the two bridges which separate the bay from the river. The beginning of the channel is marked by a small green daymark "1" **[WP-185]** that is hard to spot until you're practically on top of it. Your best bet is to travel a course parallel to a line between red flasher "4" and nun "6" **[WP-186]** at Black Rock until you spot the entrance daymarker. Remember to stay well west of both buoys to avoid White Rock. If you're coming from the west, put Threefoot Rock dead astern and steer a course of about 54°m until you see the entrance.

CAUTION: A new bridge is under construction at the entrance to the Niantic River. Read the following instructions carefully before entering the river.

The southernmost bridge at the **Niantic River** entrance is a railroad bascule with a clearance of 11 feet, and is usually open. The northernmost bridge is that of Rte. 156, and is now being replaced by a new bridge under construction, just south of the old. The present Rte. 156 bridge is a swing affair with a clearance of 9 feet and is usually closed.

To facilitate construction of the new bridge supports, coffer dams–resembling large steel bulkheads–are built to keep the water out of a specific section of the river. Construction of the dams effectively cuts the already narrow channel in half, making the passage even trickier. Considering the strong tidal currents here, which can reach 4 to 5 knots, we suggest you enter only under power.

To open the car bridge give one long and one short blast of your horn. Both bridge tenders monitor VHF 13. The bridge tender at the auto bridge will be able to give you advice on navigating the constricted channel, and let you know what's waiting on the other side. On weekends, there should also be some sort of traffic control, provided until construction is completed, which may not be for another couple of years. If you're not used to the tricks the current can play, it's best to enter the river at slack tide, or with the current against you. Plan to spend a few hours above the bridges, taking advantage of the tides for your return.

CAUTION: When in the narrow entrance channel, you should also be alert for small buoys that mark underwater cables. There is a no-wake speed limit between the bridges, which is strictly enforced.

Beyond the bridges you'll find a privately maintained channel with a maximum depth of 3.5 feet. Most of the marinas are right next to each other inside the west end of The Bar. The hard part isn't finding the marinas, it's trying to tell which is which in the profusion of docks and yards.

From the marinas on the lower Niantic, you can go another couple of miles up river to get away from it all. The entire channel from the entrance up to Smith Cove and beyond is marked with privately maintained buoys. Though some of the markers are not charted, they should be scrupulously obeyed, since water is in short supply there.

The entrance to **Smith Cove** is marked by privately maintained aids and carries 3 to 5 feet of water. Inside, you'll find Bayreuther Boat Yard, a full-service facility, and the Smith Cove Yacht Club. When entering Smith Cove from the south, be sure not to cut green buoy "27."

There is good water for anchoring starting about 500 yards north of Smith Cove. You'll find depths of 10 to 20 feet for nearly a mile north of Sandy Point, and 8 to 11 feet in **Keeny Cove.** The inner bay at Keeny Cove is peaceful, with good holding ground below.

 ### Shoreside and Emergency Services

Airport: Groton-New London (203) 445-8549
Ambulance: 911
Bus: SEAT (203) 886-2631
Coast Guard: New London (203) 442-4471 or VHF 16
Fire: 911 or (203) 739-3449
Harbormaster: (203) 739-5446
Hospital: Lawrence & Memorial Hospital (203) 442-0711
Police: 911 or (203) 739-7007
Radio Telephone: VHF 25, 26, 86; I.D.: New London Marine Operator
Taxi: East Lyme Taxi (203) 739-7775
Tow Service: Southeastern Marine Towing, Groton, CT (203) 445-8381 or VHF 16; Saybrook Towing and Salvage, Old Saybrook, CT (203) 388-4065 or VHF 16; Marine Rescue Services, Wickford, RI (401) 295-8711 or VHF 16   ✦

New London Harbor and Groton

All That Life Can Afford

You must admit, the first American settlers had guts; not only did they invade hostile territory and take the land, they also named the places after their old homes. Take, for example, New London. Some colonists moved into an area along a 12-mile-long river and decided to call it *Thames*. Short on imagination, perhaps; but it took spine to survey their meager little settlement with its few miserable log cabins and call it *New London*–as in London, greatest city on earth, monetary capital of the world, cultural center extraordinaire, home of the King. Optimistic blokes, these.

Even today, New London harbor can't quite rival its famous namesake; but it has come a long way since those early days. In fact, if those first settlers were to show up now, they might well feel their vision had been fulfilled. The city has become a major shipping, military, and educational center, teeming with activity. As Dr. Johnson may have said, "When a man is tired of [New] London, he is tired of life; for there is in [New] London all that life can afford." Hyperbole, yes; but still, you need never have a dull minute while in New London.

New London Ledge Light, the last manned offshore lighthouse on the Sound.

© *Jack McConnell*

The Thames, on the other hand, remains as it was, meager in comparison to its forebear–but still a fine river for shipping. Draining across old crystalline rocks in a narrow, crooked valley, the river remains almost sandless.

Marine Facilities and Services	Phone	No. Transient Moorings	No. Transient Berths	Seasonal/Year-round	Largest Vessel Accommodation	Marked Entry Channel	Approach Depth (in feet)	Dockside Depth in feet at MLW	Gas/Diesel Fuel	Fuel Brand	Ramp/Dinghy Dock/Launch Service	Railway/Lift: Capacity (in tons)	Propeller/Hull Repairs	Engine Repairs: Gas/Diesel	Pump-out Station	Showers/Laundromat	Marine Supplies/Groceries/Bait/Ice	110V★ 220V▲ Maximum Amps	MasterCard/VISA/Diners Club/American Express	Restaurant/Snack Bar	Monitors VHF Channel
1 Shenecosset Yacht Club	(203) 445-9976	8	2	S	50	●	9	7	GD	MOB	R	L30				S	I	★30			
2 Spicer's Groton Marina	(203) 536-4978	6	4	Y	40	●	7	5			RDL	L15	PH	GD		S	SIB	★▲30	MVA		9
3 Thames Yacht Club	(203) 443-9933	7		S	60	●	15	10								S	I	▲		S	9
4 Thames Port Marina	(203) 443-8502	5		S	50	●	14	8	GD							S	I	★20		RS	
5 Burr's Yacht Haven	(203) 443-8457	25	10	S	125	●	12	9	GD			L20	PH	GD		SL	S	★50	MV	RS	9
6 A & W Marina	(203) 443-6076	2	2	S	25	●	5	3						D			B				
7 Ferry Slip Dockominiums	(203) 536-8162	20		Y	47	●	10	13			*PRIVATE CLUB - MEMBERS ONLY*						I	★▲60			16
8 Fort Trumbull Marina*	(203) 443-9729																				
9 Hellier Yacht Sales	(203) 442-1154			Y	*YACHT SALES*																
10 Crocker's Boatyard	(203) 443-6304	25		Y	90	●	12	12	GD	MOB		L75	PH	GD		SL	SIG	★▲50	MV	R	16
11 New London City Pier	(203) 442-1777	10		Y	350	●	21	21									I	★		R	16
12 **Groton Oil Co. & Marina (p. 237)**	**(203) 445-5336**	3		Y	50	●	15	12	GD	MOB							I	▲20	MVA		16
13 Groton Marine Dock	(203) 445-4994			S	35	●	20	15										★			
14 Hel-Cat Dock	(203) 535-2066			S		●													MV	R	
15 Thames Harbor Inn	(203) 445-8111	4		S	80	●	15	15								SL	GBI	★30	MVA		13

Information in these listings is provided by the facilities themselves. An asterisk (*) indicates that the facility did not respond to our most recent requests for information.

It seems the glacier left the lower Thames broad and deep, a perfect channel for big ships to come and go. Testament to the harbor's commercial promise, New London's first customs master was appointed in 1659, a short 13 years after the town was first deeded to Governor John Winthrop, Jr. It was only another year before shipbuilding began along the harbor shores.

By the time of the Revolution, New London had become a busy port. The privateers licensed by the revolutionary government to harass British ships liked to hide out in New London. And their enormous success–capturing more than 500 British ships during the war–filled the burgeoning city's warehouses with valuable booty.

The British retaliated, of course, under the leadership of Benedict Arnold, who had lived in Norwich and was familiar with the area as well as the Continental Army's routine. He sent 400 men in a two-pronged attack against both Fort Griswold and Fort Trumbull. When the British were spotted by colonial militiamen, two cannon shots were fired as an alarm. Arnold, however, confused the signal by firing a third shot of his own and then proceeded to overrun both forts once their guard was down. Many colonists were killed in the attack and Arnold succeeded in burning much of New London and Groton–43 warehouses and homes in all–to the ground, gaining a reputation for having spread "desolation and woe throughout the region."

Since those down days, New London has never relinquished its position as a major shipping port. At one point during the 1880s, the city lay claim to the second largest whaling fleet in the nation, with a total of 72 ships, only one less than New Bedford. More important, still, has been the presence of American armed services in the area. In addition to the Coast Guard Academy, located above the bridges, the river also sports the Electric Boat submarine facility in Groton and the Naval Underwater Communications Center at Fort Trumbull. The latter specializes in sonar communications development and research. The high arches on the west shore of the river are part of a submarine antenna testing system which simulates the orbits of communication satellites over a model submarine floating in a six-foot tank below.

Across the river, Groton is known as the "submarine capital of the world." *Nautilus,* the first nuclear sub, was built here during the early 1950s and launched from this site in 1955. In 1981, Electric Boat launched the first of the new Trident-class nuclear attack subs. Each of these 560-foot subs carries 24 missiles that can land within 20 feet of a target located 4,000 miles away.

Of equal interest to boaters in this area is the New London Ledge Light, built in 1909. A square, red-brick, three-story building with a basement, the lightkeeper's house is notorious for its ominous presence as well as its ghost. A former keeper of the light named Ernie apparently jumped from the top balcony after his wife eloped with a ferryboat captain. The light is now automated, but some claim that Ernie still plays tricks with local ferries.

Another interesting light is on Avery Point, on the campus of the University of Connecticut. Built by local shipping magnate Morton Plant to decorate his mansion, the light shone only during the 1940s and 1950s. For the most part, Plant enjoyed standing on the balcony watching the boats practice for the America's Cup. The property now belongs to the University's Marine Science Institute, where students study the viability of harvesting kelp and other seaweeds from the waters around New London Ledge.

 What To See and Do

The City of New London has been undergoing major refurbishing. The railroad station has been restored, as has a large part of the waterfront and some of the grand old homes in the area. Among the places worth visiting are the Hempstead House (203) 443-7949, oldest in the city, and the Huguenot House, which dates from 1751. The Shaw Mansion (1756), once home of Captain Nathaniel Shaw, is now home to the New London County Historical Society (203) 443-1209.

The handsome New London County Courthouse, built in 1784, is also worth a visit, as are the four Greek Revival houses on Whale Oil Row, and the Monte Cristo Cottage on Pequot Avenue (203) 443-0051, boyhood home of dramatist Eugene O'Neill. A fair walk from there is the schoolhouse where Nathan Hale taught in 1775, just across from the train station. You can pick up a free map of New London and a listing of commercial services at the Downtown Association (203) 444-1879.

Ocean Beach Park (203) 447-3031 at the foot of Ocean Avenue has a beautiful bathing beach, a water slide, and a mile-long boardwalk. Like Napatree Point in Watch Hill, RI, Ocean Beach was originally lined with private homes; and, as at Napatree, all those homes were washed away by the hurricane of 1938.

To the west of Avery Point is the equally nice but less developed Bushy Point Beach. You can anchor just off the steep, pebbly beach and swim or row a dinghy ashore for a stroll along the shore or through the woods at the park. There's even a rise of land where you can see all the way to Watch Hill. It's a great place for the kids to burn off some steam, but you should check them carefully for ticks afterward, especially the tiny ones that carry Lyme disease.

The party boat *Hel-Cat II* (203) 535-2066 can take you deep-sea fishing from its pier on Thames Street in Groton. The *River Queen* (203) 445-9516 sails from the city pier on a one-hour harbor tour and also has special "Lobster in the Rough" and "Dixieland Jazz" cruises in the evenings. The downtown area, a short walk from the docks, contains many fine restaurants and all the services you may need.

The big event in New London and Groton each summer is the annual Sail Festival (203) 443-8331, culminating in a terrific fireworks display on the weekend after July 4th. Due to the number of boats, the late hour, and the amount of alcohol consumed, the harbor often gets a bit too exciting

The 1892 Yale-Harvard Regatta on the Thames River, probably photographed from the Groton side. (For the record, Yale won.) The railroad bridge in the photo no longer exists.
Photographer unknown. Photo courtesy of Yale University Library Archives.

IVY LEAGUE ON THE HALF-SHELL

During the midst of the Great Depression, President Franklin Delano Roosevelt kept his own particular date with destiny. He had an appointment with his son, young Franklin Jr., a student at Harvard University, the president's alma mater. The unusual feature of this appointment was that Mr. Roosevelt chose to keep it not at the White House or in Cambridge, MA, but in the middle of the Thames River in New London.

Young Franklin Jr. was an oarsman pulling for the Harvard junior varsity team on June 21, 1935, and Franklin Sr. was just one among the cheering crowd that lined the river's banks or filled the flotilla of boats anchored in the Thames to watch the Yale-Harvard Regatta.

During the century the two universities have raced on the Thames River, millionaires, presidents, and industrialists have been among the thousands of men and women watching from ashore or anchored yachts.

In 1879, the square-rigged Man 'O War, *Saratoga* sailed up the Thames for the spectacle. During the 1920s, the magnate J.P. Morgan watched from his 400-foot *Corsair*. Morton F. Plant, a shipping and railroad magnate with a summer home at Avery Point in Groton, invited guests from all over the country to stay at his mansion for the race.

For land-bound viewers, the New London Northern and New Haven railroads provided special observation cars that traveled up and down the rails following the race from Winthrop Neck in New London to Bartlett's Cove in Montville. The flatbed cars had chairs that provided an unobstructed view of the river.

For those who could not afford a yacht, the railroad bridge built across the river in 1889 allowed a bird's eye but stationary look at the competition. Remnants of this first bridge, which after 1910 was transformed for automobiles, can be seen just south of the current twin spans of the Gold Star Memorial Highway.

Today, the race is but a shadow of its former self. The thousands of spectators have dwindled to hundreds. The private yachts have been replaced by company-run ferries and schooners, and small power boats. But the rivalry remains. And, as always, will be played out again this spring.

Contributed by Linda M. Rancourt, a freelance writer from Groton, CT.

during this event. You may get just as good a view, while not risking your boat, if you watch the fireworks from your slip or on foot in downtown New London. Both sides of the harbor sponsor interesting concerts and other events, and there are sail races in the harbor all weekend. For the best view of New London and the harbor, climb up to the high ground at Fort Griswold State Park (203) 445-1729 in Groton. Here, you'll have the added benefit of watching the reenactment of Fort Griswold's last stand, when Colonel Ledyard surrendered to the British commander, who then promptly ran Ledyard through with his own sword.

 ### Where To Eat

As with most cities, New London and Groton have plenty of restaurants, many of which are within a mile of the harbor. The Gondolier (203) 447-1781 at 92 Huntington Street serves Italian and American food. Ye Olde Tavern (203) 442-0353 in the historic district, offers excellent American food. For fine seafood, try the Sea Dragon (203) 443-1317 on Pequot Avenue. Paul's Pasta (203) 442-5276 also serves Italian food, while the Lorelei (203) 449-9515 in Groton serves steak and seafood. For something more exotic, try the Szechuan food at Tin Tsin (203) 444-7411.

 ### Navigation and Anchorages

Use NOAA Charts 13213 (1:10,000), 13212 (1:20,000), 12372 (1:40,000), and 13205 (1:80,000). Use tide tables for New London. Mean tidal range is 3.0 feet.

The paired flashers marking the entrance to the New London Harbor channel are 4.5nm by boat east of the entrance to Niantic Bay, 3.3nm by boat north-northwest of Race Rock, and 4.5nm by boat west of the approach to Mystic at Morgan Point.

You're going to run into a lot of commercial shipping traffic in the **New London Harbor** area. Always give the right-of-way to the larger and less maneuverable vessels, especially submarines, which will be on the surface until they reach the open Atlantic.

For all of their awesome capabilities, subs aren't as maneuverable in tight quarters as you are. One of our readers, who once served on subs out of New London, tells us they would stop their forward thrust at New London Ledge Light and would still have to reverse the turbines to

© Steven R. Krous

bring the sub to a stop at Electric Boat, more than 3 miles upriver. On rare occasions you may notice a "pinging" sound running through your hull from sonar transmitters. You may also experience sporadic electrical interference with your instruments.

CAUTION: *If you look carefully at the chart for New London Harbor, you'll notice lots of "Security Zone" warnings, which should be taken seriously. The Navy and Coast Guard do not take kindly to waterborne photographers in the vicinity of the sub base or the shipyards, so tell the shutterbugs in your crew to put away their cameras.*

The main channel into the harbor begins at the paired 4sec flashers "1" and "2" **[WP-196].** Buoy "1" is now a green 2.5sec flasher, instead of the white 4sec shown on the charts. Red flasher "2" is now 2.5sec, and can "3" is now a 4sec green flasher. Similar changes have been made on many of the other channel markings. Between flasher "2" and Race Point on Fishers Island, two new ship anchorages, "E" and "F" have been established.

As you head into the wide-open harbor, you'll see **New London Ledge Light,** a square brick Victorian building atop a white pier, marking a series of ledges that block the harbor. The group-flashing, red and white light 58 feet above the water is visible for 19 miles and has a continuous fog signal. Farther up to port, to the west, is the beacon of the **New London Harbor Light** (also known as "Pequot Light"), 89 feet above the water, with a red sector marking the nearby shoals. Note that the green flasher "5" **[WP-197]** on the channel now flashes 2.5sec, and red flasher "6" is now 2.5sec.

Other prominent features are the microwave tower atop a building in downtown New London and the large sheds of the shipyard on the east side of the river opposite Fort Trumbull. Ferries run in and out of the harbor, moving fast and leaving large wakes. The main entrance has 36 to 40 feet of water, with a mean tidal range of only 3 feet, so fixed docks are the rule.

If you're coming from the west, you need not enter the channel at flashers "1" and "2," unless your boat is an oil tanker. Don't cut inside the red and green nun "R" **[WP-195]** at Rapid Rock, or can "7" off Ocean Beach on the west entrance to the harbor, as there are numerous rocky patches and boulders. Also note that **Sarah Ledge,** 600 yards southeast of can "7," is now marked by red and green can "SL."

From the east, **Pine Island Channel** cuts between Black Ledge, marked on the north by green can "3," and the red 4sec flasher "2" off Pine Island. (Red nun "6," marking the west side of Black Ledge, has been relocated slightly to the west.)

CAUTION: Pine Island channel has a 10-foot controlling depth and is used by small boats running between New London and Fishers Island, but it is best left to those who are familiar with the area. If you do use it, stand well out from Eastern Point to avoid Black Rock as you come into the main channel. Note that can "F" at Frank Ledge is now green and red.

The currents follow the direction of the channel, and are generally not strong. To the east, between Avery Point and Pine Island, is an enticing small anchorage, home of the Shennecossett Yacht Club, which has a launch service and is also the home port for the Groton Police boat.

The marinas in the **Avery Point** area offer moorings or slips. Supplies are available at a convenience store about a half-mile away; there is also access to public tennis courts, a golf course, and a beach. Just to the east of Shennecossett is the Groton/New London Airport. Depending on the winds and which runway the planes are using for takeoffs, you may not notice the airport at all, or you may find it glaringly obvious.

The first good anchorage on the west side of the river in everything but a strong southerly is **Greens Harbor,** marked by White Rock just off the main channel. There's a 5-mph speed limit throughout the harbor. The green flasher "7" on the channel opposite Greens Harbor is now a 6sec flasher.

City Pier in New London offers dockage at reasonable rates and is certainly convenient for downtown shopping or browsing. However, due to the ferries that dock nearby, the channel wash can be severe.

Upriver, beyond Fort Trumbull, is **Shaw Cove,** with 11 to 15 feet of water, entered through a railroad swing bridge. Sound one long and one short blast to open the bridge.

If you want to anchor away from the noise of New London, there are several coves out on the Sound to the east. When heading east toward them and passing in the neighborhood of the 28-foot 4sec flashing **Seaflower Reef Light [WP-198],** be careful of the lobster pots. There's a strong current in the area, so remember that the lines down to the pots may not be directly under the buoys.

 ### Shoreside and Emergency Services

Airport: Groton-New London (203) 445-8549
Ambulance: 911 or (203) 442-2345
Bus: SEAT (203) 886-2631
Coast Guard: New London (203) 442-4471 or VHF 16
Ferry: To Montauk, NY (516) 668-5709
    To Orient Point, NY (203) 443-5281
    To Fishers Island, NY (203) 442-0165
    To Block Island, RI (203) 442-9553
Fire: 911 or (203) 442-2345
Harbormaster: (203) 443-4431 or VHF 13
Hospital: Lawrence and Memorial (203) 442-0711
    Pequot Treatment Center (203) 446-8265
Police: 911 or (203) 442-4444
Radio Telephone: VHF 25, 26, 86; I.D.: New London
    Marine Operator
Taxi: Yellow (203) 443-4321
    Blue (203) 443-4303
Tow Service: Southeastern Marine Towing, Groton, CT
    (203) 445-8381 or VHF 16; Saybrook
    Towing and Salvage, Old Saybrook, CT
    (203) 388-4065 or VHF 16; Marine Rescue
    Services, Wickford, RI (401) 295-8711
    or VHF 16
Train: Amtrak 1-800-USA-RAIL ◆

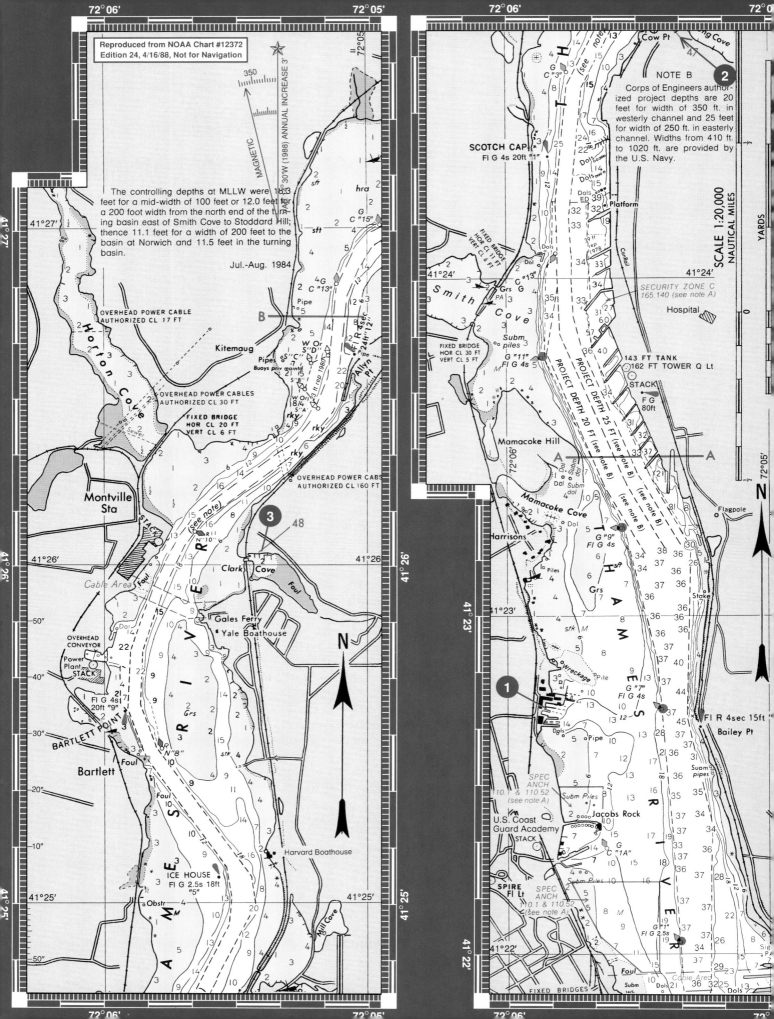

The Thames River to Norwich

Old and New Along the Thames

The out-of-the-future nuclear subs that ply the waters of the Thames before heading to the Sound have nothing over the bark *Eagle*, just across the river. The Coast Guard maintains this 295-foot, three-masted sailing ship in perfect condition, and with her grand red strip across the fore-hull and a mainmast of 143 feet, she's hard to overlook. When carrying her full 21,000 square feet of sail, the *Eagle* cuts the waters easily at 17 knots. Every Coast Guard cadet trains on the *Eagle*, and some believe a cadet's performance on board reveals a lot about his future potential as an officer.

The Coast Guard Academy, which owns and maintains the *Eagle*, was founded on board the cutter *Chase*, a fast sloop which spent some time in Maryland before moving north to New London. Established in 1910 at Fort Trumbull, the Academy didn't move to its present location above the Gold Star Bridge until 1929. The Georgian red brick buildings are still an impressive landmark on the river, though they're hard to see until you have them abeam.

New London Harbor is part of the Thames River tidewater estuary, a 12-mile stretch of river with various mixes of fresh and salt water. The watershed from this estuarine river comprises 1,500 square miles of streams, woodlands, meadows, and high ridges: nearly one-quarter of Connecticut's land, all told. Forty-three towns lie within the watershed area, which is monitored by the Thames River Watershed Association (203) 445-1868 in hopes that the resource can eventually be restored to a healthy state. At the moment, most of the water in the river is heavily polluted and has a quality rating of "C," meaning fish still swim in it, but you shouldn't.

At the head of the river is a small city named Norwich. During the Colonial period, Norwich was a major port, serving as a transfer point for produce from farms in the back country before later developing into a shipbuilding center. The coming of the railroad in 1840 cut deeply into the shipping business, however, leaving mostly passenger steamships in the harbor. Travelers would come from New York by ship and then head north to Boston on the train.

Today, the waterfront of Norwich is rebounding after a long period of decline. There is renewed interest in the harbor since the construction of American Wharf, a large marina, restaurant, and office complex being built on Holly Hock Island. With the new developments, the area is once again becoming popular with cruising boaters, though the distance upriver from the Sound will deter some sailors.

Oh, Buoy!

© *Clyde Smith*

 What To See and Do

Traveling up the Thames River is an interesting mish-mash of sights. Part of New London is heavily industrialized, with

Marine Facilities and Services		Number of Transient Berths	Number of Transient Moorings	Seasonal/Year-round	Largest Vessel Accommodation (in feet)	Approach Depth in feet	Marked Entry Channel	Dockside Depth in feet at MLW	Ramp/Dinghy Dock/Launch Service	Gas/Diesel Fuel	Fuel Brand	Railway/Lift: Capacity (in tons)	Propeller/Hull Repairs	Engine Repairs: Gas/Diesel	Pump-out Station	Showers/Laundromat	Marine Supplies/Groceries/Bait/Ice	110V★ 220V▲ Maximum Amps	MasterCard/VISA/Diners Club American Express	Restaurant/Snack Bar	Monitors VHF Channel
① Thames Shipyard	(203) 442-5349								*COMMERCIAL SHIPBUILDING/REPAIRS*												
② Long Cove Landing	(203) 464-7033	5	4	S	34	4		6		G	TEX	R	PH	G			SI	★	MV		72
③ Gales Ferry Marina	(203) 464-2146	5	3	Y	45	4	•	7		GD	TEX	L35	PH	GD		S	SBI	★30	MV	S	16
④ The Marina at American Wharf (p. 241)	(203) 886-6363	25		Y	140	11	•	8		GD	TEX	L50	P	GD	•	SL	SGI	★50	MVA	RS	68

Information in these listings is provided by the facilities themselves. An asterisk (*) indicates that the facility did not respond to our most recent requests for information.

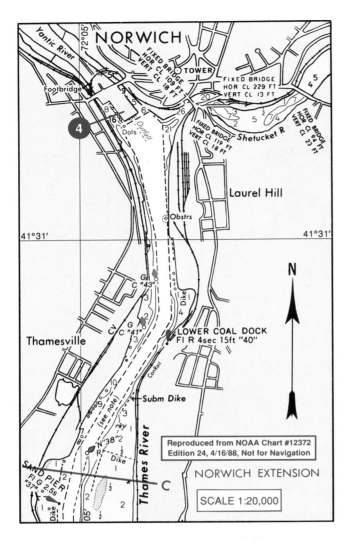

Pfizer Chemical and the naval shipyard dominating the waterline. Other sections, however, are on the rise, with old brick buildings being refurbished and whole street blocks rebuilt.

Coming up the river, be sure to keep an eye out for the tall masts of the *Eagle*. She's one sight you won't want to miss. When in port, the *Eagle* is open to visitors from 12:00 to 5:00 on weekends. The Academy campus is also worth a visit, especially to see the mural in the administration building. From May to October the Visitors' Pavillion is open from 9:00 to 5:00 and offers a map for self-guided toursof the school.

Across the highway, you'll find the Lyman Allen Museum (203) 443-2545 on the Connecticut College campus. This museum highlights a number of beautiful doll houses made by an old master. The children may also enjoy the Thames Science Center (203) 442-0391 right next to campus, with hands-on exhibits.

History and ship buffs will love the *Nautilus* Memorial and Submarine Force Library and Museum (203) 449-3174, located next to the sub base. Christened in 1954, the USS *Nautilus* was the first nuclear-powered submarine. Now docked at the museum on permanent display, the submarine is an immensely popular attraction. The wait at the entrance is often more than an hour during the summer. Unfortunately, there are no tie-up facilities for recreational boaters at the sub base or at the museum, so you'll have to get there by foot or by wheel.

About four miles above the bridges are the boathouses used by Yale and Harvard during their yearly regatta on the Thames. The first annual regatta was held more than 100 years ago and now normally occurs on the first Saturday in June. Though the fanfare has diminished over the years, the race remains an intense and stirring sight. Neither team regularly practices on the river, because of its distance from campus, but that doesn't seem to slow the boats down. Call (203) 432-1456 for more information.

Even further up river, in Norwich, you can attend city-sponsored concerts each week, and the special Harborday, held in late August, at the Howard P. Brown Memorial Park (203) 886-2800. Located along the river, the park is just a short walk from downtown. There are also a number of community events held during the summer at the Marina at American Wharf. These include music, arts and crafts shows, and children events, and you may pick up a calendar secheduling the specific dates at the marina.

If you'd rather listen to nature make music, you might want to visit Mamacoke Island across from the sub-base. This little, rounded island is a wildlife refuge owned by Connecticut College and is open to picnickers of all shapes and sizes, provided they step softly and pack out whatever they pack in.

Where To Eat

When traveling the Thames River, you'll have many choices for food. For restaurant suggestions in New London and Groton, please see the previous chapter on those two cities.

When in Norwich, however, be sure to head for the Chelsea Landing Pub & Galley (203) 889-9932, which serves excellent steak and seafood. The River Café (203) 889-5666 at American Wharf serves a variety of entrees, all of which can be enjoyed while overlooking the waterfront. For pizza, we suggest Yantic Pizza (203) 887-6152 or Olympic Pizza (203) 887-0196, both of which offer take-out and are just two of the many pizza pubs in this area.The Prince of Wales Dining Room at the Norwich Inn & Spa (203) 886-2401 serves fine American cuisine and offers the luxury of eating on an outdoor terrace. For a stick-to-the-ribs meal, try Wild Bill's BBQ (203) 886-8397, and don't hesitate to call beforehand, as they offer free delivery.

Navigation and Anchorages

Use NOAA Chart 12372 (1:40,000). Use tide tables for New London. High tide at Norwich is 13 minutes later; low tide is 25 minutes later. Multiply by 1.2 for height at high or low water. Mean tidal range is 3.4 feet.

The I-95 bridges across the Thames River are 3.5nm by boat north of the New London Ledge Light and 7.8nm by boat north of The Race. Holly Hock Island in Norwich is 10.0nm by boat to the north. About 2 miles above the bridges on the east shore is the U.S. Naval Submarine Base, marked by the 143-foot-high tank used to train sailors to escape from submarines.

CAUTION: There have been many buoy changes in this area. We have noted the most important below, but be alert for others.

A bascule railroad bridge just above downtown New London separates the upper river from **New London Harbor.** Give the usual one long and one short blast on your horn, or contact the bridge tender on VHF 13 to open the bridge. Unless your masts are extremely tall, you won't have trouble passing under the next two bridges, with clearances of 135 and 75 feet respectively. The *Eagle,* with a foretruck height of 147.3 feet, has to house, or lower, her top masts to get under the bridge–and at that she has only a 2 foot clearance–but we suspect you'll have an easier time making this passage.

CAUTION: A careful look at the chart for New London Harbor reveals many "Security Zone" warnings. These should be taken seriously, as the Navy and Coast Guard do not take kindly to photographers in the vicinity of the sub base or the shipyards, so please encourage your shipborne shutterbugs to stow their cameras before arriving.

The trip from **New London Ledge Light** to **Norwich** will take anywhere from 2 to 3 hours, though the trip back down river takes only half the time. You'll find brackish water all the way upriver, but it's fresh enough that the trip offers the lazy man a good way to kill off the marine growth on the bottom of his boat.

CAUTION: Both Connecticut College and the Coast Guard Academy regularly row on the river. Whenever you see the sleek and unstable crew shells, proceed with extreme caution as not to flip them. Remember, you are legally responsible for any damage caused by your wake.

Tidal range in the upper Thames River is 3.6 feet, and the 5-mph speed limit is strictly enforced. The channel is well-marked and runs at least 11 feet deep all the way to Norwich. The only boating facility between New London and Norwich is Gales Ferry Marina at **Clark Cove.** Further up river the commercial traffic thins out, and the river narrows. Nature reasserts itself with trees, somewhat cleaner water, and flocks of birds; boating facilities disappear until you reach Norwich. You'll see many local boats trying their luck for bunker, blues, and mackerel. The warm water

© American Wharf Marina

The American Wharf Marina Complex in Norwich, CT.

produced by the Connecticut Light and Power plant in Montville is especially attractive to fish, and its two tall stacks are a conspicuous landmark.

Below **Poquetanuck Cove,** a new green can "19" has been added by the Coast Guard. This cove would be an inviting spot for exploration if it weren't for the fixed railroad bridge across the entrance, with its clearance of 2 feet. There's been talk of replacing this bridge with a taller one or a bascule, but so far no luck; if you have the gumption, put a word in with your state representative. Above Poquetanuck Cove, red flasher "22" at Walden Island, and red flasher "32" at Burnt House Pier are now both flashing 2.5sec beacons.

With prevailing summertime winds out of the southwest, sailors will find an easy broad reach all the way up river. The channel is well-marked with buoys and range lights, and there are no problems until you pass beneath the 65-foot-high **Mohegan-Pequot Bridge.** Above this bridge, you must be careful of the sea walls and dikes which are invisible at anything over half-tide. These walls were originally built to keep steamships from silting up the channel with erosion from their wash; and while the dikes were once above water except at unusually high tides, the

level of the river has risen by nearly a foot in the last century, putting the dikes under water and forming a distinct and unusual hazard to navigation. If you follow the channel markers, however, the dikes will pose no problem. Newcomers are advised to head upriver at low tide to get a good look at the location of these obstacles.

Norwich Harbor, at the confluence of the Thames, Shetucket, and Yantic rivers, is well protected by the high hills around it and makes an excellent haven in all bad weather. Small boats can anchor above the Norwich bridges, with its clearance of 13 feet, but larger boats will have to look for space further south.

The new harbor-revitalization project, on the site of an old coal depot, is already attracting boaters (mostly power) to what was until recently a dying waterfront. More than 200 slips are planned at the American Wharf Marina, some able to accommodate boats up to 100 feet. All the conveniences and amenities a boater could ask for–including a swimming pool, telephone and cable-TV hookups, laundry service, fuel, and a pump-out station–are available. At green can "43," head straight for the gold CBT building until you pick up the privately maintained buoys leading into the marina.

CRUISING INSTRUCTIONS 1850s STYLE

Oh, how cruising guides have changed. If you think things can get complicated today, with LORAN and SATNAV and such, send yourself back in time about 130 years and imagine a pleasant Sunday with the family, cruising from Stratford, CT , toward Sands Point on Long Island. Your mate reads you the "Sailing Directions by the North Shore" below, helpfully provided by the U.S. Coast Survey Office in 1855.

By the North Shore: Approaching Stratford Point from the East keep the lead in hand. The bottom never changes from soft to hard, and the land should not be approached nearer than in 3-1/2 fathoms, giving the Light a berth of 1-3/4 to 2 miles to clear the shoals making out from Stratford Point. When Charles Island ranges with Stratford Point the light bearing N.E. 1/4 E. steer W.S.W. until up with Sands' Point.

Not only are you busy translating the above, you're also taking frequent soundings with a lead line and handling a sailboat without that handy diesel down below to pull you out of a jam.

You might want to take the southern route, although it sounds a little more complicated and dangerous. Simply proceed as follows:

By the South Shore: From Fisher's Island Sound, continue the course W. by S. towards Eaton's Point Light passing 1-1/4 miles South of the Light Boat on the Middle Ground, and 2-1/2 miles North of Old Field Point Light House till this light bears (true) S. 86-3/4 degrees E. Then steer (true) S. 83-1/2 degrees W. passing not more than 1 miles North of Eaton's Point Light leaving the 2 buoys off that Point the one 400 yards on the Starboard, the other the same distance on the Port hand to clear the two shoals; keep this course till Eaton's Point Light bears (true) S. 85 degrees E. then haul to W.S.W. (true S. 61-1/4 degrees W.) and continue to Sands' Point as before directed from the Northern shore.

But of course! Clear as today's bottom at 3 fathoms—and enough to make you think a little more kindly about all that electronic gadgetry you paid so dearly for.

These and other instructions can be found in the Long Island Sound section (Western Sheet) of the 1855 *Survey of the Coast of the United States.* While modern-day mariners have greatly improved on that survey's content, they still can't beat the price: In the corner it says you can get your own copy from authorized dealers for 75 cents.

Contributed by Captain Paul Connolly, President of Connecticut Coastline, a marine instruction and publishing firm in Rowayton, Connecticut.

 Shoreside and Emergency Services

Airport: Groton-New London (203) 445-8549
Ambulance: 911 or (203) 886-1463
Bus: SEAT (203) 886-2631
Coast Guard: New London (203) 442-4471 or VHF 16
Ferry: To Montauk, NY (516) 668-5709
To Orient Point, NY (203) 443-5281
To Fishers Island, NY (203) 442-0165
To Block Island, RI (203) 442-9553
Fire: New London 911 or (203) 442-2345
Norwich (203) 887-2521
Harbormaster: (203) 443-4431/8331 at City Pier
or VHF 13
Hospital: William W. Backus (203) 889-8331
Pequot Treatment Center (203) 446-8265
Police: New London 911 or (203) 442-4444
Norwich (203) 886-2411
Radio Telephone: VHF 25, 26, 86; I.D.: New London
Marine Operator
Taxi: Yellow (203) 443-4321
Blue (203) 443-4303
Tow Service: Southeastern Marine Towing, Groton, CT
(203) 445-8381 or VHF 16
Train: Amtrak 1-800-USA-RAIL   ◆

SCALE 1:40,000

Fishers Island
and The Race

Dare Not Tread Beyond These Gates
For Fear Your Boat The Race Will Take

In its retreat from Montauk Point more than 25,000 years ago, the great glacier paused between Rhode Island and the north shore of Long Island just long enough to leave behind a recessional moraine of clay, sand, and boulders. From this huge, uneven deposit of earth came several islands, including Fishers, Little Gull, Great Gull, and Plum. Also left behind were the submerged threats we now know as Watch Hill Reef and Catumb Rocks, to the east of Fishers Island, as well as Race and Valiant Rocks, to the west.

While the most spectacular creation in these parts may be Plum Gut, the most hospitable is surely Fishers Island. John Winthrop, Jr., who had recently been named "the first governor of the river Connecticut," obtained a grant to Fishers Island from the Connecticut colony in 1641. After witnessing the massacre of the Pequots at Mystic in 1637, Winthrop was careful not to take advantage of any other tribes in the area and took pains to purchase the island from local natives. By 1646, the governor had moved his family

to the island, and was able to raise a few goats and to introduce the horse to Connecticut before he and his family returned to New London.

In 1662, Governor Winthrop secured a charter from King Charles II for the Connecticut colony including Fishers Island. The Duke of York believed, however, that Fishers was part of his domain. The question of which state–New York or Connecticut–had legal possession of Fishers Island was not settled until 1878-79, when a joint committee from both states decided that this island–like Gardiners and Shelter–belonged to New York. Fishers now has the same area code as Long Island, though the mail still goes through Connecticut, which is closer.

Descendants of Governor Winthrop owned Fishers Island until 1863 when it was sold to a New York manufacturer. The wealthy retiree continued to raise sheep, cattle, and horses on the island for many years, but by the late 1870's he had begun selling off lots. In 1889, Edmund and Walt Ferguson bought the island and began developing a summer resort for the wealthy. Over the years, Fishers has been broken up and sold to private owners and is now mostly off-limits to the public.

As you sail past the island, sneak a glance at the houses lining the shores–their size and beauty are spectacular–but don't take your eyes from the water for too long or you'll surely run into trouble, especially when coming through The Race–the treacherous passage marked by Race Rock Light. Rising a majestic 67 feet above the turbulent water, the "Castle" is a remarkable feat of engineering. Built in the 1870s, the light stands right on the reef. After a year of trying to raise a platform of boulders, engineers realized that the rocks would never remain in place. Finally, stones from the reef itself were used to make a breakwater around the intended site, and concrete was then poured into this basin to form a secure base. The completed project took more than six years and cost nearly $300,000.

© Robert G. Bachand

The legendary Race Rock Light off Fishers Island, NY took six years to build at the cost of $278,716 in 1879.

Marine Facilities and Services		Number of Transient Berths	Number of Transient Moorings	Seasonal/Year-round	Largest Vessel Accommodation	Approach Channel	Marked Entry Channel	Dockside Depth in feet at MLW	Depth in feet at MLW	Gas/Diesel Fuel	Fuel Brand	Ramp/Dinghy Dock/Launch Service	Railway/Lift: Capacity (in tons)	Propeller/Hull Repairs	Engine Repairs: Gas/Diesel	Pump-out Station	Showers/Laundromat	Marine Supplies/Groceries/Bait/Ice	110V ★ 220V ▲ Maximum Amps	MasterCard/VISA/Diners Club American Express	Restaurant/Snack Bar	Monitors VHF Channel
① **Pirates Cove Marine** (p. 247)	(516) 788-7528			Y	35	●	9	7				R	L15	PH	G			S		★	MVA	16
② Fishers Island Yacht Club	(516) 788-7245	6	8	S	100	●	11	11									SL	I	★▲30	MV		16
③ **Fishers Island Mobil** (p. 249)	(516) 788-7311	7		Y	60	●	14	14	GD	MOB	RD						S	I	★▲30	MV		16

Information in these listings is provided by the facilities themselves. An asterisk (*) indicates that the facility did not respond to our most recent requests for information.

East Harbor and the surrounding golf course on Fishers Island, NY from the east.

 What To See and Do

Unless you have friends on the island, there isn't much to do on Fishers. A walk or bike ride offers a view of the beautiful countryside, but even these activities are restricted by the "pearly gates"–a barrier crossing the main road south of Pirates Cove Marina, intended to prevent the public from exploring the eastern two-thirds of the island. On the west end, there isn't much of a downtown, but you will find an excellent grocery store, as well as a few antique shops, boutiques, and a post office.

Your best bet when visiting Fishers is to remain aboard your boat. The waters around the island make for a good cruise, revealing beautiful surf beaches along the south shore and snug coves along the north. Passing the island to the south, you'll see the remains of Fort Wright, which was built as a naval artillery post during the first World War and then beefed up for the second. The old concrete gun emplacements look like man-made caves, dotting the hills.

Look for fluke and flatfish around Wilderness Point and Isabella Beach. Some of the best bluefishing on Long Island Sound comes in the jaws of the rough-watered Race. The heavy turbulence makes it easy for the vicious blues to catch weaker bait fish. Make sure you bring a bat.

Under water, most of Long Island Sound is a dark morass of silt and seaweed, but the depths around Fishers Island are often clear enough for good snorkeling–just be sure to stay in calm waters close to protected shores.

 Where To Eat

You've only a few choices for food on Fishers Island. Many people like to pack a picnic, in which case you can make your own sandwich or head to the deli in town. Otherwise, you'll have to choose between elegant outdoor dining on the docks at Goose Island (516) 788-7311, or indoor dining at the charming Pequot Inn (516) 788-7246. Both serve excellent seafood, but you may want to head for the "Quot," if only for a drink, as it has been around longer, and tends to attract many of the locals.

 Navigation and Anchorages

Use NOAA Charts 13214 (1:20,000), 12372 (1:40,000), and 13205 (1:80,000). Use tide tables for New London. High tide at Silver Eel Pond is 16 minutes earlier; low tide is 4 minutes earlier. Multiply by 0.9 for height at high or low water. Mean tidal range is 2.6 feet.

The channel into West Harbor on Fishers Island, beginning at Hawks Nest Point, is 3.9nm by boat southeast of New London Ledge Light and 2.8nm by boat southwest of Morgan Point in Noank. The entrance to Lake Montauk on the tip of Long Island is 11.1nm by boat south-southeast of Race Rock.

Your LORAN unit will auto-select the 43 and 26 lines while in Fishers Island Sound, because these provide the strongest signals; however, many local boaters manually select the 43 and 14 signal lines, because the crossing angle for these lines is closer to perpendicular and therefore preferable. For this reason we have included, in our LORAN Index at the back of the book, numbers for all three of these signal lines for each waypoint in Fishers Island Sound.

Fishers Island is the plug on the east end of Long Island Sound. Tides entering the Sound must first pass by the island's south shore, contending with the shallows and rocks and heading through **The Race.** For boaters, the area offers both risk and beauty: if you don't take The Race seriously, you're bound to pay; but a safe trip through these waters reveals the spectacular shores of Fishers Island. Passing the island to the other side, through **Fishers Island Sound,** offers scarcely less of a challenge. On a nice summer day, the sound is packed with boaters, especially sailors, and because of its narrow passage, this area suffers its fair share of nasty chop. In addition to the currents in both The Race and Fishers Island Sound, keep an eye out for submarines. They will be traveling on the surface in these waters, but their wakes can still be dangerous.

CAUTION: Treat The Race with utmost respect. Tidal currents and opposing winds create treacherous conditions in this area, as 25 billion gallons of water swirl through here with every tide. Currents routinely run 4 to 5 knots and sometimes reach 6. If the wind is strong and blowing across the current, the chop will be even worse. No matter how calm the conditions, the water shoals so quickly at Valiant Rock that there will always be chop there, so proceed cautiously.

Approaching **Fishers Island** from the west and heading for **West Harbor,** you have a clear course until you reach South Dumpling; here, you will pass between the flashing red bell "2" **[WP-231]** and green can "3" off of South Dumpling. Continuing on, you will keep both red nun "6" and flashing red 4sec "8" off Hawks Nest Point to starboard before entering the channel into the harbor.

Boats heading to and from **Block Island** often choose Fishers Island Sound over the rougher waters of **The Race.**

To enter or leave Fishers Island Sound at its eastern end, you must head through one of five passages: **Wicopesset, Lords, Catumb, Sugar Reef,** or **Watch Hill.** For detailed descriptions of these areas see the chapter on Watch Hill.

Coming from the east, your first view of Fishers Island will be **East Harbor.** It's a small cove with a good deal of foul ground, but is a decent gunkhole for exploration by dinghy or shallow-draft boat. The entrance is well marked, but you'll have to keep an eye out for the many lobster pots in this area. There are no public facilities or access points ashore, and the old Coast Guard Station is now privately owned. When anchoring in here, be sure to stay at least 150 yards offshore to avoid the rocks. You'll find this a quiet spot–it's surrounded by a golf course–and nice for swimming from the boat. At low tide, you may even want to do some musseling along the rocks.

Continuing west, keep an eye out for several obstructions. **The Clumps–East, Middle, and West**–are each well marked on the chart and visible from the water. Pulpit Rock, near West Clump, is difficult to see, however, because it doesn't often break the water's surface. The rock is marked to the west by green can "1," which used to be black, and should be given wide berth. Green can "17" marking East Clump was also formerly black.

You may pass safely between the Clumps and Fishers Island, but be sure to make your way between red nun "2W" and green can "1W" off Brooks Point. From here, Chocomount Cove will be just to your south. You may anchor in this bight between Clay Point and Brooks Point, but it is exposed to the north. Chocomount Hill, southeast of the cove, rises 136 feet and makes for an excellent landmark as it is the highest point on the island.

Continuing toward West Harbor, you will want to round Clay Point by passing between red nun "4" (off Pulpit Rock) and green can "5." Best to stay as close to the center of this passage as traffic will allow. From here, West Harbor will open just to the south. The entire area between Hawks Nest Point and Clay Point offers decent protection from the weather, except when the winds come from the north or the west. The bottom here is a composite of grass, gravel, and mud.

LADY FENWICK'S FAVORITES

For a one-week cruise in eastern Long Island Sound the skipper is blessed with many options. Having a shallow draft, under six feet, extends the possibilities. *Lady Fenwick*, my 1967 Dickerson ketch based in Old Saybrook, draws only 4.6 feet with board up. Over the years she has been sailed often to Block Island, Newport, Marion, the Vineyard, and Nantucket, and once to Maine, but old age, laziness and the overcrowding of harbors to the east have dampened my enthusiasm for venturing so far. Now my preferences are a smaller horizon, shorter distances, and plenty of room to anchor.

My ideal cruise is a circuit encompassing the area from Saybrook to Stonington or Mystic, and from there to Shelter Island, a route which can be taken clockwise or counter-clockwise. Leaving the Connecticut River, I take advantage of the prevailing southwesterly and head 15 miles east to West Harbor on Fishers Island. Before entering, in calm weather, it's fun to drop the hook on the east side of Flat Hammock for a swim and lunch.

The next day it's a short run to Stonington, where the best anchorage is behind the breakwater to avoid the swell from Block Island Sound. Walking the length of Water Street in the borough is always a delight, topped off by a lobster dinner at one of the two fine restaurants. If you have a reservation, wind your way up the Mystic River to the Seaport. The tranquility of a night here, with no landlubbers on the grounds, amid the eerie shadows of a 19th-century maritime village, is well worth the price.

The third day leave early, because you're headed for Long Island–specifically Three Mile Harbor. Three Mile is never crowded, has several marinas and restaurants, and–best of all–lets you moor or anchor in snug solitude in its southwestern corner. There is a strict 5-mph speed limit–once I almost got arrested by the harbor police for *sailing* out in a strong breeze at seven knots!

No need for an early departure on the fourth day. Savor the charms of Three Mile all morning, since the afternoon southwester will whisk you into Coecles Harbor on Shelter Island, five miles to the northeast, in an hour. Usually I favor the protection of the marked anchorage on the wooded southerly side, but I also recommend picking up one of the guest moorings at the Ram's Head Inn on the north side and sampling the excellent cuisine.

Reaching your next anchorage on the following day will probably require a good deal of engine time. Head south, passing between the abandoned lighthouse on

The author on board Lady Fenwick *in an Off Soundings race. In the background is first mate J. Murray Marshall.*

Cedar Point and Mashomack Point. If you have kids aboard yearning to run around, spend a couple of hours in Sag Harbor and tour the Whaling Museum. From there, a truly unique experience awaits you in Smith Cove, with its shell-strewn beach and tidal creek that winds into the forest; just lie on your back and let the warm current carry you blissfully up or down...depending on its direction.

If you don't care to spend the night here, continue around Shelter Island, past the grand summer homes and their sweeping lawns, to Dering Harbor. Sure, it's full of yachts, a club mooring is expensive, but the ferry ride to Greenport and a meal at Claudio's make a fitting climax for your last night. If the southwester holds, you'll be back in Old Saybrook tomorrow afternoon.

Contributed by Ellsworth S. Grant, a sailor, historian, and Editor Emeritus of *Embassy's Complete Boating Guide to Long Island Sound*. He resides in West Hartford, CT.

West Harbor itself is the best anchorage at Fishers Island. The entrance to the harbor is quite wide and is surrounded to the east by large estates, to the west by the small village. The port channel, marked by private buoys, leads to the inner harbor and a small shipyard. The starboard channel leads to the yacht club, marked by a white building, and the commercial marina, both of which sell fuel. Anchoring is limited to the area north of **Goose Island,** which is usually jam-packed during the summer months. All the moorings are privately owned, so you'll probably have to hunt for a spot to drop your hook–the town tries to discourage visitors from anchoring here, which raises questions of ownership over the harbor, and makes it all that more difficult to find space.

In favorable weather, you may want to lay over on the east side of **Flat Hammocks Island.** Keep an ear to the weather channel, however, in case something creeps up. Be sure not to cut between the red 2.5sec flasher "2" **[WP-203],** which was formerly a nun, and the islet or you'll run aground. North Dumpling Light, just west of here, has been turned into a home and was recently up for sale, though we're sure it cost more than most can afford.

On the west end of Fishers Island, you'll find **Silver Eel Cove,** used by the ferry from New London to drop off passengers. You may duck in here during bad weather, but it's particularly difficult to enter during a stiff westerly. There isn't much room, either, and none for anchoring

unless you don't mind being flattened by the ferry as it maneuvers to a stop. The channel entrance is marked by the red 4sec flasher "2" and a series of pilings. Stay as near mid-channel as possible or risk running aground.

 Shoreside and Emergency Services

Airport: Elizabeth Field (516)·788-7249
Ambulance: 911
Coast Guard: New London (203) 442-4471 or VHF 16
Ferry: To New London (516) 788-7463
Fire: 911 or (516) 788-7375
Harbormaster: (516) 788-7828 or 7326 or 7760 or 7734
  Long Island Bay Constable (516) 788-7734
  or 7585
Hospital: Groton (203) 446-8265
Police: 911 or (516) 788-7600 (summer) or VHF 16
Radio Telephone: VHF 25, 26, 86; I.D.: New London
  Marine Operator
Tow Service: Southeastern Marine Towing, Groton, CT
  (203) 445-8381 or VHF 16; Marine Rescue
  Services, Wickford, RI (401) 295-8711
  or VHF 16 ◆

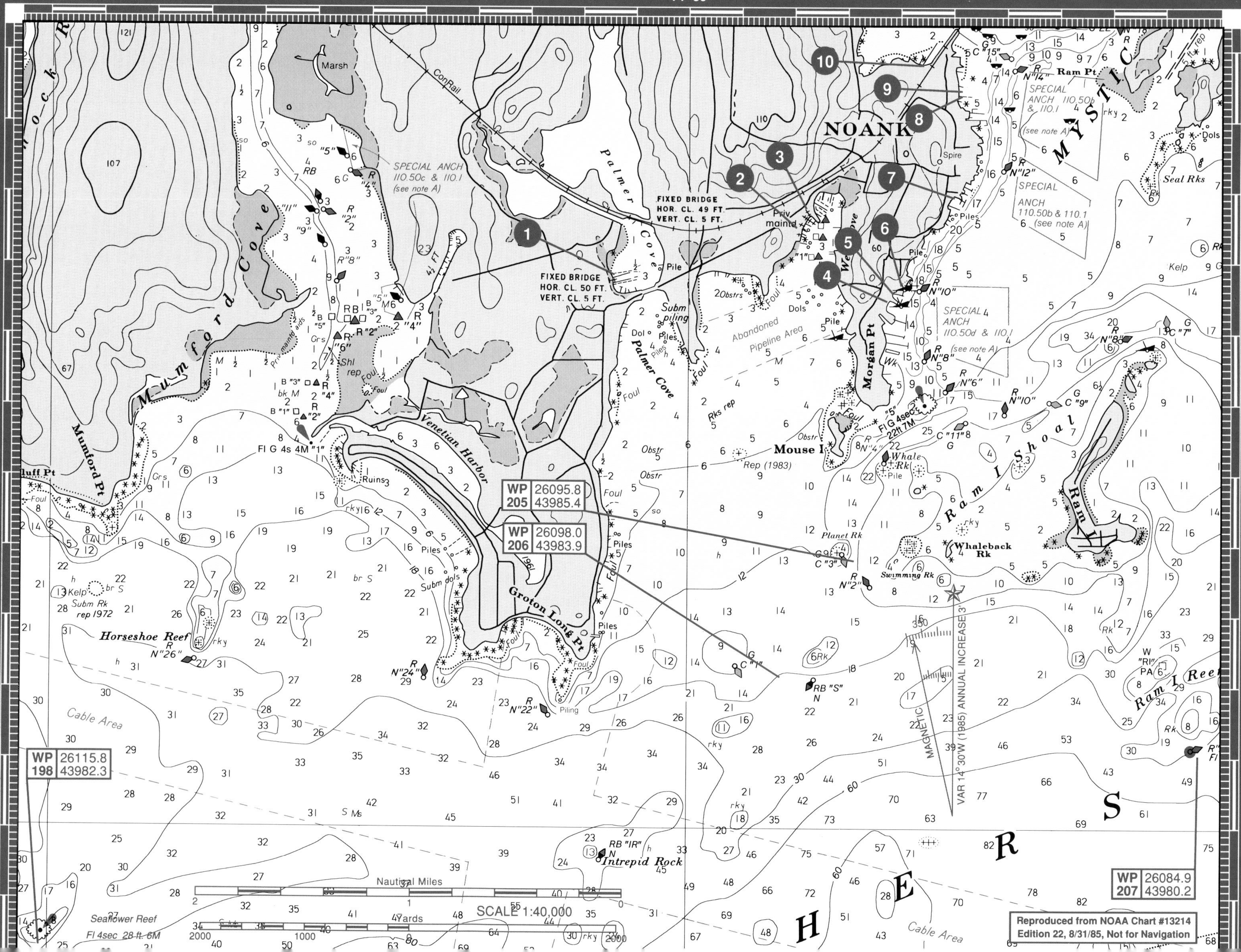

71° 59'

72° 00'

MYSTIC

Ram Pt.

Seal Rks

Kelp

SPECIAL ANCH 110.50e & 110.1 (see note A)

SPECIAL ANCH 110.50b & 110.1 (see note A)

SPECIAL 4 ANCH 110.50d & 110.1 (see note A)

NOANK

Morgan Pt.

West Cove

Mouse I.

Abandoned Pipeline Area

Palmer Cove

FIXED BRIDGE HOR. CL. 49 FT. VERT. CL. 5 FT.

FIXED BRIDGE HOR. CL. 50 FT. VERT. CL. 5 FT.

ConRail

Palmer Cove

SPECIAL ANCH 110.50c & 110.1 (see note A)

Marsh

Mumford Cove

Mumford Pt.

Bluff Pt.

Venetian Harbor

Groton Long Pt.

Horseshoe Reef

Ram I.

Ram I. Reef

Whaleback Rk

Whale Rk

Swimming Rk

Planet Rk

Intrepid Rock

Seaflower Reef

VAR 14°30'W (1985) ANNUAL INCREASE 3'

MAGNETIC

Cable Area

Cable Area

R A M
I S L A N D

S O U N D

FISHERS

WP 26084.9
207 43980.2

WP 26095.8
205 43985.4

WP 26098.0
206 43983.9

WP 26115.8
198 43982.3

SCALE 1:40,000

Nautical Miles

Yards

Meters

FI 4sec 28 ft 6M

Noank and the Mystic Harbor Entrance

The Accent Here's On Yankee

Noank is out of the way, and that's the way the villagers like it. Not long ago, an outsider sold them a bill of goods and sided many of the fine, old homes in town with asbestos. Though most of that stuff has come down by now, the locals have lost no love for the siding man. In fact, there's been talk of tar and feathers for anyone who's ever touched siding–other than wood clapboards or shingles–so, if you sell such goods, we suggest you tread lightly while visiting.

In fact, anyone visiting Noank should keep a low profile; that way, with any luck, you'll run into an old timer from these parts. Though he or she might not talk to you outright, you might catch a word or two under the breath. If you do, be sure to note the rounded corners–that's the voice of a Yankee. With an accent not unlike that of the Mainer or the folk of central New Hampshire, Noank's Yankees also share a few other distinguishing characteristics, namely an independence of spirit and and extreme dislike of authority. As for language, they tend to drop the *r's* at the ends of syllables; this means you hear *hahba*, instead of *harbor*. They pronounce *I* more like *oi*, and tend to add an extra syllable to simple words. *Trees* sounds more like *tree-uhs*, *Norwich* like *Norrich*, and *Stonington* is almost always pronounced *Stun'n'ton*. While diligent teachers and rock music have destroyed much of this regional dialect, a keen ear will still catch the tune. Just don't stay too long; no self-respecting Yankee likes a loiterer.

West Cove at Noank, CT from the north. Spicer's Noank Marina is in the center foreground.

© Spicer's Noank Marina

★ What To See and Do

Noank is a small town on a peninsula, and you'll soon find that most of the activities here have to do with the outdoors: gunkholing, fishing, swimming, or sometimes hiking through the woods. The town itself centers around an old church on the green and is entirely residential, with streets that criss-cross their way up and around the hills. A walk along these narrow streets will take you to several country stores, one of which is an historic site.

Marine Facilities and Services

Facility	Phone	No. Transient Berths	No. Transient Moorings	Seasonal/Year-round	Largest Vessel Accommodation (ft)	Approach Depth (ft)	Marked Entry Channel	Dockside Depth (ft at MLW)	Gas/Diesel Fuel	Fuel Brand	Ramp/Dinghy Dock/Launch Service	Railway/Lift: Capacity (tons)	Engine Repairs: Gas/Diesel	Propeller/Hull Repairs	Marine Supplies/Groceries Bait/Ice	Pump-out Station	Showers/Laundromat	110V ★ 220V ▲ Max Amps	MasterCard/VISA/Diners Club · American Express	Restaurant/Snack Bar	Monitors VHF Channel
1 Palmer's Cove Marina	(203) 536-6207			Y	25	3	●	3	G	CHE			G	PH	SI		S		MV		72
2 Golden Era Boats	(203) 536-1005			Y	41	7	●	7						H				★30			
3 Spicer's Noank Marina	(203) 536-4978	15	12	Y	45	7	●	7			RD	L20	GD	PH	SBI	●	SL	★30	MVA		9
4 Noank Shipyard	(203) 536-9651	30	2	Y	80	14	●	8	GD			L35	GD	PH	SI		SL	▲	MV	S	9
5 Maxwell Boat Yard	(203) 535-3905	2	2	S	45	15	●	15			R						S	★▲30			
6 Abbott's Lobster-in-the-Rough	(203) 536-7719		6	S	100	9	●												MV	R	
7 Haring's Marine & Ford's Lobsters	(203) 536-2842			Y	150	9		8.5	GD	MOB					I			★	MVA		79
8 Ram Island Yacht Club	(203) 536-9014	3	3	S	50	9		4			R						S	★10			
9 Noank Village Boatyard	(203) 536-1770	2	20	Y	45	8	●	6			R	L20	GD	PH	I	●	S	★50			16
10 Beebe Cove Marina	(203) 536-0221	7	7	Y	40	7		7			RD	L20	G	PH				★			

Information in these listings is provided by the facilities themselves. An asterisk (*) indicates that the facility did not respond to our most recent requests for information.

The town recreation center has a small beach, located near the town landing at the foot of Pearl Street. You'll also find tennis and basketball courts as well as a playground for the kids. The tennis courts are popular with local skateboarders, who set up their ramps on the smooth surface.

There are two state parks in the Noank area. Haley Farm State Park near the north end of Palmer Cove offers good hiking trails, while the tidal pools at Bluff Point State Park on Mumford Point–a 750-acre coastal nature preserve–are a great draw for school field trips. You can pull up to the park in a dinghy from Mumford Cove, and you'll probably be undisturbed, as the road is 2 miles away.

Mumford, Palmer, and Beebe coves are great spots for exploration by dinghy, and each has a reputation for excellent bird-watching. The marshy Sixpenny Island, which forms the eastern boundary of Beebe Cove, is a popular spot with nesting seabirds. Palmer Cove sports a public park and beach with a snack stand. Esker Point Beach, run by the town of Groton, is also good for sunbathing but not good for swimming, because of the silt.

Where To Eat

It's Noank's good fortune that most people pass it by; but for those who choose to visit, the town offers excellent marinas and facilities, and some fine seafood restaurants. Those staying at Spicer's in West Cove will want to try the Seahorse Restaurant (203) 536-1670 across the street. Also nearby is The Fisherman (203) 536-1717, serving duck and veal, as well as seafood, for dinner.

During the boating season, Abbott's Lobster-in-the-Rough (203) 536-7719, on Morgan Point, will pack fresh lobsters for you. Ford's Lobsters (203) 536-2842 will do the same–so you can steam dinner on board your boat.

Navigation and Anchorages

Use NOAA Charts 13214 (1:20,000), 12372 (1:40,000), and 13205 (1:80,000). Use tide tables for New London. High tide at the Mystic River entrance is 22 minutes earlier; low tide is 8 minutes earlier. Multiply by 0.9 for height at high or low water. Mean tidal range is 2.8 feet.

Most cruising boaters–on their way to Mystic for the charm or New London for the action–pass Noank by, thinking it's just another landmark. Those who stop and visit, however, are pleasantly surprised by the town's combination of solitude and good marine facilities.

Morgan Point in Noank is 2.9nm by boat north-northeast of the entrance to West Harbor on Fishers Island, and 4.5nm by boat east of New London Ledge Light. The breakwater at Stonington Harbor is 4.6nm by boat east.

CAUTION: *There have been many buoy changes in this area. We have noted the most important below, but be alert*

for others. Also be sure to keep an eye out for lobster pots. The current pulls many of the lines to stretching, so it's easy to get a hidden painter wrapped around your propellor.

Between New London and Mystic, you'll find several gunkholes and anchorages. **Mumford Cove** and **Venetian Harbor**, located between Mumford Point and Groton Long Point, are accessible to shallow draft boats and dinghies. The approach to Mumford Cove is straightforward: Stay halfway between red nun "26" marking Horseshoe Reef and nun "24;" from here, you have a clear shot north to the green 4sec flasher "1" at the entrance to Venetian Harbor. Venetian Harbor is a privately dredged cove hidden behind a bar and filled with small boats. There isn't much room, but this is an interesting place to explore.

Continuing into **Mumford Cove,** keep green flasher "1" well to starboard, and proceed slowly, watching all the while for red buoys "2" and "4." Even dinghies will have to wait for higher tides to get through here, as there is only about 2 feet of water at low tide, and the tidal range is only about 2.7 feet–larger boats don't have a prayer.

Once you reach red buoy "6," there is a narrow channel with 7 to 9 feet of water, but not much on either side. You can drop a hook wherever there's room. There's also a "special anchorage" area on the east shore inside can "5" and red nun "4," but this is difficult to reach. This narrow channel is privately owned, but almost all of the western shore, which belongs to Bluff Point State Park, remains undeveloped. The pebbly beaches here are seldom crowded with people, but you will see a fair amount of wildlife.

On the east side of Groton Long Point, **West Cove** is packed with moorings–particularly in the northeast corner, so pay attention to the privately maintained markers in the area. You may be able to pick up an unoccupied mooring by calling the dockmaster at Spicer's. The approach depth in West Cove is only about 7 feet.

Palmer Cove, just to the west, is a nice place to explore by dinghy, but there are some shallow spots here at low tide that will cause trouble for even a canoe. Palmer Cove Marina is a small-boat facility located just inside the bridge connecting Groton Long Point to Noank. The bridge has a vertical clearance of only 5 feet at mean high water, so it's only accessible to small power boats and dinghies.

From the west, the approach to **Palmer** and **West** coves is pretty straightforward. Keep red nun "22" off Groton Long Point to port and turn to the northeast. You may pass green can "1" to either side. Coming from the east is also straightforward, though you'll have to resist the temptation to cut between Whaleback Rock and either red nun "2" or green can "3" **[WP-205]** at Planet Rock. Swimming Rock, just 0.2nm to the west of Whaleback, is unmarked and may be submerged at high tide; so it's safest to keep green can "3" marking Planet Rock to starboard, giving it wide berth as you head north toward West Cove.

The channel leading to **Mystic** begins at the 22-foot green 4sec flashing **Morgan Point Light.** From New

London and points west, the approach is quite easy. Follow a straight-line course from the 28-foot Seaflower Reef Light **[WP-198]** to red nun "22" off Groton Long Point, and then up to the Morgan Point Light. Be sure to leave green can "1," east of Groton Long Point, and green can "3" **[WP-205]** at Planet Rock well to starboard. Most facilities in **Noank** are located on the east side of **Morgan Point,** just outside of the channel to Mystic; so if you're heading into Mystic, watch for boaters coming in and out of the Noank yards.

From **West Harbor** on Fishers Island, you will begin your approach by passing between the red 2.5sec flasher "2" at **Flat Hammock [WP-203]** and green can "1" at Pulpit Rock. Note that flasher "2" at Flat Hammock used to be a nun. From Flat Hammock, head for the green and red (formerly black and red) channel buoy "S" and green can "1" **[WP-206]** 0.8nm east of Groton Long Point. From here you may pass Planet Rock, marked by green can "3" **[WP-205],** to either side. If you choose to pass the can to starboard, however, be sure to give it wide berth, as the rock itself is northwest of the can.

When coming from **East Harbor,** you can either head north toward Mason Island before turning to port around Ram Island and following the main channel toward Morgan Point; or you can head south of the red 4sec flashing bell "20" **[WP-207]** at Ram Island Reef and then join the main channel at red nun "2" **[WP-205]** near Planet Rock.

CAUTION: Do not attempt to cut through the special anchorage between Noank and Mason Island. There are many obstructions, both visible and hidden, and the eel grass on the bottom may cause your depth sounder to show false readings.

Entering the channel to **Mystic** can be intimidating, as it is long and twists through many shoals and reefs; but if you honor the buoys and stay toward the center of the channel, you should have no trouble.

When coming from the west, leave Morgan Point Light to port. This short turn around the light can sometimes be difficult, as you may not be able to see red nun "6" ahead until you're right on top of it–the riprap of the light makes this buoy difficult to pick out. You may see local boaters cutting west of the light when heading south; but you should avoid this side of the light in order not to cross traffic in the channel more than once and to avoid a dangerous rock on this side. For more detailed information about the trip to Mystic, see the following chapter.

Coming from the east, you'll find that the channel running north of **Ram Island** is well marked. There is a small anchorage on the east side of the island which offers some protection from southwest winds; but you may be tossed about by the wakes of other boats in this area. The bottom is mostly grassy and should provide a decent hold for your anchor. You'll also find this area is popular with fishermen in search of blues.

The primary anchoring area in this part of the river is between Noank and Mason Island. This area is often crowded during the summer, but there should be enough water for you to set anchor with adequate scope. Try to stay as far east in the channel as possible in order to avoid the heaviest wakes from passing powerboats.

Shoreside and Emergency Services

Airport: Groton (203) 445-8549
Ambulance: 911
Bus: SEAT (203) 886-2631
Coast Guard: New London (203) 442-4471 or
VHF 16 or 83
Fire: 911 or (203) 536-7366
Harbormaster: Noank (203) 536-7115
Mystic (203) 536-1677
Stonington (203) 535-0770
Hospital: Pequot Treatment Center, Groton
(203) 446-8265
Police: 911 or (203) 445-9721
Radio Telephone: VHF 25, 26, 86; I.D.: New London
Marine Operator
Taxi: Plaid Cab Co. (203) 536-8888
Ryan's Taxi Service (203) 535-4548
Tow Service: Southeastern Marine Towing, Groton, CT
(203) 445-8381 or VHF 16 ◆

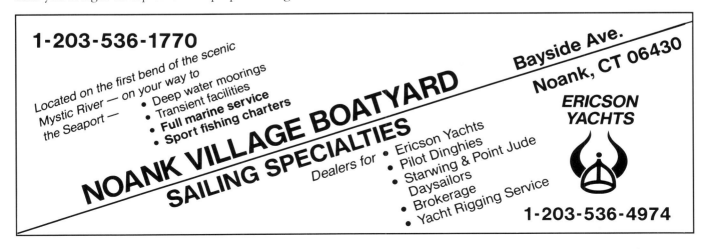

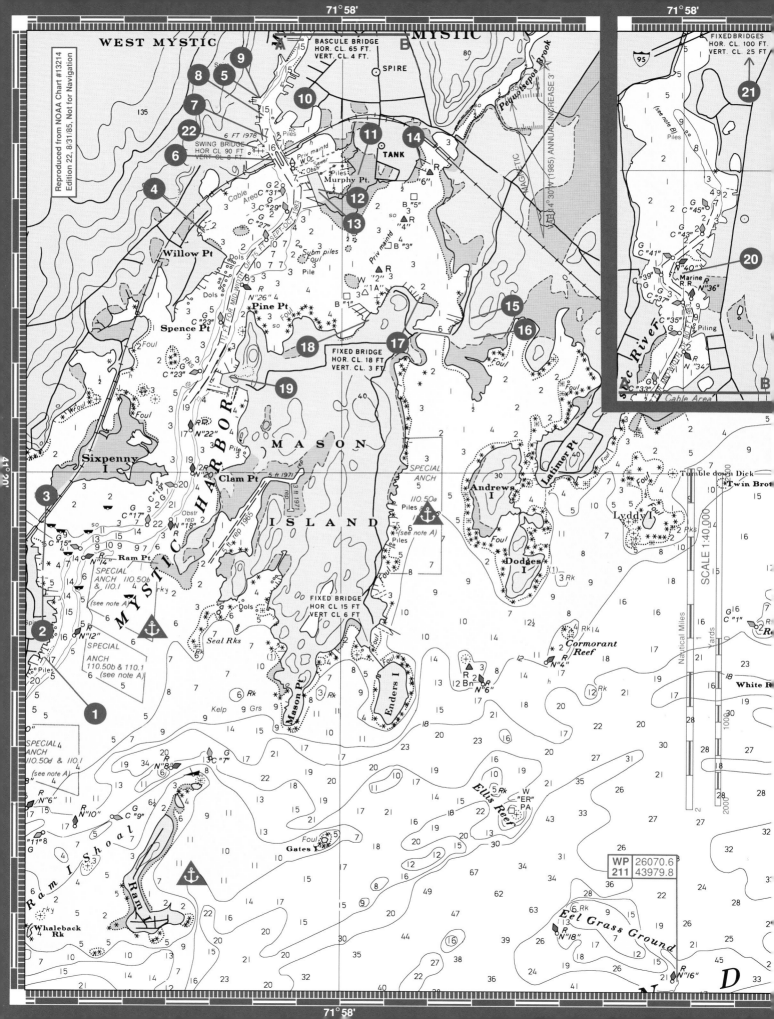

Along the River of Wooden Boats

Stretching a good 4 miles from mouth to shallows, the Mystic River has as fine and diverse a collection of boats as you'll find anywhere: one designs, sailing yachts, 12 meters, power cruisers, even the *Charles W. Morgan*, the last surviving wooden whaleship in the world. Interestingly, Mystic village itself doesn't properly exist, or at least isn't incorporated. The west shore actually belongs to Groton, while the east is legally part of Stonington. The mail still gets sent to Mystic, CT, however, zip code 06355.

The English first captured Mystic in 1645, and though they kept the original name–which meant tidal river or estuary in the native dialect–they destroyed the tribe who used it. The Pequots were, perhaps, the fiercest tribe on the

© Gene Mitchell

Sculling on the Mystic River, below the bascule bridge.

Marine Facilities and Services

#	Facility	Phone	Transient Berths	Transient Moorings	Seasonal/Year-round	Largest Vessel (ft)	Approach Depth (ft)	Marked Entry Channel	Dockside Depth at MLW	Gas/Diesel Fuel	Fuel Brand	Ramp/Dinghy Dock/Launch Service	Railway/Lift: Capacity (tons)	Propeller/Hull Repairs	Engine Repairs: Gas/Diesel	Pump-out Station	Showers/Laundromat	Marine Supplies/Groceries/Bait/Ice	110V★ 220V▲ Max Amps	MC/VISA/Diners/AmEx	Restaurant/Snack Bar	Monitors VHF Channel
1	Haring's Marine & Ford's Lobsters	(203) 536-2842			Y	150	9		8.5	GD	MOB							I	★	MVA		79
2	Ram Island Yacht Club	(203) 536-9014	3	3	S	50	9		4			R					S		★10			
3	Noank Village Boatyard	(203) 536-1770	2	20	Y	45	8	●	6			R	L20	PH	GD	●	S	I	★50			16
4	**Mystic Shipyard (p. 257)**	**(203) 536-9436**	30		Y	130	12	●	6			D	L35	PH	GD	●	SL	SI	★▲50			16
5	High-Tech Marine	(203) 572-8273	7		Y	80	12	●	8.5					PH	GD		SL	SI	★▲30	MV		9
6	Fort Rachel Marine Service	(203) 536-6647	2		Y	44	7	●	6				L30		GD		S	I	★20			
7	John I. Carija & Son Boatworks	(203) 536-9440	2		Y	76	12	●	9						GD		S		★▲50			
8	**Yacht Rigging East (p. 258)**	**(203) 572-8286**	1	2	Y	44	15	●	9								S		★30	MV		
9	Mystic Marine Railway	(203) 536-8441	2		Y	70	10	●	8				L20	H	GD		S	SI	★▲30			16
10	Seaport Marine	(203) 536-9681	5		Y	125	12	●	12				L60	PH	GD		S	S	★▲100			
11	Gwenmor Marina	(203) 536-0281			Y	46	6	●	6				L35	PH	GD		S	SI	▲60	MV		16
12	Brewer Yacht Yard at Mystic	(203) 536-2293	6		Y	120	12		9	GD	MOB		L35	PH	GD	●	SL	SI	★▲50	MV		16
13	Sterling Yacht Sales	(203) 572-8810	—					*YACHT BROKER & CHARTERS*														16
14	Mystic Cove Marina Dockominiums	(203) 572-8939	2		S	38	5	●	5				L20	PH	GD	●	S	SI	★30	MV		
15	Shaffer's Boat Livery	(203) 536-8713	5	5	S	26	2	●	2	G	MOB	R		H	G			SI		MV		68
16	Mystic Harbor Boatworks	(203) 572-9314			Y									PH	G							68
17	Whittle's Marina	(203) 536-3144	5	5	Y	40	3	●	4	GD	HSS	R	L20	PH	GD		S	SI	★30	MV		16
18	**Mason Island Marina (p. 260)**	**(203) 536-2608**	6	2	Y	45	4.5	●	6			DL	L25	PH			S	SIG	★30	MV		9
19	Mystic River Marina	(203) 536-3123	35		Y	100	15	●	6	GD	TEX		L35	PH	GD		SL	SI	★▲50	MVAD	R	
20	**Mystic Seaport Museum (p. 258)**	**(203) 572-0711**	40		S	200	12	●	12								SL	I	★▲50	MV	SR	9
21	**Mystic Marine Basin (p. 261)**	**(203) 572-7547**	4		Y	42	3.5	●	5			L	L20	PH	GD		S	SB	★20			16
22	**Mystic Harbor Marine (p. 261)**	**(203) 536-1210**	15		Y	70	10	●	10					P			S		s50	MV		16

Information in these listings is provided by the facilities themselves. An asterisk (*) indicates that the facility did not respond to our most recent requests for information.

© Clyde Smith

The Mystic River and bascule bridge from the northeast.

east coast of America; and rather than take any chances, the colonists surrounded the Indians in 1637 and wiped out nearly every member of the tribe. The few Pequots who survived the attack were later tracked down and killed in the Great Swamp Battle near Southport, CT. The settlers, on the other hand, turned to fishing and farming before finally becoming shipbuilders.

By the time the British dared attack the United States in 1812, Mystic had become a fierce fighting town. In fact, the Brits referred to the place as a "cursed hornet's nest" and lived in cautious respect for the local privateers and their "devilish torpedoes." In retaliation against one British attack, the "Mystickers" fitted out a double-banked galley with 12 oars and went hunting for loot and revenge. Sneaking through a heavy fog bank, the locals were able to capture three ships by ramming them unexpectedly. One of the prizes turned out to be an English smuggler, loaded with silks, tin, and medicine, which were promptly put up for auction.

Over the next hundred years, almost everyone in Mystic would be connected with shipbuilding. The town produced every type of wooden vessel from coastal sloops to clipper ships, of which Mystic was a major builder; one local clipper, the *Andrew Jackson,* made the trip from New York City around Cape Horn to San Francisco in only 89 days, 4 hours. Until the hurricane of 1938 wreaked havoc

on local yards and filled in much of the harbor, Mystic remained a great shipbuilding town. Even today, the Seaport Shipyard employs some of the finest wooden shipsmiths in the world.

 ## What To See and Do

Downtown Mystic is a series of waterside streets with shops, boutiques, galleries, and restaurants all packed into a small area just west of the bascule bridge. Since so many people enjoy exploring the town during the summer, the Chamber of Commerce (203) 572-9578 offers local maps at the railroad depot and Bank Square.

Many people will want to head further up-river to the Mystic Seaport Museum (203) 572-0711, which is clearly the town's greatest attraction. The Seaport captures the essence of maritime New England. Preserving the history of wooden sailing ships in the attempt to recapture the spirit of a mid-19th century sea town, the seaport maintains more than 100 buildings, located on an ever-expanding 40 acres. Most of the buildings are more than a century old, and some are much older than that. They have been collected from many New England sea towns and brought to Mystic for restoration, preservation, and display.

The Museum maintains one of the world's largest collections of wooden boats, ranging from skiffs to the three-

masted whaleship, *Charles W. Morgan*. If you're around on the third weekend in July, expect to see even more wooden boats at the Antique and Classic Boat Rendezvous, sponsored by the Museum.

Visitors to the Seaport will also see a world-class maritime library and a fully operational planetarium. Most exhibits are manned by trained guides who will show you how figureheads were carved, riggings maintained, and sails sewn. During the summer, the 1908 steamboat *Sabino* offers day and evening cruises lasting half an hour, including special trips featuring Dixieland jazz bands and barbershop quartets. Completing the Seaport's commitment to education are programs in maritime history, marine biology, sailing, and boat building.

The privately owned windjammers, *Mystic Whaler* and *Mystic Clipper* (203) 536-4218 offer one-day sails, cruises to the Goodspeed Opera House in East Haddam, CT, and 4 or 5-day cruises to Chesapeake Bay. A fleet of smaller sailing yachts operated by Voyager Cruises (203) 536-0416 take 1/2 to 2-day cruises and are also available for charter.

The Mystic Marinelife Aquarium (203) 536-3323, located a short distance north of the Seaport, is one of the most-visited attractions in Connecticut. More than 6,000 specimens of marine life are displayed in 45 live exhibits. Whether you prefer hermit crabs or sharks, you'll find your favorite sea-beastie here. Among the most exciting exhibits are the whale, dolphin, and sea lion training shows.

 ### Where To Eat

There are many fine restaurants within walking distance or taxi ride of the marinas in Mystic. On Rte. 1, near Brewer Yacht Yard or Gwenmor Marina, you'll find the Flood Tide Inn (203) 536-8140 with its continental menu. Across the Pequotsepos Brook are Pier 27 (203) 536-7300 and Angie's (203) 536-7300, serving everything from seafood to pizza.

On the west side of the river is Margaritaville (203) 536-4589 on Water Street, just south of Rte. 1. Two blocks away you'll find Mystic Pizza (203) 536-3700–where the movie of the same name was filmed–as well as many delis and pubs. For your money and time, the best stop, especially for

lunch, is Two Sisters Deli (203) 536-1244, just a short walk across Main Street to 4 Pearl Street, serving incredible sandwiches and even more incredible desserts.

Nearer the Seaport is the Seaman's Inne (203) 536-9649, serving lunch and dinner in an elegant, colonial atmosphere with an excellent but costly menu. Also try Kitchen Little (203) 536-2122 for a hearty, inexpensive breakfast.

Even further out, near the Aquarium, is the Golden Phoenix (203) 536-4956, serving Chinese food. Just next door you'll find The Mooring (203) 572-0731 at the Hilton with excellent American nouvelle cuisine. The Steak Loft (203) 536-2661 in Olde Mystick Village serves great surf 'n' turf at reasonable prices.

 ### Navigation and Anchorages

Use NOAA Charts 13214 (1:20,000), 12372 (1:40,000), and 13205 (1:80,000). Use tide tables for New London. High tide at the Mystic River entrance is 22 minutes earlier; low tide is 8 minutes earlier. Multiply by 0.9 for height at high or low water. Mean tidal range is 2.8 feet.

The trip up the Mystic River, if you follow it as far as possible, will take at least an hour. There is a no wake speed limit for most of the trip, and if you get caught waiting for the bridge, your patience will surely be tried. There are

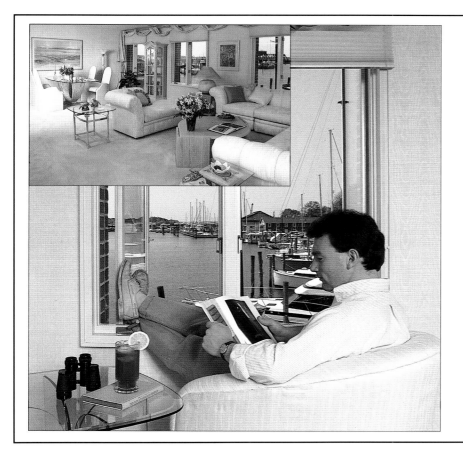
many marinas all along the river, but you may want to look for space down by the mouth and take a taxi from there; though the trip past the seaport is lovely by water.

The beginning of the channel up to Mystic, at Morgan Point in Noank, is 2.9nm by boat north-northeast of the entrance to West Harbor on Fishers Island, and 4.5nm by boat east of New London Ledge Light. The breakwater at Stonington Harbor is 4.6nm by boat to the east of Morgan Point, while Murphy Point, at the entrance to the Mystic River, is 4.2nm by boat to the north-northeast.

CAUTION: *There have been many buoy changes in this area. We have noted the most important below, but be alert for others.*

When speaking of **Mystic,** you must first define your terms. What's charted as "Mystic Harbor" is known locally as "out there where all the boats are moored" and actually lies between **Noank** and **Mason Island.** Most people think of Mystic, however, as the area north of Mason Island, around the bridges, and up to Mystic Seaport.

The channel up to either of these harbors begins at the 22-foot green 4sec flashing **Morgan Point Light.** Most of the Noank facilities are on the east side of Morgan Point, right off the channel to Mystic, so keep an eye out for boaters coming out of the Noank yards. Entering the channel for the first time can be daunting. The long passage

twists and turns through many shoals and reefs, but it proves simple enough if you honor the buoys and stay as close to the center of the channel as traffic will allow.

For detailed information on the approaches to **Mystic Harbor** from the south or west, see the previous chapter on Noank and the Mystic Harbor entrance.

When approaching Mystic from East Harbor on **Fishers Island** you have two courses from which to choose. Either head north toward Mason Island, turn to port around Ram Island, and then follow the main channel toward Morgan Point (being continually cautious of tiny Gates Island, 0.4nm south of Mason Point, on your way). Or head south of the red 4sec flashing bell "20" **[WP-207]** at Ram Island Reef and then join the main channel at red nun "2" **[WP-205]** near Planet Rock.

CAUTION: *Do not attempt to cut through the special anchorage between Noank and Mason Island. The number of moorings in this area has increased steadily, making passage through here difficult and dangerous. There are many obstructions, visible and hidden, and the eel grass on the bottom may cause your depth sounder to show false readings.*

Approaching **Mystic** from the west, you'll round **Morgan Point Light,** leaving it to port. It's a short turn around the light; but you won't be able to see red nun "6" until it's right in front of you, as it will be blocked by the rip-rap of the light. You may see boaters cutting west of the light on their way south, but don't try this when heading north, because you'll have to cross the traffic in the channel twice. Note that red nun "10" between Ram Island and **Noank** has been relocated slightly to the northeast. The channel north of **Ram Island** is well marked by a row of nuns and cans.

Coming from **Stonington** and other points east, you'll begin your trip at the 31-foot green 4sec flasher **[WP-214]** on the breakwater off Wamphassuc Point. Keep south of both the unmarked White Rock—named for the sea gulls that visit here so frequently—and green can "1" at Red Reef. Leave nuns "4" and "6" at Cormorant Reef to starboard and make for green can "7" at the north end of Ram Island; this course will keep you well north of Ellis Reef, which is marked by a spindle but still catches a number of boats each year. From Ram Island you can either follow the channel over to Morgan Point and then up to **Mystic,** or head for the anchorages on the west side of **Mason Island.**

When coming in from Watch Hill, Wicopesset, or any of the other eastern passages into **Fishers Island Sound,** stay south of the 55-foot 6sec flashing bell **[WP-226]** at **Latimer Reef.** Once past Latimer Reef, leave red nuns "16" and "18" at Eel Grass Ground to starboard and head for the north end of Ram Island and the approach to the main channel. You can pass on either side of Gates Island, which sticks way up but has deep water all around it.

Along with its many marinas, Mystic also lays claim to a number of anchorages. There is a nice, quiet spot on the east side of Ram Island, protected from prevailing southwest winds. The island is low in the middle, so this area gets enough breeze to cool things off but not enough to rock the boat. The island has a house, a barn, and a lot of sheep—from which the name may have come—and is right in the middle of a high traffic area, so you can get a good rocking from the wakes of powerboats as they pass. The weedy-grass bottom will give a decent hold for your hook, but keep an eye on the line. Anglers will find many blues and weakfish in this area, as the current is quite heavy.

The east side of **Mason Island** also has some nice anchorages, particularly between Mason Point and the

monastery on Enders Island. This area is somewhat exposed to the weather, particularly that from the south, but offers a nice break from the hectic main anchorage.

As for **Dodges Island,** you may want to take a picnic here, but don't bring your boat in close to shore. There's deep water all around, but it's dotted with rocks, so stay at least 100 yards offshore and take a dinghy in to land.

The primary anchorage is located between **Noank** and **Mason Island.** There are usually many boats here, and a number of new permanent moorings, so finding a spot may be difficult, especially on a busy weekend. Due to heavy traffic in the channel, you should drop your hook as far east as possible in order to get away from the wakes. The closer you are to shore, the better view you'll have of the wildlife. We suggest you drop a kedge anchor to the grassy bottom here, though a plow will also serve you well. There is also an anchorage on the north side of **Mason Island,** north of red nun "26;" but the water in this area is too shallow for most boats at low tide.

CAUTION: You may see boats anchored south of Sixpenny Island, but you should be cautious about using this area in anything other than a shallow draft boat. The harbormaster warns us that large boats often go aground here.

The 3.2nm course up river to the **Seaport** runs about north by northeast. The deeper water is usually on the **Noank** side. Don't cut too close to the buoys, as the channel tends to silt up on the edges, particularly around **Sixpenny Island** where the bottom seems to grab someone every weekend. The tidal range here is 2.8 feet, so don't expect much help from Mother Nature if you stick your keel in the mud. While there are many boats in the area, you'll find surprisingly little dock space for transients. Our best advice is to make reservations well in advance. If you haven't made reservations, call the marinas before you head up river—it's a long ride back down if you get there and find out that no one has any room.

About a half-mile north of **Mason Island,** you'll come to the Amtrak railroad bridge at Fort Rachel. The fort has long since disappeared, and the old rotting barges that once choked this area are going the same way. The railroad swing bridge is usually open to river traffic but closes well in advance of approaching trains. Contact the bridge tender at (203) 444-4908 or on VHF 13, or let them know of your presence with one long and one short blast of the horn.

North of the railroad is the bascule bridge in downtown **Mystic.** During the summer, this bascule bridge opens at 15 minutes past every hour from 7:15 a.m. to 7:15 p.m.; it should open on demand at other times in season. From November 1 to April 30, the bridge will open only from 7:15 a.m. to 5:15 p.m., and the tender will require *8 hours* advance notice. Call (203) 599-4411. There's often a lot of traffic on the bridge, so you should probably call in advance, at (203) 536-7070 or on VHF 13 or 16, to tell them when you'll need the bridge opened. The boat moving with the tide has right-of-way under the bridge.

When the bascule bridge is closed, the channel can become crowded. Some boats raft up, others motor in place, and still others circle around, waiting. If you miss a scheduled opening and have to pass the time, you may be able to tie up at the town dock on the west side of the river between the two bridges.

You must have reservations, usually several months in advance, to stay at the Seaport, and the prices are steep. Be careful when approaching the docks here–it's especially embarrassing to crash in front of a crowd of tourists. The docking fee includes free entrance to the Museum, and you can even walk around at night, when the paths are empty.

The east side of the river is well-dredged, but the other side is shallow, so don't wander from the channel. Showers and washing machines are available at the New York Yacht Club Station 10 Annex and the Preservation Shipyard.

Although the charts end just above the I-95 bridges, even large powerboats and sailboats (with masts less than 25 feet) can continue up the river to a secluded boatyard in the village of Old Mystic. The channel is poorly marked, however, and until you've made it once, the experience is nerve-wracking. You may wonder along the way if someone hasn't played a nasty joke, but keep going–the quiet is worth the journey.

 Shoreside and Emergency Services

Airport: Groton (203) 445-8549
Ambulance: 911
Bus: SEAT (203) 886-2631
Coast Guard: New London (203) 442-4471 or VHF 16
Fire: Groton 911 or (203) 536-7366
    Stonington 911 or (203) 536-8221
Harbormaster: Mystic (203) 536-1677
              Stonington (203) 535-0770
Hospital: Groton (203) 446-8265
Police: Groton 911 or (203) 445-9721
    Stonington 911 or (203) 599-4411
Radio Telephone: VHF 25, 26, 86; I.D.: New London
              Marine Operator
Taxi: Plaid Cab Co. (203) 536-8888
    Ryan's Taxi Service (203) 535-4548
Tow Service: Southeastern Marine Towing, Groton, CT
        (203) 445-8381 or VHF 16; Marine Rescue
        Services, Wickford, RI (401) 295-8711
        or VHF 16
Train: (New London) Amtrak 1-800-USA-RAIL   ✦

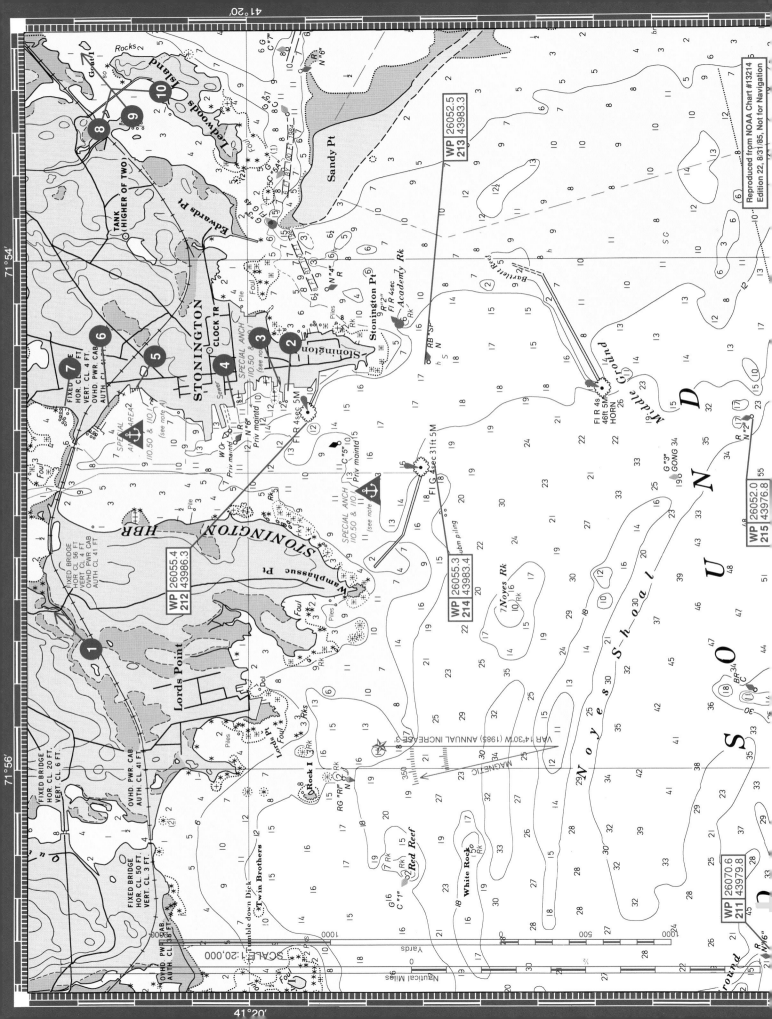

Stonington Harbor

Fighting the British, With Love and Armor

The small borough of Stonington has the distinction of being the only town in Connecticut to have defeated the British in battles during two wars–the American Revolution and the War of 1812.

The first assault came in August of 1775, when Captain Sir James Wallace and the HMS *Rose*, a 20-gun frigate, harassed colonial shipping to secure supplies for the British army. The inhabitants of Block Island heard of Wallace's mission and quietly began shipping cattle from their defenseless island to Stonington, where the animals could be protected. When word of the move got out, however, Wallace took little time before entering Stonington Harbor and demanding the cattle be turned over to the British.

The people of Stonington didn't take kindly to the Captain's demands, and his arrival was greeted with a shower of musket balls from the local militia. The *Rose* returned fire with her portside guns, flinging cannonballs at the town for more than a few hours, but Stonington suffered little damage in the attack. Finally, having failed to conquer the colonists, Wallace was forced to retreat with his vessel and crew intact.

Nearly forty years later, the British again assailed the village. Though this second onslaught was more serious than the first, it arose over an even more trivial matter. Captain Thomas Masterman Hardy, a close friend and once second in command to Admiral Lord Nelson, sailed into

© Clyde Smith

Blessing of the fleet in Stonington Harbor: bright colors and fun for all.

Marine Facilities and Services		Number of Transient Berths	Number of Transient Moorings	Seasonal/Year-round	Largest Vessel Accommodation	Approach Depth (in feet)	Marked Entry Channel	Dockside Depth in feet at MLW	Ramp/Dinghy Dock at MLW	Gas/Diesel Fuel	Fuel Brand	Railway/Lift: Capacity (in tons)	Propeller/Hull Repairs	Engine Repairs: Gas/Diesel	Pump-out Station	Marine Supplies/Groceries/Bait/Ice	Showers/Laundromat	110V ★ 220V ▲ Maximum Amps	MasterCard/VISA/Diners Club American Express	Restaurant/Snack Bar	Monitors VHF Channel
① Cardinal Cove Marina	(203) 535-0600			S	20	●	2	2	G	MOB	R		L				SIB	★			16
② Harbor View Restaurant	(203) 535-2720			Y	60	●	10	10		*DOCKAGE FOR PATRONS*											
③ Skippers Dock Restaurant	(203) 535-2000			Y	60	●	10	10		*DOCKAGE FOR PATRONS*											
④ Stonington Small Boat Assn.	(203) 535-0432			S		●	10		*FOR TOWN RESIDENTS ONLY*												
⑤ **Dodson Boat Yard (p. 267)**	**(203) 535-1507**	25	25	Y	85	●	8	7	GD	DK	DL	L35	PH	GD	●	SL	SIG	★30	MVA	SR	9
⑥ Wadawanuck Yacht Club	(203) 535-9309								*PRIVATE CLUB - MEMBERS ONLY*												
⑦ Don's Dock	(203) 535-0077	15		Y	22	●	5	5	G	MOB	R						SBI			S	
⑧ Wequetequock Cove Boat	(203) 599-5864			Y	25	●	3	3	G	TEX	R		PH	G			SI	★	MV		16
⑨ Coveside Marina	(203) 535-2276	10		S	25		2	2	G	NN	R	L4			S		SBI	★	MV		
⑩ Whewell's Marine	(203) 599-4322			Y	24		2	1			R	L	PH	G			SI				16

Information in these listings is provided by the facilities themselves. An asterisk (*) indicates that the facility did not respond to our most recent requests for information.

THE COASTS OF NEW YORK, CONNECTICUT, AND RHODE ISLAND

Looking due north along Water Street in the Borough of Stonington.

Stonington harbor in August of 1814 leading five ships with a total of 160 guns. Sitting ominously at the harbor entrance, Hardy sent village officials a message: "Since I am not wishing to destroy the unoffending inhabitants residing in the town of Stonington, one hour is given them from the receipt of this to remove out of the town."

Perhaps remembering the earlier humiliation they had handed the *Rose,* the villagers dug in and never once considered honoring the British ultimatum. When the hour was up, Hardy kept his word and opened fire. To his chagrin, however, the villagers began firing back, bombarding the ships with three small cannon. After three days of this direct intercourse, the 60 tons of shot Hardy launched on the town had only succeeded in toppling a few chimneys, airing a few walls, and killing one of the locals—not a terribly high success rate. On the other hand, the British had suffered destruction of a landing barge, loss of 21 soldiers, and injury to at least 50 more. Finally relying on good sense, Hardy retreated.

Once the smoke cleared, Stonington demanded an explanation for this unprovoked assault. The Captain claimed that he had heard rumors of torpedoes being built in town and that a British consul's wife had recently been detained in New London. Stonington, however, was innocent on both counts. Torpedos had never been built in town and local historians have since discovered that the missing lady was kept ashore only by her love of an American.

 What To See and Do

Stonington is its own best attraction. You could stay busy for days exploring the nooks and crannies of this small town. A myriad of shops and historical homes are shoe-

horned onto a tiny peninsula with charming one way streets, some of which are still cobblestoned with granite. Start your tour at the ornate library in Wadawanuck Park, and from there, walk down Water Street past Cannon Square to the Old Lighthouse Museum on the point. There is an impressive group of artists and writers in town, and many have work on display in the local galleries.

Stonington continues its intimate relationship with the sea and boasts the largest commercial fishing fleet in Connecticut. Many of the fishermen are descendants of Portuguese seafarers who came to the area from the Cape Verde Islands and Azores aboard whale and seal ships. One of the most colorful events in town is the annual Blessing of the Fleet by the bishop of Norwich. Sponsored by the Southern New England Fishermen's Association (203) 535-3903, the event includes a parade, concerts, the formal blessing ceremony, and lots of food, especially lobsters. Usually held in early July, the Blessing attracts more people each year, so plan on arriving early and staying late.

The old Stonington Lighthouse Museum (203) 535-1440 at the foot of Water Street has an excellent collection of marine art and rotating exhibits on such wide-ranging subjects as kitchen gadgets and ice-harvesting machinery.

Just down the hill from the museum on Stonington Point is DuBois Beach, which is operated by the Stonington Community Center (203) 535-2476 and is open to the public. The Community Center has four tennis courts in town, also available to visitors. The Center sponsors an annual fair, complete with hay rides, auctions, and a magic show, on the first weekend in August at Wadawanuck Park.

Those who want to sail even when in port should join the dinghy races held every Wednesday night by the Wadawanuck Yacht Club (203) 535-9309.

If you'd like to visit the Denison Pequotsepos Nature Center (203) 536-1216–with its 7 miles of trails through 125 acres of wilderness–or venture even further afield, you can rent a bike at the Stonington Sailing School (203) 535-0046 at Dodson Boatyard.

 Where To Eat

Skippers Dock (203) 535-2000 and the Harborview Restaurant (203) 535-2720 have piers for use by their customers; and fresh lobsters are available right at the dock.

The Boatyard Café (203) 535-1381 at Dodson serves breakfast and lunch. Further down along Water Street, Noah's (203) 535-3925 serves lunch and dinner in a homestyle atmosphere, while One South Broad Café (203) 535-0418 has coffee, sandwiches, and desserts.

If you're out on Wequetequock Cove–1.2nm as the crow flies northeast of Stonington Point–you'll find a small deli and a convenience store across the road from the marinas.

 Navigation and Anchorages

Use NOAA Charts 13214 (1:20,000), 12372 (1:40,000), and 13205 (1:80,000). Use tide tables for New London. High tide at Stonington is 32 minutes earlier; low tide is 41 minutes earlier. Multiply by 1.1 for height at high or low water. Mean tidal range is 3.2 feet.

Stonington is nearly as picturesque from the water as it is from land–even more so, in some ways. The shore is dotted with tightly packed homes and lined with masts; and as you approach from Fishers Island Sound, the docks seem welcome reprieve from heavy weather. Facilities and services are hardly more than a few steps away, and two of the largest docks offer direct access to food.

Stonington Point is 3.4nm by boat northwest of Watch Hill Point, 3.8nm by boat east of Morgan Point in Noank, and 5.6nm by boat northeast of Fishers Island.

Coming from **Mystic,** the most direct route to **Stonington Harbor** is by way of the north side of **Ram Island,** where you'll pass between white beacon "ER" on Ellis Reef and red nun "4" on Cormorant Reef. Further east, you can pass White Rock (named for the many seagulls that frequent its shores) to either side.

From green can "1" at Red Reef, head east for the breakwater off **Wamphassuc Point,** marked by the 31-foot 4sec green flasher "5" **[WP-214].** The breakwater creates a blind corner, so give it wide berth and watch for heavy crossing traffic. The "back door" of the harbor, between the west end of the breakwater and Wamphassuc Point, has only about 4 feet of water at low tide. If you must pass this way, stick close to the breakwater and move slowly. But we suggest you leave this passage to the locals.

Coming from farther west, you'll want to stay south of Ram Island Reef, marked by the red 4sec flashing bell "20" **[WP-207]** and Eel Grass Ground red nun "16" **[WP-211].**

BLACK MAYONNAISE IN QUIAMBOG COVE

Old-timers may remember harvesting oysters and quahogs from Quiambog Cove in Stonington, CT, but you won't hear any young people tell tales of fishing there. In 1890, the U.S. Fisheries Commission reported that Quiambog produced 140,000 pounds of flounder–more than any other cove in the state. Today, the cove is nearly dead to both finfish and shellfish.

Back when railroad bridges crossed our estuaries and bays on high trestles, the sounds of heavy traffic may have disturbed the waters below, but at least the tide ebbed and flowed freely into the coves. Tidal surges carried cleansing saltwater inland, sweeping out silt and vegetation. Then, in the early 1900s, trestles were replaced with solid causeways, which closed the estuaries and bays to tidal exchange, except for narrow, 30-foot openings.

Constrictions created by the causeways allow silt and vegetation to accumulate upstream, where they rot and form layers of muck called "black mayonnaise." Reaching depths of more than five feet, this muck often suffocates shellfish, making it impossible for oysters, clams, and scallops to reproduce. The highly acidic water, created by decomposition of leaves, causes finrot in flounder who enter the cove to spawn; moreover, it destroys the eggs laid and fertilized by the few fish who survive the disease.

A recent report of the Environmental Protection Agency argues that the vast majority of ocean finfish harvests depend on the health of our tidal wetlands. By destroying the habitats of these shellfish and finfish species, causeways have not only decimated our inland coves and estuaries, but they have negatively affected the entire coastal food chain. Wetlands provide nutrition for large pelagic fish such as tuna, swordfish, and marlin. These areas also produce food for coastal fish-eating birds, including ospreys, terns, herons, egrets, cormorants, and seagulls.

Many organizations, including The Sounds Conservancy, are working to revitalize these coastal waters. Reopening coves and inlets to a normal tidal flow will cause many shellfish and finfish habitats to return to a natural balance. Without attention to these areas, however, we will see a continuing decline in our coastal and ocean fish harvests.

Contributed by Chris Percy, President of The Sounds Conservancy, a non-profit environmental group based in Essex, CT.

"CAPTAIN NAT" PALMER

Captain Nathaniel Palmer
Engraving courtesy of Stonington Historical Society

During the 18th and 19th centuries Connecticut was famous for the number of daring sea captains it produced. One of the best known, and most highly regarded, was Nathaniel Palmer of Stonington, born in 1799. As a teenager "Captain Nat" smuggled goods through the British fleet during the War of 1812. At the age of 21 he commanded a sealing ship, making seven voyages to the islands at the end of South America. During one of these trips he discovered the Antarctic archipelago that now bears his name. He ran guns and troops to Simon Bolivar and carried cotton north from New Orleans. He was still in his thirties when he helped design the flat-bottomed transatlantic packet.

Captain Nat's greatest impact on American ship design came when he whittled out the model of the celebrated *Houqua*. Launched in 1844, she was the prototype of the true clipper ship, 143 feet long and only 32 feet in beam. She set a record of 95 days for the run from New York to China. Captain Nat commanded as well as supervised a fleet of clippers for the shipping firm of A.A. Low & Brothers. Never a bully, Captain Nat believed in giving his crew the best, including salt beef and pork. His most violent form of anger, in an age of irascible and inhumane captains, was to throw his white beaver hat on the deck and stomp on it. His retirement was peaceful. He raced, bought and sold yachts, hunted on Long Island, and was a founder of the New York Yacht Club.

Leave the 55-foot 6sec flasher **[WP-226]** at **Latimer Reef Light** to starboard. The undesignated red and black can at Latimer Reef is now a red and green nun "E." From Latimer Reef you have clear passage to the breakwaters. Deep draft sailboats should keep clear of Noyes Rock and Noyes Shoal, southwest of the west breakwater.

Coming from the **Pawcatuck River** and **Little Narragansett Bay** to the east, the channel is well marked. When approaching Stonington from this channel, remember that green buoys are to starboard and reds to port, because these waters are marked as the approach to the Pawcatuck River.

As you can see from the chart, **Sandy Point** has migrated north and east toward Stonington. There is deep water off the point, but the channel is quite narrow and crowded. When connected to Napatree Point, Sandy Point was part of Rhode Island, but has since moved into Connecticut waters and is now owned by the Mashantucket Land Trust and operated by the Community Center (203) 535-2476 as a nature preserve and undeveloped park. It's a popular swimming, sunbathing, and picnicking spot, though you'll need a Community Center membership card to use the beach, which is patrolled. Overnight camping is not allowed.

Between Fishers Island and Watch Hill Point are the five eastern passages into Fishers Island Sound: **Wicopesset, Lords, Catumb, Sugar Reef,** and **Watch Hill.** Watch Hill Passage is generally considered the easiest and the best marked, and is surely the most used. Wicopesset Passage is probably the second-most popular, as its rocks are easy to see. See the chapter on Watch Hill for more information about each of these passages.

Many boats cut inside red 4sec flashing bell "6" **[WP-220]** at **Napatree Point Ledge,** but we suggest you avoid this area as it is loaded with rocks near Napatree Point. Instead, stay south of the buoy and head for the 46-foot red 4sec flasher "4" on the end of the east breakwater. With local knowledge, it's possible to enter the harbor by going east of Middle Ground, but it's not recommended. The northeast end of the east breakwater is unmarked and disappears into Bartlett Reef (which should not be confused with the reef of the same name near Niantic).

While **Middle Ground** isn't a great place for sailors to play, it's well known for the huge flatfish and summertime blues that come from its waters. It's also a favorite spot among divers hunting for lobsters at night.

Stonington's finest anchorage is just inside the west breakwater. Turn to port after passing the green flasher **[WP-214]** and snuggle up to the rocks. Dodson Boat Yard maintains a couple of hundred moorings here and operates launch service throughout the entire harbor. The launch can take you to the waterfront restaurants as well as to the boatyard for a small round-trip charge, and is free with a mooring rental. Contact Dodson on VHF 9.

Just north of the mooring area inside the west breakwater is a "special anchorage" that's likely to be crowded. North of this anchorage, the moorings pick up again and stretch all the way to the northern part of the harbor at the railroad bridge. There are two more "special anchorage" areas just off the docks in **Stonington.**

If you want to drop your own hook, we suggest a kedge or plow anchor will hold best on Stonington's grassy bottom. Although the breakwaters add considerably to the protection offered in the harbor, big Atlantic swells still roll in when the wind comes out of the south, making parts of the anchorage uncomfortable.

Here are a few buoy changes of which you should be aware: black can "5" west of **Stonington Point** is now green can "7;" the 31-foot green 4sec flasher **[WP-214]** on the inner breakwater is now designated "5;" red nun "6" near the fishing pier is now "10;" and the privately maintained white and orange marker next to nun "10" has been removed.

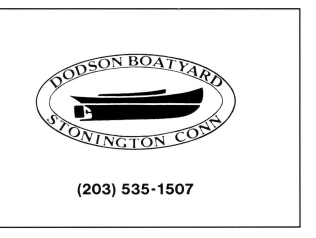

(203) 535-1507

 Shoreside and Emergency Services

Ambulance: 911
Coast Guard: New London (203) 442-4471 or VHF 16
Fire: 911 or (203) 599-4411
Harbormaster: (203) 535-0770
Hospital: Westerly Hospital (401) 596-6000
Police: 911 or (203) 599-4411
Radio Telephone: VHF 25, 26, 86; I.D.: New London Marine Operator
Taxi: Ryan's Taxi Service (203) 535-4548
Tow Service: Southeastern Marine Towing, Groton, CT (203) 445-8381 or VHF 16; Marine Rescue Services, Wickford, RI (401) 295-8711 or VHF 16
Train: Amtrak 1-800-USA-RAIL ◆

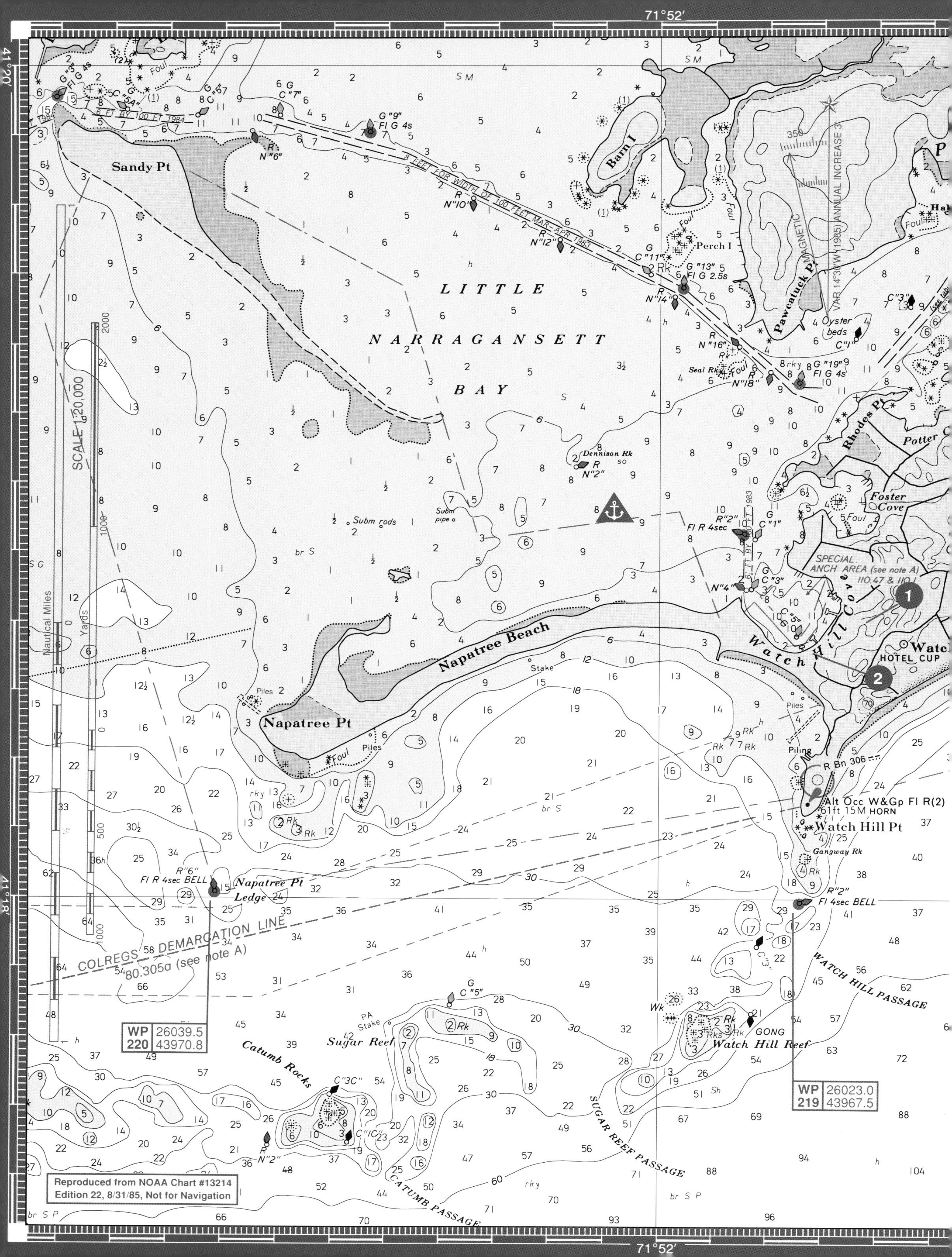

71°52'

41°20'

G"3"
FI G 4s
Foul
Foul

Sandy Pt

SM

SM

Barn I

Perch I

G"7"
C"7"

G"9"
FI G 4s

R
N"6"

N"10"

FEET FOR WIDTH OF 100 FEET MAR-APR 1983

8 FEET BY 100 FT 1984

N"12"

G
C"11"

Pawcatuck Pt

VAR 14°30'W (1985) ANNUAL INCREASE 3'

MAGNETIC

358°

RK
G"13"
FI G 2.5s

R
N"14"

Oyster
beds

C"3"

C"1"

LITTLE

NARRAGANSETT

BAY

N"16"
Rk

Seal Rk
rky 8 G"19"9
FI G 4s
N"18"

Rhodes Pt

Potter C

Foul

Foster
Cove

Dennison Rk
so
R
N"2"

SCALE 1:20,000

2000

Subm rods

Subm
pipe

br S

R"2" 6 FT BY 1983
FI R 4sec

G
C"1"

R
Foul

Napatree Beach

Stake

N"4"

G
C"3"

SPECIAL
ANCH AREA (see note A)
110.47 & 110

Watch Hill Cove

1

Watc
HOTEL CUP

Nautical Miles

Yards

Piles

Napatree Pt

Piles

Foul

Piles

2

Rk   Rk
Rk
Rk
Piling

R Bn 306

Alt Occ W & Gp FI R(2)
61ft 15M HORN
Watch Hill Pt

Gangway Rk

Rk

1000

500

rky
Rk
Rk

br S

Napatree Pt
Ledge

R"6"
FI R 4sec BELL

R"2"
FI 4sec BELL

C"3"

WATCH HILL PASSAGE

COLREGS DEMARGATION LINE
80.305a (see note A)

Wk

C"3"

WP 220 | 26039.5 43970.8

Catumb Rocks

PA
Stake
Sugar Reef

G
C"5"

Rk

GONG
Watch Hill Reef

Wk

Rk
Rks

C"3C"

Sh

WP 219 | 26023.0 43967.5

R"2"

C"C"

SUGAR REEF PASSAGE

CATUMB PASSAGE

br S P

Reproduced from NOAA Chart #13214
Edition 22, 8/31/85, Not for Navigation

br S P

41°18'

71°52'

Watch Hill Point and Napatree Beach

Mother Nature and the Kitchen Sink

More than any other spot between New York City and Block Island, Watch Hill illustrates the precarious balance between land and sea. Located at the intersection of Fishers Island and Block Island Sounds, Watch Hill has a floating island called Sandy Point, a migrating beach named Napatree, and a well-deserved reputation as the foggiest spot around. If all this gives you the feeling that man's presence here is tenuous and that Mother Nature could wash the whole thing away on whim, you're right.

Sandy Point was attached to Napatree Point until the great hurricane of '38 swooped down and tore the narrow spit away, creating an island. Since then, strong currents have been shifting the sand around, slowly choking the old channel from Stonington and opening a new channel between the island and Napatree Point.

The area north of Napatree Beach is called the "Kitchen," because of the heavy cast-iron stoves and sinks that landed there after the hurricane destroyed summer homes on the

Exploring Napatree Beach.

shore. Napatree Point is also migrating slowly to the north, having moved nearly 100 yards since the hurricane.

Way out on Napatree Point, you'll find Fort Mansfield, which was built to guard Fishers Island Sound during the Spanish-American War. The fort only fired its guns in practice, however, when the gunners blasted old whale boats which were marked by pieces of cloth and towed behind fishing trawlers. The fishermen found the experience nerve-wracking, and often complained that the gunners had notoriously bad aim. The fort shut down before the war ended when a visitor noted that even with good marksmen, the barricade would be useless against attack; a warship could easily anchor off the east side of Watch Hill Point, protected by land, and take an easy shot at the fort.

 What To See and Do

Large, weather-shingled mansions overlook sea and land, drawing us toward the sense of grand summer sprawl that grips most everyone. From the water, the hill rises slowly, providing an impressive back-drop to the endless sands. Crowds flock to Napatree during the summer to walk the long curve toward the fort, stopping to dig through the gravelly remains of a winter beach and make a small sand fort of their own. Keep an eye out for the dune grass—it's fragile, and sharp, and the only thing that keeps the beach from eroding. Also watch for the old fence stakes that stick up, here and there, waiting to catch a bare sole unawares.

Protected shallow water and long beaches make Little Narragansett Bay a haven for watersports and small boats. Take care to avoid the runabouts, jet skis, and daysailers here, and don't take your cruising boat through the shallow waters. You'll find excellent shellfishing, provided you get the proper permit from the Westerly town hall (401) 596-0341 or the local marinas in Stonington (Don's Dock, Coveside, and Wilcox, among others). For flounder and other bottom species, fish the bay and head for the Middle

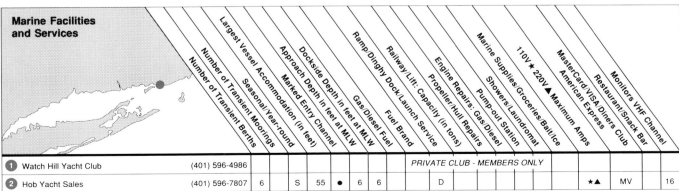

Marine Facilities and Services		Number of Transient Berths	Number of Transient Moorings	Seasonal/Year-round	Largest Vessel Accommodation (in feet)	Approach Depth in feet	Marked Entry Channel	Dockside Depth in feet at MLW	Gas/Diesel Fuel	Fuel Brand	Ramp/Dinghy Dock/Launch Service	Railway/Lift: Capacity (in tons)	Propeller/Hull Repairs	Engine Repairs: Gas/Diesel	Marine Supplies/Groceries/Bait/Ice	Pump-out Station	Showers/Laundromat	110V ★ 220V ▲ Maximum Amps	MasterCard VISA/Diners Club American Express	Restaurant/Snack Bar	Monitors VHF Channel
❶ Watch Hill Yacht Club	(401) 596-4986										*PRIVATE CLUB - MEMBERS ONLY*										
❷ Hob Yacht Sales	(401) 596-7807	6		S	55	●	6	6						D				★▲	MV		16

Information in these listings is provided by the facilities themselves. An asterisk (*) indicates that the facility did not respond to our most recent requests for information.

Ground breakwater. Napatree Point is a good spot for surf casting. Try Wequetequock Cove for trolling early summer blues and watching osprey.

From Watch Hill Cove or Napatree, you can walk into the town of Watch Hill or to Rhode Island's famous Atlantic beaches, which stretch 17 miles to the east. Sunday-morning sailors will like Watch Hill's bakeries and newsstand. Surprisingly, there is no grocery store here, but there is a convenience store and a good diner, as well as the famous Ocean House Hotel. The boardwalk across from the beach is lined with antique shops and boutiques–most open only during the summer.

The 1883 Flying Horse Carousel between the beach and the cove is supposed to be the oldest in the country, though Nantasket natives claim that their "roundabout" is older. The Watch Hill Improvement Society controls the granite lighthouse on Watch Hill Point, which is now automated; part is rented as a private residence and the rest will be turned into a museum. The rocky point at the light is popular among those casting for bluefish and bass.

 ## Where To Eat

Watch Hill boasts a few good restaurants, but you will have to wait until May to try them. Facing the cove is the Olympia Tea Room Restaurant (401) 348-8211, serving New American cuisine. Just up the road, the Watch Hill Inn (401) 348-8912 has two eateries under its gables: Positano serves Italian and seafood in a fine dining atmosphere, while the Deck Bar & Grill offers homestyle meals for those preferring a casual night out. Overlooking the Atlantic is the Ocean House Hotel (401) 348-8161, an inn with a spirited American menu. For a quick sandwich try the St. Claire's Annex (401) 348-8407 or the Bay Street Deli (401) 596-6606.

 ## Navigation and Anchorages

Use NOAA Charts 13214 (1:20,000), 12372 (1:40,000), 13215 (1:40,000), and 13205 (1:80,000). Use tide tables for Newport. High tide at Watch Hill Point is 41 minutes later; low tide is 1 hour 16 minutes later. Multiply by 0.7 for height at high or low water. Mean tidal range is 2.8 feet.

Napatree Beach is a two-sided sand spit running for more than a mile. With a fine anchorage off the north shore, beautiful beaches, and an excellent bird habitat, the area attracts many people during the summer. The holding ground in the anchorage is excellent. You'll often find more than 400 boats hooked here, their crew having long since abandoned ship by dinghy or swim stroke for the beach. Just remember that a local ordinance, strictly enforced, requires all boats to anchor at least 50 feet offshore.

The approach to Little Narragansett Bay, including the Pawcatuck River and Watch Hill Cove, begins at the red 4sec flasher "2" off Academy Rock at Stonington Point. Academy Rock is 3.0nm east of Mason Island at Mystic, and 2.2nm northeast of East Point on Fishers Island. From Academy Rock it's another 3.3nm by boat to the Pawcatuck River and the approach to Watch Hill Cove.

CAUTION: When planning a trip to Little Narragansett Bay, take into account the heavy fog which frequently rolls in from Block Island Sound. Late June and early July normally experience the worst fogs, which generally show up late in the afternoon and clear by 10 the next morning.

Approaching **Little Narragansett Bay** from Block Island Sound and the east can be tricky. There are five passages into Fishers Island Sound. From east to west, these are **Watch Hill, Sugar Reef, Catumb, Lords,** and **Wicopesset.** Each has a stiff 3 to 4 knot current and can get choppy when the wind and tide are opposed.

Coming from the east, we suggest you use **Watch Hill Passage.** It's nearest the Watch Hill Lighthouse, which is an excellent landmark, especially in the fog. On clear days, also look for the enormous yellow Ocean House Hotel, northeast of Watch Hill Point. Stay between bell "2" **[WP-219]**, now flashing red 6sec, and can "3," so that the currents don't push you into Watch Hill Reef. The gong on the east side of Watch Hill Reef is now green gong "1." Also note that (though it is not yet shown on the chart) the Coast Guard has recently marked a dangerous wreck about a quarter mile southeast of the lighthouse before you enter Watch Hill Passage.

Once through the passage, you can pass the red 4sec flashing bell "6" **[WP-220]** marking **Napatree Point Ledge** to either side, but be sure to stay within 200 yards of the marker. There are rocks extending nearly 500 yards south and west of Napatree Point, and the Coast Guard also reports a dangerous wreck about 0.3nm true east of the Napatree Point Ledge Light.

As for the remaining passages:

1. **Sugar Reef Passage** is not buoyed and is best left to those familiar with it.

2. **Catumb Rocks** are marked on the west by red nun "2" and on the east by green can "3C" and green can "1C." Because the channel is narrow–only about 200 yards wide–passing on the east side is risky. Better to pass on the west side of nun "2" where there's more water; either way, try to stay within 300 yards of the marker. Once you've left the nun to starboard, make course for bell "6" **[WP-220]** at **Napatree Point Ledge.** From here, you're home free.

3. **Lords Passage** is also well-marked. Look for black and white bell "L" **[WP-224]** to the south; red nun "2L" to the east; and can "7" at Wicopesset Rock to the west. Stay between the buoys for good water, and *do not* confuse green can "7" with can "9" to the northwest, or you'll end up high and dry. Bell "L," can "7," and the 46-foot flasher at Middle Ground line up nicely for a good range mark.

4. The western approach through **Wicopesset Passage** looks worse than it is. The rocks are real enough and close by the passage, but they are also easy to see, leaving no

doubt as to your position. You may have to punch through some standing waves upon entering, but that's par for the course on this end of Long Island Sound. Be careful that the current doesn't set you into **Seal Rocks,** which are marked at the northern end by can "13." Coming from the south, line up the black and white bell "W" **[WP-225]** and the green and red marker "WP" and keep that line to port as you pass through. Don't turn to starboard until you've passed green can "11," which should be given wide berth. There is one distinct advantage to Wicopesset Passage for sailors: when returning to Fishers Island Sound, the prevailing winds during the summer will be out of the southwest, so you will be on a reach instead of beating to weather.

CAUTION: Whichever passage you choose here, be extremely cautious. While going aground is hazardous anywhere, tricky currents and heavy seas make a grounding in this area particularly dangerous.

Resist the temptation to cut directly from **Napatree Point** to **Sandy Point.** The chart shows good water for most of the distance, but this course will get you in trouble between the east breakwater and Sandy Point. The waters around Sandy Point are popular with commercial fishermen, so keep an eye out for large boats and lobster pots.

The safest route from **Napatree Point** to the channel entrance will take you around the west end of the east breakwater off Stonington Point, marked by a 46-foot flashing red 4sec horn. From here, follow the buoys directly. The passage looks worse than it is. You'll find deep water off the point, though it's narrow and often crowded.

From Sandy Point, you'll follow the channel as it heads east and then southeast through **Little Narragansett Bay.** Don't turn south for **Napatree Beach** until you've passed Seal Rocks and nun "18." The local marinas make a lot of money on repairs each year for people who cut the last buoy or stray from the channel. Also watch for two 5-foot spots south of Seal Rocks, as well as Dennison Rock, marked by red nun "2," in the middle of the anchorage.

Vessels which choose to raft in this area ought to each drop an anchor to avoid smacking hulls when the wind shifts. With summer thunderstorms coming from the north, your boat may swing 180° with the wind. Make sure to set anchor well and leave a lot of scope. **Little Narragansett Bay** is shallow, and with the long fetch from the north, steep waves often build quickly.

When approaching **Watch Hill** from the **Pawcatuck River,** you'll find the channel well marked and easy to follow. From green 4sec flasher "19" off Pawcatuck Point, head southwest toward flashing 4sec red buoy "2" at the entrance to Watch Hill Cove. Don't swing too wide here or you'll run into a couple of unmarked shallow spots. From red flasher "2" you may head south into the cove or west across the lee side of Napatree Beach.

Both **Watch Hill Cove** and **Foster Cove,** to the north, are lined with beautiful old summer cottages. Foster Cove is the smaller of the two and is often crowded. There is also a rock in the middle of the anchorage. The large brown-shingled house on the point at the north entrance of the cove makes a good landmark. The cove entrance is unmarked but simple enough as long as you steer clear of the rocks extending north of the point. Don't turn into Foster Cove until you're close to green can "1" at the entrance to Watch Hill Cove.

The Watch Hill Yacht Club is in **Watch Hill Cove,** where there is an average of 11 feet of water. The club warns, however, that the holding ground is poor, making these crowded waters unsafe for anchoring. Before arriving, you should contact either the yacht club or Hob Yachts for a mooring or slip.

 Shoreside and Emergency Services

Airport: Westerly State (401) 596-2357
Ambulance: 911
Bus: Rhode Island Transit Authority 1-800-662-5088
Coast Guard: Point Judith (401) 789-0444 or VHF 16
    New London (203) 442-4471 or VHF 16
Fire: Watch Hill (401) 348-8933 or 911
  Pawcatuck 911
Harbormaster: (401) 348-8005 or VHF 16
Hospital: Westerly (401) 596-6000
Police: Westerly 911 or (401) 596-2022
   Pawcatuck 911
Radio Telephone: VHF 25, 26, 86; I.D.: New London
      Marine Operator
Taxi: Eagle Cab (401) 596-7300
Tow Service: Southeastern Marine Towing, Groton, CT
     (203) 445-8381 or VHF 16; Marine Rescue
     Services, Wickford, RI (401) 295-8711
     or VHF 16; Tidewater Interstate Towing
     Services, Wakefield, RI (401) 789-4300
     or VHF 16 and 7
Train: Amtrak 1-800-USA-RAIL   ◆

PAWCATUCK

WESTERLY

SPIRE

A   B

RADIO TOWER (WERI)
1230 kHz

Cable Area

Clarks
Village

TANK

Gavitt Pt

Stanton Weir Pt

Thompson Cove

SPECIAL
ANCHORAGE ARE
110.48 & 110.1
(see note A)

Pawcatuck Rk

Certain Draw Pt

Mastuxet Cove

Ram Pt

Babcock Cove

Marsh

Marine R

Avondale

P A W C A T U C K   R I V E R

Barn I

Hall I

Perch I

Graves Neck

Marsh

Pawcatuck Pt

Horace I

Colonel Willie Cove

Oyster
beds

Seal Rk

SCALE 1:20,000

Buoys 9-27A are
privately maintained

VAR 14°30'W (1985) ANNUAL INCREASE 3'

MAGNETIC

350

Nautical Miles

Yards

The Pawcatuck River to Westerly

Granite Quarries and Greenhouses

Westerly, Rhode Island has a past carved in stone. Red, grey, and white granites were found near the town long ago and have been quarried for years. The largest quarry in Westerly's history was operated by the Smith Company, which at one time owned a special narrow-gauge railroad that carried the heavy stone to schooners waiting in the harbor. The finer-grained white granite was often used in constructing monuments and for carving sculpture, such as the bear at Brown University. When demand for this high grade stone dropped off, local quarrymen were forced to cut paving blocks and cobblestones. In fact, it's said that all the streets of Philadelphia and Baltimore were paved with granite from Westerly.

While granite still figures prominently in the local economy today, the valuable pink granite used in some of the state's more fashionable building façades is quarried in Connecticut. Some of the plainer granites still come from Westerly, however; and the beautiful stones in the River Bend Cemetery on the east side of the Pawcatuck River stand in mute testimony to the town's stonecutting heritage.

The Pawcatuck River, the dividing line between Pawcatuck, CT (on the left) and Westerly, RI (on the right).

	Marine Facilities and Services		Number of Transient Berths	Number of Transient Moorings	Seasonal/Year-round	Largest Vessel Accommodation (in feet)	Marked Entry Channel	Approach Depth in feet at MLW	Dockside Depth in feet at MLW	Gas/Diesel Fuel	Fuel Brand	Ramp/Dinghy Dock/Launch Service	Railway/Lift: Capacity (in tons)	Propeller/Hull Repairs	Engine Repairs: Gas/Diesel	Marine Supplies/Groceries/Bait/Ice	Pump-out Station	Showers/Laundromat	110V ★ 220V ▲ Maximum Amps	MasterCard/VISA/Diners Club American Express	Restaurant/Snack Bar	Monitors VHF Channel
❶	Watch Hill Boat Yard	(401) 348-8748	2	2	Y	36	●	5	6				R	L15	PH	GD		S	SI	★15			16
❷	Avondale Boat Yard	(401) 348-8187	8		Y	50	●	8	3.5	GD				R35	PH	GD		S	SI	★15	MV		16
❸	Lotteryville Marina	(401) 348-8064	5	5	S	50	●	6	6				R	L10	PH	GD		S	SI	★▲30	MVA		16
❹	Frank Hall Boat Yard	(401) 348-8005	6		Y	40	●	8	6					R20	PH	GD		S	SI	★▲	MV		16
❺	Covedge Bait & Tackle	(401) 348-8888	1		S	24	●	2	2										SI		MV		16
❻	Gray's Boat Yard	(401) 348-8689	3	1	S	25	●	3	3				R	R8	P			S	SI				
❼	Westerly Yacht Club	(401) 596-7556	10		S	51	●	5		G			PRIVATE CLUB - MEMBERS ONLY					I		★30			
❽	River Bend Boat Yard *																						
❾	Pier 65 Marina	(401) 596-6350	1		Y	60	●	5	5					L25	PH	GD		S	I	★30	MV		
❿	Westerly Marina *	(401) 596-1727																					
⓫	Viking Marina	(401) 596-7390	2		Y	55	●	7	10				R	L25	PH	GD	SL	SBI		★55	MVA	R	6
⓬	Pawcatuck River Boatyard *	(203) 599-3379																					
⓭	Connors - O'Brien Marina	(203) 599-5567			Y	26	●	15	20				R		PH	G		S		★	MV		
⓮	**Norwest Marine** (p. 275, 134)	**(203) 599-2442**	20		Y	180	●	7	7	GD	TEX			L35	PH	GD	SL	SI		★▲50	MVA		68
⓯	Stonington on the River	(203) 599-8728			Y	40	●	6	6				DOCKOMINIUM				SL			★50			16

Information in these listings is provided by the facilities themselves. An asterisk (*) indicates that the facility did not respond to our most recent requests for information.

Once granite quarrying leveled off in the early part of the century, Westerly turned, like many New England towns, to textiles. At the same time, however, the town had its own, unique source of income: a large greenhouse industry. It was said that if you were searching for food or flowers, you could find them in Westerly, where everything from tomatoes to roses was grown. Westerly's northern clime was able to compete in the greenhouse industry because of its proximity to the water. Heating coal was off-loaded directly from coastal barges to the furnaces of the main plant, saving overland transportation costs.

Across the river from Westerly is Pawcatuck, Connecticut, known for many years as Pawcatuck Rock. The town was originally named for the rocky spot where the rope ferry tied up after crossing the river along the course of the Old King's Highway. People still tell stories of the time that the first Postmaster General of the United States crossed the river on the local ferry, all to visit with Mr. Smith, the local Postmaster of Pawcatuck Rock. You might wonder why one mailman visiting another would cause such a stir. All we can suggest is that while Pawcatuck was a small town, Benjamin Franklin wasn't just another mailman.

 What To See and Do

The river from Watch Hill to Westerly is quiet and lined with gracious homes set apart here and there by marshlands. If you follow the water as far as it carries, you'll find yourself in downtown Westerly, with good eating, shopping, and supplies. The twisting streets of this old Victorian town are lined with a mixture of frame houses and red brick buildings and are fine for a casual walk or an easy bike ride. For information about events in the city, call the Chamber of Commerce (401) 596-7761.

Both Pawcatuck and Westerly have been shaped by their nearness to river and sea. Crabs, clams, scallops, and fish were once harvested here in abundance and still thrive in local waters. Unfortunately, the river is now closed to shellfishing because of the effluent from two sewage-treatment plants upstream. Plans to reopen the area to shellfish beds hinge upon a scheduled upgrade of the treatment facilities.

You'll have no problem finding healthy bass and blue-fish, however. Half the boats in the river belong to people who call themselves fishermen, not boaters. The Pawcatuck River is also one of the few sites chosen for reintroduction of shad and Atlantic salmon. After a few small ladders are built, the migrating fish will once again have access to suitable spawning grounds along the river.

 Where To Eat

Unless you follow the river all the way to its source in Westerly, you'll be hard-pressed to find suitable dining arrangements. Once in downtown Westerly, the Dockside Restaurant (401) 596-6370 at the Viking Marina serves hardy breakfasts for boaters as well as excellent seafood at dinner. Happy Holliday's (401) 596-5936, also in downtown, offers steak, seafood, sandwiches, and Italian, all available as takeout for those on the run. Also try Spuchy's (401) 596-8570 for Italian, or the China Village (401) 596-2392 for Chinese-American dishes. Two Canal Street (401) 596-8330, at the same address, serves great steak and seafood in an elegant atmosphere.

On the Connecticut side of the river, the Sportsmen's Café (203) 599-4246 offers a well-stocked selection of traditional American meals. The River's Edge Café (203) 599-2447 serves seafood. And with a little effort, you'll surely run into one of the many delis and pizzerias in town.

 Navigation and Anchorages

Use NOAA Charts 13214 (1:20,000), 13215 (1:40,000), and 13205 (1:80,000). Use tide tables for New London. High tide at Westerly is 26 minutes earlier; low tide is 2 minutes later. Multiply by 1.1 for height at high or low water. Mean tidal range is 3.0 feet.

Heading up the Pawcatuck River for the first time, the channel seems narrow and tricky; but with some experience under your belt, the ride will be easy and pleasant. Keep some film in your camera and your binoculars at hand to fully enjoy the scenery. Houses line the shores between marshes where you'll see birds fly up in search of their estuarine prey. Some have tried, at times, to use the boundary between Pawcatuck and Westerly to their advantage, but speeding boaters who attempt to slip past the law in this area, with quick words about state lines, usually end up chewing on their own feet. As it turns out, the Westerly police chief is also the local harbormaster.

The entrance to the **Pawcatuck River** at Pawcatuck Point is 2.5nm by boat east of Stonington Point and 0.6nm north of Watch Hill Cove. The head of the river at Westerly is 4.5nm by boat to the north-northeast of the river entrance.

See the chapters on Stonington Harbor and Watch Hill Point for information about the approaches to the **Pawcatuck River.**

From Pawcatuck Point on, the water is tidal and brackish up to the bridge. Most of the current in the river runs less than 2 knots and comes from tidal flow, rather than river incline. Because the tidal range is only 3.2 feet, a few of the local marinas have fixed docks.

The first anchorage you'll see is on the west side of the river, between green can "1" and **Hall Island.** This is a large area with a good 8 feet of water. You'll be in a lee when the wind is out of the west, making this a good place to drop a hook night or day.

Further upriver, **Colonel Willie Cove,** inside Graves Neck on the Rhode Island shore, is a good anchorag; but much of the cove is full to capacity with boats belonging to local property owners or moored at the boatyard.

Graves Neck came by its name from a local burial ground. Sailors and fishermen lost at sea were often laid to rest here. Some of the graves are of unknown men who washed ashore and had to be buried before they could be identified. To avoid the rocks and Horace Island on the south side, stay at least 300 yards north of can "3" (which is east of Pawcatuck Point) before turning into **Colonel Willie Cove.**

From Graves Neck on, past the marinas and boatyards in Avondale, there is an enforced no-wake zone. The river widens for a short distance off Ram Point, where you'll find a shallow anchorage to the east. It then narrows once again at Pawcatuck Rock, a cedar-covered point jutting out from the Connecticut shore; this is matched by a similar point on the Rhode Island side. Because of the river's narrow width at this point, the channel remains free of silt–if you hit bottom here, you hit rock.

Just upstream from Pawcatuck Rock, you'll see the Westerly Yacht Club at **Thomson Cove** on the east side. The club welcomes cruisers from other recognized clubs, but dock space is usually scarce. A no-wake zone extends across the area in front of the yacht club, as with all the other clubs and marinas along the river.

Near the **River Bend Cemetery** opposite Gavitt Point, the channel begins to silt. Also be aware that the passage isn't as wide as it seems on the chart. Don't expect buoys at every bend in the river channel. Heading directly from one marker to the next will surely leave you in the mud. It's best to read the chart carefully and stay to the outside of each curve, where the channel will be deepest. Near the radio tower, the river narrows again and is less silty. The large mill and modern building on the west shore belong to the Hamilton Graphics Company, manufacturers of printing equipment.

Above Viking Marina, you'll find that the river narrows quickly. Time to break out the dinghy or continue in a small power boat. In the area of the **Rte. 1 bridge,** you'll notice a spire marked on chart 13214; riverside of the spire is the Main Street Shopping Center, with a pharmacy, newsstand, pizzeria, convenience store, and–for those not operating the vessel–a package store. Those in a small boat or dinghy can easily tie a line to the trees and scurry up and down the embankment for supplies.

Further upriver, again on the east shore, is a full grocery mart and a hardware store. One more lazy bend to starboard will bring you within sight of Pawcatuck Park, where you can tie up and walk around downtown.

 Shoreside and Emergency Services

Airport: Westerly State (401) 596-2357
Ambulance: 911 or (401) 596-2213
Coast Guard: Point Judith (401) 789-0444 or VHF 16
New London (203) 442-4471 or VHF 16
Fire: Westerly (401) 596-2711 or 911
Pawcatuck 911
Harbormaster: (401) 596-2022
Hospital: Westerly (401) 596-6000
Police: Westerly (401) 596-2022 or 911
Pawcatuck 911
Radio Telephone: VHF 25, 26, 86; I.D.: New London Marine Operator
Taxi: Eagle Cab (401) 596-7300
Tow Service: Southeastern Marine Towing, Groton, CT (203) 445-8381 or VHF 16; Marine Rescue Services, Wickford, RI (401) 295-8711 or VHF 16; Tidewater Interstate Towing Services, Wakefield, RI (401) 789-4300 or VHF 16 and 7
Train: Amtrak 1-800-USA-RAIL   ◆

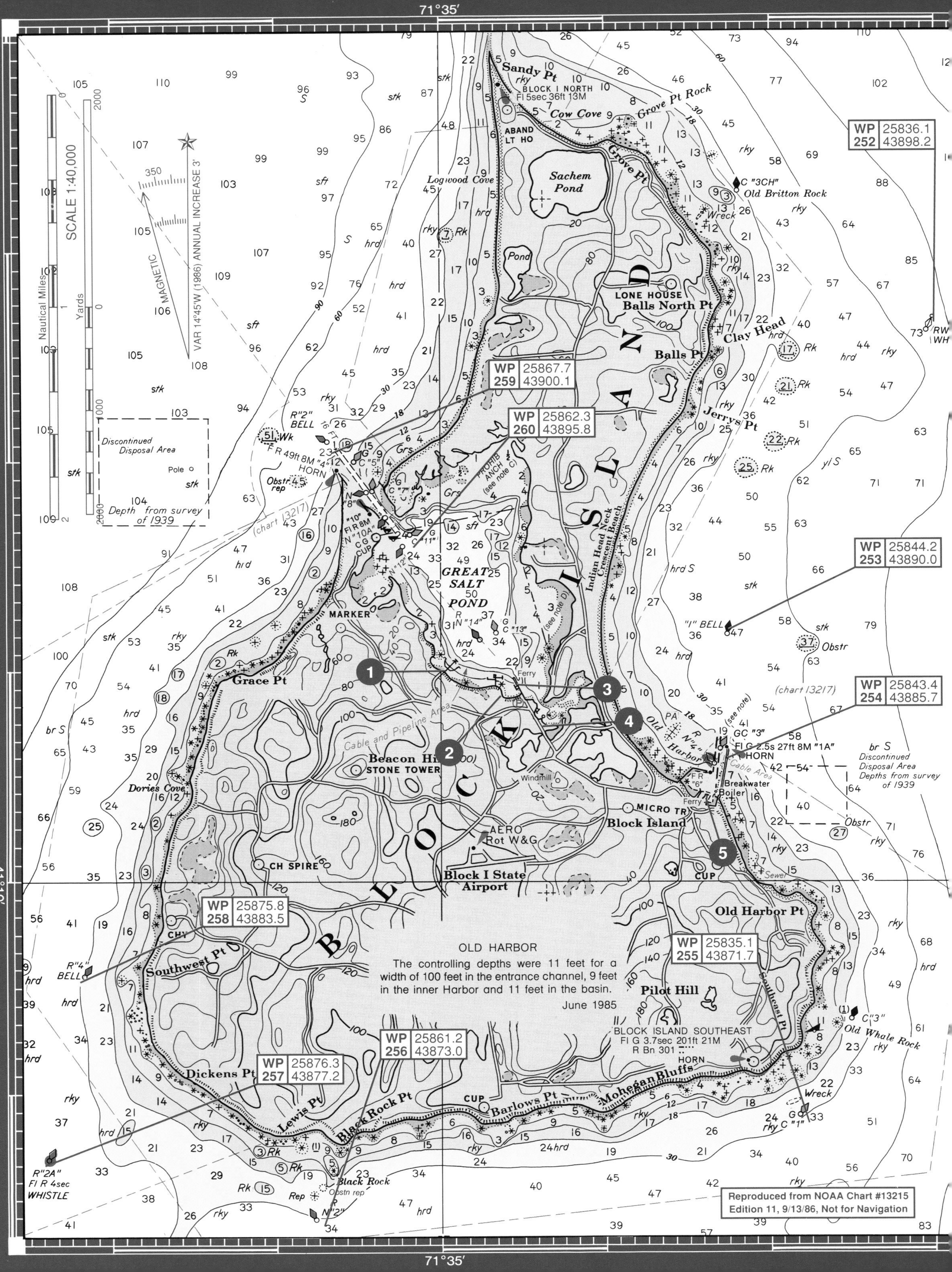

SCALE 1:40,000

VAR 14°45'W (1986) ANNUAL INCREASE 3'

MAGNETIC

Nautical Miles

Yards

Discontinued
Disposal Area

Pole

Depth from survey
of 1939

Sandy Pt
rky
BLOCK I NORTH
Fl 5sec 36ft 13M
Cow Cove
Grove Pt Rock
ABAND
LT HO

Sachem
Pond

Logwood Cove

Grove Pt

C "3CH"
Old Britton Rock

Wreck

LONE HOUSE
Balls North Pt

Clay Head

Balls Pt

Jerrys Pt

WP 259 25867.7 43900.1

WP 260 25862.3 43895.8

R "2" BELL
Fl R 49ft 8M "4"
HORN
Obstr rep

PROHIB
ANCH
(see note C)

Indian Head Neck
Crescent Beach

WP 253 25844.2 43890.0

"I" BELL

GREAT
SALT
POND

(chart 13217)

MARKER

Grace Pt

①

Ferry

③

④

Old Harbor
Fl G 2.5s 27ft 8M "1A"
HORN

WP 254 25843.4 43885.7

Cable Area
Discontinued
Disposal Area
Depths from survey
of 1939

②
Beacon Hill
STONE TOWER

Windmill

MICRO TR
Block Island

Breakwater
Boiler
Ferry

⑤

Dories Cove

AERO
Rot W&G

CH SPIRE

Block I State
Airport

CUP

Old Harbor Pt

WP 258 25875.8 43883.5

WP 255 25835.1 43871.7

OLD HARBOR

The controlling depths were 11 feet for a
width of 100 feet in the entrance channel, 9 feet
in the inner Harbor and 11 feet in the basin.

June 1985

Pilot Hill

R "4"
BELL

Southwest Pt

WP 256 25861.2 43873.0

BLOCK ISLAND SOUTHEAST
Fl G 3.7sec 201ft 21M
R Bn 301
HORN

C "3"
Old Whale Rock

Dickens Pt

WP 257 25876.3 43877.2

Lewis Pt

Black Rock Pt

Barlows Pt

Mohegan Bluffs

Wreck

R "2A"
Fl R 4sec
WHISTLE

Black Rock
Obstn rep

B L O C K   I S L A N D

41°10'

WP 252 25836.1 43898.2

Block Island

Island of the Little God

Though Adriaen Block is best known for his discovery of the Connecticut River, he left his name on an ocean isle rather than an inland tributary. Block Island was originally known to native Americans as *Manisses,* or "Island of the Little God," and was not discovered by Europeans until 1524, when the Italian explorer Verrazano christened it "Luisa." It was still another 90 years before Block charted the small island and humbly dubbed it "Adriaen's Eylant."

Six and a half miles long by three and a half wide, Block Island is, like most of Long Island, part of the terminal moraine. As the last glacier retreated, scraping together coastal-plain strata from the seabed and folding this mass on top of older glacial deposits, it left the lamb-chop shaped island with a windswept, hilly terrain of cliffs, giant ravines, freshwater ponds, and spectacular beaches.

The island was first settled in 1661 by a small group of hardy English families seeking religious freedom. While the island offered an escape from persecution, it was without a natural deep water harbor, leaving the small community economically stranded from the outside world. In those days, Great Salt Pond was almost entirely landlocked and accessible only to the Indians, who traveled a tiny outlet creek in their light canoes.

Recognizing the pond's potential, early settlers made several attempts to widen its opening. Unsuccessful, they eventually looked elsewhere, turning their attention to the east side of the island, where a harbor was cleared using teams of oxen to build a pair of riprap breakwaters.

This protected area became known as "Old Harbor," and while it alleviated some of the need to open the Salt Pond, the potential gain offered by opening the larger inland basin still drew attention. In 1749, the Town Council resolved "that the Great Salt Pond be let out in the Ocian Sea and that there be five gallons of rum allowed by this town for the encouragement of the labourers that shall lett out the same." Though the rum was potent incentive, attempts still failed to open the Pond. In fact, it would not be for another 138 years that a sufficient channel was dug to a depth of 20 feet. Within six years, however, even this passage had shoaled to a mere 2 feet. Finally, the federal government stepped in and authorized construction of a harbor of refuge, and the "New Harbor" in Great Salt Pond was opened to commerce in 1899.

With increasing activity over the years, unwary ships heading to and from the island have often been grounded on Sandy Point at its extreme northern end. A lighthouse was erected on the point in 1829 but soon washed away, as did its two replacements. Then in 1867, a stone house was built which continues to stand today. Now owned by

Anchoring at sunset in Block Island's Great Salt Pond.

	Marine Facilities and Services		Number of Transient Berths	Number of Transient Moorings	Seasonal/year-round	Largest Vessel Accommodation (in feet)	Approach Depth in feet at MLW	Marked Entry Channel	Dockside Depth in feet at MLW	Gas/Diesel Fuel	Ramp/Dinghy Dock	Fuel Brand	Railway/Lift: Capacity (in tons)	Propeller/Hull Repairs	Engine Repairs: Gas/Diesel	Marine Supplies/Groceries/Bait/Ice	Pump-out Station	Showers/Laundromat	110V ★ 220V ▲ Maximum Amps	MasterCard/VISA/Diners Club American Express	Restaurant/Snack Bar	Monitors VHF Channel
1	Champlin's Marina & Resort	(401) 466-2641	180		S	180	●	15	14	GD	MOB	L					SL	SIG	★30	MV	R	68
2	**Block Island Boat Basin (p. 279)**	**(401) 466-2631**	85		S	100	●	10	10	GD	TEX				GD	●	S	SIG	★▲50	MV	RS	16
3	**Payne's Dock (p. 279)**	**(401) 466-5572**	50		S	100	●	25	15	GD	MOB						S	I	★		S	
4	Smuggler's Cove	(401) 466-2828	14		S	58		6	10					PH	D		S	I	★	MVAD	R	68
5	Old Harbor Dock	(401) 466-2526	40		S	60	●	10	10	GD	MOB						S	SIG	★▲	MV	RS	16

Information in these listings is provided by the facilities themselves. An asterisk (*) indicates that the facility did not respond to our most recent requests for information.

the town and maintained by the North Light Commission, the Coast Guard re-activated this light in 1989, removing the tower which had been lighting the point for nearly 15 years.

 What To See and Do

Block Island is its own attraction. With a rolling landscape not unlike Scotland or Wales, you'll find the hills pleasant for biking and the rugged ravines beautiful for exploration on foot. The town itself is full of old homes and hotels, and there are plenty of shops and galleries to make a day of browsing. When it's rainy, the small movie theater will entertain both you and the kids.

Coming to the island early in the summer promises some excitement. Block Island Race Week is usually held in the last week of June and often attracts more than 250 participants. One of the Off Soundings Races consists of two legs: from Watch Hill to New Harbor on the first day and then around the island on the second. This difficult race tests competitors with a variety of conditions requiring all types of equipment and strategies. To see 200 sailboats rounding Southeast Light, spinnakers spread before the wind, is a stirring sight indeed.

If you'd rather partake of the events than watch, you've come to the right place. There is excellent swimming at Ocean Beach, extending north of Old Harbor to Jerry's Point on the eastern shore. Coming from Great Salt Pond, row your dinghy to the west shore of the harbor and then walk across the narrow spit. If you're coming at high tide, you may want to take your dinghy into the marshes at the southeast end of the Pond and do some exploring.

Those interested in diving should head for the Pinnacles. Marked "Boulders" on the chart, southwest of Block Island and under 30 feet of water, this area is one of the best dive

Old Harbor on Block Island from the south.

sites south of Cape Cod, with huge stones piled 50 to 70 feet high. In August, when the Gulf Stream cleans the water, visibility can reach 50 feet, and you can swim between the boulders, scouting tropical fish like barracuda and checking out the many wrecks which litter the area.

 Where To Eat

Block Island is well prepared to handle the influx of hungry and thirsty tourists each summer. Whether arriving in Old Harbor by ferry or searching for some free holding ground in Great Salt Pond, you won't have to walk far from the dock to fill an empty stomach or soothe a parched gullet.

Near Old Harbor you'll find McGovern's Yellow Kittens (401) 466-5855, one of the island's more famous stomping grounds. With music and dancing in the evenings, the bar attracts a great crowd, and Windfield's (401) 466-5856, the restaurant in the same building, is also popular with those looking for fine dining. Also try Finn's Seafood Bar (401)

466-2102, which has an outdoor deck, or Ernie's Old Harbor Restaurant (401) 466-2473, just upstairs.

If you've lost your friends and don't know where to look, head to Ballard's Inn (401) 466-2231. This Block Island version of Grand Central Station attracts just about everyone in the course of an evening, so if you hang out long enough, you're bound to find someone you're glad to see.

 Navigation and Anchorages

Use NOAA Charts 13217 (1:15,000), 13215 (1:40,000), and 13205 (1:80,000). Use tide tables for Newport. High tide at Great Salt Pond is 2 minutes later; low tide is 7 minutes later. Multiply by 0.7 for height at high or low water. Mean tidal range is 2.8 feet.

In recent years, Block Island has become a favorite destination for both yachters and tourists. Ferries from Point Judith and New London bring more than 10,000 visitors a day to this "Bermuda of the North," swamping the 600 natives and putting a severe strain on the island's ecology. It's also not surprising to see 2,000 boats packed into Great Salt Pond on a weekend. As a result, pollution has closed the harbor to shellfishing for several years.

The entrance to Great Salt Pond, marked by red bell "2," is 13.4nm by boat southeast of Watch Hill Point and 14.3nm by boat northeast of Montauk Point. The breakwaters at Point Judith are 10.5nm by boat to the northeast.

If you're heading to Block Island from the west, you'll be in **Block Island Sound,** akin to being in the open Atlantic. There are long swells, heavy fogs in early summer, and lots of big-ship traffic. Due to budget cuts, the Block Island Coast Guard station (401) 466-2462 was closed a couple of years ago, but has since been reopened with a much smaller staff and two boats during the summer.

Leaving Fishers Island Sound there are five passages: **Wicopesset** (close to East Point on Fishers Island), **Lords, Catumb, Sugar Reef,** and **Watch Hill.** Play it safe and use either Wicopesset (which has only one rock that you need to watch out for), or Watch Hill. You can pass on either side of can "3" in Watch Hill Passage, although most people like

a course close to the fixed landmark of the 61-foot white and red group-flashing Watch Hill Lighthouse. Stay to the south of red 4sec flasher "2" **[WP-219],** off the point.

Lords Passage is the best marked of the five and most often used by fishing boats from Stonington. Both Catumb and Sugar Reef can be spooky, even for seasoned mariners. (For more on these passages see the chapter on Watch Hill and Napatree Beach.) Once through the passages, you're virtually in the Atlantic, and the going can be rough.

Block Island looks like two separate islands from a distance because of the low-lying area of Great Salt Pond between two hills, one about 100 feet high to the north and the other 200 feet high to the south. The north end of the island is marked by the squat tower of the Block Island North Lighthouse, about 1.8nm south of the green 4sec flashing bell "1BI" **[WP-248],** off the chart. A dangerous sandy reef stretches all the way from Sandy Point to bell "1BI." The waves usually break on the reef, and so have a good number of ships over the centuries. Even today, at least 2 boats go aground there each summer. Standing waves develop around the bell buoy when the wind and tide are opposed. The bell is often used as a racing mark and can be a devil to round, since you usually have to beat back when the winds are out of the southwest.

On the southeast end of the island stands **Block Island Southeast Light,** high on Mohegan Bluff. The light itself is an elaborate 67-foot brick Victorian edifice built in 1875. The bluff raises the beacon to 201 feet above sea level, making it the highest lighthouse in New England, visible for 35 miles out to sea. A radio beacon and fog signal are at the station. It's been reported that the fog signal is indistinct when close-to but can be heard easily when several miles away. Coming from the north or west, the light will not be visible as it's on the far side of the island. You will see it, however, when approaching from Montauk.

The perimeter of **Block Island** has many boulders in the shallows and should be approached with extreme caution, even by small boats. The Coast Guard recommends keeping 0.5nm offshore except in marked channels.

The entrance to **Great Salt Pond,** on the west side of Block Island, is about 1.8nm south-southwest of Block

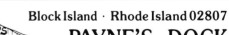

Island North Light. The entrance is marked by the 49-foot flashing red light "4" at the end of the jetty and is 16 feet deep, though once again it's beginning to shoal at the mouth. It's best to keep red bell buoy "2" to starboard even when coming from the south and west. This way, you'll be sure to avoid Charlestown Beach. Note that the Great Salt Pond Breakwater Light "10" has been removed. The channel heading in is straight: just pass down the middle toward the paired nun "12" and green can "11" **[WP-260].**

Once inside, the harbor offers good protection, with a tidal range of only 3.2 feet; though if the harbor is ever reopened to shellfishing, the anchorage area may be extended into this area.

With the varied types of holding ground in **Great Salt Pond,** you must choose your anchor carefully. Use a Danforth on the hard bottom of the middle of the anchorage, or a plow anchor in the soft areas on the perimeters. On the east side of the pond there are some spots where the bottom is covered with oyster shells and other debris–it's best to avoid this area and head out into the deeper water.

Dragging is a problem here, especially in the afternoon. When the wind gets above 15 knots, boats start to take off. A rising tide only exacerbates the situation, especially on the west side of the harbor. Rafting is allowed only in pairs.

The town of New Shoreham has strict rules about anchoring, since it already maintains 80 moorings that can

"Moped Square" in Old Harbor
Photo by Malcolm Greenaway

HOW TO SECEDE IN RHODE ISLAND

The U.S. Declaration of Independence states that if we, the people, are unhappy with our government we have the right to replace it. In 1984, more than a century after the Civil War, the residents of Block Island threatened to invoke that right and secede from Rhode Island.

This small 11-square-mile island 10 miles out in the Atlantic is considered by many to be one of the gems of southern New England.

But beauty is sometimes costly, and in this case, throngs of tourists swarm the island every year on rented mopeds. When a few businesses began renting the little motorized bicycles to tourists in the late 1970s, islanders took exception to the noisy vehicles and their riders. Local residents first tried an ordinance in 1981 limiting the number of mopeds on the island, but it was declared unconstitutional by the state supreme court, as was a 1983 ordinance prohibiting any further introduction of mopeds. Meanwhile, the island's rescue squad, who saw their calls doubled between 1982 and 1983, threatened to quit if something wasn't done about the problem.

The islanders then drafted two bills for the legislature. One regulating the number of dealers, and the other requiring that moped operators be licensed. Both bills died in committee.

Finally, faced with an unresponsive state government, residents took action. They petitioned the state: Either grant us our constitutional right of self-government and regulation of the mopeds, they said, or we will exercise our constitutional right to secede from Rhode Island.

The governors of Massachusetts and Connecticut immediately expressed interest in accepting Block Island into their respective domains. Even Colorado's Governor Richard Lamm was interested, making noises about "Colorado lobsters" and a seaport for his landlocked state.

Faced with such amorous suitors, Rhode Island gave in and allowed regulation of the mopeds. Secession fervor no longer grips the tiny island, and there is an uneasy truce between the moped dealers and the residents. The number of mopeds has been regulated, certain roads and paths are off-limits to riders, and dealers require helmets and goggles. Still, moped riders would be advised to tread lightly. Block Islanders will do what they must to maintain order, and while Colorado may have the turf, they would still enjoy having the surf.

be rented for $25 a night. These moorings, all colored green, are allotted on a first-come, first-served basis and fill up quickly. If you want to have a chance at a town mooring, arrive a day early; as the harbormaster tells us, if you show up after 3 p.m. on a Friday, forget it. Call the harbormaster on VHF 12 or 16 between 7 a.m. and 7 p.m. The moorings and anchorages also empty quickly at the end of a weekend. Starting at 8 a.m. on Sunday morning, the exodus begins as boaters head for home.

With the popularity of **Great Salt Pond** come serious pollution problems. The town has taken several steps to deal with the situation. Starting in 1989, it began running a floating pump-out station (VHF 12 or 16) that will come to a boat and empty its holding tanks. Discharge of any sewage within Salt Pond or Old Harbor is prohibited, and it's expected that by 1990 anyone breaking this rule will be subject to a stiff fine. For disposal of garbage, the town also offers free dumpsters at the Boat Basin.

Smugglers Cove, or "the Hog Pen" as the islanders call it, is south of the ferry dock and is the place to be in a storm, though it's too small for everyone. Most of the marina slips here are booked by May. Be careful of the tricky currents off Champlin's and the heavy shoaling off Payne's Dock.

Old Harbor, on the east side of Block Island, 1.4nm north of Southeast Light, is a tiny refuge occupied mainly by fishing boats and ferries. The east breakwater extends 300 yards north of the harbor entrance and is marked by a 27-foot flashing 2.5sec green light and fog signal "1A" **[WP-254].** The controlling depth of the channel was 9 feet but has just been re-dredged to 15 feet, so the ferries won't scrape as often as before.

Don't try to enter **Old Harbor** in a fresh easterly. Vessels can use only the east or south dock on a first-come, first-served basis and must have plenty of lines and bumpers ready. Anchoring can be tricky. There simply isn't enough room for everyone. On July 4 you can practically walk across the harbor from boat to boat. Because of the heavy traffic in both harbors, the harbormaster strictly enforces a 5-mph speed limit for all vessels, including dinghies. Any kids, young or old, caught speeding will be subject to a punishment of community service.

Shoreside and Emergency Services

Airport: New England Airlines (401) 466-5959
Block Island (401) 466-2422
Ambulance: 911 or (401) 466-2622
Coast Guard: Block Island (401) 466-2462 or VHF 16
Point Judith (401) 789-0444 or VHF 16
Montauk (516) 668-2773 or VHF 16
or CB 9
Ferry: To Point Judith, RI (401) 466-2261
To New London, CT (203) 442-9553
To Montauk, NY (516) 668-5709 or 2214
Fire: 911 or (401) 466-2211
Harbormaster: (401) 466-5364 or VHF 16
Hospital: Block Island Medical Center (401) 466-2125
Police: 911 or (401) 466-2622
Radio Telephone: VHF 25, 26, 86; I.D.: New London Marine Operator
VHF 28; I.D.: Riverhead Marine Operator
Taxi: (401) 466-5550
Tow Service: Marine Rescue Services, Wickford, RI (401) 295-8711 or VHF 16; Sea Tow Eastern Long Island (516) 765-3660 or VHF 16; Southeastern Marine Towing, Groton, CT (203) 445-8381 or VHF 16   ◆

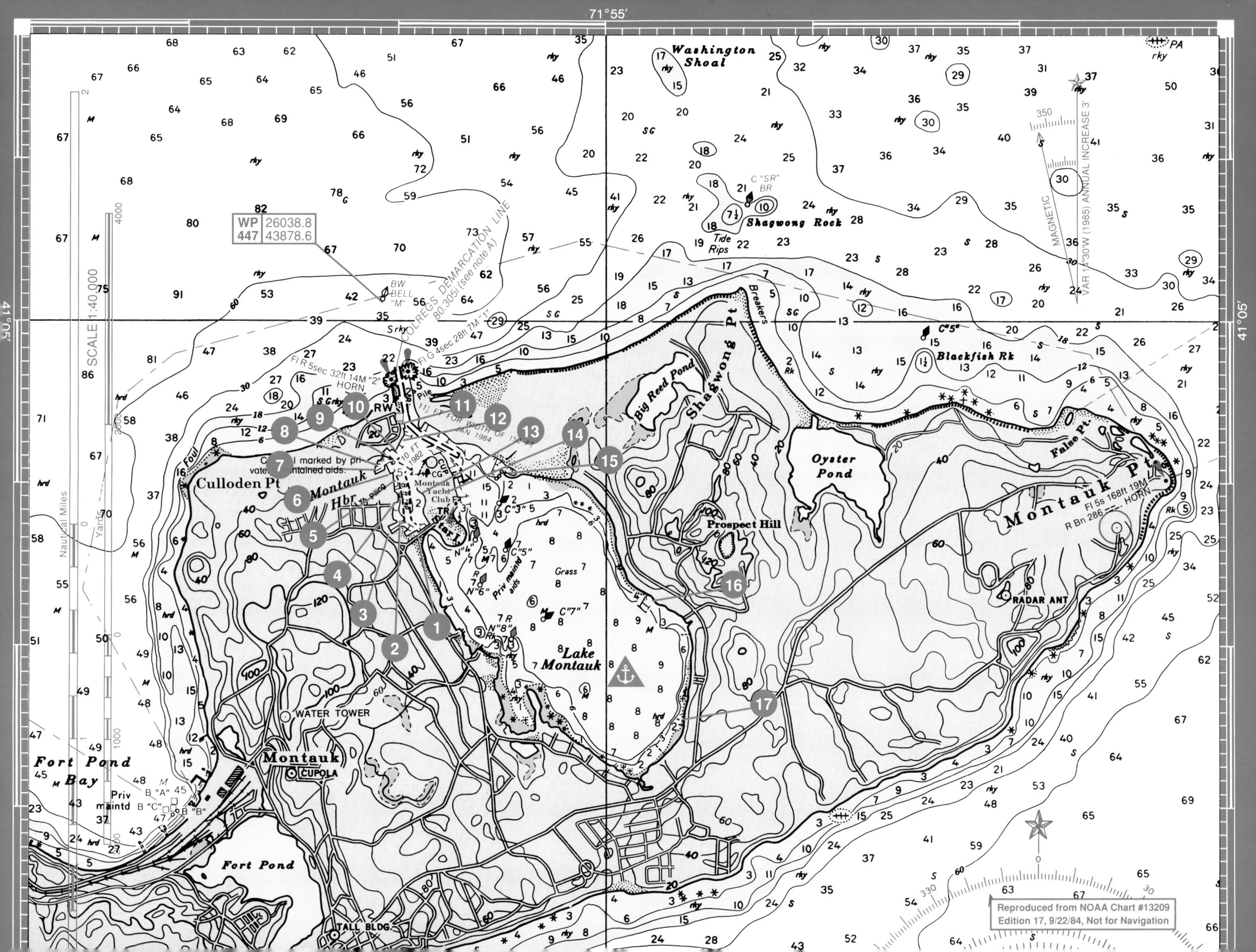
71°55′
41°05′
Washington Shoal
Shagwong Rock
Tide Rips
C "SR" BR
Blackfish Rk
C "5"
Breakers
Shagwong Pt
Big Reed Pond
Oyster Pond
Prospect Hill
False Pt.
Montauk Pt
Fl 5s 168ft 19M HORN
R Bn 286
RADAR ANT
Lake Montauk
Grass
Priv maintd aids
Montauk Hbr
Montauk Yacht Club
Star I.
Culloden Pt
Foul
Channel marked by privately maintained aids.
Fl R 5sec 32ft 14M "2" HORN
Fl G 4sec 28ft 7M "1"
COLREGS DEMARCATION LINE 80.305i (see note A)
BW BELL "M"
WP 447 26038.8 43878.6
11 FT FOR WIDTH OF 150 FT JAN 1984
10 FT 1982
WATER TOWER
Montauk
CUPOLA
TALL BLDG.
Fort Pond
Fort Pond Bay
Priv maintd
SCALE 1:40,000
Nautical Miles
Yards
VAR 14°30′W (1985) ANNUAL INCREASE 3′
MAGNETIC
Reproduced from NOAA Chart #13209 Edition 17, 9/22/84, Not for Navigation

Montauk and Napeague Harbors

On a Mighty Eagle's Beak

When Walt Whitman came east to Montauk Point, he was so moved by the sight that he wrote:

I stand on some mighty eagle's beak,
Eastward the sea absorbing, viewing,
    (Nothing but sea and sky)
The tossing waves, the foam, the ships in the distance,
The wild unrest, the snowy, curling caps–that
    inbound urge and urge of waves,
Seeking the shore forever.

Montauk Point has inspired similar, if less eloquent, feelings in thousands of visitors. Jutting into the confluence of Block Island Sound and the Atlantic, the point reveals a struggle between the land, the sea, and man. The warfare has been focused at Montauk Point Light. When the light was erected in 1795 under orders from George Washington–some say he was also the architect–it was about 300

© Steve Dunwell

The endangered Montauk Point Lighthouse from the south.

Marine Facilities and Services

#	Facility	Phone	No. Transient Berths	No. Transient Moorings	Largest Vessel Accommodation (ft)	Seasonal/Year-round	Approach Depth (ft)	Marked Entry Channel	Dockside Depth (ft at MLW)	Gas/Diesel Fuel	Fuel Brand	Ramp/Dinghy Dock/Launch Service	Railway/Lift: Capacity (tons)	Engine Repairs: Gas/Diesel	Propeller/Hull Repairs	Pump-out Station	Marine Supplies/Groceries/Bait/Ice	Showers/Laundromat	110V★ 220V▲ Max Amps	MC/VISA/Diners · Amex	Restaurant/Snack Bar	Monitors VHF Channel
1	Snug Harbor Marina and Motel	(516) 668-2860	20		50	S	6	●	6	MOTEL						●	I	SL	▲30	MVA	R	16
2	**West Lake Fishing Lodge (p. 288)**	**(516) 668-5600**	15		60	S	6	●	6	GD	GUL	R		GD	PH		SGBI	SL	★30	MVA	R	16
3	Captain's Cove Marina	(516) 668-5995	6		17	S	8	●	5	GD	EXX			GD	PH		SGI	S	★	MVA		
4	The Landing					Y				CONDOMINIUMS												
5	Offshore Sports Marina	(516) 668-2406	25		50	Y	8	●	7	GD	GUL		L50	GD	PH		SBI	SL	★30	MVA	S	16
6	**Montauk Marine Basin (p. 284)**	**(516) 668-5900**	35		80	Y	8	●	8	GD	EXX		L80	GD	PH		SGBI	SL	★▲50	MVDA		16
7	Uihlein Marina and Boat Rental	(516) 668-3799	3		40	S	17	●	7	G	GUL	R	L14	G			SGI	S	▲	MVA		
8	Viking Dock	(516) 668-5700			140	S		●		CHARTERS AND FERRY										MV		
9	Tuma's Dock	(516) 668-2707				S														MV		
10	Christman's Dock	(516) 668-9815			75	Y	10			RESTAURANT - DOCKAGE FOR PATRONS											R	
11	Gosman's Dock	(516) 668-2447				Y	12		11	SHOPS AND RESTAURANTS												
12	Salivar Dock Restaurant	(516) 668-2555		2	80	Y	6	●	6	RESTAURANT - DOCKAGE FOR PATRONS											R	
13	**Star Island Yacht Club (p. 288)**	**(516) 668-5052**	30		100	Y	10	●	6	GD	TEX		L75	GD	PH		SIG	SL	50	MVA	S	16
14	**Montauk YC Resort & Marina (p. 287)**	**(516) 668-3100**	70		250	S	11	●	10	D	TEX			GD		●	I	SL	★▲100	MVA	SR	16
15	**Gone Fishing Marina (p. 289)**	**(516) 668-3232**	30		50	S	6	●	6	GD	GUL	R	L25	GD	PH	●	SIG	S	★	MV		16
16	Montauk Lake Club & Marina	(516) 668-5705			120	Y	8	●	8	PRIVATE CLUB - MEMBERS AND GUESTS ONLY									▲		R	16
17	Bridgeford Colony & Marina	(516) 668-2273								SUMMER RESORT CABINS												

Information in these listings is provided by the facilities themselves. An asterisk (*) indicates that the facility did not respond to our most recent requests for information.

feet from the edge of the bluffs. Today, the tower stands less than 60 feet from the steadily eroding precipice.

In 1970, the 108-foot octagonal tower was in danger of slipping into the sea, so the Coast Guard debated abandoning it. Lighthouse devotees rallied and persuaded the Coast Guard to protect the point and terrace the bluff. Preservation efforts have centered on the construction of erosion barriers at key points along the Montauk coast. Today, the Montauk Historical Society is seeking the additional funds that will assure the safety of the lighthouse.

A smaller conservation attempt is underway at Napeague Harbor, 6.5nm southwest of Montauk. Apart from the eco-logical considerations, the Town of East Hampton has begun a scallop reseeding effort on the harbor bed. Anchoring has since been prohibited, for obvious reasons.

Just as there have been efforts to keep the sea at bay, there have also been attempts to bring the sea closer. Montauk Harbor, for instance, was created by cutting a channel from Lake Montauk to Block Island Sound, in 1926. This union of waters has effectively turned Montauk into the gateway to deep-sea fishing in the northeast.

There was even a time when a few developers feverishly imagined Montauk Harbor as a great shipping center, rivaling even New York. Others, such as Carl Fisher, thought he could turn Montauk into a pleasure land on par with his previous creation: Miami Beach. Montauk, however, has been spared the ravages of development, and as a result, a wild bit of seascape has been preserved only 96 miles from New York City. Its rugged handsomeness is made of scrubby, windswept pines, undulating stretches of sand, and a restless surf–amid which are "Mineshaft Modern" summer houses of people who, like Whitman's waves, have sought the shore, and have found it here.

 What To See and Do

Carl Fisher may have been somewhat disappointed that Montauk never made it to the glittering status of Miami Beach, but Montauk is a choice summer vacation spot for

Lake Montauk from the north. Star Island is in the center.

many. Its seaside wilderness is tamed by sprawling summer homes, salt-stained motels, and a busy port-of-call.

Recreation takes an active tone in Montauk, where you can sport fish, ride on horseback, golf, swim, surf, and even fly. There are, of course, the more leisurely pursuits, such as strolling the breathtaking Atlantic beaches and sightseeing.

As you come into the harbor you will see how firmly entrenched fishing is. Most of the boats are power cruisers outfitted for sport fishing. There is also no shortage of fishing charters, and you can find them just outside any of the marinas. Uihlein Marina (516) 668-3799 has boat rentals for people who are also looking to water-ski as well as fish.

Other boats such as the *Finback II* (516) 728-4522 will take you on a whalewatching cruise where the only catch you can bring home is the one you get on film. Run from May to September, the cruises are sponsored by the Okeanos Ocean Research Foundation, which also organizes a sea-mammal rescue program. If you find a sea mammal in trouble, call the sea stranding hotline collect (516) 728-8103.

Ever-popular, sightseeing can be done from two levels. Viking Ferry Lines (800) MON-TAUK offers cruises around Montauk every Wednesday in the summer, as well as passenger-bicycle ferries to Block Island and New London, CT. Or you may want to take to the wild, blue sky in a small plane; call Long Island Airlines at (516) 694-0671.

Montauk Downs State Park (516) 668-5000 is on the west side of the harbor, where you can take part in a civilized game of tennis or golf, or swim at the pool. In the summer there is bus service between the park, lighthouse, and the docks, among other places.

Since Montauk Village is 2.5 miles west of the harbor, at Fort Pond, you'll need a taxi to get to the shopping, restaurants, pharmacy, post office, and other amenities. (There are, however, many dockside restaurants in the harbor from which to choose.)

A taxi will also put you in touch with the other summer attractions in town, such as Indian Field Ranch (516) 668-2744, the oldest cattle ranch in the United States. You can rent a horse and be a dude for a day on this 4,000-acre spread.

Montauk Point Light is also a cab ride away. A museum dedicated to the light, run by the Montauk Historical Society (516) 668-5340, is at Montauk Point.

Walking the beaches, especially on the Atlantic side, is certainly an attraction that may be difficult to miss. You can go at it on your own or contact the Suffolk County Park Nature Trails (516) 668-5022 for the guided walks through the dunes and other trails. (Stay clear of the bushes on the beach; they are a favorite breeding spot for ticks.)

While the long tracts of beach may offer some peace and quiet, the place to go if you really want seclusion is

Napeague Harbor, 6.5nm by boat southwest of Montauk. An intimate and secluded harbor with a nice stretch of beach, Napeague was once one of the best kept secrets in Suffolk County. Throughout the years, unfortunately, anchors have torn up the harbor bed and visitors have, shall we say, not been mindful of the fragile wilderness there. Since an effort to reseed the harbor bed with scallops is underway, anchoring has been banned. The harbor remains popular with windsurfers. You are free to come and contemplate the placid and spare scenery–and leave once you have.

 ### Where To Eat

Finding a place to eat in Montauk Harbor is not a problem. But you better like seafood, because–like most dockside restaurants–that's pretty much what they serve. The seafood you'll get here is the freshest you'll find anywhere. Christman's Dock (516) 668-9815 and the Salivar Dock (516) 668-2555 are among the few harbor restaurants where you can dock and dine. Next door is Gosman's Dock (516) 668-2447, specializing in lobster.

If you're on Star Island you'll find a restaurant at the Montauk Yacht Club Resort & Marina (516) 668-3100 called Zeigfeld's, serving a Continental menu. Nearby, on the mainland, is the West Lake Fishing Lodge (516) 668-5600 with another very good seafood menu.

 ### Navigation and Anchorages

Use NOAA Charts 13209 (1:40,000) and 13205 (1:80,000). Use tide tables for New London. High tide at the Montauk Harbor entrance is 24 minutes earlier; low tide is 16 minutes earlier. Multiply by 0.7 for height at high or low water. Mean tidal range is 2.0 feet.

High tide at Promised Land, 2.4nm by boat southwest of the entrance to Napeague Harbor, is 13 minutes earlier, and low tide is 8 minutes earlier. Multiply by 0.9 for height at high or low water. Mean tidal range is 2.6 feet.

The entrance to Montauk Harbor is 17.3nm by boat southwest of the entrance to Great Salt Pond on Block Island, 13.8nm by boat southeast of Plum Gut and Orient Point, and 14.0nm south-southwest of Watch Hill Point, RI.

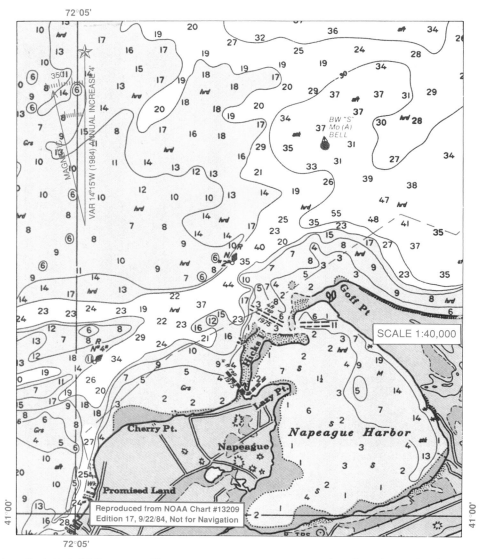

SCALE 1:40,000

Reproduced from NOAA Chart #13209
Edition 17, 9/22/84, Not for Navigation

The entrance to Napeague Harbor lies 6.5nm by boat southwest of Montauk Harbor and 7.4nm by boat east of Three Mile Harbor.

From the green 4sec flashing bell "7SR" **[WP-451]** marking Shagwong Reef, a course of about 225°m will bring you to the approach buoy "M" **[WP-447]** just off the entrance to Montauk Harbor.

CAUTION: *There have been many buoy changes in the Montauk Harbor area and the Promised Land Channel to Napeague Harbor. We have noted the most important ones below, but be alert for others.*

If you're planning a cruise to Montauk, especially on a weekend, have a slip or mooring reserved in advance. Lake Montauk can be a mob scene during summer weekends, and it's an awfully long trip to get there, so be sure you have some place to dock, anchor, or moor once you arrive.

Montauk Point Light has a fog signal, rises 168 feet above the water, and can be seen for 24nm. Beside the light is a simple white building. A radio beacon is located 0.3nm

south-southwest, and can also be seen well over the horizon. If you are coming in from the east at sunrise, the cliffs that come down from these two landmarks take on a bright reddish hue because of their high iron content.

On the north side of the point is a shoal area that extends about 4nm to the northwest, on which the tidal current usually breaks. In an ebb current, westbound sailors heading for **Montauk Harbor** may find the going slow as they will be fighting the tide. Note that bell "1" at Great Eastern Rock, due east of Montauk Point, is now green.

The approach to **Lake Montauk** is wide-open from any direction, with the only serious obstruction being **Shagwong Reef,** marked by the flashing 4sec bell "7SR" **[WP-451]** about 2.5nm to the northeast of the entrance. The approach bell "M" **[WP-447]** just outside the harbor entrance has been changed from black and white to red and white.

The entrance to **Montauk Harbor** is between two stone breakwaters marked by the 32-foot 5sec red flasher "2" and the 28-foot 4sec green flasher "1." In fog you will hear the horn on the west breakwater. While the current at the harbor entrance is evident–generally 1 to 2 knots–it diminishes dramatically inside. The channel carries 11 feet.

Since Montauk is a busy fishing town, watch out for local fishing boats, which tend to run a bit faster than the no-wake limit allows since they know the harbor by heart. With all the fishing docks jutting in and out, boats can suddenly swing out at you like a moray eel. These boats also tend to kick up a good wake, so it's even more important that you keep a slow and steady pace.

After passing through the breakwaters, you will see **Star Island** dead ahead, connected to the mainland by a causeway. The Coast Guard station is on the northern end of the island, next to a town dock where commercial fishing boats tie up. The most conspicuous landmark on the eastern side of Star Island is the lighthouse tower of the Montauk Yacht Club Resort & Marina. On the mainland to the west, you'll find a heavy concentration of marinas, restaurants, motels, and charter boats. Follow the privately marked channel, which has a reported depth of 8 feet at mlw.

If you're heading for one of the marinas on the eastern side of Lake Montauk or the designated anchorage area, keep Star Island to starboard and stay close to it to avoid the sandbar (marked by can "3") that reaches out from the eastern shore of the mainland.

The channel to the anchorage area is clearly marked and you should stay in the middle of it, as there are some suddenly shallow spots–some as low as 3 feet–just off the buoys. The East Hampton Bay Constable, however, reports that the channel has more than the reported 4 feet of water on the chart, but if you have any draft or doubts call him through the radio telephone operator on VHF 28.

After passing can "7" follow the privately maintained buoys and swing to port, at which you'll find about 8 feet of water and a charming anchorage. The muddy bottom of the harbor is considered poor holding ground.

In contrast to Montauk, **Napeague** is not marked at all, save for misleading stakes and "Tick Infested Area" signs. The approaches, however, are buoyed clearly. Before visiting Napeague Harbor there are two rules of thumb to go by: Come only if you must, and then only on a rising tide.

CAUTION: *When we first collected LORAN waypoints for the area between Gardiners Island and Napeague Harbor, we encountered severe land-mass distortion of our readings. Our most recent attempts, on the other hand, yielded much* *better numbers, which are listed in the "LORAN Index" in the back of this book. However, because of our earlier experience, we recommend you be extremely cautious when using LORAN in this area, collect your own LORAN numbers as you go through, and do without LORAN if at all possible.*

If you're coming in from the west, follow the **Promised Land Channel,** the buoyed passage southward of Gardiners and Cartwright Islands. From the east, note that red nun "6" south of Cartwright island has been slightly relocated to the southwest. Also, lighted bell "S" north of Goff Point is now red and white. Tidal velocity in the channel averages 1.5 knots.

The entrance to **Napeague Harbor** is as difficult to spot and negotiate as the harbor is beautiful. Approaching from the east or west, wait until you're at least 400 yards southwest of red nun "2" before heading toward the entrance. It is very shallow off Goff Point, so don't enter from the north. The harbor's mouth is marked by a large sign—the size of a small billboard—spelling out "No Anchoring" in no uncertain terms.

CAUTION: *The currents in and out of this harbor are quite strong and should not be underestimated; in an opposing wind they can be downright hellacious. Be ready to compensate quickly in your turns.*

Keep your speed way down when entering the harbor, and cautiously feel your way in the 4-foot-deep, privately dredged channel, turning hard to port when going around the bar. Use extreme care because as of October 1989, the narrow part of the channel seems to have silted in a bit.

The bottom contours on the chart for Napeague Harbor are not entirely in concordance with the actual depth, so if you have a depth sounder on board or a spare hand to watch the bottom at the bow—use 'em.

If your boat draws less than 5 feet you can enter on a rising tide, but keep at least 125 feet from shore and follow the shore's curve. Even under the best conditions the channel is only 12 feet wide, so don't be a cowboy.

There's another entrance on the west side of Hicks Island, dredged to a depth of about 4 feet. The channel is very narrow and at the change of tides, the current is swift. The entrance is mainly for local boaters who use the town ramp on Lazy Point. It is best to enter here at half or full tide.

Once inside you'll find shoals and marsh to the west. Stay at least 200 yards off the eastern shore and you'll find plenty of deep water.

Acabonack Harbor, just west of Cartwright Island, has a narrow channel with privately maintained markers. You'll be making your turn from the Promised Land Channel about 600 yards northwest of nun "8," taking care for the rock to port at the entrance. The channel is 2.5 feet deep, but there is more water inside.

📞 Shoreside and Emergency Services

Airport: Montauk (516) 668-3738
           Montauk Seaplane Base (516) 878-1125
Ambulance: (516) 668-2464
Coast Guard: Montauk (516) 668-2773 or VHF 16
Fire: (516) 668-2464
Harbormaster: (516) 329-3079
Hospital: Southampton General (516) 283-2600
Police: (516) 324-0024
Radio Telephone: VHF 28; I.D.: Riverhead
           Marine Operator
Taxi: Montauk Taxi (516) 668-5511
Tow Service: Harbor Ready Marine, Wickford, RI
           (401) 295-8711 or VHF 16; Tidewater
           Interstate Towing Services, Wakefield, RI
           (401) 789-4300 or VHF 7 and 16;
           Southeastern Marine Towing, Groton, CT
           (203) 445-8381 or VHF 16
Train: Long Island Railroad (516) 758-LIRR   ◆

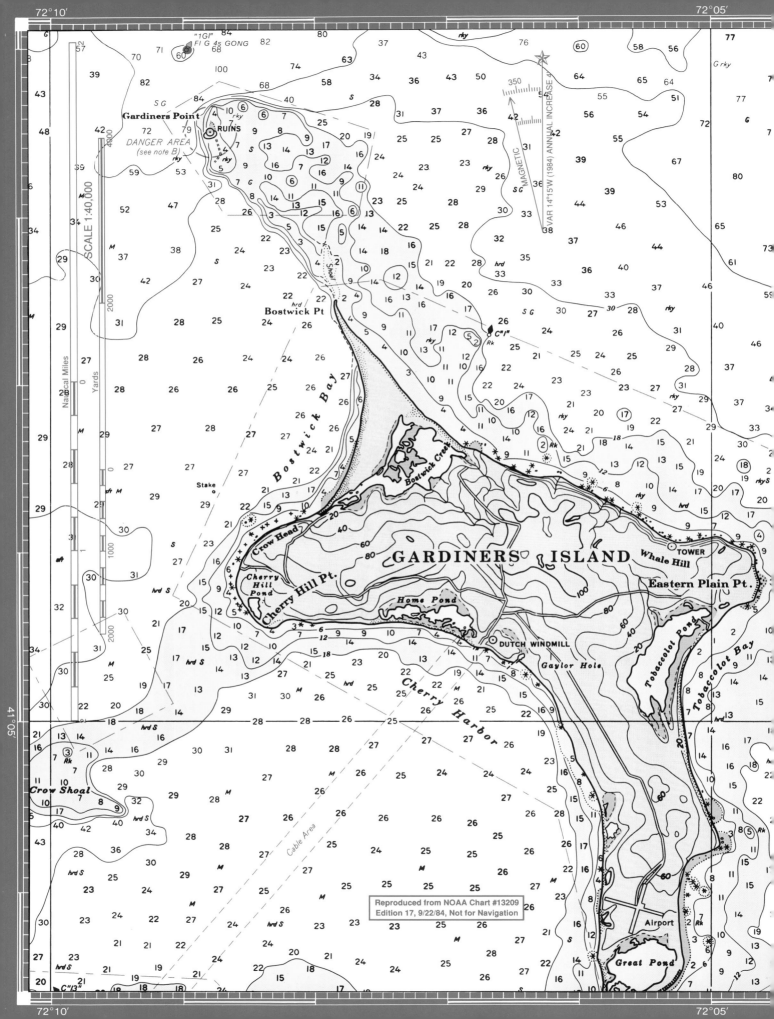

GARDINERS ISLAND

Gardiners Point
RUINS
DANGER AREA
(see note B)

Bostwick Pt

Bostwick Bay

Bostwick Creek

Crow Head

Cherry Hill Pond

Cherry Hill Pt.

Home Pond

DUTCH WINDMILL

Gaylor Hole

TOWER
Whale Hill

Eastern Plain Pt.

Tobaccolot Pond

Tobaccolot Bay

Cherry Harbor

Crow Shoal

Stake

Cable Area

Airport

Great Pond

"1GI"
FI G 4s GONG

SCALE 1:40,000

Nautical Miles
Yards

VAR 14°15'W (1984) ANNUAL INCREASE 4'
MAGNETIC

72°10'   72°05'
41°05'

Gardiners Island

Faith's Fortress in Dispute

The tidings of Salvation dere
  comes to our Ears from hence
the fortress of our faith is here
  the shield of our Defense.

—From a prayer Lion Gardiner copied onto the back page of a paper giving an account of his arrival in America.

Hanging like a question mark on the western edge of Block Island Sound is Gardiners Island, a virtually untouched 3,300-acre jewel of land. The island has been in the Gardiner family since 1639, making them the oldest non-Indian landowners in North America.

The dynasty was founded by Lion Gardiner, who bought the island from the Montauket Indians for "ten coates of trading cloth and some other articles worth 20 pounds in all." He then received a royal grant which stipulated that the property must remain in the Gardiner family.

John Gardiner, the third proprietor, was a salty reincarnation of his grandfather, and he loved his drink, Indian girls, and his land—all in equal measure, but not necessarily in that order. Asked to describe his lord's character, a servant replied, "On the main [land] he might pass for a good man, but on the island he was a devilish rogue." Every inch the lord, John Gardiner outlasted three wives; he married a fourth in his 72nd year.

It was during his tenure as owner that Captain Kidd is said to have made landfall on the island, given some of his treasure to John, and buried the rest, warning Gardiner that "If I call for it and it's gone, I will take your head and your sons."

John Gardiner died with his head, and his sons lived to marry.

The seventh landlord of the island was John Lion Gardiner, a shy and sensitive scholar who married one Sarah Griswold of Lyme, Connecticut. One of his other chief amusements was bird-watching, ospreys in particular; there are more osprey nests on Gardiners Island than on any other bird sanctuary along the Atlantic seaboard. Their daughter Julia Gardiner, born in 1820, was a damsel who would dazzle high society from New York to Saratoga Springs, thusly bringing her into the White House. She married the then-widowed President John Tyler, when she was 24.

By 1910 the island was being leased as a hunting preserve-cum-executive retreat. Deer were imported, became fruitful, and multiplied. For a while, Gardiner's Island was a small paradise. Today, however, it is ground-zero in a feud between its present occupants, Robert Gardiner and

The lush green fields of Lion Gardiner's private island. The old windmill on the west side is a good navigational landmark.

his niece, Alexandra Creel Goulet—a dispute which, at times, has been rougher than the Sound on a stormy day. The island is legally owned by U.S. Trust for the late Sarah Gardiner, mother of Robert and grandmother of Sarah.

The island itself is as it was when Lion Gardiner first set foot upon it, fresh and unspoiled as, in later years, Julia Gardiner was said to be—largely due to the fact that no one save the Gardiners and their guests are allowed to land. Approaching the island, its limestone cliffs and 5 centuries-old stand of oak rise to meet you, and it almost looks glorious. It is easy to see how, like America, it could have bolstered his faith—not just in God and freedom, but in family as well.

 Where To Eat

On your boat.

 Navigation and Anchorages

Use NOAA Charts 13209 (1:40,000), 13205 (1:80,000), and 12354 (1:80,000). Use tide tables for New London. High tide at the Three Mile Harbor entrance is 22 minutes later; low tide is 2 minutes later. Multiply by 0.9 for height at high water or low water. Mean tidal range is 2.8 feet.

Cherry Hill Point, the westernmost point on Gardiners Island, is 4.1nm northeast of the entrance to Three Mile Harbor and 5.5nm southeast of Plum Gut. Coecles Harbor on Shelter Island is 6.5nm to the west.

From the green flashing 4sec gong "9" **[WP-452]** marking Cerebus Shoal, steering 245°m will bring you to Tobaccolot Bay, on the eastern side of Gardiners Island.

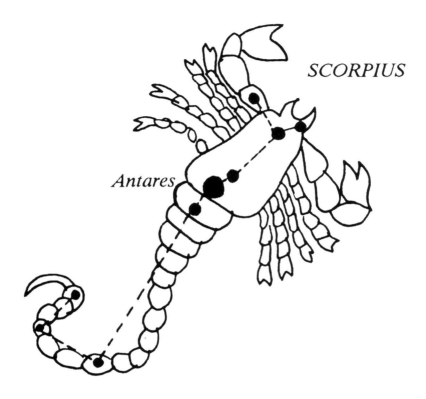

SCORPIUS

Antares

AUGUST SKIES:
The Scorpion and Shooting Stars

Low in the south after sunset this month, you'll find a hooked pattern of stars. This is Scorpius, whose poisonous sting killed the mythic hero, Orion. Supposedly, Orion's bravado landed him a duel with the scorpion, and he lost.

Scorpius is one of the zodiac constellations visited by the sun in late autumn, when the sting of impending winter is in the air. But this time of year, the scorpion's body sweeps low across the southern horizon, fierce as the heat of an August night.

Near the heart of the scorpion is a bright red star called Antares. Its name means the "rival of Mars," since it is often confused with the red planet. It rides low on the horizon and flashes red, blue, and green. This color show results from atmospheric boil.

On clear nights at sea this pattern of stars seems to rise in the southeast and drag along the ocean like a giant fish hook. Many fascinating myths are associated with it. The most charming is the Polynesian belief that this was the great fish hook used by Maui to pull the Hawaiian Islands up from the floor of the Pacific.

Watch for the Perseid Meteor Shower during this month. It peaks around August 12. This celestial display of natural fireworks results when a dense area of comet debris is scooped up by earth's gravity. Once the debris is pulled into earth's atmosphere, it heats up and burns in a fiery show of light and color.

Popularly called shooting stars, as many as sixty of these meteors are sighted each hour during the Perseid peak. They're named for the constellation Perseus, from which they seem to originate.

Contributed by Elinor DeWire, assistant at the Mystic Seaport Planetarium and a freelance writer.

CAUTION: When circumnavigating Gardiners, keep well away from the spot marked "Ruins" 1.2nm northwest of the island, at the end of the shoal. Not only is there rubble about, but the area within 300 yards is also dangerous because of the possibility of undetonated explosives. The area was a target range during the second World War.

Many find that it's always windy in **Gardiners Bay,** even if the Sound is becalmed. Gardiners has as much fetch as the open Sound, and since it is shallow (an average depth of 35 feet), short, steep waves can build up in a blow.

The ruins, a mass of concrete and iron, is an abandoned Army fort that was later used as a Navy bombing target in World War II. The old fort (and the lighthouse that preceded it) were originally connected to the island by a long sandy neck of land, parts of which are still visible at low tide. Your best course is to stay close to the flashing green 4sec gong "1GI" **[WP-453]** 0.5nm north of the ruins. *Again, be careful. This is no place to mess around.*

Take care going around Cartwright Island, extending in a series of shoals and bars south from Gardiners Island about a mile. The general geography of Cartwright Island and the shoals around it can be changed considerably by storms. The currents surrounding the island are very strong, enough to put you onto the shoals on either end of this wisp of land if you're not careful. The Town of East Hampton's Bay Constables, who patrol these waters, tell us they regularly pull 30 or 40 sailboats off the shoals each season. (Note that red nun "6" south of Cartwright Island has been relocated slightly to the southwest.)

CAUTION: When we first collected LORAN waypoints south of Gardiners Island, in the vicinity of Cartwright Island and Napeague Harbor, we encountered severe distortion of our readings–some off by more than a mile–probably caused by the landforms surrounding the area. Our most recent trip yielded much better numbers, which we have published in the LORAN Index at the back of this book. However, you may encounter the same problems with distortion, so you might not want to rely too heavily on your LORAN when navigating south of Gardiners Island. If you do, trust no one's numbers but your own.

As the entire island is privately owned, there are no harbors at Gardiners Island where visiting yachters can tie

©*Ellsworth S. Grant*

The Gardiners Island windmill, built in 1815.

up or seek refuge. However, the island itself will offer some protection from offshore winds. Given the prevailing southwest winds, the nicest place to drop a hook and watch the wildlife on the island is Tobaccolot Bay on the east side. During flood tide, however, the currents on the east side of the island can set you toward the shore, so keep an eye on your tide tables and check periodically to make sure you aren't dragging.

The view from Cherry Harbor affords nice shots of the mansion and the windmill, although the area is wide-open and exposed. The only shelter is a small cut south of the windmill to accommodate the owner's launch. You, however, are not invited to tie up.

 ### Shoreside and Emergency Services

None. Please see chapters on Shelter Island, Orient Point, and Three Mile Harbor.

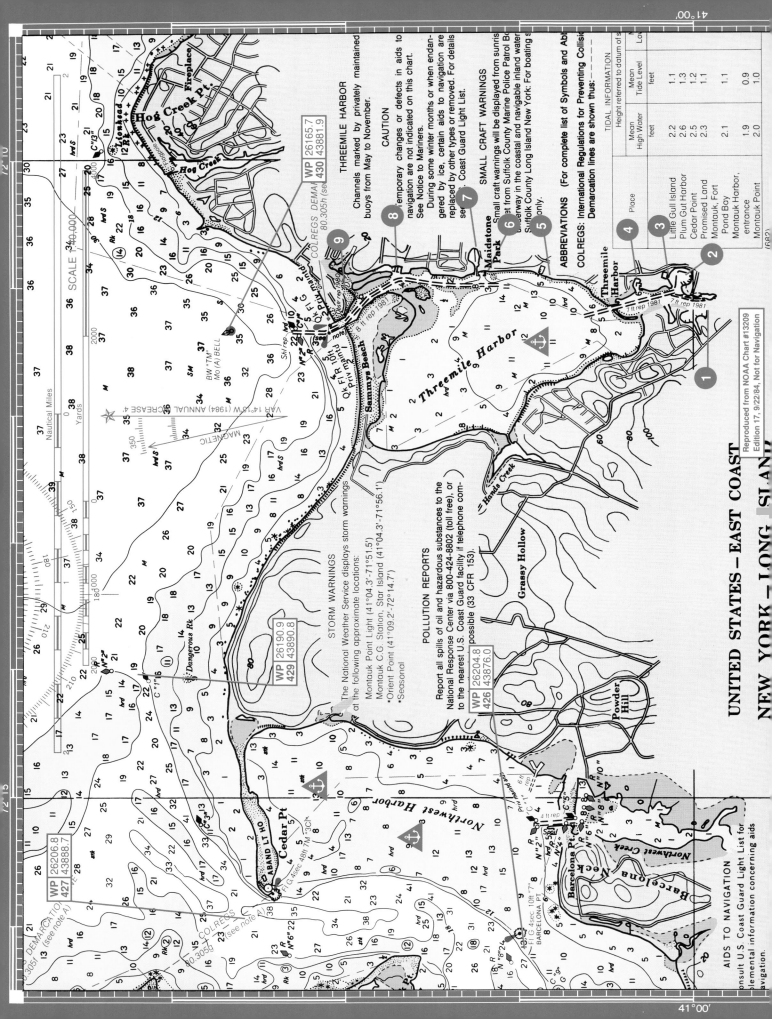

Home Sweet Home

"Home," a writer once said, "is where one starts from." In the 1820s, however, home was certainly where you were grateful to be at the end of the day, at least in East Hampton, the town just south of Three Mile Harbor. In the most idyllic situations we imagine a framed piece of needlepoint over the mantle, reading "Home Sweet Home," the title to a popular song of the times written by East Hampton poet-actor, John Howard Payne.

Originally called "Maidstone," for the English town whence most of the first residents came, the Village of East Hampton has always been a home away from home to many. In the 19th century, farm houses took in guests. By the turn of the century the fashionable and wealthy began to arrive, and lavish summer homes–"cottages," they were called–began to ring the shores of East Hampton as well as the cash registers in town.

As a result, East Hampton does not rank among the more inexpensive towns on Long Island. The village is chic with cafés and pricey, international boutiques, a far cry from its beginnings when the land was purchased from the Montauk Indians for an assortment of farming implements, musty coats, and 100 muxes (small metal drills used to make wampum). Today you must have cash, sweet cash.

To start your vacation here is to start in a place that is central to the other harbors on both forks of Long Island. And if you start here, you may find yourself infected by the harbor's and town's comfortable and welcoming disposition, and you may also find yourself coming back.

The southern tip of Three Mile Harbor, NY from the northwest.

 What To See and Do

Visitors to Long Island may be confused about the names of the places they find here. Apart from the counties, the major political units on Long Island are the townships, or "towns," which are comprised of villages. Distinguishing between the "Town of East Hampton," which includes everything from Montauk Point to the east side of Sag Harbor, and the "Village of East Hampton," the smaller settlement on the Atlantic shore, can be confusing. The situation can be more than a semantic dilemma, however, if you happen to live in the *Village* of East Hampton: since

	Marine Facilities and Services		Transient Berths	Transient Moorings	Seasonal/Year-round	Largest Vessel Accommodation (feet)	Approach Depth (feet)	Marked Entry Channel	Dockside Depth (feet at MLW)	Gas/Diesel Fuel	Fuel Brand	Ramp/Dinghy Dock/Launch Service	Railway/Lift: Capacity (tons)	Propeller/Hull Repairs	Engine Repairs: Gas/Diesel	Pump-out Station	Marine Supplies/Groceries/Bait/Ice	Showers/Laundromat	110V★ 220V▲ Max Amps	MasterCard/VISA/Diners Club · American Express	Restaurant/Snack Bar	Monitors VHF Channel
1	East Hampton Marina	(516) 324-4042			Y	30	5		10	G				H	G			S	★50	MV		16
2	Three Mile Harbor Boatyard (p. 297)	(516) 324-1320	5		Y	65	7	●	7	G	GLF		L40	PH	GD		SI		★▲50	MVA		
3	Gardiners Marina	(516) 324-9894			Y	45	7	●	4	GD	GLF							SL	▲	MV		16
4	Halsey's Marina	(516) 324-9847	3		S	82	7	●	7									SL	★▲50			16
5	Shagwong Marina	(516) 324-9605	6		Y	52	7	●	7	GD	GLF						SI	SL	★50			16
6	Wings Point Yacht Club (p. 297)	(516) 324-8400	12	10	Y	98	7	●	7	GD			L25	PH	GD	●	SI	SL	★▲50	MVA	R	16
7	Duck Creek Marina	(516) 329-2651	10		Y	65	7	●	7							●	I	SL	★▲50		R	16
8	Harbor Marina (p. 296)	(516) 324-5666	10		Y	50	12	●	6	GD	AMC		L15	PH	GD		SIG		★15	MV	SR	16
9	Sunset Cove Marina *	(516) 324-5326																				

Information in these listings is provided by the facilities themselves. An asterisk (*) indicates that the facility did not respond to our most recent requests for information.

the village is inside the *Town* of East Hampton, residents pay taxes to both! We should also mention that the locals and the road-map-makers call the harbor "Three Mile," even though NOAA uses "Threemile" on the charts.

Nit-picking aside, the Village of East Hampton is a full 3 miles south of the harbor, but catching a taxi or bus there from any of the marinas is not a problem.

Once in town, the possibilities for a fine day are nearly limitless, which is astounding, given the size of the town.

History aficionados often start at John Howard Payne's own Home Sweet Home (516) 324-0713, now a museum of Americana. Contacting the East Hampton Historical Society at the same number, however, puts you in contact with other historical attractions, such as The Marine Museum on Bluff Road in Amagansett, and the Boat Shop on Gann Road at Three Mile Harbor. The latter is dedicated to preserving wooden boat building techniques.

At the cemetery in the center of town you'll see the elaborate grave of Lion Gardiner, the first lord of Gardiners Island. Nearby is Hook Windmill, also run by the Historical Society, and which you'll come upon unexpectedly–it's surprisingly placed in a traffic island between two major roads; it is open to the public at a slight charge.

The Guild Hall Museum and John Drew Theater (516) 324-0806/4050, beside the flagpole at the other end of town, has changing art exhibits and stage presentations.

Out at Three Mile Harbor, the water is clean and good for swimming. The best swimming area, other than off the side of your boat, is the north side of Sammy's Beach, just to the west of the entrance jetties. You can come into the port, row your dinghy ashore, and walk across to the beach. Unfortunately, clamming is not allowed.

Cedar Point, a long spit, sandy on one side and stony on the other, is a county park 3 miles west of the Three Mile Harbor entrance. It's a great place for quiet bathing and beaching. There are also campsites and a nearby store.

By local tradition, fireworks are set off right over the harbor on Bastille Day in mid-July, making a spectacular display reflected in the water. July 4 fireworks are launched from the Devon Yacht Club, 3 miles southeast, and at the main beach at East Hampton, 3 miles to the south.

 ### Where To Eat

Although the nearest large commercial area is in the Village of East Hampton, there are plenty of restaurants right around Three Mile Harbor. For fine food in an elegant setting try the Wings Point Yacht Club (516) 324-6100, which used to be Maidstone Boat Yard; they serve a Continental menu with a number of seafood specialties.

For more medium-priced dining (with a water view) try the seafood at Little Rock Lobster (516) 324-7040 at Harbor Marina, or the Sea Wolf (516) 324-1650 at Duck Creek Marina. Nearby on Flaggy Hole Road there's Michael's (516) 324-0725, offering a Long Island seafood menu apart from such staples as pasta and steak.

 ### Navigation and Anchorages

Use NOAA Charts 13209 (1:40,000), 12358 (1:40,000), 12354 (1:80,000), and 13205 (1:80,000). Use tide tables for New London. High tide at Three Mile Harbor entrance is 22 minutes later; low tide is 2 minutes later. Multiply by 0.9 for height at high or low water. Mean tidal range is 2.8 feet.

The entrance to Three Mile Harbor is 6.6nm by boat east-northeast of Sag Harbor, 7.9nm by boat south of Plum Gut, and 13.3nm by boat west of Lake Montauk.

From the green flashing 4sec gong "1GI" **[WP-453]** north of Gardiners Island, a course of about 210°m will bring you to the harbor entrance.

The approach to **Three Mile Harbor** (called "Threemile Harbor" on the NOAA charts) is easy with few obstructions. If you're coming from the east around Hog Creek Point, note that can "13" at Lionhead Rock is now green.

The **Three Mile Harbor** channel entrance is marked by a seasonal lighted red and white bell buoy "TM" **[WP-430]** (formerly black and white) about 0.6nm offshore, and begins between red nun "2" and can "1," now green. There are usually a number of fishermen on the jetties at the entrance, the jetties being marked at the outer ends with privately maintained lights. When you approach at night the channel is so well marked you feel you're heading down a runway. There is a current in the entrance channel of up to 3 knots–enough to make you cautious.

The channel is charted as 8 feet deep to **Wings Point** (erroneously labeled **"Maidstone Park"** on the NOAA chart). However, the local boaters will tell you the depth is more like 6.5 to 7 feet at mlw, still enough for most cruising boats. South of Wings Point, there is 10 to 13 feet in the channel and in the anchorage area to starboard. The channel is well marked, but narrow and crowded on weekends. You may want to motor in rather than sail, or at least have the engine on for extra steerage.

A 5-mph speed limit is enforced throughout the harbor and especially in the channel. Just past the entrance on the west are the remains of an old wooden bulkhead that has fallen into the side of the channel, so keep clear.

Just south of Sammy's Beach to starboard is tiny **Keyes Island,** easily recognized by the small house built on it. Directly across the channel from Keyes Island, near Harbor Marina, is a town dock with a public restroom. It's mostly used by commercial fishermen, but in an emergency you can tie up for a short period.

CAUTION: A sandbar extends at least 0.5nm farther south from Sammy's Beach than is marked on the chart, and is unforgiving to those who try to cut it. Do not turn to starboard until you've passed red nun "22," about 100 yards south of the Wings Point Yacht Club. (The buoys inside Three Mile Harbor are maintained by the town.)

Stay within the channel markers, favoring the starboard side until you pass nun "22" and then heading into the anchorage. At **Wings Point** you'll find the Wings Point Yacht Club (formerly Maidstone Boat Yard) and Duck Creek Marina.

CAUTION: Just south of Wings Point you'll see a dolphin. There is an unmarked shoal extending about 30 yards west of the dolphin (toward the channel), so be very careful heading into either one of these marinas. As long as you stay well north of the dolphin there should be no problem.

You can catch a bus to East Hampton at any of the marinas. There you'll have access to almost anything you need–groceries and supplies but no laundromat.

Once past nun "22" you can make a slow turn into the anchorage and find deep water as far as the western shore. The mud bottom is good holding ground throughout, and there is a large area for anchoring, well protected by the hills to the south. Another channel at the southern end of the harbor, marked with a big dolphin, leads to more marinas and a gorgeous, totally protected inlet.

To the west and around Cedar Point, **Northwest Harbor** is 5.5nm by boat to the west of Three Mile Harbor. Northwest Harbor makes a good anchorage when the southwesterlies are quiet. You'll have to round **Cedar Point,** 3.7nm by boat west of Three Mile Harbor, and then south to the shelter of Barcelona Neck. Cedar Point is easy to spot, with its 48-foot green flasher at the westernmost end and an abandoned lighthouse.

If you draw more than 4 feet, be careful entering Northwest Harbor, as there are boulders on the bottom. Some boats go farther south into Northwest Creek, which has a marked channel into a small gunk hole. Once inside, turn east for deeper water and the anchorage, where you'll also find a town ramp, open to non-residents with a permit. (Call the East Hampton Town Clerk (516) 324-4143 for permit information.) The entire creek is an undeveloped nature preserve, full of wildlife.

Shoreside and Emergency Services

Airport: East Hampton Airport (516) 537-1130
Ambulance: (516) 324-6767
Bus: Suffolk County Transit (516) 360-5700
Coast Guard: Montauk (516) 668-2773 or VHF 16
Fire: "0" (Operator) or (516) 324-0124
Harbormaster: Bay Constable (516) 324-0024 or VHF 16
Hospital: Southampton Hospital (516) 283-2600
      Good Friend Clinic (516) 329-0200
Police: (516) 324-0024 or VHF 16
Radio Telephone: VHF 85; I.D.: Bay Shore
          Marine Operator
          VHF 28; I.D.: Riverhead
          Marine Operator
Taxi: Village Coach (516) 324-0077
Tow Service: Sea Tow Eastern LI, Southold, NY
          (516) 765-3660 or VHF 16; Marine Rescue
          Services, Wickford, RI (401) 295-8711
          or VHF 16; Saybrook Towing and Salvage,
          Old Saybrook, CT (203) 388-4065
          or VHF 16
Train: Long Island Railroad (516) 234-LIRR   ◆

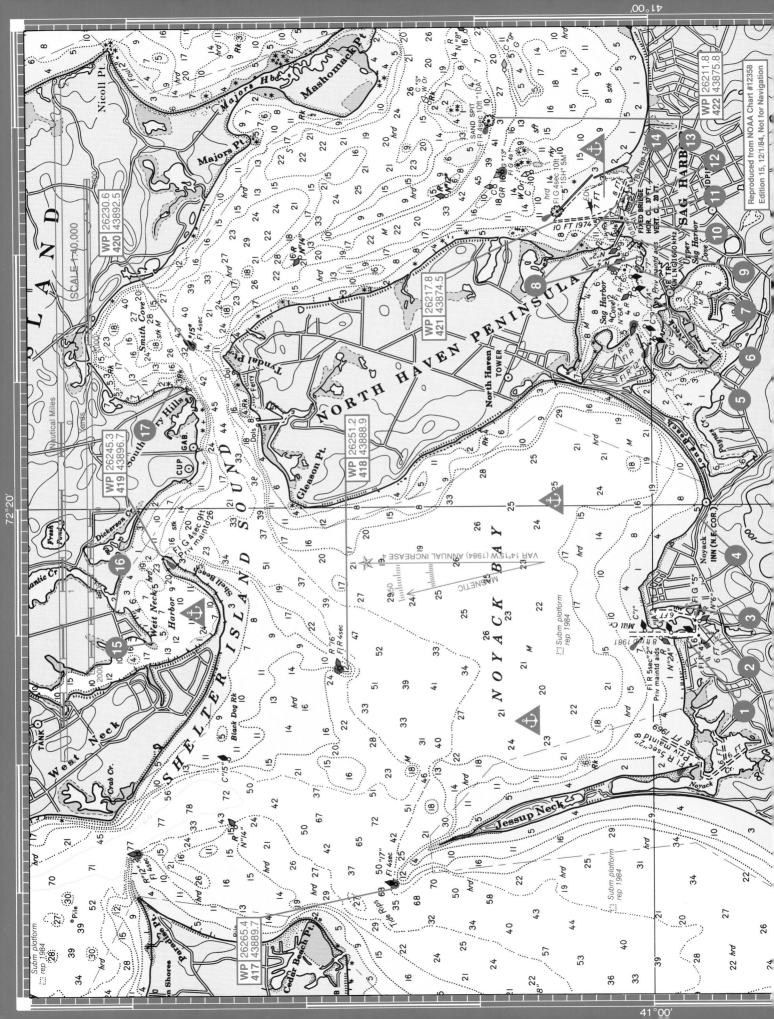

Sag Harbor and Noyack Bay

Where the Ground Nuts Grew

In the early days before the English came in 1640, the Indians harvested a kind of wild potato in these parts. It was called a "ground nut" and the reaping ground, *Sagaponack*–"Where the Ground Nuts Grow." Realizing they needed access to the Peconic Bays, Sagaponack farmers cut a road to The Great Meadows, 5 miles north, and called it the Harbor of Sagaponack, eventually paring away the last syllables of its name, leaving Sag Harbor.

In the 1760s shipbuilding was on its way to being an established industry, and a lively trade had begun with the West Indies. Thirty years later George Washington would approve an act establishing Sag Harbor as a port of entry, ensuring that it would be one of Long Island's more significant villages. People began looking at Sag Harbor and saw another New York on the rise; in fact, for a period at the end of the 18th century Sag Harbor was not only clearing more tonnage than New York, but had more ships than that city.

Sag Harbor, NY from the southwest. Mashomack Point on Shelter Island is in the center background. To the right is Cedar Point.

#	Marine Facilities and Services	Phone	Number of Transient Berths	Number of Transient Moorings	Seasonal/year-round	Largest Vessel Accommodation	Approach Depth (in feet)	Marked Entry Channel	Dockside Depth in feet at MLW	Gas/Diesel Fuel	Fuel Brand	Ramp/Dinghy Dock/Launch Service	Railway/Lift: Capacity (in tons)	Propeller/Hull Repairs	Engine Repairs: Gas/Diesel	Pump-out Station	Showers/Laundromat	Marine Supplies/Groceries/Bait/Ice	110V ★ 220V ▲ Maximum Amps	MasterCard/VISA/Diners Club · American Express	Restaurant/Snack Bar	Monitors VHF Channel
1	North Hampton Colony Yacht Club					*PRIVATE CLUB - MEMBERS ONLY*																
2	Mill Creek Marina	(516) 725-1351	2		S	40	4	●	3	G	GUL		L25	PH	GD		S	I	★30	MVA	SR	
3	Noyac Marina	(516) 725-3333	5	5	S	23	6	●	6	G	GUL			P	G			SI			S	
4	Salty Dog Restaurant	(516) 725-0840				*DOCKAGE FOR PATRONS*																
5	Redwood Boat Basin	(516) 725-0138			Y	36	4	●	4	G	GUL			P	G		S		★110			
6	Ship Ashore Marina	(516) 725-3755			Y	42	4	●	6	G	EXX		L30	PH	GD		S	S	★30	MV		16
7	Baron's Cove Marina	(516) 725-3939	20		S	55	4	●	3	GD	GUL						SL	I	★▲50	MV	R	16
8	Sag Harbor Village Docks	(516) 725-2368	20		S	60	11	●	11								S		★30			16
9	Whaler's Marina *	(516) 725-1605																				
10	Long Wharf					*VILLAGE PIER - NO DOCKAGE*																
11	**Bayview Marine & Tackle (p. 302)**	(516) 725-0740				*MARINE SUPPLIES & TACKLE*												SGBI		MV		
12	**Waterfront Marina (p. 302)**	(516) 725-3886	12		S	130	9	●	4	GD							S	I	★▲50	MV	R	16
13	Sag Harbor Yacht Club	(516) 725-0567	15		S	180		●	9	GD	GUL						S	I	★▲100	MV		16
14	**Sag Harbor Yacht Yard (p. 300)**	(516) 725-3838		2	Y	45	6	●				L	L25	PH	GD	●	L	S		MV		16
15	Menantic Yacht Club					*PRIVATE CLUB - MEMBERS ONLY*																
16	**The Island Boatyard & Marina (p. 309)**	(516) 749-3333	27		Y	45	6	●	6	GD						●	SL	GI	★30	MV	S	16
17	Shelter Island Marina	(516) 749-1030	2		S	45	6	●	6	G	MOB	R		PH	GD		SL	SBI	★30			

Information in these listings is provided by the facilities themselves. An asterisk (*) indicates that the facility did not respond to our most recent requests for information.

Whaling only aided the harbor's spectacular climb, and by 1840 a fleet of 63 whaleships jammed the already tight harbor. The prosperous village had a population of about 4,000 which rose and dropped like the sea swell because nearly half that population were seamen on ships. Herman Melville used one whaling Capt. David Hand as the source for Ahab in *Moby Dick*. James Fenimore Cooper found characters like Leather Stocking among these men and wrote his first novel, *Precaution*–on a dare from his wife–while living in town as an agent for a whaling company.

Many harbors and ports were symbiotic with the whaling industry, and when whaling declined, so did they. In a way, like its name, Sag Harbor was compacted. Sag Harbor did not become the New York-style city that a few envisioned it to be. In fact, it had to wait until after the second World War to be rejuvenated by the tourist trade (although in the 1920s and 30s rum running helped a bit).

Main Street in Sag Harbor is where the past–or various bits of it–is most keenly alive. Colonial brick buildings disappear into twisting trees beneath which are benches. At night the street is brightened with replica iron lamps that once were gaslit. There is a persistent sense of elegance and worldliness–whaling's legacy, no doubt–and it finds its way even to the menu of one classy restaurant that has taken some "ground nuts" (the Idaho kind) and made a torte.

 ### What To See and Do

There are few ports-of-call on Long Island that are polished like Sag Harbor. The village is small, manageable, and if you enjoy a good walk through calm and pleasant streets, Sag Harbor will not disappoint you. If you start at the information booth in the mock windmill just off Long Wharf, you can get a walker's map of the town, courtesy of the Chamber of Commerce (516) 725-0011. The tourist center can also provide you with a list of the historical houses in town that are open to the public.

Whaling's significant influence on the town has left a few memorable impressions, one being the Whaling Museum at the Benjamin Hunting House (516) 725-0770. After making a fitting entrance through the massive jawbones of a whale that arch over the main door, you will find an engaging collection of flensing knives, blubber spades, harpoons, and "try-works," the huge vats used to boil whale blubber.

An architectural momento from the whaling days is the Whalers Church, a unique creation with Egyptian overtones which was originally topped with a spyglass steeple that was blown off in the hurricane of 1938 and never replaced. The trim is supposed to have been carved by the town's whalers.

Sag Harbor is also a shoppers town. On Main Street, right off the waterfront, you'll find antique shops, boutiques, art galleries, and restaurants. There are also the conveniences such as a liquor and grocery store, laundromat, and pharmacy.

 ### Where To Eat

After a cold, hard, and long day–or sometimes longer–asea, a sailor wants a couple of things; one is food. In Sag Harbor, then, there is no shortage of restaurants, and you will find the best ones on Main Street.

Right on Long Wharf, however, is Studley's Long Wharf Restaurant (516) 725-0176 with its fine seafood menu. At Baron's Cove Marina is the Chart Inn (516) 725-3332, another steak, seafood, and chops place. Once in town and hungry and in a hearty, American mood, the Webb City Bar and Grill (516) 725-9628 should be right up your alley. Apart from the just-this-morning catch of seafood is the BBQ, which is done very well and very plentifully here.

Across the street from the Fire Department is J.W. Ryerson's (516) 725-3530. The restaurant serves almost everything from burgers to roast lamb in a casual atmosphere. Down the street is the American Hotel (516) 725-3535 where you can dress up to dine well in a perfectly classic setting. On some nights, especially in the off-season, the restaurant offers dinner with a movie at the local cinema, following desert. You'll also come across Il Capuccino Ristorante (516) 725- 2747; this is a good place to go if you're looking to dress up a bit and dine on Northern

© *Mary Jane Hayes*

High tide at Noyack Bay is 2 hours 6 minutes later; low tide is 1 hour 44 minutes later. Multiply by 0.9 for height at high water or low water. Mean tidal range is 2.6 feet.

CAUTION: *There have been many buoy changes in this area. We have noted the most important below, but be alert for others.*

Sag Harbor is 4.2nm by boat from West Neck Harbor on Shelter Island, and 2.5nm by boat southwestward of the light at Cedar Point, where a picturesque abandoned lighthouse guards the approach.

When a northeast wind blows across **Gardiners Bay,** very rough seas can build up around Cedar Point as the waves converge on the shallower and more constricted passage.

If you're headed for **Sag Harbor** from the east, make sure to leave nun "8" and the 10-foot 4sec red flasher "10A" **[WP-422],** both south of Mashomack Point on Shelter Island, to starboard in order to avoid the sand spit and rocks that they mark. There is very shallow water south of green can "9," so honor the markers and stay in the channel.

If you're headed past Sag Harbor toward **Smith Cove** or **West Neck Harbor** on Shelter Island, however, you can stay to the north of the sand spit. Leave nun "8" and the white and orange can "S" well to port and head directly for the green 4sec flasher "15" **[WP-420]** off Tyndal Point on North Haven.

Coming towards Sag Harbor from Smith Cove to the north and points west, keep the green (formerly white) 4sec flasher "15" **[WP-420]** off the northeast tip of North Haven Peninsula to starboard, and then keep red nuns "14" and "12" to port as you head southeast.

None of these passages should be attempted in the dark, and even in daytime you must steer carefully between the markers. From either direction, look for the green 4sec flasher "11" (numbered "13" on the chart) 0.4nm northeast of the Sag Harbor breakwater, and the green and red mid-channel marker 200 yards to the west of the flasher. Between these buoys lies the only acceptably safe approach to the harbor. Trying to save time by cutting buoys, especially if you're coming from the east, is not useful

Italian cuisine and a robust chianti. Il Capuccino, however, is only open for dinner.

If you're staying around Mill Creek in Noyack, you might try the Inn at Mill Creek (516) 725-1116 or the Salty Dog Restaurant (516) 725-0840, both for the seafood.

 Navigation and Anchorages

Use NOAA Charts 12358 (1:40,000) and 12354 (1:80,000). Use tide tables for New London. High tide at Sag Harbor is 1 hour later; low tide is 48 minutes later. Multiply by 1.0 for height at high or low water. Mean tidal range is 2.8 feet.

because you'll just lose even more time waiting for your hull repairs at a local boatyard.

The 10-foot green flasher "1SH" **[WP-421]** (charted as "4sec," it is now 2.5sec) on the port side of the long Sag Harbor breakwater marks the harbor entrance. Keep clear of the rocks, marked with an orange and white can, also to port, as you make your way to the breakwater.

Do not round the breakwater too closely—keep 10 to 15 feet away—as the water is only about 6 feet deep near its end, though the main channel has 8 to 10 feet of water. Dead ahead you'll see Long Wharf, between you and the windmill.

Part of the town marina stretches east from Long Wharf. Transient berths with piles and slips are available on a first-come, first-served basis, as at the Sag Harbor Yacht Club. The harbormaster can be reached on VHF 16 to find out if space is available. (Since there are no finger piers, and the ladders from the water up to the main pier are built into the bulkhead, be sure to back into the berth.)

There's not much room in the harbor, but the best and only anchorage is between Long Wharf and the breakwater, with a 5-foot depth. The harbormaster tells us that the charted wreck in the middle of this anchorage is no longer there, but that the depth just off the town marina may be less than the 8 feet indicated on the chart. The Town of Southampton (of which Sag Harbor is a part) allows free anchoring here for the first 72 hours, after which you'll be charged $25 for each additional 72 hours.

CAUTION: *One of our readers tells us he was not allowed to anchor in the lower half of the area between Long Wharf and the breakwater, and had to find a spot in the far northern section of the anchorage, hard by flasher "1SH" on the end of the breakwater. It's a good idea to check with the harbormaster before dropping your hook, to see if the anchoring regulations have changed.*

Sag Harbor Cove, to the west of Long Wharf, is fine for power boats that can go under the 20-foot fixed bridge, following a privately maintained seasonal set of buoys to the marinas inside. There's another section of the town marina here, 300 yards inside of the bridge.

Three ferries run back and forth across the channel between the North Haven Peninsula and South Ferry Hills on Shelter Island, and don't give way for recreational boaters.

Noyack Bay, on the western side of North Haven Peninsula, provides unobstructed deep water as long as you stay a half mile from shore. The northwest corner of Noyack Bay is marked with the green 4sec flasher "17" **[WP-417]** (formerly white).

Noyack Bay provides no protection in a northerly wind, but there is plenty of room to escape from a southerly. The water quality here is very good, so if you've been dying to take a dip, here's your chance.

Mill Creek, at the southern end of Noyack Bay, is a cozy little anchorage, with several marine facilities. The approach is a straight shot south from Shelter Island Sound, but don't cut too close to Gleason Point if you're coming around from the east, or too close to Jessup Neck from the west. Mill Creek is entered by an 8-foot-deep channel marked by private seasonal lights and buoys. Inside is a town dock and ramp, on the east side directly opposite the green flasher "5." Transients may tie up for 2 hours, but a permit is needed to use the ramp. Call the Southampton Town Hall (516) 283-6000 for permit information.

The Morton Wildlife Refuge is on **Jessup Neck,** manned full-time by a naturalist from the U.S. Fish and Wildlife Service who will be glad to answer any question you may have about the place. The Neck has a varied wooded terrain with many kinds of flora and, of course, good beach walking. It's a prime spot for watching warbler migration in the spring when the woods are also beautiful with daffodils.

The shellfishing is good in **Noyack Creek** at the base of the point, but no facilities will be found there. Also, anchoring in Noyack Creek is for residents only, with a town permit.

For more on nearby anchorages at Shelter Island, please see the next chapter.

A LIGHT IS A LIGHT IS A SHIPWRECK

On Jan. 2, 1796 George Washington authorized the construction of a lighthouse at Montauk Point. It's said he had it built 300 feet from the bluff, to stave off the gradual advance of erosion–and still be there for mariners a couple of hundred years later.

The Light was designed by Ezra L'Hommedieu, and constructed by a New York bricklayer. When completed in 1797, it was armed with 9 cedar cisterns which held whale oil to fuel the light: not much light, but better than the dark for mariners battling the elements.

Since its construction, mariners have relied heavily on Montauk Light when navigating the northeast coast. But it took one tragic incident to emphasize that a light is a light is a light unless you can distinguish it from other lights.

On February 18, 1858, Captain Harding of the *John Milton* and his crew ran into a snow storm off the southern coast of Long Island. Spotting Montauk Light to port, he soon turned north into what he thought were the open waters of Block Island Sound. In fact, he had mistaken the steady beam of the newly erected Poquonogue (or Shinnecock) Light for the light at Montauk Point (which had since been changed to a flashing signal). With all sails set at dawn on the 20th, the *John Milton* crashed onto rocks along the south shore of Long Island, 5 miles west of Montauk Point. No one survived.

The *John Milton's* fate demonstrated the importance of maintaining the uniqueness of aids such as the Montauk Point Light and having up-to-date charts and navigational information.

But if it's any consolation to the long-dead Captain Harding–wherever he may be– there are plenty of modern-day mariners who *still* can't tell one beacon from another, or navigate properly even with the latest space-age equipment.

Just ask any major oil company.

Contributed by Ian Quarrier, a freelance writer from Essex, CT.

 Shoreside and Emergency Services

Airport: East Hampton (516) 537-1130
Ambulance: (516) 725-0058
Bus: Suffolk County Transit (516) 360-5700
Coast Guard: Montauk (516) 668-2773 or VHF 16
Ferry: South Ferry to North Haven Peninsula
         (516) 749-1200
         Sag Harbor to Marine Park, Haddam, CT
         (203) 345-4507
Fire: (516) 324-6550
Harbormaster: (516) 725-2368 or VHF 16
Hospital: Southampton (516) 283-2600
Police: (516) 725-0058
Radio Telephone: VHF 85; I.D.: Bay Shore
                   Marine Operator
                   VHF 28; I.D.: Riverhead
                   Marine Operator
Taxi: East End Taxi (516) 725-2500
Tow Service: Sea Tow Eastern LI, Southold, NY
         (516) 765-3660 or VHF 16; Saybrook
         Towing and Salvage, Old Saybrook, CT
         (203) 388-4065 or VHF 16
Train: Long Island Railroad (516) 234-LIRR   ◆

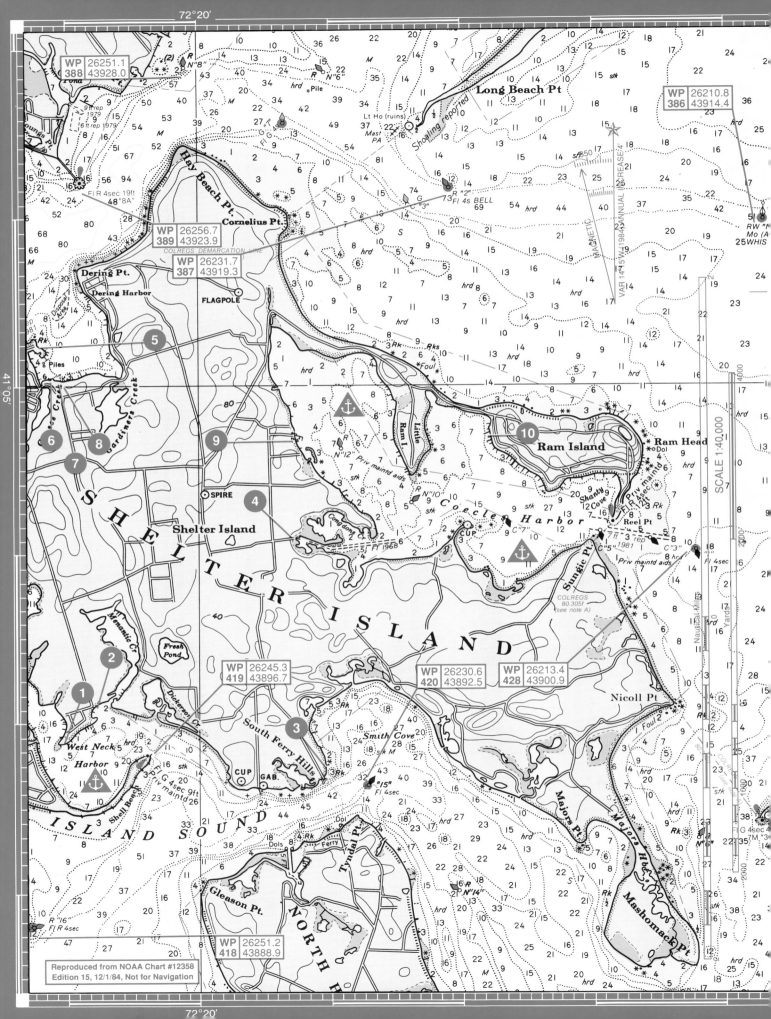

Island Sheltered By Islands

It is rare to find a place on Long Island Sound so aptly named as Shelter Island. The Indians first gave the island its name, drawing from its geography: *Manhansacka-haquashawamock,* they called it, meaning "island sheltered by islands." English settlers pruned this mouthful to its present form, but the island has lost none of its protective qualities.

Coecles Harbor on Shelter Island from the west. From foreground to background: Coecles Harbor Marina, Little Ram Island, and Ram Island.

One of the the island's earliest settlers was Nathaniel Sylvester, a sugar merchant from Barbados. In 1652 Sylvester, Thomas Rouse, and Thomas Middleton bought the island because of its great stands of oak, needed to make hogsheads for shipping sugar. What Sylvester is remembered for, however, is how he welcomed and harbored Quaker refugees on the island when they were being persecuted throughout New England.

Sylvester's wife was also the daughter of the King's Auditor, and she interceded with King Charles on behalf of the Quakers, leading to the "King's Missive," the order that put an end to the persecution; later, George Fox, founder of the Quaker faith, also came to the island and talked about brotherly love with another persecuted group of people: The Indians.

The Sylvester name is itself a kind of stronghold on the island mostly because it is so historically pervasive, fixing itself nearly everywhere, and in many disguises: One of Sylvester's descendants, for example, married a prominent Boston merchant named Thomas Dering, who came to live on the island in Sylvester Manor. It is from him that Dering Harbor gets its name.

Marine businesses also found Shelter Island to be a haven of sorts, because of its safety from and proximity to the open sea. Throughout the years, shipbuilding, whaling, and fishing–especially for menhaden–prospered on the island. Attracted by the relative calm, the tourist industry

Marine Facilities and Services

# Facility	Phone	Transient Berths	Transient Moorings	Seasonal/Year-round	Largest Vessel Accommodation	Marked Entry Channel	Dockside Depth (ft at MLW)	Approach Depth (ft at MLW)	Gas/Diesel Fuel	Fuel Brand	Ramp/Dinghy Dock/Launch Service	Railway/Lift Capacity (tons)	Propeller/Hull Repairs	Engine Repairs: Gas/Diesel	Pump-out Station	Showers/Laundromat	Marine Supplies/Groceries/Bait/Ice	110V★ 220V▲ Max Amps	Cards (M/V/A/D)	Restaurant/Snack Bar	Monitors VHF Channel
1 Menantic Yacht Club									*PRIVATE CLUB - MEMBERS ONLY*												
2 **The Island Boatyard & Marina (p. 309)**	**(516) 749-3333**	40		Y	55	●	6	7	GD	GUL					●	SL	SGBI	★30	MV	S	16
3 Shelter Island Marina	(516) 749-1030		2	S	45		6	6	G	MOB				GD		SL	SGI	★30			
4 Town Dock/Coecles Harbor					24		3	3			R							★20			16
5 Shelter Island Yacht Club	(516) 749-0888		10	S	75	●	8	6	*PRIVATE CLUB - MEMBERS ONLY*								I	★30	MVA	R	9
6 Jack's Marine	(516) 749-0114	3	10	S	60	●	10	10			D						SGRI	★30			68
7 Town Dock/Dering Harbor					60		12	12	*2 HR TIE-UP LOADING & UNLOADING*												16
8 Picozzi's Dering Harbor Marina	(516) 749-0045	30	13	Y	250	●	12	12	GD	MOB						SL	SGI	★▲50	MVA	SR	16
9 Coecles Harbor Marina & Boatyard	(516) 749-0700	40	50	Y	65	●	6	6	GD	MOB	D	L30	PH	GD	●	SL	SI	★30	MV	S	16
10 Ram's Head Inn	(516) 749-0811								*RESORT - DOCKAGE FOR PATRONS*												

Information in these listings is provided by the facilities themselves. An asterisk (*) indicates that the facility did not respond to our most recent requests for information.

also began to flourish here. Daily steamers out of New York brought a steady flow of summer folk eager to escape the sweltering metropolis.

The city people, however, were quickly confronted with a malodorous surprise: the sea breezes carried the distinctive smell of menhaden as they were hauled up to local factories to be processed for their oil content and use in glue. Protests–some of them even stinkier than the fish–eventually closed the factories.

Today, there is only the smell of cedar and salt water, and, if you're in town, perhaps the scent of some fashionable perfume. True to its form in the pre-Revolutionary War days, Shelter Island is still a refuge of sorts: it is one of the most beautiful–if not most expensive–places to live near Long Island Sound. There's a minimum of commercial development and an abundance of wooded areas in which you'll find some very big and beautiful homes. These are the telltale signs of the island's exclusivity, and maybe why it remains clean, quiet, and peaceful.

 What To See and Do

You will notice a sense of calm as you pull into Dering Harbor on the northwest side of Shelter Island, or into any other harbor or cove on the island for that matter. The hills are layered with woods and stunning houses with big windows that look out over the surrounding waters.

The roads that wind their way through all this are great for bicycling, and bikes–if you don't have your own with you–can be rented at Picozzi's (516) 749-0045 in Dering Harbor or Coecles Harbor Marina (516) 749-0700. A brisk game of tennis can be had at the tennis courts run by the Shelter Island Heights Association (516) 749-8897, just up the road from Picozzi's; call to reserve a court. If golf is your game, 9 holes of it can be had at the Shelter Island Country Club (516) 749-8841. Windsurfing? Call the Bay Breeze at (516) 749-3314.

The more nature-oriented pursuits on Shelter Island can be found on the 2,000-acre Mashomack Preserve (516) 749-1001 on the southwestern point of the island, about 4 miles from Dering Harbor. Operated by the Nature Conservancy, you will find over 15 miles of trails taking you through woodland, beaches, and salt marshes. Guided tours are offered every other Sunday throughout the year. Boaters should note that coming ashore from Majors Harbor is prohibited, and that there are ticks in the area.

Fishing, however, is allowed anywhere you can get close enough to the water to drop a hook.

The water and beaches around Shelter Island are terrific for swimming, also. You will find a long and inviting stretch of sand known as Crecent Beach, running from Jennings Point to Shelter Island Heights, on the northwest side of the island, which is also thronged with resort-type inns. ("A note of advice," one of our readers from the island writes us, "an old pair of sneakers might come in handy...because a lot of the beaches are not exactly 'sandy'.")

If you are looking to delve into the history of Shelter Island, you can visit the Manhanset Chapel Museum (516) 749-1116 or the Havens House (516) 749-0025 with its period rooms and pungent herb garden. Or you may decide on a peaceful stroll through the Quaker burial grounds, just up the road from Dering Harbor. Meetings are held outdoors on Sundays–as they were originally intended–in the summer. (The Sylvester Manor, however, is closed to the public: it is presently and happily occupied by a family.)

 Where To Eat

Landing at Dering Harbor puts you near a number of restaurants, among which is the Chequit Inn (516) 749-0018, serving good, home-cooked meals at reasonable prices. On Bridge Street is The Dory (516) 749-8871 with its hearty American menu. Nearby, with similar fare, is Coogan's Country Restaurant (516) 749-2129.

Out on Ram Island is the Ram's Head Inn (516) 749-0811 and its excellent restaurant of the same name; the inn also maintains a few moorings for the use of its patrons. Apart from this and Coecles Harbor Marina, there are no landings in Coecles Harbor, so cooking aboard is the only other option.

A good thing to keep in mind is that spring and summer are the restaurant seasons on the island; otherwise most places are shut tighter than mud-fresh clams until April.

 Navigation and Anchorages

Use NOAA Charts 12358 (1:40,000) and 12354 (1:80,000). Use tide tables for New London. High tide at Greenport is 1 hour and 5 minutes later; low tide is 49 minutes later. Multiply by 0.9 for height at high or low water. Mean tidal range is 2.8 feet.

CAUTION: *There have been many buoy changes in this area. We have noted the most important ones below, but be alert for others.*

Shelter Island is an island of many harbors. Three, to be exact.

At its entrance on the northwest side of the island, Dering Harbor is 10.1nm by boat southwest of Plum Gut, 6.9nm by boat north by northwest from Coecles Harbor, and 15.7nm by boat northwest of the Shinnecock Canal.

Coecles Harbor is 6.5nm by boat south-southwest of Plum Gut and 4.3nm by boat northwest of Three Mile Harbor.

The entrance to West Neck Harbor on the south side of the island is 7.5nm by boat roughly south-southwest from Dering Harbor, and 9nm by boat east-southeast, then north-northwest from Coecles Harbor.

Directly opposite Greenport, **Dering Harbor** usually has a handsome complement of yachts. The harbor is pictur-

Dering Harbor on Shelter Island from the northwest. The Shelter Island Yacht Club is on the peninsula in the foreground.

esque enough so that imagining it in a postcard setting is no trouble at all. Nor is there a problem making its entrance. If you're coming from the east, just be sure to keep a good margin between you and Long Beach Point, as the reported shoaling extends a bit further than the charts let on. Follow the waterway to the harbor–not cutting any of the markers–and you have it made. (Note that red nun "8" **[WP-388],** just east of Cleaves Point, has been relocated slightly to the north.)

The entrance to **Dering Harbor,** however, is partially blocked by a shoal extending beyond the west shore–so most boats enter in mid-channel. It's best to stay at least 100 yards off Dering Point to avoid the riprap there. Apart from being exposed to the north, Dering Harbor is well protected from the east.

Once in the harbor you should be able to pick up a mooring at the yacht club or one of the marinas; anchoring, however, is prohibited. Make reservations for a mooring or berth with the facility of your choice well in advance, because the harbor can get quite crowded, especially in the summer. Launch service is available from the yacht club for a fee, and is included in the price of a mooring rental.

Next to Piccozzi's Dering Harbor Marina is the town dock where you can tie up for 2 hours, enough time to restock your larder at the general store just off the dock. Jack's Marine, a complete chandlery, has a floating dinghy dock where you can also tie up the small boat.

A short walk from the yacht club is the ferry to **Greenport,** which runs every 20 minutes, putting you in touch with–among other things–a supermarket and more restaurants.

Southwest from Dering Harbor is **Coecles Harbor,** one of the most pleasant places on the island. If you are coming in from the west, as from Greenport or Dering Harbor, stay well to the north of the green 4sec flasher "7" off Cornelius Point. The shoals to the south of it collect a regular crop of sun-struck early risers who think they know where they are and wake up too late. Again, leave a good margin between you and Long Beach Point. Follow the curve of the northwest side of Shelter Island to starboard, keeping at least 400 yards from shore. You should have no trouble rounding Ram Head and then spotting the green 4sec flasher "1" **[WP-428]** directly south.

Flasher "1" marks the entrance channel, at which point you will turn west into the harbor. This dredged passage is narrow and has a tendency to shoal; the privately maintained navigational aids can be difficult to see when Gardiners Bay sets up a chop; they are also small and sometimes out of order. Upon entering, favor the starboard side of the channel, which carries a reported depth of 7 feet at low water.

Once inside the harbor, you'll see can "7" dead ahead, and the abandoned and dilapidated lighthouse on a point called Taylor Island by the local residents, but marked CUP (for "CUPOLA") on the chart; give the point and the surrounding rocks a wide berth. Can "7" is well-placed, marking the end of a rocky shoal off the point. The sandbar connecting it to the mainland is submerged at high tide, so stay clear of this at all times.

Inside **Coecles Harbor** are several choices for anchoring. **Shanty Cove,** immediately to starboard as you enter the harbor, offers excellent protection from winds from the north and east. The bight south of the channel, between Sungic Point and the CUPola, is a designated anchorage, marked off at four corners by small red balls.

CAUTION: A common mistake made by boaters who enter this harbor for the first time is that they travel past can "7," and then turn back towards this anchorage area, cutting between the CUPola and can "7." This is a good way to lose the bottom of your boat.

If you draw less than 6 feet you can go behind **Little Ram Island,** up in the northern bight. Keep nun "10" to starboard and give it a wide berth–at least 200 feet–since

there's only 4 feet of water immediately surrounding it. From nun "10" there are privately maintained markers to the marina and the anchorage area north of nun "12."

There is a small, town marina inside **Congdons Creek** in the southwest corner of the harbor, used mainly by residents with small boats. While the marked channel has a reported depth of about 5 feet, the water can be as low as 3 feet at dockside.

Coecles Harbor has generally good holding ground of grass and mud, and is a popular anchoring area. Weekends, you will certainly have company, but you shouldn't have any trouble finding room to swing at anchor. The northwest-southeast axis of the harbor means that it can get

THE LORD OF SHELTER ISLAND

There's a great old story they tell on Shelter Island:

In 1804 England and France were embroiled in one of their interminable wars, and this time Napoleon held the upper hand. The French held England in check with a blockade, and none could sail into or out of British ports. The call went out for captains willing to run the blockade. The risk was great – death or imprisonment by the French – but the rewards were substantial.

The word spread in Norfolk, Virginia, that a cargo of 1,000 barrels of flour had to be carried to Liverpool. The owners let it be known that any captain willing to run the French blockade would receive a guinea per barrel, a price to tempt even the most cautious.

Enter Captain Sam Lord. The wealthy, crusty head of the Lord family from Shelter Island, Captain Sam was in Norfolk with his swift schooner, *Paragon,* when the call went out. He didn't really need the money, but the prospect of a guinea a barrel was too much for his proud Yankee heart to refuse.

The captain came from a long line of seafaring folk. The Lords had been shipbuilders for generations in Connecticut. Searching for reliable supplies of timber, around 1800 they bought 500 acres on Shelter Island, built a shipyard on West Neck Creek, and lived in feudal fashion on the island. "They were Lords by name and Lords by nature," said the islanders of the prideful clan.

Captain Sam was the oldest of the three Lord brothers, all confirmed bachelors who lived with their two equally unencumbered sisters at the Lord Manor. Upon completion of a ship, one brother would sail her away with cargo, leaving the other two at home to run the shipyard. Of all the boats built by the Lords, none was more prized than the sleek, swift *Paragon.*

The very night the flour was loaded, *Paragon* sailed for Britain with Captain Sam and a doughty and devoted crew of ten. The fifteenth night out was black, a blockade runner's best friend. All lights aboard were extinguished, and not a word passed between the men.

Suddenly a French frigate loomed ahead in the darkness. Captain Sam steered the *Paragon* hard to starboard and swiftly past the French vessel. By dawn the Shelter Island men were in the Irish Sea headed for Liverpool. They had run the blockade!

Determined to make a proper entrance at Liverpool, Captain Sam allowed no slack discipline or raucous celebrating. *Paragon's* decks were spotless, her brass shone and her sails were full as she came to anchor in Liverpool.

Soon all England was abuzz, and Captain Sam was invited to a banquet with the Lord Mayor and all the brightest lights of Liverpool.

The next day the *Paragon* left for home, 1,000 guineas safely stored in Captain Sam's cabin. Running the blockade again was easy, but on the third day out a man 'o war was sighted in pursuit. The *Paragon* nearly showed her heels to the unidentified pursuer, but the winds died and the frigate began gaining on her. Sam Lord, having no wish to lose his thousand guineas to a scurvy pirate, went below and stashed the cache in the bilges, where only he could find it.

When the chase was over, the mysterious ship proved to be British. Her commander demanded to know whom she had caught. "The *Paragon* from New York, three days out of Liverpool!" cried Captain Sam.

"You lie, sir!" came the sharp reply.

Sam Lord flushed with anger and roared back, "Sir, I invite you to come aboard my ship and examine my sailing papers, and TAKE BACK THAT WORD."

The British captain was astonished when handed a Liverpool newspaper from the day *Paragon* sailed. Never had he known a ship to come so far so fast.

Apologies were immediately given, the British man 'o war went on her way, and the *Paragon* made her way home to Shelter Island, arriving 21 days out from Liverpool. Sam Lord and his crew were given another hero's welcome, "not so grand but twice as welcome to his patriotic sailor heart, as the Liverpool one."

choppy when the wind blows along the same direction, especially in an opposing tide. In such a case, head into one of the bights for a smoother night. (On warm summer nights, however, keep the bug-spray handy.)

Keeping the water clean is important to Shelter Islanders–as it should be to all of us–and the town's Chief of Police is quite strict with polluters. "When we catch someone littering or discharging into the water," he told us with a smile, "we'll go out of our way to ruin his day."

While **Coecles Harbor** is popular with windsurfers, the preferred activity here seems to be beachcombing, especially on the sandy stretch around Sungic Point. You may see a few people clamming inside the point, but the privilege is extended to New York residents only. Swimming in the harbor can be good, but watch out for jellyfish that sometimes drift in.

West Neck Harbor is another protected and peaceful spot to drop anchor. If you are coming from Dering Harbor, the traffic and currents can be quite heavy, so be alert, as always. Please refer to the Greenport and Southold chapter chart for a detail of the following passage. The jaunt between Shelter Island Heights and Jennings Point is thoroughly pleasant, as Greenport is left to starboard and the woods, beaches and inns rise to port. After you've picked up the green 4sec flasher "11" **[WP-394]** off Jennings Point, leave it to port and make for the red 4sec flasher "12" **[WP-396]** between Paradise Point and West Neck, which you should leave to starboard. Do not cut between Paradise Point and the number "12" **[WP-396]**, or you'll be one of the 7 or 8 boaters that have to be pulled off the **Paradise Point** shoal every year.

You can now head directly for the red 4sec flasher "16" **[WP-418]** which you should leave to port, since you are leaving–however briefly–Long Island. Do not think "red-right-returning" here, or else you may end up stirring up some bottom if the tide is low enough. (Note that can "15" off Black Dog Rock has been relocated slightly west, and flasher "16" slightly south.) The harbor entrance is an easy shot from here.

West Neck Harbor has plenty of good depth inside, but there is a bar at the entrance, narrowing an otherwise wide opening considerably. The entrance is very close to the seaward end of the gravel point, locally called Shell Beach. There is an uncharted buoy just off the point. (Note that the green flashing 9-foot tower was no longer in service since the fall of '89.)

The harbor may look as though you will never get into it if you draw more than 2 feet, but yachtsmen with 5-foot-or-deeper drafts regularly pass over the bar. To do this, they come in on a rising tide and come in very carefully–as you should, too. On entering, hug the port side, as there isn't much water near the red buoy. (If you can spit on the land you're about close enough. When we put our bow on the beach, our transom was in 14 feet of water–and that was at low tide!) About 300 yards inside the point, to starboard, is a privately maintained and very well-marked channel to the marinas there.

☎ Shoreside and Emergency Services

Ambulance: 911
Coast Guard: Montauk (516) 668-2773 or VHF 16
New London (203) 442-4471 or VHF 16
Ferry: To Sag Harbor from South Ferry (516) 749-1200
To Greenport from Dering Harbor (516) 749-0139
Fire: 911
Hospital: Eastern Long Island Hospital (516) 477-1000
Shelter Island Medical Center (516) 749-2232
or (516) 749-3149
Police: 911 or (516) 749-0600
Marine Unit VHF 16
Radio Telephone: VHF 85; I.D.: Bay Shore
Marine Operator
VHF 28; I.D.: Riverhead
Marine Operator
Taxi: Fleetwood (516) 477-0078
Tow Service: Sea Tow Eastern LI, Southold, NY
(516) 765-3660 or VHF 16; Saybrook
Towing and Salvage, Old Saybrook, CT
(203) 388-4065 or VHF 16
Train: Long Island Railroad (516) 234-LIRR   ◆

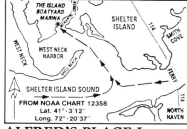

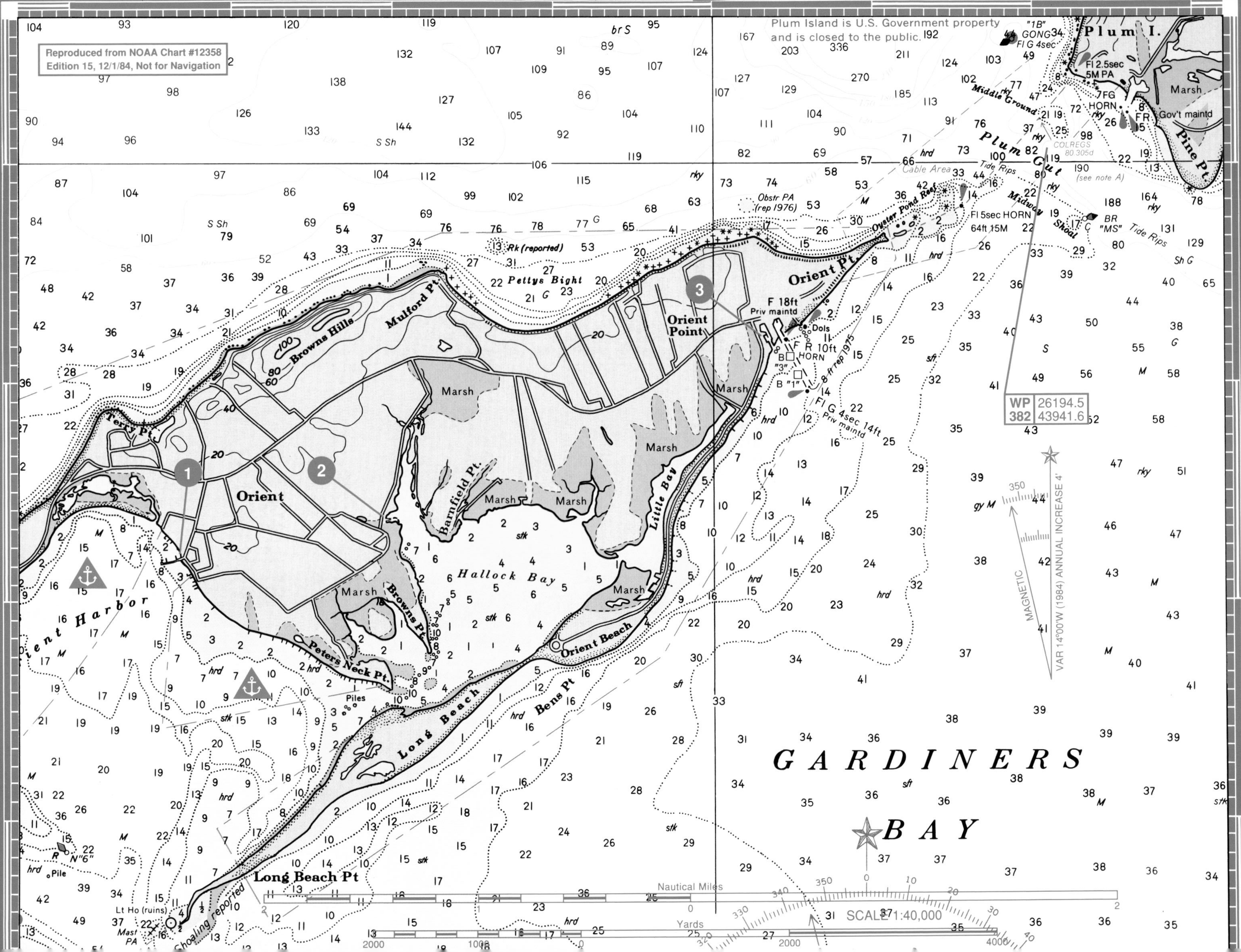

41°10'

72°15'

41°10'

Pine Pt

Plum I.

Marsh

Plum Gut

Plum Island is U.S. Government property and is closed to the public. 192

Middle Ground

Midway

Orient Pt

Orient Point

Orient

Browns Hills

Mulford Pt

Terry Pt

Orient Harbor

Marsh

Pettys Bight

Barnfield Pt.

Hallock Bay

Browns Pt.

Peters Neck Pt.

Marsh

Little Bay

Orient Beach

Bens Pt

Long Beach

Long Beach Pt

Lt Ho (ruins)

G A R D I N E R S

B A Y

VAR 14°00'W (1984) ANNUAL INCREASE 4'

MAGNETIC

WP 26194.5
382 43941.6

SCALE 1:40,000

Nautical Miles

Yards

Plum Gut and Orient Point

No Quiche in Plum Gut

It's said that when you go east as far as you can, you end up in the Orient. While this book doesn't go even as far east as the Mediterranean, we do go to the easternmost point on the north shore of Long Island, or Orient Point.

The town of Orient is a picturesque fishing village of modest, weathered houses surrounded by sincere pumpkin patches, corn fields, and marsh. Set back several miles from the tip of the point, the secluded town was a favorite hideaway for honeymooners early in the century. A large tract of land in Orient Point was acquired in 1988 by Suffolk County as part of an effort to preserve scenic and environmentally fragile areas and is open to the public (a similar project has been undertaken at Montauk Point); there is a footpath to the point itself.

Rising out of the point is another testament to the town's preservation efforts: the cast iron Orient Point Light–also called the "Coffee Pot" by sea-weary navigators–was beginning to rust through in the 1970s. When the Coast Guard decided to demolish it, concerned citizens successfully rallied to save the historic light. Now rehabilitated, it operates automatically.

Tapering toward The Race, Plum Island was purchased when real estate prices were much more reasonable: it was bought from the Indians for a coat, a container of biscuits, and 100 fish hooks. Because of its strategic location, the Government eventually obtained it and built Fort Terry during the Spanish-American War.

Still in the Government's possession, Plum Island is now used by the Department of Agriculture for its Animal Disease Laboratory, where research is conducted on contagious animal diseases such as swine fever and hoof-and-mouth. The public is not allowed on the island.

The neighboring Great Gull Island is a healthy sanctuary for a large population of common and roseate terns, an endangered species. The island is co-owned by the American Museum of Natural History and the Linnean Society. The birds need peace and space to propagate, so landing is prohibited there, too.

Back in the 1920s, in the dry days of Prohibition, the landing (and imbibing) of alcohol was, of course, forbidden everywhere. But that didn't stop the regular shipments of rum from the West Indies. Ships laden with the potent cargo would hang offshore and unload to fishing boats, which would take the sweet, cure-all elixir to Orient where it was transferred onto the Long Island Railroad and sent westward to New York City, packed with the day's catch.

★ What To See and Do

The American Heritage Dictionary lists several definitions for "orient," one of which is "having exceptional luster." The town of Orient is an unassuming pearl of a town, full of charming, antique houses.

The ferry *MV Cape Henlopen* from New London arriving at Orient Point, NY. From bottom to top: Orient-by-the-Sea Marina; the U.S. Government depot for the ferries from Plum Island; and the New London ferry depot.

Marine Facilities and Services		Number of Transient Berths	Number of Transient Moorings	Seasonal/Year-round	Largest Vessel Accommodation (in feet)	Approach Depth in feet at MLW	Marked Entry Channel	Dockside Depth in feet at MLW	Gas/Diesel Fuel	Ramp/Dinghy Dock/Launch Service	Fuel Brand	Railway/Lift: Capacity (in tons)	Engine Repairs: Gas/Diesel	Propeller/Hull Repairs	Pump-out Station	Marine Supplies/Groceries/Bait/Ice	Showers/Laundromat	110V ★ 220V ▲ Maximum Amps	MasterCard/VISA/Diners Club	American Express	Restaurant/Snack Bar	Monitors VHF Channel
❶ Orient Point Yacht Club	(516) 323-9767								*PRIVATE CLUB - MEMBERS ONLY*													
❷ Narrow River Marina	(516) 323-2660	10		Y	28		●	3	3				R	L5	PH	GD		SL	★30			16
❸ Orient by the Sea	(516) 323-2424	12		S	50	6		10	GD	AGW		R	L50	PH	GD	S	I	★30	MV	R	16

Information in these listings is provided by the facilities themselves. An asterisk (*) indicates that the facility did not respond to our most recent requests for information.

The town is somewhat off the beaten path, so there is a minimum of boutiques, restaurants, and the like. There is, however, the Oysterponds Historical Museum (516) 323-2480, a seven-house complex that includes exhibits of marine paintings and scrimshaw, among other things. The museum is a hike enough away to warrant a cab or bike ride. On the same street is the quaint Country Store.

While there isn't a bicycle rental shop in Orient, you're

THE TERNS OF GREAT GULL

From a distance, the white boxes rising off of Great Gull Island look like so many mushrooms. Anyone venturing too close to get a better look at those boxes–actually blinds–will be warned away by signs erected by the American Museum of Natural History. Great Gull Island is, after all, a research station, not a stopover for tourists.

Despite the forbidding message, the island can be a welcome place, especially for the scores of volunteers who each year work to preserve one of the largest colonies of common terns in North America. Under the direction of Project Director Helen Hays, the volunteers collect information about the nesting and mating habits of the tern.

From 50 terns more than 30 years ago, the colony has grown to more than 12,000 thanks to the efforts of Hays, her volunteer staff, and the island's two owners: the American Museum and the Linnaean Society, a non-profit group dedicated to the study of the birds.

Ms. Hays knows the history of nearly every tern living on Great Gull Island, or so it seems. Ask her a question about where one of the sleek birds nested two years ago and she could probably tell you. If not, she could check one of the thousands of data cards she keeps.

The terns, gray and white with a distinctive black cap, have not always enjoyed such sanctuary. In the early part of the 20th century, the birds fell prey to the fashion industry. Millions of terns, gulls and herons were killed for hats, and the millinery industry's demand for feathers seemed insatiable.

Then during World War II, the terns of Great Gull Island received another blow. The U.S. Government moved more than 500 soldiers to the island, filled a freshwater swamp, and built huge gun emplacements. By 1949, there were no terns left on the island, and the U.S. Government sold Great Gull for $1 to the present owners.

Since 1969 the birds have made a spectacular comeback. Their population has grown steadily in the last 20 years, and the importance of the island as a nesting sanctuary intensifies.

Says Ms. Hays, who, like the terns, returns to the island each spring: "You either make a place safe for the birds or you lose them. In a city there is not much you can do. There, people are a priority. Here, is a tern colony."

Contributed by Linda M. Rancourt, a freelance writer from Groton, CT.

in luck if you've brought your own bike along. Once away from town the roads meander through farmland, along marshes, and past a vineyard or two. Since there is hardly ever a glut of cars in the area, the biking is as peaceful as the view is relaxing.

Another restful panorama is the one seen from Orient Beach State Park. The 342-acre park is a long sand spit on the south side of Orient Point, and has deep water off the beach, so it is easy for visiting boaters to pull up for a swim. You may have to slowly pick your way between fish stakes as you approach the beach, however. Deer frequent Long Beach Point, but they're hard to spot from the water.

If the pastoral scenes start short-circuiting your senses, the Cross Sound Ferry (516) 443-7394 can take you from Orient Point to New London, CT, and a chance to tour a nuclear sub. (See the chapter on the Thames River to Norwich for details on what to see and do in New London.)

 Where To Eat

The restaurant in town is right at the Cross Sound Ferry dock, at the Orient-by-the-Sea Marina (516) 323-2424. They serve a wide variety of seafood specials which culminate in their Friday night lobsterfest: two 1-pound lobsters for the price of one.

If a sandwich is more to your palate there is a small deli in Orient Village.

For a wider range of options your best bet would be to hail a cab down to Greenport, which has all the amenities and attractions for the touring boater. (See the next chapter for restaurant suggestions in Greenport.)

 Navigation and Anchorages

Use NOAA Charts 12358 (1:40,000), 13209 (1:40,000), and 12354 (1:80,000). Use tide tables for New London. High tide at Plum Gut is 28 minutes later; low tide is 16 minutes later. Mean tidal range is 3.0 feet.

High tide at Orient Harbor is 37 minutes later than New London; low tide is 36 minutes later. Mean tidal range is 2.8 feet.

Having crossed the Sound, chances are you'll choose to go through Plum Gut to get to Orient Point. Plum Gut is 9.9nm by boat southwest of New London and 10.4nm by boat northeast of Dering Harbor on Shelter Island. Three Mile Island is 7.8nm by boat to the south.

From the red flashing 4sec bell "8" **[WP-168]** marking the Saybrook bar, a course of about 150°m will take you between the lighted daymarks on Plum Island and Orient Point.

CAUTION: *All boats should use extreme care when entering Plum Gut, being particularly careful of the tide rips that can be worse than The Race, though more short-lived. Be sure you know the tide and wind conditions before entering,* *and pick a clear, calm day if you're going through here for the first time.*

If you're sailing in from **Long Island Sound,** it is absolutely necessary to check the tide tables in order to time your passage through for slack water or for ebb tide, so that you don't end up sailing backward. Pay close attention to the wind and current: pick a time when they're not fighting each other, because in the Gut it can turn into a brawl.

When approaching from **Gardiners Bay,** take the passage at slack or flood tide. Give yourself as much distance as possible from the lee shore–at least 0.2nm.

The channel through **Plum Gut** is 0.6nm wide and plenty deep; there is one spot where the bottom plunges from about 35 feet to nearly 200, and it can look spectacular as well as scary on the depth sounder.

The average velocities of flood and ebb tide in the Gut are 3.5 and 4.3 knots respectively, but can go much higher. The flood sets northwestward and the ebb, southeastward. During floodtime a countercurrent develops along the north shore of **Plum Island,** and it gets quite nasty within half a mile of shore.

Watch the wind also, because it can do hair-raising things; be careful you don't lose your steerage as you lose headway in the chop. Keep an eye out for what the water does, too: it is not uncommon to encounter an 8-foot standing wave poised in front of you like a fist.

Orient Point is marked by a 64-foot 5sec flashing white light and fog signal, but the fog horn can be difficult to hear in a rumbling easterly wind. Don't cut inside this light because Oyster Pond Reef is well strewn with boulders, and only about 2 feet deep at low water. As if the wind and currents weren't enough of a hazard, you'll have to watch out for fishermen in this area, especially around Middle Ground off Plum Island, and Midway Shoal, just south of Plum Gut. Also be on the lookout for commercial trawlers, which will usually identify themselves with a metal basket hanging from the mast: keep in mind that they may be trailing nets as much as 50 yards astern, and that they have right-of-way over you, even if you're sailing.

Stay clear of the ferryboats. They travel the channel so regularly that they have little patience with small craft. Their sheer size makes for a great lack of maneuverability, so it's up to you to steer around them and through their wake. (If you happen to be passing through the Gut in a high sea, and are in a power boat, follow the ferry through close to its stern, as its wake flattens the water considerably.)

Be careful of sailing parallel to the shores anywhere in this area. You should stand out a good distance and know which way the tides are running so that you aren't sucked into the rocks and shoals off Orient Point.

As you round Orient Point and come into **Gardiners Bay,** you'll see the ferry slips just southwest of the point. The marinas in the area are good, but often crowded because of their proximity to the traffic at Plum Gut and the

lack of other facilities nearby. You can anchor anywhere along the sandy spit of Orient and Long Beach for a swim, but note that the depths decrease suddenly, not gradually, as you approach the shore.

Heading southwest directly toward **Shelter Island,** stay at least 500 yards offshore to keep from running over the many fish weirs close to the beaches.

Also, keep clear of **Long Beach Point,** as a shoal extends south from it and has built up enough to be a danger even to small boats. The best course is to steer between the red flashing 4sec bell "2" and green can "3" south of Long Beach Point.

From red bell "2," head directly for the green 4sec flasher "7" off Cornelius Point on Shelter Island. This is also the gateway to Greenport, Southold, and Dering Harbor. If you're heading for anchorage north of **Long Beach Point,** follow the same course and make sure you clear the point by at least 800 yards. The currents are also strong here, so be sure you aren't drawn up to the shoal. Once around the point and heading northeast, there's a pleasant anchorage dead ahead. Keep clear of the fish stakes, some of which may be broken off below water. You should also know, however, that this is a fair-weather anchorage and is entirely exposed to the southwest. Across the bay is **Orient Harbor** proper, well-protected to the north, but wide-open to the south.

To the east, between Long Beach and Peters Neck Point, is the entrance to **Hallock Bay.** The bay is shallow and the entrance is tight, blocked with pilings and shoals, so it should be attempted only in a dinghy or a boat with very shallow draft. It is, however, quite peaceful and has good holding ground. There is a channel marked by pilings that hugs the western shore, along Browns Point.

Transient slip space is available at Narrow River Marina, inside the bay. It's a moderate walk to town from there.

 Shoreside and Emergency Services

Ambulance: 911
Coast Guard: Montauk (516) 668-2773 or VHF 16
New London (203) 442-4471 or VHF 16
Fire: 911 or (516) 765-2600
Harbormaster: (516) 765-2600
Hospital: Eastern Long Island (516) 477-1000
Police: 911 or (516) 765-2600 or VHF 16
Radio Telephone: VHF 85; I.D.: Bay Shore
Marine Operator
VHF 28; I.D.: Riverhead
Marine Operator
VHF 25, 26, 84; I.D.: New York
Marine Operator
Taxi: Fleetwood (516) 477-0078
Tow Service: Sea Tow Eastern LI, Southold, NY
(516) 765-3660 or VHF 16; Saybrook
Towing and Salvage, Old Saybrook, CT
(203) 388-4065 or VHF 16   ◆

Sub Busters and Shipbuilders

Greenport is a town of boats. Its history is awash with ships and wind-driven stories of what feats they accomplished, some of which are legendary. One such ship was the *Flying Cloud*, the Yankee clipper that made the 1854 record journey from New York to San Francisco in only 89 days. Crewed mostly by Greenport men, it has taken 135 years to break her record–which was done in 1989, when *Thursday's Child* completed the trip in 81 days.

Greenport's nautical glory came when it was the home port of the *Enterprise*, the successful America's Cup de-

The waterfront at Greenport, N.Y.

Marine Facilities and Services	Phone	Number of Transient Berths	Number of Transient Moorings	Seasonal/Year-round	Largest Vessel Accommodation (ft)	Marked Entry Channel	Approach Depth (ft)	Dockside Depth (ft at MLW)	Gas/Diesel Fuel	Fuel Brand	Ramp/Dinghy Dock	Railway/Lift: Capacity (tons)	Propeller/Hull Repairs	Engine Repairs: Gas/Diesel	Pump-out Station	Showers/Laundromat	Marine Supplies/Groceries/Bait/Ice	110V ★ 220V ▲ Maximum Amps	MasterCard/VISA/Diners Club, American Express	Restaurant/Snack Bar	Monitors VHF Channel
1 Southold Marine Center	(516) 765-3131	5		Y	25	●	3	3				L35	PH	G		S		★30	MVA		
2 Goldsmiths Boat Shop	(516) 765-1600			Y	30	●	2.5	5	G			L10	PH	G		S			MVA		16
3 Albertson Marina	(516) 765-3232			Y	40	●	5	5				L25	PH	GD	●	S		★30	MVA		16
4 Port of Egypt Marine	(516) 765-2445	12		Y	36	●	4.5	4.5	GD	GLF	R	L8	PH	G		S	SI	★	MV	R	
5 Mill Creek Inn	(516) 765-1010	30		Y	54	●	5	7								S	I	★▲60	MVAD	R	
6 Young's Boatyard & Marina	(516) 477-0830	10		Y	45	●	6	6	G	GLF	R	L30	PH	GD		S	S	★30			
7 William. J. Mills, Inc.	(516) 477-1500			Y	*SAILMAKERS & BOAT COVERS*														MVA		
8 A.P. White Bait Shop	(516) 477-0008				30		6	4									SI				67
9 **Claudio's Restaurant & Marina (p. 321)**	**(203) 477-0355**			S	200		25	8	GD	TEX						SL	I	★▲30	MVA	SR	16
10 **S.T. Preston & Son (p. 318)**	**(516) 477-1990**	20		Y	40		10	6	*CHANDLERY*							S			MVA		
11 Greenport Yacht & Shipbuilding	(516) 477-2277	20		Y	120	●	14	12	GD			L50	PH	GD	●	SL		▲30	M		16
12 Harbor Haven/Stirling Harbor	(516) 725-4333	8		S	30	●	12	12								S		★30	A		
13 Hanff's Boat Yard	(516) 477-1550			Y	*RENOVATION & RESTORATION*																
14 **Townsend Manor Marina (p. 320)**	**(516) 477-2000**	50		Y	50	●	8	8	G	AGW						S	I	★30	MV	SR	
15 Triangle Yacht Club*																					
16 **Stirling Harbor Shipyard & Marina (p.317)**	**(516) 477-0828**	30		Y	100	●	20	15	GD	GLF		L50	PH	GD		SL	I	★▲50	MVA	R	
17 Brewer Yacht Yard	(516) 477-9594	5		Y	50	●	7	7			D	L70	PH	GD		S	S	★30	MV		16
18 Shelter Island Yacht Club	(516) 749-0888		10	S	75	●	8	6	*PRIVATE CLUB - MEMBERS ONLY*								I	★30	MVA		
19 Jack's Marine	(516) 749-0114	3	10	S	60	●	10	10	*CHANDLERY / FISHING STATION*							L	SIG			R	68
20 Town Dock/Dering Harbor					*2 HR TIE-UP LOADING & UNLOADING*																
21 Picozzi's Dering Harbor Marina	(516) 749-0045	30	13	Y	250	●	12	12	GD	MOB						SL	SIG	★▲50	MVA	SR	16
22 **The Island Boatyard & Marina (p. 309)**	**(516) 749-3333**	35		S	50	●	6	6	GD						●	SL	SI	★	MV	S	16
23 Menantic Yacht Club					*PRIVATE CLUB - MEMBERS ONLY*																

Information in these listings is provided by the facilities themselves. An asterisk (*) indicates that the facility did not respond to our most recent requests for information.

fender in 1930, commanded by Commodore Harold S. Vanderbilt and crewed with Greenport men. "Almost every merchant in town," wrote one Greenporter, "had a hand in fitting out *Enterprise*." She is truly a Greenport ship.

In the years following the *Flying Cloud's* success–especially during the years of Prohibition–that clipper's swiftness was echoed by the rumrunners who shipped in their contraband from the Caribbean. Their stealth, however, was countered by the Coast Guard, who set up a station in town. The jails soon filled up with offenders as a brig might with water in a storm. The local shipyards did well, apparently, busily repairing the busted boats of both.

The Coast Guard's presence in Greenport has always been impressive, so much so that Greenport is the only town on Long Island that can lay claim to having had its own navy during the second World War.

"The Hooligan Navy," as it was known locally, was a hodgepodge of dandy boats–schooners, ketches, motorsailers, and other such yachts–lent by their owners in the Greenport area to the U.S. Coast Guard. With their brightwork and peacetime colors painted over with navy gray, the flotilla was outfitted with submarine-detection devices and commissioned

© Steve Dunwell

to patrol the offshore shipping lanes, looking for German U-Boats. Wind-powered and made of wood, this fleet–officially called "The Corsair Fleet"–was virtually undetectable by the enemy.

The war effort was, of course, also vigorous ashore. At one point the Greenport Shipyard alone employed as many as 2,000 men–an incredible total considering the size of the town–to build minesweepers, sea sleds, and landing barges. In Southold the John Hollins Shipyard, which turned out some of the first practical submarines, eventually became the Electric Boat Company, and now builds Trident-class nuclear-powered submarines in Groton, CT.

The war would leave Greenport a quieter town. The shipbuilding factories shut down, and the boats from the makeshift navy were returned to their rightful owners. The harbor, however, invited another industry: leisure.

A small creek used to run roughly southwest out of town, toward Young's Point. It was dredged out in the 1960s and you will know it today as Stirling Basin, home of several marinas and boatyards. Among the small fleet of

commercial fishing vessels based in Greenport–fishing has always figured big in this town–you'll find party fishing boats ready for chartering. It's only a short run to the fertile grounds off Block Island and Montauk for tuna, flounder, bluefish, mackerel, and the occasional swordfish.

Greenport is the major marine center on the north fork of Long Island, and continues to be a popular destination with the boating set. In the summers, the harbor is often crowded with gorgeous boats, many of them from places across the Sound and even further. Unconscripted, they can still be seen as a navy of sorts, a fleet of boats that, like the *Flying Cloud* and the *Enterprise*, are piloted by those for whom setting records or winning a race is perhaps only a fraction of the enchantment of being out there, on the wide water.

 What To See and Do

Greenport is very much the seaside town, even if the sea is not quite at its side. There is, however, the unmistakable

You could end up spending your entire cruise here.
(It happens all the time!)

Some people just decided to stop in at the last minute. Still others had read the Offshore Magazine review which gave Stirling Harbor its highest rating. It called us "...one of those special places that is kept nestled in your memory. It is worth a visit." Either way, they ended up staying a lot longer than planned.

The reasons were many. A park-like setting with scores of trees and fieldstone fireplaces. A three-star restaurant and pool in a country club setting. Full security and privacy. Plus every important feature any cruising boater could ever need including complimentary electricity, water and ice, plus full-service shipyard facilities and more.

All situated in a spot often called the "crossroads of boating." A place where fishing villages meet farm fields and vineyards. Just one visit will convince you that Stirling Harbor is not just a place to stop, but a destination.

Photos: H.L. Redfield

For more information for the coming season, please write or call:

STIRLING HARBOR MARINA

**1440 Manhanset Avenue
Greenport, New York 11944
(516) 477-0828**

look of the influence the water has upon the place. Look around the town and you'll see all the trappings of a nautical past and present.

There are many fine, old houses in town, captains' houses, some of them used to be; today they hold art and crafts galleries, nautical and antique shops, restaurants and apartments. Small churches gleam in the back streets of this small town, among modest residences and big trees.

In Greenport all the streets seem to let out at the water. Main Street is no exception; it ends at the heart of town, which is also the main waterfront area, right where S.T. Preston & Son is. You will find all the conveniences you might need within a 5-minute walking distance from the dock where, if you choose, you can also watch the commercial fishermen unload their catch, some of which will go to the local restaurants.

It is difficult not to think of food in Greenport, as there seems to be a restaurant on every street. To compound the matter, the town is right in Long Island's wine country. There are 26 wineries and vineyards within a short cab ride west of town. Pindar Vineyards (516) 734-6200 is a perennial favorite, although 15 minutes away by car. For more information on the other wineries you can call the Long Island Grape Growers Association at (516) 727-6464.

Southold, just down Rte. 25 to the west, is more spread out and suburban than Greenport, but has an adequate selection of restaurants and stores. Although the town doesn't have quite the concentrated nautical flavor of the *Enterprise's* home port, there is a distinct maritime edge. Sight-seeing cruises leave from the town waterfront (516) 477-9629, and the *Star Star* (516) 777-9508 provides open-boat fishing trips to The Race and Block Island Sound.

If you'd rather stay on land, the New York State Archaeological Association runs the Indian Museum (516) 765-5577, offering "A Flashback to Indian Days," as the brochure claims. Aside from an impressive collection of artifacts, some of which date back 10,000 years, the exhibits also show how the Algonquins "hunted, fished, farmed...[and] gambled."

The Southold Historical Society (516) 765-5500 maintains the Horton Point Lighthouse and museum on the Sound side, two miles from the docks at Mill Creek. The light is quite picturesque and nicely adorned by the ever-present beach anglers, complementing the scene like earrings on a woman. What heightens the experience–especially at sunset–is walking among the giant boulders that were strewn over the beach by a glacier before we were born.

Walking the beachscape may set you wishing for another and less rocky beach to contemplate. Cedar Beach Point, on the southeast tip of Great Hog Neck, is a county preserve and just what you might be looking for. The beach is crowded in the summer–as are all beaches unless you have your own–but titillating because of the thousands of

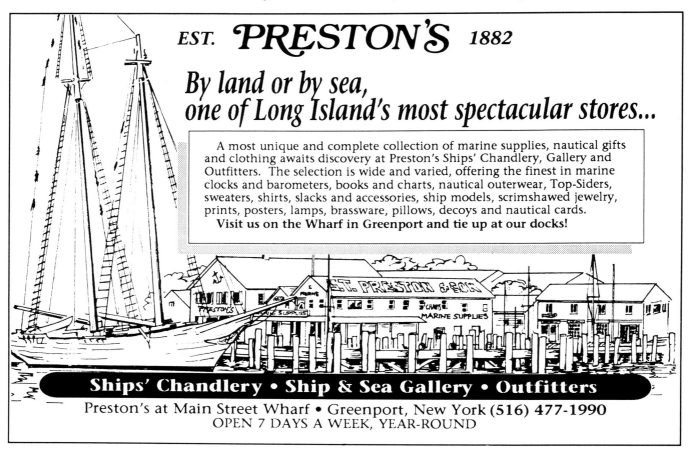

shells that wash ashore: They come in practically every color of the spectrum. There are also a lot of gulls here, no doubt interested in the pretty mollusks. Wear a hat. Please.

 ## Where To Eat

Greenport is not only a boater's haven, but also a restaurant-goer's. The establishments here serve straight-forward, no-nonsense, hearty meals in cozy, familiar settings—familiar in the way that friendliness and good home-cooking is.

A true Greenport institution—it has been in business since 1870—is Claudio's (516) 477-9800, a sizeable family-style eatery with nautical memorabilia from such ships as the *Enterprise* hanging on the walls. Seafood is the main fare here, with lobster, in all its various renditions, as the specialty. Claudio's is right on the water, by the docks, and offers free dockage to patrons.

A block over on Front Street is Gene's Dockside Inn (516) 477-9824, which is as close to a French bistro as you'll get on the north fork. It may not have a patio with "Cinzano" umbrellas, but the helpings here are so B.I.G. (Big, Inexpensive, and Good) that you might consider sharing, unless you're absolutely starved, as we were. There are no ancient mariner trappings on the walls; instead, they are plain. There is, however, a polished bar that goes on for a mile or two, as do the portions there.

Set back from Main Street in a brick courtyard called Stirling Square is the Cinnamon Tree (516) 477-0012, a relatively "upscale," shiny-everything restaurant. It serves a Continental menu punctuated by local seafood specialties. Sunday brunch is particularly hearty.

In Southhold, around the marinas at Hashamomuck Pond, you'll find the much touted La Gazalle (516) 765-2656, the *restaurant français*. Other Southold eateries include the Original Barge (516) 765-2691, for seafood with a view, and the Mill Creek Inn (516) 765-1010, where you can tie up to dine on steak and seafood.

 ## Navigation and Anchorages

Use NOAA Charts 12358 (1:40,000) and 12354 (1:80,000). Use tide tables for New London. High tide at Greenport is 1 hour 5 minutes later; low tide is 49 minutes later. Multiply by 0.9 for height at high or low water. Mean tidal range is 2.9 feet.

The entrance to Greenport, opposite Dering Harbor on Shelter Island, is 7.8nm by boat southwest of Plum Gut, and 3.2nm by boat northeast of Mill Creek in Southold.

The 19-foot red 4sec flasher "8A" **[WP-389]** on the breakwater off **Youngs Point** marks the entrance to **Stirling Basin** from the east, and there is good water up to the many docks south of Stirling Basin. The port is not really an anchorage since it is too busy and too open, but it is a good place to tie up to see the old fishing town.

Preston's Chandlery has free dockage during the day, but you should know there is heavy channel wash. Some people, however, find docking more comfortable next door at Claudio's—at the cost of a meal.

If you're heading toward one of the marinas west of **Stirling Basin** at night, note that the charted, privately maintained range lights at the Mobil dock have been removed.

"CAPTAIN, THERE BE WHALES... AND TURTLES!"

From the end of fall to January the north shores of Long Island become stranding grounds for huge turtles. Unfortunately, most of the stranded animals are found dead or dying; the ones that do live will almost certainly survive because of the vigilance of the Okeanos Ocean Research Foundation.

"O-kay-ah-nos," from the ancient Greek meaning "father of all life in the sea," is dedicated to the preservation and study of marine mammals and sea turtles, with an emphasis on Long Island. Since 1979 the foundation has rescued and released nearly 500 beached animals, most of them turtles—many of which were survivors of a mass stranding in 1985.

The Center also conducts invaluable scientific analyses on those animals which do not survive. Tissues are sent to other research organizations around the world for study, and the skeletons are often given to museums and educational institutions.

The centerpiece of this program is a Marine Center presently in the planning stage; groundbreaking is scheduled for1990. Rising on an 11-acre site leased from Suffolk County, it will sport a museum devoted to whaling artifacts. Along with classrooms and a laboratory, the building will house a stranding facility with a number of rehabilitation tanks for marine mammals and sea turtles.

Since the cost of such research, rehabilitation and expansion is immense, Okeanos funds its projects mainly through tourist and educational programs. Guided Harbor seal walks are given during the winter by volunteer staffers. The more popular and warmer trips are the whale-watch cruises offered every summer. Groups are taken out to the deep sea off Montauk on the *Finback II*, a 90-foot research and sightseeing vessel.

As many as 200 volunteers keep a lookout for stranded animals on Long Island's shores, but much of the program's effectiveness is in the hands (and eyes) of you, the beachgoer. Okeanos can be notified through their 24-hour hotline at (516) 728-8013, collect.

If you want to know more about Okeanos and their Whale Watch, write to the Okeanos Ocean Research Foundation, Inc. at 216 East Montauk Highway, P.O. Box 776, Hampton Bays, NY 11946. Or call (516) 728-4522.

The best place for an overnight stay in Greenport itself, if you can find room, is inside **Stirling Basin** on the northeast side, with a depth in the channel of 8 feet. The harbormaster (516) 477-2385 controls mooring and anchoring; reservations are a must for weekends. You'll find a pair of privately maintained buoys at the Stirling Basin entrance; green can "1" and red nun "2." Can "1" marks foul ground; once beyond it, turn to port and stay close to the west shore. Farther up in town are piers, marinas, and anything else you need. There is a town ramp on the east side of **Youngs Point,** usable by anyone.

Stirling Basin offers more protection than **Dering Harbor** but isn't as quiet, and larger boats may have difficulty navigating in the confined area. Most cruising yachtsmen anchor in Dering Harbor on Shelter Island and take the ferry across to Greenport to shop or visit a restaurant. The three ferries operate continuously, so if you are staying at one of the marinas in Greenport, try to get a slip away from the channel wash and noise.

West about two miles from Greenport, between Conkling and Jennings points, is the entrance to **Southold Bay. Mill Creek,** opposite Jennings Point, is a pleasant little anchorage with a marina and a small restaurant. Keep well off

A PENNY FOR A THOUSAND DOLLARS

Like many another Long Island boy of the late 18th century, Joshua Penny went to sea and in Liverpool signed up on a slave ship. In Jamaica a press gang from a British frigate captured him, forcing him into service in the Royal Navy. But in Cape Town, South Africa, he managed to escape and lived a year among the Hottentots. He was finally caught, brought back to the fleet, and flogged. On the fourth of June the sailors were allowed to get drunk to celebrate the King's birthday, so when the fourth of July arrived, Penny asked for the same privilege. "I want the liberty," he had the courage to say, "to rejoice on my nation's birthday." Amused, the captain ordered that two gallons of wine and one of brandy be given to the 30 members of the Yankee mess in the forecastle. They all sang "Hail Columbia, Happy Land."

Once more Penny escaped and after an absence of 15 years returned to Orient Point. During the war of 1812 he was the lighthouse keeper at Cedar Island in Northwest Harbor. Eager to get even with the British, he sailed about in a fast sloop trying to blow up Commodore Hardy's flagship with a floating mine, a la David Bushnell. Hardy demanded that a sharp lookout be kept for "these damned Yankee barnacles," and offered a reward of $1,000 for Penny's capture. Eventually Penny was caught. "Someone in Sag Harbor," he later wrote, "sold a Penny for a thousand dollars." Penny languished for nine months in a chilly Halifax dungeon but was finally exchanged and sent home to write his memoirs.

Jennings Point, which is surrounded by rocks extended out 150 yards. The channel narrows at this point to as little as 700 yards, and the traffic can be very heavy, as can the currents. Keep your eye on the chart and your wits about you. The Town of Southold, which includes Greenport and Orient Point, enforces a 5-mph speed limit within 500 yards of the shore.

The channel into **Mill Creek** is 4 feet deep and then 3.5 feet farther inside. Follow the privately maintained markers and lights. East of Mill Creek is a small unnamed inlet with a reported depth of 6 feet up to the marina inside. The channel is marked by privately maintained aids.

To the northeast of Southold Bay, **Pipes Cove,** between Greenport and Conkling Point, is OK for lunch, but is ringed with shallows and wide open to wakes from the nearby channel. Don't stay here overnight.

Jockey Creek and **Town Creek,** which make up Southold Harbor, share the same entrance with bulkheads and sandy beaches on each side. A white tower on the south side of Jockey Creek is a good range to head for after rounding Jennings Point, but as you get closer look for red nun "2" paired with can "1" **[WP-395],** which marks the entrance. (Both buoys are seasonal and privately maintained.)

Stay close to can "1" to avoid the shoal on the north side of the entrance. The channel may be less than the 6 to 8 feet shown on your chart. Several marinas and marine service centers are around the harbor.

Goose Creek, a little farther south, has a fixed bridge with a height of 9 feet, and with shallow water within, is suitable only for small boats. You can drop a lunch hook anywhere in **Southold Bay,** but the open anchorage suffers from the same problems as Pipes Cove. You'll want to head for a more secure anchorage at night.

 Shoreside and Emergency Services

Airport: Mattituck Airbase (516) 298-8330
Ambulance: 911
Bus: Suffolk County Transit (516) 360-5700
Coast Guard: Montauk (516) 668-2773 or VHF 16
   New London (203) 442-4471 or VHF 16
   Shinnecock (516) 728-1171 or VHF 16
Ferry: Greenport to Shelter Island (516) 749-0139
   Excursion boat to the Connecticut River,
   Haddam, CT (203) 345-4507
Fire: Southold 911 or (516) 765-3270
   Greenport 911 or (516) 924-5252
Harbormaster: Southold Bay Constable (516) 765-2600
   Greenport (516) 477-2385 or VHF 16
Hospital: Eastern Long Island (516) 477-1000
Police: Southold 911 or (516) 765-2600
   Greenport 911 or (516) 477-0160
Radio Telephone: VHF 85; I.D.: Bay Shore
   Marine Operator
   VHF 28; I.D.: Riverhead
   Marine Operator
   VHF 25, 26, 84; I.D.: New York
   Marine Operator
Taxi: Fleetwood (516) 477-0078
Tow Service: Sea Tow Eastern LI, Southold, NY
   (516) 765-3660 or VHF 16; Saybrook
   Towing and Salvage, Old Saybrook, CT
   (203) 388-4065 or VHF 16
Train: Long Island Railroad (516) 234-LIRR   ◆

Great Peconic Bay and the Shinnecock Canal

The Punctures in the Whale's Tail

Think of Long Island as a giant whale, beached on the shores of the Atlantic. Between the two great flukes of its tail–the 50-mile-long north and south forks of the island–lie the Peconic Bays. Little Peconic Bay, about 5 miles long, is ringed with many fascinating creeks and gunk holes. Great Peconic Bay, rounder and about 5 miles in diameter, has extensive shoals along its southern and northern shores, especially the latter.

The village of Southampton, to the southeast of Great Peconic Bay, was settled in 1640 and is one of the oldest towns on Long Island. In the mid-19th century it began to draw summer visitors. The coming of the railroad in 1870 attracted thousands more, who bought land and built estates. The village has managed to retain much of the past with road names like Ox Pasture and Meeting House Lane.

The 3/4-mile long Shinnecock Canal connects Great Peconic Bay with Shinnecock Bay to the south, and hence, the Atlantic Ocean. As early as the 1650s the residents of Southampton and Canoe Place–the little hamlet on the west side of the present-day canal–recognized the commercial potential of making Shinnecock Bay, then landlocked, into a saltwater bay suitable for commercial fishing. (Canoe Place is so named because the local Indians portaged their canoes from bay to bay across the narrow strip of land.

Some have even suggested that the Indians dug a primitive canal of their own here at one time.)

Over the centuries, several futile attempts were made to either cut a canal to Shinnecock Bay from Great Peconic Bay, or to cut an inlet across the sandy beaches separating Shinnecock from the Atlantic. In 1826 a state's engineer proposed a canal–with a lock–that would serve a dual purpose: not only would it allow saltwater to flow south from Great Peconic Bay into Shinnecock Bay, but the lock

The Shinnecock Canal, Shinnecock Bay, and the Atlantic from the north.

Marine Facilities and Services

Facility	Phone	Number of Transient Berths	Number of Transient Moorings	Seasonal/Year-round	Largest Vessel Accommodation (in feet)	Marked Entry Channel	Approach Depth in feet at MLW	Dockside Depth in feet at MLW	Gas/Diesel Fuel	Fuel Brand	Ramp/Dinghy Dock/Launch Service	Railway Lift: Capacity (in tons)	Propeller/Hull Repairs	Engine Repairs: Gas/Diesel	Pump-out Station	Showers/Laundromat	Marine Supplies/Groceries/Bait/Ice	110V★ 220V▲ Maximum Amps	MasterCard/VISA/Diners Club American Express	Restaurant/Snack Bar	Monitors VHF Channel
1 Modern Yachts (p. 326)	(516) 728-2266	4		Y	60	●	10	5	GD	GLF	L	L40	PH	GD		S	SI	★▲30	MVA		
2 Corrigan Yacht Yard	(516) 728-4189	10		Y	53	●	8	5	GD	TEX		L30	PH	GD		SL	SGI	★30	MVA		
3 Indian Cove Marina	(516) 728-2800	6		Y	45																
4 Mariner's Cove Marina (p. 327)	(516) 728-0286	25		Y	60	●	6	6	G	GLF	R		PH	GD		S	SGBI	★30	MV		16
5 Jackson's Marina (p. 327)	(516) 728-4220			Y	80	●	6	6	GD	TEX			PH	GD		S	SGBI	★▲50	MVA	S	68
6 Shinnecock Canal Boat Basin		64		S	65	●	10	8								S		★30		S	
7 The Lobster Inn	(516) 283-1525	8		Y	35	●	3.5	4.5	DOCKAGE FOR PATRONS									★	MVA	R	
8 Spellman's Marine	(516) 283-7907			Y					BOAT SALES & MARINE SUPPLIES							S			MV		
9 Bullhead Yacht Club	(516) 283-9403	2		S	43	●	4	6	PRIVATE CLUB - MEMBERS ONLY							S			MV		16
10 Dave Bofill Marine	(516) 283-4841			Y	35	●	4	3	G	GLF		12						★30	MVA		
11 Conscience Pt. Marina (p. 325)	(516) 283-8295	26		S	46	●	5.5	5.5	GD	NOV	R		PH	GD	●	SL	I	★15			16
12 Peconic Marina	(516) 283-3767	3		S	30	●	6	6	GD	TEX		R30	P	GD		S	SBI	★30	MV	R	

Information in these listings is provided by the facilities themselves. An asterisk (*) indicates that the facility did not respond to our most recent requests for information.

could also be used to keep the water level high in the latter. Should an inlet from the ocean ever be dug, the tides could be manipulated to keep the inlet from filling with sand.

Sixty-six years later, after a decade of half-hearted attempts, the state succeeded in opening the Shinnecock Canal–without a lock, a feature that wouldn't be added until 1919. Seeing a dramatic rise in the shellfish population in Shinnecock Bay, local fishermen were delighted.

The final act–described by one as a "left-handed miracle"–in the Shinnecock Canal drama, came in September 1938 when the great hurricane created the Shinnecock Inlet and opened the southern bay to the ocean.

Over the years the canal has been rebuilt and improved, and today is traveled by thousands of boaters. Sailors, however, are galled from time to time because they must unstep their masts to pass under the 22-foot-high bridge over the canal.

 ## What To See and Do

The old Halsey Homestead (516) 283-3527 in Southampton Village, about 5 miles southeast of the Shinnecock Canal, is considered the oldest frame house in the state. Built in 1648, it's open to the public, as is an early silversmith shop. The Southampton Historical Museum (516) 283-2494, housed in the home of a whaling captain, offers exhibits highlighting local history. The museum grounds also contain a one-room schoolhouse and a pre-Revolutionary War barn.

The Parrish Art Museum and Arboretum (516) 283-2118 specializes in American art of the 19th and 20th centuries and holds more than 2,500 paintings in its permanent collection. The centerpieces of the museum are collections of two renowned residents of Southampton, William Merritt Chase and Fairfield Porter.

The Morton National Wildlife Refuge on Jessup Neck is a feeding and resting area for migratory birds, particularly the piping plover and the least tern. The descendants of the Shinnecock Indians own a reservation adjacent to the village at the south end of the canal and hold an annual powwow in September (516) 283-3775.

There is a small beach about a mile to the west of the north end of the canal. Be careful when approaching it, and dink to shore. There are rocks just offshore (marked on the charts) that give the marinas lots of lower unit repair work.

 ## Where To Eat

If you're staying at the Peconic Marina you will find the Coast Grille (516) 283-3767, where you can tie up free while you're sampling the lobster and clam specialties.

Right around the Shinnecock Canal, within walking distance of Modern Yachts or Corrigan's, there are several seafood restaurants: The Indian Cove (516) 728-8833, the Lock House (516) 728-7373 (you can tie up at the dock while dining), and The Canal (516) 728-1717. For a sandwich or burger try O'Malley's (516) 728-9593.

For more seafood in a casual setting, it's a short cab ride to the Fish Net (516) 728-0115. Villa Paul (516) 728-3261 offers hearty Italian, and Johnny Chi's (516) 728-8811 specializes in Chinese cuisine.

 ## Navigation and Anchorages

Use NOAA Charts 12358 (1:40,000), 12352 (1:40,000), and 12354 (1:80,000). Use tide tables for New London. High tide at the Shinnecock Canal is 2 hours 34 minutes later; low tide is 2 hours 31 minutes later. Multiply by 0.9 for height at high or low water. Mean tidal range is 2.8 feet.

At the Shinnecock Inlet, use tide tables for Sandy Hook. High tide is 51 minutes earlier; low tide is 1 hour 6 minutes earlier. Multiply by 0.6 for height at high or low water. Mean tidal range is 3.0 feet.

CAUTION: *There have been many buoy changes in this area. We have noted the most important below, but be alert for others.*

The Shinnecock Canal, on the south side of Great Peconic Bay, is 4.7nm by boat east of Riverhead, 7.0nm by boat south-southwest of Cutchogue Harbor, and 3.0nm by boat north of the Shinnecock Inlet, which connects Shinnecock Bay to the Atlantic.

It's good to bear in mind that all the harbors in both Little and Great Peconic Bays are artificial, so that the depth at the entrances varies according to the accumulation of sand and the frequency of dredging. The creeks are fun to explore but be prepared for a little bump and grind, even in a dinghy. Because of the size of Great Peconic Bay and its shallow water, a steep chop can build up quickly when the winds start to blow hard.

Since the area is totally enclosed, one of the best and easiest ways of navigating is by dead reckoning. Just pick out a few significant landmarks and write them down when plotting and running your course. Remember to pick marks that will be recognizable from a distance and from many different angles. (Dead reckoning is especially useful because the land masses that surround the Peconics can distort LORAN readings.)

When heading through **Little Peconic Bay** from the east, you'll pass the red 4sec flasher "22" **[WP-412]** off the high bluffs of Nassau Point, and you can find protection from an easterly on the west side of green can "1" **[WP-372],** tucked in between Nassau Point and Robins Island.

The southwest side of **Little Peconic Bay** has several anchorages. **Wooley Pond,** 2.1nm southeast of Nassau Point and just off our chart, is difficult because of its concealed entrance, swift currents, and visible shoals, but the harbor is cozy and well protected. The channel is marked by private seasonal buoys and a private light on the north side of the entrance. Marine services are available for boats drawing under 5 feet. The marine police will not allow overnight anchoring without a sewage holding tank.

To the west, **North Sea Harbor** also appeals mostly to small craft seeking a place of refuge. Holmes Hill, a prominent sandy bluff just west of the entrance, makes an easy landmark. The 4-foot channel is marked by can "1" and red 5sec flasher "2," about 300 yards outside the entrance. Inside, the bottom is soft, with good holding ground, though very shallow.

You'll find 2 marinas on **Conscience Point,** the small, bird's-head shaped point at the southwest corner of **North Sea Harbor.** The town of Southampton (not to be confused with the village of Southampton) maintains a ramp on Conscience Point and a town dock on Towd Point, to port as you enter the harbor. You may tie up for 2 hours for loading or unloading. The center of Southampton is 3 miles away, so a cab will be needed.

To enter **Great Peconic Bay** you'll pass **Robins Island.** Two marked channels surround the island, the preferred one being the southerly. Stay south of the red 2.5sec flasher "26" **[WP-408]** off the southern tip of the island to avoid the tide rips and shallow spots north of the flasher. Note that the lighted red buoy "30," charted to the west of Cow Neck Point, has been removed.

On the south shore of Great Peconic Bay, Sebonac Creek is the entrance to **Bullhead Bay,** and is the nearest you'll get to the village of Southampton, the most famous of all Long Island summer resorts. There's at least 5 feet of water inside the privately dredged channel, which has an entrance marked by the red 5sec flasher "2" and can "1" **[WP-407].** Because of a serious shoal on either side of the channel, stay at least 250 yards off the entrance buoys until you've lined them up on a range with the green 5sec flasher "3." Then turn into the channel and stay inside the row of buoys, or you'll be stuck waiting for the tide to rise. Also, if you've been using the green flasher "3" as a range to this point, you should now leave it well to port.

Inside **Sebonac Creek,** the Bullhead Yacht Club has slips and moorings, and there's a town dock at **West Neck,** northeast of Ram Island and just opposite can "7." You can

1976 NORTH SEA ROAD SOUTHAMPTON NY 11968 P.O. BOX 2789 516-283-8295

SLIPS 26-46 FT. • FLOATING DOCKS 16-26 FT. • GAS PUMPS • CABLE TV • TELEPHONE • WATER • ELECTRIC • CABANNA SHOWERS • PATIO

tie up for 2 hours for loading or unloading. The best anchorage is also in this area.

Cold Spring Pond, about 1.6 miles southwest of Sebonac Creek and 1.1nm east of the Shinnecock Canal, is shallow—no more than 2 feet at low tide and only used by runabouts. Stay out of Cold Spring Pond, even in a small powerboat. This is dinghy and canoe territory.

Southwestward 1.1nm from the Cold Spring Pond entrance is the entrance to the 3/4-mile-long Shinnecock Canal and the eastern end of the 29-mile inland water route along the south shore of Long Island.

When approaching the **Shinnecock Canal** from anywhere in Great Peconic Bay, look for the jetty that extends 300 yards from the canal entrance. (One of our readers tells us he can see the jetty with binoculars from Robins Island.) Closer in, you'll see the 4sec green flasher "1" **[WP-405]** off the end of the jetty, paired with red nun "2." There's good water throughout the canal (6 to 10 feet), but make sure you understand the currents in the canal before entering.

Many boaters are intimidated by the currents and the lock, but getting through the Shinnecock Canal can be quite simple if done at the right time.

CAUTION: *Before going through the Shinnecock Canal, there are three important facts to remember.*

First, if you're in a sailboat you'll have to unstep your mast to pass through because of the 22-foot clearance of the lowest bridge; there is a self service "mast-unstepper" located in the Boat Basin, for your convenience.

Second, the elevation of Great Peconic Bay is greater than that of the ocean, so that the current in the canal is always flowing south.

Third, because of the tidal action, the safest time to go north or south through the canal is when the locks are closed, not open. The currents may be less of a problem if you're going south, but still a force to be respected.

North of the lock, there is a basin on the east side at which you can tie up and wait, and several marinas and restaurants are located in the area. At the basin (and also at the southern end of the canal, at Jackson's Marina) there's a self-serve public crane with a manual winch for unstepping your masts. Meschutt Beach County Park is on the northeast side of the canal next to the basin. Don't be surprised to see shoulder-to-shoulder fishermen standing on the banks of the canal. The local fishermen tell us the flounder (in April) and the weakfish (especially in early May) are plentiful here.

The lock is located about midway down the canal, between the 2 bridges, and has a red and green "traffic light" on the east side. Enter only on the green.

The large steel gates of the lock are controlled by tidal action. When the tide in **Great Peconic Bay** is high enough (i.e. when the differential in water levels between the two

bays is great enough) the gates open automatically. When the tides in Great Peconic Bay and in **Shinnecock Bay** reach a rough equilibrium, the gates close automatically. Each phase lasts about 6 hours.

While the locks are closed, the lock tender can open one gate for you to pass into the lock, and then let you out the other end in the same way. Inside, you can tie up or simply hold onto one of the many steel rungs attached to the bulkheads while waiting to motor out of the lock. (You needn't worry about the current inside the lock at this point–it's like a mill pond.) Because the water level in the lock can be manipulated when it's closed, this is the safest time to go through the canal.

When the lock is open, however, ferocious currents can make your trip south very fast, but potentially dangerous. Current speeds of up to 9 knots are common right after the lock opens, and the lock tender once reported a current of 12 knots in the canal. If you'd rather not quicken your pulse so much, just wait an hour or two until the currents are manageable. South of the lock, at the railroad bridge, you may encounter some tricky whirlpools.

The currents are especially important if you're headed north. When the lock is open and the current going south through the canal is at its peak, you need to have a boat capable of 15 or 20 knots, or you'll be going nowhere. One of our readers, going north through the canal at 7 knots with the locks open, reports being turned around and nearly sent bow-on to a concrete bulkhead by the currents.

You can call the lock house (516) 728-2360 or VHF 13 or 20 for more information or some friendly advice. The lock tender will probably just tell you when the lock opened and that you should add 6 hours to find the time it will close. Another way to know the status of the lock is to employ a trick the local fishermen use: The gates will close 3-1/2 hours before high water at Sandy Hook, and open 2-1/2 hours after high water at Sandy Hook.

Although not many sailors use the canal because they must unstep their masts, a circumnavigation of the island is something like 22 hours, but at a more leisurely and enjoyable pace you will probably want to take four days to a week. One of the nice things about the trip is that when the weather is good, you can shoot out of one of the inlets and cruise on the open **Atlantic.** If the weather isn't so good, you can duck into the protected waters of the inland waterway. Two things you will want to consider before taking such a cruise: The state channel is dredged to a depth of 6 feet, and most of it has a speed limit of 5 to 10 mph because of the problem of wakes.

 ### Shoreside and Emergency Services

Airport: Suffolk County (516) 288-3600
Ambulance: (516) 728-3400
Bus: Suffolk County Transit (516) 360-5700
Coast Guard: Shinnecock (516) 728-1171/0078 or VHF 16
Fire: Southampton (516) 728-3400
Harbormaster: Bay Constable (516) 725-3357
                    or (516) 734-6022
Hospital: Southampton (516) 283-2600
Police: Southampton (516) 728-3400
Radio Telephone: VHF 85; I.D.: Bay Shore
                    Marine Operator
                    VHF 28; I.D.: Riverhead
                    Marine Operator
                    VHF 25, 26, 84; I.D.: New York
                    Marine Operator
Taxi: Hampton Coach (516) 728-0050
         Jackson's Taxi (516) 727-2605
Tow Service: Sea Tow-Eastern L.I., Southold, NY
                (516) 765-3660 or VHF 16; Saybrook
                Towing and Salvage, Old Saybrook, CT
                (203) 388-4065 or VHF 16
Train: Long Island Railroad (516) 758-LIRR   ✦

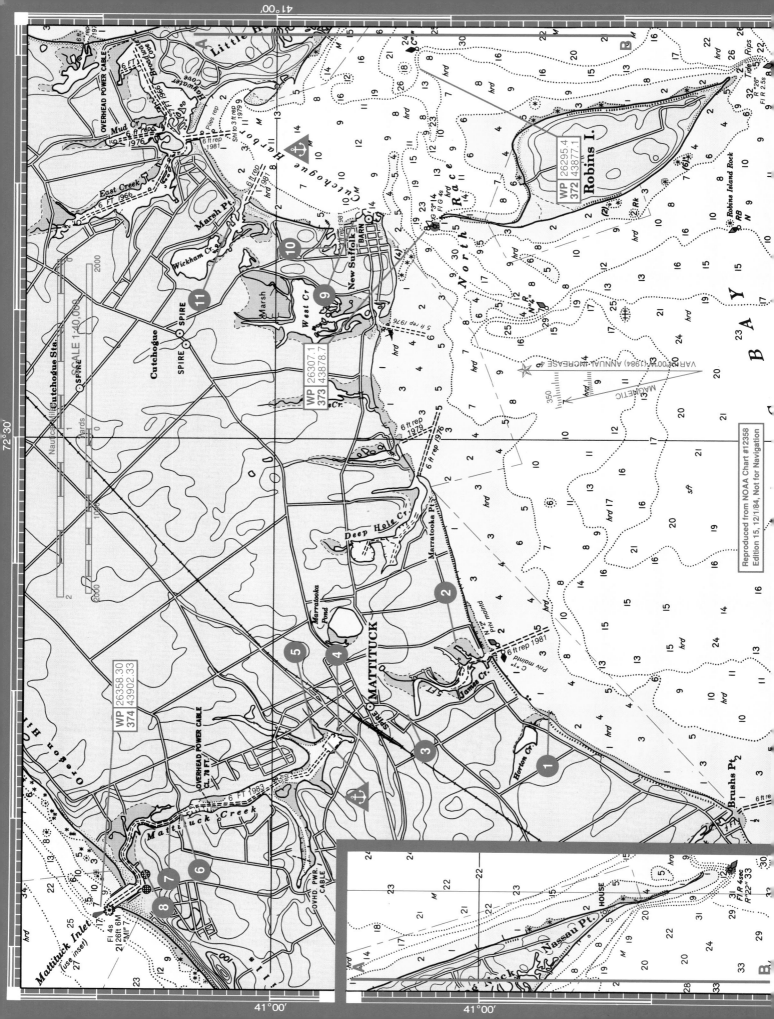

41°00'

41°00'

41°00'

72°30'

72°30'

Little H

Robins I.

WP 26295.4
372 43877.1

North Race

B A Y

Robins Island Rock
RB
N 9

VAR 13°00'W (1984) ANNUAL INCREASE 4'

MAGNETIC

Cutchogue

SPIRE

Cutchogue Sta.

SPIRE

SPIRE

New Suffolk

BARN

WP 26307.1
373 43878.7

West Cr.

Marsh

Wickham Cr.

Marsh Pt.

East Creek

Mud Cr.

Broadwater Cove

OVERHEAD POWER CABLE

SCALE 1:40,000

Marratooka Pond

Deep Hole Cr.

Marratooka Pt.

MATTITUCK

SPIRE

James Cr.

Priv maintd

N "2"

Priv maintd

Brushs Pt.

Horton Cr.

WP 26358.30
374 43902.33

OVERHEAD POWER CABLE
CL. 76 FT.

Oregon Hill

Mattituck Creek

OVHD PWR.
CABLE

Mattituck Inlet

(use inset)

Fl 4s
26ft 6M "MI" 7

Nassau Pt.

HOUSE

Fl R 4sec
R "22" 33

1
2
3
4
5
6
7
8
9
10
11

Mattituck Inlet and Cutchogue Harbor

Keeping the Land

Mattituck is the only town on the north shore that can be reached by boaters from both sides of the northern "fluke" of the "whale's tail." Some people wonder why a canal hasn't been cut across the 500-yard stretch of land from Mattituck inlet to James Creek, thereby joining Long Island Sound and Great Peconic Bay. Although a marriage of such waters would have made traveling between them less time-consuming and convenient, it would have also caused all kinds of ecological trouble. Today the idea is even more preposterous, as it would cut right through the center of town, right through the delis and Rte. 25.

As far as preservation efforts in Mattituck go, there is a steady current, and is best seen in the case of Robins Island, another one of New York's mysterious islands.

During the Revolutionary War, Robins was owned by one Parker Wickham. A loyalist to the King, Wickham was not well-liked by the local residents. Although the Treaty of Paris assured no action would be taken against Loyalists, a vengeful New York State Legislature threw Wickham off his land and sold it to the current chain of title. In the early 1900s the island was bought by a wealthy merchant who began building a house for himself and his wife. Unfortunately, the lady died before the house was completed. Today, the would-be mansion stands unfinished and unoccupied, a sad testament to the man who started it.

New Suffolk, NY and Cutchogue Harbor from the southeast.

Robins Island was last sold to a West German-controlled company in 1979. Ever since the sale, there has been constant debate over the future of the island. The zoning is restrictive—one dwelling per 10 acres—and public interest groups are trying to turn it into a park or nature preserve. Landing on the island is not permitted. There are "No Trespassing" signs to warn you and, we're told, a caretaker to chase visitors away with a shotgun.

There are, however, other places that are equally placid and inspiring, and which aren't out-of-bounds. Cutchogue

Marine Facilities and Services	Phone	Number of Transient Berths	Number of Transient Moorings	Seasonal/Year-round	Largest Vessel Accommodation	Marked Entry Channel	Approach Depth (in feet)	Dockside Depth in feet at MLW	Gas/Diesel Depth in feet at MLW	Gas/Diesel Fuel	Fuel Brand	Ramp/Dinghy Dock/Launch Service	Railway/Lift: Capacity (in tons)	Propeller/Hull Repairs	Engine Repairs: Gas/Diesel	Pump-out Station	Showers/Laundromat	Marine Supplies/Groceries/Bait/Ice	110V★ 220V▲ Maximum Amps	MasterCard/VISA/Diners Club / American Express	Restaurant/Snack Bar	Monitors VHF Channel
1 Mattituck Yacht Club	(516) 298-8974	*PRIVATE CLUB - MEMBERS ONLY*																				
2 Strong's Marineland	(516) 298-4770	10		Y	36	●	8	6		G	TEX	R	L30	PH	G			SBI	★30	MV		68
3 Village Marine	(516) 298-5800	6		Y	35	●	6	6				R		PH	GD		S		★30	MVA		
4 Mattituck Park District Marina	(516) 298-8637			S	30			10				R					S					
5 Matt-A-Mar Marina	(516) 298-4739	30		Y	75	●	8	7		GD	TEX	D	L50	PH	GD	●	S	SI	★▲50	MVA	R	16
6 **Mattituck Inlet Marina (p. 331)**	**(516) 298-4480**	3		Y	100	●	15	15		GD	GLF		L75	PH	GD				★▲50	MVA		9
7 Rosie's Old Mill Inn	(516) 298-8979	4		Y	80	●	15	10													R	
8 Mattituck Fishing Station & Marina *	(516) 298-8399																					
9 New Suffolk Fishing Station	(516) 734-6852			S	20	●	3	2		G	GET			P	G			SI	▲	MV	S	
10 New Suffolk Shipyard & Marina	(516) 734-6311	5		Y	44	●	5	5		G	MOB	D	L15	PH	GD		S	SI	★30	MVA		16
11 Boatmens Harbor Marina	(516) 734-6993	10		S	60	●	8	4		G	GLF	R		PH	GD		SL	SGI	★		S	

Information in these listings is provided by the facilities themselves. An asterisk (*) indicates that the facility did not respond to our most recent requests for information.

Harbor is punctuated with quiet little gunkholes, tiny creeks and inlets, and marine facilities. On the west side of Cutchogue Harbor is the town of New Suffolk, which resembles a Maine fishing village in size and character, looking as if it had come down from the rocky north, maybe even through a canal or two.

 What To See and Do

Mattituck is a modest, straightforward town where the transient boater will be able to get basic provisions and marine supplies. It is also a fishing town with a small fleet of trawlers. For all its charming provincialism, there is something almost refined and urbane about Mattituck, the way those towns that grow good wine carry themselves.

For a long time potatoes were dominant in these parts, but over the last decade wine grapes have become popular. The well-drained sandy soil and the moderate temperatures are perfectly suited for growing grapes. Today, there are more than a dozen vineyards, most offering free tours and wine tastings. Although Pindar Vineyards (516) 734-6200 in the village of Peconic is the largest with a 200-acre spread, Peconic Bay Vineyards (516) 734-7361 and Hargrave Vineyards (516) 734-5111 are closer.

The most unusual sight in Mattituck—and you do not need a cab for this one—is the heavy artillery museum on, of all places, Love Lane. The American Armored Tank Museum (516) 588-0033 is just off the end of the inlet, guarding the waterway with a collection of 50 tanks from World War I to the present. Inside, the museum is a veritable armory stockpiled with cannons, machine guns, and other such things with triggers.

If you've brought the dinghy with you, fishing or exploring the numerous smaller creeks at Cutchogue Harbor would be an ideal way to get into nature for a while.

 Where To Eat

On the Sound side, right up Mattituck Inlet, is Rosie's Old Mill Inn (516) 298-8979, and you can pull up right alongside to dock and dine. Rosie's specializes in seafood that the army of fishing boats brings in daily. Toward the end of the inlet is the Touch of Venice (516) 298-5851, right off the spiffy docks of Matt-A-Mar Marina. This is one of the better (and pricier) Italian restaurants in town, and recommended by many local residents.

If you aren't looking for a sit-down meal, there are a number of inexpensive delis in town along Love Lane. Coming ashore at James Creek doesn't land you at a restaurant, but you can call a cab and make your way to Rte. 25, where you'll find Amici's Pizzeria (516) 298-5303 and the Halfshell Republic (516) 298-4180, another Italian seafood place.

In Cutchogue, ask for the Fisherman's Rest (516) 734-5155 on Main Street. Like most of the other restaurants in this area it, too, serves a lot of seafood and Italian dishes.

 Navigation and Anchorages

Use NOAA Charts 12358 (1:40,000) and 12354 (1:80,000). Use tide tables for Bridgeport. High tide at Mattituck Inlet is 4 minutes later; low tide is 4 minutes earlier. Multiply by 0.8 for height at high or low water. Mean tidal range is 5.6 feet.

For Cutchogue Harbor, use tide tables for New London. High tide at New Suffolk is 2 hours 27 minutes later; low tide is 2 hours 11 minutes later. Mean tidal range is 3.0 feet.

Mattituck Inlet is 14.5nm by boat south of Clinton, CT, or 6.8nm southwest of Horton Point Light. The entrance at James Creek is about 16nm by boat southwest of Greenport, and 4.5nm by boat southeast of Riverhead.

Cutchogue Harbor is 7.2nm by boat northwest and north of the Shinnecock Canal, and about 3.5nm by boat east by southeast from the James Creek entrance.

At the risk of gross understatement, Mattituck Inlet is hard to spot from the Sound. From the red 6sec flashing bell "TE" **[WP-168]** south of Sixmile Reef, steer a course of about 210°m to reach the entrance to Mattituck Inlet.

CAUTION: *As you approach the Mattituck Inlet entrance you may chance to notice the huge battleship-like structure directly east of Ronoake Point Shoal. It's an oil platform with pipelines running to the shore at Jacobs Point. There is a 500-yard restricted area around the pipeline head.*

While gong "3A" **[WP-378]** is located a mile offshore to help you locate the inlet, it will still be quite difficult for the boater unfamiliar with the area to spot the 26-foot tower "MI" **[WP-374]** atop the western breakwater, especially in the morning with the sun in your eyes. A better landmark is the long break in the bluffs and two large oil tanks on the west side of the entrance. In a fresh northerly or westerly, you may find the entrance a rough experience, especially with an outgoing tide. Though shoaling is apt to occur at the entrance, the sandy channel carries 5 to 7 feet of water. The channel is unmarked and, thus, not so easy to find either, so proceed slower than the 5-mph limit. Don't be put off by the initial "industrialness" of the inlet; it quickly wears off into modest houses, neat marinas, and lots of trees.

The channel is marked well only after you pass Rosie's Old Mill Inn to starboard. The current at this point will hit you suddenly and strong, like a diminutive Hell Gate. This is because the channel bottom plunges to 40 feet, rises suddenly to 15, and drops again to 40; it's this damming effect that can damn your boat if you're not careful, especially in bad weather with the tide and wind opposed. We've heard stories about 4-foot standing waves at this junction in angry weather.

The channel continues to a free federal anchorage offering perfect protection and 7 feet of clean water. At the head of navigation is a transient dock and bathing beach operated by the Mattituck Park Commission. While there is fresh water available here at the bath house nearby, there is no dockmaster. You can stay up to three hours.

Off the main channel there are tiny inlets with up to 6 feet of water. Once you've anchored, docked, or moored your boat, the town is a short dinghy ride or walk away.

On the **Great Peconic Bay** side, Nassau Point is 5.6nm southwest of James Creek. The red 4sec flashing buoy "22" off Nassau Point marks the eastern approach to **Cutchogue Harbor.** Don't cut between the flasher and Nassau Point due to the shoals that stretch 0.5nm south of the point. Cutchogue Harbor is well-enclosed, although a southeasterly can make it uncomfortable.

Robins Island divides the 5-mile wide Great Peconic Bay to the west from Little Peconic Bay to the east. Given the prevailing southwest winds, the bight on the north side of the island makes a very nice anchorage. Do not try landing on the 2-mile long, seemingly deserted island. It isn't. There are "No Trespassing" signs posted and an ever vigilant caretaker wielding, it's said, a shotgun.

When rounding the north side of **Robins Island,** keep the green 4sec flasher "3" **[WP-373]** to port, as a long sand spit extends well into the North Race.

If you are headed for the Shinnecock Canal or Riverhead from Nassau Point (6.0nm and 11nm by boat, respectively) you will want to continue southwest past Robins Island and through the deeper water of the **South Race.**

CAUTION: Tide rips can develop near the southern tip of Robins Island, especially when tide and wind are opposed, so you'll also want to favor the Cow Neck side while keeping an eye out for the charted rocks and shoals.

The village of **New Suffolk** is mostly residential, though you'll find a marina, a fishing station, and a grocery there.

For anchoring, **Haywater** and **Broadwater coves** are ideal, as are **Mud Creek** and **East Creek;** all share the same entrance on the north side of Cutchogue Harbor. None of these channels are marked.

CAUTION: Although the narrow channels at these four little creeks are generally 4 to 6 feet deep, their common entrance tends to shoal, so only explore here in a shallow-draft boat. The positions and depths of these channels vary considerably, depending on recent storm activity.

There are a number of other creeks and inlets between Mattituck and Riverhead, 4.5nm by boat to the southwest. Most are successfully tackled only by the local residents, who keep boats at their private docks in their back yards.

 Shoreside and Emergency Services

Airport: Mattituck Airbase (516) 298-8330
Ambulance: 911
Bus: Suffolk County Transit (516) 360-5700
Coast Guard: New London (203) 442-4471 or VHF 16
New Haven (203) 773-2400 or VHF 16
Shinnecock (516) 728-1171/0078 or VHF 16
Fire: 911 or (516) 298-8833
Harbormaster: Bay Constable (516) 765-2600
or 734-6022 or VHF 16
Hospital: Eastern Long Island (516) 477-1000
Central Suffolk (516) 548-6000
Police: 911 or (516) 734-6022
Radio Telephone: VHF 85; I.D.: Bay Shore
Marine Operator;
VHF 28; I.D.: Riverhead
Marine Operator;
VHF 25, 26, 84; I.D.: New York
Marine Operator
Taxi: Riverhead Taxi (516) 727- 6088
Genie Taxi & Limousine Service (516) 369-1766
Fleetwood East Limousine & Taxi Service
(516) 477-0078
Tow Service: Saybrook Towing and Salvage,
Old Saybrook, CT (203) 388-4065
or VHF 16
Train: Long Island Railroad (516) 234-LIRR ◆

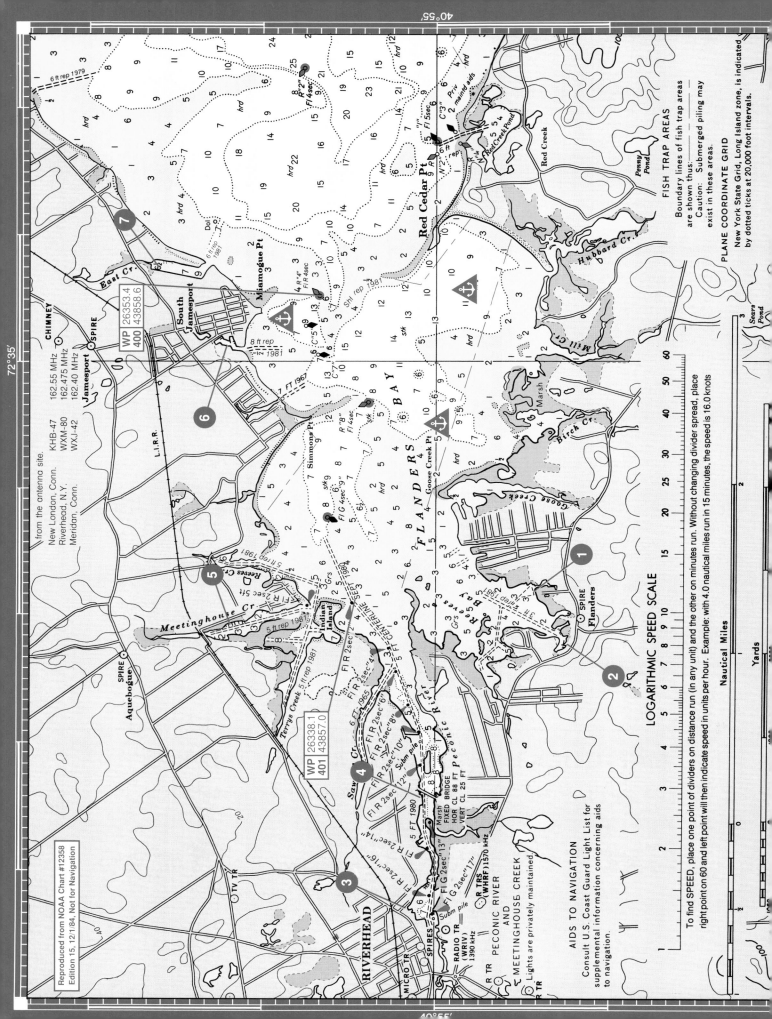

Flanders Bay and Riverhead

At the Pastoral End of Long Island

Flanders Bay, lying at the junction of the two "flukes" of the great whale that is Long Island, is the outlet for the Peconic River and innumerable small creeks. The town, Riverhead, was once called "Occabog." (You can imagine an Indian slipping off a log into the Flanders Bay mud and swearing, "Occ! A bog!" Rhymes with "log" too.)

The town was settled about 1690 and is now the seat of Suffolk County. As such, you'll find plenty of government buildings here, as well as the people who work in them. This civic activity contributes to Riverhead's status as the most densely-populated area on the "whale's fluke." Riverhead, with its busy streets, shopping, fast-food restaurants and overall urban feel, seems like a small outpost of New York amidst the pastoral New England-style villages scattered around the east end.

The town used to be a center for potato and cauliflower farming and for raising the famous Long Island ducks that were so popular on the tables of New York. The vegetable farms remain–indeed, Riverhead is surrounded by farmland–but the duck business has lost most of its feathers. The last large-scale commercial duck farm left is on Meetinghouse Creek in Aquebogue.

What To See and Do

The Suffolk County Historical Museum (516) 727-2881, close to the docks in Riverhead, offers an introduction to Eastern Long Island traditions and local genealogy. Included are dioramas that tell the story of Suffolk County from the time of the Indians to the Revolution, a gun room,

Meetinghouse Creek and Larry's Lighthouse Marina at Aquebogue, NY, from the northwest.

and collections of ship models, whaling artifacts, dolls and toys.

Canoes can be rented from the Peconic Paddler (516) 727-9895 for a very nice trip up and down the river, or kayaks to venture out into the Bay. They will take you 8 miles up the river by car, so you can paddle back down.

The shallow waters of Flanders Bay are suitable for windsurfing or jet-skiing, but be careful where you do it. The border between Riverhead (to the north) and Southampton (to the south) runs right down the middle of Flanders Bay and the Peconic River. In Southampton waters, no water skiing or jet skiing is allowed within 500 feet of the shore, and jetskis may only be launched from town of Southampton ramps.

Marine Facilities and Services		Number of Transient Berths	Number of Transient Moorings	Seasonal/Year-round	Largest Vessel Accommodation (in feet)	Marked Entry Channel	Approach Depth in feet at MLW	Dockside Depth in feet at MLW	Gas/Diesel Fuel	Fuel Brand	Ramp/Dinghy Dock/Launch Service	Railway/Lift: Capacity (in tons)	Engine Repairs; Propeller/Hull Repairs	Marine Supplies/Groceries; Bait/Ice	Pump-out Station	Showers/Laundromat	110V ★ 220V ▲ Maximum Amps	MasterCard/VISA/Diners Club; American Express	Restaurant/Snack Bar	Monitors VHF Channel
❶ B & E Marine	(516) 727-8619			S	25	●	3	3					R			PH	GD			
❷ Gateway Marine	(516) 727-8619	5		Y	35		4	3	G				R	L15	PH	G			S	★
❸ Peconic River Yacht Basin	(516) 727-8386	10		Y	60	●	7	7	G	TEX		R		P	G	●	SL	SI	▲50	MVA	S	19
❹ Riverhead Yacht Club	(516) 727-9657									*PRIVATE CLUB - MEMBERS ONLY*										
❺ Larry's Lighthouse Marina	(516) 722-3400	20		Y	65	●	6	12	GD	MAG		L30	PH	GD		S	SI	★50	MVA	S	
❻ Great Peconic Bay Marina	(516) 722-3565	10		Y	60	●	6	6	G	AGW		L25	PH	GD		S	SI	▲60		
❼ East Creek Marina	(516) 722-4842	20		Y	50	●	6	6	G				R		PH	GD		S	SBI	★30	MVA	S	16

Information in these listings is provided by the facilities themselves. An asterisk (*) indicates that the facility did not respond to our most recent requests for information.

Unfortunately, swimming is allowed only for the area residents.

Fishing is good for weakfish, blues, and flounder. Oystering and clamming used to be excellent, but conditions vary widely, so you'll have to talk to local fisherfolk to find out the state of things this summer.

 Where To Eat

The Poopdeck (516) 722-4220, serving seafood, is just across from Larry's Lighthouse Marina in Aquebogue—quite convenient, since it is the only restaurant within walking distance in that area.

Once in South Jamesport, you'll find what some local residents refer to as the "world famous" Cliff's Elbow Room (516) 722-3292 with a selection of steaks and seafood.

The Osborne Inn (516) 727-2330 is a bit out of the way, but draws the crowds with thin-crust pizza and soft shell crabs. In the town proper, a short cab ride away, there are a number of places where you can get takeout.

 Navigation and Anchorages

Use NOAA Charts 12358 (1:40,000) and 12354 (1:80,000). Use tide tables for New London. High tide at South Jamesport is 2 hours 33 minutes later; low tide is 2 hours 40 minutes later. Mean tidal range is 3.0 feet.

CAUTION: *There have been many buoy changes in this area. We have noted the most important below, but be alert for others.*

The entrance to Flanders Bay, between Red Cedar and Miamogue points, is 4.1nm by boat northwest of the Shinnecock Canal, and 12.8nm by boat west-southwest of Shelter Island. The entrance to the Peconic River is 2.0nm by boat to the west.

Before you come into **Flanders Bay** proper, you'll pass **Red Creek Pond** just east of Red Cedar Point. Red Creek Pond is a lovely little gunkhole with a 6-foot dredged channel and 4 to 5 feet in the harbor. The channel entrance is marked by the white 5sec flasher "1" and red nun "2." Nuns "2" and "4" are well off the channel to starboard, so favor the port side of the channel. Inside are a number of private moorings.

On the other side of the entrance to Flanders Bay, just north of Miamogue Point, is **East Creek,** dredged open to 8 feet. There is a state launching ramp and beach there as

well as a marina where you can rent sailboards and small boats. When on the beach, try not to disrupt the nesting roseate terns, an endangered species.

Flanders Bay is paradise for the small boats that can go skipping over its shoals, and a somewhat discouraging maze for those with deeper drafts. If you draw more than 4 to 5 feet, stay out of Flanders Bay except at half or full tide. Most of the bottom is soft mud or sand, with only a few rocks and no strong currents.

Wherever you go, unless you're in a small outboard or dinghy, follow the twisting channels and keep an eye on your depth finder. Most of the creeks are best navigated by dinghy.

South Jamesport and **Riverhead** can both be reached easily if you follow the buoys and take frequent soundings. Approach South Jamesport by leaving the red 4sec flasher "4" **[WP-400]** to starboard and can "5" port. There is an anchorage west of Miamogue Point, and the channel carries a reported depth of 8 feet, although the marina inside tells us the approach depth is more like 6 feet.

If you're looking for anchorages, there is good protection and plenty of water in the area west of **Red Cedar Point,** a little less than a mile south of red flasher "4." You can also drop a hook as much as 1,000 yards south of red flasher "8," although you should watch for a couple of 6-foot spots in the area.

Further south you'll find Birch, Mill and Hubbard creeks, which the Southampton Bay Constable aptly described to us as "dinghy water."

Proceeding past South Jamesport, leave can "7" to port, and head south-southwest towards the red 4sec flasher "8" off of Simmons Point. Don't cut it unless you're interested in mud. Lots of it. All over your keel.

At red flasher "8" turn hard to starboard and look for green 4sec flasher "9," which marks the entrance to the Flanders Bay channels. As you pass flasher "9," you'll see **Reeves Creek, Meetinghouse Creek,** and **Terry's Creek** off the starboard bow. Meetinghouse Creek, which leads to the village of Aquebogue, has piles and a 5-foot high, red 2sec flasher to guide you in. Three cans lead up the creek to a big marina with about 6 feet of water alongside the docks. A restaurant right next door to the marina is open during the boating season.

Terry's Creek will soon be dredged to 8 feet to accommodate the boats at the new condos being built. **Reeves Bay,** on the southwest side, leads into the town of Flanders via a privately dredged channel with a controlling depth of 4 feet. At the head of the creek there is a huge old oak tree that is said to have been a landmark and meeting place all the way back to Indian times. To this day, farmers in the vicinity routinely plow up arrowheads.

On the western end of the bay is **Riverhead.** The Riverhead channel, about 3 miles long, is narrow and built up, but well-marked by a series of red 2sec flashers and a couple of green ones. The river is impassable for sailboats after the first mile because of a 25-foot fixed bridge. The town maintains a basin about 0.7nm west of the bridge, with 6 feet of water, where overnight slips are available.

 ## Shoreside and Emergency Services

Airport: Mattituck Airbase (516) 298-8330
Ambulance: 911
Bus: Suffolk County Transit (516) 360-5700
Coast Guard: Shinnecock (516) 728-1171/0078 or VHF 16
Fire: Flanders "0" Operator
    Riverhead (516) 727-2750 or (516) 728-3400
Harbormaster: Bay Constable (516) 283-6000 x259
Hospital: Central Suffolk (203) 548-6000
Police: 911 or (516) 727-4500
Radio Telephone: VHF 85; I.D.: Bay Shore
        Marine Operator;
        VHF 28; I.D.: Riverhead
        Marine Operator;
        VHF 25, 26, 84; I.D.: New York
        Marine Operator
Taxi: Riverhead Taxi (516) 727-6088
Tow Service: Saybrook Towing and Salvage,
        Old Saybrook, CT (203) 388-4065
        or VHF 16; Sea Tow Eastern L.I. Southold,
        NY (516) 765-3660 or VHF 16
Train: Long Island Railroad (516) 234-LIRR ◆

MT SINAI HARBOR

CEDAR BEACH

Smack on Moses

How would you like to be a young, restless, and woman-wooing man in the early 1800s, and say to your date that you came from a town called Old Man? "Hello, I'm from Old Man." That would surely win the lovelies over, especially if they had a hearing problem and thought the prospective beau was politely disclosing some handicap or something.

The men gathered in the church and grumbled, "Why, anybody could pick a better name than that by opening the Bible and sticking his finger anywheres upon a page!" That's exactly what someone did, and the finger landed smack on Moses descending from Mount Sinai, commandments in hand. ("Hello, I'm from Moses?" they might have chortled.) Going from Old Man to Moses was clearly not a good idea, so they chose "Mount Sinai" instead.

Capping 40 miles of unbroken bluffs, Mount Sinai is the only harbor on the North Shore between Port Jefferson and Mattituck. Most of the north section of the harbor is man-

Mount Sinai Harbor, NY from the southwest.

made, and in the 1950s it was the jousting ground between sand-and-gravel companies, environmentalists, fishermen, boaters, and the town, over what was to be done with the surrounding salt marsh. To appease everyone, two-thirds of the marshland was kept as a nature preserve, and the remainder dredged. Beaches were also created, as were fishing piers, ramps, and even a marina.

It isn't known whether the town's name ever helped anyone's amorous designs, but–as you will notice upon sailing in–the development of a recreational outpost has certainly made for a lot of happy couples and their children.

 What To See and Do

While Mount Sinai does offer a great deal of outdoor recreational opportunities, it is isolated. There is only one restaurant within a mile of the harbor. "When you stay in Mount Sinai," a friend of ours remarked, "you *stay* there." Unfortunately, there isn't much room to stay either. It's a good harbor of refuge, but the marinas and moorings are likely to be jammed.

Cedar Beach gets its name from the dense growth of cedar trees to the east of the town marina parking lot. At the western end is a fishing pier. Between the pier and the parking lot is a nature preserve with indoor and outdoor exhibits on Old Man and the salt marsh.

At the nature preserve, you can pick up a map for a bicycle tour of Mount Sinai , following part of the route taken by Major Benjamin Tallmadge and his troops in 1780 as they marched from Mount Sinai Harbor to attack the British in Mastic and Coram. En route, you'll see a glacially formed kettle-hole lake, an Indian encampment area, and the pine barrens where the trees grow barely above eye level because of the poor soil.

Marine Facilities and Services		Number of Transient Berths	Number of Transient Moorings	Largest Vessel Accommodation	Seasonal/Year-round	Approach Depth (in feet)	Marked Entry Channel	Dockside Depth in feet at MLW	Gas Diesel Fuel	Ramp/Dinghy Dock/Launch Service	Fuel Brand	Railway/Lift: Capacity (in tons)	Engine Repairs: Gas/Diesel	Propeller/Hull Repairs	Marine Supplies/Groceries/Bait/Ice	Pump-out Station	Showers/Laundromat	110V ★ 220V ▲ Maximum Amps	MasterCard/VISA/Diners Club American Express	Restaurant/Snack Bar	Monitors VHF Channel
①	Ralph's Fishing Station	(516) 473-9785			S	42	●	20	4	GD	CIT			P	G		SI		MV	S	16
②	Old Man's Boatyard	(516) 473-7330		10	Y	50	●	6	6			L20	PH	GD	●		S				
③	Mt. Sinai Yacht Club	(516) 473-2993		4	Y	20	●	20	8	GD					S	I	★			S	16
④	Mt. Sinai Town Marina	(516) 928-0199	3		S	45					R				S		★			S	16

Information in these listings is provided by the facilities themselves. An asterisk (*) indicates that the facility did not respond to our most recent requests for information.

The Battle of Long Island, 1776.
Illustration from a magic lantern slide, circa 1900, by Joseph Boggs Beale.

LONG ISLAND'S REVOLUTIONARY WAR MISERY

Isolated and under enemy control during the Revolutionary War, Long Island suffered more than any other rural area in the Colonies. Looted by the British and the Americans, much of the countryside was laid waste and thousands of residents lost everything they owned as a result of the conflict.

The hardship began in 1776 with the Battle of Long Island in Brooklyn. The Colonial Army, far outnumbered, was forced to retreat, and Long Island and New York City were abandoned to British occupation. Soon the exodus began. Out of a population of 25,000-30,000 living on Long Island, as many as 5,000 fled to the mainland.

The British lost no time in setting up operations and antagonizing the residents. They demanded material and physical aid from the inhabitants; those who resisted were expelled, their property confiscated. The occupiers forced residents to build fortifications on Lloyd Neck, and even raided the local cemetery for gravestones to be used as tables and brick ovens.

According to one, "From that moment (the abandonment of Long Island) the two coasts were hostile; and an inveterate system of smuggling, marauding, plundering and kidnapping took place on both sides, in comparison with which a common state of honorable warfare might be taken for peace and good neighborhood."

Raiders in whaleboats from Connecticut harassed the British, but their targets weren't limited to the British or Loyalists; anyone was fair game. For many Long Islanders, war meant only suffering; for others, only profit.

While these "Predatory Excursions" took their toll, the governor and the courts of Connecticut gave their blessing to the raids. The looting of Long Island soon became a profitable business known as the "Illicit Trade."

Much as they hated the British, many Colonists were not above trading with the enemy. Colonists wanted tea and silk. The British needed supplies.

Many clever schemes were used to meet the demand. Long Island merchants would arrange to be "robbed" by privateers, who would sell the British goods in Connecticut, with all parties splitting the profits; ships' captains would arrange to be "captured" and their cargoes sold for profit. There was collusion between all sides: Because the mixed cast of characters involved included rebels, Tories, refugees, and British and American soldiers, officials shied away from prosecuting the traders, afraid of uncovering friends involved in the trade. The Continental Congress and Colonial Governors even participated, using it to secure clothing and food for the army.

After the war, those who had fled Long Island returned, only to find their property ruined. Long Islanders then suffered a final indignity: Since they had been unable to contribute to the war effort (thanks to the British occupation), they were heavily taxed to compensate the northern part of the state for its expenses.

If you want to shake your sea legs off, Port Jefferson is only about 3.5 miles away; a bike ride perhaps, but there are also taxis.

 Where To Eat

The only restaurant in the harbor area is Savino's (516) 928-6510, serving Italian staples and steaks in a relaxed atmosphere. (For more restaurant suggestions, please see the chapter on Port Jefferson.)

 Navigation and Anchorages

Use NOAA Charts 12362 (1:10,000), 12364 (1:40,000), and 12354 (1:80,000). Use tide tables for Bridgeport. High tide at Mount Sinai Harbor is 4 minutes later; low tide is 18 minutes later. Multiply by 0.9 for height at high or low water. Mean tidal range is 6.4 feet.

The entrance to Mount Sinai Harbor is 3.0nm by boat east of the Port Jefferson Harbor entrance, 22.2nm west of Mattituck Inlet, and 17.0nm south-southwest of the break-waters at New Haven, CT.

From the red flashing 4sec bell "2" **[WP-363]** at the southern tip of Middle Ground Shoal, a course of 165°m should bring you to the entrance of Mount Sinai Harbor.

Mount Sinai is easily approached from both the east and west, but hard to spot from a distance. From the east, stay 0.5nm offshore to avoid the occasional rocks until you are opposite the 20-foot 5sec green flasher that marks the eastern breakwater. Coming from the west, stay to the north of can "11" **[WP-360]** at Mount Misery Shoal, 2.2nm to the northwest, and then head for the breakwater. About 0.3nm north of the breakwater you'll find red and white can "M" **[WP-368]**, which is a good reference point because the harbor entrance can be very difficult to see from a distance.

CAUTION: Make sure you identify can "M" [WP-368] properly. When we were here we found a small, very shabby white buoy, uncharted and apparently signifying nothing, 1.0nm northwest of "M," on a heading of 322° m.

Another problem is that the privately maintained flasher on the east breakwater has been known to go out. A red daymark "2" is on the western side of the channel. The entrance, about 11 to 20 feet deep between the breakwaters, is marked by a low break in the beach. Along the east side of the entrance is a fishing pier, usable by non-residents for a $10 fee.

The two breakwater jetties are awash at high water, so use caution when rounding them. Furthermore, the southwestern point of **Cedar Beach** ends in a shoal which extends further into the channel than the chart suggests; be mindful of it, and pay attention to the depth sounder–as long as you're in 10 feet of water you'll be fine.

CAUTION: There is a 6-foot tidal rise and fall in the harbor, with strong currents between the breakwaters at the change of tides, so expect a bit of a push.

As you round the point at the southern end of the eastern breakwater and head into the harbor, you will want to stay as far to port as traffic will allow to keep off the shallows to the south. The channel is buoyed by a row of red nuns and a few green cans maintained by the town, and the fishing pier is lighted during the summer.

You'll be well protected in the harbor, and you can anchor almost anywhere you can find room out of the channel. If the spot you've found is tight, first set your anchor using as much scope as possible–a common measure is seven times the depth at high tide–then back down on the scope to reduce the swing. If you need to limit the swing even more, or need greater holding power, two anchors should be used.

There's good dinghy exploring in the marshes south of the town marina, but the mud can be very treacherous, so even in your dink you should wait until high tide to go into the marshes. There is more good anchoring south of red nun "2A," inside the entrance.

No landing is allowed anywhere in the harbor, apart from the marinas. Current swirls develop south of the entrance channel, where there is a popular anchorage.

Again, if you want a mooring or a slip at the town marina, contact the harbormaster (516) 928-0199 or VHF 16, but don't get your hopes up. No advance reservations are accepted, and there are no transient moorings. There is a 6-mph speed limit, so water skiing is prohibited.

 Shoreside and Emergency Services

Airport: MacArthur (516) 588-8062
Ambulance: 911
Bus: Suffolk County Transit (516) 360-5700
Coast Guard: New Haven (203) 773-2400 or VHF 16
　　　　　　　Eatons Neck (516) 261-6868/6910
　　　　　　　or VHF 16
Fire: "0" Operator
Harbormaster: (516) 928-0199 or VHF 16
Hospital: St. Charles (516) 473-2800
　　　　　　John T. Mather Memorial (516) 473-1320
Police: 911 or (516) 451-4400
Radio Telephone: VHF 85; I.D.: Bay Shore Marine
　　　　　　　Operator; VHF 28; I.D.: Riverhead
　　　　　　　Marine Operator; VHF 25, 26, 84; I.D.:
　　　　　　　New York Marine Operator; VHF 27;
　　　　　　　I.D.: Bridgeport Marine Operator
Taxi: Port Taxi (516) 475-5959
Tow Service: Saybrook Towing and Salvage,
　　　　　　　Old Saybrook, CT (203) 388-4065
　　　　　　　or VHF 16
Train: Long Island Railroad (516) 234-LIRR ◆

SCALE 1:16,000

Mt Misery Pt

Foul Area

Wrecks

Ruins

Spoil Area

Spoil Area

VAR 14°00'W (1984) ANNUAL INCREASE 4'

MAGNETIC

Fl 4sec 35ft 6M "3"

WP 26629.0
349 43929.8

Fl R 4sec 26ft
5M "2A"

R "2"
Fl R 2.5sec
BELL

MARKERS

Marsh

P O R T

Fl G 4sec BELL

R N"4"

(see tabulation)

Grs

Grs

Old Field Point
and Mount Misery Cove

Sand For a City

You would never think it, but behind all that sparkling glass and gleaming chrome, New York City is made of sand. No, nothing metaphorical here; a main component in concrete is sand, and much of that sand came from "sand holes" all over Long Island. Mount Misery is just such a one.

Charted as a "spoil area" and also known as Pirates Cove, the artificial basin was carved out of Mount Misery (and other such sand pits on the north shore) by sand-and-gravel companies, which fueled the concrete suppliers who literally laid the foundations for the big cities and the Long Island Expressway. Local legend has it that Long Island sand was so good that some of it was shipped all the way to South America for use in one of Henry Ford's exotic enterprises.

(You would also never think that legendary ships were built here, but you they were. The *Wanderer* was built here, as was the *Palatine*, which sank off Block Island.)

All this hollowing-out eventually made for good protection from the Sound's frequent blusters, and boaters have taken advantage of it as an anchorage even if they have no intention of actually visiting Port Jefferson.

 ## What To See and Do

Although the anchorages behind Old Field Point and in Mount Misery Cove offer beautiful gunkholes with excellent swimming, sunbathing, and bird-watching opportunities, the boater in search of supplies, services, or activities of a more commercial sort should proceed on to Port Jefferson, 1.8nm down the harbor to the south. (Please see the following chapter on Port Jefferson).

In this part of the world, sand is king, and you will often see kids spelling out their names on the dunes in big letters, as though they were writing rescue messages on a deserted island. These dunes are not the fragile windblown dunes you'll find on Cape Cod. They're made of glacial till, and the sand is mixed with rocks and gravel. Nonetheless, they are unstable and damaged by foot traffic, so you should admire them only at a distance.

There are a few old wrecks from dredging days left in the cove that are also fun to explore. The concrete jetties or groins on the east bank south of the cove are also left over from the sand-mining days.

Due to the different rates at which air warms over land and water, onshore/offshore breezes can develop in Port Jefferson Harbor when there isn't a breath of wind out on the Sound. These gentle breezes make the harbor a terrific area for sailing small boats, or windsurfing if you stay clear of the main channel. In a dink you will also be able to poke

Mount Misery Cove, or "Pirates Cove" on the east side of Port Jefferson Harbor, NY.

around the shallows on the west side of the harbor and go a little way into Conscience Bay for good birding, but be careful not to disturb the terns that nest along the beach on both sides of the jetties.

 ## Where To Eat

The glaciers brought the sand. You bring the lunch.

 ## Navigation and Anchorages

Use NOAA Charts 12362 (1:10,000), 12364 (1:40,000), and 12354 (1:80,000). Use tide tables for Bridgeport. High tide at the Port Jefferson Harbor entrance is 2 minutes later; low tide is 1 minute later. Mean tidal range is 7.0 feet.

CAUTION: *There have been many buoy changes in this area. We have noted the most important ones below, but be alert for others.*

The entrance to Port Jefferson is 8.1nm by boat east of Stony Brook Harbor and 4.0nm by boat west of Mount Sinai Harbor.

From the red flashing 4sec bell "2" **[WP-363]** at Middle Ground (Stratford Shoal), a course of 190°m should bring you to the buoys marking the Port Jefferson Harbor entrance channel.

In approaching **Port Jefferson,** it's best to stay well offshore to clear the rocks and shoals off Old Field and Mount Misery points. The current runs very quickly past both points and has scooped away the sand, leaving large and dangerous piles of boulders which are no longer marked by buoys. **Mount Misery Shoal** shows a charted

THE SAND, THE WIND, AND THE WAVES

Every other winter or so there's a wild Pacific storm and we see beach houses in Malibu, CA pounded by giant waves or washed into the sea. It's easy to laugh about a movie star's house falling from atop a bluff, but it isn't so funny when it happens to us.

Storms on the East Coast are seldom as spectacular, but coastal erosion is no less serious. Just west of Port Jefferson Harbor sits the Old Field Point Lighthouse. In 1964, New York state built two stone groins and a revetment on the beach, to halt erosion of the bluffs on which the 120-year-old lighthouse stands. Before then, the action of waves and the occasional storm were taking away almost a foot of the bluff every year. In 1972 the revetment was extended and since then the eroding action of the waves has been under control. The bluffs are now thickly covered with stabilizing vegetation.

The remarkable part isn't the building of structures to reduce or eliminate erosion, but that those solutions worked. For centuries men have been building groins, jetties, revetments and seawalls in a costly effort to fight off the eroding waves—usually in vain. In many coastal areas, the solutions put in place by men worsened the problem.

Today, many traditional ideas for saving coastal areas are clashing with a better understanding of erosion and a philosophy of working with, rather than against, the ocean. Behind the changing attitudes are the failures of the past and, more compelling, the world's rising sea level. Predictions vary, but there's no doubt the seas are rising and will continue to do so. If beachfront property owners don't believe it now, they will when there's water in their basements and waves are breaking over their porches.

Given that knowledge, some serious planning needs to be done. The traditional approach has long been epitomized by the Army Corps of Engineers: Build something! To their credit, even the Corps is starting to change their attitude.

Conservationists argue for a more enlightened approach, admitting that man-made structures often do more harm than good. They advocate either letting the sea take what it wants, or using newer techniques like the artificial replenishment of beaches, to protect property.

Using jetties, seawalls and other such structures to stop erosion often ignores the impermanent nature of the coastline. The two basic sources of beach sand–eroding bluffs and "littoral drift," or movement of sand by waves parallel to the coastline–can easily be disrupted by man-made structures. Groins and jetties, extending outward into the surf perpendicular to shore, are good for enlarging a beach up-current by trapping the littoral drift. But they can ruin the beach on the down-current side by eliminating a source of sand.

The Old Field Point Lighthouse
Photo © Robert G. Bachand

A classic catch-22 occurs when we try to stabilize eroding bluffs by building revetments, or walls, at their base. The protected bluffs can no longer supply sand to the beach, resulting in an eroding beach. The narrower beach can then no longer protect the bluffs, which are then pounded even harder by the waves and erode anyway.

Everything pales compared to the power of storms. On Long Island, it isn't so much the occasional hurricane as it is the less spectacular, but longer-lasting "nor'easters" that are the great levelers. Bluffs wash away, dunes and spits are created or destroyed, and inlets are cut. Most of the north shore of Long Island owes its form to the effects of storms, not gradual tidal action.

If all the dire forecasts of rising sea level bear fruit, major and minor coastal cities around the world will have to decide whether to fight for a few acres of land or let the sea take over what it will. Billions or trillions of dollars in waterfront real estate could be lost and some humility gained.

Out of this cloudy forecast could come one ray of hope for smart real estate speculators: Just think of the money to be made in buying "almost beachfront" property!

depth of 7 feet, but during new and full moons, the depth can be significantly reduced. Fishermen find these areas very rewarding, but cruising boats should stay away.

Depending on your course, your first landmark may be Old Field Point Light, with an alternating red and green flasher atop a 74-foot black skeleton tower. The old stone structure standing beside the new tower was originally built in 1823, but decommissioned in 1933 when the present light went into service. Old Field Point gong "11A," 0.5nm north of the point, is now green.

Coming from the east or northeast, other landmarks are the 60-foot-high sand bluffs of **Mount Misery** to the east of the entrance jetties. Also clearly visible are the three smokestacks of the Long Island Lighting Company power plant at the south end of Port Jefferson Harbor.

CAUTION: Be careful not to confuse these 3 stacks with the 4 stacks of the power plant at Northport, 12 miles to the west. The central stack has red and white horizontal bands: the other two are grey.

Following the new standard international buoy system, the Port Jefferson Harbor entrance buoy and whistle "PJ" which was black and red, has been repainted red and white and flashes Mo(A).

If the tide is running out, and the winds are out of the north (prevailing winds are from the southwest in the summer), rough seas can build up outside the jetties, with currents up to 2.6 knots. If you're under sail, you'll probably want to motor in. The old black can "1" **[WP-349]** is now a green 2.5sec flasher.

Once inside the jetties, you be in a well-protected, deep-water harbor. Flashing green 4sec bell "5" is now painted green to match the color of its strobe. From the jetties south to the first moorings marked on the chart there is a 12-mph speed limit, then 5-mph down to the docks at "Lower Landing" in **Port Jefferson.** The daily tidal range is 7.6 feet, so floating docks are the rule in Port Jefferson.

To the west of the entrance is a very popular anchorage behind **Old Field Point** and **Old Field Beach.** You're liable to find many rafting parties here on the weekends. You can make your turn to the west on either side of red nun "4," but be sure to make it sharp, in order to avoid the shoal about 500 yards south of the grassy point. Don't look at the chart and think there's plenty of water right off Old Field Beach at the entrance; many boats are hung up here every season.

You can go all the way up to the entrance of the grass-filled **Conscience Bay** at the Narrows. There is, however, no marked channel, so you will want to pick your way carefully. It is wisest to try it for the first time on a rising tide. The closer you get to Conscience Bay, the quieter it gets. You'll be well protected except in a southeasterly, due to the fetch across the harbor.

Although the chart does not give any soundings, **Mount Misery Cove** has an average depth of 11 to 15 feet at mlw.

If you draw a lot of water, your best route in is to round bell buoy "5" and approach from the south to avoid the shoals between the jetty and the buoy. You'll see boats anchored 100 yards east of the channel, but there's shoaling between them and the channel, so make sure you clear bell "5." Often you will see sailors leave the anchorage to the west, cross the channel and raise their sails in this area before heading out of the harbor. The cove offers good all-around protection, and the holding ground is okay. You will get the best grip on the sandy bottom with a danforth anchor.

If you are not interested in beaches or birds, and just want to get out of a blow, you can anchor anywhere out of the channel. There is plenty of room and deep water in the "Upper Landing" section of Port Jefferson Harbor.

 Shoreside and Emergency Services

Airport: MacArthur (516) 588-8062
Ambulance: 911
Bus: Suffolk County Transit (516) 360-5700
Coast Guard: Eatons Neck (516) 261-6868/6910 or VHF 16 or CB 9
Ferry: To Bridgeport, CT (516) 473-0286
Fire: 911 or (516) 941-4441
Harbormaster: (516) 331-3567
Hospital: John T. Mather Memorial (516) 473-1320
Police: 911 or (516) 451-4400
Radio Telephone: VHF 25, 26, 84; I.D.: NY Marine Operator;
VHF 86; I.D.: Mariphone Marine Operator;
VHF 28; I.D.: Riverhead Marine Operator;
VHF 27; I.D.: Bridgeport Marine Operator
Taxi: All-American (516) 736-2815 Omdurman (516) 732-0390
Tow Service: Saybrook Towing and Salvage, Old Saybrook, CT (203) 388-4065 or VHF 16
Train: Long Island Railroad (516) 234-LIRR

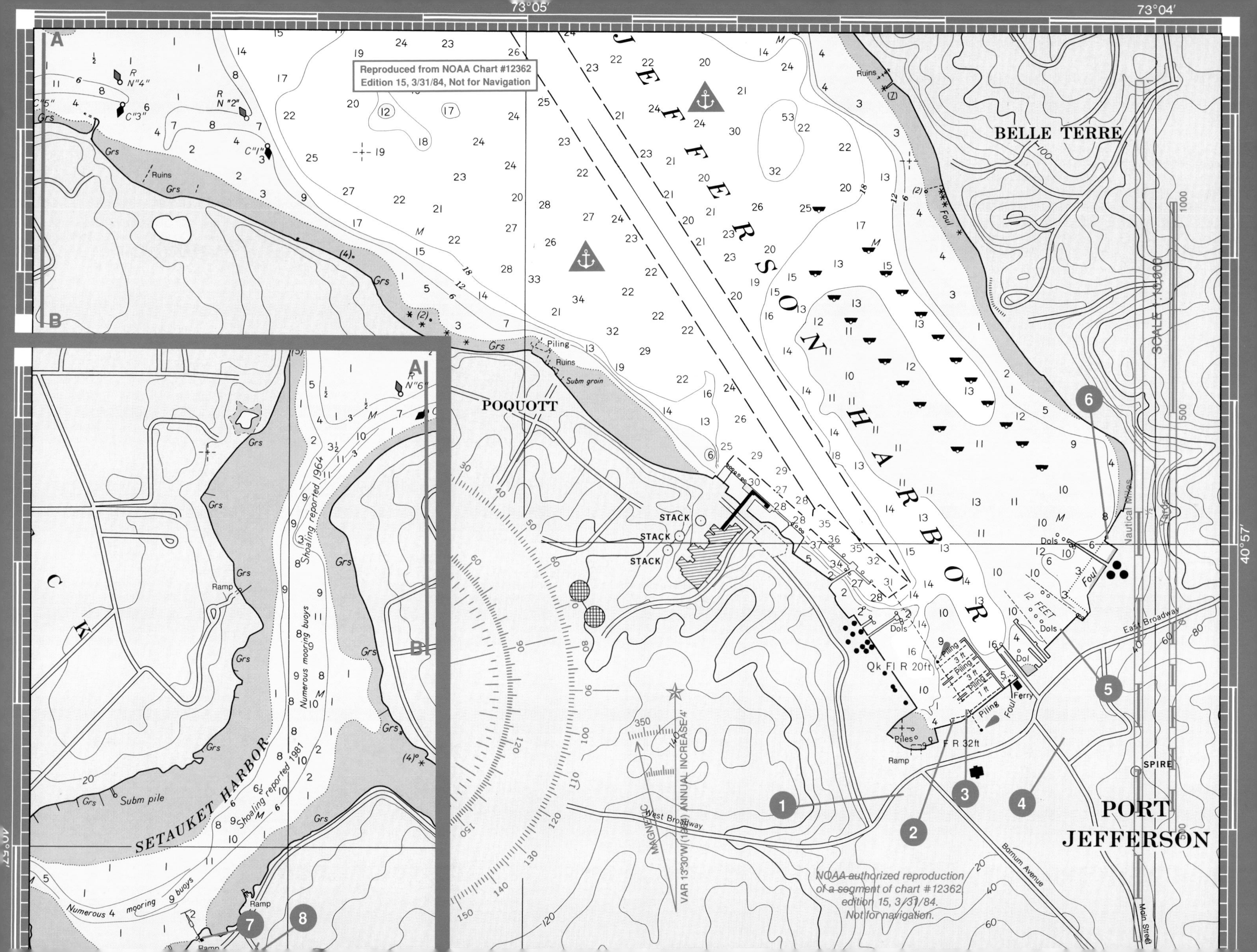

73°04'

BELLE TERRE

J E F F E R S O N   H A R B O R

J E F F E R S O N

POQUOTT

PORT
JEFFERSON

SPIRE

Main Street

Barnum Avenue

West Broadway

East Broadway

Ferry

FR 32ft

Qk Fl R 20ft

Ramp

Piles

Dols

12 FEET

Foul

STACK
STACK
STACK

VAR 13°30'W (1983) ANNUAL INCREASE 4'

MAGNETIC

SCALE 1:10,000
1000
500
Yards
Nautical Miles

Foul

Ruins

Grs

Subm groin

Piling

Ruins

Submpile

A
B
C
K

A
B
N "6"

SETAUKET HARBOR

Numerous mooring buoys

Shoaling reported 1964
Shoaling reported 1981

Numerous mooring buoys

Ramp
Ramp
Ramp

Grs

C "5"
R N "2"
R N "4"
C "3"

Ruins

1
2
3
4
5
6
7
8

Some Town, Some Meadow, Some Drowned

Back in the burly days of 1655 when Port Jefferson was a small town called "Drowned Meadow," few suspected it would ever be inundated with anything more than marsh and water. The 19th century, however, would find the place–by this time renamed Port Jefferson–built up into a thriving harbor flooded with whalers and coastal schooners, and the docks and shipyards so full they looked as though they were jammed with gorgeous wooden debris after a big storm.

"Port Jeff," as it is colloquially known, has kept a strong maritime heritage. The sails for *America,* the yacht that changed the name of the Louis Vuitton Cup to the "America's Cup," were made here by R.H. Wilson and Sons in 1856. Even before this, the great showman, P.T. Barnum, was a major backer of a burgeoning ferry service that began in the early 1800s between Port Jeff and Barnum's base of operations in Bridgeport, CT, 14 miles distant. Many of the ferries, including the original *MV Park City* (1898) were built right in Port Jeff. (Later on, after he built a house in town, Barnum wanted to overwinter his circus animals here; his plans were dashed, however, when the town rejected the idea–perhaps fearing the animals might drown out a few more meadows again.)

In the 1950s and '60s, Port Jeff became more and more industrial and less and less appealing. But about ten years ago, a major and remarkably successful revitalization effort began. The harbor has been cleaned up, the docks repaired and expanded, and the charm of the old fishing village preserved. The power plant on the southwest side of the harbor and the fuel tanks on both sides are a reminder of Port Jefferson's industrial past. (Most or all of the fuel tanks are scheduled for removal.) But Port Jeff also has interesting shops, excellent restaurants, and a first-class hotel and conference center, as well as most marine supplies and services, all on or within reach of the docks.

For the boater, Port Jefferson is one of the best harbors on the Sound, and offers great shelter. It's nearly 2 miles long, with deep water and good holding ground.

With the concentration of businesses around the waterfront and the daily sight of the huge ferries at the dock, Port Jeff presents an extremely busy façade. But walk a few blocks inland and you'll see that it's also a quiet and beautiful residential town.

The ferry from Bridgeport, CT, docking in Port Jefferson, NY.

Marine Facilities and Services	Phone	Number of Transient Berths	Number of Transient Moorings	Seasonal/Year-round	Largest Vessel Accommodation (ft)	Approach Depth (ft)	Marked Entry Channel	Dockside Depth (ft at MLW)	Gas/Diesel Fuel	Fuel Brand	Ramp/Dinghy Dock/Launch Service	Railway Lift: Capacity (tons)	Engine Repairs: Gas/Diesel	Propeller/Hull Repairs	Marine Supplies: Groceries/Bait/Ice	Pump-out Station	Showers/Laundromat	110V★ 220V▲ Maximum Amps	MasterCard/VISA/Diners/Amex	Restaurant/Snack Bar	Monitors VHF Channel
1 Gudzik Marine	(516) 473-0612			Y	45								GD	PH			S		MVA		
2 Port Jefferson Yacht Club	(516) 473-9864	2	20	S	38	4		4			R						S	★30	MV	R	68
3 Port Jefferson Town Marina	(516) 331-3567	10		S	42						R							★			16
4 Caraftis Fishing Station	(516) 473-2288			S		4	●	4				*MARINE SUPPLIES & MOTOR SALES*				I					
5 Danford's Inn at Bayles Dock (p. 346)	(516) 928-5200	75	30	S	300	11	●	10	GD				D		SI	●	SL	★▲125	MVAD	R	9
6 Setauket Yacht Club	(516) 473-9850		20	S	56	25	●	10			R				SI		S	★▲			68
7 Setauket Harbor Boat Basin *	(516) 941-9681																				
8 Marine Center Setauket	(516) 941-4640		5	Y	38	4	●	3	G		R		GD	PH	SI			★	MV		

Information in these listings is provided by the facilities themselves. An asterisk (*) indicates that the facility did not respond to our most recent requests for information.

DANFORDS

Inn, Marina, Executive Conference Center
Located at Bayles Dock
Port Jefferson, Long Island, New York

BON APPÉTIT

Danfords superb restaurant. Breakfast, lunch and dinner on the harborfront.

A LUXURY COUNTRY INN

80 rooms and suites and balconied waterviews. Fireplaces in selected suites.

THE SHOPS AT MARINERS END

Interesting shops and unhurried browsing — from Icelandic sweaters, antiques, to marine supplies and boutiques. Boaters' amenities in the hotel lobby gift shop.

BAYLES DOCK AT DANFORDS

75-slip full service transient marina. Tie up and relax.

HISTORIC PORT JEFFERSON VILLAGE

Danfords at Bayles Dock is located on the Harborfront of the charming village nestled on the north shore of Long Island. Boutiques, antique shops, live theatre, and galleries are all just a pleasant 5-minute stroll from Danfords Inn.

DANFORDS BUSINESS CONFERENCE & SEMINAR CENTER

Long Island's newest and most up-to-date business center and Inn.

"THE ONLY THING WE OVERLOOK IS THE HARBOR" SM

DANFORDS
25 EAST BROADWAY
PORT JEFFERSON, N.Y. 11777
516-928-5200
800-332-6367
Monitor Channels 16 & 9
FAX (516) 928-3598

Port Jefferson is a feisty town, lively with special events throughout the year, and if you're intent on timing your visit to match any of these fêtes, the Chamber of Commerce (516) 473-1414 will tell you what's happening when. Located on West Broadway next to the ferry slips, the Chamber gives out a free map and brochure for a walking tour of town, including the commercial and culinary attractions. The map is also available at the ferry terminal.

Every Memorial Day weekend Port Jefferson brings out the colors and celebrates the coming of summer with a street fair; on July 4 there are fireworks and a parade. Call the Chamber of Commerce for more information.

Apart from the happenings, Port Jeff is more of a browser's paradise. Shopping and eating are a joy to do here, with compelling shops and restaurants to suit most tastes Respite from a day's indulgence can be had at Theater Three (516) 928-9100 on Main Street, one of Long Island's better-known repertory theaters.

Another map, for a walking tour of the old ship captain's houses and the Barnum house, can be found at the Historical Society of Greater Port Jefferson (516) 473-2665 (or the Chamber of Commerce). At the Society's Museum on Prospect Street, a few blocks from the harbor, there is a charming collection of paintings by William M. Davis, a 19th-century genre painter from Port Jefferson. If you'd rather stroll by historical places than visit them, a walk down East Main Street is certainly in order.

Many of the restaurants in town offer takeout, so you can enjoy a good meal on your boat without having to prepare it yourself. If you want to work for your dinner, the party fishing boat *Port Jeff Ace* (516) 744-1626 makes daily excursions into the Sound for blues and whatever else is biting.

 Where To Eat

It's only natural that a place as historical as Port Jefferson should have an establishment as quaint as Danford's Inn (516) 928-5000 at Bayles Dock, right next to the ferry landing. Danford's is a sizeable and comfortable stopping place filled with antiques and a fine restaurant which

Nearby Setauket was settled in 1655 by a small group of emigres from Connecticut, and for a long time was part of the Hartford (Connecticut) Colony. Setauket, like other Long Island coastal towns, was active in fishing and shipbuilding, but really distinguished itself by spying.

After the capture and execution of Nathan Hale during the American Revolution, the need for better intelligence and surveillance of the British became clear. Setauket Patriots set up a spy ring right under the noses of a group of local Tories. Longboats made midnight excursions up and down the Sound to check on British troop movements. Messages were signaled to other Patriots by a local woman who strung a certain number and combination of red or black petticoats and white handkerchiefs on a clothesline.

These days, Setauket is like its position in Port Jefferson Harbor—tucked away and secluded. On warm, sunny days, laundry hangs in backyards, but signals nothing save that this is a peaceful town with a few meadows, some still drowned.

CRUISING BY RAIL

Many boaters spend their winters dreaming of distant ports, but they actually spend their summer weekends very much like a yo-yo: going out one day, anchoring, and coming back to their marina the next. When the two- or three-week vacation rolls around at last, they take off hell-bent for distant ports. Long Island Sound cruisers tend to shoot for the islands–Block or Nantucket or the Vineyard–or Newport, trying to cover long distances to compensate for their frustrations the rest of the time.

Fortunately, there is an alternative to the yo-yo routine, allowing the cruiser to travel far and wide on Long Island Sound anytime, without missing a day of work. The agent of this freedom is the iron horse; fortunately, Long Island Sound is well served by the Metro-North Railroad in Connecticut and by the Long Island Railroad on the Island.

Especially in the western Sound, you can cruise north or south on Saturday, anchor overnight, leave the boat in a local marina on Sunday, and take the train home. Come the next weekend, your boat will be waiting for you, ready for the next leg of your journey.

Here's an example. I'm a member of Shattemuc Yacht Club in Ossining, New York. We launch from there, sail down the Hudson with a favorable tide, and try to catch the flood at the Battery to go up the East River through Hell Gate. We usually manage to tie up at Louie's in Port Washington for dinner, and having made previous arrangements at a friendly yacht club, we leave the boat until the next weekend.

The harbors we select are served by good transportation. On Long Island, they include Hempstead Harbor, Oyster Bay, Northport, and Port Jefferson. In Connecticut, we make an intermediate stop at Greenwich and leave the boat at Stamford or Norwalk. Both are just a short taxi ride to the railroad station. Westport and Southport are also convenient to the train, despite limited marina services.

In Bridgeport, you'll find an unexpected harbor and convenient train service. One of my favorite spots is Johnson's Creek, at the starboard entrance. It's hidden from view by the railroad bridge, which opens on the half hour. You might find a slip at one of the yacht clubs there. (Slips are also available at Black Rock Harbor, which is also served by the Bridgeport train station–a short taxi ride away). The Bridgeport-Port Jefferson Ferry is convenient for traveling between the two towns; its docks are a short walk to the Bridgeport railroad station on one end, and an inexpensive cab ride to the Port Jeff railroad station on the other.

It's not necessary to hop harbor-to-harbor on the Connecticut shore; we frequently cross the Sound, and even in light airs we find no difficulty getting into a Long Island marina in time to catch a train to Manhattan. This

The author takes the helm.

allows us to try other delightful anchorages to the east: Charles Island at Milford, the Thimble Islands, and Duck Island at Westbrook.

Back on Long Island, Hempstead Harbor has the Glen Cove Yacht Club and a number of marinas. Oyster Bay, featuring a beautiful and completely protected anchorage, is full of rafting parties in the summer. If you get a slip or mooring at one of the facilities, the train station is practically right on the waterfront. The next important harbor–and one that gets a lot of clubs rafting up–is Northport, interconnected with Centerport and Huntington harbors. You can catch a train at Northport or Huntington.

No matter where you're based in Long Island Sound, you can enjoy sailing east or west anytime, hitting all the stops along the way. At night, rafted or anchored, sitting in the cockpit with drink in hand, the setting sun brings peace and satisfaction. At the end of the season, when there's a nip in the air and the day wanes early, you can head for home and eagerly await the next season.

Take my advice. Leave the yo-yo routine to the racers.

I. Martin Spier is a member of several local and international cruising clubs, and has sailed in New England, Europe, and the Caribbean for 50 years. A Manhattan resident and engineer, he holds patents for a permanent antifouling system and a high-performance keel.

predates the inn. This waterfront restaurant serves up American and seafood specialties, and (our readers tell us) a terrific Sunday brunch. Docking is available for patrons at the marina.

Across from the ferry terminal is the Steamroom (516) 928-6690. Its fast-food atmosphere is the setting for the best fried seafood, steamers and boiled lobsters in this town. So what if the big servings here boost your cholesterol to new heights—this place is good. A specialty is the "Onion Loaf," a golden nest of onion rings fried in batter to a crisp heavenly perfection.

A couple of blocks from the harbor is Savories (516) 331-4747, with its Northern Italian and French cuisine. Another favorite is the Elks Hotel Restaurant (516) 473-0086, with a widely varied "soup to nuts" menu. Also in town, you'll find East of Athens (516) 473-9007, with a Greek menu, and Ho Kee (516) 331-5335, a small chinese restaurant.

If you want to cook for yourself you'll find some excellent fish markets and grocery stores in Port Jefferson, all near the waterfront.

 Navigation and Anchorages

Use NOAA Charts 12362 (1:10,000), 12364 (1:40,000), and 12354 (1:80,000). Use tide tables for Bridgeport. High tide at Port Jefferson is 6 minutes later; low tide is 5 minutes later. Mean tidal range is 7.0 feet.

For information on the approaches to Port Jefferson Harbor and anchorages in the northern part of the harbor, please see the preceding chapter on Old Field Point and Mount Misery Cove.

The marinas and yacht clubs in Port Jefferson can accommodate overnight stays, and Danford's at Bayles Dock, the large new marina on the east side of the harbor, is the only completely transient marina on the Sound. The harbormaster can be reached at the Port Jefferson Town Marina.

Nothing could be easier than anchoring in **Port Jefferson Harbor,** though it may be crowded at times. You can drop your own hook anywhere outside the channel. Launch service is offered by Diesel Marine Service (516) 331-2049 or VHF 16, which also has mechanics on duty.

Don't go near the **Bridgeport-Port Jefferson ferry slip.** While it may look tempting for a quick run into town when the ferry is away, you'll have a horde of angry

crewmen yelling at you, and risk having your boat crushed when the ferry comes back. While on the subject of the ferries, give them and the barges a wide berth. They are not double-ended, and so must turn around inside the harbor before heading out.

Setauket Harbor is a snug but shallow anchorage between Tinkers Point and Strongs Neck, reached by a narrow, crooked channel marked by privately maintained seasonal buoys. All of the old black channel cans have been painted green in accordance with the new international standard. Unfortunately, Setauket is apt to be crowded with local moored boats. Deep-draft boats should enter only at high tide, and keep faithfully to the channel. Strongs Neck is all private, but you can get gas at the long pier and ramp at the south end of Setauket Harbor.

If you decide to sample **Setauket Harbor,** you'll be pleased with the water's calmness and cleanliness. Watch out for clammers and the Bridgeport-Port Jefferson ferry, especially when you're leaving the harbor.

 Shoreside and Emergency Services

Airport: MacArthur (516) 588-8062
Ambulance: 911
Bus: Suffolk County Transit (516) 360-5700
Coast Guard: Eatons Neck (516) 261-6868/6910
 or VHF 16
Ferry: To Bridgeport, CT (516) 473-0286
Fire: 911 or (516) 941-4441
Harbormaster: (516) 331-3567 or VHF 16
Hospital: John T. Mather Memorial (516) 473-1320
Police: 911 or (516) 451-4400
Radio Telephone: VHF 25, 26, 84; I.D.: NY
 Marine Operator;
 VHF 86; I.D.: Mariphone
 Marine Operator;
 VHF 28; I.D.: Riverhead
 Marine Operator;
 VHF 27; I.D.: Bridgeport
 Marine Operator
Taxi: All-American (516) 736-2815
 Omdurman (516) 732-0390
Tow Service: Saybrook Towing and Salvage,
 Old Saybrook, CT (203) 388-4065
 or VHF 16
Train: Long Island Railroad (516) 234-LIRR ◆

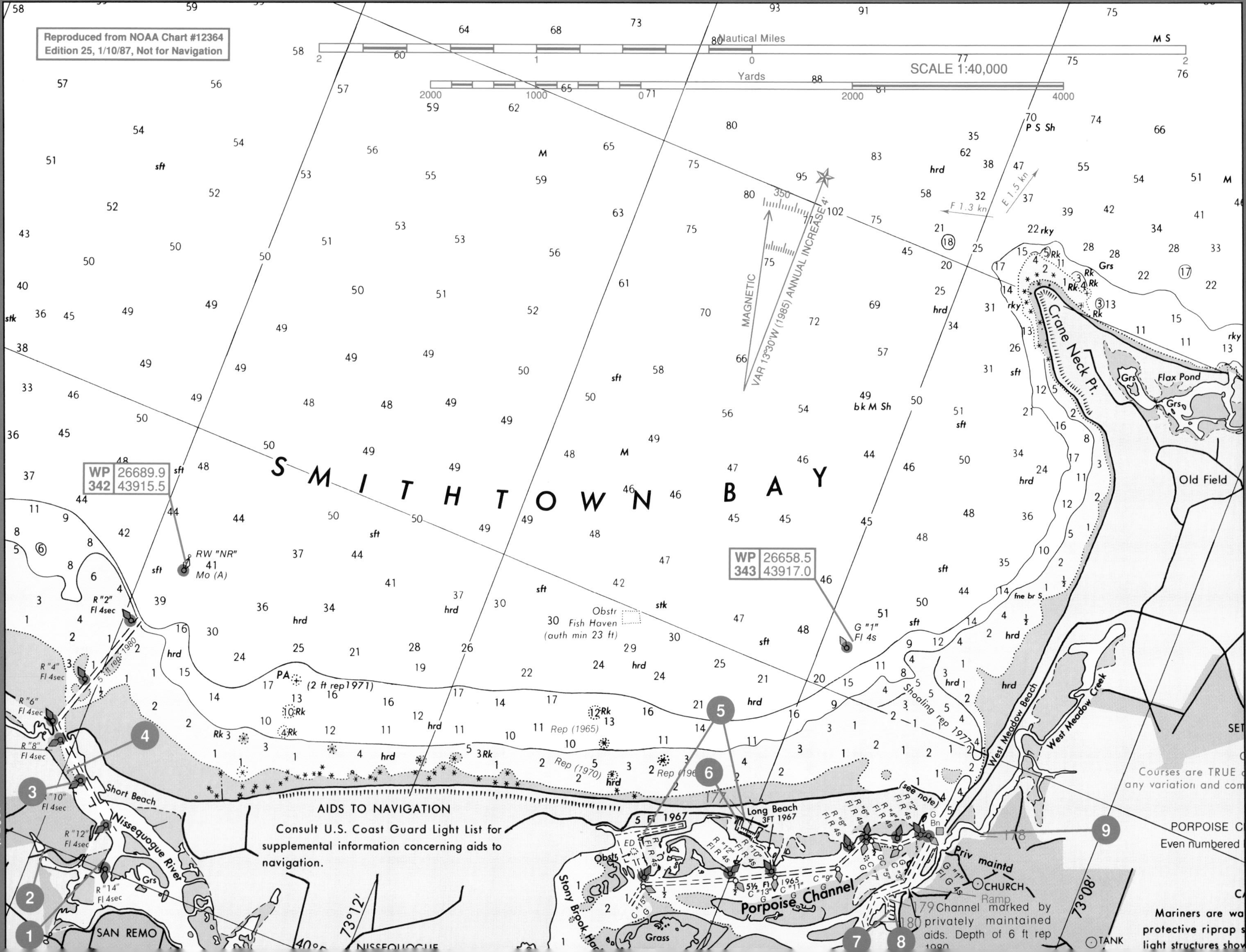
Reproduced from NOAA Chart #12364
Edition 25, 1/10/87, Not for Navigation
73°14′
73°12′
73°10′
40°56′
40°54′
40°58′
Nautical Miles
Yards
SCALE 1:40,000
SMITHTOWN BAY
MAGNETIC
VAR 13°30′W (1985) ANNUAL INCREASE 4′
WP 342 26689.9 43915.5
WP 343 26658.5 43917.0
RW "NR" Mo (A)
G "1" Fl 4s
Obstr Fish Haven (auth min 23 ft)
Crane Neck Pt.
Flax Pond
Old Field
West Meadow Beach
West Meadow Creek
Long Beach
Porpoise Channel
Stony Brook Har
Short Beach
Nissequogue River
SAN REMO
Grass
CHURCH
TANK
Priv maintd
Shoaling rep 1977
Rep (1965)
Rep (1970)
(2 ft rep 1971)
AIDS TO NAVIGATION
Consult U.S. Coast Guard Light List for supplemental information concerning aids to navigation.
Channel marked by privately maintained aids. Depth of 6 ft rep 1980
Courses are TRUE
any variation and com
PORPOISE C
Even numbered
Mariners are wa
protective riprap s
light structures show

Smithtown Bay and Stony Brook Harbor

Planned Beauty Meets the Bureaucratic Beast

Stony Brook's Colonial-style village is one of the most beautiful places on Long Island Sound. While the character of many towns can be traced to the influence of a particular group of settlers or to a particular industry, rarely will you find a town that owes so much of its present form to one person. In the case of Stony Brook, that one man was Ward Melville, who made his fortune from the line of Thom McCann shoe stores that he created, and spent it on such good works as the Museums at Stony Brook, the State University of New York at Stony Brook, and Stony Brook itself.

The Smithtown Long Beach Marina on the Porpoise Channel in Stony Brook Harbor, NY.

Melville wanted a classic New England town to call home, so he donated all the land on which the town is centered, putting into the deed of gift many restrictions on what the buildings could look like and what could be done with the land.

Mr. Melville also contributed much of the cash used to establish the State University of New York at Stony Brook: he wanted to build a classic ivy-covered college. Unfortunately he died before the plans for the college were complete, and with him out of the way, the state bureaucrats built what they wanted, a gargantuan and–it is universally agreed–strikingly ugly campus. No one in Stony Brook, least of all Mr. Melville's widow, has ever forgiven the state. The only good thing that can be said for the campus is that the medical school is so big it can be seen all the way across the Sound, making a good landmark for mariners headed for Smithtown Bay.

 What To See and Do

Stony Brook is so beautiful that just a walk around town is reason enough to visit. On the short walk from the harbor to the center of town you will go through a park that follows the millstream and is filled with wading birds and ducks.

On your way you will pass many fine old houses and the Hercules Pavilion, where you will see a large wooden figurehead of the Greek hero that was taken from the USS *Ohio*, a 74-gun ship of the line that served in the U.S. Navy from 1820 to 1880. The figurehead was originally displayed

Marine Facilities and Services		Number of Transient Berths	Number of Transient Moorings	Seasonal/Year-round	Largest Vessel Accommodation (in feet)	Marked Entry Channel	Approach Depth (in feet)	Dockside Depth in feet at MLW	Gas/Diesel Fuel	Fuel Brand	Ramp Dinghy Dock/Launch Service	Railway/Lift: Capacity (in tons)	Propeller/Hull Repairs	Engine Repairs: Gas/Diesel	Pump-out Station	Showers/Laundromat	Marine Supplies/Groceries/Bait/Ice	110V ★ 220V ▲ Maximum Amps	MasterCard/VISA/Diners Club American Express	Restaurant/Snack Bar	Monitors VHF Channel
❶ Kings Park Yacht Club	(516) 269-9723							*PRIVATE CLUB - MEMBERS ONLY*													
❷ Nissequogue Yacht Club								*PRIVATE CLUB - MEMBERS ONLY*													
❸ Canoe/Kayak Rentals	(516) 269-9761			S			●	3	*SMALL BOAT RENTALS*												
❹ Kings Park Bluff								*TOWN DOCK/RAMP - RESIDENTS ONLY*													
❺ Smithtown Long Beach Marina	(516) 862-6663	25		Y	50	●	3.5	8	G	GUL	R				●	S	GB	★50		S	16
❻ Smithtown Bay Yacht Club	(516) 584-9680							*PRIVATE CLUB - MEMBERS ONLY*													
❼ Stony Brook Boat Works	(516) 751-1230			Y	35	●	3	6			R	14	PH	GD		S		★30			9
❽ Stony Brook Yacht Club	(516) 751-9873			Y	50	●	2	4	GD		R					S	I		MV		9
❾ Wells Shipyard	(516) 751-2082			Y	45		2	2				L25				S		★			

Information in these listings is provided by the facilities themselves. An asterisk (*) indicates that the facility did not respond to our most recent requests for information.

across from the Canoe Place Inn at the Shinnecock Canal before being brought to Stony Brook.

There are a number of shops clustered around the green and an excellent country inn and restaurant. The post office at the head of the green has a mechanical eagle over the door that flaps its wings every hour on the hour.

The main attraction in town is The Museums at Stony Brook (516) 751-0066, a complex that includes a working 1751 grist mill, a blacksmith shop, extensive collections of decoys, and early American paintings. The centerpiece of the Museums, however, is its amazing carriage collection, now 250 strong, housed in a spanking-new 3-level building. The core of the collection was donated by–you guessed it–Ward Melville.

The Three Village Historical Society (516) 928-9534 has available a brochure and map of the historic sights to see in Old Field, Setauket, and Stony Brook.

A variety of events go on in town over the course of the year, including a horse show at the fairgrounds on West Meadow Beach on Labor Day weekend. Call (516) 451-6100 for more information about these and other events.

The Museum of Long Island Natural Sciences at SUNY Stony Brook (516) 632-8230 is free and designed for kids. Hands-on exhibits and programs introduce youngsters to dinosaurs, glaciers, marine animals, and the constellations; a fine place to visit in bad weather. Since the museum isn't immediately accessible from the harbor, take a cab.

 ## Where To Eat

Hungry seafarers boating in this area don't have far to walk to sate their appetites. Across the street from the marinas are the Three Village Inn (516) 751-0555, serving an American and seafood selection, and the Harbor View (516) 689-7755, with its Continental menu.

For the boater on the go there is also a sandwich shop called The Brook House (516) 751-4617.

 ## Navigation and Anchorages

Use NOAA Charts 12364 (1:40,000), 12363 (1:80,000), and 12353 (1:80,000). Use tide tables for Bridgeport. High tide at Smithtown Bay is 7 minutes later; low tide is 10 minutes later. Multiply by 0.9 for height at high or low water. Mean tidal range is 6.4 feet.

Smithtown Bay stretches for 10.5nm by boat between Crane Neck Point and Eatons Neck. The entrance to Stony Brook Harbor is 1.8nm south of Crane Neck Point and 8.1nm east of the 4 stacks of the LILCO power plant at Northport, the best landmark for boaters heading here. The four stacks of the Northport power plant line up almost exactly on a bearing of due north and south magnetic.

From the red flashing 4sec bell "2" **[WP-363]** at the southern tip of Middle Ground (Stratford Shoal), a course of about 225°m will take you past Crane Neck Point. To the

south will be the green 4sec flasher "1" **[WP-343]**, your main marker into the harbor.

Strong currents produce tide rips around both Eatons Neck and Crane Neck points, so give each plenty of room. The large boulders in this area play host to a variety of marine life, so much so that divers consider **Crane Neck** one of the best scuba sites in the western Sound. The waters off Crane Neck Point are a favorite haunt of fishermen in search of flounder and bass. A good summer anchorage, sheltered from easterly winds, can be found in the bay a mile south of Crane Neck Point.

Crane Neck Point is unmarked and can obscure the light on Old Field Point. Some older charts show a cluster of four privately maintained white and orange obstruction buoys 1.1nm northeast of Crane Neck Point. If you're hoping to use this cluster of buoys as a landmark, don't. They've been removed.

About a mile west of the green 4sec flasher "1" **[WP-343]** marking the entrance to **Stony Brook Harbor,** there's a man-made "fish haven" where you may see a few anglers. The artificial reef was built in 1978 for use by SUNY marine biologists studying reef-building. The harbormaster can show you a diagram of its components–sunken barges, various other boats, and *14,000* tires. It's not much used for research anymore, but is a great spot to find blackfish, porgies, flounder, bluefish, weakfish, and lobsters–which love testing their claws on the tires.

Stony Brook Harbor can be a nasty navigational problem. If you haven't been here before, don't expect a serene trip into peaceable marshland. The shoaling is terrible, exacerbated by a vigorous current. It's worse during a full or new moon, with an outgoing tide.

Before battling a current or negotiating the shallows, you will have to find the harbor entrance, which is no picnic either, as it is poorly marked. NOAA charts indicate a green daymark at the harbor entrance; there isn't one, unless you call a broken plaque atop a meager stake a daymark. The harbor must be entered over a bar extending out almost a mile from land. At mean low water, the depth is about 3 feet, and a fresh nor'wester can wipe out most of that.

CAUTION: *The tidal range is 7 feet, so getting in or out is easy enough as long as you do it within 3 hours on either side of high water.*

From the green 4sec flasher "1" **[WP-343],** steer east to the first of five uncharted cans; then southeast to the last can off **West Meadow Beach;** then turn south into the harbor. You may see some local boaters passing on the inside of the green cans with their hull on a step, indicating that the sand flat extending east out of Long Beach has shoaled further into the bay than the chart indicates. Follow them at your own risk.

CAUTION: *This row of markers can cause considerable confusion. The most common mistake is made by boaters* *who leave these buoys too far to port and run aground. The channel is narrow and the buoys are right on its edge, so hug them closely. You can almost touch the sandy beach on your port side when entering. Also, the buoys are pulled between November 30 and April 30, so if you're going in during the winter, you'll really need to keep your wits about you.*

Your problems aren't over once you have made the entrance. If the tide is going out, you've come at the wrong time, since a 3- to 4-knot current starts collecting as soon as you pass the half-baked daymark to port. Navigating these shallows can be tricky even if they're marked, because the current can easily push you to the shore. As in Napeague Harbor near Montauk, it might help to have someone at the bow keeping a look-out for the bottom, because the shallowness sometimes renders the depth sounder ineffective.

The channel divides after the last can, one part going south toward the town, and the other, the **Porpoise Channel,** heading west behind **Long Beach.** Heading south, you'll come to the town ramp next to the Stony Brook Yacht Club, which can accommodate a few visitors at a float.

You can anchor anywhere out of the channel, but beware of shoaling, especially at low tide. You will find more room to anchor farther west in the **Porpoise Channel,** which is marked by a row of red 4sec flashers and green cans. All the channel marker lights, formerly 1-2 mile, have been upgraded to 3-5 mile intensity; they are also removed over the winter.

You can also anchor in the southern end of **Stony Brook Harbor,** but keep an eye on the depth sounder and come in at high water because of the shallow entrance, which begins at can "15." There is 6 feet of water in parts of the anchorage. (You will also see some pretty sizeable sailboats here, but rest assured that the water is deep enough for their 5-foot-plus drafts only in very narrow places, most of which are accessible only at high tide.)

Throughout the harbor there is a 5-mph speed limit, radar-enforced. The presence of jetskiers in the harbor can make the channel even more dangerous. The town is hoping to solve the problem by building a jetski ramp on the Sound side of **Long Beach,** between the marina docks and the boat basin.

Not all of the marinas are a short walk from town, unless you're at the marinas on the southern channel. If you've gone westwards to, say, the Smithtown Long Beach Marina, you'll either have to take your boat or a taxi to get groceries.

The **Nissequogue River** is 4.5nm by boat west of Stony Brook and separated from it by a high sand bluff. The Northport Basin is about 5.2nm by boat to the east of the Nissequogue River.

As at Stony Brook, shoals extend almost three-quarters of a mile offshore, so you must stick to the dredged channel. The channel runs for about 1.4nm, with about 5

feet of water and strong tidal currents. There is a town dock with a 10-minute tie-up limit, but there are no guest moorings or services available. Good anchorages can be found in the river, however. The launching ramp is for residents only. A prominent landmark is the red brick, green-roofed buildings of the SUNY hospital complex.

The **Nissequogue** is a very beautiful river, and popular with canoeists. Would-be paddlers can rent canoes near the town dock. Farther south, next to the huge SUNY hospital complex, are two small private yacht clubs. The extensive salt marshes surrounding the river offer refuge to a great deal of wildlife, particularly wading birds and their favorite hors d'oeuvres, mosquitoes. The harbor is very well protected, but big enough that some onshore winds develop in the valley, making for nice small-boat sailing among the many grassy islands. Keep an eye on the changing tides or you may find yourself sailing nowhere fast in the mud. Clamming is not allowed.

☎ Shoreside and Emergency Services

Airport: MacArthur (516) 588-8062
Ambulance: 911
Bus: Suffolk County Transit (516) 360-5700
Coast Guard: Eatons Neck (516) 261-6868/6910
         or VHF 16
Fire: 911 or (516) 751-3434 (Emergency) or 751-0460
Harbormaster: (516) 360-7643 or VHF 16
Hospital: Community Hospital of Western Suffolk
         (516) 979-9800
         University Hospital (516) 689-8333
Police: 911 or (516) 451-4400
         Suffolk Marine 10 (516) 673-8167 or VHF 16
Radio Telephone: VHF 25, 26, 84; I.D.: NY
            Marine Operator;
            VHF 86; I.D.: Mariphone
            Marine Operator;
            VHF 28; I.D.: Riverhead
            Marine Operator;
            VHF 27; I.D.: Bridgeport
            Marine Operator
Taxi: Lindy's Taxi (516) 265-2727
      Tootsie Taxi (516) 751-1300
Tow Service: Sea Tow Services, Northport, NY
         (516) 754-1545 or VHF 16
Train: Long Island Railroad (516) 234-LIRR   ◆

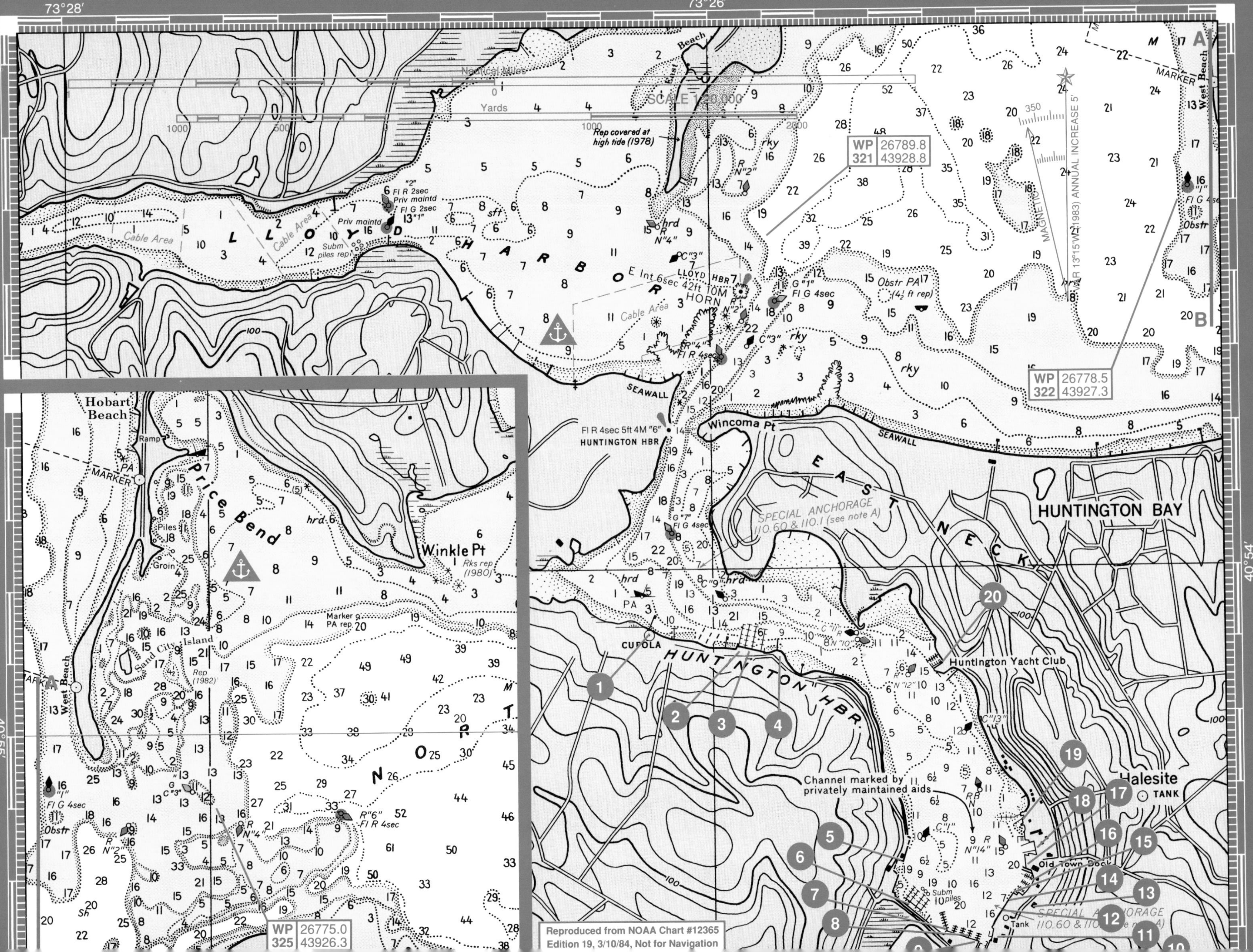

HUNTINGTON BAY

HUNTINGTON YACHT CLUB

EAST NECK

HUNTINGTON HBR.

Halesite

TANK

Old Town Dock

SPECIAL ANCHORAGE (110.60 & 110.1 see note A)

Channel marked by privately maintained aids

CUPOLA

West Beach

MARKER

MAGNETIC VAR 13°15'W (1983) ANNUAL INCREASE 5'

WP 322 26678.5 43927.3

WP 321 26789.8 43928.8

SCALE 1:20,000

Nautical Miles

Yards

EAST HARBOR

Wincoma Pt

SEAWAIL

SEAWALL

Rep covered at high high tide (1978)

Cable Area

LLOYD HARBOR

LLOYD NECK

Priv maintd

FI R 2sec

FI G 2sec

Priv maintd

Subm piles rep

Cable Area

LLOYD HBR 7 6sec 42ft 10M

HORN

HUNTINGTON HBR

FI R 4sec 5ft 4M "6"

FI R 4sec

15 Obstr PA 17

G "9" FI G 4sec

Winkle Pt

Rks rep (1980)

Price Bend

Hobart Beach

West Beach

MARKER

Club Island

Ramp

Groin

Piles rep

Marker 9 PA rep 20

WP 325 26775.0 43926.3

FI R 6sec

FI R 4sec

Reproduced from NOAA Chart #12365

73°26'

73°28'

40°54'

40°55'

Legacies From a Western Harbor

From a few hundred miles up in the atmosphere, Lloyd Neck and Eatons Neck must look like bulges of land trying to pare themselves away from Long Island. In fact, the opposite is true. Ages ago, both necks were a group of four separate islands, until the combination of tide, currents, and man connected them to Long Island.

Mariners acquainted with these waters also know that the strong tides can just as easily attach a boat to the land, or at least upon the reefs extending offshore. Huntington Bay has played host to many nautical disasters in the past, the worst of which occurred just before Christmas in 1811: 60 ships–some say 100–were lost in zero-degree weather. The most infamous disaster, however, was the wreck of the steamer *Lexington* in 1840, when 120 people were lost in an inferno, later immortalized in a Currier and Ives print.

The Coast Guard Station at Eatons Neck (foreground) and the towers of the LILCO plant at Northport, NY.

Marine Facilities and Services

#	Facility	Phone	Transient Berths	Transient Moorings	Seasonal/Year-round	Largest Vessel (ft)	Marked Entry Channel	Approach Depth (ft)	Dockside Depth MLW (ft)	Gas/Diesel Fuel	Fuel Brand	Ramp/Dinghy Dock/Launch	Railway/Lift Capacity (tons)	Propeller/Hull Repairs	Engine Repairs Gas/Diesel	Pump-out Station	Showers/Laundromat	Marine Supplies/Groceries/Bait/Ice	110V★/220V▲ Max Amps	Credit Cards	Restaurant/Snack Bar	VHF
1	Castle Cove Marina	(516) 673-3299		10	S	40	●	10	10			R		PH	GD			I	★			68
2	Harbor Boating Club	(516) 351-9312					●	15		*PRIVATE CLUB - MEMBERS ONLY*												
3	Wyncote Club	(516) 351-9521	2	2	S	42	●	14	3	G	TEX	DL					S	I	★20			
4	Dornic Marina	(516) 385-0622	1	15	Y	50	●	18	12			RDL	L15	PH	GD			BI	▲		S	16
5	**West Shore Marina (p. 358)**	**(516) 427-3444**	50		Y	125	●	20	20				L35	PH	GD	●	SL	SIG	★▲100		S	16
6	Mill Dam Marina and Ramp	(516) 351-3255			Y		●	6	6			RL										16
7	Willis Marine Center	(516) 421-3400	20	15	Y	60	●	15	14	GD	TEX	L	L20	PH	GD		S		★110	MVA		
8	**Knutson Marine Supply (p. 357)**	**(516) 673-4144**			Y		●	*MARINE RETAIL*													MVA		
9	Spencer Sails	(516) 549-3639			Y			*YACHT SAIL MANUFACTURERS & REPAIRS*														
10	Sport Boats	(516) 421-3717			Y	26	●	12	8	*BOAT SALES AND REPAIRS*							S			MV		
11	Coneys Marina	(516) 421-3366		10	Y	42	●	16	8			L	L35	PH	GD		S	S		MV		9
12	Tee T.'s Landing	(516) 421-1330			Y	60	●	8	8	*RESTAURANT*										MVA	R	
13	**Long Island Yacht Services (p. 361)**	**(516) 549-4687**	3	2	Y	40	●	6	6			R	L20	PH	GD	●						
14	Huntington Town Docks	(516) 351-3255			S			5	5	*3 HR. TEMPORARY TIE-UP*												
15	Ketewomoke Yacht Club	(516) 351-9762		2	S	45	●	15	8					D			S					16
16	Halesite Marina	(516) 351-3255			Y		●	6	6							●						16
17	Huntington Town Docks	(516) 351-3255			S			5	5	*3 HR. TEMPORARY TIE-UP*												
18	Knutson's Marina	(516) 673-0700	6	6	Y	120	●	8	8	GD	TEX	R	L35	PH	GD		S	SIG	★▲60		R	9
19	Knutson's West Marina	(516) 549-7842		25	Y	80	●	15	10	GD	TEX		L50	PH	GD		S	I	★▲50	MVA		16
20	Huntington Yacht Club	(516) 427-4949			S	70	●	10	5	GD	MOB	L					S	I	▲50	MVA	R	9

Information in these listings is provided by the facilities themselves. An asterisk (*) indicates that the facility did not respond to our most recent requests for information.

Eatons Neck Light is the second oldest lighthouse in New York. Built in 1799 to forestall such shipwrecks, the light rises 73 feet above the ground and 144 feet above the water.

Not only the waters were turbulent here. During the Revolutionary War, anti-British sentiment began to reach its boiling point when Huntington was among the first towns to proclaim a Declaration of Rights and to burn King George in effigy.

In 1776 Nathan Hale landed here on his way to uncover British plans for the Battle of Long Island, but was captured almost immediately and hanged for spying. His most precious legacy is his final statement: "I only regret that I have but one life to give for my country." (By comparison, the most significant British bequest seems to be Target Rock on East Fort Point, which was used for target practice by the British Navy.)

Another, no less patriotic man has left a similar eloquence. Walt Whitman, the "Bard of Huntington," was born in West Hills, just south of the village, in 1819. Aside from crafting intense poetry, he also founded *The Long Islander,* a newspaper still being published. Its circulation may not reach past Huntington, or Long Island for that matter, but its founder's poems have gone well beyond that.

★ What To See and Do

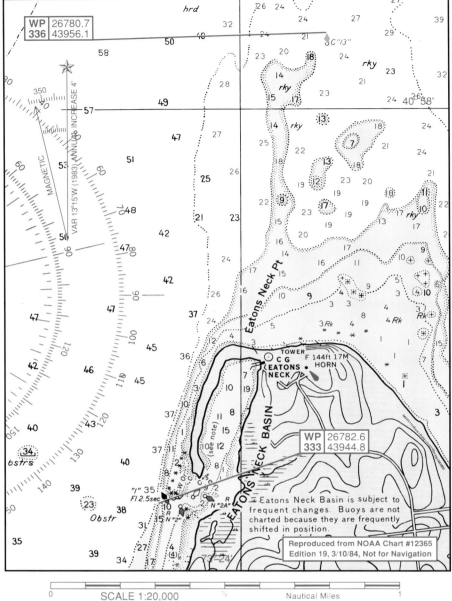

Reproduced from NOAA Chart #12365
Edition 19, 3/10/84, Not for Navigation

SCALE 1:20,000   Nautical Miles

Huntington and the surrounding areas are packed with museums, restaurants, and shops. If you'd like to go water-skiing, swimming, fishing, or exploring in your dinghy, there's plenty of options in the area, but not in Huntington Harbor itself.

Among the attractions in Huntington is Walt Whitman's Birthplace (516) 427-5240, which also includes a museum and an extensive library devoted to Whitman's career.

Every Sunday afternoon in the Town Arsenal (516) 351-3244, up to 80 people in period costume recreate the lives of Revolutionary War soldiers and their wives. The Arsenal also offers lectures on everything from musketry to military cooking, all done in period costume.

The Heckscher Museum (516) 351-3250 has a fine collection of American and European paintings and sculptures. A half mile down the road, on New York Avenue, the IMAC (Inter-Media Arts Center) (516) 351-9511 sponsors jazz and folk music concerts.

Along the lines of showmanship is the New Community Cinema (516) 423-7419 on the village green. This moviehouse screens little-known masterworks, foreign films, and work by contemporary filmmakers. They've even been known to show a movie series on boating.

If you are looking for something to do outdoors, you should know that most of Huntington Bay's beaches are restricted to local residents, but there are beaches open to the public on the eastern end of Lloyd Harbor, and West Beach to the south of Eatons Neck. There are, however, other possibilities outside Huntington.

Caumesett State Park (516) 423-1770 in Lloyd Harbor was formerly the estate of Marshall Field III. The 1,500-acre park has trails for hiking and biking. Picnicking is allowed as long as you take your trash with you. Camping, swimming, and pets are prohibited; and the buildings aren't open, either. It's still a great place to visit because the grounds are quite beautiful.

The Target Rock National Wildlife Refuge (516) 271-2409 on the eastern end of Lloyd Neck includes a 10-acre formal garden open to the public.

There's great fishing for bass and blues on the east side of Eatons Neck. (Proceed with caution: swift currents and submerged boulders make the area dangerous, especially for sailboats.) Target Rock, on the west side of Huntington Bay, offers excellent fishing for flounder year round.

Where To Eat

Near Knutson's Marina is T.K.'s Galley (516) 227-2250, serving a varied American menu in a pub atmosphere. Next door is Junior's Pizza (203) 423-9006, which delivers, and Ship Ashore (516) 549-3422, serving excellent seafood.

Across the street is Tee T.'s Landing (516) 421-1330, known for its fine American food and upper end prices. You can tie up at the dock; reservations are suggested.

If you're in the mood for flavorful Italian seafood–and hearty portions–you should try Nina's (516) 549-9214 on the west shore. A short cab ride will get you to Dragon Gate (516) 385-8100 a Chinese restaurant, or to some sushi and other Japanese delicacies at Bon Bori (516) 673-0400.

Navigation and Anchorages

Use NOAA Charts 12365 (1:20,000), 12364 (1:40,000), and 12363 (1:80,000). Use tide tables for Bridgeport. High tide at the Lloyd Harbor entrance in Huntington Bay is 2 minutes later; low tide is 3 minutes later. Multiply by 1.1 for height at high or low water. Mean tidal range is 8.0 feet.

High tide at Eatons Neck Point is 2 minutes after Bridgeport; low tide is 8 minutes later. Mean tidal range is 7.8 feet.

CAUTION: There have been many buoy changes in this area. We have noted the most important below, but be alert for others.

The wide entrance to Huntington Bay is 13.5nm by boat from Stony Brook Harbor, 5.1nm east of Oyster Bay, and 7.0nm southeast of Stamford, CT.

From the red flashing 4sec bell "28C" **[WP-334]** south of **Cable and Anchor Reef,** a course of about 195°m will bring you to the red flashing 4sec bell "8" **[WP-317]** that marks Target Rock.

Huntington Bay, the largest on the north shore of Long Island, has a wide entrance between two wooded headlands. This is the gateway to Northport Bay and to Lloyd, Huntington, Centerport, and Northport Harbors. Even with the high tidal range in this area, tidal velocity is low, generally about 0.5 knots. Around **Eatons Neck,** however, it can reach 2 knots.

Approaching **Huntington Bay** from the east, keep to the north of green can "13" **[WP-336]** north of Eatons Neck Point, to avoid shoals extending north of the point. Hundreds of smart seamen have foundered here; you don't want to add another notch to the Eatons Neck tally. It's safest to go out around green can "13." (The green flashing 4sec buoy "11B" **[WP-335],** farther to the north, has recently been changed from a bell to a gong.)

Approaching **Huntington Bay** from the west is easy as long as you stay off the rocky, shallow waters of the north coast of **Lloyd Neck.** The shoals are well marked by 3 nuns–"2" **[WP-314],** "4" **[WP-315],** and "6" **[WP-316],** and by the red flashing 4sec bell "8" **[WP-317]** off Target Rock at East Fort Point.

As you head south into **Huntington Bay,** you'll pass **Eatons Neck Basin** (also called Eatons Neck Cove) on the northwestern tip of Eatons Neck. Once a popular swimming spot, the beach is now a bird sanctuary for the endangered least tern, and closed to the public.

Make sure you enter **Eatons Neck Basin** from the west in order to avoid the sandbar on one side, and the reef that is exposed only at low tide on the other. Put the green (formerly white) 2.5sec flasher "1" **[WP-333]** to port as you come into the extremely narrow entrance between the jetties, which are covered at half tide. (Red nun "2" has been removed.)

The channel carries 7 feet, but the green cans in the basin are uncharted because the fierce tides change the channel regularly. Just because they are not charted don't think you can ignore them. Those who cut corners run into trouble. The west shore offers the best anchorage.

At the end of the basin is a 144-foot lighthouse that has been operating for almost 200 years, as well as the **Eaton's Neck Coast Guard Station** that now controls most of the lighthouses in the eastern Sound. In thick weather the fog signal is so loud that an overnight stay is unbearable.

At the southern end of Huntington Bay lies the very busy and crowded **Huntington Harbor.** A lot of dredging has been done in the harbor since the last NOAA chart was issued. You'll find a good 20 feet of water in the channel most of the way down. At the harbor's foot, there's 12 feet.

To enter **Huntington Harbor,** first pass between the Huntington Light (formerly called "Lloyd Harbor Light")–a square concrete tower attached to what looks like a dwelling–and green 4sec flasher "1." You'll pass 2 more red buoys–nun "2" and the 4sec flasher "4."

The entrance to the harbor is between West Neck and **Wincoma Point,** a narrow passage with a strong current. Watch out for a sandbar that extends west from the point; it's best to favor the starboard side when entering. Dead ahead, on top of a hill you'll see the old mansion once owned by George McKesson Brown, founder of Brown Pharmaceuticals.

The channel is about 100 feet wide at the entrance, and well marked. Make sure you don't cut the green 4sec flasher "7" south of the harbor entrance, or you'll be aground before you can say "George McKesson Brown."

The harbor can be unbelievably crowded, so there is little room for anchoring. There are many marinas, including the new West Shore Marina (NOAA has not yet charted the docks), which caters to transients, on the west side.

Along with three yacht clubs, there are two town docks, about 2 miles from the harbor entrance, with some tie-up space. The town of Huntington also runs the Halesite and Mill Dam marinas, for residents only.

Back out in **Huntington Bay, Price Bend** is a bight behind the spit of **West Beach** that extends south from Eatons Neck. This dredged-area, known locally as **Sand City,** for a local mining operation, is popular with weekend boaters, with good swimming and camping on West Beach. On the southern tip of West Beach is an old structure used for sand-and-gravel mining. It's now a bird sanctuary.

To reach **Price Bend,** pick up 4sec green flasher "1" **[WP-322]** south of the spit and head east. (Can "1A" has been discontinued.) Swing north after rounding can "3" **[WP-325],** but not northwest. If you head northwest in your eagerness to get to the beach, you may hit the seabed first, as there are several unmarked shoals.

CAUTION: *Sand City Island used to be a dredging center, hence its name. An old mining structure appears irresistible to kids, but is extremely dangerous. Just a few years ago a boy was paralyzed when he dove off the old structure into an uncharted shallow spot. This is no place to mess around.*

There is good holding ground around **Sand City,** but be cautious of the rocks. Boats with more than a 3-foot draft should be careful because of the extreme tidal range.

You can anchor east of **Sand City Island** or north as far as the spit that creates the small cove. Keep an eye out for the water-skiers that often appear in **Price Bend.** Just north of that spit is a small-boat ramp with a clearly marked channel, open to the public. If you're headed into this cove, be aware of the charted wreck off the spit. Like the waters around Sand City Island, give this area a wide berth.

Lloyd Harbor is shaped like a champagne glass turned on its side. It's a highly rated anchorage, except in an easterly wind since there is quite a fetch across the bays. It runs westward from Huntington Bay nearly to Oyster Bay, and is surrounded by large, tree-hidden estates.

Enter **Lloyd Harbor** north of the Huntington Light and stay between can "3" and nun "4" to avoid some nasty reefs south of East Beach. There's a good anchorage, reserved for transients only, to the south along the **West Neck** shore, well protected from the prevailing southwesterlies. It is bordered on the north by green can "3" and on the east by Huntington Light, and extends roughly 400 yards east of the

A MAN, A PLAN, A MARITIME CENTER

Back in 1984 William Perks got a deal. *Little Jennie,* an 86-foot bugeye ketch built in 1884, sat neglected in Huntington Harbor; he bought the ship for $1.00. The new owner then founded a non-profit group called Operation *Little Jennie* to restore the boat. Just two years later she was in sailing condition, in time for the tall-ship parade at the Statue of Liberty's centennial, where she was the oldest American-built ship in the procession.

Operation *Little Jennie* is now called the Maritime Center On Long Island, and the organization has expanded its concerns to include the preservation of Long Island Sound. The *Little Jennie* is regularly at sea again, but this time as a floating classroom where kids learn about basic marine science and Long Island's maritime heritage. Other programs include an introductory class to sailing ships, and video presentations on conserving the Sound.

The young organization's efforts extend ashore as well. Leading the agenda is the renovation of the Coindre Boathouse. The boathouse—and the mansion on the hill behind it—are the first things a boater sees upon entering Huntington Harbor. The buildings were once owned by George McKesson Brown, the founder of Brown Pharmaceuticals.

The mansion is now the Kissam House, a school for children with learning disabilities, but the boathouse has fallen into great disrepair and is now used to store the rowing shells of the Sagamore Rowing Club. The Maritime Center's goal is to complete renovations of the building in the spring of 1992; it will then serve as the center's headquarters, a research lab, a meeting-room for large groups, and an aquarium.

In 1989, however, the Maritime Center's showpiece was the Lloyd Harbor Lighthouse. The Coast Guard was ready to dismantle the historic stone structure, built in the early 1900s, when the residents of the town organized and won a long-term lease from the town for $1.00.

Plans for renovation are afoot, and on July 4, 1989 the light was formally renamed the "Huntington Light" in a special celebration. The lighthouse will continue to operate as a beacon, but the center hopes to renovate the lighthouse to also serve as a museum for maritime artifacts and a one-couple bed-and-breakfast. (Rates for the latter will probably be more than a dollar.)

As a fundraiser, the Maritime Center has purchased the *Jean,* one of the first combustion-powered cabin cruisers built in this country. The 47-foot craft, built in 1913, was scheduled to begin operations in 1989, offering dinner cruises from Huntington Harbor to Port Jefferson.

The Maritime Center has come a long way from being little more than a dilapidated old ship and a good idea. The people involved stress the importance of creating an educational and environmental center on Long Island, observing that most of the innovative marine-related institutions on Long Island Sound are on the Connecticut side.

As a non-profit and publicly-funded organization, the Maritime Center On Long Island depends on volunteers and financial help from the public, and can't accomplish its goals without that help. If you'd like to know more about the center or would like to volunteer or contribute, write to Operation *Little Jennie* at P.O. Box 481, Centerport, NY 11721, or call (516) 754-2864.

Illustration courtesy of Save Huntington's Lighthouse, Inc., Huntington, NY.

lighthouse. If you anchor outside this area without a resident permit you will be ticketed by the marine patrols.

To reach the transient anchorage, turn to port after you pass can "3." You can anchor just inside in depths of 7 to 11 feet, with a good mud bottom. A 5-mph speed limit is enforced everywhere except in the water-skiing area, and no rafting is allowed after sundown.

In the northeastern "rim" of **Lloyd Harbor,** near **East Beach,** is an area packed with local moorings. This is only for residents with permits. As in Price Bend, keep an eye out for the water-skiers that take advantage of the water-skiing area in the northwest part of Lloyd Harbor.

The western arm of **Lloyd Harbor** begins at the green 2sec flasher "1" and red 2sec flasher "2," both privately maintained. You can *paddle* a dinghy up the harbor through a quiet, beautiful, and narrow passage to the thin strip of land that separates Lloyd Harbor from Oyster Bay, hop over the causeway, and take a dip in Cold Spring Harbor. It's so quiet in Lloyd Harbor, because no power-boats are allowed in this area; you'll be quickly nabbed by the Lloyd Harbor Patrol if you go up here under power. If you want to land and stretch your legs, try **East Beach,** which marks the east end of Lloyd Harbor.

☎ Shoreside and Emergency Services

Airport: MacArthur (516) 588-8062
　　　　　Port Authority of NY/NJ 1-800-AIR-RIDE
Ambulance: 911
Bus: Suffolk County Transit (516) 360-5700
Coast Guard: Eatons Neck (516) 261-6868/6910
　　　　　or VHF 16
Fire: 911 or (516) 427-7250
Harbormaster: (516) 351-3255 or VHF 16
Hospital: Huntington (516) 351-2000
Police: 911 or (516) 351-4400
　　　　　Suffolk Marine Police VHF 16
Radio Telephone: VHF 25, 26,84;I.D.: NY
　　　　　Marine Operator;
　　　　　VHF 86;I.D.:Mariphone Marine Operator;
　　　　　VHF 28; I.D.: Riverhead Marine Operator;
　　　　　VHF 27; I.D.:Bridgeport Marine Operator
Taxi: Arrow Taxi (516) 385-9771
Tow Service: Sea Tow Services, Northport, NY
　　　　　(516) 754-1545 or VHF 16
Train: Long Island Railroad (516) 234-LIRR　　◆

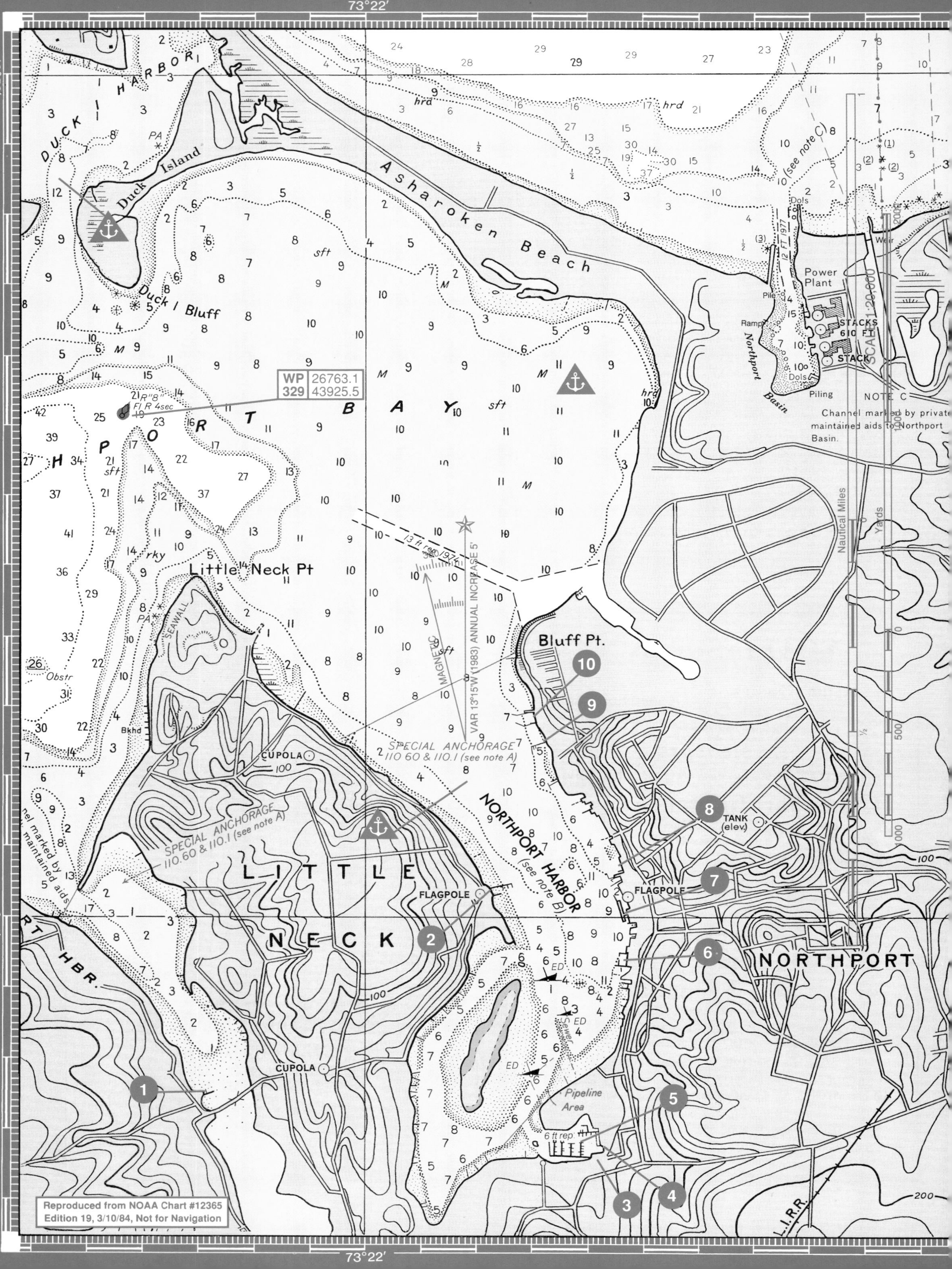

73°22'

40°56'

DUCK HARBOR

Duck Island

Duck I Bluff

PA

Asharoken Beach

hrd

NORTHPORT BAY

WP 329 | 26763.1 | 43925.5

Fl R 4sec

sft

M

Little Neck Pt

SEAWALL

PA

Obstr

Bkhd

rky

(3 ft rep 1971)

VAR 13°15'W (1983) ANNUAL INCREASE 5'

MAGNETIC

SPECIAL ANCHORAGE
110.60 & 110.1 (see note A)

Bluff Pt.

10

9

CUPOLA

SPECIAL ANCHORAGE
110.60 & 110.1 (see note A)

LITTLE

NECK

FLAGPOLE

2

NORTHPORT HARBOR (see note B)

TANK (elev)

8

FLAGPOLE

7

6

NORTHPORT

CUPOLA

1

ED

ED

ED

Pipeline Area

6 ft rep

5

3   4

L.I.R.R.

Power Plant

Northport Basin

STACKS 610 FT

STACK

Piling

Dols

Weir

Ramp

Pile

NOTE C

Channel marked by private maintained aids to Northport Basin.

(see note C)

SCALE 1-20,000

Nautical Miles

Yards

40°54'

PORT HBR.

RT HBR.

nel marked by maintained aids

73°22'

Head of the Gold Coast

As you round Little Neck Point, Northport Harbor appears as graciously as a curtsying lady. On either side of the harbor elegant colonial houses are glimpsed between veils of deep green trees. If Long Island can be said to have a "Gold Coast," Northport Harbor could very well be the spot from which it radiates.

America's wealthiest summered here, and the most prominent among them was William Kissam Vanderbilt II, who built "Eagle's Nest," a mansion on Little Neck. An avid and adept sailor, Vanderbilt owned the fabulous yacht *Alva,* named after his mother. He was also a great explorer and a collector of specimens of all types of birds, fish, and plants as he traveled around the world; an artist was often brought along to make color renderings of the finds brought up from the ocean before the sunlight faded the colors.

The village of Northport, especially the downtown waterfront, is reminiscent of Sag Harbor–albeit on a smaller scale–with its shops, restaurants, and historically preserved feel. Coming here today, you will be struck by the friendliness of the place, and be glad that while curtsying has gone out of style, gentility hasn't.

 ### What To See and Do

Right off the Northport Village Docks is a park which seems to summarize the entire demeanor of this village. The modest swatch of green bordered by oaks on one side and the harbor on the other is crowned by what seems to be the perfect gazebo–a simple whitewashed octagonal structure with a red roof: This is the most genteel park you will see anywhere on the North Shore of Long Island.

Curving away from the docks and running down the center of Main Street is a set of tram tracks, a remnant from the time when Northport actually had a tram. Main Street is a row of shops and a few good restaurants, providing a pleasant day of browsing and indulging.

© Steve Dunwell

Northport Harbor by rocking chair.

	Marine Facilities and Services	Phone	Number of Transient Berths	Number of Transient Moorings	Seasonal/Year-round	Largest Vessel Accommodation (in feet)	Marked Entry Channel	Approach Depth (in feet)	Dockside Depth in feet at MLW	Gas Diesel Fuel	Fuel Brand	Ramp/Dinghy Dock Launch Service	Railway/Lift: Capacity (in tons)	Engine Repairs: Gas/Diesel	Propeller/Hull Repairs	Marine Supplies/Groceries/Bait/Ice	Pump-out Station	Showers/Laundromat	110V★/220V▲ Maximum Amps	MasterCard/VISA/Diners Club/American Express	Restaurant/Snack Bar	Monitors VHF Channel
1	Centerport Marina	(516) 757-6151	2	5	Y	50	●	6	3			DL	L20	GD	PH			SL	★30	MV		68
2	Centerport Yacht Club	(516) 261-5440		3	Y	50	●	6	6				R			S		I	★		RS	68
3	Fred Chall Marine Supply	(516) 754-0160			Y							*MARINE SUPPLIES*						S		MVAD		
4	Long Island Yacht Sales	(516) 757-4303			Y							*YACHT BROKERAGE*										
5	Northport Marine	(516) 261-5600	30		Y	65	●	6	8	GD	TEX		L30	GD	PH	SIG		S	★30	MV	S	16
6	Woodbine Marina	(516) 351-3255			S	50	●	8	6								●					
7	Northport Village Docks	(516) 261-7502			Y	150	●						R					L				
8	Seymour's	(516) 261-6574	5	12	S	65	●	8	6	GD			R30	GD	PH	SI	●		★30	MVA		68
9	Karl's Mariners Inn (p. 365)	(516) 261-8111	10	15	Y	90	●	10	6										★110	MVAD	R	16
10	Northport Yacht Club	(516) 261-7633		6	Y	45	●	13	5	GD						S		I	★110		RS	71

Information in these listings is provided by the facilities themselves. An asterisk (*) indicates that the facility did not respond to our most recent requests for information.

An attraction you won't want to miss is the Vanderbilt Museum (516) 262-7888, formerly the "Eagle's Nest." Part of Little Neck, separating Centerport and Northport harbors, used to be owned by the Vanderbilts. The mansion complex, built on a 43-acre estate, has been turned into a public exhibit and a planetarium.

For more on the history of the area, particularly shipbuilding, visit the Northport Museum (516) 757-9859, open every day except holidays, and only a five-minute walk from the town dock.

The best swimming anywhere in the area is at Asharoken Beach, due north of Northport Harbor, and at West Beach at the entrance to Northport Bay.

Huntington is nearby, so if you'd like more information on what to see and do in that town, please see the chapter on Eatons Neck, Lloyd Harbor, and Huntington Harbor.

Northport Harbor from the south. In the center foreground is Northport Marine, Fred Chall Marine Supply, and Long Island Yacht Sales.

 Where To Eat

Now here is a deal and an adventure: The Australian Country Inn and Gardens (516) 754-4400 will fetch you at your boat, wine you, dine you, and sing to you, Australian style, and then drive you back to your boat.

If you'd rather stay closer to the water, try Pumpernickles (516) 757-7959, a German eatery complete with an accordionist. Right on the water is Karl's Mariners Inn (516) 261-8111, where you can tie up while dining on steaks and seafood.

In Centerport, across from Centerport Marine, is Rock Hoppers (516) 754-6507, offering Continental food at reasonable prices, and a deli for takeout.

 Navigation and Anchorages

Use NOAA Charts 12365 (1:20,000), 12364 (1:40,000), and 12363 (1:80,000). Use tide tables for Bridgeport. High tide at Northport Bay is 2 minutes later; low tide is 8 minutes later. Multiply by 1.1 for height at high or low water. Mean tidal range is 7.8 feet.

The village dock in Northport is 3.0nm by boat east and south of West Beach at the entrance to Northport Bay. Huntington Harbor is 4.4nm west of Northport.

See the chapter on Eatons Neck, Lloyd Harbor, and Huntington Harbor for the approaches to Huntington Bay and thence to Northport Bay.

The green 4sec flasher "1" **[WP-322]** off the long spit of West Beach marks the entrance to **Northport Bay,** due

east of Lloyd Harbor. Northport Bay gives access to Price Bend (see the preceding chapter), Centerport Harbor, Northport Harbor, and Duck Island Harbor (not to be confused with Duck Island Roads in Westbrook, CT). While the tidal range in the area is a hefty 7.8 feet, the tidal velocity is only about 0.5 knots because the area is so open.

When coming into **Northport Bay** from the west, be sure to avoid the shallow spot just west of nun "4" south of Price Bend. The first anchorage area is in **Duck Island Harbor.** To reach it, just pass green flasher "1" **[WP-322]** and can "3," and then head for the quartet of red and white 600-foot-tall stacks of the LILCO power plant east of the bay. (If you can't see *them,* you're either hopelessly lost or in a very thick fog.)

A shallow cove between Duck Island and Eatons Neck, **Duck Island Harbor** can be a dream of an anchorage—that is, when there are no waterskiers around—though open to the southwest. From the east side of the red 4sec flasher "8" **[WP-329],** head due north magnetic towards the southern tip of **Duck Island,** and then turn west when you're 250 yards off the point. This way you'll avoid the nasty rocks and shoals surrounding Duck Island, as well as the rocky shoal extending 0.4nm east of **Winkle Point.** Follow the chart carefully, stay in the deep water and don't anchor close to shore. The harbormaster may check to see if you have a holding tank, and no landing is allowed. The perimeter of the harbor is set aside for waterskiers, whose wakes can send you rocking.

Asharoken Beach, on the northeast side of Northport Bay, provides a good open anchorage. There's a town ramp open to the public on the east end of Asharoken Beach. Use of holding tanks is required.

Centerport Harbor, due south of Duck Island Harbor and across the Little Neck peninsula from Northport, is deep enough (6 feet) for keel boats all the way down to where the charted channel stops. This is roughly even with Camp Alvernia, a summer camp for boys located on Little Neck about 550 yards north of the auto bridge. You can't miss the camp's huge sign facing the water.

From there the channel carries three feet all the way to Centerport Marine at the head of the harbor. There's a restaurant, drug store, and a deli within easy walking distance of the marina.

The entrance to **Northport Harbor** is wide and easy. If you have a deep-draft boat you'll need to hug the east side, but otherwise it's open water to the dock.

The village dock is marked by the charted flagpole and by an amber light, which may be impossible to see if there are enough boats anchored in the harbor. The dock, right smack in the middle of the village, is open for two hour tie-ups until 8:00 p.m. Use fender boards to guard against too much bump-and-grind while you are gone. The Centerport Yacht Club on Little Neck allows only a 15-minute tie-up at the docks, but both the Centerport and Northport yacht clubs usually have transient moorings available to members of reciprocating clubs.

You can also anchor in the southwest corner of **Northport Harbor,** but be sure to follow the chart closely. The bottom is soft but adequate except in a nor'wester, when the wind whistles down the harbor. If you're headed down the channel from the village dock to the facilities and wharves at the south end of the harbor, you should have no trouble. The channel was dredged during the winter of 1989.

The pipeline area marked on the chart is also a hazard. The spot marked "sewer" marks an outflow pipe that sits just below the surface, and the charted wrecks are very real. The island is a bird sanctuary (appropriately named "Bird Island" by the local residents), so should be admired but not trod through.

If you want a closer look at that monstrous **LILCO power plant**–the largest oil-fired power plant in the U.S.–there is a small-boat basin and town launching ramp right at the plant. Approach from Long Island Sound, and look for the Northport oil-pumping station where the big

tankers tie up to offload their cargoes. The station is about 1.7nm due north of the power plant and 2.4nm east of Eatons Neck Point, and is surrounded by large, ominous-looking mooring buoys.

The channel into the basin begins at the 15sec green flasher "1" **[WP-338].** Inside, there is ample parking for the many boaters who use the ramps, with a permit attainable from Huntington Town Hall (516) 351-3089. The basin does not serve as an anchorage except in emergencies. By the way, those big towers will give you an almost perfect magnetic north-south bearing when they're aligned.

Shoreside and Emergency Services

Airport: MacArthur (516) 588-8062
Port Authority of NY/NJ 1-800-AIR-RIDE
Ambulance: 911
Bus: Suffolk County Transit (516) 360-5700
Coast Guard: Eatons Neck (516) 261-6868/6910
or VHF 16
Fire: 911 or (516) 261-7504
Harbormaster: (516) 351-3255 or VHF 16
Hospital: Huntington (516) 351-2000
Police: 911 or (516) 261-7500
Marine Unit (516) 261-7400 or VHF 16
Radio Telephone: VHF 25, 26,84; I.D.: NY
Marine Operator;
VHF 86; I.D.: Mariphone
Marine Operator;
VHF 28; I.D.: Riverhead
Marine Operator;
VHF 27; I.D.: Bridgeport
Marine Operator
Taxi: Quinlan's (516) 261-0235
Tow Service: Sea Tow Services, Northport, NY
(516) 754-1545 or VHF 16
Train: Long Island Railroad (516) 234-LIRR ✦

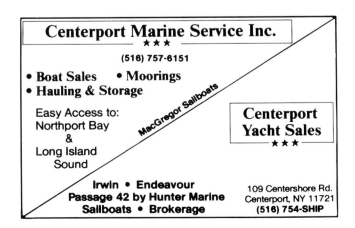

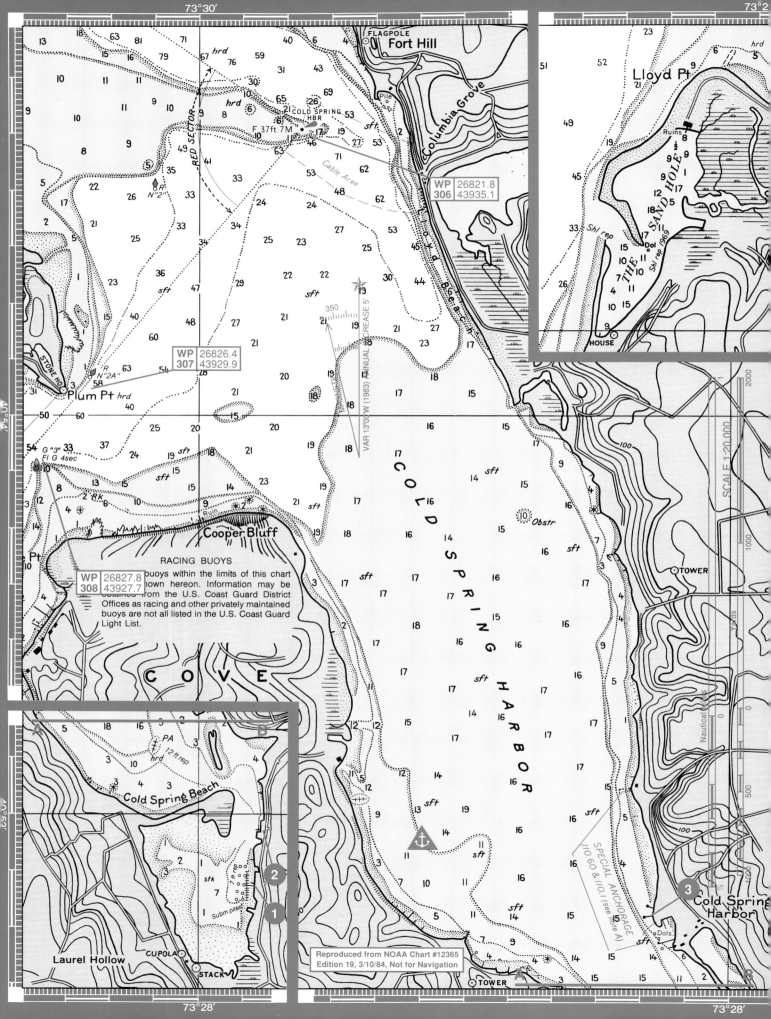

FLAGPOLE
Fort Hill

Lloyd Pt

THE SAND HOLE

RED SECTOR

COLD SPRING HBR
F 37ft 7M

Columbia Grove

Cable Area

WP 306 | 26821.8 / 43935.1

N"2"

WP 307 | 26826.4 / 43929.9

Plum Pt hrd

STONE HO

G "3"
Fl G 4sec

C O L D   S P R I N G   H A R B O R

Obstr

Cooper Bluff

RACING BUOYS

...buoys within the limits of this chart ...own hereon. Information may be ...ained from the U.S. Coast Guard District Offices as racing and other privately maintained buoys are not all listed in the U.S. Coast Guard Light List.

WP 308 | 26827.8 / 43927.7

C O V E

SCALE 1:20.000

TOWER

VAR 13°00'W (1983) ANNUAL DECREASE 5'

Cold Spring Beach

A

B

PA
hrd

Laurel Hollow

CUPOLA

STACK

SPECIAL ANCHORAGE
J110.60 & I110.1 (see note A)

Cold Spring Harbor

Dols

TOWER

Cold Spring Harbor and the Sand Hole

A Few Rumors From Wigwam Swamp

Leave it to the British and their knack for Anglicizing most things they come across. Rumor has it they were so taken with the fine quality of the local water in a place called *Wigwam Swamp* that when they bought it from the Indians in 1653 they renamed it Cold Spring Harbor, for the cold springs all along the eastern shore of the harbor that made fresh water easily obtainable.

During the Revolutionary War, a hundred years later, a new and different wave of Englishmen came to town and exploited it for much the same reasons it was settled in the first place. Soon the harbor became a base for their military operations in the area. The British Navy was fond of Cold Spring Harbor because it was a large deep-water bay, good for sheltering a fleet of warships, yet open enough so that the Americans could not bottle them up so easily.

If the water of Cold Spring Harbor attracted the first settlers, it was the ruggedness and vistas of the land that brought the wealthier personages of American society here. Cove Neck, forming the western shore of Cold Spring Harbor, was once the site of many luxurious estates, including the Roosevelts' famous Sagamore Hill. Teddy Roosevelt was known for impressive horseback riding stunts, like galloping his horse down the harrowing Cooper Bluff, on the north side of the cove. (Another rumor has it that Teddy went down this bully bluff one day, and continued going–right into the water, horse and all.)

One of the more interesting architectural relics in the Cold Spring Harbor area is not any important man's house, but a squat, wooden lighthouse just south of the stream on the east side of Centre Island. Built in 1889, it was decommissioned in 1965 by the Coast Guard, who intended to demolish it. The Guard got as far as pitching it into the water when a local family spied the then-floating structure and promptly offered to buy it. The Coast Guard was only too happy to rid themselves of the problem and

The Cold Spring Harbor Beach Club on the east side of Cold Spring Harbor.

sold it for a dollar. The floating hulk was towed to its present site and after substantial renovations, converted to a boathouse.

If you walk along the beaches of Cold Spring today at high tide you won't find the springs, but come back a few hours later and you'll see the cold, fresh water bubbling up through the ground. The springs and deep water make the harbor unusually cold, and people who should know say that it's like swimming in Maine, in October. Another rumor has it that if you do take to the water you'll find it an invigorating experience–good for the circulation. With or without a horse.

 What To See and Do

Once nicknamed "Bedlam Street" in honor of the rowdy behavior of sailors that frequented it, Main Street in Cold Spring Harbor is now one of the most civilized avenues you'll find. And if you can't find what you need there, the

Marine Facilities and Services		Number of Transient Berths	Number of Transient Moorings	Seasonal/Year-round	Largest Vessel Accommodation (in feet)	Approach Depth in feet	Marked Entry Channel	Dockside Depth in feet at MLW	Gas/Diesel Fuel at MLW	Fuel Brand	Ramp/Dinghy Dock/Launch Service	Railway Lift: Capacity (in tons)	Engine Repairs: Gas/Diesel	Propeller/Hull Repairs	Marine Supplies/Groceries/Bait/Ice	Pump-out Station	Showers/Laundromat	110V ★ 220V ▲ Maximum Amps	MasterCard/VISA/Diners Club/American Express	Restaurant/Snack Bar	Monitors VHF Channel
❶ Whalers Cove Yacht Club	(516) 367-9822			S		*PRIVATE CLUB - MEMBERS ONLY*															
❷ H & M Powles	(516) 367-7670	5		S	40	●	30	4	G	SUN	R			P	GD			SI	★		S
❸ Cold Spring Harbor Beach Club	(516) 367-9824					*PRIVATE CLUB - MEMBERS ONLY*															

Information in these listings is provided by the facilities themselves. An asterisk (*) indicates that the facility did not respond to our most recent requests for information.

mini-metropolis of Huntington is just a quick cab-ride down Rte. 25A.

The main attractions in Cold Spring Harbor are the excellent shopping and the Whaling Museum (516) 367-3418 on Main Street. The Museum includes a fully equipped whaleboat, scrimshaw, ship models, and a hands-on marine mammal bone display. It's surrounded by a row of antique and handicrafts shops and boutiques.

South of Cold Spring Harbor, on Rte. 25A, is the Cold Spring Harbor Fish Hatchery (516) 692-6768, which was once owned by New York State. Founded in 1883, the hatchery hatched trout by the thousands until recently. Now privately owned, the complex includes an aquarium and offers educational programs. Most of the complex is out in the open and looks something like a public park.

At the southwest corner of Cold Spring Harbor is the campus of Cold Spring Labs (516) 367-8397, a major biological and cancer research institution headed by the Nobel Prize-winning James Dewey Watson, one of the discoverers of DNA. Tours are available on weekends only.

If you'd rather be in nature than learning about its genetic building blocks, there are many beaches in the area that are generally free and open to all. If you come to a private section, the law allows you to walk along the wet-sand portion of the beach.

 Where To Eat

Amid the quaint shops in Cold Spring Harbor you'll find two eateries: The Wyland Country Kitchen (516) 692-5655, serving old-fashioned American food, and Creme de La Creme Café (516) 367-8558, serving–get this–tea and crumpets each afternoon at 4:00. (Huntington village is just a short cab ride away, where you'll find plenty more to eat. Please see the chapter on Eatons Neck, Lloyd Harbor, and Huntington Harbor for restaurant suggestions in Huntington.)

 Navigation and Anchorages

Use NOAA Charts 12365 (1:20,000), 12364 (1:40,000), and 12363 (1:80,000). Use tide tables for Bridgeport. High tide at Cold Spring Harbor is 7 minutes later; low tide is 8 minutes later. Multiply by 1.1 for height at high or low water. Mean tidal range is 8.0 feet.

Oyster Bay, about 4.5nm westward of Eatons Neck Light, serves as the entrance to both Cold Spring Harbor and Oyster Bay Harbor. The green (formerly white) 4sec flashing gong "15" off Lloyd Point is 4.2nm west of Eatons Neck Light. The green gong "1" off Whitewood Point (labeled "N.W. Bluff" on some charts), is another 2.3nm south-southwest; the lighthouse off Fort Hill is about 0.8nm to the southeast.

From the red flashing 2.5sec bell "32A" **[WP-300]** marking the Twenty-Six Foot Shoal, a course of about

155°m should bring you to the 37-foot lighted tower **[WP-306]** also known as Cold Spring Harbor Light.

When coming from the east, it's wise to stay more than 0.5nm off the high yellow bluff of Lloyd Neck. A rocky shoal extends northerly from Lloyd Point.

CAUTION: Morris Rock, about 0.5nm east of Lloyd Point, is covered by only 2 feet of water, and is poorly marked by a white and orange obstruction buoy. A 6-foot spot slightly to the north and west is not marked at all. The latter is usually forgotten about–and hence more often hit–as mariners concentrate on missing Morris Rock.

If you are not familiar with the area, we recommend you follow the buoy line for Huntington out to green gong "15" **[WP-313],** then turn southwards and into **Oyster Bay.** Local boaters will often cut inside **Morris Rock** to save a few minutes and get away from the currents. If you're new to the area and insist on cutting a buoy, do it right at red nun "2" **[WP-314]** north of Morris Rock, but don't go any farther south.

If you're heading in from the west, green bell "17" **[WP-301]** off **Rocky Point** is 5.1nm east of Matinicock Point. Beware of the foul area that runs for about a mile northward of Rocky Point out to bell "17" **[WP-301].** Traveling another 1.9nm to the southeast will bring you to the 37-foot light off Fort Hill **[WP-306],** and the approaches to Oyster Bay Harbor and Cold Spring Harbor.

CAUTION: Beware of the large (6-foot-diameter) unlighted steel mooring buoys for the sand barges–only one is marked on the chart–between the Sand Hole and green gong "1" [WP-302].

On the northwest side of Lloyd Neck is the **Sand Hole,** a great gunkhole also known as "Sand Diggers." From a distance the Sand Hole would be difficult to spot if it were empty, but it rarely is, so all you have to do is look for a group of masts sticking out of the sand like a stand of dead pines.

CAUTION: The bar on the north of the Sand Hole channel entrance extends much farther west than the chart indicates. If you're coming from the north, be sure to swing wide to starboard, or stay at least 400 yards off the coast, before heading due east into the channel.

The entry is not marked, and although the chart shows one dolphin off the point inside the harbor, there were no buoys last time we were there. Again, watch out for the reef on the north side and swing wide around it before you turn east. Then hug the northern point as you enter and on your turn back north.

The best time to enter the **Sand Hole** is at high water, but unfortunately that's when the breakwater that forms the southwest side of the harbor probably won't be visible.

There is also a sandbar that extends north of the breakwater, so whatever you do, stay close to that northern point! (If the dolphin is in place, pass between it and the point, since there is shallow water just to the east of where the dolphin is shown on the chart.)

If you're here for the first time, don't be surprised if you're confused by this entrance. It's hard to spot, very tricky, and unmarked. You may want to wait until you can follow someone else in and let him take the risk.

The entry to the channel is not very deep, so if you draw more than 4 feet you may have trouble getting through the inlet at low tide. There is plenty of water inside the basin, so if you have a deeper draft boat, it's best to go in at half or full tide.

Inside the **Sand Hole** are two places to anchor–one on the south side and another around the point to the north. The depths drop off sharply just off the beach, so if you keep an eye on your depth sounder and go slowly, you may be able to scoot in very close to the shore.

On weekends you'll find the **Sand Hole** jammed with motorboats, in spite of the fact that it is now a bird sanctuary and you can no longer land. The holding ground is good, with depths running from 4 to 22 feet. You will have more company in the northern end, but if you like exploring by dink you will also be close to the tidal creeks and all the little critters and birds you can find in the marshes.

Heading south down Oyster Bay, you'll find a shoal marked at its eastern end by **Cold Spring Harbor Light,** a large iron caisson, off Fort Hill. The 37-foot light **[WP-306],** which marks a wrecked barge of bricks as well as the shoal, has fixed red and white sectors that are helpful for night approaches. (You'll see the red sector marked on the chart.) Most boats that have a draft of 6 feet or less and are heading for **Oyster Bay Harbor** will cut inside the light. (For more information on Oyster Bay Harbor, see the next chapter.)

You can pass on either side of red nun "2" west of the light, but you will want to split the distance between the buoy and the shore, or the buoy and the light. Remember that the buoy is not right over the 5-foot spot it marks, but to the south of it, so stay away from the northern side.

Oyster Bay is a lovely area, with unspoiled beaches and wooded hills. It's also one of the cleanest harbors on the Sound. The mean tidal range is 8 feet, and because the harbor is so deep and wide with an unrestricted entrance, the tidal velocity at Cold Spring Harbor Light is only 0.6 knots.

The Cold Spring Harbor Beach Club on the east side of **Cold Spring Harbor** is 2.5nm south of the harbor light. From the beach club it is about a mile and a half to town, and the good restaurants and shopping you'll find there. Although there's a good complement of large yachts moored at the club, it is more active in small-boat racing and shoreside diversions such as tennis.

Cold Spring Harbor lies about 3 miles south of Lloyd Point and is separated from Oyster Bay Harbor by Cove Neck. It offers plenty of room and good protection except in a northerly wind. You'll notice the lack of buoys–they're not much needed because of the harbor's depth, size, and few facilities.

You can anchor almost anywhere and find good holding ground. You may see boats anchored off **Cooper Bluff** to the north, but this is a pretty wide-open spot and subject to some channel wash. A favorite spot is off the north side of **Cold Spring Beach,** a 600-yard-long sand pit extending across the southern tip of the harbor.

The dredged inner harbor below **Cold Spring Beach** is even better protected. It can get a little tight for cruising boats but is well-used by runabouts. There's a new town launching ramp directly opposite the eastern tip of Cold Spring Beach, as well as a small yacht club and an even smaller marina, H & M Powles. (H & M Powles is operating, even though its main building was gutted by fire in 1988. The marina office now occupies a trailer next to the charred ruins.)

If you're headed for Main Street in Cold Spring, this is the most convenient place to leave your boat, if you can find a slip, mooring, or anchorage.

 ## Shoreside and Emergency Services

Airport: MacArthur (516) 588-8062
Port Authority of NY/NJ 1-800-AIR-RIDE
Ambulance: 911
Bus: Suffolk County Transit (516) 360-5700
Nassau County Bus (516) 222-1000
Coast Guard: Eatons Neck (516) 261-6868/6910 or VHF 16
Fire: 911
Harbormaster: Huntington (516) 351-3255
Oyster Bay (516) 921-7347
(M-F 9:00-4:45) or VHF 16
Hospital: Huntington (516) 351-2000
Police: 911 or (516) 351-4416
Radio Telephone: VHF 25, 26, 84; I.D.: NY
Marine Operator;
VHF 86; I.D.: Mariphone
Marine Operator;
VHF 28; I.D.: Riverhead
Marine Operator;
VHF 27; I.D.: Bridgeport
Marine Operator
Taxi: Orange & White (516) 271-3600
Tow Service: Sea Tow Services, Northport, NY
(516) 754-1545 or VHF 16
Train: Long Island Railroad (516) 234-LIRR   ◆

73°32'

Nautical Miles

Centre Island Reef

Rocky Pt.

SCALE 1:20,000

Grassy I

Wreck

stk

rky

sft

2 ft
rep

NOAA authorized reproduction
of a segment of chart #12365,
edition 19, 3/10/84,
Not for navigation

① ②

BASCULE BRIDGE
HOR. CL. 76 FT.
VERT. CL. 9 FT.

③

Cable
Area

WP 307 26826.4
43929.9

hrd

⑨

MAGNETIC

VAR 13°00'W (1983) ANNUAL INCREASE 5'

Centre Island FS.

Plum Pt

W   E   S   T   H   A   R   B   O   R

Stone Ho.

sft

④

sft

anchor

anchor

C   E   N   T   R   E   I.

Cove Pt

WP 308 26827.8
43927.7

G "3" FI G 4sec

2 Rk

hrd

Rk

SPECIAL ANCHORAGE
110.60 & 110.1 (see note A)

WP 309 26830.1
43922.0

CUP

Moses Pt.

Brickyard Pt.

O   Y   S   T   E   R   B   A   Y   H   B   R

SPECIAL ANCHORAGE
110.60 & 110.1 (see note A)

R N"4"

sft

hrd

N"2" R N"8" stk R N"4" R
C"11" FI G 2sec "9" "7" C"5" C"3" GR G"B" I Qk FI
C"15" C"13" RB "A"
C"17" C"1A" Buoys priv maintd C"3"
Cable Area C"19" R N"2A" N"4" C"3" hrd anchor
R RB "C" 28 FI R 2sec "6" N"8" C"5"
C"21" hrd N"4A" C"9" C"7" C"5"
Dols PA Wrecks
Ramp Dols

SPECIAL ANCHORAGE
110.60 & 110.1 (see note A)

sft

⑤ ⑥ ⑦ ⑧

CH.
SP.

The Cove

73°32'

40°54'

Oyster Bay Harbor

Inglorious Bridges and "Bully" Teddy

Reaching into Oyster Bay Harbor like a bent arm is Centre Island, home of the Seawanhaka Corinthian Yacht Club. Formed in 1871, it is, along with the North Shore Yacht Club in Port Washington, the oldest yacht club on the Sound. *Seawanhaka* is Indian for "eater of clams." During the 1960s, however, there was at least one person who wanted to make it and a few other yacht clubs eat something else.

Robert Moses–no relation to Moses Point on Centre Island–the transportation tycoon of New York, was not allowed membership in any of the local yacht clubs for reasons that were never made public. An irate and somewhat discombobulated Moses retaliated by deciding to condemn the land they were on and pave them over. ("Eat dirt," he may have said.)

Moses had another idea: to build a bridge from Oyster Bay across the Sound to Rye or Port Chester–a distance of over 7 miles. This, of course, caused an uproar on both sides of the Sound, and the town of Oyster Bay promptly transferred wetlands at the proposed bridge's landfall to the Interior Department, creating a wildlife preserve through which no roads or bridges could be built. The cross-Sound bridge proposal (just one of many, incidentally) died an inglorious death a few years later.

Robert Moses–eating his heart out in the meantime–wasn't the only one who was particularly well known in Oyster Bay. Teddy Roosevelt lived here, and his home, Sagamore Hill, on Cove Neck is about 1.5 miles from the village, as

Oyster Bay Marine Center, Sagamore Yacht Club, and the Roosevelt Memorial Park Marina in Oyster Bay Harbor, NY.

the crow flies. Sagamore Hill was the summer White House during his presidency. The house has been preserved and is open to the public.

 ## What To See and Do

The village of Oyster Bay is robust with shops and restaurants–which nicely eclipse its industrial area, centered mostly around the oil depot on the waterfront. This is almost as far west as you can get on Long Island without being absolutely sure you're in a New York City Suburb.

Marine Facilities and Services		Number of Transient Berths	Number of Transient Moorings	Seasonal/Year-round	Largest Vessel Accommodation (in feet)	Marked Entry Channel	Approach Depth (in feet)	Dockside Depth in feet at MLW	Gas/Diesel Fuel	Ramp/Dinghy Dock/Launch Service	Railway/Lift: Capacity (in tons)	Propeller/Hull Repairs	Engine Repairs: Gas/Diesel	Marine Supplies/Groceries/Bait/Ice	Pump-out Station	Showers/Laundromat	110V ★ 220V ▲ Maximum Amps	MasterCard/VISA/Diners Club — American Express	Restaurant/Snack Bar	Monitors VHF Channel
❶ Soundview Marine Service	(516) 628-1100			Y	32							PH	GD					MV		21
❷ Bayville Marine	(516) 628-8686			Y					*YAMAHA OUTBOARD DEALERSHIP*							S		MVAD		16
❸ Soundview Marine	(516) 628-8688			Y	41		13	13		RDL	L	PH	GD	SBI			▲40		S	16
❹ Mill Neck Bay Marine	(516) 671-5621			Y	36	●						PH	GD	S						
❺ Jakobson Shipyard	(516) 922-4500			Y	235	●	18	18			R150	PH	GD				★▲			71
❻ Roosevelt Memorial Park Marina	(516) 922-7948			S	45	●	6	5							●		★30			16
❼ Sagamore Yacht Club	(516) 922-0555	3		Y	45		17	12			R	PH	GD		●	S	▲	MVAD		9
❽ Oyster Bay Marine Center (p. 375)	(516) 922-6331	10		Y	60	●	20	20	GD	CIT	L	PH	GD	S		I	★▲30	MV	S	71
❾ Seawanhaka Corinthian Yacht Club	(516) 922-6305			Y	90		8	8			R			S		I	★		R	9

Information in these listings is provided by the facilities themselves. An asterisk (*) indicates that the facility did not respond to our most recent requests for information.

Every October the town celebrates Teddy Roosevelt's birthday with an Oyster Festival, a two-day street festival featuring lots of activities and gobs of food–roughly 25,000 oysters are consumed at the event.

Theodore Roosevelt's Sagamore Hill (516) 922-4447 is now a museum, designed to recall "to the American people Mr. Roosevelt's personality and achievements." It is filled with the furnishings and memorabilia of a national family at play. Roosevelt's grave, a memorial park, and Old Orchard Museum are nearby.

Another landmark is Raynham Hall (516) 922-6808, which was built in 1740 by a Quaker merchant and was later the headquarters for the British army of occupation during the Revolution. If you're a student of exquisite irony you'll love this one: Robert Townsend, whose father owned Raynham Hall while the British occupied it, was the head of a large and effective American spy ring during the Revolution (Nathan Hale was one of his more unsuccessful underlings). It was Townsend who uncovered Benedict Arnold's plot to turn over West Point to the British.

There are not one, but two, arboretums within a short cab ride of Oyster Bay. Planting Fields Arboretum (516) 922-9201 sits on 409 landscaped acres of greenhouses, gardens, and natural habitat. The rhododendron and azalea collections contain more than 600 species. A Tudor Revival mansion called Coe Hall is also on the grounds. Bailey Arboretum (516) 676-4497 is much smaller, but has a more exotic collection of flora. The grounds are open from November to April. Admission, a buck.

Swimming at Centre Island Beach (516) 795-1000 is not exactly open to the public: you'll need a pass to get in, but you can always anchor your boat off shore and swim in.

At the very head of Mill Neck Creek is a ravine that forms the 200-acre Quogue Wildlife Refuge (516) 653-4771, a preserve notable for a stand of giant old tulip trees. These tulips, some 150 years old and 4 feet in diameter, are the kind of trees the Indians used to make the dugout canoes by which they traveled the inlets of Long Island. Since the area is fenced in, you should call ahead to have the gate opened.

From any of the marinas around Mill Neck Bay, it's a pleasant bicycle ride through the town of Bayville, which is mostly residential but includes a few modest restaurants and nightclubs, as well as a convenience store or two. If you want to work on the old hand-eye coordination, you'll find a miniature golf course and baseball batting cages to the west on Bayville Avenue, on the Sound side. They're located across the road from Ransom Beach, a town beach for residents only, along with a snack bar and restaurant.

 Where To Eat

You won't find any eateries on the water in Oyster Bay, so you'll have to head inland to Uwe's (516) 922-5044, serving Continental, and Canterbury Ales (516) 922-3614, an English-style pub and restaurant.

West of Oyster Bay, a short distance by cab, is the village of Locust Valley, where you can dine at Barney's (516) 671-6300, a three-star restaurant, the Country Inn (516) 671-1357 for Continental, and Marbles (516) 676-3524, a casual spot that's open until 4 a.m.

 Navigation and Anchorages

Use NOAA Charts 12365 (1:20,000), 12364 (1:40,000), and 12363 (1:80,000). Use tide tables for Bridgeport. High tide at Oyster Bay Harbor is 7 minutes later; low tide is 13 minutes later. Multiply by 1.1 for height at high or low water. Mean tidal range is 7.8 feet.

High tide at Bayville Bridge is 12 minutes after Bridgeport; low tide is 20 minutes later. Multiply by 1.1 for height at high or low water. Mean tidal range is 8.0 feet.

The wide entrance to Oyster Bay, the gateway to Oyster Bay Harbor and Cold Spring Harbor, is 9.4nm by boat from Hempstead Harbor to the west, 5.8nm by boat from Huntington Bay to the east, and 5.5nm south of Stamford, Connecticut.

From the flashing green 2.5sec bell "32A" **[WP-300]** a course of about 155°m will bring you in sight of the Cold Spring Harbor Light **[WP-306].** From here, rounding Plum Point is easy, by spotting the green 4sec flasher "3" **[WP-308],** marking the shoal's edge, north of Cove Point.

For many yachtsmen, **Oyster Bay Harbor** ranks as the queen of harbors on Long Island. It resembles a long, crooked arm on the west side of Oyster Bay, and is big enough for a navy.

From the green (formerly white) 4sec flashing gong "15" **[WP-313]** off Lloyd Point it is 2.3nm south-southeast to gong "1" **[WP-302]** off Whitewood Point (labeled on some charts as "N.W. Bluff") and 0.8nm southeast to the lighthouse off Fort Hill.

When coming from the east, it's wise to stay more than 0.5nm off the high yellow bluff of Lloyd Neck. A rocky shoal extends northerly from Lloyd Point.

CAUTION: *Morris Rock, about 0.5nm east of Lloyd Point, is covered by only 2 feet of water, and is poorly marked by a white and orange obstruction buoy. A 6-foot spot slightly to the north and west is not marked at all. It is usually forgotten about (and hence more often hit) as mariners concentrate on missing Morris Rock.*

Newcomers should follow the buoy line for Huntington out to gong "15" **[WP-313],** then turn south and into Oyster Bay, although the local boaters will often cut inside **Morris Rock** to save a few minutes and get away from the currents. If you're new to the area and insist on cutting a buoy, do it at red nun "2" **[WP-314]** north of Morris Rock, but don't go any farther south.

If you're heading in from the west, green bell "17" **[WP-301]** off **Rocky Point** is 5.1nm east of Matinicock Point.

TEDDY ROOSEVELT AND HIS NOT-SO-ROUGH RIDERS

This photograph of the President and some of his children was taken in 1902 at the Roosevelt's home in Oyster Bay. Seated on horseback left to right: Archie, 8; Quentin, 4; Theodore, 43; his wife Edith, 40; and Kermit, 12. Those in the background were probably household staff members. The boy on the ground at the right is probably Theodore Jr., 14. Built by Roosevelt in 1884-85, Sagamore Hill was named "from the old Sagamore Mohannis, who as Chief of his little tribe, signed away his rights to the land." Today the 23-room frame and brick house is open to the public as a National Historic Site (516) 922-4447.

Photo courtesy of the National Park Service

Beware of the foul area that runs for about a mile northward of Rocky Point out to bell "17" **[WP-301]**. Traveling another 1.9nm to the southeast will bring you to the 37-foot light off Fort Hill **[WP-306]**, and the approaches to **Oyster Bay Harbor** and **Cold Spring Harbor.**

On the northwest side of Lloyd Neck is the **Sand Hole,** a great gunkhole also known as "Sand Diggers." (For information on navigating the Sand Hole, please see the chapter on Cold Spring Harbor).

CAUTION: *Beware of the large (6-foot-diameter) unlighted steel mooring buoys for the sand barges (only one is marked on the chart) between the Sand Hole and green gong "1" [WP-302]. Hit one of these things at dusk and you'll gong, too.*

Eastward from **Rocky Point,** reaching nearly all the way across Oyster Bay, is a shoal marked at its eastern end by **Cold Spring Harbor Light [WP-306],** a large iron caisson, off Fort Hill.

The 37-foot light, marking the shoal and a wrecked barge of bricks, has fixed red and white sectors that are helpful for night approaches. (You'll see the red sector marked on the chart.) Most boats that have a draft of 6 feet

or less and are heading for Oyster Bay Harbor will cut inside the light.

You can pass on either side of red nun "2" west of the light, but you will want to split the distance between the buoy and the shore, or the buoy and the light. Remember that the buoy is not right over the 5-foot spot it marks, but to the south of it, so stay away from the northern side.

The entrance to **Oyster Bay Harbor** really begins with nun "2A" **[WP-307]** off Plum Point to starboard and the green 4sec flasher "3" **[WP-308]** north of Cove Point. Here the inner bay splits—one arm going southeast to Cold Spring Harbor; the other, southwest around **Centre Island,** which separates Oyster Bay from West Harbor. From green buoy "3" **[WP-308],** just aim for the big, brightly-colored oil tanks at Oyster Bay Village, and you'll end up right at the main channel entrance.

The channel into **Oyster Bay Harbor** carries 40 feet of water to **Moses Point;** west of the point the channel narrows and has less than 10 feet, but is well-marked with a row of nuns and cans. At the east end of this channel, look for the green and red Qk flasher "B" that marks the beginning of the channel down to the village wharf. This channel, like the main east-west channel, is also marked with rows of nuns and cans.

CAUTION: *There is a no-wake speed limit in this area, and it's strictly enforced. It's important to remember, especially in a busy area like this, that you are liable for any damage caused by your wakes.*

There are several good anchorages in this uncrowded and unspoiled harbor; one is the bight west of **Plum Point,** on the east side of **Centre Island,** marked by a small stone tower. You may be able to find some room to anchor near the yachts of the Seawanhaka Corinthian Yacht Club on Centre Island, but advance reservations are suggested. Picking up just any empty mooring is not a good idea. If the harbormaster nabs you he will tell you to move on if you don't have a written letter of authorization from the owner to use the mooring. Except for the yacht club, there are no boating facilities on the island, so if you want to go ashore for something to eat or stock other supplies, you will have to go ashore at the village.

The bight between **Cove Neck** and the Oyster Bay wharf offers another good tree-lined anchorage, just off the channel to Oyster Bay Village. There's a jetty on Cove Neck, on the east side of this anchorage, where you can land your dink and walk up to Sagamore Hill, less than a mile away.

On the east side of the wharf, near the oil tanks, is a row

SOMETHING AFOOT

So you say you're ready to stretch your sea legs on land? Luckily for you, citizens on both sides of Long Island Sound had the foresight to preserve some waterfront for hiking, picnicking, and swimming. Some of these areas are easily accessible by boat, some a little trickier. It's best to play it safe and call ahead for some advice.

Waterfront walking in an undeveloped setting is a rare find anywhere, but it is almost nonexistent in the Northeast. **Bluff Point Coastal Reserve, Groton, CT,** offers about six miles of it and gets our vote as the best hiking along the Connecticut side of Long Island Sound. Bluff Point's diverse 806 acres include rocky beaches, sandy beaches, wetlands, wildflowers, forest, and abundant bird life. There's no official boat access here, but cruisers can pull shallow-draft boats onto the sandy shores of Bushy Point, a peninsula at low tide and an island at high tide on the western side of the park. For more information call Ft. Griswold State Park (203) 445-1729.

Other parks of interest on the Connecticut side of the Sound:

Pelham Bay Park, Bronx, NY (212) 430-1890: New York City's largest park includes golf courses, beaches, horseback riding, and more than 4 miles of hiking trails. Anchor to the east of Rodman Neck, or walk across the causeway from City Island.

Hammonasset State Park, Madison, CT (203) 245-2785: 930 acres of woods, camping facilities, shore fishing, bike riding, and scuba facilities. Meigs Point, at the extreme east end of the park, offers access for dinghies or windsurfers.

Selden Neck State Park, Lyme, CT (203) 526-2336: 528 acres on the east shore of the Connecticut River between Hadlyme and Hamburg Cove. The park offers woodland walking and primitive camping sites, and tidal inlets and wetlands for canoeists. Come ashore at one of two sandy pickets on the west side of Selden Neck.

Rocky Neck State Park, East Lyme, CT (203) 739-5471: Some of the sandiest, safest swimming beaches in the state, plus 710 acres of walking and picnic areas. No direct boat access, but the park is adjacent to a state boat launch on the Four Mile River.

On Long Island, **Caumsett State Park (516) 423-1770** occupies the center portion of Lloyd's Neck. It also includes a popular weekend boater's destination–the Sand Hole. This park gets our vote for the best hiking on the south shore of Long Island Sound. Its 1,500 acres of diverse terrain is undeveloped, making it a naturalist's delight. The best anchorage for the park is in the Sand Hole. For approaches, see our "Lloyd Point and Cold Spring Harbor" chapter.

Other parks of interest on Long Island:

Sands Point Preserve, Port Washington, NY (516) 883-1612: 230 acres on the eastern side of Sands Point near Manhasset Bay. The park offers about 4 miles of walking trails, some of them topping 100-foot sand cliffs. Call for access information.

Sunken Meadow State Park, Kings Park, NY (516) 360-0753: Here you get a two-fer. The park has 2.5 miles of trails, but it is also the trailhead for the 34-mile "Greenbelt" trail that ends at Heckscher State Park on the south side of Long Island. Anchor off the parking area west of the Nissequogue River entrance, or anchor in the river and come ashore at the state launch area.

Orient Beach State Park, Orient, NY (516) 323-2440: 363 acres fronting Gardiners Bay. Developed as a beach park, offering some walking, great sand, and good swimming. Anchor north of Long Beach and dink ashore.

Happy trails!

Contributed by Paul and Kathy Connolly of Connecticut Coastline, a marine instruction and publishing firm in Rowayton, CT.

of sunken barges. Another channel, with about 6 feet, leads westward to the Roosevelt Memorial Marina, run by the town of Oyster Bay. Gas and diesel are available, and there is also a free pump-out station, a launching ramp, picnic tables and tennis courts. One of the reasons Oyster Bay is so clean is that the harbormaster strongly encourages boaters to use the pump-out station. You can't beat the price, so please take advantage of it. Contact the marina on VHF 16 for more information.

The Long Island Railroad station is practically a stone's throw away from the wharf, as is downtown Oyster Bay. Oyster Bay Marine Service and the Sagamore Yacht Club both offer launch service (at Sagamore, for members only).

Southeast of Moses Point, at the south end of Centre Island is an anchorage area between the island and the special anchorage marked on the chart, but most are taken up with moorings. Keep at least 0.2nm off Brickyard Point to avoid unmarked rocks. Some oystering continues in Oyster Bay, but not at the level of former years. The oyster stakes remain a danger, however; the less the areas are used, the more likely there are to be oyster stakes broken off below the waterline. Stay clear of marked areas.

In **West Harbor,** west of **Centre Island,** you'll be heading north again and can drop your hook just about anywhere–off Mill Neck to port, or off Centre Island to starboard. As one of our readers put it, this is a "hurricane hole extraordinaire," usually jam-packed with boats. You can sail well up into the harbor and then dink over to the beach at the head of the bay. Don't try landing on Centre Island, however; you are not welcome.

Mill Neck Creek, in the northwest corner of the harbor, has a bascule bridge with a clearance of 9 feet. The area westward of the bridge has depths of 6 to 16 feet. Not many cruising boats frequent this area, but it is popular with small motor boats and fishermen. Just outside the entrance to the creek is a special mooring area for Bayville residents only.

 ## Shoreside and Emergency Services

Airport: MacArthur (516) 588-8062
Port Authority of NY/NJ 1-800-AIR-RIDE
Republic Airport (516) 752-7707
Ambulance: 911
Bus: Suffolk County Transit (516) 360-5700
Coast Guard: Eatons Neck (516) 261-6868/6910 or VHF 16
Fire: 911
Harbormaster: (516) 921-7347 or VHF 16
Hospital: Huntington (516) 351-2000
Police: 911 or (516) 364-0500
Radio Telephone: VHF 25, 26, 84; I.D.: NY
Marine Operator;
VHF 86; I.D.: Mariphone
Marine Operator;
VHF 28; I.D.: Riverhead
Marine Operator;
VHF 27; I.D.: Bridgeport
Marine Operator
Taxi: Oyster Bay (516) 922-2188
Tow Service: Sea Tow Services, Northport, NY
(516) 754-1545 or VHF 16
Train: Long Island Railroad (516) 794-LIRR ◆

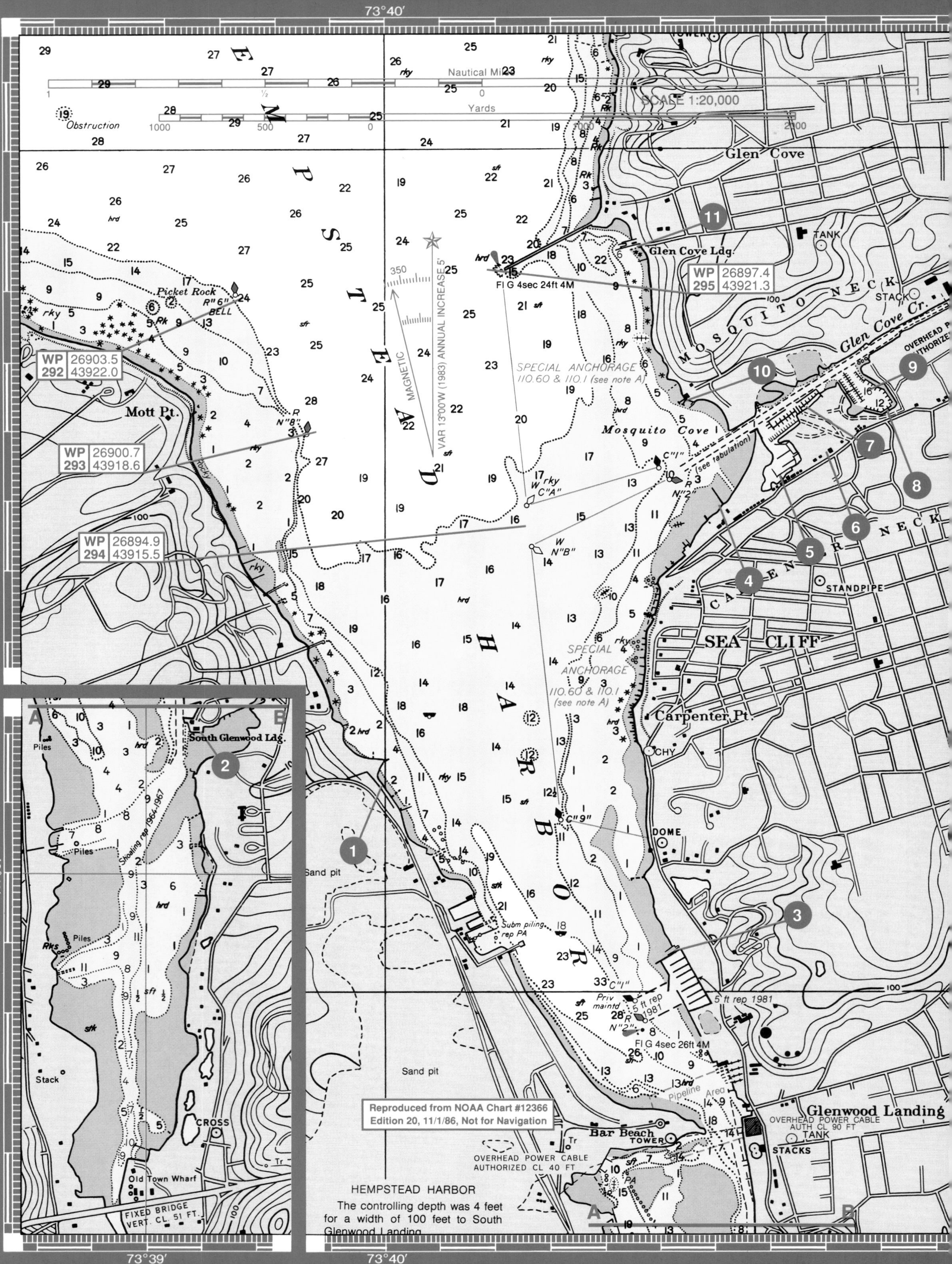

73°40'

73°39'

73°40'

40°50'

40°49'

SCALE 1:20,000

Nautical Mile

Yards

Obstruction

1000   500   0   1000   2000

MAGNETIC

VAR 13°00'W (1983) ANNUAL INCREASE 5'

350

Glen Cove

TANK

STACK

MOSQUITO NECK

Glen Cove Ldg.

FI G 4sec 24ft 4M

WP 292 | 26903.5 | 43922.0

WP 293 | 26900.7 | 43918.6

WP 294 | 26894.9 | 43915.5

WP 295 | 26897.4 | 43921.3

Glen Cove Cr.

OVERHEAD POWER AUTHORIZE

Picket Rock
R"6"
BELL

Mott Pt.

E M P S T E A D

SPECIAL ANCHORAGE
110.60 & 110.1 (see note A)

Mosquito Cove

R N"8"

W rky C"A"

W N"B"

C"I"

R N"2"

(see tabulation)

STANDPIPE

CARPENTER NECK

SEA CLIFF

SPECIAL ANCHORAGE
110.60 & 110.1
(see note A)

Carpenter Pt.

CHY

H A R B O R

C"9"

DOME

Subm piling rep PA

C"I"

Priv maintd

N"2"

FI G 4sec 26ft 4M

5 ft rep 1981

5 ft rep 1981

Pipeline Area

Glenwood Landing

OVERHEAD POWER CABLE
AUTH CL 90 FT

TANK

STACKS

Bar Beach
TOWER

OVERHEAD POWER CABLE
AUTHORIZED CL 40 FT

Reproduced from NOAA Chart #12366
Edition 20, 11/1/86, Not for Navigation

HEMPSTEAD HARBOR
The controlling depth was 4 feet
for a width of 100 feet to South
Glenwood Landing

Piles

South Glenwood Ldg.

Sand pit

Sholing rep 1964-1967

Piles

Piles

Rks

sft 1/2

stk

Stack

Sand pit

CROSS

Old Town Wharf

Tr

FIXED BRIDGE
VERT. CL. 51 FT.

A

B

A

B

11
10
9
8
7
6
5
4
3
2
1

Hempstead Harbor and Glen Cove

Grassy Flats and Grinding Glaciers

Imagine you're a glacier, slowly grinding south. Before you, to starboard, lies the hard highland of Manhasset Neck; to port, the soft, tempting Hempstead stream valley. Which do you choose?

You don't choose, of course, since you're a glacier and therefore not very smart. But you *would* follow the path of least resistance, which is precisely what happened when the last glacier moved southward. As the glacier shouldered its way into the valley of the drainage system that helped to carve out Long Island Sound, it widened the stream valley and shoved glacial debris up onto the necks to either side. That created the complex "ice-shove" geology that is typical of the east side of Manhasset Neck, which you can now see exposed in the sandpits opposite Sea Cliff.

The glacier did a fine job—creating deep unobstructed water, sandy beaches, and a spectacular view. The Indians used the area for a campsite, calling what is now Glen Cove *Musketo*, meaning "grassy flats," but it is also where you find the whining insect of that English name. The work of the glacier has been continued in modern times by the sand-and-gravel mining companies that have dug out vast quantities of the western side of the harbor.

Glen Cove was founded in 1668 when a lumber mill was built on Glen Cove Creek. The real excitement didn't begin until the 18th century, when Hempstead Harbor became one of the area's foremost smuggling ports.

In the 19th century the harbor drew the likes of J. Pierpont Morgan and his famous yacht *Corsair*, the first of four so named and owned by old J. Pierpont and then by J.P., his son. *Corsair IV* (a measly 343 feet) was the largest steam yacht of its day. The story goes that an acquaintance of Morgan's asked him what it cost to keep such an enormous yacht (crew of 60) running, prompting Morgan's famous remark, "If you have to ask, you can't afford it." Morgan also kept the *Navette*, a smaller steamer (a mere

Glen Cove Creek on the east side of Hempstead Harbor, NY.

Marine Facilities and Services	Phone	Number of Transient Berths	Number of Transient Moorings	Seasonal/Year-round	Largest Vessel Accommodation (in feet)	Marked Entry Channel	Approach Depth in feet	Dockside Depth in feet at MLW	Gas/Diesel Fuel	Fuel Brand	Ramp/Dinghy Dock/Launch Service	Railway/Lift: Capacity (in tons)	Propeller/Hull Repairs	Engine Repairs: Gas/Diesel	Marine Supplies/Groceries/Bait/Ice	Pump-out Station	Showers/Laundromat	110V ★ 220V ▲ Maximum Amps	MasterCard/VISA/Diners Club	American Express	Restaurant/Snack Bar	Monitors VHF Channel
① Beacon Hill Boat House	(516) 883-5050	4	5	S	35	●	6	5			R		PH		G I							16
② Burtis Boat Works	(516) 676-4201			Y								L50	PH	GD			S		MV			
③ Tappen Marina	(516) 671-0484			Y	45	●	5	5	GD	OKP	R					●		★30	MV			
④ Sea Cliff Yacht Club	(516) 671-7374		10	S	50		4	3.5			DL	L4					S			A	RS	9
⑤ Brewer Yacht Yard	(516) 671-5563			Y	45	●	7	8				L30	PH	GD			S	★30		A		
⑥ Quality Marine Service	(516) 676-7588			Y	*ENGINES - SALES & SERVICE*																	
⑦ Glen Cove Yacht Service & Repair	(516) 676-0777			Y	70	●	10	7	GD	TEX		L60	PH	GD	SI	●	S	▲50	MV	A		
⑧ Ackerly Marine Co. (p. 379)	(516) 676-1377			Y	*MARINE SUPPLIES*																	
⑨ Glen Cove Marina Associates	(516) 759-3129	15		Y	80	●	8	5	GD	NVL		L10	PH	GD	SI		S	★50	MV			16
⑩ Hempstead Harbour Club	(516) 761-0600			S	80		6															68
⑪ Glen Cove Yacht Club	(516) 676-9450		2	S	40		18	5			DL						S					

Information in these listings is provided by the facilities themselves. An asterisk (*) indicates that the facility did not respond to our most recent requests for information.

dinghy at 114 feet), in Glen Cove for those days when he wanted to go to work by boat. Life's hard, no?

Just as Walt Whitman was the "Bard of Huntington," so the poet William Cullen Bryant graced Roslyn, south of Hempstead Harbor. Bryant, who was also editor of The *New York Evening Post,* is best known for his philosophical poem "Thanatopsis," among others.

Hempstead's more modern claims to fame are its two airfields, Mitchell and Roosevelt. In 1924 the first transcontinental airmail left Mitchell for San Francisco; in 1927 Charles Lindbergh took off from Roosevelt on his historic flight to Paris. (Lindbergh had his own suite at the Guggenheim Mansion, where he wrote his books.)

Nearby is Garden City, founded in 1869 by the philanthropist A.T. Stewart of New York, who spent part of his fortune to create a utopia. Like most such ventures, Garden City never lived up to his expectations, though the restrictions on property that he imposed still hold, and help to give the town its special character.

Hempstead Harbor marks a cultural border of sorts, between the urban "bedroom communities" around New York City and the more laid-back parts of eastern Long Island. Spend some time in the area and you'll see an interesting mixture of types of development, attitudes, and accents.

 ## What To See and Do

At Glen Cove Creek you'll find the Garvies Point Museum and Preserve (516) 671-0300, devoted to the culture of Long Island Indians and the area's fascinating geology. A self-guiding nature trail lets you work off your sea legs and learn in the process. Particularly fascinating is the rocky beach, characteristic of glacial terrain, and the cliffs above–one of the few places on Long Island where you can see the sedimentary soil beneath the glacial moraine that created the island.

Also in Glen Cove is the Webb Institute of Naval Architecture (516) 671-2213, one of the finest such schools in the world. The 26-acre campus has facilities for 80 to 90 young men and women studying modern ways of the sea.

Right next door is the 200-acre Welwyn Preserve, where you can hike beautiful nature trails. Camping or cooking out is discouraged, however.

In 1904 the 238-foot sidewheel steamer *Glen Island* caught fire off Matinecock Point, burned, and sank. If you have scuba gear you can dive to the wreck, but be careful of the tidal currents off the point, as they can be quite strong.

On the south side of Glen Cove Creek is the mile-square village of Sea Cliff. Originally the site of a Methodist camp meeting, Sea Cliff was part of the popular 19th-century movement to encourage revivals away from the sins of the city. Individual tent sites blossomed into tiny houses; many have been maintained and today complement their grander cousins. The terrain is steep–Sea Cliff once had a cable

car–and the streets are narrow and winding, but not yet totally clogged with antique shops. Visit Sea Cliff on a foggy day, and the water, the hills, and the Victorian houses built on them will remind you of San Francisco.

The Afro-American Museum (516) 485-0470 at Hempstead offers extensive exhibits of African-American artists' paintings, as well as programs about African-American culture and history. Admission is free.

If you're in the area on July 4th, there are spectacular fireworks at Glen Cove Landing, south of the breakwater. You will, of course, have a whole lot of company.

 ## Where To Eat

In Glen Cove proper is an array of international restaurants within walking distance of each other, but a cab ride away from any of the marinas. For fine French cuisine try La Pace (516) 671-2970. For Continental try Winfield's (516) 676-0800, just a few blocks away. For Chinese, you have several choices: the Golden Woks (516) 759-3037, specializing in Hunan and Szechuan; Sino Express (516) 676-8407; or Yin's (516) 671-3223. Sino Express and Yin's both offer takeout. Expensive, elegant French and Northern Italian cuisine is available at the Veranda Restaurant (516) 759-0394 (make reservations and wear a tie). For more plebian tastes, basic Italian fare and pizza is available at Delicious (516) 676-3488, offering takeout.

 ## Navigation and Anchorages

Use NOAA Charts 12366 (1:20,000), 12364 (1:40,000), and 12363 (1:80,000). Use tide tables for Willets Point. High tide at Glen Cove is 5 minutes earlier; low tide is 8 minutes earlier. Mean tidal range is 7.8 feet.

CAUTION: There have been many buoy changes in this area. We have noted the most important below, but be alert for others.

The 24-foot 4sec green flasher "5" on the breakwater at Glen Cove Landing is 10.0nm by boat west of the Cold Spring Harbor Light, 6.2nm east of Plum Point in Manhasset Bay, and 4.6nm south-southeast of Mamaroneck Harbor.

From the green 4sec gong "21" **[WP-299]** off Matinecock Point, a course of about 225°m will take you past Weeks Point and into the broad entrance to **Hempstead Harbor.**

The harbor offers an excellent anchorage with good holding ground in everything but a strong northerly wind. This may not be a problem during the summer, but if you're coming into the harbor during the fall or winter months, with their prevailing northerly winds, you could be in for a beating. Like Manhasset Bay next door, the harbor gets narrower and shallower as you go south, leaving those big waves nowhere to go but up.

The mean tidal range is 7.8 feet, with weak currents except at the channel at **Bar Beach,** where the velocity is

0.8 knots. Note that some charts may show a can "1" off Weeks Point, but it has been removed.

If you are headed in from the east, it is wisest to stay outside of the green 4sec flashing gong "21" **[WP-299]** off Matinecock Point.

If you are coming in from Execution Rocks and the west, it is best to stay outside all the buoys from the green 4sec flasher "23" **[WP-282]** at **Sands Point** all the way into red nun "8" **[WP-293]** off Mott Point in order to clear the many boulders along the shore. Coming from Manhasset Bay or Throgs Neck, some boats cut inside the green 2.5sec flasher "25" **[WP-280]**, splitting the distance to the breakwater day marker off Sands Point. We don't recommend this if you don't know the area–too many rocks. A good landmark for **Prospect Point** is a large white house with columns, designed by the famous architect Stanford White.

Mott Point provides a favorite anchorage, just inside the line from the point to the breakwater at Glen Cove Landing, which is marked by a 24-foot 4sec green flasher **[WP-295].** (The flasher is now designated "5.") Small boats can anchor behind the breakwater in ample water, but not in the south end of the harbor, in the pipeline area between Glenwood Landing and Bar Beach. This is a free federal mooring field, one of the last around.

On the western side of the harbor, above and below **Bar Beach,** you will see the large sand-and-gravel pits that supply commercial barges. There are a lot of old rotting barges sunk along the beach. All the dredged channels off to the west of the harbor are there to allow the barges to come in close to the sand pits for loading.

Glen Cove Creek, about a half mile south of the breakwater, has a channel from Mosquito Cove up 0.6nm by boat to the head. The creek entrance has a reported depth of 8 to 10 feet, but don't believe it. There is considerable shoaling, especially on the north side of the creek. Occasionally the local barge pilots will clear the channel by intentionally hitting the sandy shoals. The best course is to stay in the middle of the channel. The creek contains several marinas and a marine supply store, and attracts many boaters. There is a ramp just north of the creek entrance for residents only.

At Glen Cove Marina Associates you'll see the *Thomas Jefferson,* (516) 744-2353, an 80-foot replica of a 19th-century side-wheel paddle steamer, available for public and private charter. We're told the 150-passenger steamer is a popular wedding place.

There are anchorages inside each of the yellow buoys "A" (a can) and "B" **[WP-294]** (a nun) marking the approach to **Glen Cove Creek.** If you want to anchor southeast of nun "B," watch the chart carefully. Go too far south and you'll be one of the many boaters who have to be pulled off the mud around Carpenter Point.

From **Sea Cliff** southerly to the town marina at **Glenwood Landing,** a shoal extends 300 yards out, marked by a can and a light. (Buoys "10" to "18," marked on some charts, have been removed, and can "9" off Carpenter Point

is now green.) The eight stacks of the large power plants at Glenwood Landing are easy to spot. The wharves have good water for tying up. For most boats, Burtis Boatyard at **South Glenwood Landing** can be reached only at high water.

From Glenwood a dredged channel continues south, but the shallow water (less than 4 feet), industrial and warehouse sites, and commercial traffic make it unappealing. The channel was also unmarked when we were last there. If you want to explore, do it by dink only.

The Glen Cove Harbor Patrol operates as a mini-Coast Guard, monitors VHF 16, and is attentive to the needs of yachters.

 Shoreside and Emergency Services

Airport: MacArthur (516) 588-8062
  Port Authority of NY/NJ 1-800-AIR-RIDE
Ambulance: 911
Bus: Nassau County Bus (516) 222-1000
Coast Guard: Eatons Neck (516) 261-6868/6910
  or VHF 16 or CB 9
  Fort Totten (718) 352-4422/4423
  or VHF 16 or CB 9
Fire: "0" Operator
Harbormaster: Harbor Patrol (516) 671-4263 or VHF 16
Hospital: Glen Cove Community (516) 676-5000
Police: 911 or (516) 676-1000
Radio Telephone: VHF 25, 26, 84; I.D.: NY
  Marine Operator;
  VHF 86; I.D.: Mariphone
  Marine Operator;
  VHF 27; I.D.: Bridgeport
  Marine Operator
Taxi: Cove Taxi (516) 671-1913
Tow Service: Sound Tow Co., Bronx, NY (212) 885-3420
  or VHF 16; Sea Tow Manhasset Bay, Port
  Washington, NY (516) 944-9483 or VHF 16
Train: Long Island Railroad (516) 794-LIRR ✦

Manhasset Bay and Port Washington

Cows, Scows, and Irish Castles

Manhasset Bay, which used to be called Cow Bay, boasts of having more yacht clubs than any other port on the Sound. The oldest started out on Staten Island as the New York Canoe Club in 1871, and by 1940 ended up in Manorhaven as the North Shore Yacht Club. Manhasset Bay Yacht Club, formed in 1891, is an outgrowth of an earlier club first established at Little Neck Bay and then moved due to silting of the harbor and the presence of mines during the Spanish-American War. Known as the Douglaston Yacht Club, that first club was an unpretentious affair–an old scow with a house on it, a bar and a piano within–yearly dues, five bucks. Gazing at the MBYC today it is hard to imagine such humble beginnings, but the club is properly reverential about its origins. All the yacht clubs on the bay take turns sponsoring year-round small-boat racing.

If you sailed into Manhasset Bay 50 years ago you'd not only be busy dodging racing boats, but also a few aircraft. The old Pan-American Airlines "Clippers" landed on Long Island Sound and taxied into Manhasset Bay to their docks on Tom Point. (The enormous old hangars are still sitting on Tom Point.) Even today you'll see the odd seaplane land

Rowing out to the moorings.

here and taxi to the fuel depot in Manorhaven just east of Capri Marina.

Sands Point, named for one of the original settlers of Block Island, is part of the fabled gold coast, where the

Marine Facilities and Services		Number of Transient Berths	Number of Transient Moorings	Seasonal/Year-round	Largest Vessel Accommodation (in feet)	Marked Entry Channel	Approach Depth in feet)	Dockside Depth in feet at MLW	Gas/Diesel at MLW	Fuel Brand	Ramp/Dinghy Dock/Launch Service	Railway/Lift: Capacity (in tons)	Engine Repairs: Propeller/Hull Repairs	Marine Supplies/Groceries Bait/Ice	Showers Laundromat	Pump-out Station	110V ★ 220V ▲ Maximum Amps	MasterCard/VISA/Diners Club American Express	Restaurant/Snack Bar	Monitors VHF Channel
❶ Capri Marina East & West (p. 383)	(516) 883-7802	25	25	Y	150	●	8	8	GD	TEX	DL	L40	PH	GD	●	SL	SI	★▲100	MVA	SR	16
❷ North Shore Yacht Club	(516) 883-9823			S	50	●	5	5				L				S	I	★			68
❸ Ventura Yachts	(516) 944-8415			Y	45		6	5			*YACHT SALES*										
❹ Joe White's Marine Service	(516) 944-9200	3	3	Y	60		6	6	D			L20	PH	GD			I	★▲50			
❺ Tom's Point Marina	(516) 883-6630	10		Y	40		4	4					PH	GD		SL		★30			
❻ Doyle Sailmakers	(516) 944-5660			Y							*SAILMAKERS & CANVAS WORK*							▲			
❼ Manhasset Bay Sportsmen's Club	(516) 883-9689	2		Y	85		4	4										▲			68
❽ North Bay Marina (p. 385)	(516) 767-0110	5		Y	60	●	5	6				L35	PH	GD		SL	S	★▲50	MVA		
❾ Manhasset Bay Marina (p. 386)	(516) 883-8411	10		Y							*REPAIR FACILITY*										
❿ The Rigging Locker	(516) 883-3756	4	8	Y	50	●	2	2				L20					S		MVA		16
⓫ D & D Marine	(516) 944-6142			Y							*MARINE SUPPLIES*						S		MVA		
⓬ Cow Bay Marine Service (p. 387)	(516) 883-1200	5		Y	60	●	10	10				L35	PH	GD		SL	S	★30	MVA		
⓭ Gulfway Marine	(516) 767-0113			S	32	●	10	10				L20	PH	GD							
⓮ Fearon Marine Service	(516) 767-0806	2		S	80	●	12	8				L25	PH					▲100			

Facilities listings continued on next page...

very, very rich once showed the nation how to live well in Irish castles and Norman mansions built high on the imposing bluffs. One of the mansions, owned by Harry Guggenheim, sheltered young Charles Lindbergh when he was being hounded by the press after his famous 1927 flight across the Atlantic.

Nearby, during the late 1930s and through World War II, the Navy tested PT boats and torpedoes. The Navy abandoned the site some years ago, and some of the land was sold to the Museums at Stony Brook and the Helen Keller School.

The "Otto Mast" marked on the chart between Sands Point and Barker Point is the mast from Sir Thomas Lipton's yacht *Shamrock*, the 1899 challenger for the America's Cup. It was placed on the property by Carl Fisher (a major developer of Miami Beach, FL and Montauk Point, NY) but gets its charted designation from the present owner, who petitioned Congress to have it named after himself.

Stepping Stones Light, originally built in 1877 and automated in the 1960s, presumably gets its name from the almost continuous line of rocks stretching from Elm Point to the light–seemingly close enough together to be able to walk across the tops all the way out. We don't recommend trying this stunt.

 ## What To See and Do

Don't let the likelihood of being one among many deter you from visiting this magnificent bay. This is a very popular spot where you'll find one of the greatest concentrations of marinas, yacht clubs, restaurants, and fine shopping anywhere.

Port Washington is a very busy place, but the waterfront and commercial districts are surrounded by quiet residential areas, ranging from middle-class to the very wealthy. It's a nice suburban area, and it has the indelible stamp of New York City on it, as you'll discover soon after going ashore.

For a glimpse at the lifestyles of the rich (and sometimes famous), you might want to take in the Sands Point Preserve (516) 883-1612, which contains the restored Guggenheim family homes and a 209-acre forest. Castlegould, built in 1902, is a huge stone castle (the Irish one) that once served as a stable; it now houses a new dinosaur exhibit. Falaise was built by Captain Harry F. Guggenheim in 1923, and is an elegant manor house (the Norman one), with original furnishings and the owner's aeronautical memorabilia. Tours are by escort only, so be sure to call ahead. Hempstead House is the former main residence. (It's Tudor!)

Execution Rocks is a favorite fishing spot, but the current is strong enough to set you onto the rocks if you're not careful, and there's much commercial traffic. To anchor and fish come in close on the south side. Don't try the west side, especially at low tide when you are likely to bang your bottom on the rocks.

The passion for racing in Manhasset Bay is truly a year-round phenomenon. The Cow Bay Racing Association, founded in the 1960s by the Knickerbocker, Manhasset

Marine Facilities and Services

#	Facility	Phone	Number of Transient Moorings	Number of Transient Berths	Seasonal/Year-round	Largest Vessel Accommodation (in feet)	Marked Entry Channel	Approach Depth (in feet)	Dockside Depth in feet at MLW	Gas/Diesel Fuel	Fuel Brand	Ramp/Dinghy Dock/Launch Service	Railway/Lift: Capacity (in tons)	Propeller/Hull Repairs	Engine Repairs: Gas/Diesel	Pump-out Station	Marine Supplies/Groceries/Bait/Ice	Showers/Laundromat	110V ★ 220V ▲ Maximum Amps	MasterCard/VISA/Diners Club/American Express	Restaurant/Snack Bar	Monitors VHF Channel
15	North Hempstead Town Dock	(516) 328-8500			Y	35	•	12	4							•						16
16	Louie's Shore Restaurant	(516) 883-4242	10		Y	50	•	7	4										l	MVAD	R	
17	**Northstar Marine (p. 386)**	**(516) 944-7828**			Y	40	•	8	6			*RETAIL ACCESSORIES*								MVAD		
18	Jimmy's Back Yard	(516) 944-3070	8		Y	50	•	8	6			*RESTAURANT*								MVAD	R	
19	Knickerbocker Yacht Club	(516) 883-7655		5	S	50	•	6	6									S	★		RS	9
20	Lager Yacht Service	(516) 767-9350	6	12	Y	50	•	7	7			D	L20	PH	GD			S	★50			68
21	Manhasset Bay Yacht Club	(516) 767-2163										*PRIVATE CLUB - MEMBERS ONLY*										
22	Sigsbee Marine Co.	(516) 767-0944		20	Y	60		8	8			R		PH			S	S		MVA		16
23	Port Washington Yacht Club	(516) 767-1614		20	Y	80	•	11	8									S			RS	9
24	Shelter Harbor Marina	(516) 482-9085										*PRIVATE CLUB - MEMBERS ONLY*										
25	Broadlawn Harbor Yacht Club	(516) 482-9793										*PRIVATE CLUB - MEMBERS ONLY*										
26	Kennilwood Yacht Club				S							*PRIVATE CLUB - MEMBERS ONLY*										
27	Randazzo Yacht Mechanics Inc.	(516) 767-1666	2	3	Y	60	•	8	7.5			D	L15	P	GD							

Information in these listings is provided by the facilities themselves. An asterisk (*) indicates that the facility did not respond to our most recent requests for information.

The Pan Am airbase on Tom Point from the west, circa 1939. The two large hangars still stand; the basin at the far right is now occupied by Tom's Point Marina and North Bay Marina.
Photo courtesy of Pan American World Airways, Inc.

PLANE OLD BOATS

On June 18, 1937 an oddly shaped aircraft lifted itself out of Manhasset Bay and climbed into a cool morning, carrying 24 passengers to the Azores. As she rose, Port Washington and the bon-voyage crowd shrank steadily, then evaporated altogether as the craft banked east and sped out over Long Island Sound.

There were plenty of waterfront towns on the Sound that could have accommodated commercial air travel, a novel and aristocratic means of transportation back then. Port Washington, however, had an edge: the smooth and sheltered waters of Manhasset Bay, which these big planes needed to get aloft and land. Moreover, there was already a seaplane facility at Tom Point; the American Aeoronautical Company kept two huge hangars there as a testing center for the single-engined seaplanes they manufactured. Pan Am acquired the site in 1933 and, with the advent of the airline age, converted it to an airbase in 1937.

The first Pan Am Clipper to inaugurate the service was built by the Sikorsky Aero Engineering Corporation, of Bridgeport, Connecticut. Designated as the *S-42,* it cruised at an average speed of 157 miles per hour with a 2,000-mile range. The 24 passengers sat on Queen Anne-style seats in a teak-lined cabin, and ate on bone china and white table cloths.

In 1939, almost two years after that first flight in the Sikorsky seaplane, Pan Am took delivery of the first production Boeing 314, the *Yankee Clipper,* a plane commissioned by the airline and designed to span the globe. Legend has it that the plane was christened with a bottle filled with water from all seven seas.

She may have looked somewhat ungainly to those who saw her moored at Port Washington; this was not exactly a dashing ship, but there was certainly a sense of romance about her, the kind associated with adventure, travel and luxury. Capable of cruising at 183 miles per hour for up to 3,500 miles, her imposing hull contained a spacious and clubby lounge as well as sleeping compartments for some of its 40 passengers.

The trade was short-lived: less than a year later, the four ships left Port Washington to contribute to the war effort in the Pacific. While none were lost in combat, two were involved in landing accidents; beyond salvage or repair, they were hauled out to sea and junked by firing squad–over 1,300 rounds of 20mm ammunition were need to sink them. The two remaining seaplanes were either cannibalized for spare parts or scrapped.

Aside from old photos and a few other documents from the heady days of the flying boats, all that remains of that era in Port Washington are the two hangars on Tom Point. The enormous buildings have changed hands a few times since Pan Am sold them to Grumman at the end of World War II. They are presently owned by Thypin Steel, but stand unused.

Bay, and Port Washington Yacht Clubs, runs the "Thirsty Thursday" regatta each spring, open to the public for a fee. Since the local racers don't get their fill during the warm weather months, the Manhasset Bay Yacht Club hosts the "Frostbite Regatta" (with dinghies!) every winter during the New Year's holiday.

A cab ride will take you to Rte. 25A at the foot of the harbor, and the "Miracle Mile," a strip of expensive shops where a sailor and his money take different tacks. If your means are more modest, however, fear not: there are plenty of very nice shops and restaurants a short walk from the water, if you don't want to go so far.

 ## Where To Eat

Port Washington is jam-packed with restaurants and delis, so you'll find no shortage of edibles. Louie's Shore Restaurant (516) 883-4242 is the local institution for the boating crowd; they have a dock for transient customers and are recommended by nearly everyone. Both Capri East and Capri West marinas have restaurants, Lattitudes (516) 767-7400 and The Barge (516) 944-9403, respectively. Just to the east you can try the steaks and seafood at Bill's Harbor Inn (516) 883-3554, next to Joe White's Marine Service. Also on Manorhaven Boulevard is Marianne's (516) 883-4660 for Northern Italian. Andy's (516) 883-1406, on New Shore Road across the street from Manorhaven Park, offers reasonably priced Italian food in a comfortable, homestyle atmosphere.

Not far from the town dock is the Main Street Restaurant (516) 944-6236 on the street of the same name, serving contemporary American, or you can try the spicy Szechuan food at Sweet Chinese (516) 944-3388.

 ## Navigation and Anchorages

Use NOAA Charts 12366 (1:20,000), 12364 (1:40,000), and 12363 (1:80,000). Use tide tables for Willets Point. High tide at Port Washington is 5 minutes later; low tide is 9 minutes later. Mean tidal range is 7.8 feet.

The Barker Point headland that marks the east entrance to Manhasset Bay is 5.1nm by boat west of the Glen Cove breakwater in Hempstead Harbor, and 3.6nm by boat east and north of the Throgs Neck Bridge. City Island is 2.1nm by boat west, and Mamaroneck Harbor is 4.1nm by boat north.

From the green 6sec flasher "27A" **[WP-276]** at Gangway Rock, a course of about 195°m will bring you into the broad entrance to **Manhasset Bay.**

To reach Barker Point from the east, stay well off Prospect Point, as the shoal extends about 0.4nm northward of the point, and then falls off quickly to a depth of 60 feet. The north end is marked by the green 4sec flasher "23" **[WP-282]**, which is 0.8nm east of Execution Rocks Light. Leave this green flasher to port and also the green 2.5sec flasher "25" **[WP-280]** west of **Sands Point.** A reef marked by a green and white daybeacon extends about 0.3nm off Sands Point, and at low water the boulders show for a distance of some 300 yards. You can't miss the brownstone tower of the old Sands Point Lighthouse, built in 1809 and now privately owned.

In the bight between Sands Point and Barker Point is **Half Moon Beach,** one of the best on the Sound. Though the area is too exposed for a night anchorage, you can sail in, drop a hook, and swim or dink to shore. Since the current runs across the two points, the bight is also a good area to tack into in order to get away from the tides.

Barker Point itself, 1.0nm south-southwest of Sands Point, is a high bluff on the northeast side of **Manhasset Bay.** If you are bound for the bay, avoid going inside **Gangway Rock,** marked by a 40-foot 6sec green flasher "27A" **[WP-276]** that is on the northwest end of a rocky shoal extending 0.6nm out from Barker Point. On the chart there appears to be room to cut the buoy, but the local navigators have enormous respect for Barker Point, and you should, too. If you insist on tempting fate, watch out for Success Rock, about 0.2nm to the southeast and awash at low water. The charted daybeacon near Success Rock is now an orange and white can. There is also a 6-foot spot about 200 yards in to the southeast. Don't try to run a rhumb line from Gangway Rock to Plum Point. You will "rub" much too close to the rocks off Barker Point.

The approach to **Manhasset Bay** from the 46-foot green flashing **Stepping Stones Light [WP-266]** and the west is straightforward. Always stay to the west of the light, and always go outside of the green 4sec flasher "29" **[WP-271]** off Hewlett Point. (There is an inside route on the east side of Stepping Stones, south of red nuns "4" **[WP-265]** and "2" off Kings Point, but this route is not recommended for boaters new to the area.)

During the summer when the prevailing winds are southwesterly, **Manhasset Bay** is well-protected and easy to enter by day or night. However, if you're crazy enough (like we were) to go in during November, the prevailing northerlies and shallow water may conspire to make you question your sanity. In a good blow, the vicious chop can make the bay even more uncomfortable than the Sound itself.

The depths in the northern part of **Manhasset Bay** range from 12 to 17 feet, and 7 to 12 feet in the southern part, with little current. The extreme south end is shallow with extensive mudflats, although 2 to 6 feet can be carried in the natural channel almost to the head of the bay.

About a mile in you will pass **Plum Point,** marked by green 4sec flasher "1" **[WP-275],** about 150 yards south of the point. If you're coming in after dark, keep an eye out for the large unlighted speed limit sign off the point. Running into it will slow you down, but quick.

Plum Point was the site of the old Sands Point Beach and Tennis Club, shown as a cupola on charts. It burned down several years ago; the future of the site is still in question. Around Plum Point, to the east is Manorhaven, one of the bay's two yachting centers. The marinas here are large, well equipped, and always busy.

Less than a mile east of Plum Point is Tom Point, guarding the entrance to **Port Washington.** There is an 8-foot unmarked channel to the town docks, and also northeastward of the point to a bight. You can tie up for a half hour with permission from the harbor patrol (VHF 16)

 **Shoreside and Emergency Services**

Airport: MacArthur (516) 588-8062
Port Authority of NY/NJ 1-800-AIR-RIDE
Ambulance: 911
Bus: Nassau County Bus (516) 222-1000
Coast Guard: Eatons Neck (516) 261-6868/6910 or VHF 16 or CB 9
Fort Totten (718) 352-4422/4423 or VHF 16 or CB 9
Fire: 911 or (516) 466-4411
Harbormaster: Marine Patrol (516) 627-0590 x365 or VHF 16
Hospital: North Shore University (516) 562-0100
Police: 911 or (516) 365-8000
Radio Telephone: VHF 25, 26, 84; I.D.: NY Marine Operator;
VHF 86; I.D.: Mariphone Marine Operator;
VHF 28; I.D.: KLU 786;
VHF 27; I.D.: Bridgeport Marine Operator
Taxi: Deluxe Cab (516) 883-1900
Tow Service: Sound Tow Co., Bronx, NY (212) 885-3420 or VHF 16; Sea Tow Manhasset Bay, Port Washington, NY (516) 944-9483 or VHF 16
Train: Long Island Railroad (516) 794-LIRR ◆

on the west and south sides of the town dock. Plans are afoot to install a new pump-out station there in 1990. There may also be some new dredging, to a 5-foot depth, at the town dock. Port Washington offers an array of facilities to satisfy every need.

The least crowded anchorages are on the south end of the bay or on the west side off **Great Neck,** which has several yacht clubs lying at the foot of impressive estates. The anchorage between Plum Point and Tom Point is good, though much of the space is taken up with moorings. The bay's soft bottom affords good holding ground.

CAUTION: Watch out for the commuting seaplanes that frequently take off or land in special no-anchoring areas clearly marked on the charts. Although seaplanes rarely have the right-of-way over any type of vessel, colliding with one will still ruin your day.

Little Neck Bay

Twinkling Lights and Tidal Mills

The lights of the Throgs Neck Bridge, 157 feet above the water, twinkle in the night and define the western end of Long Island Sound. With the bridge overhead, the Big Apple to the west, and a vast shopping complex on Great Neck to the east, Little Neck Bay is not quiet, but the noise and lights of the city are not oppressive, either. The bay has silted up over the years, and though dredged, still has an average depth of only 6 to 8 feet, so most of the boats that use the special anchorage near Douglaston tend to be of the shallow-draft variety.

The Douglaston Yacht Club was organized in 1891, and actively encouraged racing on the Sound. But because of the silting of the bay and the danger of mines around Fort Totten during the Spanish-American War, the club changed its name to Manhasset Bay Yacht Club and moved one bay to the east in 1899. The old Navy fort on Willets Point is now the home of the U.S. Coast Guard.

While the 7- to 9-foot tides in Little Neck Bay are something of an annoyance to mariners, one local entrepreneur made good use of them by building the Saddle Rock Grist Mill on Udall's Mill Pond on the east side of the bay. A dam across the inlet to the pond forced the tides through a narrow channel and under a waterwheel. No matter which way the tide was flowing, the mill would have power, except, of course, at slack tide when the tides are reversing direction. With the coming of steam, oil, and electrical power, the mill was neglected and deteriorated badly, but is now undergoing restoration and is scheduled to be open to the public in spring of 1989.

 What To See and Do

The United States Merchant Marine Academy (516) 773-5515 on Kings Point in Great Neck trains officers for the merchant marine and welcomes visitors to tour its facilities

The United States Merchant Marine Academy on Kings Point at the entrance to Little Neck Bay, NY.

from August through June. While on campus, be sure to visit the mansion of the late Walter P. Chrysler, now the Academy's administration building, and the American Merchant Marine Museum, which was once the home of William Barstow, inventor of the electric meter and the illuminator of the Brooklyn Bridge. The museum features ship models, rare navigational instruments, marine art, and a gallery on the wartime merchant marine. Only alumni are allowed to dock at the academy.

Swimming in Little Neck Bay is not recommended, but Stepping Stones Park, just north of the Academy, has a nice beach and a nifty playground for the kids. There is no docking at the beach, so you'll have to dink ashore.

The U.S. Coast Guard station at Fort Totten on Willets Point is open to visiting groups with advance reservations (718) 352-4422 or VHF 16. On the tour you will see the 9 acres of the fort and the Coast Guard's 41-foot rescue boat.

If you're thinking of leaving your boat and venturing into the Big Apple, you can call the New York City Travel

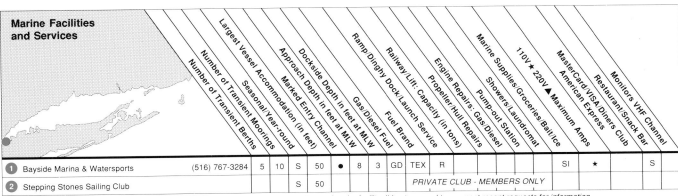

Marine Facilities and Services		Number of Transient Berths	Number of Transient Moorings	Seasonal/Year-round	Largest Vessel Accommodation (in feet)	Marked Entry Channel	Approach Depth in feet	Dockside Depth in feet at MLW	Gas/Diesel Fuel	Fuel Brand	Ramp/Dinghy Dock/Launch Service	Railway/Lift: Capacity (in tons)	Propeller/Hull Repairs	Engine Repairs: Gas/Diesel	Marine Supplies/Groceries/Bait/Ice	Pump-out Station	Showers/Laundromat	110V ★ 220V ▲ Maximum Amps	MasterCard/VISA/Diners Club American Express	Restaurant/Snack Bar	Monitors VHF Channel
❶ Bayside Marina & Watersports	(516) 767-3284	5	10	S	50	●	8	3	GD	TEX	R						SI	★			S
❷ Stepping Stones Sailing Club				S	50					*PRIVATE CLUB - MEMBERS ONLY*											

Information in these listings is provided by the facilities themselves. An asterisk (*) indicates that the facility did not respond to our most recent requests for information.

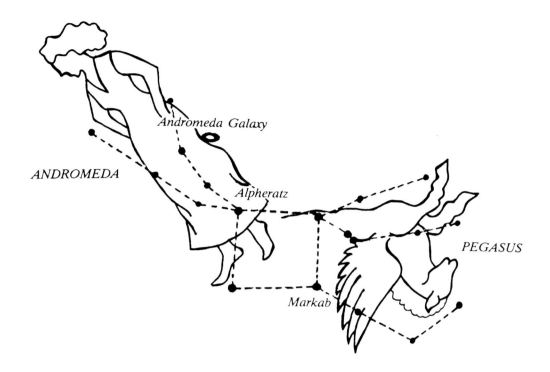

SEPTEMBER SKIES:
Pegasus and Andromeda

Look East after sunset in September, and you'll find Pegasus, the flying horse. It's identified by a Great Square of four stars of near equal brightness. This window in the heavens is almost devoid of naked eye stars. Scan it with a pair of binoculars, and many stars come into view. On September 21, the autumnal equinox, the Great Square will be directly overhead at midnight.

The Great Square forms the body of the stellar horse Pegasus as it flies upside down in the night sky. The two southern stars of the square run along Pegasus' back and join its neck in the west. The upper two stars of the square outline the horse's belly and join to its front legs, which paw the western sky.

In myth, Pegasus has played many roles, including carrying thunder and lightning to the ground from Mt. Olympus. It is also credited with pawing the earth until the Fount of Hippocrene sprang forth. These waters supposedly served as inspiration for poets of antiquity.

Trailing off Pegasus' hindquarters is Andromeda, the princess of the heavens. This constellation shares the star Alpheratz with Pegasus and forms a V-shape. Draw an imaginary line connecting Markab, the star at the base of Pegasus' neck, and Alpheratz. Double the distance of the line to find Andromeda Galaxy, a neighboring elliptical star system. The galaxy can be seen with the naked eye on very clear, moonless nights but is better viewed with binoculars. It appears as a white smudge of light containing over 200 billion distant stars.

Contributed by Elinor DeWire, assistant at the Mystic Seaport Planetarium and a freelance writer.

Authority (718) 330-1234 for information on public transportation in the five boroughs.

 ## Where To Eat

The only place to come ashore (unless you're one of the aforementioned Merchant Marine Academy alumni), is at the small marina on the west shore of Little Neck Bay; once there, you can't get to any restaurants without a cab. On Northern Boulevard (at the foot of the bay) you'll find La Baraka (718) 428-1461, for French cuisine, or Ray's Italian Restaurant (718) 225-0336, serving you-know-what. Further east is Dynasty (516) 621-1870, for Chinese.

On the west side of the harbor you'll find more Chinese food at the Golden Panda (718) 224-5200, Spanish and Continental food (complete with flamenco guitarists) at Marbella (718) 423-0100, or the Pasta House (718) 279-0050 for steaks, seafood and Italian.

 ## Navigation and Anchorages

Use NOAA charts 12366 (1:20,000), 12364 (1:40,000), and 12363 (1:80,000). Use tide tables for Willets Point. Mean tidal range is 7.6 feet.

Willets Point, marking the western entrance to Little Neck Bay, is 0.8nm east of the Throgs Neck Bridge, 2.5nm south of City Island, and 4.4nm by boat from Plum Point in Manhasset Bay.

If you're heading into or out of **New York Harbor,** see the chapter on Throgs Neck and the East River.

Approaching **Little Neck Bay** from Hewlett Point and Manhasset Bay, it is safest to pass to the north of **Stepping Stones Light,** a 46-foot red brick Victorian structure with a green flasher **[WP-266],** about halfway between Elm Point and City Island.

***CAUTION:** The stretch of foul ground between the light and nuns "4" [WP-265] and "2" has been the graveyard of many unwary captains over the years, and both the Coast Guard and the New York City Harbor Police, who also patrol in the area, tell us that it is still the place where visitors have the most trouble. If you take the southern passage along the shore just off Elm Point, honor those nuns. This passage may save you some time if traveling along the north shore of Long Island, but don't try it until you are familiar with the area, and then watch out for the tide rips.*

A little south of Elm Point is **Kings Point,** the home of the Merchant Marine Academy. A good landmark is the academy's steel flagpole, which is supposed be the country's tallest: The top is 216 feet above the water.

All of **Little Neck Bay** is a restricted anchorage, so caution is required, especially at night when moored and anchored boats may not be lighted. Depths in the bay are 10 to 12 feet, decreasing gradually to the head of the harbor, about 2 miles to the south, where the bay divides into muddy flats.

The harbor offers a convenient jumping-off place for a trip up the Sound, but it is open to weather from the north. Though thickly settled with many private boat landings, **Little Neck Bay** is not much used as an anchorage. There is a small marina on the west side that offers launch service, and the only place to land. Watch out for boulders close to shore, especially in the southern part of the bay.

 ## Shoreside and Emergency Services

Airport: Port Authority of NY/NJ 1-800-AIR-RIDE
Ambulance: 911
Bus: NYC Travel Authority Information (718) 330-1234
Coast Guard: Eatons Neck (516) 261-6868/6910
or VHF 16 or CB 9
Fort Totten (718) 352-4422/4423
or VHF 16 or CB 9
Fire: 911 or (718) 847-6600
Hospital: Deepdale General (516) 485-6265
Police: 911 or (718) 670-0360
NYPD Harbor Unit: (212) 993-0950 or VHF 16
Radio Telephone: VHF 25, 26, 84; I.D.: NY
Marine Operator
VHF 86; I.D.: Mariphone
Marine Operator
VHF 28; I.D.: WHU 738
Taxi: Little Neck (718) 229-5454
Great Neck (516) 482-0077
Tow Service: Sound Tow Co., Bronx, NY
(212) 885-3420 or VHF 16
Train: Amtrak 1-800-USA-RAIL
Long Island Railroad (516) 794-LIRR ◆

Embassy's LORAN Index

LORAN-C is currently the most popular electronic navigation system in use by mariners in the Northeast, and has greatly expanded the cruising range of many boaters. On a foggy day near Block Island, all one can hear on the VHF is captains comparing "numbers" to determine their relative positions. LORAN-C is a wonderful aid to navigation when used properly. However, it is not a primary navigational system and should never be viewed as such. When used with depth soundings, lights, buoys, radar, up-to-date charts, and proper plotting techniques, LORAN-C will enhance your abilities as a navigator.

This introduction and the data in the LORAN Index are not intended to serve as a treatise on the LORAN system or its use. There are several excellent books about the LORAN system available from the U.S. Coast Guard and from private publishers which go into detail about the theory and operation of the system. You should also consult the owner's manual supplied with your LORAN unit for its particular specifications and operating procedures.

The LORAN-C information presented in this edition of *Embassy's Complete Boating Guide to Long Island Sound* was gathered on-site by our editors on board the *Gamekeeper*, Outdoor Recreation Service's 24-foot Rampage. The LORAN-C unit used to collect the information was a 1988 Micrologic model ML-8000S. Embassy editors first collected LORAN waypoints in November and December 1988, for publication in the Second Edition of this guide. In October 1989 Embassy editors went out again and double checked every waypoint listed in this index, and added some new waypoints to the list. All positions were recorded with the boat dead in the water after the LORAN unit was allowed to settle for 2 minutes and the LORAN showed no motion over the bottom. The signal-to-noise-ratio reading was observed and in all cases was not less than 80 on the scale used by this unit, indicating very high reliability.

The on-site readings were then plotted by our editors on the charts and cross-checked with other published sources to guarantee the highest accuracy and reliability possible. When significant variations were found, we have not published those TDs and have noted in the appropriate Harbor Chapter where local conditions do not produce accurate or reliable readings. Since all observations were made directly, no additional secondary-factor corrections were applied. Attempts to plot this information on the chart may show substantial offset from actual positions on some fixes, particularly those close to land.

To save space, TDs are truncated to one decimal when presented on the Harbor Charts. The full TD readings are included in the LORAN Index. Generally, the TDs were taken as close to the mark on the channel or "safe" side as

prudently possible, with the approximate distances and directions noted in the LORAN Index.

The LORAN-C chain covering the Long Island Sound area is the Northeast U.S. #9960.

Transmitter Identification	Smallest TD
Master: Seneca, NY	N/A
Whiskey: Caribou, ME #10	11000.0
Xray: Nantucket, MA #24	25000.0
Yankee: Carolina, SC #38	39000.0
Zulu: Dana, IN #53	54000.0

The secondaries used in Long Island Sound were X and Y, because they are the most frequently used in the area, and because the LORAN unit was set to auto-select for the highest reliability for the fixes recorded.

In Fishers Island Sound, X and Y secondaries were also used, although some local mariners prefer to use W and Y. In the area to the northeast of Block Island, the unit auto-selected X and W as the secondaries. X and W were found to be accurate although the crossing angle was not optimum. Y numbers were calculated from the above.

CAUTION: *This information was gathered in the winter when it was cold and clear with reception conditions being optimum. There will be a shift in values due to seasonal weather changes. This data should be used for reference purposes only and mariners should collect their own readings on site as they become familiar with the area.*

It should also be noted that the United States Coast Guard has established the Geodetic Accuracy of the LORAN-C to be 1/4 mile 95 percent of the time, with a signal-to-noise-ratio of 1:3. The Coast Guard has not established a standard for the repeatable accuracy of LORAN-C. The repeatable accuracy is the ability to return to a fix that has been directly observed. Repeatable accuracy is usually within 100 feet, and often better.

However, the accuracy you can achieve depends upon your expertise, the quality and age of the LORAN unit, the quality of the installation, local weather conditions and topography, radio interference, signal quality, time of year, and speed of the boat. For these reasons, Embassy cannot guarantee the accuracy of the information contained herein, and will in no way be responsible for any loss or damage caused by the use or misuse of this information.

Many thanks to Captain John H. Jensen of Outdoor Recreation Services, who captained *Gamekeeper* and contributed the information in this article.

WAY PT. #	Light List #	Guide PG #	NAME AND LOCATION	DISTANCE FROM AIDE	CHARACTERISTICS	LATITUDE	LONGITUDE	TD 1	TD 2	TD 3	USER READINGS
1	20260	76	Throgs Neck lighted bell	E 50'	R "48" Fl R 4s Bell	N 40°-48.34	W 073°-47.42	26949.93	43898.49		
2	20255	76	Locust Pt.	S 50'	R "46A"	N 40°-49.42	W 073°-47.35	26952.52	43909.01		
6	24409	LIS	Cuban Ledge lighted buoy	W 50'	R "2" Fl R 4s	N 40°-50.61	W 073°-48.35	26964.89	43921.55		
8	24385	76, 82	City Island lighted buoy	S 50'	R "2" Fl R 4s	N 40°-50.13	W 073°-47.44	26955.41	43915.84		
9	24270	82	Chimney Sweeps, light	E 50'	G "1" Fl G 4s	N 40°-51.92	W 073°-46.84	26955.88	43932.03		
10	24260	82	South Nonations Reef lighted bell "4"	S 50'	R "4" Fl R 4s Bell	N 40°-52.01	W 073°-46.34	26952.03	43932.11		
15	24300	90	Machaux Rock lighted bell	Between	R "6" Fl R 4s Bell & C "7"	N 40°-52.57	W 073°-46.75	26957.08	43937.98		
16	24215	90	Huckleberry Is. lighted "2"	S 50'	R "2" Fl R 4s	N 40°-53.58	W 073°-45.40	26949.04	43945.60		
17	24225	90	Davids Island & Davenport Neck	Between	R "4" & G "5" Fl G 4s	N 40°-53.63	W 073°-46.11	26955.02	43947.07		
18	24210	90	Emerald Rock buoy	S 50'	GR Junction Buoy	N 40°-53.88	W 073°-45.83	26953.48	43949.02		
19	24175	90	Bailey Rock lighted buoy	Between	G "3BR" Fl G 4s & N "4"	N 40°-54.41	W 073°-45.70	26953.95	43953.78		
20	24130	90	Hick's Ledge junction buoy	SW 75'	GR "HL"	N 40°-54.31	W 073°-45.16	26949.23	43952.10		
24	24125	LIS	Hens and Chickens South	S 50'	R "2" Fl R 4s	N 40°-54.33	W 073°-44.35	26942.60	43951.07		
28	24115	96	East Larchmont Harbor Breakwater	E 100'	R "2" Fl R 4s	N 40°-55.07	W 073°-43.97	26941.61	43957.40		
29	23970	96	Mamaroneck Harbor Entrance	SE 50'	G "3"	N 40°-55.48	W 073°-43.23	26936.78	43960.16		
30	23995	96	Outer Steamboat Rock	Between	G "5" Fl G 4s & R "8"	N 40°-56.43	W 073°-42.96	26937.18	43968.52		
32	20180	96	Due south West Rock & Scotch Caps	S 50'	R "42" Fl R 2.5s Bell	N 40°-55.64	W 073°-42.13	26928.09	43959.94		
33	20175	96	East of Milton Point	SW 50'	R "40A"	N 40°-56.27	W 073°-41.29	26922.94	43964.52		
37	20165	LIS	Parsonage Pt.	S 50'	R "40" Fl R 6s	N 40°-56.96	W 073°-40.48	26918.29	43969.67		
38	20160	LIS	Rye Beach	S 50'	R "38" Fl R 4s Bell	N 40°-57.65	W 073°-39.61	26913.05	43974.73		
39	20155	LIS	Blue Fish Shoal Bell	SW 50'	R "36" Bell	N 40°-58.28	W 073°-38.78	26907.99	43979.24		
43	23925	102	Great Captain Rocks	SW 50'	R "2"	N 40°-59.11	W 073°-39.07	26912.95	43987.39		
44	23750	102	Jones Rocks Light	SE 100'	Fl G 4s	N 40°-59.42	W 073°-38.07	26905.45	43988.65		
45	23755	102	North of Cormorant Reef	NW 35'	R "4"	N 40°-59.63	W 073°-37.86	26904.34	43990.19		
46	23870	102	Entrance Greenwich Harbor	W 50'	R "2"	N 41°-00.06	W 073°-37.24	26900.41	43993.15		
50	23725	108	Newfoundland Reef	W 50'	R "4" Fl R 4s	N 41°-00.49	W 073°-35.99	26891.16	43995.15		
51	23715	108	Little Captain Island, East Reef Bell	E 200'	G "1" Fl G 2.5s	N 40°-59.77	W 073°-35.80	26887.45	43988.27		
52	20145	108	Woolsey Reef	S 50'	R "34"	N 41°-00.09	W 073°-33.88	26872.19	43988.08		
56	23565	114	Entrance Stamford Harbor	Between	G "1" Gong & N "2"	N 41°-00.85	W 073°-32.18	26860.04	43992.25		
57	20115	LIS	The Cows-Lighted bell buoy	S 100'	R "32" Fl R 6s	N 41°-00.35	W 073°-31.44	26852.37	43986.60		
58	23500	114	Westcott Cove-East Entrance	NE 200'	G "1" Fl G 4 s	N 41°-01.83	W 073°-30.45	26848.32	43998.33		
60	23465	122	Good Wives River Entrance	Between	G "1" Fl G 4s & N "2"	N 41°-02.40	W 073°-28.96	26837.28	44001.09		
61	20105	LIS	Smith Reef lighted buoy	S 50'	R "30" Fl R 4s	N 41°-01.63	W 073°-29.49	26839.57	43995.03		
62	20090	122	Greens Ledge Light	W 275 yd	Alt Fl W/R 24s	N 41°-02.61	W 073°-26.74	26819.06	43999.28		
63	23450	122	Five Mile River Entrance mid-channel	Between	G "3" Fl G & R "4"	N 41°-03.47	W 073°-26.77	26821.91	44007.13		
64	20085	LIS	Great Reef Buoy	S 50'	R "28"	N 41°-02.56	W 073°-25.49	26808.15	43996.79		
65	23435	126	E Norwalk channel, mid-channel	Between	R "2" Fl R & C "3"	N 41°-03.62	W 073°-25.06	26807.73	44005.66		
66	23395	130	Light Tower West of Round Beach	W 75'	R "14" Fl R	N 41°-04.69	W 073°-24.00	26802.13	44014.55		
67	23310	126	Raymond Rocks Shoal	NE 100'	G "11"	N 41°-04.50	W 073°-23.80	26799.52	44011.38		
68	23300	126, 136	Grassy Hammock Light	S 50'	R "8" Fl R 4s	N 41°-04.69	W 073°-22.99	26793.12	44011.72		
69	20055	LIS	Off East end of Norwalk Islands	S50'	R "26" Fl 4s Bell	N 41°-03.78	W 073°-21.99	26781.80	44002.03		
71	23295	136	Peck Ledge Light	NE 150'	Fl 4s	N 41°-04.78	W 073°-22.14	26786.15	44011.13		
72	23285	136	Channel Rock–SW end of reef	SW 150'	R "4"	N 41°-04.69	W 073°-21.75	26782.58	44009.68		
73	23280	LIS	East approach Cockenoe Harbor	SW 50'	R "2"	N 41°-04.50	W 073°-21.75	26773.16	44006.47		
74	20050	LIS	Cockenoe Shoal Lighted Buoy	S 50'	R "24" Bell	N 41°-04.62	W 073°-19.76	26765.23	44005.78		
75	23190	LIS	Georges Rock Buoy	E 50'	C "1"	N 41°-05.35	W 073°-19.47	26764.86	44011.64		
76	23195	LIS	Saugatuck River Entrance buoy	NE 50'	G "3" Fl G 4s	N 41°-05.97	W 073°-21.21	26781.54	44020.16		
77	23205	136	Saugatuck River Channel Entrance	Between	R "6" & G "5"	N 41°-06.06	W 073°-21.49	26784.21	44021.31		
81	23145	140	Southport channel entrance	W 50'	R "2"	N 41°-07.27	W 073°-17.13	26750.16	44024.51		
82	20045	140	Pine Creek Pt.	S 50'	R "22" Fl R 4s Bell	N 41°-06.56	W 073°-15.76	25736.41	44016.09		

WAY PT. #	Light List #	Guide PG #	NAME AND LOCATION	DISTANCE FROM AIDE	CHARACTERISTICS	LATITUDE	LONGITUDE	TD 1	TD 2	TD 3	USER READINGS
86	20040	144	Penfield Reef Light	S 300'	Fl R 6s Horn	N 41°-06.99	W 073°-13.27	26716.15	44015.56		
87	22920	LIS	Bridgeport Whistle buoy	S 50'	RW "BH" Mo(A) Whistle	N 41°-06.30	W 073°-11.73	26701.00	44007.09		
88	23050	144	Black Rock Harbor Entrance	SW 75'	Daymark "2A" Fl R 4s	N 41°-08.26	W 073°-13.05	26717.73	44026.15		
89	23120	144	Ash Creek Entrance	Between	R "2" & G "5"	N 41°-08.54	W 073°-13.83	26725.29	44029.89		
90	20000	LIS	Stratford Pt.	S 50'	R "18" Fl R 6s Bell	N 41°-06.85	W 073°-08.15	26671.59	44005.89		
91	22965	150	Bridgeport Harbor Entrance	Between	R "10" Fl R 2.5s & C "11"	N 41°-08.98	W 073°-10.87	26700.91	44028.67		
92	23005	150	Inner Bridgeport Harbor	Between	R "16" Fl R 2.5s & C "15"	N 41°-09.72	W 073°-10.62	26700.76	44034.49		
96	22755	154	Housatonic River Entrance	SW 50'	G "1" Fl G 2.5s	N 41°-09.42	W 073°-05.40	26654.27	44022.93		
100	19985	160	Charles Island lighted buoy	S 50'	R "16" Bell	N 41°-11.06	W 073°-03.11	26638.49	44032.67		
101	22720	160	Charles Island-to East	E 50'	G "1"	N 41°-11.68	W 073°-03.13	26640.37	44037.94		
102	22725	160	Milford Harbor Entrance	W 50'	R "4" Fl R 4s	N 41°-12.32	W 073°-03.01	26641.16	44043.09		
103	22715	160	Welches Point	W 50'	R "2"	N 41°-11.96	W 073°-02.27	26633.53	44038.74		
107	19980	LIS	Pond Pt. Shoal	S 50'	R "12"	N 41°-11.99	W 073°-01.14	26623.69	44037.01		
108	22490	LIS	West end jetty New Haven Harbor	NW 75'	R "2" Fl R 6s	N 41°-13.59	W 072°-57.50	26596.54	44044.14		
112	22475	164	Betw/ Middle & West Breakwaters	Between	Fl G 4s & Fl R 4s	N 41°-13.39	W 072°-56.37	26586.09	44040.49		
113	22460	164	New Haven Harbor Main Entrance	Between	G "7" & R "6"	N 41°-14.03	W 072°-55.06	26576.53	44043.58		
114	22550	164	Inner New Haven Harbor	Between	G "15" & N "16"	N 41°-16.37	W 072°-54.79	26580.72	44062.31		
118	22425	LIS	New Haven entrance buoy	S 50'	RW "NH" Mo(A) Whistle	N 41°-12.14	W 072°-53.84	26560.63	44025.85		
119	19950	LIS	Townshend Ledge	S 50'	R "10A" Fl R 4s	N 41°-12.53	W 072°-51.85	26544.28	44025.67		
123	20380	170	Cow and Calf	S 75'	R "34" Fl R 2.5s	N 41°-14.31	W 072°-50.58	26538.09	44038.11		
124	22385	170	East Indies	E 50'	G "1"	N 41°-14.47	W 072°-51.56	26547.09	44041.10		
125	22360	170	Blyn Rock	W 50'	R "2" Fl R 4s	N 41°-14.82	W 072°-49.95	26533.94	44041.23		
126	20375	170	Five Foot Rock	W 50'	R "32"	N 41°-14.45	W 072°-49.98	26533.22	44038.27		
127	19945	LIS	Branford Reef Light	S 300'	Fl W 6s 30ft.	N 41°-13.05	W 072°-48.03	26515.66	44025.32		
128	20365	LIS	Brown's Reef	S 50'	R "26"	N 41°-13.81	W 072°-46.27	26498.95	44026.67		
130	22315	174	Pine Orchard Approach	NW 50'	R "4A" Fl R 4s	N 41°-14.57	W 072°-46.73	26505.00	44033.60		
131	22330	174	Pine Orchard Approach	W 75'	R "8" Fl R 4s	N 41°-15.30	W 072°-46.29	26503.16	44038.74		
132	22215	174	Thimble Shoals	W 50'	R "4"	N 41°-14.98	W 072°-44.58	26487.23	44033.21		
136	20360	180	Goose Rock Light	S 50'	R "22" Fl R 4s	N 41°-14.38	W 072°-43.48	26475.95	44026.46		
140	19935	184	Goose Island Light	S 50'	R "10GI" Fl R 4s Bell	N 41°-12.14	W 072°-40.51	26443.87	44003.31		
141	20340	184	N Faulkner Island	N 50'	G "15" Fl G 4s Gong	N 41°-13.25	W 072°-38.94	26436.28	44011.48		
142	22160	184	Guilford Harbor Half Acre Rock	S 50'	R "4" Fl R 4s	N 41°-15.02	W 072°-39.22	26440.08	44024.33		
143	22180	184	Guilford Harbor Entrance	E 50'	G "7" Fl G 4s	N 41°-15.73	W 072°-39.83	26447.42	44031.08		
147	20335	LIS	Charles Reef	S 50'	R "14"	N 41°-14.83	W 072°-37.44	26423.90	44019.77		
148	19925	LIS	Kimberly Reef buoy	E 50'	R FL "6" & RG "KR" Horn	N 41°-12.86	W 072°-37.41	26418.45	44003.92		
149	20330	190	Hammonasset Point Reef	S 50'	R "10"	N 41°-14.74	W 072°-33.21	26386.35	44011.88		
153	22100	190	Wheeler Rock	E 50'	G "3" Fl G 4s	N 41°-15.38	W 072°-31.67	26374.33	44014.32		
154	22090	190	Kelsey Point Breakwater	SW 150'	Fl W 2.5	N 41°-14.51	W 072°-30.58	26362.49	44005.65		
158	20320	LIS	Duck Island Reef	S 50'	R "6"	N 41°-14.63	W 072°-28.21	26344.66	44004.38		
159	22050	194	Westbrook Patchogue River	SW 75'	R "2" Fl R 4s	N 41°-15.95	W 072°-28.39	26346.77	44013.28		
163	19915	LIS	Six Mile Reef Buoy	S 50'	R "8C" Fl R 4s Bell	N 41°-10.72	W 072°-29.54	26343.70	43973.80		
164	19905	LIS	Long Sand Shoal West End Buoy	W 50'	RG "W" Horn	N 41°-13.38	W 072°-27.34	26333.72	43993.21		
165	20315	LIS	Crane Reef	E 50'	N "4"	N 41°-14.88	W 072°-25.37	26317.27	43999.80		
166	20280	LIS	Cornfield Pt. Shoal	S 75'	R "2" Fl R 4s Bell	N 41°-15.02	W 072°-22.99	26296.52	43996.89		
167	19880	200	Saybrook Breakwater Nun	Due S 100'	N "2"	N 41°-15.67	W 072°-20.51	26276.12	43997.85		
168	19920	LIS	South of Six Mlie Reef	On mark	RB "TE" 1 Qk Fl R Bell	N 41°-09.26	W 072°-30.45	26348.24	43963.66		
171	21185	200	CT River Saybrook, Lynde Pt.	Range w/light	G "5" Fl G 4s	N 41°-16.29	W 072°-20.44	26277.08	44002.49		
172	21200	200	CT River Saybrook	NW 50'	R "8" Fl R 4s	N 41°-16.66	W 072°-20.61	26279.58	44005.67		
173	21210	200	CT River Saybrook	SW 50'	R "14" Fl R 4s	N 41°-17.27	W 072°-21.00	26284.61	44011.04		
177		206	Old Lyme Drawbridge	SW 150'		N 41°-18.45	W 072°-20.94	26287.19	44020.11		

WAY PT. #	Light List #	Guide PG #	NAME AND LOCATION	DISTANCE FROM AIDE	CHARACTERISTICS	LATITUDE	LONGITUDE	TD 1	TD 2	TD 3	USER READINGS
181	19870	LIS	Saybrook Bar lighted buoy	W 50'	R "8" Fl R 4s Bell	N 41°-14.84	W 072°-18.89	26259.62	43988.70		
182	19895	LIS	Mid Long Sand Shoal	S 50'	R "8A" Qk Fl R Bell	N 41°-13.52	W 072°-23.14	26294.07	43985.43		
183	19865	LIS	Hatchett Reef	S 50'	R "6"	N 41°-15.89	W 072°-15.99	26236.51	43992.01		
184	19830	LIS	Bartlett Reef	S 50'	R "4" Fl R 4s Bell	N 41°-15.58	W 072°-08.34	26167.45	43976.93		
185	20970	228	Bell south of Niantic River Entrance	SSW 50'	G "1" Daymark	N 41°-18.92	W 072°-10.66	26199.68	44008.22		
186	20950	228	Black Rock Niantic Bay	W 75'	R "6"	N 41°-18.53	W 072°-10.73	26196.30	44003.36		
187	20940	228	White Rock Niantic Bay	W 150'	R "4" Fl R 4s Bell	N 41°-17.91	W 072°-10.55	26193.05	43998.33		
191	19835	LIS	Bartlett Reef Light	S 150'	Fl W 4s Horn	N 41°-16.38	W 072°-08.18	26167.99	43982.73		
195	20495	232	Rapid Rock	S 50'	RG "R"	N 41°-17.22	W 072°-06.10	26151.64	43985.76		
196	20515	232	Mid New London Harbor Entrance	Between	R "2" Fl 2.5s & G "1" Fl 2.5s	N 41°-17.60	W 072°-04.68	26139.92	43986.28	14709.91	
197	20570	232	New London channel	Between	G "5" & R "6"	N 41°-19.27	W 072°-04.90	26146.16	43999.21	14706.03	
198	18735	232, 250	Seaflower Reef	S 300'	Fl W 4s	N 41°-17.67	W 072°-01.97	26115.80	43982.33	14692.17	
202	18725	244	North Dumpling Light	N 300'	Fl W Red Sector	N 41°-17.41	W 072°-01.29	26109.11	43979.27	14688.76	
203	19785	244	Flat Hammock	E 50'	R "2"	N 41°-17.17	W 072°-00.36	26100.14	43975.94	14683.69	
205	19075	250	Planet Rock	SE 75'	G "3"	N 41°-18.63	W 071°-58.46	26095.79	43985.40	14673.34	
206	19065	250	Mystic Harbor West Approach	Between	G "1" & RG "S"	N 41°-18.35	W 071°-59.78	26097.97	43983.88	14675.89	
207	18690	244, 250	Ram Island Reef	S 50'	R "20" Fl R 4s Bell	N 41°-18.17	W 071°-58.37	26084.92	43980.19	14667.93	
211	18675	254, 262	Eel Grass Ground	S 50'	R "16"	N 41°-18.48	W 071°-56.68	26070.59	43979.79	14655.96	
212	18765	262	Stonington Pt. Inner Breakwater	W 75'	Fl R 4s	N 41°-19.81	W 071°-54.60	26055.37	43986.25	14658.43	
213	18760	262	Stonington Pt. junction buoy	N 30'	RG "SP"	N 41°-19.47	W 071°-54.38	26052.45	43983.33	14637.89	
214	18755	262	Stonington Breakwater West	S 300'	G "5" Fl G 4s	N 41°-19.41	W 071°-54.71	26055.29	43983.44	14640.38	
215	18740	262	Stonington Harbor Approach	W 50'	R "2"	N 41°-18.54	W 071°-54.59	26052.01	43976.84		
219	18605	268	Gangway Rock, Watch Hill Passage	SW 50'	R "2" Fl R 6s Bell	N 41°-17.96	W 071°-51.52	26022.99	43967.51	14624.58	
220	18625	268	Napatree Ledge	SW 50'	R "6" Fl R 4s	N 41°-18.00	W 071°-53.35	26039.47	43970.75	14636.28	
224	18585	244	Lord's Passage	S 50'	RW "L" Mo(A) W	N 41°-17.39	W 071°-54.31	26046.63	43967.81	14644.26	
225	18595	244	Wicopesset Passage	On mark	RW "W" Bell	N 41°-17.48	W 071°-54.96	26052.64	43969.49	14642.98	
226	18665	244	Latimer Reef Light	S 100'	Fl W 6s	N 41°-18.16	W 071°-56.00	26063.65	43976.28	14652.69	
227	19750	244	East Harbor	Between	R "2E" & G "1E"	N 41°-17.30	W 071°-56.98	26070.30	43971.47	14661.75	
228	19760	244	Brooks Pt.	S 100'	R "2W"	N 41°-17.29	W 071°-58.18	26081.01	43973.30	14669.31	
229	19765	244	Clay Pt.	Between	R "4" & G "5"	N 41°-17.00	W 071°-59.51	26092.19	43973.32	14678.51	
230	19805	244	West Harbor Entrance lighted buoy	E 50'	R "8" Fl R 4s	N 41°-16.33	W 072°-00.33	26097.83	43969.58	14685.88	
231	19790	244	West approach West Harbor	NE 50'	R "2" Fl R 2.5s Bell	N 41°-16.83	W 072°-01.36	26108.25	43974.99	14691.72	
232	19820	244	Silver Eel Pond Entrance	N 50'	R "2" Fl R 2.5s Bell	N 41°-15.58	W 072°-02.23	26112.94	43966.96	14718.43	
233	18395	244	Race Rock Light	SW 375'	Fl R 10s Horn	N 41°-14.43	W 072°-03.02	26117.19	43959.54	14710.34	
237	18405	LIS	Valiant Rock-The Race, lighted bell	E 100'	G "1A" Qk Fl G Bell	N 41°-13.81	W 072°-03.90	26123.56	43956.24	14715.81	
238	18385	LIS	Watch Hill-offshore buoy Mo(A) Wh.	S 50'	RW "WH" Whistle	N 41°-15.82	W 071°-50.91	26012.32	43950.66	14627.23	
242	18065	LIS	Nebraska Shoal	S 50'	R "2NS"	N 41°-21.06	W 071°-34.49	14506.55	25878.07	43961.93	
243	18095	LIS	Pt. Judith-West Entrance	Between Brk.	R "2" Fl R 4s	N 41°-21.97	W 071°-30.80	14480.19	25847.25	43962.19	
244	18105	LIS	South Lump Buoys	S 50'	RG	N 41°-21.93	W 071°-30.40	14477.81	25843.56	43961.57	
245	18080	LIS	Pt. Judith-East Harbor Breakwater	Between	Entrance, mid-channel	N 41°-21.71	W 071°-29.71	14474.29	25836.75	43958.79	
246	18060	LIS	South of Pt. Judith	S 100'	R "4" Bell	N 41°-21.06	W 071°-30.38	14480.75	25841.06	43955.09	
247	18055	LIS	Pt. Judith	N 50'	R "2" Fl R 4s Whistle	N 41°-19.41	W 071°-28.49	14474.63	25819.76	43941.01	
248	18070	LIS	Block Island North Reef	N 50'	G "1BI" Fl G 4s	N 41°-15.51	W 071°-34.55	25864.84	43923.06	14524.79	
252	18265	276	Clay Head, Northeast Whistle	N 50'	RW "NE" Whistle	N 41°-12.60	W 071°-32.06	25836.09	43898.20	14518.60	
253	18270	276	Old Harbor Channel	N 50'	G "1" Bell	N 41°-11.24	W 071°-33.27	25844.19	43890.02	14530.82	
254	18275	276	Old Harbor Breakwater	E 25'	G "3"	N 41°-10.64	W 071°-33.32	25843.44	43885.67	14535.66	
255	18295	276	Southeast Pt.	S 75'	C "1"	N 41°-08.84	W 071°-32.77	25835.07	43871.69	14555.61	
256	18310	276	Black Rock Pt.	S 50'	N "2"	N 41°-08.43	W 071°-35.78	25861.16	43873.01	14564.34	
257	18315	276	Dickens Point lighted buoy	W 50'	R "2A" Fl R 4s Whistle	N 41°-08.68	W 071°-37.42	25876.29	43877.21		
258	18320	276	Southwest Point	W 50'	R "4" Bell	N 41°-09.58	W 071°-37.17	25875.78	43883.48		

WAY PT. #	Light List #	Guide PG #	NAME AND LOCATION	CHARACTERISTICS	DISTANCE FROM AIDE	LATITUDE	LONGITUDE	TD 1	TD 2	TD 3	USER READINGS
259	18325	276	Great Salt Pond	R "2" Bell	SE 50'	N 41°-12.14	W 071°-35.69	25867.70	43900.11		
260	18360	276	Great Salt Pond	N "12" & C "ll"	Between	N 41°-11.64	W 071°-35.20	25862.32	43895.78		
262	660	LIS	Southwest Ledge	R "2" Fl R 4s	W 75'	N 41°-06.72	W 071°-40.33	25898.72	43867.13	14589.16	
264	25580	388	Little Neck Bay mid-channel	RW C "LN"	On the mark	N 40°-47.38	W 073°-45.89	25934.54	43887.54		
265	25565	388	Elm Point	R "4"	W 50'	N 40°-49.18	W 073°-46.22	26942.53	43905.07		
266	20250	76, 388	Stepping Stones Light	F G 46ft 12M-Horn	N 200'	N 40°-49.79	W 073°-46.67	26948.07	43911.58		
270	20245	LIS	Hart Island-southern tip	R "46" Fl R 5s 23ft 10M	SE 50'	N 40°-50.84	W 073°-46.05	26946.12	43920.65		
269	24250	LIS	East side Hart Is.	G "1" Gong	E 50'	N 40°-51.59	W 073°-45.88	26946.35	43927.45		
271	20240	LIS	Hewlett Point	G "29" Fl G 4 s	N 100'	N 40°-50.72	W 073°-45.39	26940.33	43918.56		
275	25520	380	Plum Point-Manhasset Bay	G "1" Fl G 4s	W 50'	N 40°-50.09	W 073°-43.84	26925.76	43910.38		
276	20230	380	Gangway Rock Gong	G "27" Gong	W 50'	N 40°-51.66	W 073°-44.89	26939.00	43926.69		
280	20220	LIS	Sands Point Reef	G "25" & Gong "44A"	Between	N 40°-52.42	W 073°-44.29	26936.35	43933.00		
281	20195	LIS	Execution Rock Light	G "1"	N 50'	N 40°-53.64	W 073°-44.20	26939.26	43944.37		
282	20185	LIS	Prospect Pt. lighted buoy	G "23" Fl G 4s Gong	N 75'	N 40°-52.93	W 073°-43.22	26929.04	43936.21		
283	25455	LIS	West side Hempstead Harbor	R "2"	E 50'	N 40°-52.58	W 073°-42.54	26922.33	43931.92		
284	25460	LIS	West side Hempstead Harbor	R "4"	E 50'	N 40°-52.39	W 073°-42.08	26918.04	43929.49		
292	25465	LIS	Mott Pt.	R "6" Bell	E 50'	N 40°-51.84	W 073°-40.53	26903.52	43922.04		
293	25475	376	West side Hempstead Harbor	R "8"	E 50'	N 40°-51.50	W 073°-40.30	26900.65	43918.56		
294	25480	376	Mosquito Creek-Anchorage A	G "A" & R "B"	Between	N 40°-51.27	W 073°-39.68	26894.87	43915.50		
295	25470	376	East side Hemp Harbor Breakwater	G "4M" Fl G 4s 24ft	W 75'	N 40°-51.87	W 073°-39.78	26897.44	43921.25		
296	20140	LIS	Oak Neck Pt.	G "19"	N 100'	N 40°-55.67	W 073°-34.25	26826.34	43948.19		
299	20170	LIS	Matinecock Point Shoal	G "21" Fl G 4s Gong	N 50'	N 40°-54.71	W 073°-38.18	26892.46	43945.31		
300	20130	LIS	Twenty Six-foot spot lighted bell	R "32A" Fl R 2.5s Bell	S 50'	N 40°-58.26	W 073°-32.78	26857.52	43969.64		
301	20135	LIS	Centre Island Reef Bell	G "17" Bell	N 50'	N 40°-56.13	W 073°-31.71	26842.39	43948.50		
302	25270	LIS	Oyster Bay	G "1"	W 50'	N 40°-55.72	W 073°-30.32	26829.57	43942.65		
306	25275	366	Cold Spring Harbor Light	Fl W (Outside Red Sector)	E 100'	N 40°-55.01	W 073°-29.63	26821.76	43935.13		
307	25285	366, 370	Plum Pt., Oyster Bay	R "2A"	S 50'	N 40°-54.30	W 073°-30.42	26826.40	43929.88		
308	25290	366, 370	Oyster Bay	G "3" Fl G 4s	N 50'	N 40°-54.02	W 073°-30.68	26827.79	43927.65		
309	25295	370	Oyster Bay	R "4"	E 50'	N 40°-53.32	W 073°-31.19	26830.13	43922.00		
313	20110	LIS	Lloyd Point Shoal	G "15" Fl G 4s Gong	N 50'	N 40°-57.86	W 073°-29.29	26826.99	43960.53		
314	24845	LIS	Huntington Bay Approach	R "2"	N 25'	N 40°-57.40	W 073°-28.91	26822.49	43955.79		
315	24855	LIS	Huntington Bay Approach	R "4"	E 50'	N 40°-56.94	W 073°-27.62	26810.33	43949.64		
316	24860	LIS	Huntington Bay Approach	R "6" Fl R 4s	E 50'	N 40°-56.70	W 073°-26.39	26799.28	43945.61		
317	24865	LIS	Huntington Bay	R "8" Fl R 4s Bell	E 50'	N 40°-56.00	W 073°-25.45	26789.38	43937.76		
321	25050	354	Lloyd Harbor Entrance Light	R "2" & Iso W 6s Horn	Between	N 40°-54.93	W 073°-25.85	26789.82	43928.76		
322	25075	354	Northport Bay Entrance	G "1" Fl G 4s	SW 50'	N 40°-55.00	W 073°-24.48	26778.46	43927.27		
325	25085	354	Northport Bay	G "3" & R "4"	Between	N 40°-54.96	W 073°-24.09	26775.03	43926.29		
329	25100	362	Northport Harbor	R "8" Fl R 4s	NE 50'	N 40°-55.12	W 073°-22.62	26763.07	43925.50		
333	24795	356	Eatons Neck CG Station	G "1" Fl G 2.5s	W 100'	N 40°-56.97	W 073°-24.33	26782.63	43944.81		
334	20080	LIS	Cable & Anchor Reef	R "28C" Fl R 4s Bell	N 50'	N 41°-00.70	W 073°-25.13	26799.48	43979.65		
335	20060	LIS	Eatons Neck Pt.	G "11B" Fl G 4s Bell	N 50'	N 41°-00.16	W 073°-23.67	26785.88	43972.40		
336	20070	LIS	Eatons Neck Pt.	G "13"	N 50'	N 40°-58.34	W 073°-23.66	26780.74	43956.12		
337	25100	LIS	Northport Platform West	In line w/ stacks	N 180'	N 40°-57.44	W 073°-20.50	26751.53	43943.17		
338	24750	LIS	Basin Entrance	G "1" Fl G 5s	NW 50'	N 40°-55.86	W 073°-20.80	26749.72	43929.43		
342	24700	350	Nissequogue River	RW "NR" Mo(A)	N 50'	N 40°-55.48	W 073°-13.86	26689.94	43915.54		
343	24615	350	Stony Brook Harbor Entrance	G "1" Fl G 4s	N 50'	N 40°-56.32	W 073°-09.91	26658.51	43917.02		
347	20035	LIS	Oldfield Point	G "11A" Gong	N 50'	N 40°-59.33	W 073°-07.34	26644.27	43939.37		
348	24520	LIS	Port Jefferson Approach	RW "PJ" Mo(A) Whistle	N 50'	N 40°-59.37	W 073°-06.48	26637.05	43938.40		
349	24535	340	Entrance to Port Jefferson Harbor	R "2" Fl 2.5s Bell & C "1"	Between	N 40°-58.51	W 073°-05.80	26628.99	43929.82		
360	20025	LIS	Mt. Misery Shoal	G "11"	N 50'	N 40°-59.31	W 073°-04.81	26622.56	43935.25		

WAY PT. #	Light List #	Guide PG #	NAME AND LOCATION	DISTANCE FROM AIDE	CHARACTERISTICS	LATITUDE	LONGITUDE	TD 1	TD 2	TD 3	USER READINGS
362	20020	LIS	Middle Ground lighted	S 50'	R "2" Fl G 4s Bell	N 41°-03.11	W 073°-06.24	26644.81	43970.49		
363	20010	LIS	Stratford Shoal	N 50'	G "3"	N 41°-04.65	W 073°-06.28	26649.30	43983.80		
368	24460	LIS	Mt. Sinai Approach	NW 50'	RW "M"	N 40°-58.31	W 073°-02.73	26602.12	43923.38		
372	26895	328	North Race	N 50'	G "1"	N 40°-59.24	W 072°-27.01	26295.44	43877.12		
373	26900	328	North Race lighted buoy	N 50'	G "3" Fl G 4s	N 40°-59.19	W 072°-28.36	26307.11	43878.67		
374	20400	328	Mattituck-Breakwater Entrance	Center N 100'	Fl W 4s "MI"	N 41°-01.08	W 072°-33.78	26358.30	43902.33		
378	20395	LIS	Mattituck	N 50'	G "3A" Gong	N 41°-01.95	W 072°-34.05	26362.60	43909.88		
382	26370	310	Plum Gut	Depth 134'-bear 240° off coffee pot		N 41°-10.06	W 072°-12.85	26194.45	43941.61		
386	26370	304	Shelter Island Sound N. Channel	S 25'	RW Mo (A) "N"	N 41°-06.00	W 072°-15.71	26210.81	43914.37		
387	26375	304	Shelter Island Sound N. Channel	S 50'	R "2" Fl R 4s Bell	N 41°-06.17	W 072°-18.04	26231.68	43919.31		
388	26395	304	Shelter Island Sound N. Channel	S 50'	N "8"	N 41°-06.87	W 072°-20.06	26251.06	43928.01		
389	26400	304, 314	Greenport Harbor lighted buoy	S 75'	Daymark "8A" w/red light	N 41°-06.19	W 072°-20.87	26256.70	43923.85		
393	26420	314	Research Basin-Fanning Pt.	SE 50'	N "10"	N 41°-05.45	W 072°-21.70	26262.32	43919.26		
394	26455	314	Shelter Isl. Jennings Pt.	N 50'	G "11" Fl G 4s	N 41°-04.38	W 072°-23.23	26273.41	43913.06		
395	26460	314	Town Creek Entrance	SE 25'	G "1"	N 41°-03.56	W 072°-24.81	26285.47	43908.89		
396	26500	314	Shelter Island Sound N. Channel	SE 50'	R "12" Fl R 4s	N 41°-03.00	W 072°-22.72	26266.02	43901.24		
400	27075	332	Flanders Bay Entrance	SE 50'	R "4" Fl 4s	N 40°-55.65	W 072°-34.55	26353.42	43858.60		
401	27070	332	Riverhead Channel	On Mark	R "2" Fl R 2.5s	N 40°-55.77	W 072°-32.75	26338.10	43857.00		
405	27030	322	Shinnecock Canal	Between	G "1" Fl G 4s & N "2"	N 40°-53.96	W 072°-30.35	26313.79	43838.59		
406	27020	322	Cold Spring Pond Approach	Between	G "1" Fl G 5s Light & R "2"	N 40°-54.01	W 072°-28.85	26300.80	43836.71		
407	26990	322	Sebonac Creek	Between	R "2" Fl R 5s & R "2"	N 40°-55.18	W 072°-27.57	26292.68	43844.68		
408	26940	322	South Race, Great Peconic Bay	NE 50'	R "26" Fl R 2.5s	N 40°-57.15	W 072°-27.17	26292.55	43860.27		
412	26840	LIS	Little Peconic Bay	On mark	R "22"	N 40°-58.57	W 072°-25.87	26284.12	43869.95		
413	26805	LIS	Little Peconic Bay	On mark	N "18"	N 41°-00.68	W 072°-23.98	26272.02	43884.31		
417	26800	298, 314	Little Peconic Bay	N 50'	G "17"	N 41°-01.54	W 072°-22.97	26265.43	43889.73		
418	26745	298, 314	West Neck Pt. Shoal	S 25'	R "16" Fl R 4s	N 41°-01.74	W 072°-21.34	26251.16	43888.90		
419	26730	298, 304	West Neck Harbor	S 25'	R "22" Fl R 4s (Priv mntd)	N 41°-02.88	W 072°-20.38	26245.25	43896.71		
420	26725	298, 304	Shelter Island Sound S. Channel	W 25'	G "15" Fl G	N 41°-02.67	W 072°-18.78	26230.56	43892.46		
421	26645	298	Sag Harbor Breakwater	W 50'	G "1SH" Fl G 2.5s	N 41°-00.60	W 072°-17.80	26217.84	43874.51		
422	26630	298	Sand Spit Rock	SE 100'	R "10A" Fl R 4s	N 41°-00.90	W 072°-17.04	26211.78	43875.77		
426	26575	294	Barcelona Point	N 50'	G "10A" Fl G 4s & R "8"	N 41°-01.08	W 072°-16.21	26204.84	43875.99	14785.61	
427	26565	294	Cedar Island Light	"3CL" Fl G 4s	200-300 yds off 167° m	N 41°-02.70	W 072°-16.06	26206.84	43878.61	14693.89	
428	26520	304	Coecles Harbor	On mark	G "1" Fl G 4s	N 41°-04.15	W 072°-16.45	26213.41	43900.90	14627.80	
429	26550	294	Shelter Island S. channel	Between	R "2" & G "1"	N 41°-03.34	W 072°-14.10	26190.87	43890.78	14678.78	
430	26180	294	Three Mile Entrance	N 25'	"TM" RW Bell Mo(A) W	N 41°-02.73	W 072°-11.37	26165.70	43881.85	14683.04	
434	26175	LIS	Crow Shoal-Gardiner's Island	On mark	N "14"	N 41°-04.62	W 072°-10.66	26163.25	43895.73		
447	18450	282	Montauk Entrance	On mark	RW "M" Bell	N 41°-05.15	W 071°-56.45	26038.79	43878.61		
448	18425	LIS	Endeavor Shoals	NE 75'	G "3" Fl G 4s Gong	N 41°-06.10	W 071°-46.25	25950.25	43870.73		
451	18445	LIS	Shagwong Reef	N 50'	G "7sR" Fl G 2.5 Bell	N 41°-07.06	W 071°-54.90	26029.03	43891.07		
452	18390	LIS	Cerberus Shoal	On mark	G "9" Fl G 4s Gong	N 41°-10.47	W 071°-57.12	26055.61	43920.22		
453	26075	LIS	Gardiner's Island	N 75'	G "1GI" Fl G 4s	N 41°-09.06	W 072°-08.97	26157.78	43927.74		
454	26070	LIS	Constellation Rock	SE 100'	R "2"	N 41°-10.52	W 072°-06.54	26139.51	43935.22		
455	18415	LIS	Little Gull Island Reef	NE 100'	C "1"	N 41°-12.55	W 072°-06.12	26140.41	43950.16		
456	19845	LIS	Plum Island-Mo(A) Whistle	NE 50'	RW "PI"	N 41°-13.31	W 072°-10.85	26184.30	43963.60	14744.42	
460	26140	LIS	Napeague Bay	On mark	RW "S" Mo(A) Bell	N 41°-02.22	W 072°-03.16	26092.38	43865.78		
461	26145	LIS	Napeague Bay	On mark	R "2"	N 41°-01.52	W 072°-03.86	26097.35	43861.33	14750.51	
462	26150	LIS	North of Promised Land	On mark	R "4"	N 41°-00.92	W 072°-04.90	26105.39	46858.19	14758.99	
463	26155	LIS	South of Cartwright Is.	On mark	R "6"	N 41°-00.84	W 072°-06.94	26121.53	43860.68	14770.56	
464	26160	LIS	West of Cartwright Is.	On mark	R "8"	N 41°-01.37	W 072°-07.26	26126.86	43865.09	14772.75	
465	26165	LIS	North of Acabonack Harbor	On mark	G "11"	N 41°-02.82	W 072°-07.99	26136.13	43877.57	14773.47	

TIDAL DIFFERENCES & OTHER CONSTANTS

(on NEW LONDON / on BRIDGEPORT)

Location	Time High (h m)	Time Low (h m)	Height High (multiply by)	Height Low (multiply by)	Range Mean (ft)	Range Spring (ft)	Mean Tide Level (ft)
on NEW LONDON							
Westerly, Pawcatuck River	-0 26	+0 02	1.05	1.05	2.7	3.2	1.5
Stonington, Fishers Island Sound	-0 32	-0 41	1.05	1.05	2.7	3.2	1.5
Noank, Mystic River entrance	-0 22	-0 08	0.89	0.90	2.3	2.7	1.4
West Harbor, Fishers Island, N.Y.	0 00	-0 06	0.97	0.97	2.5	3.0	1.4
Silver Eel Pond, Fishers Island, N.Y.	-0 16	-0 04	0.89	0.89	2.3	2.7	1.3
Thames River							
New London, State Pier	Daily predictions						1.5
Smith Cove Entrance	0 00	+0 10	0.97	0.95	2.6	3.0	1.5
Norwich	+0 13	+0 25	1.16	1.15	3.0	3.6	1.7
Millstone Point	+0 09	+0 01	1.05	1.05	2.7	3.2	1.5
Connecticut River							
Saybrook Jetty	+1 11	+0 45	1.36	1.35	3.5	4.2	2.0
Saybrook Point	+1 11	+0 53	1.24	1.25	3.2	3.8	1.8
Lyme, Highway bridge	+1 25	+1 10	1.20	1.20	3.1	3.7	1.7
Essex	+1 39	+1 38	1.16	1.15	3.0	3.6	1.7
Connecticut River							
Hadlyme	+2 19	+2 23	1.05	1.05	2.7	3.2	1.5
East Haddam	+2 42	+2 53	1.12	1.10	2.9	3.5	1.6
Haddam	+2 48	+3 05	0.97	0.95	2.5	3.0	1.4
Higganum Creek	+2 55	+3 25	1.01	1.00	2.6	3.1	1.5
Portland	+3 51	+4 28	0.85	0.85	2.2	2.6	1.3
Rocky Hill	+4 44	+5 44	0.78	0.80	2.0	2.4	1.2
Hartford	+5 30	+6 52	0.74	0.75	1.9	2.3	1.1
Plum Gut Harbor, Plum Island	+0 28	+0 16	1.01	1.01	2.6	3.1	1.5
Little Gull Island	+0 13	-0 22	0.85	0.85	2.2	2.6	1.3
Shelter Island Sound							
Orient	+0 37	+0 36	0.97	0.97	2.5	3.0	1.4
Greenport	+1 05	+0 49	0.93	0.95	2.4	2.9	1.4
Southold	+1 44	+1 33	0.89	0.89	2.3	2.7	1.3
Peconic Bays							
New Suffolk	+2 06	+1 44	1.00	1.00	2.6	3.1	1.5
South Jamesport	+2 27	+2 11	1.05	1.05	2.7	3.2	1.5
Shinnecock Canal	+2 33	+2 40	1.05	1.05	2.7	3.2	1.4
Noyack Bay	+1 00	+0 48	0.97	0.97	2.5	3.0	1.4
Sag Harbor	+0 45	+0 27	0.97	0.95	2.5	3.0	1.4
Threemile Harbor ent., Gardiners Bay	+0 22	+0 02	0.93	0.93	2.4	2.9	1.3
Promised Land, Napeague Bay	-0 13	-0 08	0.89	0.92	2.3	2.7	1.0
Montauk Harbor entrance	-0 24	-0 16	0.74	0.75	1.9	2.3	1.2
Montauk, Fort Pond Bay	-0 30	-0 26	0.82	0.85	2.1	2.6	1.2
Montauk Point, north side	-1 12	-1 31	0.78	0.80	2.0	2.4	1.2
on BRIDGEPORT							
Westbrook, Duck Island Roads	-0 24	-0 32	0.61	0.60	4.1	4.7	2.2
Duck Island	-0 26	-0 35	0.67	0.68	4.5	5.2	2.4
Madison	-0 21	-0 30	0.73	0.72	4.9	5.6	2.6
Falkner Island	-0 14	-0 25	0.80	0.80	5.4	6.2	2.9
Sachem Head	-0 11	-0 15	0.80	0.80	5.4	6.2	2.9
Money Island	-0 12	-0 23	0.83	0.84	5.6	6.4	3.0
Branford Harbor	-0 08	-0 18	0.88	0.88	5.9	6.8	3.1
New Haven Harbor entrance	-0 09	-0 14	0.92	0.92	6.2	7.1	3.3
New Haven (city dock)	+0 01	-0 01	0.89	0.89	6.0	6.9	3.3
Milford Harbor	-0 08	-0 10	0.98	0.96	6.6	7.6	3.5
Stratford, Housatonic River	+0 26	+1 01	0.82	0.80	5.5	6.3	2.9
Shelton, Housatonic River	+1 35	+2 44	0.74	0.72	5.0	5.8	2.7
Bridgeport	Daily predictions				6.8	7.7	3.6
Black Rock Harbor entrance	-0 04	-0 03	1.02	1.04	6.9	7.9	3.7
Saugatuck River Entrance	-0 02	+0 01	1.04	1.04	7.0	8.0	3.8

(on BRIDGEPORT continued / on WILLETS POINT / on NEWPORT)

Location	Time High (h m)	Time Low (h m)	Height High (multiply by)	Height Low (multiply by)	Range Mean (ft)	Range Spring (ft)	Mean Tide Level (ft)
on BRIDGEPORT continued							
South Norwalk	+0 09	+0 15	1.05	1.04	7.1	8.2	3.8
Greens Ledge	-0 02	-0 01	1.07	1.08	7.2	8.3	3.9
Stamford	+0 05	+0 08	1.07	1.08	7.2	8.3	3.9
Cos Cob Harbor	+0 05	+0 11	1.07	1.08	7.2	8.3	3.9
Greenwich	+0 01	+0 01	1.10	1.08	7.4	8.5	4.0
Great Captain Island	0 00	+0 01	1.08	1.08	7.3	8.4	3.9
Oyster Bay							
Oyster Bay Harbor	+0 07	+0 13	1.08	1.08	7.3	8.4	3.9
Bayville Bridge	+0 12	+0 20	1.10	1.08	7.4	8.5	4.0
Cold Spring Harbor	+0 07	+0 08	1.10	1.08	7.4	8.5	4.0
Eatons Neck Point	+0 02	+0 08	1.05	1.04	7.1	8.2	3.9
Lloyd Harbor entrance, Huntington Bay	+0 02	+0 03	1.10	1.08	7.4	8.5	4.0
Northport, Northport Bay	+0 02	+0 08	1.08	1.08	7.3	8.4	3.9
Nissequogue River entrance	-0 04	-0 04	1.04	1.04	7.0	8.0	3.8
Stony Brook, Smithtown Bay	-0 07	-0 10	0.90	0.90	6.1	7.0	3.2
Stratford Shoal	-0 06	-0 07	0.98	0.98	6.6	7.6	3.5
Port Jefferson Harbor entrance	+0 02	-0 01	0.98	0.98	6.6	7.6	3.5
Port Jefferson	+0 06	+0 05	0.98	0.98	6.6	7.5	3.5
Setauket Harbor	+0 03	+0 11	0.99	0.99	6.7	7.7	3.5
Conscience Bay entrance (Narrows)	+0 01	+0 04	0.99	1.00	6.7	7.7	3.5
Mount Sinai Harbor	+0 04	+0 18	0.89	0.88	6.0	6.9	3.2
Herod Point	-0 08	-0 14	0.89	0.88	5.9	6.8	3.1
Northville	-0 03	-0 03	0.79	0.79	5.4	6.2	2.9
Mattituck Inlet	-0 04	-0 04	0.77	0.76	5.2	6.0	2.8
Horton Point	-0 21	-0 33	0.59	0.60	4.0	4.6	2.1
Hashamomuck Beach	-0 03	-0 13	0.64	0.64	4.2	4.8	2.3
Truman Beach	-0 43	-0 50	0.50	0.50	3.4	3.9	1.8
on WILLETS POINT							
Port Chester	-0 03	-0 14	1.01	1.01	7.2	8.5	3.9
Rye Beach	-0 22	-0 31	1.01	1.01	7.2	8.4	3.9
Mamaroneck	-0 02	-0 13	1.02	1.04	7.3	8.6	3.9
New Rochelle	-0 18	-0 21	1.02	1.04	7.3	8.4	3.9
Davids Island	-0 04	-0 09	1.01	1.00	7.2	8.5	3.9
City Island	+0 03	-0 05	1.01	1.00	7.2	8.5	3.9
Throgs Neck	+0 08	+0 12	0.98	0.98	7.0	8.2	3.8
Whitestone	+0 04	+0 06	1.00	1.00	7.1	8.3	3.8
Old Ferry Point	+0 10	+0 14	0.99	0.99	7.1	8.3	3.7
College Point, Flushing Bay	+0 14	+0 13	0.95	0.96	6.8	7.9	3.7
Northern Blvd. Bridge, Flushing Creek	+0 29	+0 35	0.95	0.95	6.8	8.0	3.7
Westchester, Westchester Creek	+0 16	+0 14	0.98	0.98	7.0	8.3	3.8
Hunts Point	+0 11	+0 10	0.97	0.96	6.9	8.1	3.7
Westchester Ave. Bridge, Bronx River	+0 16	+0 15	0.97	0.97	6.9	8.1	3.7
North Brother Island	+0 15	+0 15	0.92	0.92	6.6	7.8	3.6
Port Morris (Stony Point)	+0 19	+0 14	0.89	0.89	6.3	7.4	3.3
Lawrence Point	+0 03	+0 11	0.90	0.90	6.4	7.6	3.5
Wolcott Avenue	+0 03	+0 11	0.85	0.86	6.1	7.2	3.2
Willets Point	Daily predictions				7.1	8.4	3.8
Hewlett Point	+0 03	+0 03	0.99	1.00	7.1	8.3	3.8
Port Washington, Manhasset Bay	+0 05	+0 09	1.02	1.02	7.3	8.6	3.9
Execution Rocks	0 00	-0 10	1.02	1.04	7.3	8.6	3.9
Glen Cove, Hempstead Harbor	-0 05	-0 08	1.02	1.04	7.3	8.6	3.9
on NEWPORT							
Point Judith Harbor of Refuge	-0 10	+0 17	0.88	0.86	3.1	3.9	1.6
Block Island (Great Salt Pond)	+0 02	+0 07	0.74	0.71	2.6	3.2	1.4
Block Island (Old Harbor)	-0 17	+0 12	0.83	0.86	2.9	3.6	1.5
Watch Hill Point	+0 41	+1 16	0.74	0.71	2.6	3.2	1.4

All Tides in Feet above Mean Lower Low Water (MLLW). Times Corrected to Daylight Savings Time

High Tides are shown in BOLD

TIDES

March 1990

Day	Time	Height	Day	Time	Height	Day	Time	Height
Thu 1	**01:27**	**8.3**	Mon 12	06:29	-0.5	Fri 23	02:14	0.9
	08:14	-0.6		**12:22**	**7.4**		**08:00**	**7.3**
	13:56	**7.3**		18:44	-0.1		14:53	0.5
	20:17	-0.2					**20:34**	**7.4**
Fri 2	**02:17**	**8.0**	Tue 13	**00:31**	**7.6**	Sat 24	03:11	0.3
	09:16	-0.2		07:06	-0.3		**08:53**	**7.6**
	14:52	**6.8**		**12:53**	**7.2**		15:38	0.0
	21:10	0.3		19:06	0.2		**21:19**	**7.9**
Sat 3	**03:13**	**7.6**	Wed 14	**00:53**	**7.5**	Sun 25	04:00	-0.2
	10:43	0.2		07:35	0.0		**09:42**	**7.8**
	16:01	**6.3**		**13:14**	**6.9**		16:19	-0.4
	22:27	0.8		19:16	0.4		**22:03**	**8.3**
Sun 4	**04:22**	**7.1**	Thu 15	**01:15**	**7.4**	Mon 26	04:47	-0.7
	12:05	0.4		07:54	0.3		**10:28**	**8.0**
	17:44	**6.1**		**13:38**	**6.7**		17:00	-0.6
				19:36	0.6		**22:47**	**8.6**
Mon 5	00:17	1.0	Fri 16	**01:43**	**7.3**	Tue 27	05:35	-1.0
	06:14	**6.9**		08:15	0.6		**11:15**	**8.0**
	13:17	0.3		**14:12**	**6.6**		17:42	-0.7
	19:12	**6.2**		20:12	0.9		**23:32**	**8.8**
Tue 6	01:33	0.8	Sat 17	**02:19**	**7.2**	Wed 28	06:24	-1.1
	07:39	**7.1**		08:50	0.9		**12:03**	**7.9**
	14:21	0.1		**14:52**	**6.4**		18:26	-0.6
	20:18	**6.6**		20:54	1.2			
Wed 7	02:39	0.5	Sun 18	**03:03**	**7.0**	Thu 29	**00:18**	**8.7**
	08:42	**7.3**		09:36	1.2		07:14	-1.0
	15:15	-0.2		**15:39**	**6.2**		**12:53**	**7.6**
	21:12	**7.1**		21:42	1.5		19:14	-0.3
Thu 8	03:33	0.1	Mon 19	**03:53**	**6.9**	Fri 30	**01:08**	**8.5**
	09:35	**7.6**		10:29	1.4		08:12	-0.6
	16:04	-0.4		**16:36**	**6.2**		**13:46**	**7.2**
	22:02	**7.4**		22:38	1.6		20:07	0.1
Fri 9	04:25	-0.3	Tue 20	**04:50**	**6.8**	Sat 31	**02:03**	**8.0**
	10:25	**7.7**		11:36	1.5		09:21	-0.2
	16:50	-0.5		**17:37**	**6.3**		**14:49**	**6.8**
	22:45	**7.7**		23:45	1.7		21:16	0.6
Sat 10	05:10	-0.5	Wed 21	**05:50**	**6.8**			
	11:07	**7.7**		13:00	1.3			
	17:32	-0.5		**18:42**	**6.5**			
	23:24	**7.8**						
Sun 11	05:52	-0.6	Thu 22	01:00	1.4			
	11:45	**7.6**		**06:56**	**7.0**			
	18:10	-0.3		14:05	0.9			
	23:59	**7.7**		**19:44**	**6.9**			

April 1990

Day	Time	Height	Day	Time	Height	Day	Time	Height
Sun 1	**04:04**	**7.5**	Thu 12	**01:14**	**7.6**	Mon 23	04:35	-0.4
	11:38	0.2		08:03	0.2		**10:14**	**7.7**
	17:14	**6.5**		**13:45**	**6.9**		16:41	-0.2
	23:50	1.0		19:37	0.7		**22:32**	**8.6**
Mon 2	**05:35**	**7.1**	Fri 13	**01:34**	**7.6**	Tue 24	05:31	-0.8
	12:51	0.4		08:18	0.4		**11:07**	**7.8**
	18:48	**6.5**		**14:06**	**6.8**		17:31	-0.4
				20:03	0.9		**23:22**	**8.8**
Tue 3	01:12	1.0	Sat 14	**02:06**	**7.5**	Wed 25	06:24	-1.1
	07:15	**7.0**		08:40	0.6		**11:57**	**7.8**
	13:57	0.4		**14:39**	**6.8**		18:21	-0.5
	19:59	**6.8**		20:40	1.1			
Wed 4	02:21	0.8	Sun 15	**02:45**	**7.5**	Thu 26	**00:11**	**8.9**
	08:25	**7.2**		09:15	0.8		07:16	-1.1
	14:57	0.3		**15:20**	**6.7**		**12:49**	**7.7**
	20:57	**7.1**		21:24	1.3		19:12	-0.3
Thu 5	03:19	0.4	Mon 16	**03:29**	**7.4**	Fri 27	**01:02**	**8.8**
	09:26	**7.4**		10:02	1.0		08:13	-1.0
	15:50	0.1		**16:06**	**6.7**		**13:45**	**7.5**
	21:50	**7.5**		22:13	1.5		20:07	0.0
Fri 6	04:14	0.0	Tue 17	**04:16**	**7.2**	Sat 28	**01:55**	**8.4**
	10:17	**7.5**		10:52	1.2		09:12	-0.6
	16:39	0.0		**16:58**	**6.7**		**14:44**	**7.3**
	22:38	**7.7**		23:09	1.6		21:12	0.3
Sat 7	05:02	-0.2	Wed 18	**05:11**	**7.1**	Sun 29	**02:54**	**8.0**
	11:02	**7.6**		11:48	1.2		10:16	-0.2
	17:23	-0.1		**17:54**	**6.8**		**15:57**	**7.0**
	23:20	**7.9**					22:28	0.7
Sun 8	05:47	-0.4	Thu 19	00:11	1.5	Mon 30	**04:07**	**7.5**
	11:45	**7.6**		**06:11**	**7.1**		11:24	0.1
	18:04	0.0		12:51	1.1		**17:16**	**6.9**
	23:57	**7.9**		**18:53**	**7.1**		23:45	0.9
Mon 9	06:28	-0.4	Fri 20	01:21	1.2			
	12:24	**7.4**		**07:16**	**7.1**			
	18:38	0.1		13:54	0.9			
				19:54	**7.4**			
Tue 10	**00:32**	**7.8**	Sat 21	02:33	0.8			
	07:06	-0.3		**08:21**	**7.3**			
	12:57	**7.3**		14:55	0.5			
	19:09	0.3		**20:50**	**7.8**			
Wed 11	**00:57**	**7.7**	Sun 22	03:40	0.2			
	07:38	-0.1		**09:18**	**7.5**			
	13:24	**7.1**		15:51	0.1			
	19:24	0.6		**21:42**	**8.3**			

May 1990

Day	Time	Height	Day	Time	Height	Day	Time	Height
Tue 1	**05:40**	**7.2**	Sat 12	**01:05**	**7.7**	Wed 23	05:20	-0.7
	12:29	0.3		07:55	0.5		**10:48**	**7.4**
	18:29	**7.0**		**13:41**	**6.9**		17:11	-0.1
				19:38	1.1		**23:02**	**8.8**
Wed 2	00:54	0.9	Sun 13	**01:37**	**7.7**	Thu 24	06:15	-1.0
	06:57	**7.1**		08:18	0.6		**11:47**	**7.5**
	13:30	0.4		**14:13**	**7.0**		18:08	-0.2
	19:33	**7.2**		20:16	1.1		**23:55**	**8.8**
Thu 3	01:57	0.7	Mon 14	**02:18**	**7.7**	Fri 25	07:11	-1.0
	08:02	**7.1**		08:51	0.7		**12:44**	**7.5**
	14:27	0.4		**14:54**	**7.0**		19:09	-0.1
	20:31	**7.4**		20:59	1.2			
Fri 4	02:55	0.4	Tue 15	**03:01**	**7.6**	Sat 26	**00:51**	**8.6**
	08:58	**7.2**		09:35	0.8		08:06	-0.9
	15:18	0.4		**15:36**	**7.1**		**13:42**	**7.5**
	21:21	**7.7**		21:51	1.3		20:09	0.1
Sat 5	03:48	0.1	Wed 16	**03:50**	**7.5**	Sun 27	**01:50**	**8.3**
	09:50	**7.3**		10:23	0.8		09:04	-0.6
	16:08	0.4		**16:27**	**7.1**		**14:45**	**7.4**
	22:07	**7.8**		22:42	1.3		21:14	0.3
Sun 6	04:36	-0.1	Thu 17	**04:42**	**7.4**	Mon 28	**02:54**	**7.9**
	10:36	**7.3**		11:14	0.8		10:02	-0.3
	16:51	0.4		**17:19**	**7.4**		**15:49**	**7.3**
	22:50	**7.9**		23:42	1.1		22:18	0.5
Mon 7	05:20	-0.2	Fri 18	**05:40**	**7.2**	Tue 29	**04:05**	**7.6**
	11:18	**7.2**		12:09	0.8		11:01	0.0
	17:32	0.5		**18:18**	**7.6**		**16:57**	**7.3**
	23:29	**7.9**					23:24	0.6
Tue 8	06:02	-0.2	Sat 19	00:49	0.9	Wed 30	**05:19**	**7.3**
	11:57	**7.2**		**06:42**	**7.1**		11:58	0.3
	18:08	0.6		13:09	0.7		**18:00**	**7.3**
				19:15	**7.8**			
Wed 9	**00:02**	**7.8**	Sun 20	02:01	0.6	Thu 31	00:27	0.7
	06:40	-0.1		**07:45**	**7.1**		**06:27**	**7.1**
	12:34	**7.0**		14:07	0.5		12:56	0.5
	18:36	0.8		**20:14**	**8.1**		**19:00**	**7.4**
Thu 10	**00:27**	**7.7**	Mon 21	03:15	0.1			
	07:13	0.1		**08:48**	**7.2**			
	13:01	**6.9**		15:10	0.2			
	18:51	0.9		**21:10**	**8.4**			
Fri 11	**00:42**	**7.7**	Tue 22	04:19	-0.4			
	07:39	0.3		**09:50**	**7.3**			
	13:20	**6.9**		16:11	0.0			
	19:06	1.0		**22:07**	**8.6**			

All Tides in Feet above Mean Lower Low Water (MLLW). Times Corrected to Daylight Savings Time

High Tides are shown in BOLD

June 1990

Day	Time	Height	Day	Time	Height	Day	Time	Height
Fri 1	01:27	0.6	Tue 12	01:53	7.8	Sat 23	07:03	-0.9
	07:29	**6.9**		**08:32**	0.4		**12:44**	**7.5**
	13:51	0.7		**14:30**	**7.4**		19:08	0.0
	19:56	**7.5**		20:42	0.9			
Sat 2	02:25	0.5	Wed 13	02:38	7.8	Sun 24	**00:52**	**8.4**
	08:25	**6.9**		**09:12**	0.4		07:56	-0.8
	14:43	0.7		**15:12**	**7.5**		**13:39**	**7.6**
	20:47	**7.6**		21:30	0.9		20:06	0.0
Sun 3	03:16	0.4	Thu 14	03:25	7.7	Mon 25	**01:49**	**8.2**
	09:16	**6.9**		**09:54**	0.4		08:46	-0.6
	15:30	0.8		**15:59**	**7.7**		**14:35**	**7.6**
	21:34	**7.6**		22:21	0.8		21:01	0.1
Mon 4	04:06	0.3	Fri 15	04:16	7.5	Tue 26	**02:45**	**7.9**
	10:06	**6.9**		**10:44**	0.5		09:36	-0.3
	16:16	0.8		**16:50**	**7.8**		**15:28**	**7.6**
	22:19	**7.7**		23:18	0.8		21:57	0.3
Tue 5	04:53	0.2	Sat 16	05:13	7.2	Wed 27	**03:46**	**7.6**
	10:48	**6.9**		**11:35**	0.5		10:29	0.0
	16:57	0.9		**17:45**	**7.9**		**16:26**	**7.5**
	22:59	**7.7**					22:55	0.5
Wed 6	05:36	0.2	Sun 17	00:23	0.7	Thu 28	**04:45**	**7.2**
	11:31	**6.9**		**06:13**	**7.0**		11:21	0.4
	17:36	1.0		12:33	0.5		**17:21**	**7.4**
	23:34	**7.7**		**18:44**	**8.0**		23:53	0.6
Thu 7	06:14	0.2	Mon 18	01:37	0.5	Fri 29	**05:48**	**6.9**
	12:09	**6.9**		**07:17**	**6.9**		12:13	0.7
	18:07	1.0		13:35	0.5		**18:17**	**7.3**
				19:46	**8.1**			
Fri 8	**00:02**	**7.6**	Tue 19	03:02	0.2	Sat 30	00:51	0.8
	06:48	0.3		**08:26**	**6.9**		**06:46**	**6.7**
	12:39	**6.9**		14:44	0.5		13:06	1.0
	18:27	1.0		**20:49**	**8.2**		**19:13**	**7.3**
Sat 9	**00:16**	**7.7**	Wed 20	04:11	-0.2			
	07:18	0.4		**09:37**	**7.0**			
	12:59	**7.0**		15:58	0.4			
	18:49	1.0		**21:50**	**8.4**			
Sun 10	**00:39**	**7.7**	Thu 21	05:13	-0.5			
	07:37	0.4		**10:43**	**7.1**			
	13:18	**7.0**		17:07	0.2			
	19:21	1.0		**22:51**	**8.5**			
Mon 11	**01:14**	**7.8**	Fri 22	06:10	-0.8			
	07:58	0.4		**11:45**	**7.3**			
	13:50	**7.2**		18:10	0.1			
	19:58	1.0		**23:53**	**8.5**			

July 1990

Day	Time	Height	Day	Time	Height	Day	Time	Height
Sun 1	01:49	0.8	Thu 12	**02:16**	**8.0**	Mon 23	**00:51**	**8.3**
	07:46	**6.5**		08:46	0.1		07:38	-0.7
	13:59	1.2		**14:46**	**8.0**		**13:24**	**7.8**
	20:08	**7.3**		21:10	0.4		19:52	-0.2
Mon 2	02:41	0.8	Fri 13	**03:03**	**7.8**	Tue 24	**01:41**	**8.1**
	08:41	**6.5**		09:28	0.1		08:24	-0.5
	14:50	1.3		**15:31**	**8.1**		**14:11**	**7.8**
	21:00	**7.3**		22:00	0.4		20:42	-0.1
Tue 3	03:33	0.7	Sat 14	**03:54**	**7.5**	Wed 25	**02:29**	**7.9**
	09:32	**6.6**		10:16	0.3		09:06	-0.2
	15:37	1.3		**16:23**	**8.0**		**14:56**	**7.8**
	21:46	**7.4**		22:56	0.5		21:30	0.1
Wed 4	04:22	0.6	Sun 15	**04:50**	**7.2**	Thu 26	**03:17**	**7.5**
	10:19	**6.7**		11:08	0.5		09:51	0.2
	16:23	1.3		**17:19**	**8.0**		**15:43**	**7.6**
	22:30	**7.5**					22:20	0.4
Thu 5	05:05	0.5	Mon 16	00:04	0.6	Fri 27	**04:05**	**7.1**
	11:04	**6.8**		**05:50**	**6.8**		10:34	0.6
	17:03	1.3		12:06	0.7		**16:29**	**7.4**
	23:07	**7.6**		**18:19**	**7.9**		23:11	0.7
Fri 6	05:45	0.4	Tue 17	01:35	0.6	Sat 28	**04:57**	**6.7**
	11:42	**6.9**		**06:59**	**6.6**		11:19	1.0
	17:38	1.2		13:14	0.8		**17:24**	**7.2**
	23:36	**7.6**		**19:25**	**7.9**			
Sat 7	06:21	0.4	Wed 18	03:00	0.4	Sun 29	00:07	1.0
	12:13	**7.0**		**08:17**	**6.6**		**05:57**	**6.4**
	18:06	1.1		14:44	0.9		12:07	1.4
	23:52	**7.7**		**20:39**	**7.9**		**18:20**	**7.0**
Sun 8	06:52	0.3	Thu 19	04:07	0.0	Mon 30	01:06	1.2
	12:33	**7.2**		**09:42**	**6.8**		**06:58**	**6.3**
	18:33	0.9		16:08	0.6		13:02	1.6
				21:55	**8.1**		**19:21**	**7.0**
Mon 9	**00:20**	**7.9**	Fri 20	05:07	-0.3	Tue 31	02:02	1.3
	07:15	0.3		**10:48**	**7.1**		**07:59**	**6.3**
	12:54	**7.4**		17:12	0.3		14:02	1.8
	19:05	0.8		**23:02**	**8.2**		**20:20**	**7.0**
Tue 10	**00:53**	**8.0**	Sat 21	06:00	-0.6			
	07:38	0.2		**11:45**	**7.4**			
	13:24	**7.6**		18:08	0.1			
	19:42	0.6						
Wed 11	**01:34**	**8.0**	Sun 22	**00:00**	**8.3**			
	08:09	0.1		06:49	-0.7			
	14:03	**7.8**		**12:37**	**7.7**			
	20:24	0.5		19:01	-0.1			

August 1990

Day	Time	Height	Day	Time	Height	Day	Time	Height
Wed 1	02:57	1.3	Sun 12	03:33	7.4	Thu 23	**02:03**	**7.7**
	08:57	**6.4**		09:52	0.3		08:32	0.1
	14:57	1.8		**15:57**	**8.2**		**14:18**	**7.9**
	21:11	**7.2**		22:42	0.5		20:59	0.1
Thu 2	03:47	1.1	Mon 13	04:31	7.0	Fri 24	**02:41**	**7.4**
	09:47	**6.6**		10:45	0.7		09:04	0.5
	15:47	1.6		**16:55**	**7.9**		**14:54**	**7.7**
	21:55	**7.3**					21:39	0.5
Fri 3	04:32	0.9	Tue 14	00:04	0.7	Sat 25	**03:17**	**7.0**
	10:30	**6.8**		**05:35**	**6.6**		09:31	0.9
	16:30	1.4		11:47	1.1		**15:27**	**7.4**
	22:36	**7.5**		**18:01**	**7.7**		22:21	0.9
Sat 4	05:12	0.7	Wed 15	01:43	0.8	Sun 26	**03:57**	**6.7**
	11:10	**7.1**		**06:58**	**6.4**		09:54	1.2
	17:07	1.2		13:32	1.3		**16:05**	**7.2**
	23:04	**7.7**		**19:23**	**7.5**		23:08	1.3
Sun 5	05:47	0.5	Thu 16	02:57	0.5	Mon 27	**04:45**	**6.4**
	11:37	**7.3**		**08:39**	**6.6**		10:26	1.6
	17:41	0.9		15:05	1.1		**16:49**	**7.0**
	23:26	**7.9**		**21:00**	**7.7**			
Mon 6	06:18	0.3	Fri 17	03:58	0.2	Tue 28	00:07	1.6
	11:59	**7.6**		**09:50**	**7.0**		**05:48**	**6.2**
	18:13	0.6		16:11	0.7		11:19	1.9
	23:55	**8.1**		**22:09**	**7.9**		**17:44**	**6.8**
Tue 7	06:45	0.1	Sat 18	04:54	-0.1	Wed 29	01:12	1.7
	12:24	**7.8**		**10:45**	**7.4**		**07:08**	**6.2**
	18:49	0.3		17:08	0.2		12:22	2.1
				23:04	**8.1**		**19:06**	**6.8**
Wed 8	**00:33**	**8.2**	Sun 19	05:44	-0.4	Thu 30	02:10	1.7
	07:12	-0.1		**11:36**	**7.7**		**08:13**	**6.4**
	12:59	**8.1**		18:00	-0.1		13:57	2.1
	19:26	0.1		**23:55**	**8.2**		**20:23**	**6.9**
Thu 9	**01:13**	**8.2**	Mon 20	06:32	-0.5	Fri 31	03:05	1.5
	07:45	-0.1		**12:21**	**8.0**		**09:05**	**6.6**
	13:37	**8.3**		18:48	-0.3		15:02	1.9
	20:08	0.0					**21:14**	**7.2**
Fri 10	**01:57**	**8.1**	Tue 21	**00:42**	**8.2**			
	08:21	-0.1		07:14	-0.4			
	14:21	**8.4**		**13:04**	**8.1**			
	20:54	0.0		19:33	-0.3			
Sat 11	02:43	7.8	Wed 22	**01:23**	**8.0**			
	09:03	0.0		07:55	-0.2			
	15:07	**8.4**		**13:44**	**8.0**			
	21:42	0.2		20:16	-0.2			

All Tides in Feet above Mean Lower Low Water (MLLW). Times Corrected to Daylight Savings Time

High Tides are shown in BOLD

TIDES

September 1990

Day	Time	Height	Time	Height	Time	Height	Time	Height
Sat 1	03:50	1.2	**09:48**	**7.0**	15:53	1.5	**21:53**	**7.4**
Sun 2	04:32	0.9	**10:25**	**7.3**	16:35	1.0	**22:25**	**7.7**
Mon 3	05:06	0.6	**10:48**	**7.7**	17:12	0.6	**22:56**	**8.0**
Tue 4	05:38	0.2	**11:17**	**8.0**	17:48	0.1	**23:33**	**8.2**
Wed 5	06:07	0.0	**11:52**	**8.4**	18:25	-0.2		
Thu 6	**00:11**	**8.3**	06:39	-0.2	**12:29**	**8.6**	19:06	-0.4
Fri 7	**00:53**	**8.2**	07:16	-0.3	**13:12**	**8.8**	19:50	-0.4
Sat 8	**01:38**	**8.1**	07:57	-0.2	**13:57**	**8.7**	20:38	-0.3
Sun 9	**02:26**	**7.7**	08:43	0.1	**14:45**	**8.5**	21:31	0.1
Mon 10	**03:19**	**7.3**	09:35	0.6	**15:39**	**8.2**	22:44	0.5
Tue 11	**04:18**	**6.9**	10:37	1.0	**16:39**	**7.7**		
Wed 12	00:19	0.8	**05:35**	**6.6**	12:12	1.4	**17:59**	**7.4**
Thu 13	01:38	0.8	**07:26**	**6.6**	13:54	1.3	**19:52**	**7.3**
Fri 14	02:46	0.6	**08:41**	**6.9**	15:05	0.9	**21:08**	**7.6**
Sat 15	03:43	0.3	**09:40**	**7.4**	16:06	0.5	**22:06**	**7.9**
Sun 16	04:36	0.0	**10:32**	**7.8**	16:56	0.0	**22:56**	**8.0**
Mon 17	05:25	-0.2	**11:18**	**8.0**	17:44	-0.3	**23:44**	**8.1**
Tue 18	06:07	-0.2	**12:00**	**8.2**	18:30	-0.4		
Wed 19	**00:24**	**8.0**	06:49	-0.1	**12:39**	**8.2**	19:12	-0.4
Thu 20	**01:02**	**7.8**	07:25	0.1	**13:11**	**8.1**	19:51	-0.2
Fri 21	**01:39**	**7.5**	07:57	0.4	**13:41**	**7.9**	20:25	0.2
Sat 22	**02:07**	**7.2**	08:18	0.7	**14:06**	**7.7**	20:56	0.5
Sun 23	**02:35**	**7.0**	08:30	1.0	**14:35**	**7.5**	21:20	0.9
Mon 24	**03:07**	**6.8**	08:59	1.3	**15:09**	**7.3**	21:48	1.3
Tue 25	**03:46**	**6.6**	09:41	1.6	**15:52**	**7.1**	22:29	1.6
Wed 26	**04:36**	**6.4**	10:30	1.9	**16:42**	**6.9**	23:27	1.8
Thu 27	**05:29**	**6.4**	11:30	2.1	**17:38**	**6.9**		
Fri 28	00:51	1.8	**06:45**	**6.5**	12:33	2.1	**18:45**	**6.9**
Sat 29	02:02	1.7	**07:56**	**6.8**	13:59	1.8	**19:51**	**7.1**
Sun 30	02:55	1.3	**08:45**	**7.1**	15:08	1.3	**20:50**	**7.3**

October 1990

Day	Time	Height	Time	Height	Time	Height	Time	Height
Mon 1	03:37	0.9	**09:22**	**7.6**	15:55	0.8	**21:37**	**7.6**
Tue 2	04:15	0.5	**10:01**	**8.0**	16:41	0.2	**22:21**	**7.9**
Wed 3	04:51	0.1	**10:40**	**8.4**	17:23	-0.3	**23:04**	**8.1**
Thu 4	05:31	-0.2	**11:20**	**8.8**	18:06	-0.6	**23:49**	**8.1**
Fri 5	06:09	-0.3	**12:04**	**9.0**	18:51	-0.8		
Sat 6	**00:34**	**8.1**	06:53	-0.3	**12:48**	**9.0**	19:39	-0.7
Sun 7	**01:22**	**7.9**	07:39	-0.1	**13:36**	**8.8**	20:32	-0.5
Mon 8	**02:14**	**7.6**	08:30	0.3	**14:27**	**8.5**	21:36	0.0
Tue 9	**03:09**	**7.2**	09:28	0.7	**15:25**	**8.0**	22:53	0.4
Wed 10	**04:18**	**6.9**	10:53	1.2	**16:34**	**7.5**		
Thu 11	00:12	0.6	**05:59**	**6.7**	12:32	1.3	**18:24**	**7.2**
Fri 12	01:23	0.6	**07:23**	**6.9**	13:48	1.0	**19:51**	**7.3**
Sat 13	02:26	0.5	**08:26**	**7.3**	14:51	0.6	**20:55**	**7.5**
Sun 14	03:22	0.3	**09:21**	**7.6**	15:47	0.2	**21:50**	**7.6**
Mon 15	04:12	0.1	**10:11**	**7.9**	16:38	-0.2	**22:38**	**7.7**
Tue 16	04:59	0.0	**10:56**	**8.1**	17:25	-0.4	**23:23**	**7.7**
Wed 17	05:41	0.0	**11:37**	**8.2**	18:10	-0.5		
Thu 18	**00:04**	**7.6**	06:19	0.2	**12:14**	**8.1**	18:47	-0.4
Fri 19	**00:41**	**7.4**	06:56	0.4	**12:44**	**8.0**	19:26	-0.1
Sat 20	**01:13**	**7.2**	07:21	0.7	**13:08**	**7.8**	20:00	0.2
Sun 21	**01:42**	**7.0**	07:33	0.9	**13:28**	**7.6**	20:22	0.5
Mon 22	**02:03**	**6.9**	07:52	1.1	**13:56**	**7.5**	20:38	0.8
Tue 23	**02:32**	**6.8**	08:27	1.3	**14:32**	**7.4**	21:07	1.0
Wed 24	**03:09**	**6.7**	09:09	1.5	**15:14**	**7.3**	21:48	1.3
Thu 25	**03:52**	**6.7**	09:57	1.7	**16:02**	**7.1**	22:37	1.4
Fri 26	**04:42**	**6.7**	10:53	1.8	**16:55**	**7.0**	23:30	1.5
Sat 27	**05:40**	**6.8**	11:56	1.7	**17:54**	**6.9**		
Sun 28	00:29	1.4	**05:38**	**7.0**	12:03	1.5	**17:56**	**7.0**
Mon 29	00:32	1.1	**06:33**	**7.4**	13:12	1.0	**18:57**	**7.1**
Tue 30	01:29	0.8	**07:29**	**7.8**	14:16	0.5	**19:57**	**7.3**
Wed 31	02:21	0.4	**08:16**	**8.2**	15:11	-0.1	**20:48**	**7.6**

November 1990

Day	Time	Height	Time	Height	Time	Height	Time	Height
Thu 1	03:11	0.0	**09:06**	**8.6**	16:02	-0.6	**21:38**	**7.7**
Fri 2	03:57	-0.2	**09:52**	**8.9**	16:53	-0.9	**22:29**	**7.8**
Sat 3	04:46	-0.3	**10:41**	**9.0**	17:42	-1.0	**23:19**	**7.8**
Sun 4	05:35	-0.3	**11:30**	**8.9**	18:35	-0.9		
Mon 5	**00:10**	**7.6**	06:29	-0.1	**12:21**	**8.7**	19:35	-0.7
Tue 6	**01:06**	**7.4**	07:27	0.2	**13:17**	**8.3**	20:39	-0.3
Wed 7	**02:09**	**7.2**	08:41	0.6	**14:20**	**7.8**	21:45	0.0
Thu 8	**03:26**	**7.0**	10:03	0.8	**15:42**	**7.3**	22:53	0.3
Fri 9	**04:51**	**7.0**	11:21	0.8	**17:19**	**7.1**	23:58	0.4
Sat 10	**06:02**	**7.1**	12:27	0.6	**18:31**	**7.1**		
Sun 11	00:58	0.4	**07:02**	**7.4**	13:29	0.3	**19:31**	**7.1**
Mon 12	01:53	0.3	**07:57**	**7.6**	14:26	0.0	**20:26**	**7.2**
Tue 13	02:45	0.2	**08:45**	**7.8**	15:15	-0.2	**21:15**	**7.2**
Wed 14	03:31	0.2	**09:30**	**7.9**	16:02	-0.4	**22:02**	**7.2**
Thu 15	04:15	0.3	**10:12**	**7.9**	16:45	-0.4	**22:40**	**7.1**
Fri 16	04:54	0.4	**10:49**	**7.8**	17:26	-0.3	**23:21**	**7.0**
Sat 17	05:31	0.6	**11:21**	**7.7**	18:03	-0.1	**23:54**	**6.9**
Sun 18	05:56	0.8	**11:42**	**7.6**	18:35	0.1		
Mon 19	**00:21**	**6.8**	06:06	0.9	**12:01**	**7.5**	19:01	0.4
Tue 20	**00:41**	**6.8**	06:28	1.0	**12:27**	**7.5**	19:14	0.5
Wed 21	**01:06**	**6.8**	07:03	1.1	**13:03**	**7.4**	19:40	0.7
Thu 22	**01:40**	**6.9**	07:45	1.2	**13:44**	**7.4**	20:17	0.7
Fri 23	**02:22**	**6.9**	08:31	1.2	**14:31**	**7.2**	21:03	0.8
Sat 24	**03:08**	**7.0**	09:23	1.2	**15:20**	**7.1**	21:49	0.8
Sun 25	**03:58**	**7.1**	10:18	1.2	**16:17**	**6.9**	22:43	0.8
Mon 26	04:51	0.5	**11:19**	**7.8**	17:16	0.2	**23:39**	**6.9**
Tue 27	**05:49**	**7.5**	12:27	0.6	**18:16**	**6.8**		
Wed 28	00:36	0.5	**06:45**	**7.8**	13:41	0.2	**19:18**	**6.9**
Thu 29	01:34	0.3	**07:41**	**8.1**	14:47	-0.3	**20:19**	**7.1**
Fri 30	02:37	0.0	**08:37**	**8.4**	15:46	-0.7	**21:18**	**7.2**

EMBASSY'S TIDE GUIDE© - BRIDGEPORT, CT

All Tides in Feet above Mean Lower Low Water (MLLW). Times Corrected to Daylight Savings Time

High Tides are shown in BOLD

March 1990

Day	Time	Height	Day	Time	Height	Day	Time	Height
Thu 1	**01:31** / 07:57 / **14:03** / 20:11	7.6 / -0.8 / 6.7 / -0.3	Mon 12	05:43 / **11:50** / 17:58	-0.5 / 6.8 / -0.2	Fri 23	**01:54** / **08:04** / 14:22 / **20:30**	0.6 / 6.9 / 0.3 / 7.0
Fri 2	**02:24** / 08:53 / **14:58** / 21:08	7.3 / -0.4 / 6.2 / 0.2	Tue 13	**00:04** / 06:22 / **12:26** / 18:33	7.1 / -0.4 / 6.6 / 0.0	Sat 24	**02:46** / **08:54** / 15:10 / **21:17**	0.1 / 7.2 / -0.1 / 7.4
Sat 3	**03:24** / 09:56 / **16:02** / 22:12	7.0 / 0.0 / 5.9 / 0.6	Wed 14	**00:39** / 06:59 / **13:02** / 19:10	7.0 / -0.2 / 6.4 / 0.2	Sun 25	**03:35** / **09:41** / 15:54 / **22:03**	-0.4 / 7.4 / -0.4 / 7.7
Sun 4	**04:30** / 11:05 / **17:13** / 23:23	6.7 / 0.3 / 5.7 / 0.8	Thu 15	**01:15** / 07:38 / **13:39** / 19:46	6.9 / 0.1 / 6.2 / 0.5	Mon 26	**04:21** / **10:29** / 16:39 / **22:47**	-0.9 / 7.5 / -0.7 / 8.0
Mon 5	**05:42** / 12:18 / **18:26**	6.6 / 0.4 / 5.8	Fri 16	**01:55** / 08:19 / **14:21** / 20:26	6.7 / 0.4 / 6.0 / 0.9	Tue 27	**05:09** / **11:17** / 17:24 / **23:33**	-1.2 / 7.4 / -0.7 / 8.1
Tue 6	00:37 / **06:55** / 13:25 / **19:35**	0.8 / 6.6 / 0.3 / 6.0	Sat 17	**02:35** / 09:01 / **15:06** / 21:12	6.6 / 0.7 / 5.9 / 1.2	Wed 28	**05:58** / **12:04** / 18:11	-1.3 / 7.3 / -0.6
Wed 7	01:45 / **08:01** / 14:25 / **20:33**	0.6 / 6.8 / 0.2 / 6.4	Sun 18	**03:22** / 09:53 / **15:57** / 22:05	6.5 / 1.0 / 5.8 / 1.4	Thu 29	**00:22** / 06:46 / **12:54** / 19:00	8.0 / -1.1 / 7.0 / -0.4
Thu 8	02:44 / **08:57** / 15:16 / **21:23**	0.2 / 7.0 / 0.0 / 6.7	Mon 19	**04:16** / 10:46 / **16:53** / 23:02	6.4 / 1.1 / 5.8 / 1.5	Fri 30	**01:12** / 07:41 / **13:50** / 19:55	7.8 / -0.8 / 6.7 / 0.0
Fri 9	03:36 / **09:47** / 16:01 / **22:08**	-0.1 / 7.1 / -0.2 / 7.0	Tue 20	**05:13** / 11:44 / **17:50**	6.4 / 1.1 / 5.9	Sat 31	**02:08** / 08:40 / **14:48** / 20:56	7.5 / -0.4 / 6.4 / 0.4
Sat 10	04:23 / **10:32** / 16:43 / **22:49**	-0.4 / 7.1 / -0.3 / 7.1	Wed 21	00:03 / **06:13** / 12:39 / **18:49**	1.4 / 6.5 / 1.0 / 6.2			
Sun 11	05:05 / **11:12** / 17:22 / **23:26**	-0.5 / 7.0 / -0.3 / 7.1	Thu 22	01:00 / **07:09** / 13:35 / **19:40**	1.1 / 6.7 / 0.7 / 6.6			

April 1990

Day	Time	Height	Day	Time	Height	Day	Time	Height
Sun 1	04:09 / **10:43** / 16:53 / **23:03**	7.1 / 0.1 / 6.2 / 0.8	Thu 12	**01:08** / 07:30 / **13:35** / 19:38	7.2 / 0.0 / 6.4 / 0.6	Mon 23	04:07 / **10:15** / 16:21 / **22:33**	-0.5 / 7.2 / -0.3 / 8.1
Mon 2	**05:18** / 11:51 / **18:03**	6.8 / 0.4 / 6.1	Fri 13	**01:43** / 08:08 / **14:12** / 20:13	7.1 / 0.2 / 6.3 / 0.9	Tue 24	04:58 / **11:04** / 17:11 / **23:21**	-0.9 / 7.3 / -0.4 / 8.3
Tue 3	00:17 / **06:30** / 12:59 / **19:13**	0.9 / 6.6 / 0.5 / 6.2	Sat 14	**02:20** / 08:47 / **14:50** / 20:55	7.0 / 0.4 / 6.3 / 1.1	Wed 25	05:49 / **11:56** / 18:00	-1.2 / 7.3 / -0.5
Wed 4	01:27 / **07:40** / 14:04 / **20:16**	0.8 / 6.6 / 0.5 / 6.5	Sun 15	**03:00** / 09:29 / **15:34** / 21:37	6.9 / 0.7 / 6.2 / 1.3	Thu 26	**00:11** / 06:39 / **12:47** / 18:51	8.3 / -1.2 / 7.2 / -0.3
Thu 5	02:33 / **08:45** / 15:02 / **21:12**	0.6 / 6.7 / 0.4 / 6.8	Mon 16	**03:47** / 10:14 / **16:23** / 22:28	6.8 / 0.9 / 6.2 / 1.5	Fri 27	**01:03** / 07:33 / **13:40** / 19:45	8.2 / -1.0 / 7.0 / -0.1
Fri 6	03:30 / **09:38** / 15:51 / **21:59**	0.2 / 6.8 / 0.3 / 7.0	Tue 17	**04:37** / 11:05 / **17:15** / 23:26	6.7 / 1.0 / 6.3 / 1.5	Sat 28	**01:57** / 08:27 / **14:36** / 20:42	8.0 / -0.7 / 6.8 / 0.3
Sat 7	04:18 / **10:26** / 16:36 / **22:42**	-0.2 / 6.8 / 0.1 / 7.2	Wed 18	**05:32** / 12:00 / **18:10**	6.6 / 1.1 / 6.4	Sun 29	**02:55** / 09:27 / **15:37** / 21:45	7.6 / -0.3 / 6.7 / 0.6
Sun 8	05:02 / **11:08** / 17:15 / **23:21**	-0.2 / 6.8 / 0.1 / 7.3	Thu 19	00:25 / **06:33** / 12:56 / **19:07**	1.3 / 6.6 / 0.9 / 6.7	Mon 30	**03:56** / 10:28 / **16:40** / 22:52	7.2 / 0.1 / 6.5 / 0.8
Mon 9	05:41 / **11:47** / 17:53 / **23:58**	-0.3 / 6.8 / 0.2 / 7.3	Fri 20	01:24 / **07:31** / 13:51 / **20:01**	1.0 / 6.7 / 0.7 / 7.0			
Tue 10	06:18 / **12:22** / 18:27	-0.3 / 6.7 / 0.3	Sat 21	02:21 / **08:27** / 14:42 / **20:53**	0.5 / 6.9 / 0.4 / 7.4			
Wed 11	**00:33** / 06:55 / **12:58** / 19:03	7.3 / -0.2 / 6.5 / 0.4	Sun 22	03:15 / **09:22** / 15:33 / **21:42**	0.0 / 7.0 / 0.0 / 7.8			

May 1990

Day	Time	Height	Day	Time	Height	Day	Time	Height
Tue 1	**05:03** / 11:31 / **17:45**	6.9 / 0.4 / 6.5	Sat 12	**01:16** / 07:42 / **13:46** / 19:49	7.3 / 0.3 / 6.5 / 1.1	Wed 23	04:36 / **10:42** / 16:47 / **23:00**	-0.8 / 7.0 / -0.1 / 8.3
Wed 2	00:02 / **06:10** / 12:34 / **18:48**	0.9 / 6.7 / 0.6 / 6.7	Sun 13	**01:53** / 08:20 / **14:26** / 20:27	7.2 / 0.5 / 6.5 / 1.2	Thu 24	05:31 / **11:37** / 17:40 / **23:53**	-0.9 / 7.1 / -0.1 / 8.3
Thu 3	01:08 / **07:17** / 13:34 / **19:48**	0.8 / 6.6 / 0.7 / 6.8	Mon 14	**02:33** / 09:00 / **15:08** / 21:12	7.1 / 0.6 / 6.6 / 1.3	Fri 25	06:24 / **12:32** / 18:35	-1.0 / 7.1 / -0.1
Fri 4	02:09 / **08:19** / 14:29 / **20:43**	0.6 / 6.6 / 0.7 / 7.0	Tue 15	**03:16** / 09:44 / **15:53** / 22:01	7.0 / 0.7 / 6.6 / 1.3	Sat 26	**00:48** / 07:19 / **13:27** / 19:32	8.2 / -0.8 / 7.1 / 0.1
Sat 5	03:05 / **09:11** / 15:19 / **21:31**	0.4 / 6.6 / 0.6 / 7.2	Wed 16	**04:04** / 10:30 / **16:41** / 22:54	6.9 / 0.8 / 6.7 / 1.3	Sun 27	**01:43** / 08:13 / **14:23** / 20:31	8.0 / -0.6 / 7.0 / 0.3
Sun 6	03:51 / **09:57** / 16:02 / **22:11**	0.2 / 6.6 / 0.6 / 7.3	Thu 17	**04:58** / 11:21 / **17:34** / 23:51	6.8 / 0.8 / 6.9 / 1.1	Mon 28	**02:39** / 09:08 / **15:19** / 21:31	7.6 / -0.2 / 7.0 / 0.5
Mon 7	04:36 / **10:39** / 16:43 / **22:51**	0.0 / 6.6 / 0.5 / 7.3	Fri 18	**05:54** / 12:13 / **18:28**	6.7 / 0.7 / 7.1	Tue 29	**03:40** / 10:04 / **16:17** / 22:33	7.3 / 0.1 / 6.9 / 0.7
Tue 8	05:15 / **11:20** / 17:22 / **23:29**	-0.1 / 6.5 / 0.6 / 7.4	Sat 19	00:51 / **06:54** / 13:09 / **19:23**	0.8 / 6.7 / 0.6 / 7.4	Wed 30	**04:41** / 11:03 / **17:17** / 23:36	6.9 / 0.4 / 6.9 / 0.8
Wed 9	05:53 / **11:57** / 17:57	0.0 / 6.5 / 0.7	Sun 20	01:50 / **07:54** / 14:04 / **20:19**	0.4 / 6.7 / 0.4 / 7.7	Thu 31	**05:43** / 12:01 / **18:17**	6.6 / 0.6 / 6.9
Thu 10	**00:04** / 06:29 / **12:32** / 18:34	7.4 / 0.0 / 6.5 / 0.8	Mon 21	02:48 / **08:51** / 14:59 / **21:14**	-0.1 / 6.8 / 0.2 / 7.9			
Fri 11	**00:40** / 07:05 / **13:09** / 19:09	7.3 / 0.1 / 6.5 / 0.9	Tue 22	03:43 / **09:47** / 15:52 / **22:07**	-0.5 / 6.9 / 0.0 / 8.2			

All Tides in Feet above Mean Lower Low Water (MLLW). Times Corrected to Daylight Savings Time

High Tides are shown in BOLD

TIDES

June 1990

Day	Time	Height	Day	Time	Height	Day	Time	Height
Fri 1	00:39	0.8	Tue 12	02:09	7.3	Sat 23	06:11	-0.7
	06:44	6.4		08:34	0.4		12:19	7.1
	12:58	0.8		14:42	6.9		18:24	0.0
	19:13	6.9		20:47	1.0			
Sat 2	01:37	0.7	Wed 13	02:52	7.2	Sun 24	00:35	8.1
	07:41	6.3		09:15	0.4		07:04	-0.6
	13:50	0.9		15:24	7.0		13:12	7.2
	20:04	7.0		21:35	1.0		19:19	0.1
Sun 3	02:32	0.6	Thu 14	03:37	7.1	Mon 25	01:28	7.9
	08:37	6.2		09:58	0.5		07:56	-0.5
	14:41	0.9		16:11	7.1		14:05	7.2
	20:53	7.1		22:25	0.9		20:15	0.2
Mon 4	03:21	0.4	Fri 15	04:28	6.9	Tue 26	02:23	7.6
	09:27	6.2		10:46	0.5		08:46	-0.2
	15:27	0.9		17:02	7.2		14:57	7.2
	21:38	7.2		23:21	0.7		21:11	0.3
Tue 5	04:05	0.3	Sat 16	05:24	6.7	Wed 27	03:16	7.2
	10:09	6.3		11:38	0.5		09:37	0.1
	16:09	0.9		17:56	7.3		15:48	7.1
	22:18	7.4					22:06	0.5
Wed 6	04:46	0.3	Sun 17	00:21	0.6	Thu 28	04:11	6.8
	10:51	6.3		06:24	6.5		10:28	0.4
	16:50	0.9		12:33	0.5		16:43	7.0
	23:00	7.4		18:52	7.5		23:02	0.7
Thu 7	05:27	0.3	Mon 18	01:23	0.3	Fri 29	05:06	6.4
	11:30	6.4		07:26	6.4		11:22	0.7
	17:30	0.9		13:33	0.5		17:36	6.9
	23:37	7.5		19:52	7.7			
Fri 8	06:03	0.2	Tue 19	02:25	0.0	Sat 30	00:00	0.8
	12:07	6.5		08:29	6.5		06:02	6.1
	18:08	1.0		14:32	0.4		12:14	0.9
				20:51	7.9		18:30	6.9
Sat 9	00:14	7.4	Wed 20	03:25	-0.2			
	06:42	0.2		09:29	6.6			
	12:45	6.6		15:33	0.3			
	18:47	1.0		21:49	8.0			
Sun 10	00:51	7.4	Thu 21	04:21	-0.5			
	07:19	0.3		10:27	6.7			
	13:24	6.7		16:31	0.2			
	19:24	1.0		22:45	8.1			
Mon 11	01:28	7.4	Fri 22	05:18	-0.6			
	07:56	0.3		11:24	6.9			
	14:01	6.8		17:28	0.1			
	20:05	1.0		23:40	8.2			

July 1990

Day	Time	Height	Day	Time	Height	Day	Time	Height
Sun 1	00:58	0.9	Thu 12	02:28	7.3	Mon 23	00:22	7.9
	06:59	6.0		08:46	0.1		06:46	-0.5
	13:07	1.1		14:56	7.4		12:54	7.3
	19:23	6.9		21:10	0.4		19:04	-0.1
Mon 2	01:52	0.9	Fri 13	03:13	7.1	Tue 24	01:12	7.7
	07:55	5.9		09:27	0.2		07:32	-0.4
	13:58	1.2		15:42	7.4		13:41	7.4
	20:14	6.9		22:01	0.4		19:54	0.0
Tue 3	02:43	0.8	Sat 14	04:04	6.8	Wed 25	02:01	7.4
	08:46	6.0		10:16	0.3		08:18	-0.2
	14:48	1.2		16:33	7.4		14:27	7.3
	21:02	7.0		22:57	0.4		20:44	0.1
Wed 4	03:33	0.7	Sun 15	04:59	6.5	Thu 26	02:47	7.0
	09:34	6.1		11:09	0.5		09:03	0.1
	15:34	1.1		17:28	7.4		15:13	7.2
	21:48	7.2		23:58	0.4		21:35	0.3
Thu 5	04:16	0.6	Mon 16	06:00	6.3	Fri 27	03:35	6.6
	10:19	6.3		12:07	0.6		09:50	0.4
	16:20	1.1		18:28	7.4		16:03	7.0
	22:29	7.3					22:25	0.6
Fri 6	04:58	0.4	Tue 17	01:03	0.4	Sat 28	04:26	6.3
	11:01	6.5		07:06	6.2		10:38	0.8
	17:03	1.0		13:13	0.7		16:51	6.8
	23:09	7.4		19:32	7.5		23:17	0.9
Sat 7	05:37	0.3	Wed 18	02:08	0.3	Sun 29	05:18	6.0
	11:40	6.6		08:12	6.2		11:27	1.1
	17:43	0.9		14:17	0.7		17:44	6.7
	23:49	7.5		20:35	7.6			
Sun 8	06:14	0.2	Thu 19	03:12	0.1	Mon 30	00:12	1.1
	12:18	6.8		09:17	6.4		06:14	5.8
	18:22	0.8		15:22	0.6		12:21	1.3
				21:38	7.8		18:36	6.7
Mon 9	00:27	7.6	Fri 20	04:10	-0.2	Tue 31	01:08	1.2
	06:52	0.1		10:17	6.7		07:10	5.7
	12:57	7.0		16:23	0.3		13:16	1.5
	19:01	0.7		22:36	7.9		19:32	6.7
Tue 10	01:06	7.6	Sat 21	05:06	-0.4			
	07:28	0.1		11:12	6.9			
	13:36	7.1		17:19	0.1			
	19:41	0.6		23:31	7.9			
Wed 11	01:45	7.5	Sun 22	05:57	-0.5			
	08:05	0.1		12:04	7.2			
	14:13	7.3		18:12	0.0			
	20:26	0.5						

August 1990

Day	Time	Height	Day	Time	Height	Day	Time	Height
Wed 1	02:03	1.1	Sun 12	03:43	6.7	Thu 23	01:34	7.2
	08:06	5.9		09:50	0.3		07:48	0.0
	14:10	1.5		16:08	7.5		13:56	7.4
	20:24	6.9		22:37	0.3		20:15	0.0
Thu 2	02:56	1.0	Mon 13	04:40	6.4	Fri 24	02:18	6.8
	08:57	6.1		10:48	0.6		08:28	0.3
	15:01	1.4		17:07	7.4		14:37	7.2
	21:12	7.1		23:41	0.5		20:58	0.3
Fri 3	03:41	0.8	Tue 14	05:44	6.1	Sat 25	03:00	6.5
	09:46	6.3		11:52	0.9		09:10	0.6
	15:49	1.2		18:13	7.2		15:21	7.0
	21:59	7.3					21:44	0.6
Sat 4	04:26	0.6	Wed 15	00:49	0.6	Sun 26	03:45	6.2
	10:29	6.6		06:54	6.0		09:53	1.0
	16:34	1.0		13:02	1.0		16:06	6.8
	22:40	7.5		19:21	7.2		22:33	1.0
Sun 5	05:06	0.3	Thu 16	01:58	0.5	Mon 27	04:33	5.9
	11:11	6.9		08:04	6.2		10:43	1.3
	17:15	0.7		14:11	0.9		16:57	6.7
	23:21	7.6		20:29	7.4		23:26	1.2
Mon 6	05:44	0.1	Fri 17	03:01	0.3	Tue 28	05:28	5.8
	11:48	7.2		09:09	6.5		11:35	1.6
	17:57	0.4		15:17	0.7		17:50	6.6
				21:31	7.5			
Tue 7	00:01	7.7	Sat 18	04:00	0.1	Wed 29	00:22	1.4
	06:21	-0.1		10:07	6.8		06:26	5.8
	12:25	7.4		16:16	0.3		12:34	1.7
	18:35	0.2		22:28	7.7		18:46	6.6
Wed 8	00:41	7.7	Sun 19	04:52	-0.1	Thu 30	01:18	1.4
	06:58	-0.2		11:00	7.1		07:23	5.9
	13:06	7.6		17:09	0.0		13:31	1.7
	19:17	0.0		23:19	7.7		19:42	6.8
Thu 9	01:22	7.6	Mon 20	05:39	-0.3	Fri 31	02:14	1.2
	07:37	-0.2		11:46	7.4		08:19	6.2
	13:45	7.7		18:00	-0.2		14:27	1.5
	20:01	-0.1					20:35	7.0
Fri 10	02:05	7.3	Tue 21	00:07	7.6			
	08:17	-0.1		06:24	-0.3			
	14:30	7.7		12:30	7.5			
	20:47	-0.1		18:47	-0.2			
Sat 11	02:52	7.1	Wed 22	00:53	7.4			
	09:02	0.1		07:06	-0.2			
	15:16	7.6		13:14	7.5			
	21:39	0.1		19:30	-0.2			

All Tides in Feet above Mean Lower Low Water (MLLW). Times Corrected to Daylight Savings Time

High Tides are shown in BOLD

September 1990

Day	Time	Height	Day	Time	Height	Day	Time	Height
Sat 1	03:01	1.0	Wed 12	**05:36**	**6.1**	Sun 23	**02:26**	**6.4**
	09:07	**6.5**		11:45	1.1		08:31	0.8
	15:15	1.2		**18:02**	**7.1**		**14:41**	**7.1**
	21:23	**7.2**					21:08	0.7
Sun 2	03:46	0.7	Thu 13	00:39	0.7	Mon 24	**03:08**	**6.2**
	09:51	**6.9**		**06:48**	**6.2**		09:15	1.2
	16:02	0.8		12:59	1.2		**15:24**	**6.9**
	22:08	**7.4**		**19:15**	**6.9**		21:52	1.0
Mon 3	04:29	0.3	Fri 14	01:47	0.7	Tue 25	**03:56**	**6.1**
	10:34	**7.3**		**07:58**	**6.4**		10:01	1.5
	16:46	0.4		14:08	1.0		**16:12**	**6.7**
	22:51	**7.6**		**20:22**	**7.2**		22:43	1.3
Tue 4	05:09	0.0	Sat 15	02:49	0.5	Wed 26	**04:46**	**6.0**
	11:14	**7.6**		**08:59**	**6.7**		10:54	1.8
	17:28	0.0		15:12	0.6		**17:05**	**6.6**
	23:33	**7.7**		**21:23**	**7.3**		23:36	1.4
Wed 5	05:48	-0.2	Sun 16	03:44	0.3	Thu 27	**05:42**	**6.0**
	11:55	**7.8**		**09:54**	**7.1**		11:52	1.9
	18:10	-0.3		16:07	0.2		**18:01**	**6.6**
				22:18	**7.4**			
Thu 6	**00:15**	**7.7**	Mon 17	04:34	0.1	Fri 28	00:33	1.5
	06:27	-0.3		**10:42**	**7.4**		**06:39**	**6.2**
	12:36	**8.0**		16:56	-0.1		12:51	1.8
	18:53	-0.5		**23:04**	**7.4**		**18:59**	**6.7**
Fri 7	**00:59**	**7.6**	Tue 18	05:19	0.0	Sat 29	01:29	1.3
	07:08	-0.3		**11:25**	**7.5**		**07:35**	**6.4**
	13:18	**8.0**		17:41	-0.2		13:48	1.5
	19:38	-0.5		**23:48**	**7.3**		**19:55**	**6.9**
Sat 8	**01:42**	**7.3**	Wed 19	05:59	0.0	Sun 30	02:18	1.0
	07:51	-0.2		**12:05**	**7.6**		**08:25**	**6.8**
	14:04	**8.0**		18:23	-0.3		14:40	1.1
	20:28	-0.4					**20:45**	**7.1**
Sun 9	**02:32**	**7.0**	Thu 20	**00:28**	**7.1**			
	08:39	0.1		06:37	0.1			
	14:54	**7.8**		**12:45**	**7.6**			
	21:21	-0.1		19:05	-0.2			
Mon 10	**03:27**	**6.7**	Fri 21	**01:08**	**6.9**			
	09:32	0.5		07:16	0.2			
	15:50	**7.5**		**13:23**	**7.4**			
	22:22	0.3		19:45	0.0			
Tue 11	**04:27**	**6.3**	Sat 22	**01:46**	**6.7**			
	10:35	0.9		07:54	0.5			
	16:53	**7.3**		**14:02**	**7.3**			
	23:28	0.6		20:25	0.3			

October 1990

Day	Time	Height	Day	Time	Height	Day	Time	Height
Mon 1	03:06	0.7	Fri 12	00:25	0.7	Tue 23	**02:39**	**6.3**
	09:12	**7.2**		**06:37**	**6.4**		08:42	1.3
	15:30	0.6		12:52	1.1		**14:50**	**7.0**
	21:33	**7.3**		**19:03**	**6.9**		21:16	0.9
Tue 2	03:49	0.3	Sat 13	01:31	0.7	Wed 24	**03:21**	**6.2**
	09:57	**7.6**		**07:43**	**6.7**		09:27	1.5
	16:15	0.1		14:00	0.8		**15:34**	**6.8**
	22:20	**7.5**		**20:11**	**6.9**		22:04	1.1
Wed 3	04:31	0.0	Sun 14	02:30	0.5	Thu 25	**04:09**	**6.2**
	10:39	**7.9**		**08:43**	**7.0**		10:17	1.7
	17:00	-0.4		15:01	0.5		**16:25**	**6.7**
	23:06	**7.6**		**21:09**	**7.0**		22:53	1.2
Thu 4	05:14	-0.3	Mon 15	03:24	0.4	Fri 26	**05:02**	**6.3**
	11:22	**8.2**		**09:33**	**7.3**		11:13	1.7
	17:45	-0.7		15:53	0.1		**17:18**	**6.6**
	23:50	**7.6**		**22:01**	**7.1**		23:45	1.3
Fri 5	05:57	-0.4	Tue 16	04:10	0.3	Sat 27	**05:55**	**6.4**
	12:07	**8.3**		**10:19**	**7.5**		12:09	1.6
	18:31	-0.8		16:39	-0.1		**18:13**	**6.6**
				22:47	**7.0**			
Sat 6	**00:36**	**7.4**	Wed 17	04:52	0.2	Sun 28	00:38	1.1
	06:43	-0.3		**11:01**	**7.6**		**05:50**	**6.7**
	12:53	**8.3**		17:21	-0.2		12:06	1.3
	19:19	-0.8		**23:27**	**6.9**		**18:10**	**6.7**
Sun 7	**01:25**	**7.2**	Thu 18	05:32	0.2	Mon 29	00:32	0.9
	07:29	-0.1		**11:40**	**7.6**		**06:42**	**7.0**
	13:43	**8.2**		18:02	-0.2		13:02	0.8
	20:12	-0.6					**19:04**	**6.8**
Mon 8	**02:17**	**7.0**	Fri 19	**00:06**	**6.8**	Tue 30	01:21	0.6
	08:22	0.2		06:11	0.3		**07:32**	**7.4**
	14:36	**7.9**		**12:17**	**7.5**		13:54	0.3
	21:07	-0.2		18:40	-0.1		**19:57**	**7.0**
Tue 9	**03:13**	**6.7**	Sat 20	**00:43**	**6.7**	Wed 31	02:09	0.3
	09:19	0.6		06:46	0.5		**08:20**	**7.7**
	15:35	**7.5**		**12:53**	**7.4**		14:44	-0.2
	22:09	0.2		19:17	0.1		**20:49**	**7.1**
Wed 10	**04:17**	**6.4**	Sun 21	**01:20**	**6.5**			
	10:25	1.0		07:23	0.7			
	16:41	**7.2**		**13:30**	**7.3**			
	23:15	0.5		19:55	0.4			
Thu 11	**05:26**	**6.3**	Mon 22	**01:57**	**6.4**			
	11:39	1.1		08:01	1.0			
	17:53	**7.0**		**14:09**	**7.1**			
				20:34	0.6			

November 1990

Day	Time	Height	Day	Time	Height	Day	Time	Height
Thu 1	02:57	0.0	Mon 12	01:03	0.6	Fri 23	**02:35**	**6.5**
	09:09	**8.1**		**07:17**	**7.0**		08:43	1.3
	15:34	-0.6		13:38	0.4		**14:48**	**6.8**
	21:37	**7.2**		**19:46**	**6.6**		21:12	0.8
Fri 2	03:44	-0.3	Tue 13	01:56	0.5	Sat 24	**03:22**	**6.5**
	09:55	**8.3**		**08:09**	**7.2**		09:34	1.3
	16:23	-0.9		14:31	0.1		**15:38**	**6.6**
	22:27	**7.3**		**20:37**	**6.6**		22:02	0.8
Sat 3	04:32	-0.4	Wed 14	02:41	0.4	Sun 25	**04:12**	**6.6**
	10:44	**8.4**		**08:52**	**7.3**		10:30	1.1
	17:12	-1.0		15:18	0.0		**16:31**	**6.5**
	23:18	**7.2**		**21:23**	**6.5**		22:53	0.8
Sun 4	05:21	-0.3	Thu 15	03:24	0.4	Mon 26	**05:06**	**6.8**
	11:34	**8.4**		**09:36**	**7.4**		11:27	0.9
	18:03	-0.9		16:01	-0.1		**17:30**	**6.5**
				22:05	**6.5**		23:45	0.6
Mon 5	**00:09**	**7.1**	Fri 16	04:05	0.4	Tue 27	**05:59**	**7.1**
	06:13	-0.1		**10:14**	**7.4**		12:25	0.5
	12:27	**8.2**		16:40	-0.1		**18:27**	**6.5**
	18:57	-0.7		**22:42**	**6.4**			
Tue 6	**01:04**	**7.0**	Sat 17	04:44	0.5	Wed 28	00:39	0.4
	07:09	0.2		**10:51**	**7.4**		**06:53**	**7.4**
	13:22	**7.9**		17:18	0.0		13:21	0.1
	19:54	-0.3		**23:19**	**6.4**		**19:24**	**6.6**
Wed 7	**02:03**	**6.8**	Sun 18	05:21	0.6	Thu 29	01:33	0.2
	08:11	0.5		**11:28**	**7.3**		**07:48**	**7.7**
	14:23	**7.5**		17:54	0.1		14:17	-0.3
	20:53	0.0		**23:56**	**6.4**		**20:20**	**6.7**
Thu 8	**03:04**	**6.6**	Mon 19	05:58	0.8	Fri 30	02:25	0.0
	09:17	0.8		**12:04**	**7.3**		**08:41**	**8.0**
	15:28	**7.1**		18:30	0.3		15:10	-0.7
	21:57	0.3					**21:15**	**6.8**
Fri 9	**04:09**	**6.6**	Tue 20	**00:33**	**6.4**			
	10:26	0.9		06:35	1.0			
	16:36	**6.8**		**12:41**	**7.2**			
	23:03	0.5		19:07	0.4			
Sat 10	**05:17**	**6.7**	Wed 21	**01:13**	**6.4**			
	11:34	0.8		07:15	1.1			
	17:45	**6.6**		**13:20**	**7.1**			
				19:47	0.6			
Sun 11	00:05	0.6	Thu 22	**01:52**	**6.4**			
	06:19	**6.8**		07:57	1.2			
	12:41	0.6		**14:02**	**6.9**			
	18:50	**6.6**		20:29	0.7			

REFERENCE

All Tides in Feet above Mean Lower Low Water (MLLW). Times Corrected to Daylight Savings Time

High Tides are shown in BOLD

TIDES

March 1990

Day	Time	Height	Time	Height	Time	Height	Time	Height
Thu 1	**06:32**	-0.3	**12:11**	2.5	18:36	-0.1		
Fri 2	**00:37**	3.2	07:30	-0.2	**13:09**	2.2	19:32	0.1
Sat 3	**01:37**	3.0	08:34	-0.1	**14:15**	2.1	20:35	0.2
Sun 4	**02:44**	2.9	09:40	0.0	**15:27**	2.0	21:41	0.3
Mon 5	**03:54**	2.8	10:44	0.1	**16:42**	2.0	22:49	0.3
Tue 6	**05:05**	2.8	11:45	0.0	**17:48**	2.1	23:53	0.2
Wed 7	**06:09**	2.8	12:38	0.0	**18:47**	2.3		
Thu 8	00:49	0.1	**07:06**	2.7	13:27	0.0	**19:33**	2.4
Fri 9	01:42	0.0	**07:55**	2.7	14:10	-0.1	**20:15**	2.6
Sat 10	02:30	-0.1	**08:37**	2.7	14:51	-0.1	**20:56**	2.7
Sun 11	03:15	-0.1	**09:16**	2.6	15:31	0.0	**21:32**	2.8
Mon 12	03:58	-0.1	**09:53**	2.5	16:10	0.0	**22:10**	2.8
Tue 13	04:41	0.0	**10:30**	2.4	16:49	0.1	**22:46**	2.8
Wed 14	05:26	0.1	**11:07**	2.3	17:31	0.2	**23:25**	2.8
Thu 15	06:11	0.2	**11:47**	2.2	18:13	0.3		
Fri 16	**00:03**	2.7	07:00	0.3	**12:29**	2.0	19:00	0.5
Sat 17	**00:48**	2.6	07:51	0.4	**13:19**	1.9	19:51	0.6
Sun 18	**01:38**	2.5	08:46	0.5	**14:18**	1.8	20:49	0.7
Mon 19	**02:34**	2.4	09:43	0.5	**15:22**	1.8	21:48	0.8
Tue 20	**03:34**	2.4	10:38	0.4	**16:23**	1.9	22:44	0.7
Wed 21	**04:34**	2.5	11:27	0.3	**17:16**	2.1	23:37	0.5
Thu 22	**05:30**	2.6	12:14	0.2	**18:06**	2.3		
Fri 23	00:27	0.3	**06:20**	2.7	12:58	0.1	**18:49**	2.6
Sat 24	01:15	0.1	**07:07**	2.8	13:39	-0.1	**19:31**	2.9
Sun 25	02:01	-0.2	**07:53**	2.9	14:21	-0.2	**20:14**	3.2
Mon 26	02:49	-0.4	**08:39**	3.0	15:02	-0.2	**20:58**	3.4
Tue 27	03:36	-0.5	**09:25**	3.0	15:44	-0.3	**21:42**	3.5
Wed 28	04:25	-0.5	**10:13**	2.9	16:30	-0.2	**22:30**	3.6
Thu 29	05:17	-0.5	**11:04**	2.7	17:19	-0.1	**23:20**	3.5
Fri 30	06:13	-0.3	**11:57**	2.5	18:13	0.1		
Sat 31	**00:16**	3.4	07:11	-0.2	**12:58**	2.4	19:14	0.2

April 1990

Day	Time	Height	Time	Height	Time	Height	Time	Height
Sun 1	**01:19**	3.2	09:14	0.0	**15:04**	2.2	21:20	0.4
Mon 2	**03:26**	2.9	10:19	0.1	**16:18**	2.2	22:30	0.4
Tue 3	**04:40**	2.8	11:22	0.2	**17:31**	2.2	23:37	0.4
Wed 4	**05:53**	2.7	12:21	0.2	**18:36**	2.4		
Thu 5	00:40	0.3	**06:59**	2.6	13:12	0.2	**19:28**	2.6
Fri 6	01:36	0.2	**07:54**	2.6	13:59	0.2	**20:13**	2.7
Sat 7	02:27	0.1	**08:36**	2.6	14:42	0.2	**20:53**	2.8
Sun 8	03:12	0.1	**09:16**	2.5	15:21	0.2	**21:28**	2.9
Mon 9	03:54	0.0	**09:53**	2.5	15:59	0.2	**22:03**	3.0
Tue 10	04:36	0.0	**10:26**	2.4	16:38	0.3	**22:37**	3.0
Wed 11	05:17	0.1	**11:01**	2.4	17:17	0.3	**23:12**	3.0
Thu 12	05:59	0.1	**11:40**	2.3	17:56	0.4	**23:48**	2.9
Fri 13	06:42	0.2	**12:18**	2.3	18:38	0.6		
Sat 14	**00:26**	2.9	07:28	0.3	**12:59**	2.2	19:26	0.7
Sun 15	**01:08**	2.7	08:17	0.4	**13:50**	2.1	20:18	0.8
Mon 16	**01:53**	2.6	09:10	0.5	**14:46**	2.1	21:15	0.9
Tue 17	**02:46**	2.5	10:04	0.5	**15:46**	2.1	22:14	0.9
Wed 18	**03:50**	2.5	10:56	0.5	**16:44**	2.2	23:14	0.8
Thu 19	**04:51**	2.5	11:47	0.4	**17:37**	2.4		
Fri 20	00:08	0.6	**05:52**	2.6	12:33	0.3	**18:25**	2.7
Sat 21	01:01	0.3	**06:46**	2.7	13:17	0.2	**19:14**	3.0
Sun 22	01:51	0.1	**07:38**	2.8	14:02	0.1	**20:00**	3.3
Mon 23	02:39	-0.2	**08:26**	2.9	14:45	0.0	**20:44**	3.6
Tue 24	03:28	-0.4	**09:15**	2.9	15:30	-0.1	**21:31**	3.8
Wed 25	04:17	-0.5	**10:04**	2.9	16:16	-0.1	**22:20**	3.9
Thu 26	05:06	-0.5	**10:56**	2.8	17:06	-0.1	**23:09**	3.8
Fri 27	06:01	-0.4	**11:48**	2.7	17:59	0.1		
Sat 28	**00:02**	3.7	06:55	-0.3	**12:44**	2.6	18:57	0.2
Sun 29	**01:00**	3.5	07:53	-0.1	**13:45**	2.5	19:59	0.4
Mon 30	**02:03**	3.2	08:54	0.1	**14:51**	2.5	21:07	0.5

May 1990

Day	Time	Height	Time	Height	Time	Height	Time	Height
Tue 1	**03:10**	2.9	09:54	0.2	**16:01**	2.5	22:15	0.5
Wed 2	**04:21**	2.7	10:54	0.3	**17:09**	2.6	23:23	0.5
Thu 3	**05:32**	2.6	11:50	0.4	**18:11**	2.7		
Fri 4	00:23	0.4	**06:36**	2.5	12:40	0.4	**19:01**	2.8
Sat 5	01:18	0.4	**07:29**	2.4	13:27	0.4	**19:43**	2.9
Sun 6	02:06	0.3	**08:11**	2.4	14:09	0.4	**20:24**	3.0
Mon 7	02:50	0.2	**08:50**	2.4	14:50	0.4	**20:57**	3.1
Tue 8	03:32	0.2	**09:25**	2.4	15:28	0.4	**21:33**	3.1
Wed 9	04:10	0.2	**10:01**	2.4	16:06	0.5	**22:06**	3.1
Thu 10	04:52	0.2	**10:37**	2.4	16:47	0.5	**22:40**	3.1
Fri 11	05:33	0.2	**11:16**	2.4	17:29	0.6	**23:17**	3.1
Sat 12	06:15	0.3	**11:54**	2.3	18:11	0.7	**23:54**	3.0
Sun 13	07:00	0.3	**12:39**	2.3	18:57	0.8		
Mon 14	**00:36**	2.9	07:47	0.4	**13:26**	2.3	19:48	0.9
Tue 15	**01:19**	2.8	08:35	0.5	**14:17**	2.3	20:44	0.9
Wed 16	**02:11**	2.7	09:26	0.5	**15:10**	2.4	21:44	0.9
Thu 17	**03:12**	2.6	10:15	0.5	**16:04**	2.5	22:44	0.8
Fri 18	**04:14**	2.6	11:04	0.5	**16:58**	2.7	23:40	0.6
Sat 19	**05:14**	2.6	11:52	0.4	**17:50**	3.0		
Sun 20	00:35	0.3	**06:12**	2.6	12:40	0.3	**18:40**	3.1
Mon 21	01:27	0.1	**07:07**	2.7	13:27	0.2	**19:28**	3.3
Tue 22	02:17	-0.1	**08:03**	2.7	14:13	0.1	**20:18**	3.8
Wed 23	03:09	-0.3	**08:53**	2.8	15:03	0.0	**21:08**	3.9
Thu 24	03:59	-0.4	**09:45**	2.8	15:53	0.0	**22:00**	3.9
Fri 25	04:50	-0.4	**10:39**	2.8	16:46	0.1	**22:52**	3.9
Sat 26	05:43	-0.3	**11:33**	2.8	17:44	0.1	**23:46**	3.7
Sun 27	06:36	-0.2	**12:30**	2.7	18:43	0.3		
Mon 28	**00:44**	3.4	07:31	-0.1	**13:29**	2.7	19:44	0.4
Tue 29	**01:44**	3.1	08:27	0.1	**14:31**	2.7	20:49	0.5
Wed 30	**02:47**	2.9	09:23	0.3	**15:34**	2.7	21:54	0.5
Thu 31	**03:54**	2.6	10:19	0.4	**16:36**	2.8	22:59	0.6

All Tides in Feet above Mean Lower Low Water (MLLW). Times Corrected to Daylight Savings Time

High Tides are shown in BOLD

TIDES

June 1990

Day	Time	Height	Time	Height	Time	Height	Time	Height
Fri 1	**04:58**	2.4	11:12	0.5	**17:36**	2.8	23:57	0.5
Sat 2	**05:58**	2.3	12:03	0.5	**18:27**	2.9		
Sun 3	00:53	0.5	**06:54**	2.3	12:50	0.6	**19:09**	3.0
Mon 4	01:41	0.4	**07:38**	2.2	13:34	0.6	**19:50**	3.0
Tue 5	02:23	0.4	**08:20**	2.2	14:16	0.6	**20:27**	3.1
Wed 6	03:06	0.3	**08:58**	2.3	14:58	0.6	**21:03**	3.1
Thu 7	03:46	0.3	**09:35**	2.3	15:39	0.6	**21:38**	3.2
Fri 8	04:27	0.2	**10:14**	2.3	16:19	0.6	**22:14**	3.2
Sat 9	05:08	0.2	**10:53**	2.4	17:02	0.7	**22:52**	3.1
Sun 10	05:51	0.2	**11:33**	2.4	17:46	0.7	**23:31**	3.1
Mon 11	06:33	0.2	**12:15**	2.4	18:33	0.8		
Tue 12	**00:10**	3.0	07:16	0.5	**13:00**	2.5	19:23	0.8
Wed 13	**00:57**	2.9	08:01	0.4	**13:46**	2.6	20:16	0.8
Thu 14	**01:47**	2.8	08:47	0.4	**14:37**	2.7	21:14	0.7
Fri 15	**02:40**	2.7	09:34	0.4	**15:28**	2.8	22:13	0.6
Sat 16	**03:42**	2.5	10:24	0.5	**16:22**	2.9	23:12	0.5
Sun 17	**04:43**	2.5	11:15	0.4	**17:16**	3.2		
Mon 18	00:09	0.3	**05:44**	2.5	12:05	0.4	**18:11**	3.4
Tue 19	01:06	0.1	**06:43**	2.5	12:58	0.3	**19:06**	3.6
Wed 20	01:59	0.0	**07:41**	2.5	13:50	0.2	**19:59**	3.8
Thu 21	02:51	-0.2	**08:36**	2.6	14:43	0.1	**20:52**	3.8
Fri 22	03:42	-0.3	**09:31**	2.7	15:38	0.1	**21:45**	3.8
Sat 23	04:34	-0.3	**10:24**	2.8	16:33	0.1	**22:39**	3.7
Sun 24	05:24	-0.2	**11:17**	2.8	17:30	0.1	**23:32**	3.5
Mon 25	06:15	-0.1	**12:10**	2.8	18:26	0.2		
Tue 26	**00:27**	3.3	07:05	0.0	**13:06**	2.9	19:24	0.3
Wed 27	**01:23**	3.0	07:57	0.1	**14:03**	2.9	20:24	0.4
Thu 28	**02:19**	2.7	08:49	0.3	**15:01**	2.9	21:25	0.5
Fri 29	**03:17**	2.5	09:41	0.4	**15:57**	2.8	22:25	0.6
Sat 30	**04:19**	2.3	10:33	0.5	**16:52**	2.9	23:25	0.6

July 1990

Day	Time	Height	Time	Height	Time	Height	Time	Height
Sun 1	**05:16**	2.2	11:24	0.6	**17:45**	2.9		
Mon 2	00:19	0.6	**06:11**	2.1	12:13	0.6	**18:32**	2.9
Tue 3	01:09	0.5	**07:02**	2.1	13:01	0.7	**19:17**	3.0
Wed 4	01:57	0.5	**07:47**	2.2	13:47	0.7	**19:57**	3.0
Thu 5	02:39	0.4	**08:29**	2.2	14:30	0.7	**20:34**	3.1
Fri 6	03:21	0.3	**09:11**	2.3	15:13	0.6	**21:13**	3.1
Sat 7	04:01	0.2	**09:50**	2.4	15:56	0.6	**21:51**	3.2
Sun 8	04:41	0.2	**10:28**	2.5	16:40	0.6	**22:30**	3.2
Mon 9	05:22	0.1	**11:07**	2.6	17:24	0.6	**23:09**	3.2
Tue 10	06:03	0.2	**11:49**	2.7	18:10	0.6	**23:51**	3.1
Wed 11	06:45	0.2	**12:30**	2.8	18:58	0.5		
Thu 12	**00:36**	3.0	07:26	0.6	**13:13**	2.9	19:50	0.5
Fri 13	**01:23**	2.8	08:09	0.3	**14:01**	3.0	20:46	0.5
Sat 14	**02:17**	2.6	08:57	0.4	**14:54**	3.1	21:47	0.5
Sun 15	**03:13**	2.5	09:49	0.4	**15:50**	3.2	22:46	0.4
Mon 16	**04:17**	2.4	10:42	0.5	**16:49**	3.3	23:47	0.3
Tue 17	**05:22**	2.3	11:40	0.4	**17:51**	3.4		
Wed 18	00:46	0.2	**06:27**	2.3	12:39	0.4	**18:50**	3.5
Thu 19	01:43	0.1	**07:27**	2.4	13:35	0.3	**19:47**	3.6
Fri 20	02:35	0.0	**08:24**	2.5	14:31	0.2	**20:42**	3.6
Sat 21	03:25	-0.1	**09:17**	2.7	15:26	0.1	**21:35**	3.6
Sun 22	04:14	-0.1	**10:08**	2.8	16:21	0.1	**22:27**	3.5
Mon 23	05:01	-0.1	**10:59**	2.9	17:13	0.1	**23:17**	3.3
Tue 24	05:49	0.0	**11:49**	3.0	18:07	0.2		
Wed 25	**00:06**	3.1	06:36	0.1	**12:36**	3.0	19:03	0.3
Thu 26	**00:54**	2.9	07:22	0.2	**13:27**	3.0	19:56	0.4
Fri 27	**01:45**	2.6	08:11	0.4	**14:18**	2.9	20:52	0.5
Sat 28	**02:35**	2.4	09:01	0.5	**15:11**	2.9	21:50	0.6
Sun 29	**03:31**	2.2	09:52	0.6	**16:07**	2.8	22:46	0.7
Mon 30	**04:31**	2.1	10:45	0.7	**17:00**	2.8	23:44	0.7
Tue 31	**05:29**	2.1	11:37	0.8	**17:53**	2.8		

August 1990

Day	Time	Height	Time	Height	Time	Height	Time	Height
Wed 1	00:37	0.6	**06:27**	2.1	12:30	0.8	**18:41**	2.8
Thu 2	01:23	0.5	**07:17**	2.1	13:20	0.7	**19:26**	2.9
Fri 3	02:09	0.4	**08:00**	2.3	14:06	0.7	**20:07**	3.0
Sat 4	02:51	0.3	**08:42**	2.4	14:50	0.6	**20:47**	3.1
Sun 5	03:30	0.3	**09:21**	2.5	15:34	0.5	**21:27**	3.2
Mon 6	04:10	0.1	**09:59**	2.7	16:16	0.4	**22:06**	3.2
Tue 7	04:50	0.1	**10:38**	2.8	17:00	0.3	**22:48**	3.2
Wed 8	05:29	0.1	**11:17**	3.0	17:46	0.1	**23:30**	3.1
Thu 9	06:09	0.1	**11:58**	3.1	18:34	0.3		
Fri 10	**00:14**	3.0	06:50	0.2	**12:42**	3.2	19:26	0.3
Sat 11	**01:02**	2.8	07:34	0.3	**13:31**	3.3	20:23	0.3
Sun 12	**01:53**	2.6	08:24	0.4	**14:25**	3.3	21:25	0.3
Mon 13	**02:51**	2.4	09:20	0.5	**15:24**	3.3	22:27	0.4
Tue 14	**03:59**	2.3	10:22	0.5	**16:30**	3.3	23:30	0.3
Wed 15	**05:10**	2.3	11:25	0.5	**17:36**	3.3		
Thu 16	00:29	0.3	**06:17**	2.3	12:27	0.5	**18:40**	3.3
Fri 17	01:27	0.2	**07:18**	2.5	13:27	0.4	**19:41**	3.4
Sat 18	02:18	0.1	**08:15**	2.6	14:24	0.2	**20:34**	3.4
Sun 19	03:07	0.1	**09:04**	2.8	15:17	0.1	**21:24**	3.3
Mon 20	03:52	0.1	**09:51**	3.0	16:08	0.1	**22:11**	3.2
Tue 21	04:37	0.1	**10:36**	3.1	16:57	0.1	**22:57**	3.1
Wed 22	05:19	0.1	**11:20**	3.1	17:46	0.2	**23:40**	2.9
Thu 23	06:02	0.2	**12:04**	3.1	18:34	0.3		
Fri 24	**00:25**	2.7	06:47	0.4	**12:47**	3.1	19:24	0.4
Sat 25	**01:07**	2.5	07:32	0.5	**13:33**	3.0	20:16	0.6
Sun 26	**01:55**	2.4	08:21	0.7	**14:22**	2.9	21:11	0.7
Mon 27	**02:46**	2.2	09:14	0.8	**15:15**	2.8	22:07	0.8
Tue 28	**03:47**	2.1	10:09	0.9	**16:11**	2.7	23:06	0.8
Wed 29	**04:51**	2.1	11:07	0.9	**17:10**	2.7	23:58	0.7
Thu 30	**05:50**	2.1	12:00	0.9	**18:03**	2.7		
Fri 31	00:48	0.6	**06:45**	2.2	12:53	0.8	**18:51**	2.8

All Tides in Feet above Mean Lower Low Water (MLLW). Times Corrected to Daylight Savings Time

High Tides are shown in BOLD

TIDES

September 1990

Day	Time	Height	Day	Time	Height	Day	Time	Height
Sat 1	01:35	0.5	Wed 12	**03:50**	**2.3**	Sun 23	**00:31**	**2.5**
	07:28	**2.4**		10:08	0.6		06:55	0.6
	13:41	0.7		**16:16**	**3.2**		**12:49**	**3.0**
	19:38	**2.9**		23:11	0.4		19:42	0.6
Sun 2	02:18	0.4	Thu 13	**05:03**	**2.4**	Mon 24	**01:18**	**2.3**
	08:10	**2.6**		11:16	0.6		07:45	0.6
	14:26	0.5		**17:26**	**3.1**		**13:34**	**2.9**
	20:20	**3.1**					20:35	0.7
Mon 3	02:57	0.3	Fri 14	00:11	0.4	Tue 25	**02:09**	**2.2**
	08:48	**2.8**		**06:11**	**2.5**		08:37	0.9
	15:08	0.4		12:21	0.5		**14:25**	**2.7**
	21:00	**3.1**		**18:35**	**3.1**		21:28	0.7
Tue 4	03:36	0.2	Sat 15	01:08	0.3	Wed 26	**03:07**	**2.2**
	09:27	**3.0**		**07:11**	**2.6**		09:36	1.0
	15:52	0.2		13:21	0.4		**15:22**	**2.6**
	21:42	**3.2**		**19:33**	**3.1**		22:26	0.8
Wed 5	04:15	0.1	Sun 16	01:57	0.3	Thu 27	**04:12**	**2.1**
	10:05	**3.2**		**08:02**	**2.8**		10:35	1.1
	16:36	0.1		14:15	0.3		**16:24**	**2.6**
	22:24	**3.2**		**20:26**	**3.1**		23:20	0.7
Thu 6	04:54	0.1	Mon 17	02:44	0.2	Fri 28	**05:14**	**2.2**
	10:45	**3.4**		**08:48**	**3.0**		11:31	1.0
	17:22	0.0		15:06	0.1		**17:21**	**2.6**
	23:08	**3.1**		**21:11**	**3.0**			
Fri 7	05:34	0.1	Tue 18	03:27	0.2	Sat 29	00:11	0.6
	11:28	**3.5**		**09:30**	**3.1**		**06:06**	**2.4**
	18:12	0.0		15:53	0.1		12:25	0.8
	23:54	**3.0**		**21:54**	**3.0**		**18:15**	**2.7**
Sat 8	06:18	0.2	Wed 19	04:08	0.3	Sun 30	00:56	0.5
	12:14	**3.6**		**10:09**	**3.2**		**06:53**	**2.6**
	19:05	0.1		16:37	0.1		13:12	0.7
				22:35	**2.9**		**19:04**	**2.8**
Sun 9	00:44	2.8	Thu 20	04:48	0.3			
	07:06	0.3		**10:50**	**3.3**			
	13:04	**3.5**		17:22	0.2			
	20:01	0.2		**23:13**	**2.7**			
Mon 10	**01:37**	**2.6**	Fri 21	05:29	0.4			
	07:59	0.5		**11:30**	**3.2**			
	14:01	**3.4**		18:07	0.3			
	21:03	0.3		**23:54**	**2.6**			
Tue 11	**02:41**	**2.4**	Sat 22	06:11	0.5			
	09:02	0.6		**12:09**	**3.1**			
	15:06	**3.3**		18:54	0.4			
	22:08	0.4						

October 1990

Day	Time	Height	Day	Time	Height	Day	Time	Height
Mon 1	01:39	0.4	Fri 12	**04:54**	**2.5**	Tue 23	**00:48**	**2.3**
	07:33	**2.8**		11:06	0.6		07:09	0.9
	13:59	0.4		**17:16**	**2.9**		**12:52**	**2.9**
	19:49	**3.0**		23:48	0.4		20:00	0.6
Tue 2	02:20	0.3	Sat 13	**06:00**	**2.7**	Wed 24	**01:37**	**2.2**
	08:11	**3.1**		12:13	0.5		08:02	1.0
	14:44	0.2		**18:25**	**2.9**		**13:40**	**2.7**
	20:31	**3.1**					20:54	0.6
Wed 3	02:57	0.2	Sun 14	00:44	0.4	Thu 25	**02:33**	**2.2**
	08:52	**3.4**		**06:58**	**2.8**		09:01	1.1
	15:29	0.0		13:12	0.4		**14:33**	**2.6**
	21:17	**3.1**		**19:22**	**2.8**		21:46	0.7
Thu 4	03:39	0.1	Mon 15	01:33	0.4	Fri 26	**03:33**	**2.2**
	09:32	**3.6**		**07:47**	**3.0**		10:01	1.1
	16:13	-0.1		14:03	0.3		**15:33**	**2.5**
	22:01	**3.1**		**20:12**	**2.8**		22:39	0.6
Fri 5	04:20	0.1	Tue 16	02:16	0.4	Sat 27	**04:32**	**2.3**
	10:15	**3.8**		**08:28**	**3.1**		10:59	1.0
	17:01	-0.2		14:51	0.2		**16:37**	**2.5**
	22:46	**3.0**		**20:57**	**2.7**		23:28	0.6
Sat 6	05:03	0.1	Wed 17	03:00	0.4	Sun 28	**04:24**	**2.5**
	11:01	**3.8**		**09:07**	**3.2**		10:52	0.8
	17:51	-0.2		15:34	0.1		**16:36**	**2.6**
	23:34	**2.9**		**21:33**	**2.7**		23:14	0.5
Sun 7	05:49	0.2	Thu 18	03:39	0.4	Mon 29	**05:13**	**2.7**
	11:50	**3.8**		**09:44**	**3.3**		11:42	0.5
	18:44	-0.1		16:16	0.2		**17:27**	**2.7**
				22:10	**2.6**		23:58	0.4
Mon 8	00:26	2.8	Fri 19	04:18	0.4	Tue 30	**05:55**	**3.0**
	06:41	0.3		**10:19**	**3.3**		12:32	0.3
	12:44	**3.7**		16:58	0.2		**18:15**	**2.7**
	19:42	0.0		**22:47**	**2.5**			
Tue 9	**01:24**	**2.6**	Sat 20	04:57	0.5	Wed 31	00:41	0.3
	07:42	0.5		**10:56**	**3.2**		**06:36**	**3.3**
	13:42	**3.5**		17:40	0.3		13:18	0.0
	20:43	0.2		**23:24**	**2.5**		**19:04**	**2.8**
Wed 10	**02:30**	**2.5**	Sun 21	05:39	0.6			
	08:49	0.6		**11:33**	**3.1**			
	14:51	**3.2**		18:25	0.4			
	21:46	0.3						
Thu 11	**03:42**	**2.5**	Mon 22	00:04	2.4			
	09:58	0.6		06:23	0.7			
	16:03	**3.0**		**12:10**	**3.0**			
	22:49	0.4		19:11	0.5			

November 1990

Day	Time	Height	Day	Time	Height	Day	Time	Height
Thu 1	01:22	0.2	Mon 12	**05:37**	**2.9**	Fri 23	**01:01**	**2.2**
	07:19	**3.6**		11:55	0.3		07:27	0.9
	14:05	-0.2		**18:04**	**2.5**		**12:56**	**2.6**
	19:50	**2.9**					20:06	0.4
Fri 2	02:04	0.1	Tue 13	00:02	0.4	Sat 24	**01:54**	**2.3**
	08:05	**3.8**		**06:22**	**3.0**		08:26	0.9
	14:52	-0.3		12:46	0.2		**13:49**	**2.5**
	20:37	**2.9**		**18:51**	**2.4**		20:55	0.5
Sat 3	02:50	0.0	Wed 14	00:46	0.4	Sun 25	**02:46**	**2.4**
	08:51	**3.9**		**07:05**	**3.1**		09:25	0.8
	15:41	-0.4		13:32	0.2		**14:51**	**2.4**
	21:27	**2.9**		**19:33**	**2.4**		21:44	0.5
Sun 4	03:38	0.0	Thu 15	01:28	0.4	Mon 26	**03:39**	**2.6**
	09:40	**3.9**		**07:41**	**3.1**		10:20	0.6
	16:32	-0.4		14:14	0.1		**15:50**	**2.4**
	22:18	**2.8**		**20:09**	**2.3**		22:30	0.4
Mon 5	04:30	0.1	Fri 16	02:09	0.4	Tue 27	**04:29**	**2.8**
	10:32	**3.8**		**08:17**	**3.2**		11:13	0.4
	17:26	-0.3		14:56	0.1		**16:47**	**2.4**
	23:12	**2.7**		**20:46**	**2.3**		23:16	0.3
Tue 6	05:25	0.2	Sat 17	02:49	0.4	Wed 28	**05:16**	**3.1**
	11:27	**3.6**		**08:51**	**3.2**		12:04	0.1
	18:23	-0.1		15:36	0.1		**17:43**	**2.4**
				21:23	**2.3**			
Wed 7	00:11	2.6	Sun 18	03:28	0.5	Thu 29	00:02	0.2
	06:28	0.4		**09:28**	**3.1**		**06:06**	**3.4**
	12:27	**3.3**		16:17	0.2		12:54	-0.1
	19:22	0.0		**21:59**	**2.3**		**18:35**	**2.5**
Thu 8	**01:17**	**2.6**	Mon 19	04:11	0.6	Fri 30	00:49	0.1
	07:35	0.5		**10:03**	**3.0**		**06:54**	**3.6**
	13:34	**3.1**		16:59	0.2		13:45	-0.3
	20:23	0.2		**22:41**	**2.3**		**19:27**	**2.6**
Fri 9	**02:26**	**2.6**	Tue 20	04:55	0.7			
	08:44	0.5		**10:41**	**2.9**			
	14:45	**2.8**		17:41	0.3			
	21:23	0.3		**23:24**	**2.2**			
Sat 10	**03:35**	**2.6**	Wed 21	05:41	0.8			
	09:51	0.5		**11:20**	**2.8**			
	15:57	**2.6**		18:29	0.3			
	22:20	0.3						
Sun 11	**04:37**	**2.8**	Thu 22	00:11	2.2			
	10:57	0.4		06:32	0.9			
	17:05	**2.5**		**12:05**	**2.7**			
	23:13	0.4		19:16	0.4			

VHF Marine Radio Use

The VHF Marine Radio is not only a convenience for the boater, but an essential safety device for every vessel. This introduction is meant to clarify the use of your VHF Marine Radio. It may be supplemented by the *Maritime Radio Users Handbook*, published by the Radio Technical Commission for Maritime Services (RTCM), which details the proper use of the VHF Marine Radio. You should also consult the owner's manual supplied with your unit for the unit's particular specifications and operation. You must also have a Federal Communications Commission (FCC) ship radio license to operate your unit.

It is important to keep the airwaves from being jammed with transmissions so that messages or distress calls from others–or yourself–may be understood clearly. Use your radio only when necessary. Avoid excessive calling, and make your messages as brief as possible.

Each VHF channel has a specific use, as authorized by the FCC. All boaters with a VHF Marine Radio unit are required to monitor channel 16 at all times. Channel 16 is reserved for hailing and emergency calling only. Channel 06 is reserved for safety calling. Use of these channels for any other purpose may interfere with other boaters' efforts to place a distress call.

Channel 13 is important for contacting other boaters, bridge tenders, or commercial ships. Recreational boaters, especially those on small vessels, monitor this channel to determine the intentions of larger craft.

The following is a partial listing of the 48 marine channels available. For a complete list or for more information, please consult the *Maritime Radio Users Handbook*, which may be purchased from RTCM, Box 19087, Washington, D.C. 20036; or write to the FCC, 201 Varick Street, New York, NY 10014.

16 156.800 MHz
Distress, Safety, and Calling Ship-to-Ship and Ship-to-Shore
Channel **16** is the National Distress Frequency, and is monitored 24 hours by the Coast Guard. Except in distress situations, channel 16 should only be used to establish another working channel to switch to.

22 157.100 MHz
Primary Coast Guard Communication Channel
Channel **22** is used for communications with the U.S. Coast Guard only after establishing contact on channel 16. Weather reports and Notice to Mariners are broadcast on this channel; a schedule is announced on channel 16.

06 156.650 MHz
Safety Calling, Ship to Ship
Channel **06** is mandatory on all VHF sets, and is the Intership Safety Frequency. Use it only for communicating with the Coast Guard and other rescue vessels. This channel should only be used for *safety* messages.

13 156.650 MHz
Commercial, Ship to ship, and Bridge and Lock Tenders
Channel **13** is reserved for navigational communication. Commercial vessels must monitor it at all times. Recreational boaters may also use this channel to contact bridge and lock tenders.

68 156.425 MHz
General Calling, Ship to Ship and Ship to Shore
Channel **68** is for general communication. It is limited to pleasure craft, shore stations, and harbormasters. Use channels **09, 69, 71,** and **78** as alternates; channel **09** is also used by commercial vessels.

72 156.625 MHz
General Calling, Recreational, and Ship to Ship
Channel **72** is reserved for general communication. It is limited to pleasure craft contacting other pleasure craft.

WX-1 162.550 MHz
WX-2 162.400 MHz
WX-3 162.475 MHz
NOAA Weather Reports
Forecasts are broadcast on these channels 24 hours a day. Taped messages are updated every 3-6 hours. Weather advisories include sea conditions and detailed local forecasts.

RADIO TELEPHONE

The following is a list of the radio telephone operators that may be reached from the Long Island Sound area. It's best to make your calls collect, to avoid giving out credit card numbers over the airwaves.

25, 26, 86   **New London, CT**
Hailing I.D.: New London Marine Operator

24, 27   **Bridgeport, CT**
Hailing I.D.: Bridgeport Marine Operator

25, 26, 84   **New York, NY**
Hailing I.D.: New York Marine Operator

28   **Riverhead, NY**
Hailing I.D.: Riverhead Marine Operator

85   **Bay Shore, NY**
Hailing I.D.: Bay Shore Marine Operator

28   **Staten Island, NY**
Hailing I.D.: WHU 738

86   **Mamaroneck, NY**
Hailing I.D.: Mariphone Marine Operator

All Currents in Knots. Times Corrected to Daylight Savings Time

Flood Tides are shown in BOLD

CURRENTS

March 1990

Day	Slack	Max	Kts
Thu 1	00:20, 06:42, 12:51, 19:00	03:13, 09:40, 15:38, 22:01	-5.1, 3.7, -4.8, 3.6
Fri 2	01:12, 07:37, 13:45, 19:55	04:04, 10:33, 16:31, 22:56	-4.9, 3.5, -4.6, 3.4
Sat 3	02:09, 08:39, 14:46, 20:59	05:01, 11:34, 17:29	-4.7, 3.2, -4.3
Sun 4	03:14, 09:49, 15:53, 22:12	00:00, 06:04, 12:43, 18:36	3.2, -4.4, 3.0, -4.1
Mon 5	04:25, 11:03, 17:04, 23:26	01:15, 07:18, 14:04, 19:54	3.0, -4.4, 2.9, -4.0
Tue 6	05:37, 12:13, 18:12	02:35, 08:42, 15:17, 21:18	3.0, -4.4, 3.0, -4.1
Wed 7	00:09, 06:28, 12:35, 18:43	03:47, 10:04, 16:22, 22:29	3.2, -4.4, 3.2, -4.3
Thu 8	01:35, 07:42, 14:08, 20:05	04:48, 11:01, 17:14, 23:24	3.4, -4.5, 3.4, -4.5
Fri 9	02:27, 08:33, 14:55, 20:52	05:37, 11:48, 18:01	3.6, -4.6, 3.5
Sat 10	03:13, 09:18, 15:37, 21:35	00:04, 06:24, 12:27, 18:42	-4.7, 3.7, -4.7, 3.6
Sun 11	03:55, 10:00, 16:16, 22:15	00:41, 07:04, 13:00, 19:19	-4.8, 3.7, -4.7, 3.7
Mon 12	04:35, 10:39, 16:54, 22:53	01:16, 07:37, 13:33, 19:52	-4.8, 3.7, -4.7, 3.6
Tue 13	05:13, 11:18, 17:30, 23:31	01:49, 08:15, 14:06, 20:28	-4.8, 3.7, -4.7, 3.6
Wed 14	05:50, 11:56, 18:06	02:21, 08:47, 14:40, 21:03	-4.7, 3.6, -4.6, 3.4
Thu 15	00:09, 06:28, 12:35, 18:43	02:58, 09:24, 15:17, 21:40	-4.6, 3.4, -4.5, 3.3
Fri 16	00:49, 07:08, 13:15, 19:22	03:35, 10:04, 15:55, 22:21	-4.5, 3.4, -4.3, 3.1
Sat 17	01:30, 07:50, 13:59, 20:05	04:18, 10:47, 16:38, 23:05	-4.3, 3.0, -4.1, 2.9
Sun 18	02:16, 08:39, 14:48, 20:54	05:03, 11:34, 17:25, 23:54	-4.2, 2.8, -3.9, 2.8
Mon 19	03:09, 09:33, 15:41, 21:50	05:55, 12:27, 18:20	-4.0, 2.7, -3.9
Tue 20	04:06, 10:32, 16:39, 22:50	00:51, 06:50, 13:27, 19:17	2.8, -4.0, 2.7, -3.9
Wed 21	05:06, 11:31, 17:36, 23:49	01:54, 07:49, 14:27, 20:15	2.8, -4.2, 2.8, -4.0
Thu 22	06:03, 12:26, 18:29	02:52, 08:49, 15:21, 21:12	3.0, -4.2, 3.0, -4.3
Fri 23	00:44, 06:57, 13:16, 19:19	03:46, 09:43, 16:12, 22:09	3.3, -4.4, 3.3, -4.6
Sat 24	01:35, 07:47, 14:02, 20:07	04:39, 10:35, 17:00, 22:58	3.5, -4.7, 3.6, -4.8
Sun 25	02:23, 08:35, 14:47, 20:53	05:26, 11:24, 17:46, 23:45	3.8, -4.9, 3.8, -5.1
Mon 26	03:10, 09:22, 15:31, 21:39	06:12, 12:09, 18:32	4.0, -5.0, 4.0
Tue 27	03:57, 10:09, 16:16, 22:25	00:33, 06:58, 12:56, 19:17	-5.2, 4.0, -5.1, 4.0
Wed 28	04:45, 10:56, 17:02, 23:14	01:20, 07:45, 13:43, 20:04	-5.3, 4.0, -5.1, 4.0
Thu 29	05:35, 11:45, 17:51	02:07, 08:34, 14:31, 20:53	-5.2, 3.9, -5.0, 3.9
Fri 30	00:04, 06:27, 12:37, 18:43	02:58, 09:26, 15:22, 21:45	-5.1, 3.7, -4.8, 3.7
Sat 31	00:59, 07:25, 13:34, 19:42	03:51, 10:21, 16:17, 22:46	-4.8, 3.5, -4.5, 3.4

April 1990

Day	Slack	Max	Kts
Sun 1	01:59, 09:28, 15:36, 21:49	05:49, 12:25, 18:18	-4.5, 3.2, -4.2
Mon 2	04:05, 10:38, 16:44, 23:03	00:54, 06:54, 13:38, 19:29	3.2, -4.3, 3.0, -4.0
Tue 3	05:16, 11:49, 17:53	02:11, 08:16, 14:57, 20:56	3.0, -4.1, 2.9, -3.9
Wed 4	00:15, 06:25, 12:55, 18:57	03:27, 09:44, 16:05, 22:15	3.1, -4.1, 3.0, -4.1
Thu 5	01:20, 07:28, 13:53, 19:53	04:34, 10:53, 17:04, 23:15	3.2, -4.2, 3.2, -4.3
Fri 6	02:16, 08:23, 14:43, 20:43	05:28, 11:42, 17:51	3.4, -4.4, 3.4
Sat 7	03:05, 09:10, 15:27, 21:26	00:00, 06:17, 12:28, 18:36	-4.5, 3.5, -4.5, 3.5
Sun 8	03:48, 09:52, 16:07, 22:07	00:39, 06:56, 13:01, 19:13	-4.6, 3.6, -4.6, 3.6
Mon 9	04:28, 10:32, 16:44, 22:45	01:12, 07:33, 13:31, 19:46	-4.7, 3.7, -4.6, 3.6
Tue 10	05:05, 11:10, 17:20, 23:22	01:45, 08:08, 13:59, 20:21	-4.8, 3.7, -4.6, 3.6
Wed 11	05:42, 11:47, 17:55, 23:59	02:15, 08:41, 14:33, 20:54	-4.8, 3.6, -4.6, 3.6
Thu 12	06:19, 12:24, 18:31	02:50, 09:16, 15:06, 21:29	-4.7, 3.4, -4.6, 3.5
Fri 13	00:36, 06:56, 13:02, 19:07	03:25, 09:52, 15:43, 22:06	-4.7, 3.3, -4.5, 3.3
Sat 14	01:15, 07:35, 13:42, 19:45	04:04, 10:29, 16:24, 22:45	-4.6, 3.3, -4.3, 3.2
Sun 15	01:56, 08:16, 14:25, 20:27	04:46, 11:14, 17:07, 23:30	-4.4, 3.1, -4.2, 3.1
Mon 16	02:41, 09:02, 15:12, 21:15	05:33, 12:00, 17:52	-4.3, 2.9, -4.1
Tue 17	03:32, 09:54, 16:03, 22:10	00:19, 06:20, 12:51, 18:45	2.9, -4.2, 2.8, -4.0
Wed 18	04:28, 10:51, 16:59, 23:10	01:14, 07:15, 13:46, 19:43	2.9, -4.2, 2.8, -4.0
Thu 19	05:27, 11:49, 17:56	02:14, 08:14, 14:45, 20:42	2.9, -4.3, 2.9, -4.2
Fri 20	00:11, 06:26, 12:45, 18:51	03:13, 09:12, 15:41, 21:39	3.1, -4.3, 3.1, -4.4
Sat 21	01:10, 07:22, 13:37, 19:44	04:12, 10:07, 16:38, 22:34	3.3, -4.5, 3.4, -4.7
Sun 22	02:04, 08:15, 14:28, 20:35	05:06, 11:02, 17:29, 23:28	3.6, -4.7, 3.6, -4.9
Mon 23	02:57, 09:07, 15:17, 21:25	05:57, 11:55, 18:17	3.8, -4.9, 3.8
Tue 24	03:48, 09:57, 16:05, 22:15	00:19, 06:48, 12:44, 19:07	-5.1, 3.9, -5.0, 4.0
Wed 25	04:39, 10:46, 16:54, 23:05	01:10, 07:38, 13:34, 19:57	-5.3, 4.0, -5.1, 4.0
Thu 26	05:30, 11:37, 17:44, 23:56	02:01, 08:28, 14:23, 20:46	-5.3, 4.0, -5.0, 4.0
Fri 27	06:22, 12:29, 18:37	02:52, 09:19, 15:16, 21:41	-5.2, 3.8, -4.9, 3.8
Sat 28	00:50, 07:18, 13:23, 19:34	03:44, 10:13, 16:07, 22:36	-5.0, 3.6, -4.7, 3.6
Sun 29	01:46, 08:16, 14:21, 20:35	04:39, 11:14, 17:04, 23:37	-4.8, 3.4, -4.5, 3.4
Mon 30	02:47, 09:19, 15:23, 21:42	05:39, 12:18, 18:09	-4.5, 3.2, -4.2

May 1990

Day	Slack	Max	Kts
Tue 1	03:52, 10:25, 16:27, 22:51	00:46, 13:30, 19:22	3.2, 3.0, -4.1
Wed 2	04:58, 11:31, 17:30, 23:58	02:01, 08:06, 14:39, 20:42	3.1, -4.1, 3.0, -4.0
Thu 3	06:02, 12:32, 18:30	03:13, 09:23, 15:40, 21:53	3.1, -4.1, 3.0, -4.1
Fri 4	00:59, 07:00, 13:26, 19:23	04:10, 10:25, 16:33, 22:46	3.1, -4.2, 3.1, -4.3
Sat 5	01:52, 07:52, 14:13, 20:11	05:03, 11:10, 17:23, 23:29	3.2, -4.2, 3.3, -4.4
Sun 6	02:39, 08:38, 14:56, 20:53	05:48, 11:51, 18:02	3.3, -4.3, 3.4
Mon 7	03:21, 09:19, 15:36, 21:33	00:06, 06:25, 12:24, 18:39	-4.5, 3.4, -4.4, 3.4
Tue 8	04:00, 09:59, 16:13, 22:12	00:39, 07:02, 12:55, 19:14	-4.6, 3.5, -4.5, 3.5
Wed 9	04:38, 10:37, 16:50, 22:50	01:10, 07:37, 13:25, 19:47	-4.7, 3.5, -4.5, 3.5
Thu 10	05:15, 11:15, 17:26, 23:28	01:44, 08:10, 14:00, 20:22	-4.7, 3.5, -4.6, 3.5
Fri 11	05:53, 11:53, 18:02	02:20, 08:47, 14:37, 21:00	-4.8, 3.4, -4.5, 3.4
Sat 12	00:06, 06:31, 12:31, 18:39	02:57, 09:07, 15:14, 21:37	-4.7, 4.3, -4.5, 3.3
Sun 13	00:45, 07:10, 13:11, 19:18	03:36, 10:03, 15:55, 22:16	-4.7, 3.2, -4.4, 3.3
Mon 14	01:26, 07:51, 13:53, 20:00	04:19, 10:45, 16:39, 23:01	-4.6, 3.1, -4.4, 3.2
Tue 15	02:10, 08:36, 14:37, 20:47	05:04, 11:31, 17:24, 23:49	-4.5, 3.0, -4.3, 3.1
Wed 16	02:59, 09:24, 15:26, 21:40	05:53, 12:18, 18:15	-4.4, 3.0, -4.3
Thu 17	03:52, 10:16, 16:19, 22:38	00:42, 06:44, 13:13, 19:10	3.1, -4.4, 3.0, -4.3
Fri 18	04:49, 11:11, 17:15, 23:39	01:37, 07:40, 14:09, 20:07	3.1, -4.5, 3.1, -4.4
Sat 19	05:47, 12:07, 18:12	02:36, 08:37, 15:04, 21:07	3.2, -4.6, 3.2, -4.6
Sun 20	00:39, 06:46, 13:03, 19:09	03:36, 09:34, 16:01, 22:04	3.3, -4.8, 3.3, -4.8
Mon 21	01:38, 07:42, 13:57, 20:04	04:34, 10:31, 17:00, 22:59	3.4, -5.0, 3.4, -5.0
Tue 22	02:34, 08:38, 14:51, 20:59	05:32, 11:27, 17:51, 23:55	3.6, -4.8, 3.8, -5.1
Wed 23	03:30, 09:32, 15:44, 21:53	06:27, 12:22, 18:46	3.8, -4.9, 3.9
Thu 24	04:24, 10:25, 16:38, 22:47	00:51, 07:20, 13:15, 19:40	-5.2, 3.8, -5.0, 3.9
Fri 25	05:18, 11:19, 17:32, 23:41	01:45, 08:14, 14:08, 20:33	-5.2, 3.8, -4.9, 3.9
Sat 26	06:13, 12:13, 18:28	02:39, 09:08, 15:02, 21:29	-5.1, 3.7, -4.9, 3.8
Sun 27	07:09, 13:08, 19:26	03:35, 10:03, 15:58, 22:27	-5.0, 3.6, -4.7, 3.6
Mon 28	08:06, 14:04, 20:26	04:29, 11:01, 16:55, 23:28	-4.8, 3.4, -4.5, 3.4
Tue 29	09:05, 15:02, 21:29	05:30, 12:02, 17:59	-4.6, 3.2, -4.4
Wed 30	03:31, 10:05, 16:01, 22:31	00:31, 07:01, 13:05, 19:02	3.2, -4.6, 3.1, -4.2
Thu 31	04:30, 11:04, 16:58, 23:32	01:35, 07:35, 14:08, 20:11	3.1, -4.6, 3.0, -4.2

EMBASSY'S CURRENT GUIDE© - HELL GATE, NY

All Currents in Knots. Times Corrected to Daylight Savings Time

Flood Tides are shown in BOLD

CURRENTS

June 1990

Day	Slack	Max	Kts
Fri 1		02:38	**3.0**
	05:28	08:41	-4.1
	12:00	**15:08**	**3.0**
	17:54	21:14	-4.2
Sat 2	00:29	**03:35**	**3.0**
	06:23	09:40	-4.1
	12:52	**15:57**	**3.0**
	18:45	22:03	-4.2
Sun 3	01:21	**04:25**	**3.0**
	07:13	10:27	-4.1
	13:39	**16:44**	**3.1**
	19:33	22:51	-4.3
Mon 4	02:07	**05:13**	**3.1**
	08:00	11:06	-4.2
	14:23	**17:23**	**3.2**
	20:17	23:28	-4.4
Tue 5	02:51	**05:51**	**3.2**
	08:43	11:45	-4.3
	15:04	**18:04**	**3.2**
	20:59		
Wed 6	03:32	00:03	-4.5
	09:24	**06:30**	**3.2**
	15:43	12:20	-4.4
	21:40	**18:43**	**3.3**
Thu 7	04:11	00:39	-4.6
	10:05	**07:09**	**3.3**
	16:21	12:55	-4.5
	22:20	**19:18**	**3.4**
Fri 8	04:50	01:16	-4.7
	10:44	**07:44**	**3.3**
	16:59	13:31	-4.5
	22:59	**19:56**	**3.4**
Sat 9	05:29	01:53	-4.7
	11:24	**08:21**	**3.3**
	17:37	14:09	-4.6
	23:39	**20:33**	**3.4**
Sun 10	06:08	02:32	-4.8
	12:03	**08:59**	**3.3**
	18:15	14:48	-4.6
		21:15	**3.4**
Mon 11	00:19	03:13	-4.8
	06:47	**09:38**	**3.3**
	12:43	15:31	-4.6
	18:55	**21:54**	**3.4**
Tue 12	01:00	03:54	-4.7
	07:27	**10:19**	**3.2**
	13:23	16:14	-4.6
	19:37	**22:37**	**3.3**
Wed 13	01:44	04:38	-4.7
	08:09	**11:02**	**3.2**
	14:07	17:01	-4.6
	20:22	**23:22**	**3.3**
Thu 14	02:30	05:25	-4.6
	08:54	**11:48**	**3.2**
	14:53	17:48	-4.6
	21:13		
Fri 15	03:21	**00:13**	**3.2**
	09:42	06:14	-4.6
	15:45	**12:39**	**3.2**
	22:09	18:39	-4.6
Sat 16	04:15	**01:06**	**3.2**
	10:35	07:07	-4.5
	16:40	**13:33**	**3.2**
	23:09	19:35	-4.6
Sun 17	05:13	**02:06**	**3.2**
	11:32	08:04	-4.5
	17:39	**14:29**	**3.3**
		20:34	-4.7
Mon 18	00:12	**03:07**	**3.3**
	06:14	09:04	-4.6
	12:32	**15:33**	**3.4**
	18:40	21:35	-4.8
Tue 19	01:15	**04:08**	**3.4**
	07:15	10:03	-4.6
	13:32	**16:31**	**3.5**
	19:40	22:37	-4.9
Wed 20	02:16	**05:09**	**3.5**
	08:14	11:06	-4.7
	14:31	**17:32**	**3.6**
	20:39	23:38	-5.0
Thu 21	03:15	**06:11**	**3.6**
	09:12	12:04	-4.8
	15:29	**18:30**	**3.7**
	21:37		
Fri 22	04:12	00:36	-5.1
	10:09	**07:08**	**3.6**
	16:26	13:01	-4.9
	22:34	**19:28**	**3.8**
Sat 23	05:07	01:34	-5.1
	11:04	**08:04**	**3.7**
	17:22	13:58	-4.9
	23:29	**20:24**	**3.8**
Sun 24	06:01	02:29	-5.0
	11:58	**08:57**	**3.7**
	18:17	14:52	-4.8
		21:21	**3.7**
Mon 25	00:23	03:24	-4.9
	06:55	**09:51**	**3.6**
	12:51	15:47	-4.8
	19:13	**22:14**	**3.6**
Tue 26	01:17	04:16	-4.8
	07:48	**10:45**	**3.5**
	13:43	16:39	-4.6
	20:08	**23:11**	**3.5**
Wed 27	02:10	05:11	-4.6
	08:40	**11:37**	**3.3**
	14:36	17:34	-4.5
	21:03		
Thu 28	03:03	**00:05**	**3.3**
	09:33	06:02	-4.4
	15:28	**12:32**	**3.2**
	21:59	18:28	-4.3
Fri 29	03:56	**01:00**	**3.1**
	10:26	06:54	-4.2
	16:21	**13:28**	**3.0**
	22:54	19:22	-4.2
Sat 30	04:49	**01:55**	**3.0**
	11:18	07:50	-4.1
	17:13	**14:21**	**2.9**
	23:49	20:15	-4.1

July 1990

Day	Slack	Max	Kts
Sun 1	05:42	**02:50**	**2.9**
	12:10	08:43	-4.0
	18:04	**15:12**	**2.9**
		21:09	-4.1
Mon 2	00:41	**03:42**	**2.9**
	06:32	09:32	-4.0
	12:59	**16:01**	**2.9**
	18:54	22:02	-4.1
Tue 3	01:30	**04:31**	**2.9**
	07:21	10:21	-4.0
	13:45	**16:50**	**3.0**
	19:42	22:44	-4.2
Wed 4	02:17	**05:16**	**3.0**
	08:08	11:03	-4.1
	14:29	**17:31**	**3.1**
	20:27	23:28	-4.3
Thu 5	03:01	**05:58**	**3.1**
	08:53	11:45	-4.2
	15:12	**18:11**	**3.2**
	21:11		
Fri 6	03:43	00:08	-4.5
	09:36	**06:38**	**3.2**
	15:52	12:24	-4.4
	21:54	**18:53**	**3.3**
Sat 7	04:24	00:49	-4.6
	10:17	**07:17**	**3.3**
	16:32	13:05	-4.5
	22:35	**19:31**	**3.4**
Sun 8	05:03	01:28	-4.7
	10:58	**07:55**	**3.4**
	17:10	13:44	-4.6
	23:16	**20:09**	**3.5**
Mon 9	05:42	02:08	-4.8
	11:37	**08:33**	**3.4**
	17:49	14:27	-4.7
	23:57	**20:48**	**3.6**
Tue 10	06:20	02:47	-4.8
	12:17	**09:12**	**3.4**
	18:29	15:06	-4.8
		21:29	**3.6**
Wed 11	00:38	03:30	-4.9
	06:58	**09:51**	**3.5**
	12:57	15:49	-4.8
	19:11	**22:10**	**3.6**
Thu 12	01:21	04:13	-4.8
	07:39	**10:36**	**3.5**
	13:41	16:35	-4.8
	19:56	**22:55**	**3.5**
Fri 13	02:06	04:58	-4.8
	08:21	**11:21**	**3.4**
	14:26	17:22	-4.8
	20:45	**23:47**	**3.4**
Sat 14	02:55	05:49	-4.7
	09:09	**12:10**	**3.4**
	15:17	18:13	-4.7
	21:40		
Sun 15	03:49	**00:40**	**3.3**
	10:02	06:39	-4.6
	16:14	**13:03**	**3.3**
	22:42	19:08	-4.7
Mon 16	04:48	**01:39**	**3.2**
	11:01	07:36	-4.5
	17:16	**14:05**	**3.3**
	23:47	20:09	-4.6
Tue 17	05:52	**02:42**	**3.2**
	12:06	08:39	-4.4
	18:21	**15:08**	**3.3**
		21:13	-4.6
Wed 18	00:55	**03:49**	**3.2**
	06:57	09:42	-4.5
	13:12	**16:15**	**3.4**
	19:26	22:21	-4.7
Thu 19	02:00	**04:56**	**3.3**
	08:00	10:50	-4.5
	14:16	**17:23**	**3.5**
	20:29	23:29	-4.8
Fri 20	03:01	**06:01**	**3.5**
	09:01	11:54	-4.6
	15:17	**18:23**	**3.7**
	21:28		
Sat 21	03:59	00:30	-4.8
	09:57	**07:04**	**3.6**
	16:14	12:53	-4.7
	22:24	**19:20**	**3.8**
Sun 22	04:52	01:27	-4.9
	10:51	**07:52**	**3.5**
	17:08	13:49	-4.8
	23:18	**20:13**	**3.8**
Mon 23	05:43	02:20	-4.9
	11:42	**08:41**	**3.7**
	18:00	14:40	-4.8
		21:05	**3.8**
Tue 24	00:08	03:09	-4.9
	06:31	**09:32**	**3.7**
	12:31	15:29	-4.8
	18:50	**21:54**	**3.7**
Wed 25	00:57	03:54	-4.8
	07:19	**10:19**	**3.4**
	13:18	16:13	-4.7
	19:39	**22:41**	**3.6**
Thu 26	01:45	04:40	-4.6
	08:05	**11:04**	**3.4**
	14:06	16:58	-4.5
	20:28	**23:30**	**3.4**
Fri 27	02:33	05:21	-4.4
	08:52	**11:50**	**3.3**
	14:53	17:44	-4.3
	21:17		
Sat 28	03:21	**00:18**	**3.2**
	09:40	06:09	-4.2
	15:42	**12:37**	**3.1**
	22:07	18:32	-4.2
Sun 29	04:10	**01:04**	**3.0**
	10:29	06:54	-4.0
	16:32	**13:30**	**2.9**
	23:00	19:18	-4.0
Mon 30	05:02	**01:58**	**2.8**
	11:20	07:45	-3.9
	17:24	**14:21**	**2.8**
	23:53	20:14	-3.9
Tue 31	05:54	**02:53**	**2.8**
	12:12	08:38	-3.8
	18:17	**15:14**	**2.8**
		21:07	-3.9

August 1990

Day	Slack	Max	Kts
Wed 1	00:47	**03:46**	**2.8**
	13:03	**16:08**	**2.9**
	19:09	22:02	-4.0
Thu 2	01:38	**04:39**	**2.9**
	07:37	10:21	-3.9
	13:52	**16:57**	**3.0**
	19:59	22:54	-4.2
Fri 3	02:25	**05:26**	**3.0**
	08:25	11:10	-4.1
	14:37	**17:42**	**3.2**
	20:46	23:38	-4.3
Sat 4	03:10	**06:08**	**3.2**
	09:10	11:55	-4.3
	15:20	**18:24**	**3.4**
	21:30		
Sun 5	03:51	00:21	-4.5
	09:52	**06:48**	**3.4**
	16:01	12:36	-4.5
	22:13	**19:05**	**3.6**
Mon 6	04:31	01:02	-4.7
	10:32	**07:27**	**3.5**
	16:41	13:17	-4.7
	22:54	**19:44**	**3.7**
Tue 7	05:09	01:43	-4.8
	11:12	**08:06**	**3.6**
	17:21	14:01	-4.8
	23:35	**20:25**	**3.8**
Wed 8	05:47	02:24	-4.9
	11:52	**08:45**	**3.7**
	18:01	14:40	-4.8
		21:05	**3.8**
Thu 9	00:17	03:05	-4.9
	06:26	**09:24**	**3.7**
	12:34	15:25	-5.0
	18:44	**21:48**	**3.8**
Fri 10	01:00	03:48	-4.9
	07:06	**10:07**	**3.7**
	13:17	16:08	-4.9
	19:29	**22:33**	**3.7**
Sat 11	01:46	04:34	-4.8
	07:49	**10:52**	**3.6**
	14:04	16:57	-4.9
	20:19	**23:24**	**3.6**
Sun 12	02:35	05:21	-4.7
	08:38	**11:44**	**3.5**
	14:57	17:48	-4.7
	21:15		
Mon 13	03:31	**00:15**	**3.4**
	09:33	06:14	-4.5
	15:56	**12:41**	**3.4**
	22:18	18:46	-4.6
Tue 14	04:33	**01:19**	**3.2**
	10:37	07:13	-4.3
	17:02	**13:44**	**3.3**
	23:28	19:49	-4.4
Wed 15	05:40	**02:26**	**3.1**
	11:48	08:19	-4.2
	18:11	**14:55**	**3.2**
		21:00	-4.3
Thu 16	00:39	**03:40**	**3.1**
	06:48	09:32	-4.2
	12:59	**16:09**	**3.3**
	19:20	22:15	-4.4
Fri 17	01:47	**04:54**	**3.3**
	07:53	10:44	-4.3
	14:06	**17:19**	**3.5**
	20:24	23:26	-4.5
Sat 18	02:47	**05:55**	**3.5**
	08:53	11:51	-4.5
	15:06	**18:20**	**3.7**
	21:22		
Sun 19	03:42	00:27	-4.7
	09:46	**06:48**	**3.6**
	16:00	12:47	-4.6
	22:14	**19:12**	**3.8**
Mon 20	04:31	01:18	-4.8
	10:36	**07:37**	**3.7**
	16:50	13:38	-4.8
	23:03	**19:59**	**3.9**
Tue 21	05:18	02:04	-4.8
	11:23	**08:23**	**3.8**
	17:37	14:21	-4.8
	23:49	**20:46**	**3.9**
Wed 22	06:01	02:45	-4.8
	12:07	**09:06**	**3.8**
	18:21	15:02	-4.8
		21:27	**3.8**
Thu 23	00:33	03:25	-4.7
	06:43	**09:47**	**3.7**
	12:50	15:41	-4.7
	19:04	**22:08**	**3.7**
Fri 24	01:17	04:03	-4.5
	07:25	**10:28**	**3.5**
	13:33	16:22	-4.5
	19:47	**22:51**	**3.5**
Sat 25	02:00	04:42	-4.3
	08:07	**11:07**	**3.3**
	14:17	17:01	-4.3
	20:31	**23:33**	**3.3**
Sun 26	02:45	05:22	-4.1
	08:50	**11:49**	**3.1**
	15:03	17:43	-4.1
	21:17		
Mon 27	03:32	**00:18**	**3.0**
	09:36	06:05	-3.9
	15:52	**12:38**	**2.9**
	22:08	18:31	-4.0
Tue 28	04:23	**01:06**	**2.9**
	10:27	06:54	-3.8
	16:45	**13:29**	**2.8**
	23:03	19:22	-3.8
Wed 29	05:18	**02:04**	**2.7**
	11:22	07:48	-3.7
	17:41	**14:27**	**2.8**
		20:19	-3.8
Thu 30	00:00	**03:03**	**2.7**
	06:13	08:45	-3.7
	12:18	**15:27**	**2.9**
	18:37	21:17	-3.8
Fri 31	00:55	**03:59**	**2.9**
	07:06	09:42	-3.8
	13:11	**16:18**	**3.0**
	19:30	22:15	-4.0

EMBASSY'S CURRENT GUIDE©- HELL GATE, NY

All Currents in Knots. Times Corrected to Daylight Savings Time

Flood Tides are shown in BOLD

CURRENTS

September 1990

Day	Slack	Max	Kts
Sat 1	01:46 07:56 14:00 20:19	**04:50** 10:38 **17:09** 23:06	**3.0** -4.0 **3.2** -4.2
Sun 2	02:32 08:41 14:46 21:04	**05:35** 11:23 **17:55** 23:50	**3.3** -4.3 **3.5** -4.5
Mon 3	03:15 09:24 15:29 21:48	**06:16** 12:08 **18:36**	**3.5** -4.6 **3.7**
Tue 4	 03:55 10:05 16:11 22:30	00:33 **06:55** 12:51 **19:18**	-4.7 **3.7** -4.8 **3.9**
Wed 5	 04:35 10:46 16:53 23:12	01:14 **07:36** 13:34 **19:59**	-4.9 **3.8** -5.0 **4.0**
Thu 6	 05:14 11:27 17:35 23:55	01:56 **08:16** 14:17 **20:42**	-4.9 **3.9** -5.1 **4.0**
Fri 7	 05:54 12:10 18:20	02:39 **09:00** 15:00 **21:25**	-5.0 **3.9** -5.1 **4.0**
Sat 8	00:40 06:37 12:56 19:07	03:22 **09:43** 15:47 **22:10**	-4.9 **3.9** -5.0 **3.8**
Sun 9	01:27 07:22 13:46 19:58	04:11 **10:32** 16:35 **23:02**	-4.8 **3.8** -4.9 **3.6**
Mon 10	02:19 08:14 14:41 20:56	05:00 **11:23** 17:28 **23:59**	-4.6 **3.6** -4.7 **3.4**
Tue 11	03:17 09:13 15:44 22:03	05:57 **12:22** 18:29	-4.3 **3.4** -4.4
Wed 12	 04:23 10:23 16:54 23:15	**01:06** 06:59 **13:34** 19:36	**3.2** -4.1 **3.2** -4.2
Thu 13	 05:33 11:39 18:06	**02:20** 08:11 **14:54** 20:55	**3.1** -3.9 **3.2** -4.1
Fri 14	00:28 06:42 12:52 19:15	**03:36** 09:33 **16:12** 22:18	**3.1** -4.0 **3.3** -4.2
Sat 15	01:34 07:45 13:56 20:16	**04:47** 10:46 **17:13** 23:26	**3.3** -4.2 **3.5** -4.4
Sun 16	02:31 08:41 14:53 21:10	**05:42** 11:49 **18:08**	**3.5** -4.4 **3.7**
Mon 17	 03:22 09:30 15:43 21:58	00:17 **06:32** 12:36 **18:55**	-4.5 **3.7** -4.6 **3.8**
Tue 18	 04:07 10:16 16:28 22:43	01:02 **07:17** 13:19 **19:40**	-4.6 **3.8** -4.7 **3.9**
Wed 19	 04:49 10:58 17:11 23:24	01:41 **07:58** 13:57 **20:19**	-4.7 **3.8** -4.8 **3.9**
Thu 20	 05:29 11:39 17:51	02:16 **08:35** 14:31 **20:58**	-4.7 **3.8** -4.8 **3.8**
Fri 21	00:05 06:08 12:19 18:30	02:51 **09:12** 15:07 **21:34**	-4.6 **3.7** -4.7 **3.7**
Sat 22	00:45 06:46 12:59 19:10	03:25 **09:49** 15:45 **22:13**	-4.5 **3.6** -4.5 **3.5**
Sun 23	01:25 07:24 13:40 19:50	04:03 **10:27** 16:22 **22:51**	-4.3 **3.4** -4.4 **3.3**
Mon 24	02:08 08:05 14:24 20:34	04:43 **11:08** 17:05 **23:36**	-4.1 **3.2** -4.2 **3.1**
Tue 25	02:54 08:49 15:12 21:22	05:25 **11:52** 17:50	-3.9 **3.0** -4.0
Wed 26	 03:44 09:39 16:05 22:17	**00:25** 06:12 **12:47** 18:41	**2.9** -3.8 **2.9** -3.9
Thu 27	 04:38 10:35 17:01 23:15	**01:20** 07:07 **13:42** 19:39	**2.8** -3.7 **2.8** -3.8
Fri 28	 05:34 11:34 17:59	**02:16** 08:04 **14:41** 20:38	**2.8** -3.7 **2.9** -3.9
Sat 29	00:12 06:28 12:31 18:54	**03:17** 09:01 **15:40** 21:33	**2.9** -3.8 **3.0** -4.0
Sun 30	01:05 07:19 13:24 19:45	**04:09** 09:59 **16:31** 22:27	**3.1** -4.1 **3.3** -4.3

October 1990

Day	Slack	Max	Kts
Mon 1	01:53 08:06 14:12 20:32	**04:57** 10:50 **17:19** 23:16	**3.3** -4.4 **3.5** -4.5
Tue 2	02:38 08:50 14:59 21:17	**05:42** 11:35 **18:04**	**3.6** -4.7 **3.8**
Wed 3	 03:21 09:33 15:44 22:02	00:01 **06:23** 12:22 **18:49**	-4.7 **3.8** -4.9 **3.9**
Thu 4	 04:03 10:17 16:29 22:46	00:46 **07:07** 13:07 **19:32**	-4.9 **3.9** -5.1 **4.0**
Fri 5	 04:45 11:01 17:14 23:32	01:31 **07:50** 13:51 **20:17**	-5.0 **4.0** -5.2 **4.1**
Sat 6	 05:29 11:48 18:02	02:16 **08:35** 14:40 **21:05**	-5.0 **4.0** -5.2 **4.0**
Sun 7	00:19 06:15 12:36 18:52	03:03 **09:22** 15:27 **21:54**	-4.9 **4.0** -5.1 **3.8**
Mon 8	01:09 07:06 13:29 19:47	03:50 **10:13** 16:20 **22:47**	-4.8 **3.8** -4.9 **3.6**
Tue 9	02:04 08:02 14:28 20:48	04:42 **11:11** 17:15 **23:46**	-4.5 **3.6** -4.6 **3.3**
Wed 10	03:05 09:06 15:33 21:56	05:43 **12:15** 18:19	-4.2 **3.3** -4.3
Thu 11	 04:12 10:19 16:44 23:08	**00:57** 06:50 **13:29** 19:32	**3.1** -4.0 **3.2** -4.1
Fri 12	 05:21 11:35 17:55	**02:16** 08:07 **14:50** 20:56	**3.0** -3.9 **3.1** -4.0
Sat 13	00:17 06:28 12:44 19:00	**03:31** 09:32 **16:01** 22:12	**3.1** -4.0 **3.3** -4.2
Sun 14	01:19 07:27 13:45 19:58	**04:31** 10:46 **17:00** 23:13	**3.3** -4.2 **3.4** -4.3
Mon 15	02:13 08:20 14:37 20:49	**05:26** 11:35 **17:51** 23:58	**3.4** -4.4 **3.6** -4.4
Tue 16	03:00 09:06 15:24 21:34	**06:11** 12:20 **18:35**	**3.6** -4.6 **3.7**
Wed 17	 03:43 09:49 16:06 22:15	00:39 **06:52** 12:53 **19:12**	-4.5 **3.7** -4.7 **3.7**
Thu 18	 04:22 10:29 16:46 22:54	01:14 **07:29** 13:30 **19:53**	-4.6 **3.7** -4.7 **3.7**
Fri 19	 05:00 11:08 17:24 23:33	01:47 **08:06** 14:01 **20:27**	-4.6 **3.7** -4.7 **3.7**
Sat 20	 05:37 11:46 18:02	02:18 **08:39** 14:35 **21:03**	-4.6 **3.6** -4.7 **3.6**
Sun 21	00:11 06:14 12:24 18:41	02:53 **09:15** 15:12 **21:39**	-4.5 **3.5** -4.6 **3.4**
Mon 22	00:51 06:52 13:04 19:20	03:28 **09:51** 15:51 **22:19**	-4.4 **3.4** -4.5 **3.3**
Tue 23	01:31 07:31 13:46 20:03	04:07 **10:32** 16:32 **23:01**	-4.2 **3.2** -4.3 **3.1**
Wed 24	02:15 08:14 14:32 20:49	04:52 **11:17** 17:18 **23:47**	-4.1 **3.1** -4.2 **2.9**
Thu 25	03:02 09:02 15:22 21:40	05:37 **12:06** 18:05	-4.0 **2.9** -4.1
Fri 26	 03:53 09:56 16:17 22:35	**00:38** 06:32 **13:01** 19:00	**2.8** -3.9 **2.9** -4.0
Sat 27	 04:47 10:55 17:14 23:31	**01:33** 07:24 **13:57** 19:55	**2.8** -3.9 **2.9** -4.0
Sun 28	 04:42 10:53 17:10 23:25	**01:28** 07:21 **13:56** 19:52	**2.9** -4.1 **3.0** -4.2
Mon 29	 05:34 11:49 18:03	**02:24** 08:20 **14:52** 20:46	**3.1** -4.3 **3.2** -4.4
Tue 30	00:15 06:24 12:42 18:54	**03:15** 09:11 **15:41** 21:39	**3.3** -4.6 **3.5** -4.6
Wed 31	01:03 07:13 13:32 19:43	**04:06** 10:05 **16:32** 22:28	**3.6** -4.8 **3.7** -4.8

November 1990

Day	Slack	Max	Kts
Thu 1	01:50 08:00 14:21 20:31	**04:51** 10:54 **17:23** 23:19	**3.8** -5.1 **3.9** -4.9
Fri 2	02:37 08:48 15:10 21:19	**05:40** 11:43 **18:09**	**3.9** -5.2 **3.9**
Sat 3	 03:24 09:37 16:00 22:08	00:05 **06:27** 12:32 **18:57**	-5.0 **4.0** -5.3 **4.0**
Sun 4	 04:13 10:27 16:51 22:59	00:54 **07:16** 13:21 **19:49**	-5.0 **4.0** -5.2 **3.9**
Mon 5	 05:04 11:19 17:44 23:51	01:45 **08:08** 14:12 **20:41**	-4.9 **3.9** -5.1 **3.7**
Tue 6	 05:59 12:14 18:41	02:36 **09:03** 15:06 **21:37**	-4.8 **3.7** -4.9 **3.5**
Wed 7	00:48 06:59 13:14 19:43	03:33 **10:02** 16:05 **22:38**	-4.6 **3.5** -4.6 **3.3**
Thu 8	01:49 08:05 14:18 20:49	04:33 **11:06** 17:09 **23:50**	-4.3 **3.3** -4.4 **3.1**
Fri 9	02:53 09:15 15:25 21:56	05:44 **12:22** 18:23	-4.2 **3.1** -4.2
Sat 10	 03:58 10:25 16:32 23:01	**01:00** 07:02 **13:35** 19:42	**3.0** -4.1 **3.1** -4.1
Sun 11	 05:01 11:30 17:33 23:59	**02:09** 08:18 **14:43** 20:53	**3.1** -4.2 **3.1** -4.2
Mon 12	 05:58 12:28 18:29	**03:10** 09:21 **15:38** 21:47	**3.2** -4.3 **3.3** -4.3
Tue 13	00:51 06:49 13:19 19:18	**03:59** 10:10 **16:25** 22:34	**3.3** -4.4 **3.3** -4.4
Wed 14	01:36 07:35 14:04 20:02	**04:42** 10:51 **17:10** 23:09	**3.4** -4.5 **3.4** -4.4
Thu 15	02:18 08:17 14:45 20:43	**05:26** 11:28 **17:49** 23:42	**3.4** -4.6 **3.5** -4.5
Fri 16	02:58 08:57 15:24 21:22	**06:01** 12:01 **18:24**	**3.5** -4.7 **3.5**
Sat 17	 03:36 09:36 16:03 22:00	00:15 **06:37** 12:34 **19:01**	-4.5 **3.5** -4.7 **3.5**
Sun 18	 04:13 10:14 16:40 22:38	00:49 **07:10** 13:07 **19:36**	-4.6 **3.5** -4.7 **3.4**
Mon 19	 04:50 10:52 17:19 23:17	01:24 **07:47** 13:44 **20:11**	-4.5 **3.4** -4.7 **3.3**
Tue 20	 05:28 11:31 17:58 23:57	02:01 **08:26** 14:21 **20:50**	-4.5 **3.3** -4.6 **3.2**
Wed 21	 06:07 12:12 18:39	02:40 **09:03** 15:04 **21:29**	-4.4 **3.2** -4.6 **3.1**
Thu 22	00:38 06:49 12:55 19:23	03:23 **09:48** 15:49 **22:14**	-4.4 **3.1** -4.5 **3.0**
Fri 23	01:21 07:34 13:41 20:09	04:07 **10:33** 16:34 **22:59**	-4.3 **3.0** -4.4 **2.9**
Sat 24	02:08 08:24 14:32 20:58	04:56 **11:25** 17:21 **23:50**	-4.3 **3.0** -4.3 **2.9**
Sun 25	02:58 09:19 15:26 21:51	05:49 **12:16** 18:17	-4.3 **3.0** -4.3
Mon 26	 03:51 10:17 16:22 22:44	**00:45** 06:42 **13:13** 19:12	**3.0** -4.4 **3.0** -4.4
Tue 27	 04:46 11:16 17:19 23:38	**01:39** 07:39 **14:11** 20:07	**3.1** -4.5 **3.2** -4.5
Wed 28	 05:42 12:13 18:15	**02:36** 08:37 **15:09** 21:04	**3.3** -4.7 **3.3** -4.6
Thu 29	00:32 06:36 13:09 19:09	**03:31** 09:34 **16:03** 21:59	**3.5** -4.9 **3.5** -4.8
Fri 30	01:24 07:30 14:03 20:03	**04:26** 10:29 **16:57** 22:53	**3.7** -5.1 **3.7** -4.9

All Currents in Knots. Times Corrected to Daylight Savings Time

Flood Tides are shown in BOLD

March 1990

Day	Slack	Max	Kts
Thu 1	01:55 08:35 14:25 20:45	05:18 11:21 17:41 23:44	-4.2 3.4 -3.6 3.6
Fri 2	02:49 09:34 15:22 21:44	06:15 12:18 18:41	-3.9 3.1 -3.3
Sat 3	03:48 10:41 16:26 22:52	00:41 07:20 13:19 19:48	3.2 -3.7 2.8 -3.0
Sun 4	04:53 11:52 17:35	01:43 08:27 14:31 20:58	3.0 -3.5 2.6 -2.9
Mon 5	00:06 06:02 13:02 18:47	02:56 09:36 15:49 22:04	2.8 -3.5 2.6 -3.0
Tue 6	01:18 07:11 14:05 19:54	04:15 10:39 17:02 23:09	2.8 -3.6 2.8 -3.2
Wed 7	02:23 08:15 15:02 20:53	05:22 11:39 18:00	3.0 -3.7 3.0
Thu 8	03:21 09:12 15:52 21:43	00:04 06:23 12:30 18:51	-3.5 3.1 -3.9 3.2
Fri 9	04:12 10:02 16:38 22:28	00:55 07:12 13:19 19:36	-3.7 3.3 -3.9 3.3
Sat 10	04:58 10:46 17:19 23:08	01:41 07:55 14:02 20:13	-3.8 3.3 -3.9 3.3
Sun 11	05:41 11:26 17:57 23:45	02:22 08:31 14:43 20:46	-3.8 3.2 -3.7 3.2
Mon 12	06:21 12:04 18:32	03:05 09:04 15:23 21:17	-3.8 3.0 -3.5 3.1
Tue 13	00:20 07:00 12:40 19:07	03:44 09:37 16:00 21:51	-3.6 2.8 -3.2 2.9
Wed 14	00:55 07:38 13:17 19:41	04:22 10:13 16:38 22:26	-3.4 2.6 -2.9 2.7
Thu 15	01:31 08:18 13:55 20:18	05:01 10:54 17:17 23:07	-3.1 2.4 -2.6 2.5
Fri 16	02:09 09:02 14:38 20:59	05:40 11:37 18:00 23:50	-2.9 2.1 -2.3 2.2
Sat 17	02:52 09:51 15:25 21:48	06:29 12:22 18:47	-2.6 1.9 -2.0
Sun 18	03:40 10:48 16:20 22:47	00:40 07:23 13:17 19:48	2.0 -2.4 1.7 -1.9
Mon 19	04:36 11:48 17:21 23:53	01:35 08:21 14:15 20:52	1.8 -2.4 1.7 -1.9
Tue 20	05:38 12:47 18:22	02:34 09:24 15:16 21:52	1.8 -2.4 1.8 -2.1
Wed 21	00:56 06:39 13:40 19:18	03:35 10:21 16:15 22:46	2.0 -2.7 2.1 -2.5
Thu 22	01:53 07:36 14:27 20:09	04:34 11:09 17:06 23:35	2.3 -3.0 2.4 -2.9
Fri 23	02:43 08:29 15:10 20:56	05:26 11:58 17:54	2.7 -3.3 2.9
Sat 24	03:30 09:18 15:51 21:41	00:20 06:15 12:43 18:38	-3.4 3.1 -3.7 3.3
Sun 25	04:14 10:05 16:32 22:25	01:07 07:02 13:25 19:21	-3.9 3.5 -3.9 3.7
Mon 26	04:59 10:52 17:13 23:10	01:48 07:49 14:10 20:07	-4.3 3.8 -4.1 4.0
Tue 27	05:45 11:38 17:57 23:56	02:34 08:35 14:53 20:52	-4.6 4.0 -4.2 4.1
Wed 28	06:33 12:26 18:44	03:19 09:21 15:41 21:39	-4.7 4.0 -4.1 4.1
Thu 29	00:44 07:24 13:17 19:34	04:08 10:11 16:32 22:30	-4.6 3.8 -3.9 3.9
Fri 30	01:36 08:19 14:11 20:30	05:01 11:04 17:27 23:24	-4.4 3.5 -3.6 3.6
Sat 31	02:31 09:20 15:10 21:33	05:59 12:03 18:28	-4.1 3.2 -3.3

April 1990

Day	Slack	Max	Kts
Sun 1	04:32 11:26 17:14 23:44	00:25 08:03 14:07 20:35	3.2 -3.8 2.9 -3.1
Mon 2	05:38 12:35 18:23	02:32 09:10 15:21 21:42	2.9 -3.5 2.7 -3.0
Tue 3	00:58 06:48 13:42 19:32	03:48 10:16 16:38 22:49	2.7 -3.4 2.7 -3.1
Wed 4	02:08 07:57 14:43 20:36	05:08 11:21 17:44 23:51	2.7 -3.4 2.8 -3.3
Thu 5	03:10 09:00 15:38 21:31	06:11 12:16 18:39	2.8 -3.5 3.0
Fri 6	04:05 09:55 16:27 22:19	00:46 07:07 13:09 19:30	-3.5 3.0 -3.6 3.1
Sat 7	04:55 10:42 17:11 23:01	01:33 07:54 13:52 20:11	-3.7 3.0 -3.5 3.1
Sun 8	05:39 11:24 17:50 23:39	02:18 08:35 14:36 20:44	-3.8 3.0 -3.5 3.1
Mon 9	06:20 12:02 18:27	02:58 09:10 15:17 21:15	-3.8 3.0 -3.3 3.0
Tue 10	00:14 06:58 12:39 19:02	03:37 09:41 15:55 21:46	-3.7 2.8 -3.1 2.9
Wed 11	00:47 07:34 13:14 19:35	04:15 10:11 16:31 22:19	-3.5 2.7 -2.9 2.7
Thu 12	01:21 08:11 13:50 20:08	04:53 10:47 17:09 22:54	-3.3 2.5 -2.7 2.6
Fri 13	01:56 08:48 14:28 20:45	05:29 11:23 17:48 23:35	-3.1 2.4 -2.4 2.4
Sat 14	02:34 09:29 15:10 21:26	06:08 12:00 18:27	-2.9 2.2 -2.2
Sun 15	03:16 10:14 15:56 22:15	00:18 06:52 12:54 19:12	2.2 -2.7 2.0 -2.0
Mon 16	04:03 11:05 16:47 23:12	01:09 07:41 13:45 20:10	2.0 -2.5 1.9 -2.0
Tue 17	04:58 12:00 17:43	02:00 08:39 14:38 21:13	1.9 -2.4 1.9 -2.1
Wed 18	00:15 05:58 12:56 18:41	02:58 09:38 15:37 22:11	1.9 -2.5 2.0 -2.3
Thu 19	01:18 07:00 13:49 19:36	03:59 10:37 16:30 23:07	2.1 -2.7 2.3 -2.7
Fri 20	02:16 07:59 14:39 20:29	04:58 11:30 17:24 23:58	2.4 -2.9 2.7 -3.0
Sat 21	03:09 08:55 15:26 21:19	05:52 12:19 18:15	2.8 -3.3 3.1
Sun 22	03:59 09:48 16:12 22:08	00:47 06:45 13:07 19:04	-3.7 3.2 -3.6 3.5
Mon 23	04:48 10:38 16:58 22:56	01:33 07:34 13:56 19:52	-4.2 3.6 -3.9 3.9
Tue 24	05:36 11:28 17:45 23:44	02:21 08:23 14:44 20:40	-4.6 3.9 -4.1 4.1
Wed 25	06:25 12:18 18:33	03:10 09:12 15:33 21:28	-4.8 4.0 -4.2 4.2
Thu 26	00:34 07:16 13:09 19:25	04:00 10:03 16:24 22:21	-4.8 4.0 -4.1 4.1
Fri 27	01:25 08:09 14:02 20:19	04:52 10:56 17:17 23:13	-4.7 3.9 -3.9 3.9
Sat 28	02:19 09:05 14:58 21:19	05:48 11:51 18:15	-4.5 3.6 -3.7
Sun 29	03:16 10:05 15:58 22:24	00:11 06:46 12:49 19:16	3.5 -4.1 3.3 -3.4
Mon 30	04:16 11:08 17:00 23:33	01:12 07:47 13:53 20:20	3.2 -3.8 3.0 -3.3

May 1990

Day	Slack	Max	Kts
Tue 1	05:21 12:12 18:05	02:19 08:50 15:05 21:23	2.8 -3.5 2.9 -3.2
Wed 2	00:43 06:28 13:15 19:09	03:34 09:51 16:14 22:27	2.6 -3.3 2.8 -3.2
Thu 3	01:49 07:33 14:13 20:08	04:46 10:54 17:17 23:24	2.6 -3.3 2.8 -3.3
Fri 4	02:49 08:34 15:07 21:01	05:47 11:50 18:10	2.7 -3.2 2.9
Sat 5	03:43 09:28 15:55 21:47	00:19 06:42 12:39 18:56	-3.5 2.7 -3.2 2.9
Sun 6	04:31 10:16 16:39 22:29	01:06 07:27 13:26 19:37	-3.6 2.7 -3.1 2.9
Mon 7	05:15 10:58 17:19 23:06	01:51 08:10 14:09 20:14	-3.6 2.7 -3.1 2.8
Tue 8	05:56 11:37 17:57 23:42	02:31 08:45 14:50 20:44	-3.6 2.7 -3.0 2.8
Wed 9	06:34 12:14 18:33	03:10 09:18 15:29 21:15	-3.5 2.6 -2.8 2.7
Thu 10	00:17 07:11 12:51 19:07	03:49 09:48 16:08 21:50	-3.4 2.5 -2.7 2.6
Fri 11	00:52 07:48 13:28 19:43	04:25 10:22 16:47 22:29	-3.3 2.5 -2.5 2.5
Sat 12	01:28 08:24 14:07 20:20	05:04 11:01 17:22 23:08	-3.1 2.4 -2.4 2.3
Sun 13	02:07 09:03 14:47 21:02	05:43 11:42 18:05 23:53	-3.0 2.3 -2.3 2.2
Mon 14	02:48 09:44 15:31 21:49	06:24 12:27 18:46	-2.8 2.2 -2.2
Tue 15	03:35 10:28 16:18 22:43	00:40 07:09 13:12 19:37	2.1 -2.7 2.2 -2.3
Wed 16	04:27 11:16 17:09 23:41	01:32 08:01 14:07 20:34	2.1 -2.6 2.3 -2.4
Thu 17	05:24 12:07 18:02	02:27 08:54 14:57 21:30	2.1 -2.6 2.4 -2.7
Fri 18	00:42 06:23 13:00 18:57	03:26 09:55 15:52 22:27	2.3 -2.8 2.6 -3.0
Sat 19	01:41 07:24 13:53 19:52	04:21 10:49 16:45 23:25	2.5 -3.0 2.9 -3.4
Sun 20	02:38 08:22 14:45 20:45	05:21 11:44 17:40	2.8 -3.2 3.3
Mon 21	03:32 09:19 15:37 21:38	00:16 06:14 12:39 18:32	-3.9 3.2 -3.5 3.6
Tue 22	04:25 10:14 16:29 22:31	01:07 07:11 13:30 19:25	-4.3 3.5 -3.7 3.9
Wed 23	05:17 11:07 17:22 23:23	02:00 08:02 14:21 20:18	-4.6 3.7 -3.9 4.1
Thu 24	06:09 12:01 18:15	02:52 08:54 15:16 21:11	-4.8 3.9 -4.0 4.1
Fri 25	00:16 07:02 12:54 19:10	03:44 09:49 16:09 22:04	-4.8 3.9 -4.0 4.0
Sat 26	01:09 07:55 13:49 20:08	04:37 10:42 17:03 22:57	-4.7 3.8 -3.9 3.8
Sun 27	02:04 08:50 14:44 21:07	05:32 11:38 18:01 23:55	-4.5 3.6 -3.8 3.5
Mon 28	03:00 09:47 15:41 22:10	06:27 12:33 19:00	-4.2 3.4 -3.6
Tue 29	03:58 10:44 16:40 23:14	00:56 07:25 13:34 19:58	3.1 -3.8 3.2 -3.4
Wed 30	04:58 11:43 17:38	02:00 08:23 14:36 20:57	2.8 -3.5 3.0 -3.3
Thu 31	00:19 05:59 12:40 18:36	03:06 09:22 15:39 21:56	2.6 -3.2 2.8 -3.2

All Currents in Knots. Times Corrected to Daylight Savings Time

Flood Tides are shown in BOLD

CURRENTS

June 1990

Day	Slack	Max	Kts
Fri 1	01:22, 07:00, 13:36, 19:32	04:13, 10:20, 16:39, 22:51	2.4, -3.0, 2.7, -3.2
Sat 2	02:20, 07:59, 14:29, 20:23	05:14, 11:15, 17:32, 23:45	2.4, -2.9, 2.7, -3.3
Sun 3	03:15, 08:54, 15:19, 21:10	06:09, 12:06, 18:19	2.4, -2.8, 2.6
Mon 4	04:04, 09:44, 16:05, 21:54	00:34, 06:58, 12:55, 19:01	-3.3, 2.4, -2.7, 2.6
Tue 5	04:49, 10:29, 16:48, 22:34	01:17, 07:42, 13:38, 19:39	-3.4, 2.4, -2.7, 2.6
Wed 6	05:31, 11:11, 17:28, 23:12	02:04, 08:21, 14:21, 20:15	-3.4, 2.4, -2.7, 2.6
Thu 7	06:11, 11:51, 18:07, 23:50	02:44, 08:54, 15:03, 20:50	-3.4, 2.5, -2.6, 2.5
Fri 8	06:49, 12:29, 18:44	03:24, 09:27, 15:44, 21:27	-3.4, 2.5, -2.6, 2.5
Sat 9	00:28, 07:25, 13:07, 19:21	04:03, 10:01, 16:23, 22:06	-3.3, 2.5, -2.6, 2.5
Sun 10	01:06, 08:01, 13:45, 20:00	04:41, 10:38, 17:03, 22:46	-3.3, 2.5, -2.5, 2.5
Mon 11	01:45, 08:37, 14:24, 20:41	05:19, 11:19, 17:42, 23:31	-3.2, 2.5, -2.5, 2.4
Tue 12	02:26, 09:14, 15:05, 21:26	05:58, 12:00, 18:23	-3.1, 2.5, -2.6
Wed 13	03:11, 09:54, 15:49, 22:16	00:16, 06:37, 12:44, 19:08	2.4, -3.0, 2.6, -2.7
Thu 14	04:00, 10:38, 16:37, 23:11	01:05, 07:22, 13:33, 20:00	2.4, -2.9, 2.6, -2.8
Fri 15	04:54, 11:26, 17:28	01:58, 08:15, 14:24, 20:55	2.4, -2.9, 2.8, -3.0
Sat 16	00:09, 05:51, 12:19, 18:23	02:54, 09:14, 15:17, 21:52	2.5, -2.9, 2.9, -3.3
Sun 17	01:10, 06:52, 13:15, 19:20	03:51, 10:14, 16:14, 22:51	2.6, -3.0, 3.1, -3.6
Mon 18	02:11, 07:54, 14:13, 20:18	04:52, 11:14, 17:12, 23:50	2.8, -3.1, 3.3, -3.9
Tue 19	03:10, 08:55, 15:12, 21:15	05:51, 12:12, 18:09	3.0, -3.3, 3.5
Wed 20	04:07, 09:54, 16:10, 22:12	00:48, 06:51, 13:11, 19:04	-4.2, 3.3, -3.6, 3.7
Thu 21	05:03, 10:51, 17:07, 23:07	01:42, 07:46, 14:07, 20:01	-4.5, 3.5, -3.8, 3.9
Fri 22	05:56, 11:46, 18:03	02:37, 08:41, 15:01, 20:57	-4.7, 3.7, -3.9, 3.9
Sat 23	00:02, 06:49, 12:41, 18:59	03:29, 09:36, 15:56, 21:52	-4.7, 3.8, -4.0, 3.9
Sun 24	00:55, 07:40, 13:34, 19:56	04:22, 10:28, 16:47, 22:45	-4.6, 3.8, -4.0, 3.7
Mon 25	01:48, 08:32, 14:26, 20:52	05:13, 11:21, 17:42, 23:39	-4.4, 3.7, -3.9, 3.4
Tue 26	02:40, 09:23, 15:18, 21:49	06:05, 12:14, 18:36	-4.1, 3.5, -3.7
Wed 27	03:33, 10:15, 16:10, 22:48	00:33, 06:59, 13:05, 19:31	3.1, -3.8, 3.2, -3.5
Thu 28	04:27, 11:07, 17:03, 23:47	01:28, 07:53, 13:57, 20:26	2.8, -3.4, 2.9, -3.3
Fri 29	05:22, 12:00, 17:56	02:27, 08:46, 14:51, 21:19	2.4, -3.0, 2.7, -3.1
Sat 30	00:47, 06:19, 12:55, 18:48	03:28, 09:42, 15:46, 22:15	2.2, -2.7, 2.5, -3.0

July 1990

Day	Slack	Max	Kts
Sun 1	01:45, 07:17, 13:48, 19:40	04:29, 10:36, 16:43, 23:08	2.1, -2.5, 2.4, -3.0
Mon 2	02:41, 08:14, 14:41, 20:30	05:31, 11:29, 17:36	2.0, -2.4, 2.3
Tue 3	03:33, 09:08, 15:31, 21:18	00:00, 06:22, 12:21, 18:23	-3.1, 2.1, -2.4, 2.3
Wed 4	04:21, 09:58, 16:17, 22:02	00:48, 07:11, 13:10, 19:07	-3.1, 2.2, -2.4, 2.4
Thu 5	05:04, 10:43, 17:01, 22:45	01:35, 07:52, 13:55, 19:46	-3.2, 2.3, -2.5, 2.4
Fri 6	05:45, 11:25, 17:42, 23:25	02:17, 08:29, 14:38, 20:25	-3.3, 2.4, -2.6, 2.5
Sat 7	06:23, 12:04, 18:22	03:00, 09:03, 15:21, 21:03	-3.4, 2.5, -2.7, 2.6
Sun 8	00:05, 06:59, 12:42, 19:00	03:39, 09:37, 15:59, 21:44	-3.4, 2.6, -2.8, 2.7
Mon 9	00:44, 07:34, 13:19, 19:38	04:17, 10:14, 16:37, 22:25	-3.4, 2.8, -2.9, 2.8
Tue 10	01:24, 08:08, 13:57, 20:18	04:53, 10:51, 17:16, 23:06	-3.4, 2.9, -3.0, 2.8
Wed 11	02:05, 08:43, 14:37, 21:02	05:31, 11:32, 17:57, 23:51	-3.3, 2.9, -3.1, 2.8
Thu 12	02:48, 09:22, 15:19, 21:50	06:12, 12:17, 18:36	-3.3, 3.0, -3.2
Fri 13	03:36, 10:05, 16:06, 22:43	00:39, 06:53, 13:04, 19:28	2.7, -3.2, 3.0, -3.3
Sat 14	04:28, 10:53, 16:58, 23:42	01:30, 07:40, 13:53, 20:22	2.7, -3.0, 3.0, -3.3
Sun 15	05:25, 11:48, 17:55	02:27, 08:42, 14:49, 21:23	2.6, -3.0, 3.0, -3.4
Mon 16	00:46, 06:27, 12:48, 18:56	03:26, 09:49, 15:48, 22:29	2.6, -2.9, 3.1, -3.6
Tue 17	01:51, 07:32, 13:53, 19:58	04:27, 10:54, 16:49, 23:31	2.7, -3.0, 3.2, -3.8
Wed 18	02:55, 08:37, 14:57, 21:00	05:34, 11:57, 17:52	2.9, -3.2, 3.3
Thu 19	03:55, 09:40, 16:00, 21:59	00:32, 06:38, 12:58, 18:55	-4.1, 3.1, -3.4, 3.5
Fri 20	04:51, 10:39, 16:59, 22:56	01:30, 07:36, 13:55, 19:53	-4.3, 3.4, -3.7, 3.7
Sat 21	05:44, 11:34, 17:55, 23:50	02:23, 08:32, 14:48, 20:47	-4.5, 3.6, -3.9, 3.8
Sun 22	06:34, 12:25, 18:48	03:14, 09:25, 15:40, 21:39	-4.5, 3.7, -4.0, 3.7
Mon 23	00:41, 07:22, 13:14, 19:40	04:05, 10:12, 16:31, 22:29	-4.5, 3.7, -4.0, 3.6
Tue 24	01:30, 08:09, 14:02, 20:32	04:53, 10:57, 17:19, 23:17	-4.3, 3.6, -3.9, 3.3
Wed 25	02:17, 08:54, 14:48, 21:23	05:39, 11:43, 18:07	-4.0, 3.4, -3.7
Thu 26	03:04, 09:40, 15:35, 22:15	00:04, 06:28, 12:27, 18:56	3.0, -3.6, 3.1, -3.4
Fri 27	03:52, 10:27, 16:21, 23:10	00:52, 07:16, 13:12, 19:47	2.6, -3.1, 2.8, -3.2
Sat 28	04:42, 11:17, 17:10	01:41, 08:07, 14:03, 20:40	2.3, -2.8, 2.5, -2.9
Sun 29	00:07, 05:35, 12:09, 18:01	02:39, 08:58, 14:54, 21:34	2.0, -2.4, 2.2, -2.8
Mon 30	01:05, 06:32, 13:05, 18:55	03:39, 09:56, 15:48, 22:29	1.8, -2.2, 2.1, -2.7
Tue 31	02:04, 07:32, 14:02, 19:49	04:42, 10:53, 16:49, 23:24	1.8, -2.1, 2.0, -2.8

August 1990

Day	Slack	Max	Kts
Wed 1	02:59, 08:30, 14:57, 20:41	05:43, 11:50, 17:43	1.8, -2.2, 2.1
Thu 2	03:48, 09:24, 15:48, 21:31	00:16, 06:39, 12:39, 18:34	-2.9, 2.0, -2.3, 2.2
Fri 3	04:34, 10:12, 16:34, 22:17	01:03, 07:22, 13:26, 19:20	-3.1, 2.2, -2.5, 2.4
Sat 4	05:15, 10:55, 17:16, 23:00	01:48, 07:59, 14:12, 20:02	-3.3, 2.5, -2.8, 2.6
Sun 5	05:52, 11:34, 17:56, 23:41	02:31, 08:33, 14:52, 20:40	-3.4, 2.7, -3.0, 2.8
Mon 6	06:27, 12:11, 18:34	03:10, 09:09, 15:30, 21:19	-3.6, 2.9, -3.2, 3.0
Tue 7	00:21, 07:01, 12:49, 19:13	03:48, 09:44, 16:09, 21:59	-3.6, 3.1, -3.4, 3.1
Wed 8	01:02, 07:35, 13:27, 19:53	04:25, 10:22, 16:47, 22:42	-3.6, 3.2, -3.5, 3.2
Thu 9	01:43, 08:11, 14:07, 20:37	05:02, 11:03, 17:28, 23:27	-3.6, 3.3, -3.6, 3.2
Fri 10	02:26, 08:51, 14:51, 21:26	05:42, 11:48, 18:11	-3.5, 3.4, -3.7
Sat 11	03:14, 09:36, 15:40, 22:20	00:15, 06:27, 12:36, 19:02	3.1, -3.4, 3.3, -3.6
Sun 12	04:07, 10:27, 16:34, 23:21	01:09, 07:20, 13:29, 20:00	2.9, -3.2, 3.2, -3.5
Mon 13	05:05, 11:27, 17:33	02:04, 08:23, 14:26, 21:05	2.7, -3.0, 3.1, -3.5
Tue 14	00:28, 06:10, 12:33, 18:38	03:06, 09:33, 15:29, 22:13	2.6, -2.9, 3.0, -3.5
Wed 15	01:37, 07:19, 13:44, 19:45	04:15, 10:41, 16:37, 23:18	2.6, -2.9, 3.0, -3.7
Thu 16	02:43, 08:26, 14:53, 20:50	05:25, 11:46, 17:47	2.8, -3.2, 3.1
Fri 17	03:43, 09:30, 15:55, 21:51	00:19, 06:32, 12:48, 18:50	-3.9, 3.0, -3.4, 3.3
Sat 18	04:38, 10:27, 16:52, 22:46	01:17, 07:30, 13:41, 19:49	-4.1, 3.3, -3.7, 3.5
Sun 19	05:28, 11:19, 17:45, 23:37	02:08, 08:21, 14:34, 20:41	-4.3, 3.5, -4.0, 3.6
Mon 20	06:15, 12:06, 18:35	02:58, 09:09, 15:21, 21:24	-4.3, 3.6, -4.1, 3.6
Tue 21	00:24, 06:59, 12:51, 19:22	03:45, 09:51, 16:08, 22:10	-4.2, 3.6, -4.0, 3.4
Wed 22	01:09, 07:41, 13:33, 20:08	04:28, 10:31, 16:53, 22:51	-4.0, 3.5, -3.9, 3.2
Thu 23	01:51, 08:22, 14:14, 20:53	05:11, 11:10, 17:38, 23:32	-3.7, 3.2, -3.6, 2.9
Fri 24	02:33, 09:03, 14:55, 21:39	05:56, 11:48, 18:22	-3.3, 3.0, -3.3
Sat 25	03:16, 09:46, 15:37, 22:29	00:15, 06:40, 12:31, 19:08	2.5, -2.9, 2.6, -3.0
Sun 26	04:02, 10:31, 16:23, 23:23	00:59, 07:26, 13:15, 19:57	2.2, -2.5, 2.3, -2.7
Mon 27	04:52, 11:23, 17:13	01:50, 08:19, 14:05, 20:52	1.9, -2.2, 2.0, -2.6
Tue 28	00:22, 05:49, 12:22, 18:08	02:46, 09:15, 15:01, 21:51	1.7, -2.0, 1.9, -2.5
Wed 29	01:22, 06:50, 13:25, 19:06	03:48, 10:17, 16:00, 22:48	1.6, -1.9, 1.8, -2.5
Thu 30	02:19, 07:51, 14:24, 20:04	04:55, 11:15, 17:05, 23:43	1.7, -2.1, 1.9, -2.7
Fri 31	03:11, 08:46, 15:17, 20:58	05:54, 12:09, 17:59	1.9, -2.3, 2.1

All Currents in Knots. Times Corrected to Daylight Savings Time

Flood Tides are shown in BOLD

September 1990

Day	Slack	Max	Kts
Sat 1	03:56 09:35 16:04 21:47	00:32 **06:39** 12:54 **18:47**	-3.0 **2.2** -2.7 **2.4**
Sun 2	04:37 10:18 16:47 22:32	01:17 **07:20** 13:39 **19:31**	-3.2 **2.6** -3.0 **2.8**
Mon 3	05:14 10:58 17:27 23:14	01:58 **07:56** 14:21 **20:12**	-3.5 **2.9** -3.3 **3.1**
Tue 4	05:50 11:37 18:06 23:56	02:41 **08:35** 14:59 **20:53**	-3.7 **3.2** -3.7 **3.3**
Wed 5	06:25 12:16 18:47	03:17 **09:12** 15:37 **21:36**	-3.8 **3.3** -3.9 **3.5**
Thu 6	00:37 07:02 12:57 19:29	03:57 **09:53** 16:18 **22:17**	-3.8 **3.6** -4.1 **3.6**
Fri 7	01:20 07:41 13:40 20:15	04:36 **10:37** 16:59 **23:04**	-3.8 **3.7** -4.1 **3.5**
Sat 8	02:06 08:24 14:26 21:05	05:19 **11:22** 17:49 **23:53**	-3.7 **3.6** -4.0 **3.3**
Sun 9	02:55 09:14 15:17 22:01	06:08 **12:13** 18:44	-3.5 **3.5** -3.9
Mon 10	03:50 10:10 16:14 23:05	**00:47** 07:05 **13:08** 19:45	**3.1** -3.2 **3.2** -3.7
Tue 11	04:52 11:15 17:17	**01:46** 08:13 **14:11** 20:51	**2.8** -3.0 **3.0** -3.5
Wed 12	00:14 05:59 12:28 18:26	**02:53** 09:22 **15:17** 21:59	**2.7** -2.8 **2.8** -3.5
Thu 13	01:24 07:09 13:41 19:35	**04:06** 10:30 **16:30** 23:04	**2.6** -3.0 **2.8** -3.6
Fri 14	02:29 08:17 14:49 20:41	**05:21** 11:34 **17:45**	**2.8** -3.3 **3.0**
Sat 15	03:28 09:18 15:49 21:41	00:05 **06:26** 12:35 **18:48**	-3.8 **3.1** -3.6 **3.2**
Sun 16	04:21 10:12 16:43 22:34	01:01 **07:19** 13:26 **19:39**	-3.9 **3.3** -3.8 **3.4**
Mon 17	05:09 11:00 17:32 23:22	01:50 **08:05** 14:15 **20:28**	-4.0 **3.5** -4.0 **3.4**
Tue 18	05:53 11:43 18:18	02:37 **08:48** 14:59 **21:09**	-4.0 **3.5** -4.1 **3.4**
Wed 19	00:05 06:34 12:23 19:01	03:20 **09:26** 15:44 **21:48**	-3.9 **3.4** -4.0 **3.3**
Thu 20	00:46 07:12 13:01 19:42	04:03 **09:59** 16:24 **22:22**	-3.6 **3.3** -3.8 **3.0**
Fri 21	01:24 07:50 13:39 20:23	04:44 **10:35** 17:06 **22:58**	-3.3 **3.2** -3.5 **2.7**
Sat 22	02:03 08:27 14:16 21:05	05:22 **11:11** 17:45 **23:39**	-3.0 **2.8** -3.2 **2.4**
Sun 23	02:43 09:06 14:55 21:50	06:04 **11:50** 18:31	-2.6 **2.5** -2.9
Mon 24	03:26 09:49 15:39 22:40	**00:22** 06:49 **12:35** 19:18	**2.1** -2.3 **2.2** -2.7
Tue 25	04:15 10:41 16:27 23:36	**01:09** 07:41 **13:25** 20:10	**1.9** -2.0 **1.9** -2.4
Wed 26	05:10 11:41 17:23	**02:04** 08:39 **14:20** 21:09	**1.7** -1.9 **1.7** -2.4
Thu 27	00:36 06:09 12:46 18:24	**03:01** 09:39 **15:21** 22:09	**1.7** -1.9 **1.7** -2.4
Fri 28	01:34 07:09 13:48 19:24	**04:03** 10:37 **16:24** 23:04	**1.8** -2.1 **1.9** -2.6
Sat 29	02:26 08:04 14:42 20:21	**05:02** 11:31 **17:20** 23:54	**2.0** -2.4 **2.1** -2.8
Sun 30	03:12 08:53 15:30 21:12	**05:53** 12:19 **18:10**	**2.3** -2.8 **2.5**

October 1990

Day	Slack	Max	Kts
Mon 1	03:53 09:38 16:14 22:00	00:42 **06:39** 12:54 **18:57**	-3.1 **2.2** -2.7 **2.9**
Tue 2	04:32 10:21 16:56 22:45	01:24 **07:17** 13:46 **19:43**	-3.4 **3.1** -3.7 **3.3**
Wed 3	05:11 11:03 17:39 23:29	02:05 **08:01** 14:28 **20:24**	-3.7 **3.5** -4.1 **3.6**
Thu 4	05:50 11:45 18:22	02:47 **08:42** 15:10 **21:09**	-3.9 **3.8** -4.3 **3.7**
Fri 5	00:13 06:31 12:29 19:07	03:29 **09:25** 15:52 **21:55**	-4.0 **3.9** -4.5 **3.8**
Sat 6	01:00 07:15 13:15 19:55	04:15 **10:12** 16:39 **22:44**	-3.9 **4.0** -4.5 **3.7**
Sun 7	01:48 08:03 14:05 20:48	05:01 **11:01** 17:30 **23:35**	-3.8 **3.8** -4.3 **3.5**
Mon 8	02:40 08:57 14:59 21:46	05:56 **11:54** 18:27	-3.6 **3.6** -4.1
Tue 9	03:38 09:58 15:58 22:50	**00:30** 06:56 **12:52** 19:31	**3.3** -3.3 **3.3** -3.8
Wed 10	04:41 11:08 17:03 23:58	**01:31** 08:03 **13:57** 20:37	**3.0** -3.1 **3.0** -3.6
Thu 11	05:48 12:22 18:13	**02:42** 09:11 **15:08** 21:42	**2.8** -3.1 **2.8** -3.5
Fri 12	01:06 13:34 19:22	**03:57** 10:16 **16:27** 22:48	**2.8** -2.7 **2.8** -3.5
Sat 13	02:10 08:02 14:39 20:28	**05:08** 11:19 **17:36** 23:47	**2.9** -3.4 **2.9** -3.6
Sun 14	03:07 09:00 15:37 21:26	**06:06** 12:17 **18:35**	**3.1** -3.7 **3.1**
Mon 15	03:58 09:51 16:29 22:17	00:42 **06:57** 13:06 **19:27**	-3.7 **3.3** -3.9 **3.2**
Tue 16	04:44 10:36 17:16 23:03	01:29 **07:44** 13:55 **20:12**	-3.7 **3.3** -4.0 **3.2**
Wed 17	05:27 11:17 17:59 23:44	02:14 **08:25** 14:38 **20:51**	-3.6 **3.0** -4.0 **3.1**
Thu 18	06:07 11:55 18:40	02:56 **08:57** 15:17 **21:26**	-3.5 **2.8** -3.9 **3.0**
Fri 19	00:22 06:44 12:31 19:19	03:37 **09:28** 15:57 **21:59**	-3.2 **3.0** -3.7 **2.8**
Sat 20	01:00 07:20 13:06 19:57	04:15 **10:03** 16:38 **22:33**	-3.0 **2.8** -3.4 **2.6**
Sun 21	01:37 07:55 13:42 20:36	04:54 **10:38** 17:16 **23:10**	-2.7 **2.6** -3.2 **2.4**
Mon 22	02:16 08:33 14:20 21:17	05:35 **11:20** 17:55 **23:51**	-2.5 **2.3** -2.9 **2.2**
Tue 23	02:57 09:15 15:01 22:02	06:18 **12:03** 18:38 **24:36**	-2.2 **2.1** -2.7 **2.0**
Wed 24	03:43 10:05 15:48 22:52	**00:36** 07:05 **12:52** 19:31	**2.0** -2.0 **1.9** -2.5
Thu 25	04:34 11:02 16:42 23:46	**01:28** 08:01 **13:45** 20:26	**1.9** -2.0 **1.8** -2.4
Fri 26	05:29 12:05 17:41	**02:23** 08:58 **14:44** 21:23	**1.9** -2.0 **1.8** -2.4
Sat 27	00:41 06:25 13:06 18:42	**03:13** 09:50 **15:38** 22:13	**2.2** -2.6 **2.2** -2.7
Sun 28	01:33 07:10 13:53 19:35	**04:04** 10:41 **16:32** 23:01	**2.5** -3.0 **2.5** -3.0
Mon 29	02:06 07:58 14:41 20:26	**04:54** 11:29 **17:21** 23:47	**2.9** -3.5 **2.9** -3.3
Tue 30	02:06 07:58 14:41 20:26	**04:54** 11:29 **17:21** 23:47	**2.9** -3.5 **2.9** -3.3
Wed 31	02:50 08:45 15:27 21:15	**05:41** 12:13 **18:12**	**3.3** -3.9 **3.3**

November 1990

Day	Slack	Max	Kts
Thu 1	03:34 09:31 16:13 22:03	00:33 **06:37** 12:59 **19:00**	-3.6 **2.2** -4.3 **3.6**
Fri 2	04:18 10:18 17:00 22:52	01:18 **07:13** 13:44 **19:47**	-3.8 **3.9** -4.6 **3.8**
Sat 3	05:05 11:06 17:49 23:41	02:06 **08:02** 14:33 **20:36**	-4.0 **4.1** -4.7 **3.9**
Sun 4	05:54 11:56 18:40	02:55 **08:52** 15:22 **21:25**	-4.0 **4.1** -4.7 **3.9**
Mon 5	00:33 06:48 12:48 19:34	03:47 **09:43** 16:16 **22:20**	-3.9 **3.9** -4.5 **3.7**
Tue 6	01:27 07:45 13:44 20:31	04:43 **10:38** 17:14 **23:17**	-3.7 **3.6** -4.3 **3.4**
Wed 7	02:25 08:49 14:44 21:33	05:43 **11:37** 18:15	-3.5 **3.3** -3.9
Thu 8	03:27 09:58 15:48 22:37	**00:18** 06:47 **12:44** 19:17	**3.2** -3.4 **3.0** -3.7
Fri 9	04:32 11:09 16:55 23:41	**01:26** 07:52 **13:55** 20:22	**3.0** -3.3 **2.8** -3.5
Sat 10	05:36 12:17 18:02	**02:35** 08:57 **15:10** 21:23	**2.9** -3.3 **2.7** -3.4
Sun 11	00:42 06:38 13:21 19:06	**03:42** 09:55 **16:18** 22:22	**2.9** -3.5 **2.8** -3.3
Mon 12	01:39 07:34 14:18 20:04	**04:41** 10:54 **17:15** 23:15	**3.0** -3.6 **2.8** -3.3
Tue 13	02:30 08:25 15:09 20:55	**05:34** 11:45 **18:04**	**3.0** -3.7 **2.9**
Wed 14	03:17 09:09 15:56 21:41	00:03 **06:20** 12:30 **18:53**	-3.2 **3.0** -3.8 **2.9**
Thu 15	04:00 09:50 16:39 22:22	00:49 **06:59** 13:13 **19:32**	-3.0 **3.0** -3.8 **2.8**
Fri 16	04:41 10:27 17:19 23:01	01:31 **07:31** 13:55 **20:07**	-3.0 **2.9** -3.7 **2.7**
Sat 17	05:18 11:03 17:58 23:38	02:13 **08:04** 14:34 **20:38**	-2.9 **2.7** -3.6 **2.6**
Sun 18	05:55 11:39 18:35	02:52 **08:37** 15:12 **21:11**	-2.7 **2.6** -3.4 **2.5**
Mon 19	00:15 06:31 12:15 19:12	03:32 **09:14** 15:50 **21:48**	-2.6 **2.5** -3.2 **2.4**
Tue 20	00:53 07:09 12:52 19:49	04:10 **09:53** 16:30 **22:27**	-2.6 **2.3** -3.0 **2.3**
Wed 21	01:33 07:50 13:33 20:29	04:52 **10:36** 17:11 **23:10**	-2.3 **2.2** -2.8 **2.2**
Thu 22	02:15 08:36 14:17 21:12	05:37 **11:23** 17:52 **23:53**	-2.2 **2.1** -2.7 **2.2**
Fri 23	03:01 09:27 15:07 21:58	06:22 **12:10** 18:41	-2.2 **2.0** -2.5
Sat 24	03:50 10:24 16:01 22:47	**00:44** 07:16 **13:06** 19:35	**2.2** -2.3 **2.0** -2.5
Sun 25	04:41 11:22 16:59 23:37	**01:35** 08:12 **14:01** 20:28	**2.2** -2.5 **2.1** -2.5
Mon 26	05:34 12:21 17:59	**02:29** 09:06 **14:58** 21:26	**2.4** -2.8 **2.3** -2.7
Tue 27	00:29 06:27 13:16 18:57	**03:22** 10:02 **15:55** 22:20	**2.7** -3.2 **2.5** -2.9
Wed 28	01:20 07:20 14:10 19:53	**04:15** 10:53 **16:49** 23:13	**3.0** -3.6 **2.9** -3.2
Thu 29	02:11 08:12 15:01 20:47	**05:06** 11:44 **17:45**	**3.4** -4.0 **3.2**
Fri 30	03:03 09:04 15:52 21:41	00:07 **06:01** 12:34 **18:36**	-3.5 **3.7** -4.4 **3.5**

Embassy's Current Charts© - Western Long Island Sound show the approximate speed, direction, and times at which spring tidal currents are at maximum flow. The **BOLD** heads of the arrows are **FLOOD** tides. The light arrow heads are ebb tides. All times are referenced against "SLACK, FLOOD BEGINS AT THE RACE."

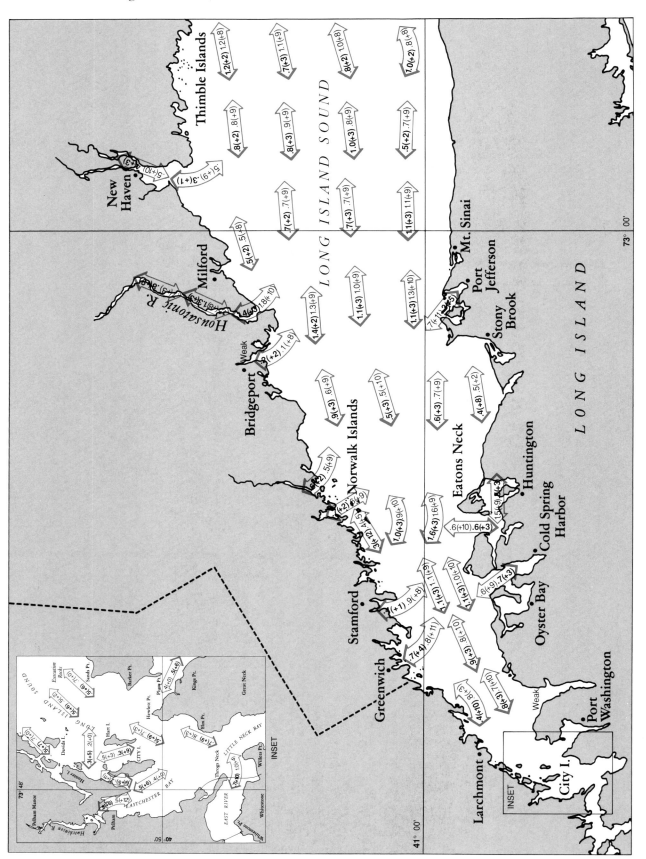

Embassy's Current Charts© - Eastern Long Island Sound show the approximate speed, direction, and times at which spring tidal currents are at maximum flow. The **BOLD** heads of the arrows are **FLOOD** tides. The light arrow heads are ebb tides. All times are referenced against "SLACK, FLOOD BEGINS AT THE RACE."

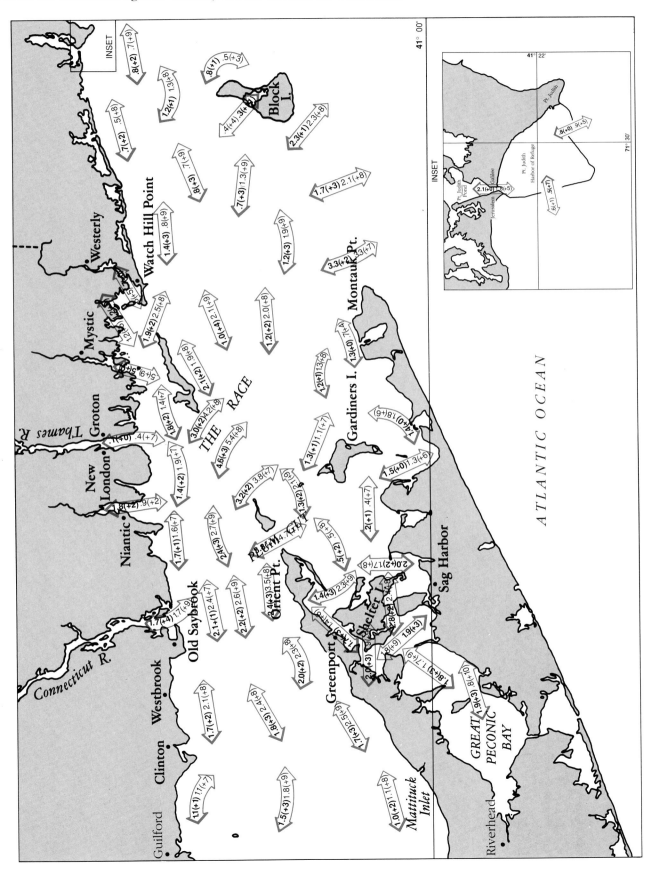

Bibliography

Adkins, Edwin P. Setauket: *The First Three Hundred Years, 1655-1955* (Second Edition). East Setauket, NY: The Three Village Historical Society.

Allen, Everett S. *A Wind To Shake the World: The Story of the 1938 Hurricane*. Boston: Little, Brown & Company, 1976.

Allyn, James H. *Swamp Yankee from Mystic*. Mystic, CT: Roy N. Bohlander, Mystic, CT, 1980.

Bachand, Robert G. *Scuba Northeast, Volume II*. Norwalk, CT: Sea Sports Publications, 1986.

Bell, Michael. *The Face of Connecticut: People, Geology, and the Land*. Hartford, CT: Connecticut Geological and Natural History Survey, 1985.

Carrick, Robert W., and Simons, George Calvert. *The Pictorial History of the America's Cup Races*. New York: The Viking Press, 1964.

Clark, Elizabeth W., editor. *Before and After 1776: A Comprehensive Chronology of the Town of Greenwich* (Second Edition). Greenwich, CT: The Historical Society of the Town of Greenwich, 1978.

Connable, Alfred. *Tigers of Tammany: Nine Men Who Ran New York*. New York: Holt, 1967.

Cooley, Susan D. *Country Walks in Connecticut: A Guide to the Nature Conservancy Preserves*. Boston, MA: Appalachian Mountain Club, 1982.

Deforest, John W. *History of the Indians of the Indians from the Earliest Known Period to 1850*. Hamden, CT: The Shoe String Press, Inc., 1964.

Delaney, Edmund T. *The Connecticut River: New England's Historic Waterway*. Chester, CT: The Globe Pequot Press, 1983.

Duvall, Ralph G. *The History of Shelter Island 1652-1952*. Shelter Island, NY: Glorian Duvall Devereux and Jean Litchy Schaldermundt, 1952.

Gordon, Bernard L., editor. *Hurricane in Southern New England: An Analysis of the Great Storm of 1938*. Watch Hill, RI: The Book & Tackle Shop, 1976.

Gottlieb, Polly Rose. *The Nine Lives of Billy Rose*. New York: Crown Publishers, 1968.

Grant, Marion Hepburn. *The Infernal Machines of Saybrook's David Bushnell*. Old Saybrook, CT: The Bicentennial Committee of Old Saybrook, CT, 1976.

Hall, Karyl Lee Kibler, and Cooper, Carolyn. *Windows on the Works: Industry on the Eli Whitney Site 1798-1979*. Hamden, CT: Eli Whitney Museum, 1984.

Hanna, Archibald. *A Brief History of the Thimble Islands in Branford, Connecticut*. Branford, CT: Archon Books, 1970.

Helander, Joel E. *Oxpasture to Summer Colony: The Story of Sachem's Head in Guilford, Connecticut*. Guilford, CT: Joel E. Helander, 1976

History of Connecticut's Coast: 400 Years of Coastal Industry and Development, A. Hartford, CT: Coastal Area Management Program, Connecticut Department of Environmental Protection, 1982.

Hugill, Stan. *Shanties From the Seven Seas: Shipboard Work-Songs and Songs Used as Work-Songs From the Great Days of Sail*. London: Routledge & Kegan Paul, 1984.

Jensen, Barbara Neff. *Mystic: Memories of a Native*. Groton, CT: Groton Public Library and Information Center, 1989.

Jones, Steven. *Noank: The Ethereal Years*. Noank, CT: Noank Historical Society, 1988.

Keyarts, Eugene. *60 Selected Short Walks in Connecticut*. Chester, CT: The Globe Pequot Press, 1974.

Knapp, Alfred P. *Connecticut Yesteryears: So Saith the Wind*. Old Saybrook, CT: Andrews, Brownell, Hill & Cate, 1985.

Light List, Volume One, Atlantic Coast. Washington, DC: Department of Transportation, U.S. Coast Guard, 1989.

Mather, Frederic Gregory. *The Refugees From Long Island to Connecticut*. Albany, NY: J.B. Lyon Company, 1913.

Middlebrook, Louis F. *Maritime Connecticut During the American Revolution*. Salem, MA: Essex Institute, 1925.

Philips-Brit, Douglas. *The History of Yachting*. Briarcliff Manor, NY: Stein and Day Publishers, 1974.

Hamilton, Harlan. *Lights & Legends*. Stamford, CT: Westcott Cove Publishing Company, 1987.

Rattray, Jeannette Edwards. *Ship Ashore! A Record of Maritime Disasters off Montauk and Eastern Long Island, 1640-1955*. Southampton, NY: Yankee Peddler Book Company, 1955.

Reaske, Christopher R. *The Compleat Clammer*. New York: Nick Lyons Books, 1986.

Snow, Edward Rowe. *Pirates and Buccanneers of the Atlantic Coast*. Boston: Yankee Publishing Company, 1944.

Stone, Herbert L., and William H. Taylor, *The America's Cup Races*. Princeton, NJ: D. Van Nostrand Company, 1944.

Summary of Corrections Volume One: East Coast of North and South America. Washington, DC: Defense Mapping Agency, 1988

Tidal Current Charts: Long Island Sound and Block Island Sound, (Seventh Editon). Rockville, MD: U.S. Department of Commerce, National Oceanic and Atmospheric Administration, National Ocean Survey, 1989

Tide Tables: East Coast of North and South America. Rockville, MD: U.S. Department of Commerce, National Oceanic and Atmospheric Administration, National Ocean Service, published annually.

United States Coast Pilot, Volume Two, Atlantic Coast: Cape Cod to Sandy Hook. Rockville, MD: U.S. Department of Commerce, National Oceanic and Atmospheric Administration, National Ocean Service, 1989

U.S. Coast Guard Academy. *Eagle Seamanship: A Manual for Square Rigger Sailing*. New York: M. Evans and Company, 1969.

Wallace, Irving. *The Fabulous Showman: The Life and Times of P.T. Barnum*. New York: Knopf, 1959.

Weigold, Marilyn E. *American Mediterranean*. Port Washington, NY: Kennikat, 1974.

Welles, Gordon and Proios, William. *Port Jefferson: Story of a Village*. Port Jefferson, NY: Historical Society of Greater Port Jefferson, 1977.

Willoughby, M.F. *The Lighthouses of New England*. Boston: Metcalf Publishing Company, 1929.

Index to Advertisers

Index

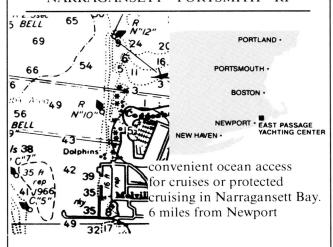

Embassy's Complete Waterproof Chart to Long Island Sound

A $52 Value... for Under $15

Embassy's Complete Waterproof Chart is printed on an incredibly tough plastic stock that can't be torn or damaged by water.

A one-of-a-kind, full-color chart of the entire Sound...that's virtually indestructible.

This 34" x 47" chart is printed on two sides and covers the entire Sound on one easy-to-use chart. It takes four standard charts to cover the same area. **Embassy's Waterproof Chart** gives you more at less than half the price!

These are just some of the reasons why we're sure that **Embassy's Complete Waterproof Chart to Long Island Sound** is the best...

We Guarantee It.

If not completely satisfied, return it to us at any time for a full refund.

EMBASSY

Tell Us What You Think...

...And What You Know

We need your help. We plan to issue revised editions of *Embassy's Boating Guides* periodically, updating them with the latest available information. We strive to keep *Embassy's Boating Guides* the best cruising guides in the world, but we can't do it without you. We hope you'll help us by telling us about your experiences this year – navigational changes, events, sightings – on the water, at marinas, anchorages, and in town.

Please join our many valued contributors in helping to make *Embassy's Boating Guides* even better with each new edition. We have prepared this postage-paid form to encourage you to contribute your ideas and suggestions. Rate us on the scales below and send us your ideas for interesting articles – or write an article yourself!

1 Which *Embassy Boating Guides* do you own? *Embassy's Complete Boating Guide to Long Island Sound*_____
*Embassy's Complete Boating Guide to Cape Cod & Rhode Island*_____

2 How would you rate each of the following aspects of *Embassy's Complete Boating Guide:*

	Excellent	Very Good	OK	Not Very Good	Poor
Overall Rating					
Introductory Chapters					
Harbor Chapters					
Harbor Highlights					
Tide, Current Tables & Charts					

3 Listed below are five cruising guides covering the coast of New England. Please rank each guide on a scale of 1 to 5 (1=The Best, 5=The Worst).

Boating Almanac_____   NYNEX Boater's Directory_____   Embassy's Boating Guide_____
Waterway Guide_____   Chart Kit/BBA_____

4 We want to make *Embassy's Complete Boating Guide* not only the best guide covering this area, but also the best guide of its type for any region in the world. How are we doing? Compared to any other cruising guide you know of at any price, how would you rate *Embassy's Complete Boating Guide?* Circle your rating below:

The Best   **Better Than Average**   **Average**   **Below Average**   **The Worst**

If you rated us **The Best**, why? If you rated us as less than **The Best**, what do we need to do to be **The Best**?

5 Do you have any specific comments, criticisms, or suggestions for improving any Harbor Chapter or other elements of the *Guide?* Did you have any special or interesting experiences this cruising season that other boaters should know about? Were there any changes in local navigational aids, landmarks, or harbor towns that we should recheck? Fold in a copy of the Harbor Chapter or an extra piece of paper if necessary.

6 What kind of boat do you have?   **Power**_____   **Sail**_____   **Length**_____

7 In which harbor do you keep your boat? _____
What are your favorite cruising destinations?_____
For what other cruising areas would you like to see us publish an *Embassy's Complete Boating Guide?*_____

Please provide your name and address so that we can keep in contact with you. This information is for *Embassy's Boating Guide* use only.

Your Name _____ Street Address _____
City _____ State _____ Zip _____ Phone _____

If you have a friend or relative who would be interested in receiving information about the *Guide,* please let us know:

Name _____ Street Address _____
City _____ State _____ Zip _____ Phone _____

——————————————————————— *Fold here, with above material inside* ———————————————————————

Thank you for your assistance.

EMBASSY

——————————————————————— *Fold here and staple or tape closed* ———————————————————————

|||||

BUSINESS REPLY MAIL

FIRST CLASS   PERMIT NO. 18   ESSEX, CT, U.S.A.

POSTAGE WILL BE PAID BY ADDRESSEE

Embassy's Complete Boating Guides
P.O. Box 338
37 Pratt Street
Essex, CT 06426-9956

Embassy's Complete Boating Guide to Long Island Sound

Updated & Improved!

Embassy's Complete Boating Guide is the only guide devoted exclusively to Long Island Sound. It brings you over 400 full-color pages of boating information in an easy-to-use 8-1/2" x 11" wire-bound book.

- ◆ Up-to-date navigational advice for every harbor along the coast. Including large-scale, full-color Harbor Charts so you can clearly see the approaches and anchorages.

- ◆ Special articles on local attractions and special events that make cruising on the Sound so exciting. You can plan ahead to get the most out of your trip.

- ◆ Fascinating background information helps you understand the area you're boating in. Special articles cover fishing...scuba diving...boating safety...and more.

Embassy's Complete Waterproof Chart to Long Island Sound

A $52 Value...only $14.95!

This exceptional waterproof chart covers the entire Sound in one easy-to-use chart – the same area it takes four standard charts to cover!

- ◆ Full-color chart printed on both sides, measures 34" x 47".

- ◆ Printed on virtually indestructible plastic – can't be torn or damaged by water.

- ◆ Easy to read – sharp and clean.

Embassy's Complete Boating Guide to Rhode Island and Massachusetts

Brand New!

Embassy's Complete Boating Guide is the only guide devoted exclusively to Rhode Island & Massachusetts. It brings you over 350 full-color pages of boating information in an easy-to-use 8-1/2" x 11" wire-bound book.

- ◆ Harbor Chapters provide up-to-date navigational advice for every harbor along the coast. Each chapter includes a large-scale, full-color Harbor Chart so you can clearly see approaches and anchorages.

- ◆ Special articles on local attractions and special events that make cruising along the coast so exciting. You can plan ahead to get the most out of your trip.

- ◆ Fascinating background information helps you understand the area you're boating in. Special articles cover fishing...scuba diving...boating safety...and more.

Embassy's Complete Boating Guide to Long Island Sound

Updated & Expanded!

Embassy's Complete Boating Guide is the only guide devoted exclusively to Long Island Sound. It brings you over 400 full-color pages of boating information in an easy-to-use 8-1/2" x 11" wire-bound book.

- ◆ Up-to-date navigational advice for every harbor along the coast. Including large-scale, full-color Harbor Charts so you can clearly see the approaches and anchorages.

- ◆ Special articles on local attractions and special events that make cruising on the Sound so exciting. You can plan ahead to get the most out of your trip.

- ◆ Fascinating background information helps you understand the area you're boating in. Special articles cover fishing...scuba diving...boating safety...and more.

COMPLETE YOUR CRUISING LIBRARY WITH THE BEST FROM EMBASSY

Don't miss out on Embassy's invaluable boating books and charts.

To Order: Call Toll-Free 1-800-999-1075 or Send Your Order To:

TITLE	QTY	PRICE EACH	TOTAL
Embassy's Complete Boating Guide to Long Island Sound, 3rd Ed.		$34.95	
Embassy's Complete Boating Guide to Rhode Island & Massachusetts, 1st Ed.		$34.95	
Embassy's Complete Waterproof Chart to Long Island Sound		$14.95	
The Complete Boating Guide to the Connecticut River, 2nd Ed.		$11.95	
1991 Tide & Current Tables for Long Island Sound or Rhode Island & Massachusetts		**FREE** $ 1.00	

Shipping & Handling ($2.50 per book, $1.50 per chart, $1.00 per set of Tide Tables)	TOTAL PRICE OF ITEMS	
	SALES TAX (CT,NY,MA,RI)	
	SHIPPING & HANDLING	
	TOTAL	

Method of payment: _____ Check Enclosed (Payable to Embassy Marine Publishing)
Charge to my: Visa _____ Mastercard _____ American Express _____
Credit Card Account Number _____ Exp. Date _____
Signature _____

Embassy Marine Publishing
P.O. Box 338
37 Pratt Street
Essex, CT 06426

Ordered By:

Name _____
Address_____
City _____
State _____ Zip_____

Ship To: (if different from above)

Name_____
Address_____
City _____
State _____ Zip_____

If you are not completely satisfied, return the item(s) at any time for a full refund of the purchase price.

EMBASSY

COMPLETE YOUR CRUISING LIBRARY WITH THE BEST FROM EMBASSY

Don't miss out on Embassy's invaluable boating books and charts.

To Order: Call Toll-Free 1-800-999-1075 or Send Your Order To:

TITLE	QTY	PRICE EACH	TOTAL
Embassy's Complete Boating Guide to Long Island Sound, 3rd Ed.		$34.95	
Embassy's Complete Boating Guide to Rhode Island & Massachusetts, 1st Ed.		$34.95	
Embassy's Complete Waterproof Chart to Long Island Sound		$14.95	
The Complete Boating Guide to the Connecticut River, 2nd Ed.		$11.95	
1991 Tide & Current Tables for Long Island Sound or Rhode Island & Massachusetts		**FREE** $ 1.00	

Shipping & Handling ($2.50 per book, $1.50 per chart, $1.00 per set of Tide Tables)	TOTAL PRICE OF ITEMS	
	SALES TAX (CT,NY,MA,RI)	
	SHIPPING & HANDLING	
	TOTAL	

Method of payment: _____ Check Enclosed (Payable to Embassy Marine Publishing)
Charge to my: Visa _____ Mastercard _____ American Express _____
Credit Card Account Number _____ Exp. Date _____
Signature _____

Embassy Marine Publishing
P.O. Box 338
37 Pratt Street
Essex, CT 06426

Ordered By:

Name _____
Address_____
City _____
State _____ Zip_____

Ship To: (if different from above)

Name_____
Address_____
City _____
State _____ Zip_____

If you are not completely satisfied, return the item(s) at any time for a full refund of the purchase price.

EMBASSY